KU-511-102

PEARSON
BACCALAUREATE

Environmental Systems and Societies

ANDREW DAVIS • GARRETT NAGLE

PEARSON

Pearson Education Limited is a company incorporated in England and Wales, having its registered office at Edinburgh Gate, Harlow, Essex, CM20 2JE. Registered company number: 872828.

www.pearsonbaccalaureate.com

Pearson is a registered trademark of Pearson Education Limited.

Text © Pearson Education Limited 2010

First published 2010

13 12 11
IMP 10 9 8 7 6 5 4

ISBN 978 0 435032 63 0

Edited by Penelope Lyons
Designed by Tony Richardson
Typeset by TechType
Original illustrations © Pearson Education Limited 2010
Illustrated by Oxford Designers & Illustrators and TechType
Cover design by Tony Richardson
Picture research by Joanne Forrest Smith
Cover photo © Digital Vision
Printed in Malaysia (CTP-VVP)

Acknowledgements

The authors and publisher would like to thank the following individuals and organisations for permission to reproduce photographs:

(Key: b – bottom; c – centre; l – left; r – right; t – top)
Alamy Images: Chris Hellier 203, Dinodia Images 151, Martin Shields 311tr, Photos 12 292, RIA Novosti 291b, Terry Fincher Photo Int 224; Andrew J Davis: 202, 209, 210, 305tl, 305tr; Bridgeman Art Library Ltd: 100t, 196, Musée des Antiquites Nationales, St. Germain-en-Laye, France / Lauros / Giraudon 99; CITES: 211; Corbis: 100c, Aas, Erlend / epa 286, Andy Rain / epa 177b, Bettmann 290t, Charles & Josette Lenars 204, Dlillc 180c, Elmer Frederick Fischer 200, Enzo & Paolo Ragazzini 311tl, Frans Lanting 195cr, G. Bowater 118, Galen Rowell 183, Hashimoto Noboru / Sygma 193, Hubert Stadler 195tl, Hulton–Deutsch Collection 177cr, Image Source 198, 201, Image Source 198, 201, James Marshall 141, Kevin Schafer 213, Made Nagi / epa 291t, Marcelo Del Pozo / Reuters 197, Michael & Patricia Fogden 199, Michael S. Yamashita 181, Miroslaw Tremebcki / PAP 295c, Natural Selection David Ponton / Design Pics 180bc, Reuters 290b, Richard Hamilton Smith 186c, Rungroj Yongrit / epa 295tc, Stephanie Maze 70b, Tom Bean 186b, Visuals Unlimited 195cl, Warren Jacobi 195b; DFO MPO: 233, 234; Dreamstime.com: 315t, Dvmsimages 315br, Gnup 300, Madartists / Dreamstime.com 288; Fearless Threads Passion T's; www.fearlessthreads.com: 315bl; FLPA Images of Nature: Desmond Dugan 71c, Mark Moffett / Minden Pictures 32b, Wayne Hutchinson 71t; Garrett E Nagle: 20c, 23, 26, 27, 32t, 38b, 42t, 69, 70t, 111, 113, 116t, 116b, 123, 126, 128, 131, 134, 138tl, 142, 145, 156, 157, 158c, 158b, 159, 176, 189t, 217, 223, 231tl, 231tc, 237, 256, 305cr, 305bl, 305br, 307, 313; Getty Images: Deborah Harrison 301t, Joel Sartore / National Geographic 312tr, Ken Lucas 310, Mike Kemp 306, Stock4B 302, Tom Brakefield 133; Glen J Kuban: 308bl, 308br; Lyons Photo Library: 178bc, 178br, 238, 276c; Pearson Education Ltd: 3b, 18, 39, 40t, 42c, 70c, 97, 138tc, 138tr, 140c, 140b, 144, 175, 250, 274, 276b, 305cl, 312tc, 312cl, 312b, 312bl, 312bc, 3b, 18, 39, 40t, 42c, 70c, 97, 138tc, 138tr, 140c, 140b, 144, 175, 250, 274, 276b, 305cl, 312tc, 312cl, 312b, 312bl, 312bc; Penguin Books Ltd: 228; Rex Features: Sutton Hibbert 273; Sanjay Molur/WILD/ZOO: 195tr; Science Photo Library Ltd: David M Schleser / Nature's Images 3c, David Parker 25, David Taylor 79, Dr Jeremy Burgess 50, Dr Keith Wheeler 271, Georgette Douwma 16, Jeff Lepore 8, Kjell B Sandved 22b, PG Adam / Publiphoto Diffusion 4, Sinclair Stammers 2, 22t, 66, Sinclair Stammers 2, 22t, 66, Sinclair Stammers 2, 22t, 66, US Geological Survey 76; www.CartoonStock.com: 301br.

All other images © Pearson Education

Dedications

For my mother, and in memory of my father, Brian Davis, who is remembered here.

With thanks to my colleagues in the Department of Biology at St Edward's for their friendship and support – Lucy Baddeley, Lewis Faulkner, Kate Kettlewell, Jo Shindler, Al Summers, Helen Warden and Kendall Williams; to John Grahame who taught me ecology at Leeds, and Stephen Sutton who introduced me to the world of rainforests and conservation for which I am eternally grateful; to friends and colleagues at Danum Valley who taught me more about ecology than can be read about in textbooks; to Jane McNicholl and Sue Lees who were my way into teaching; to Lily French, Chris Hatton, Amy Hicks and Lydia Smith who together pioneered the course at St Edward's and whose input is contained here; and to all my pupils over the years who have taught me much. This book is for my mother, who has taught me most of all.

Andrew J Davis

To Angela, Rosie, Patrick and Bethany

With thanks to staff and students at St Edward's School and to Angela, Rosie, Patrick and Bethany for their patience and good humour.

Garrett E Nagle

CONTENTS

CONTENTS

INTRODUCTION

Content

Welcome to Environmental systems and societies (ESS). We hope you enjoy the course. This book is designed to be a comprehensive course book, covering all aspects of the syllabus. It will help you prepare for your examinations in a thorough and methodical way as it follows the syllabus outline section by section, explaining and expanding on the material in the course syllabus. Each chapter deals with one topic from the syllabus and, within each chapter, the main sections are numbered and named as in the syllabus. This makes the book readily accessible for use and reference throughout the course. There are also short chapters explaining overall assessment and internal assessment (IA) and offering advice on writing the Extended Essay (EE) and developing exam strategies. In addition, there is an appendix on basic statistics and data analysis. And after the answers section, you will find a glossary of useful terms that have been emboldened in the book.

Links between different parts of the syllabus are emphasized, and key facts essential to your understanding are highlighted throughout. At the end of each section, you will find practice questions to test your knowledge and understanding of that part of the course. You can self-assess your answers using the mark-schemes in the answers section.

The ESS course is the first fully transdisciplinary course within the IB. It covers group 3 (individuals and societies) and group 4 (experimental sciences). As a group 4 subject, it demands the scientific rigour expected of an experimental science, and has a large practical component. The group 3 approach balances this with a human-centred perspective which examines environmental issues from a social and cultural viewpoint. Throughout the book, you will look at the environment from the perspective of human societies, and assess their response in the light of the scientific framework used in environmental sciences. The book therefore looks at environmental issues from economic, historical, cultural, socio-political viewpoints as well as a scientific one, to provide a holistic perspective.

The aims of the course and this book are to:
- promote understanding of environmental processes at a variety of scales, from local to global
- provide the methodologies and skills that can be used to analyse the environment at local and global levels
- enable you to apply the knowledge, methodologies and skills gained
- promote critical awareness of a diversity of cultural perspectives
- recognize the extent to which technology plays a role in both causing and solving environmental issues
- appreciate the value of local as well as international collaboration in resolving environmental problems
- appreciate that environmental issues may be controversial, and may provoke a variety of responses
- appreciate that human society is both directly and indirectly linked to the environment at a number of levels and at a variety of scales.

Information boxes

Throughout the book you will see a number of coloured boxes interspersed through each chapter. They may be in the margins or in the main text area. Each of these boxes provides different information and stimulus as follows.

> **Assessment statements**
> 2.1.1 Distinguish between biotic and abiotic (physical) components of an ecosystem.
> 2.1.2 Define the term *trophic level*.

You will find a box like this at the start of each section in each chapter. They list the numbered objectives for the section you are about to read and set out what content and aspects of learning are covered in that section.

 Global warming challenges views of certainty within the sciences. In the popular perception, global warming is having a negative impact on the world. There is, moreover, some confusion between the public perception of global warming and the greenhouse effect. The greenhouse effect is a natural process, without which there would be no life on Earth. The *enhanced* or *accelerated* greenhouse effect is synonymous with global warming. The enhanced greenhouse effect is largely due to human (anthropogenic) forces, although feedback mechanisms may trigger some natural forces, too. Lobby groups and politicians will take views which suit their own economic and political ends. In the USA, the strength of the oil companies during the Bush Administration was seen by many as an example of economic groups, and the politicians they supported, choosing a stance which was not in the long-term environmental, social or economic interest of the world. But it did benefit the oil companies and the politicians they supported.

In addition to the Theory of Knowledge chapter, there are TOK boxes like this throughout the book. These boxes are there to stimulate thought and consideration of any TOK issues as they arise and in context. Often, they will just contain a question to stimulate your own thoughts and discussion.

 The pH scale is logarithmic. This means that pH 6.0 is 10 times more acidic than pH 7.0; natural rainwater at pH 5.6 is about 25 times more acidic than distilled water at pH 7.0. Acid rain is frequently more than 20 times more acidic than natural rainwater. Rain over Scandinavia commonly has a pH of 4.2–4.3.

The yellow interesting fact boxes contain interesting information which will add to your wider knowledge but which does not fit within the main body of the text.

 Rainwater is normally a weak carbonic acid with a pH of about 5.5. Acid rain is a more acidic substance, due to the addition of sulfur dioxide and the oxides of nitrogen. Any rain with a pH below 5.5 is termed 'acid rain'.

The green key fact boxes contain key facts which are drawn out of the main text and highlighted. This makes them easily identifiable for quick reference. The boxes also enable you to identify the core learning points within a section.

 To learn more about smog levels in Los Angeles on 4 July 2008, go to www.pearsonhotlinks.com, insert the express code 2630P and click on activity 5.21.

Hotlinks boxes direct you to the publisher's website, which in turn will take you to the relevant website(s). On the web pages there, you will find additional information to support the topic, video simulations, and the like.

Blue online resources boxes indicate that online resources are available that relate to this section of the book. These resources might be extension exercises, additional practice questions, interactive online material, suggestions for IA, EE and revision, or other sources of information. Some of the content on this site may be password protected for copyright reasons. When prompted for a password, please use PearsonBaccESS exactly as shown.

 To access worksheet 4.6 on endangered species, please visit www.pearsonbacconline.com and follow the on-screen instructions.

The first effects of acid rain were noted in Scandinavian lakes in the 1960s. Over 18 000 lakes in Sweden are acidified, 4000 of them, are seriously affected. Fish stocks in about 9000 Swedish lakes, mostly in the south and the centre of the country, are also badly affected. In the Eastern USA and Canada over 48 000 lakes are too acidic to support fish.

A global perspective is important to the International Baccalaureate. These boxes indicate examples of internationalism within the area of study. The information given offers you the chance to think about how Environmental systems and societies fits into the global landscape.

ENVIRONMENTAL PHILOSOPHIES

Ultimately, the choices people make depend on their environmental philosophy. People with an anthropocentric worldview see the technological possibilities as central to solving environmental problems. An ecocentric worldview leads to greater caution and a drive to use Earth's natural resources in a sustainable way rather than rely on technology to solve the problems.

A central theme of the course is that diverse societies view the environment and environmental problems in different ways. These environmental philosophies lie on a spectrum, from cultures that have a life-centred worldview, seeing humans as being heavily reliant on nature and needing to use the Earth's resources in a sustainable way (ecocentric), to those that see nature as being for the benefit of human kind (anthropocentric) where technology is able to solve environmental problems (a technocentric approach). The cause and effect of these different environmental philosophies is covered in detail in Chapter 7.

● **Examiner's hints**

Soil pH can be measured using a universal indicator as follows.
1 Take a small soil sample from a known depth (horizon) of soil.
2 Place about 1–2 cm of soil in the bottom of a test tube.
3 Add 1–2 cm of barium sulfate (this causes the clay to settle leaving a clear solution.
4 Fill the tube with distilled water and shake.
5 Add a few drops of universal indicator to clear the solution. Compare the colour of the liquid to the colour of the chart provided. The pH can be read off to the nearest 0.5.

Examiner's hints provide insight into how to answer a question in order to achieve the highest marks in an examination. They also identify common pitfalls when answering such questions and suggest approaches that examiners like to see.

CASE STUDY

Fertility in the Arab world

The Arab performance in improving women's health is unmatched. Female life expectancy is up from 52 years in 1970 to more than 70 years in 2004. The number of children borne by the average Arab woman has fallen by half in the past 20 years, to a level scarcely higher than world norms. In Oman, fertility has plummeted from ten births per woman to fewer than four. A main reason for this is a dramatic rise in the age at which girls marry. A generation ago, three-quarters of Arab women were married by the time they were 20. That proportion has dropped by half. In large Arab cities, the high cost of housing, added to the need for women to pursue degrees or start careers, is prompting many to delay marriage until they are in their 30s.

Case studies are self-contained examples that you can use to answer questions on specific points. They are usually longer than this example and often contain photographs or other illustration.

Approaches to Environmental systems and societies

Systems approach

The nature of environmental issues demands a holistic treatment. This is why the systems approach is central to the course. This approach is explained in detail in Chapter 1, and used throughout this book. Science often uses a reductionist approach to examine phenomena, breaking a system down into its components and studying them separately. Environmental science cannot work in this way, as understanding the functioning of the whole topic (e.g. an ecosystem) is essential (i.e. a holistic approach is needed). The traditional reductionist approach of science inevitably tends to overlook or understate this important holistic quality. Furthermore, the systems approach is common to many disciplines (e.g. economics, geography, politics, and ecology). It emphasizes the similarities between all these disciplines in the ways in which matter, energy and information flow, allowing common terminology to be used when discussing different systems and disciplines. This approach therefore integrates the perspectives of different subjects. Throughout this book, the integrated nature of this subject is stressed by examining the links between different areas of the syllabus and between different disciplines.

Sustainability

Sustainability is a term that refers to the use of natural resources in a way that does not reduce or degrade them, so that they are available for future generations. The concept of sustainability is central to an understanding of the nature of interactions between environmental systems and societies. Throughout the book, we look at resource management issues and show that these are essentially ones of sustainability.

Holistic evaluation

The systems approach used throughout the course, as we have already discussed, encourages a holistic appreciation of the complexities of environmental issues. The interaction between environmental systems and societies is central to this holistic approach. The course requires you to consider the costs and the benefits of human activities, both to the environment and to societies, over the short and long term. In doing so, you will arrive at informed personal viewpoints. The book explains how you can justify your own position, and appreciate the views of others, along a continuum of environmental philosophies.

Local and global approaches

This course studies environmental systems and societies at a range of scales from local to global. Inevitably, appreciation of your local environment will enable you to appreciate these issues from a local perspective, through carrying out field-work in nearby ecosystems and research on local issues. Certain issues such as resource and pollution management require a national or regional perspective, and others an international perspective (e.g. global warming) and the book explores all these perspectives in detail. On a broader scale, the course naturally leads us to an appreciation of the nature of the international dimension, since the resolution of the major environmental issues rests heavily on international relationships and agreements – case studies and key facts are used to illustrate these points throughout the book.

Now you are ready to start. Good luck with your studies.

1 SYSTEMS AND MODELS

1.1 Concepts and characteristics of systems

Assessment statements

1.1.1 Outline the concepts and characteristics of systems.
1.1.2 Apply the systems concept on a range of scales.
1.1.3 Define the terms *open system*, *closed system* and *isolated system*.
1.1.4 Describe how the first and second laws of thermodynamics are relevant to environmental systems.
1.1.5 Explain the nature of equilibria.
1.1.6 Define and explain the principles of *positive feedback* and *negative feedback*.
1.1.7 Describe transfer and transformation processes.
1.1.8 Distinguish between flows (inputs and outputs) and storages (stock) in relation to systems.
1.1.9 Construct and analyse quantitative models involving flows and storages in a system.
1.1.10 Evaluate the strengths and limitations of models.

Outline the concepts and characteristics of systems

The title of this course can be divided into three parts – 'environment', 'systems' and 'societies'. Each part can be considered separately or **holistically** (i.e. together). This chapter examines the systems approach to the course, Chapter 2 focuses on ecosystems and the environment, and Chapter 7 on society, although each of these themes can be found throughout the course.

A system is an assemblage of parts and the relationships between them, which together constitute an entity or whole. The interdependent components are connected through the transfer of energy and matter, with all parts linked together and affecting each other. Examples of systems, with increasing levels of complexity, include particles, atoms, molecules, cells, organs, organ systems, communities, ecosystems, biomes, the Earth, the Solar System, galaxies, and the universe.

 A system is an assemblage of parts and the relationships between them, which together constitute an entity or whole.

The systems approach, central to the ESS course, emphasizes similarities in the ways in which matter, energy and information link together in a variety of different disciplines such as ecology, economics, geography, and politics. This approach, therefore, allows different subjects to be looked at in the same way, and for links to be made between them. Although the individual parts of complex systems can be looked at independently, as is often the case in scientific investigations (the reductionist approach), this overlooks the way in which these systems operate as a whole – a holistic approach is necessary to fully understand the way in which they operate together.

 The systems approach gives a holistic view of the issues, whereas the reductionist approach of conventional science is to break the system down into its components and to understand the inter-relations between them. The former describes patterns and models of the whole system, whereas the latter aims at explaining cause-and-effect relationships within it.

Systems consist of:
- storages (of matter or energy)
- flows (inputs into the system, outputs from the system)
- processes (which transfer or transform energy or matter)
- feedback mechanisms that maintain stability and equilibrium.

Using the systems approach, a tree can be summarized as shown in Figure 1.1.

Figure 1.1
Tree system showing storage, inputs and outputs.

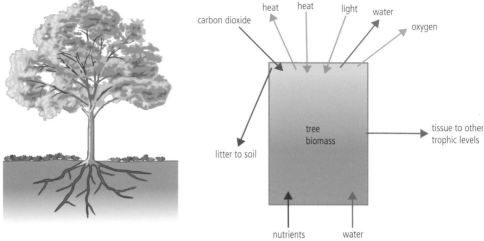

System diagrams consist of:
- boxes which show **storages** – in Figure 1.1, tree biomass (i.e. biological matter)
- arrows which show **flows** – inputs to and outputs from storages.

In addition, the diagram could be labelled with processes on each arrow. Processes in this example would include:
- photosynthesis – transforming carbon dioxide (CO_2), water (H_2O) and light into biomass and oxygen (O_2)
- respiration – transforming biomass into carbon dioxide and water
- diffusion – allowing the movement of nutrients and water into the tree
- consumption – transferring tissue (i.e. biomass) from one trophic level to another.

The ESS course especially focuses on ecosystems, although the same systems approach can be applied to other aspects of the course, including social and value systems, as well as economic systems.

ENVIRONMENTAL PHILOSOPHIES

The systems approach and the reductionist approach used by conventional science use almost identical methodologies: the difference between them may, therefore, be only one of perspective.

The systems concept on a range of scales

Bromeliads are flowering plants that are found in abundance in the canopy and on the floor of rainforest. They capture rainwater which enables a small self-contained ecosystem to exist, containing tree frogs, snails, flatworms, tiny crabs and salamanders. Animals within the bromeliad may spend their entire lives inside the plant.

The systems concept can be applied across a range of scales. We can see this if we look at, for example, an ecosystem. An ecosystem is a biological community of interdependent organisms and the physical environment they inhabit. Different ecosystems exist where different species and physical or climatic environments are found. An ecosystem may, therefore, be of any size up to global. For example, a forest contains lots of small-scale ecosystems, such as the complex web of life that exists within a bromeliad in the canopy of tropical rainforest (see photograph, left, and Global perspective, page 3). The forest itself can be viewed as an ecosystem with particular inputs (e.g. sunlight energy, nutrients and water), outputs (e.g. oxygen, soil litter and water), and stores (e.g. biomass within trees and plants; nutrients within soil). Such ecosystems can be viewed on the local scale (i.e. within one country) or more widely (in many different countries where the same climatic conditions apply). On the global scale, ecosystems due to similar climatic conditions in different parts of the world, are usually called biomes. Examples of different biomes include tundra, tropical rainforest, and desert (Chapter 2, pages 37–43).

At the largest scale, the entire planet could be seen as an ecosystem, with specific energy inputs from the Sun and containing particular physical characteristics. The Gaia hypothesis, formulated by scientist James Lovelock in the mid-1960s, proposes that our planet functions as a single living organism. The hypothesis says that the Earth is a global control system of surface temperature, atmospheric composition and ocean salinity. It proposes that Earth's elements (water, soil, rock, atmosphere, and the living component called the biosphere) are closely integrated to form a complex interacting system that maintains the climatic and biogeochemical conditions on Earth in a preferred homeostasis (i.e. in the balance that best provides the conditions for life on Earth).

To learn more about James Lovelock's Gaia hypothesis, go to www.pearsonhotlinks.com, insert the express code 2630P and click on activity 1.1.

Dendrobates pumilio, the strawberry poison dart frog, is common in the Atlantic lowland tropical forests of Central America, especially Costa Rica. The female typically lays 3 to 5 eggs on the forest floor in a jelly-like mass that keeps them moist. Once the eggs are ready to hatch, one of the parents steps into the jelly surrounding the eggs: the tadpoles respond to the movement and climb onto the parent's back, where they stick to a secretion of mucus. The parent carries the tadpoles up to the canopy where they are deposited in water caught by the upturned leaves of a bromeliad. Each tadpole is put in a separate pool to increase the likelihood that some offspring will survive predators. The bromeliad ecosystem is a vital part of the frog's life-history.

Strawberry poison-dart frog.

Systems can be applied across a range of scales, from global-scale biomes to the small scale of life contained within a bromeliad in the rainforest canopy.

The NASA missions of the 1960s and 1970s produced memorable images of the Earth from space. People had never before seen pictures of the Earth like this; they enabled a greater appreciation of the vulnerability of the planet and its uniqueness within the Solar System and more even within the universe beyond. These images prompted Lovelock to formulate his Gaia hypothesis, named after the Greek supreme goddess of the Earth.

This image of the Earth was taken on the NASA Apollo 17 mission.

To learn more about the origin and use of the systems approach, go to www.pearsonhotlinks. com, insert the express code 2630P and click on activity 1.2.

Open, closed and isolated systems

Systems can be divided into three types, depending on the flow of energy and matter between the system and the surrounding environment.

- Open systems – Both matter and energy are exchanged across the boundaries of the system (Figure 1.2a, overleaf). Open systems are organic (i.e. living) and so must interact with their environment to take in energy and new matter, and to remove wastes (e.g. an ecosystem). People are also open systems in that they must interact with their environment in order to take in food, water, and obtain shelter, and produce waste products.

An isolated system does not exchange matter or energy with its surroundings, and therefore cannot be observed. Is this a useful concept?

Figure 1.2
The exchange of matter (mass) and energy across the boundary of different systems. Open systems (**a**) exchange both; closed systems (**b**) exchange only energy, and isolated systems (**c**) exchange neither.

- Closed systems – Energy but not matter is exchanged across the boundaries of the system (Figure 1.2b). Examples are atoms and molecules, and mechanical systems. The Earth can be seen as a closed system: input = solar radiation (Sun's energy or light), output = heat energy. Matter is recycled within the system. Although space ships and meteorites can be seen as moving a small amount of matter in and out of the Earth system, they are generally discounted. Strictly, closed systems do not occur naturally on Earth, but all the global cycles of matter (e.g. the water and nitrogen cycles) approximate to closed systems.
- Isolated systems – Neither energy nor matter is exchanged across the boundary of the system (Figure 1.2c). These systems do not exist naturally, although it is possible to think of the entire universe as an isolated system.

An open system exchanges both energy and matter with its surroundings, a closed system exchanges energy but not matter, and an isolated system does not exchange anything with its surroundings.

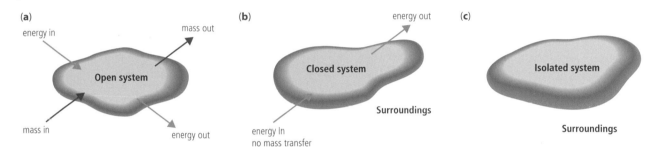

(a)

energy in

mass out

Open system

mass in

energy out

(b)

energy out

Closed system

Surroundings

energy In
no mass transfer

(c)

Isolated system

Surroundings

To learn more about Biosphere II, go to www.pearsonhotlinks.com, insert the express code 2630P and click on activity 1.3.

Systems are hierarchical, and what may be seen as the whole system in one investigation may be seen as only part of another system in a different study (e.g. a human can be seen as a whole system, with inputs of food and water and outputs of waste, or as part of a larger system such as an ecosystem or social system). Difficulties may arise as to where the boundaries are placed, and how this choice is made.

Biosphere II encloses an area equivalent to 2.5 football pitches, and contains five different biomes (ocean with coral reef, mangrove, rainforest, savannah and desert). Further areas explore agricultural systems and human impact on natural systems.

Biosphere II is an experiment to model the Earth as a closed system. It was constructed in Arizona between 1987 and 1991 and enables scientists to study the complex interactions of natural systems (e.g. the constantly changing chemistry of the air, water and soil within the greenhouses), and the possible use of closed biospheres in space colonization. It allows the study and manipulation of a biosphere without harming the Earth. The project is still running and has resulted in numerous scientific papers showing that small, closed ecosystems are complex and vulnerable to unplanned events.

Laws of thermodynamics and environmental systems

Energy exists in a variety of forms (e.g. light, heat, chemical, electrical, and kinetic). It can be changed from one form into another but cannot be created or destroyed. Any form of energy can be converted to any other form, but heat can be converted to other forms only when there is a temperature difference.

The behaviour of energy in systems is defined by the laws of thermodynamics. The first law states that energy can neither be created nor destroyed: it can only change forms. This means that the total energy in any system, including the entire universe, is constant and all that can happen is change in the form the energy takes. This law is known as the 'law of conservation of energy'. In ecosystems, energy enters the system in the form of sunlight energy, is converted into biomass via photosynthesis, passes along food chains as biomass, is consumed, and ultimately leaves the ecosystem in the form of heat. No new energy has been created – it has simply been transformed and passed from one form to another. Heat is released because of the inefficient transfer of energy (as in all other systems).

Available energy is used to do work such as growth, movement, and the assembly of complex molecules. Although the total amount of energy in a system does not change, the amount of available energy does (Figure 1.3). The transformation and transfer of energy is not 100 per cent efficient: in any energy conversion there is less usable energy at the end of the process than at the beginning. This means there is a dissipation of energy which is then not available for work. The second law of thermodynamics states that energy goes from a concentrated form (e.g. the Sun) into a dispersed form (ultimately heat): the availability of energy to do work therefore diminishes and the system becomes increasingly disordered.

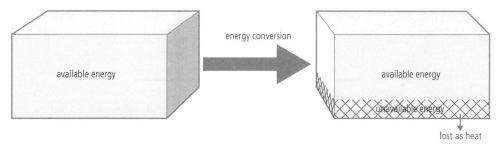

energy conversion

available energy

available energy

unavailable energy

lost as heat

Figure 1.3
The available energy in a system is reduced through inefficient energy conversions. The total amount of energy remains the same, but less is available for work. An increasing quantity of unusable energy is lost from the system as heat (which cannot be recycled into useable energy).

Energy is needed to create order (e.g. to hold complex molecules together). Therefore, as less energy becomes available, disorder (entropy) increases. In any isolated system, entropy tends to increase spontaneously. The universe can be seen as an isolated system in which entropy is steadily increasing so eventually, in billions of years' time, no more available energy will be present. Natural systems can never actually be isolated because there must always be an input of energy for work (to replace energy that is dissipated). The maintenance of order in living systems requires a constant input of energy to replace that lost through the inefficient transfer of energy. Although matter can be recycled, energy cannot, and once it has been lost from a system in the form of heat energy it cannot be made available again.

 The first law of thermodynamics concerns the conservation of energy (i.e. energy can be neither created nor destroyed); whereas the second law explains that energy is lost from systems when work is done, bringing about disorder (entropy).

The nature of equilibria

Open systems tend to have a state of balance among the components of a system – they are in a state of equilibrium. This means that although there may be slight fluctuations in the system, there are no sudden changes and the fluctuations tend to be between closely defined limits. Equilibrium allows systems to return to an original state following disturbance. Two different types of equilibrium are discussed below.

Steady-state equilibrium

A steady-state equilibrium is the common property of most open systems in nature. Despite constant inputs and outputs of energy and matter, the overall stability of the system remains. Fluctuations in the system are around a fixed path, and deviation above or below this path results in a return towards it (Figure 1.4, overleaf).

 Steady-state equilibrium is the common property of most open systems in nature. There is a tendency in natural systems for the equilibrium to return after disturbance, but some systems (e.g. succession) may undergo long-term changes to their equilibrium while keeping their integrity (Chapter 2, page 64).

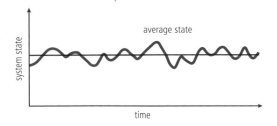

Figure 1.4
The conditions of an open system fluctuate around an average state in steady-state equilibrium.

● **Examiner's hint:**
Most open systems have steady-state equilibrium, where any change to a stable system results in a return to the original equilibrium after the disturbance. This is because there are inputs and outputs of energy and matter to the system that allow this to happen. Static equilibrium does not apply to natural systems as there is no input or output from the system, and no change occurs.

The stability of this form of equilibrium means that the system can return to the steady state following disturbance; for example, the return to closed forest canopy in tropical rainforest following the death of a canopy tree through the process of succession (page 8 and Chapter 2, page 64). Homeostatic mechanisms in animals (e.g. temperature control) maintain body conditions at a steady state – a move away from the steady state results in a return to equilibrium. The term 'dynamic equilibrium' is sometimes used to describe this phenomenon, but is not used in this course.

Static equilibrium

In **static equilibrium**, there are no inputs or outputs of matter or energy and no change in the system over time (Figure 1.5).

Figure 1.5
Static equilibrium.

Inanimate objects such as a chair or table are in static equilibrium. No natural systems are in static equilibrium because all have inputs and outputs of energy and matter.

Stable and unstable equilibrium

If a system returns to the original equilibrium after a disturbance, it is said to be **stable** (Figure 1.6a and b). Systems that do not return to the same equilibrium but form a new equilibrium are described as **unstable** (Figure 1.7a and b).

Figure 1.6
(a) Disturbance to the system results in it returning to its original equilibrium.
(b) Immediately following disturbance, conditions may be very different in the system, but eventually return to the original equilibrium.

Figure 1.7
(a) Disturbance results in a new equilibrium very different from the first (in this case the object lying horizontally rather than standing vertically).
(b) Scientists believe that the Earth's climate may reach a new equilibrium following the effects of global warming, with conditions on the planet dramatically altered.

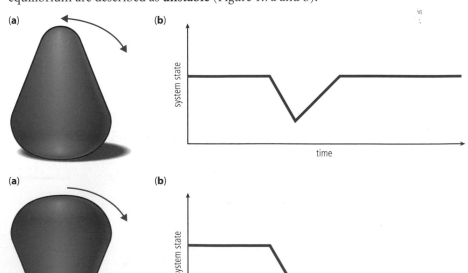

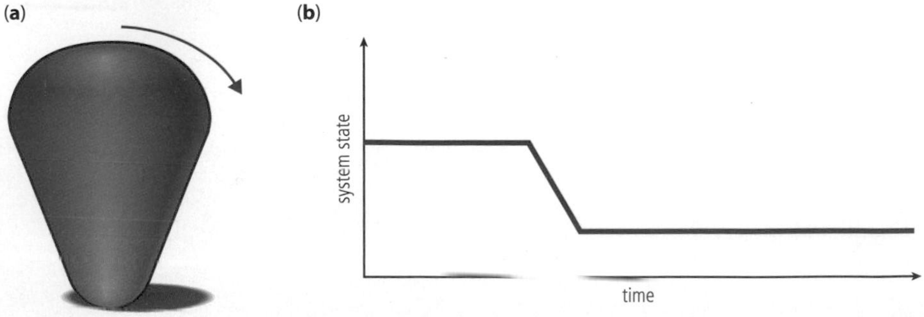

Positive and negative feedback

Homeostatic systems in animals require feedback mechanisms to return them to their original steady state. This is also true of all other systems. Such mechanisms allow systems to self-regulate (Figure 1.8). Feedback loops can be positive or negative.

Figure 1.8
Changes to the processes in a system lead to changes in the level of output. This feeds back to affect the level of input.

Positive feedback

Positive feedback occurs when a change in the state of a system leads to additional and increased change. Thus, an increase in the size of one or more of the system's outputs feeds back into the system and results in self-sustained change that alters the state of a system away from its original equilibrium towards instability (Figure 1.9). For example, increased temperature through global warming melts more of the ice in the polar ice caps and glaciers, leading to a decrease in the Earth's albedo (reflection from the Earth's surface) – the Earth absorbs more of the Sun's energy which makes the temperature increase even more, melting more ice. Exponential population growth is also an example of positive feedback.

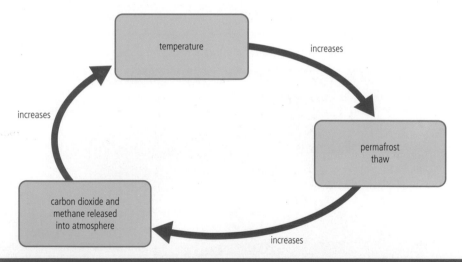

Figure 1.9
A positive feedback mechanism enhancing climate change. Such mechanisms are often linked to tipping points (i.e. the point at which the system actually becomes unstable and forms a new equilibrium).

CASE STUDY

Humans, resources and space

Human population is growing at an ever-increasing rate – more people on the planet produce more children (positive feedback) and the rate will continue to increase as long as there are sufficient resources available to support the population. Human population is growing exponentially, which means that growth rate is proportional to its present size.

Some 2000 years ago, the Earth's population was about 300 million people. Today, it is 6.8 billion. It took the human population thousands of years to reach 1 billion, which it did in 1804. However, it took only 123 years to double to 2 billion in 1927. The population doubled again to 4 billion in 1974 (after only 47 years), and if it continues at the current rate it will reach 8 billion in 2028. Doubling from our present count of 6.8 billion to 13.6 billion will have a much greater impact than previous doublings due to the increased discrepancy between the potential food supply (arithmetic growth) and population size (geometric growth).

Negative feedback

Negative feedback mechanisms work by reducing the effect of one of the system's components. This is a self-regulating method of control leading to the maintenance of a steady-state equilibrium. For example, increase in the temperature of the human body results in increased sweat release and vasodilation, thus evaporation of sweat from the skin increases. This cools the body and returns it to its original equilibrium. Similarly, increased release of carbon dioxide through the burning of fossil fuels leads to enhanced plant growth through increased photosynthesis. This reduces atmospheric levels of carbon dioxide. Negative feedback mechanisms are therefore stabilizing forces within systems. They counteract deviation. Consider, for example, the effects of a storm on a rainforest. If high winds blow down a tree, leaving a gap in the canopy, more light is let in to the forest floor. This encourages new growth: rates of growth are rapid as light levels are high, so new saplings compete to take the place of the old tree in the canopy and equilibrium is restored.

CASE STUDY

The snowshoe hare and the lynx

Predator–prey relationships demonstrate negative feedback. The lynx lives in the boreal forest of North America (Canada) and feeds on the snowshoe hare. The data in Figure 1.10 are based on skins (pelts) traded by trappers of both animals, recorded by the Hudson Bay Company over a period of almost a century. It is reasonable to assume that success in trapping each species was approximately proportional to the numbers of that species in the wild at any given time. The graph shows fluctuations in population density over time for both species. Increases in hare density, when predator numbers are low, result in more food for the lynx, whose numbers then increase. Over-hunting of the hare by the lynx leads to a reduction in hare numbers and then a corresponding drop in predator density. The cycle then repeats. There is a lag in the feedback links – this is true of all feedback mechanisms as it takes time for the system to respond to change.

Figure 1.10
Predator–prey relationship between snowshoe hare and lynx.

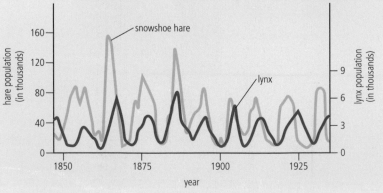

Feedback refers to the return of part of the output from a system as input, so as to affect succeeding outputs. There are two type of feedback.
- Negative – Feedback that tends to damp down, neutralize or counteract any deviation from an equilibrium, and promotes stability.
- Positive – Feedback that amplifies or increases change; it leads to exponential deviation away from an equilibrium.

A system may contain both negative and positive feedback loops resulting in different effects within the system (Figure 1.11).

 For an overview of positive and negative feedback, go to www.pearsonhotlinks. com, insert the express code 2630P and click on activity 1.4.

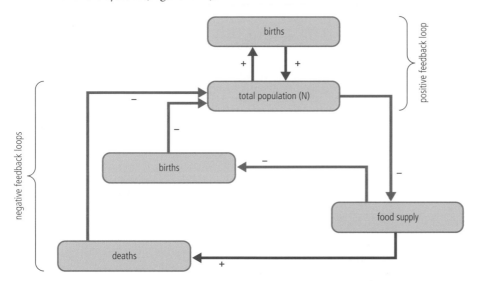

◀ **Figure 1.11**
Population control in animal populations contains both negative and positive feedback loops.

EXERCISES

1   How does the systems approach differ from that of conventional science? What are the advantages of the systems approach compared to the conventional approach?

2   Draw a table comparing and contrasting open, closed and isolated systems. Comparisons should be in terms of the exchange of matter and energy with their surroundings. Give examples for each.

3   Summarize the first and second laws of thermodynamics. What do they tell us about how energy moves through a system?

4   What is the difference between a steady-state equilibrium and a static equilibrium? Which type of equilibrium applies to ecological systems and why?

5   **(a)** When would a system not return to the original equilibrium, but establish a new one? Give an example and explain why this is the case.

   (b) Give an example of a system that undergoes long-term change to its equilibrium while retaining the integrity of the system.

● **Examiner's hint:**
Negative feedback counteracts deviation in a system and returns it to equilibrium, for example predator–prey relationships. Positive feedback accelerates deviation away from the equilibrium, for example the exponential growth of populations. Both positive and negative feedback links involve time lags.

Transfers and transformation processes

Matter and energy move through systems. If the movement does not involve a change of form or state, it is called a **transfer**; if it does involve a change of form or state, it is called a **transformation**. Both types of movement use energy: transfers are simpler so they use less energy and are more efficient than transformations.

Transfers normally flow through a system and involve a change in location. For example, energy flows from one trophic level to the next through consumption of biomass.

Transformations either lead to an interaction within a system in the formation of a new end product, or they involve a change of state. Using water as an example, run-off is a transfer process and evaporation is a transformation process. In decay processes, dead organic matter entering a lake is an example of a transfer process; decomposition of this material is a transformation process. Energy is transformed in ecosystems: solar energy is transformed into chemical energy by photosynthesis and from chemical energy to kinetic and heat energy by respiration.

 ● **Transfers** normally flow through a system and involve a change in location.
● **Transformations** lead to an interaction within a system in the formation of a new end product, or involve a change of state.

For an online quiz on the transfers and transformations of the water cycle, go to www.pearsonhotlinks.com, insert the express code 2630P and click on activity 1.5.

Examples of transfers

- Movement of material through living organisms (biomass being passed on as consumers eat organisms further down the food chain).
- Movement of material in a non-living process (precipitation and water-flow from surface water to groundwater storage in the water cycle).
- Movement of energy (energy re-radiating from greenhouse gases in the atmosphere; radiating from a warm body into a cooler atmosphere).

Examples of transformations

- Matter transformations – Amino acids converted to proteins; glucose converted to starch or glycogen.
- Energy transformations – Ultraviolet light reflected from the Earth's surface as infrared light.
- Energy-to-matter transformations – Photosynthesis in plants converting sunlight energy with carbon dioxide and water into glucose.
- Matter-to-energy transformations – Respiration breaking down glucose into water, carbon dioxide and energy.

Inputs and outputs from systems are called flows and are represented by arrows in system diagrams. The stock held within a system is called the storage and is represented by boxes.

The systems approach follows a standard protocol, using storages and flows. What are the benefits of using this framework, which is common to other disciplines such as economics and sociology?

Flows and storage

Both energy and matter flow through a system in the form of inputs or outputs. Sometimes both energy and matter are stored in the form of stocks or reservoirs. In ecosystems, energy is input in the form of sunlight energy, transformed by photosynthesis to form chemical bonds, and then output as heat energy following respiration. Matter flows from one trophic level to the next through consumption of tissues and is recycled through decomposition and decay.

The relative sizes of flows and storages can be shown in diagrams, for example the width of arrows can be made proportional with wider arrows representing greater flows.

Ecosystems may have several stores linked by many flows. Carbon, for example, is continually cycled between land, oceans, and the atmosphere.

Models and flows of storage

A model is a simplified description designed to show the structure or workings of an object system or concept. Models can be used to illustrate the flows, storages and linkages within ecosystems (Figure 1.12).

Figure 1.12
Models of ecosystems are simplified versions of reality. They can reveal much about the underlying processes in the ecosystem and show key linkages, but they are unable to show much of the complexity present within the real system.

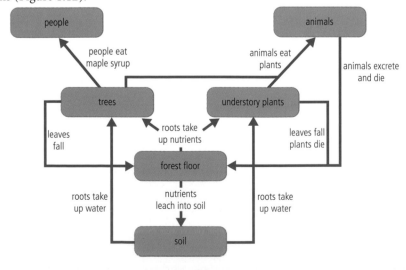

The arrows in food chains represent energy flow. Different shapes can be used to represent the energy source, producer, and consumers. Energy is dissipated (lost) along the food chain as species at each trophic level are using some of the energy for respiration and are releasing heat as a by-product (waste) to the environment. Thus, as energy is passed along a food chain, the amount of available energy decreases.

The models in Figure 1.13 offer information about the different systems by drawing flows and stores proportionally (e.g. biomass store is larger in the woodland; litter store is larger in the woodland; and there is a large output in mixed farming due to the harvested crops and livestock). The diagrams also show that legumes and fertilizers are additional inputs in mixed farming. Extra value can be given to models, even simple ones, by showing data quantitatively.

A model is a simplified description designed to show the structure or workings of an object, system or concept.

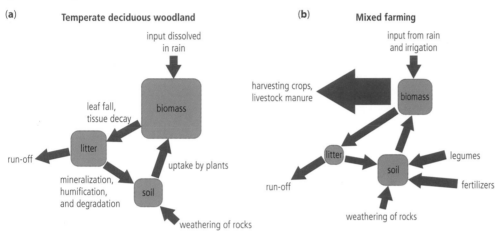

(a) Temperate deciduous woodland

input dissolved in rain

leaf fall, tissue decay

biomass

litter

run-off

uptake by plants

mineralization, humification, and degradation

soil

weathering of rocks

(b) Mixed farming

input from rain and irrigation

harvesting crops, livestock manure

biomass

litter

soil

run-off

legumes

fertilizers

weathering of rocks

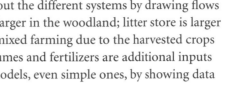

Figure 1.13
Nutrient cycles for **(a)** a temperate deciduous woodland and **(b)** for an area nearby where the woodland has been cleared for mixed farming. Biomass is all the living material in the ecosystem. Arrows are proportional to the amount of energy present (i.e. larger arrows show greater energy flow than smaller ones).

Evaluation of models

Models may be in the form of practical examples such as an aquarium or terrarium, computer models, or diagrams. Although they are meant to represent real systems, in practice some models require approximation techniques to be used. For example, predictive models of weather systems may give very different results. In contrast, an aquarium may be a relatively simple ecosystem but demonstrates many ecological concepts.

All models have positive and negative attributes. Let's consider the complex computer simulations used by scientists to model the effects of changes in the temperature of the Earth, and that can demonstrate anticipated changes to climate based on carbon emissions.

The advantages of these models are:
- they allow scientists to predict and simplify complex systems
- inputs can be changed and outcomes examined without having to wait for real events
- results can be shown to other scientists and to the public.

Disadvantages of such models are:
- they may not be accurate – climate models are hugely complex in terms of numbers of factors involved in atmospheric systems, accuracy is lost in the process of oversimplification
- they rely on the expertise of the people making them
- different people may interpret them in different ways
- vested interests may hijack them politically
- any model is only as good as the data that goes in and these may be suspect
- different models may show different effects using the same data.

In particular, the complexity and oversimplification of climate models has led to criticism of these models.

 To access worksheet 1.1 on terminology, please visit www.pearsonbacconline.com and follow the on-screen instructions.

 To learn more about the advantages and limitations of climate change models, go to www.pearsonhotlinks.com, insert the express code 2630P and click on activity 1.6.

Read the International Panel on Climate Change's evaluation of climate models. You can visit the website by going to www.pearsonhotlinks.com. Insert the express code 2630P and click on activity 1.7.

● **Examiner's hint:**
The need for models to summarize complex systems requires approximation techniques to be used: these can lead to loss of information and oversimplification. The advantage of models is that they can clearly illustrate links between parts of the system, and give a clear overview of complex interrelationships.

EXERCISES

1 What is the difference between negative and positive feedback? What characteristic is common to both mechanisms?

2 Give an environmental example of positive feedback. Draw a diagram to explain the inter-relationships within the feedback loop. Now do the same for an example of negative feedback.

3 What is meant by transfer within a system? How does this differ from transformation processes?

4 Draw a systems diagram showing the inputs, outputs and storages of a tree.

5 Draw a table listing the strengths and weaknesses of models. Your table could summarize the issues regarding one particular model (e.g. climate change) or be more generally applicable.

PRACTICE QUESTIONS

1 The graph below shows the interdependence of population size of two species of mites. *Eotetranychus sexmaculatus* serves as the food supply for *Typholodromus occidentalis*.

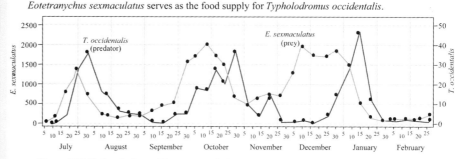

Eotetranychus sexmaculatus serves as the food supply for *Typholodromus occidentalis*.

[Source: W B Clapham Jr, *National Ecosystems*, 2nd edition, (1983), Macmillan Publishing Company, page 124 reprinted form C B Huffaker (1958), *Hilgardia*, **27**, pages 343-383]

(a) Predict when the next population maximum of *T. occidentalis* will occur. Show your working. [2]

(b) Determine the numbers of both *T. occidentalis* and *E. sexmaculatus* on September 30. [1]

(c) (i) Identify the five-day period for which the rate of increase of *E. sexmaculatus* is at its maximum. [1]

(ii) Determine when the difference in numbers between both populations is at a maximum. [1]

(d) (i) Calculate the time lag between the maximums of both species in the period from October 5 through to November 5. [1]

(ii) Suggest a reason for this time lag. [1]

(e) (i) Describe the role that negative feedback might play in this species interaction. [2]

(ii) Explain why the global human population is less prone to negative feedback control than other organisms. [3]

(f) Outline **two** examples of feedback in global warming. [2]

© International Baccalaureate Organization [2004]

2 **(a)** State the first law of thermodynamics. [1]

  (b) Calculate the amount of enrgy output in the model below. [2]

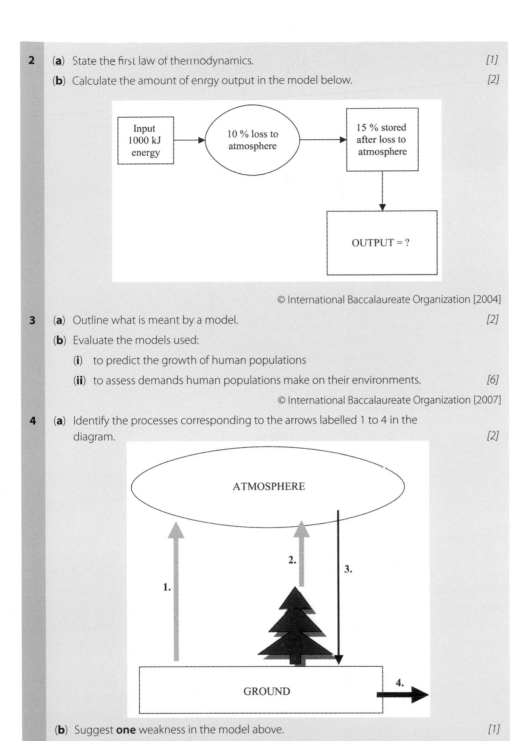

© International Baccalaureate Organization [2004]

3 **(a)** Outline what is meant by a model. [2]

  (b) Evaluate the models used:

  (i) to predict the growth of human populations

  (ii) to assess demands human populations make on their environments. [6]

© International Baccalaureate Organization [2007]

4 **(a)** Identify the processes corresponding to the arrows labelled 1 to 4 in the diagram. [2]

  (b) Suggest **one** weakness in the model above. [1]

© International Baccalaureate Organization [2004]

5 **(a)** Define the following terms

  (i) *negative feedback*

  (ii) *positive feedback*. [2]

  (b) Suggest why most ecosystems are negative feedback systems. [1]

● **Examiner's hint:**
When identifying stores within an ecosystem, specific answers are needed; for example; biomass within trees and plants / nutrient within soil, *not* just 'trees' or 'soil'. The item stored must be identified.

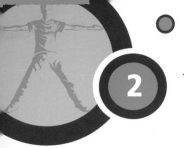

THE ECOSYSTEM

Structure

Biotic and abiotic components

Biotic refers to the living components within an ecosystem (the community). **Abiotic** refers to the non-living factors of the ecosystem (the environment).

Ecosystems consist of living and non-living components. Organisms (animals, plants, algae, fungi and bacteria) are the organic or living part of the ecosystem. The physical environment (light, air, water, temperature, minerals, soil and climatic aspects) constitute the non-living part. The living parts of an ecosystem are called the **biotic** components and the non-living parts the **abiotic** (not biotic) components. Abiotic factors include the soil (edaphic factors) and topography (the landscape). Biotic and non-biotic components interact to sustain the ecosystem. The word 'environment' refers specifically to the non-living part of the ecosystem.

To find links to hundreds of environmental sites, go to www.pearsonhotlinks.com, insert the express code 2630P and click on activity 2.1.

To learn more about all things environmental, go to www.pearsonhotlinks.com, insert the express code 2630P and click on activity 2.2.

Trophic levels, food chains and food webs

The term 'trophic level' refers to the feeding level within a food chain. Food webs are made from many interconnecting food chains

Certain organisms in an ecosystem convert abiotic components into living matter. These are the **producers**; they support the ecosystem by producing new biological matter (biomass) (Figure 2.1). Organisms that cannot make their own food eat other organisms to obtain energy and matter. They are **consumers**. The flow of energy and matter from organism to organism can be shown in a food chain. The position that an organism occupies in a food chain is called the trophic level (Figure 2.2). Trophic level can also mean the position in the food chain occupied by a group of organisms in a community.

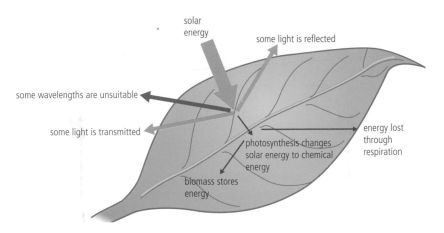

Figure 2.1
Producers covert sunlight energy into chemical energy using photosynthetic pigments. The food produced supports the rest of the food chain.

solar energy

some light is reflected

some wavelengths are unsuitable

some light is transmitted

photosynthesis changes solar energy to chemical energy

energy lost through respiration

biomass stores energy

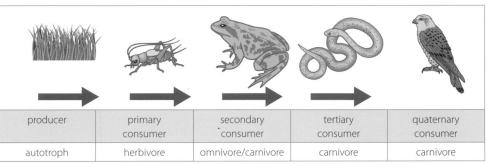

Figure 2.2
A food chain. Ecosystems contain many food chains.

producer	primary consumer	secondary consumer	tertiary consumer	quaternary consumer
autotroph	herbivore	omnivore/carnivore	carnivore	carnivore

Ecosystems contain many interconnected food chains that form food webs. There are a variety of ways of showing food webs, and they may include **decomposers** which feed on the dead biomass created by the ecosystem (Figure 2.3). The producer in this food web for the North Sea is phytoplankton (microscopic algae), the primary consumers (**herbivores**) are zooplankton (microscopic animal life), the secondary consumers (**carnivores**) include jellyfish, sand eels, and herring (each on different food chains), and the tertiary consumers (top carnivores) are mackerel, seals, seabirds and dolphins (again on different food chains).

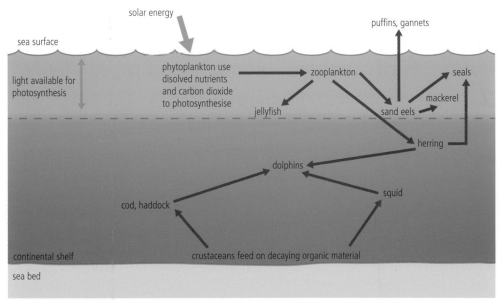

Figure 2.3
A simplified food web for the North Sea in Europe.

solar energy

sea surface

light available for photosynthesis

phytoplankton use disolved nutrients and carbon dioxide to photosynthesise

zooplankton

puffins, gannets

seals

mackerel

jellyfish

sand eels

herring

dolphins

squid

cod, haddock

crustaceans feed on decaying organic material

continental shelf

sea bed

Diagrams of food webs can be used to estimate knock-on effects of changes to the ecosystem. During the 1970s, sand eels were harvested and used as animal feed, for fishmeal and for oil and food on salmon farms: Figure 2.3 can be used to explain what impacts a

Food chains always begin with the producers (usually photosynthetic organisms), followed by primary consumers (herbivores), secondary consumers (omnivores or carnivores) and then higher consumers (tertiary, quaternary, etc.). Decomposers feed at every level of the food chain.

● **Examiner's hint:**
You will need to find an example of a food chain from your local area, with named examples of producers, consumers, decomposers, herbivores, carnivores, and top carnivores.

▶ Stromatolites were the earliest producers on the planet and are still here. These large aggregations of cyanobacteria can be found in the fossil record and alive in locations such as Western Australia and Brazil.

Pyramids are graphical models showing the quantitative differences between the tropic levels of an ecosystem. There are three types.
● Pyramid of numbers – This records the number of individuals at each trophic level.
● Pyramid of biomass – This represents the biological mass of the standing stock at each trophic level at a particular point in time.
● Pyramid of productivity – This shows the flow of energy (i.e. the rate at which the stock is being generated) through each trophic level

dramatic reduction in the number of sand eels might have on the rest of the ecosystem. Sand eels are the only source of food for mackerel, puffin and gannet, so numbers of these species may decline or they may have to switch food source. Similarly, seals will have to rely more on herring, possibly reducing their numbers or they may also have to switch food source. The amount of zooplankton may increase, improving food supply for jellyfish and herring.

An estimated 1000 kg of plant plankton are needed to produce 100 kg of animal plankton. The animal plankton is in turn consumed by 10 kg of fish, which is the amount needed by a person to gain 1 kg of body mass. Biomass and energy decline at each successive trophic level so there is a limit to the number of trophic levels which can be supported in an ecosystem. Energy is lost as heat (produced as a waste product of **respiration**) at each stage in the food chain, so only energy stored in biomass is passed on to the next trophic level. Thus, after 4 or 5 trophic stages, there is not enough energy to support another stage.

The earliest forms of life on Earth, 3.8 billion years ago, were consumers feeding on organic material formed by interactions between the atmosphere and the land surface. Producers appeared around 3 billion years ago – these were photosynthetic bacteria and their photosynthesis led to a dramatic increase in the amount of oxygen in the atmosphere. The oxygen enabled organisms that used aerobic respiration to generate the large amounts of energy they needed. And, eventually, complex ecosystems followed.

Pyramids of numbers, biomass and productivity

Pyramids are graphical models of the quantitative differences that exist between the trophic levels of a single ecosystem. These models provide a better understanding of the workings of an ecosystem by showing the feeding relationship in a community.

Pyramids of numbers

The numbers of producers and consumers coexisting in an ecosystem can be shown by counting the numbers of organisms in an ecosystem and constructing a pyramid. Quantitative data for each trophic level are drawn to scale as horizontal bars arranged symmetrically around a central axis (Figure 2.4a). Sometimes, rather than counting every individual in a trophic level, limited collections may be done in a specific area and this multiplied up to the total area of the ecosystem. **Pyramids of numbers** are not always pyramid shaped; for example, in a woodland ecosystem with many insect herbivores feeding on trees, there are bound to be fewer trees than insects; this means the pyramid is inverted (upside-down) as in Figure 2.4b. This situation arises when the size of individuals at lower trophic levels are relatively large. Pyramids of numbers, therefore, have limitations in showing useful feeding relationships.

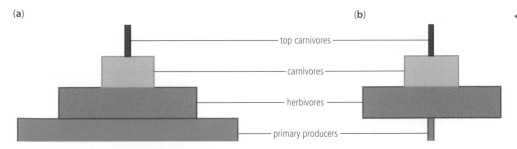

top carnivores

carnivores

herbivores

primary producers

Figure 2.4
Pyramids of numbers. **(a)** A typical pyramid where the number of producers is high. **(b)** A limitation of number pyramids is that they are inverted when the number of producers is fewer than the number of herbivores.

Pyramids of biomass

A **pyramid of biomass** quantifies the amount of biomass present at each trophic level at a certain point in time, and represents the standing stock of each trophic level measured in units such as grams of biomass per metre squared ($g\,m^{-2}$). Biomass may also be measured in units of energy, such as joules per metre squared ($J\,m^{-2}$). Following the second law of thermodynamics, there is a tendency for numbers and quantities of biomass and energy to decrease along food chains so the pyramids become narrower towards the top.

Although pyramids of biomass are usually pyramid shaped, they can sometimes be inverted and show greater quantities at higher trophic levels. This is because, as with pyramids of numbers, they represent the biomass present at a given time (i.e. they are a snap-shot of the ecosystem). The standing crop biomass (the biomass taken at a certain point in time) gives no indication of productivity over time. For example, a fertile intensively grazed pasture may have a lower standing crop biomass of grass but a higher productivity than a less fertile ungrazed pasture (the fertile pasture has biomass constantly removed by herbivores). This results in an inverted pyramid of biomass. In a pond ecosystem, the standing crop of phytoplankton (the major producers) at any given point will be lower than the mass of the consumers, such as fish and insects, as the phytoplankton reproduce very quickly. Inverted pyramids may also be the result of marked seasonal variations.

Both pyramids of numbers and pyramids of biomass represent storages.

Pyramids of productivity

The turnover of two retail outlets cannot be compared by simply comparing the goods displayed on the shelves, because the rates at which the goods are sold and the shelves are restocked also need to be known. The same is true of ecosystems. Pyramids of biomass simply represent the momentary stock, whereas pyramids of productivity show the rate at which that stock is being generated.

Pyramids of productivity take into account the rate of production over a period of time because each level represents energy per unit area per unit time. Biomass is measured in units of mass ($g\,m^{-2}$) or energy ($J\,m^{-2}$) as opposed to the more useful measurement of productivity in units of flow, mass or energy per metre squared per year ($g\,m^{-2}\,yr^{-1}$ or $J\,m^{-2}\,yr^{-1}$). Pyramids of productivity refer to the flow of energy through a trophic level and invariably show a decrease along the food chain. There are no inverted pyramids. The relative energy flow within an ecosystem can be studied, and different ecosystems can be compared. Pyramids of productivity also overcome the problem that two species may not have the same energy content per unit weight: in these cases, biomass is misleading but energy flow is directly comparable.

Pyramid structure and ecosystem functioning

Because energy is lost through food chains, top carnivores are at risk from disturbance further down the food chain. If there is a reduction in the numbers of producers or primary consumers, existence of the top carnivores can be put at risk if there are not enough organisms (and therefore energy and biomass) to support them. Top carnivores may be the first population to noticeably suffer through ecosystem disruption.

A snow leopard. ▶

CASE STUDY

Snow leopards are found in the mountain ranges of Central Asia. They feed on wild sheep and goats. Effects lower down the food chain threaten this top carnivore. Overgrazing of the mountain grasslands by farmed animals leaves less food for the snow leopard's main prey: with less food for the wild sheep and goats, fewer of these animals are available for the snow leopard, which puts its existence at risk. The snow leopard has little choice but to prey on the domestic livestock in order to survive. But this leads the herdsmen to attack and kill the snow leopards.

The total wild population of the snow leopard is estimated at between 4100 and 6600 individuals, and they have now been designated as endangered by the International Union for Conservation of Nature (IUCN).

Top carnivores can also be put at risk through other interferences in the food chain. Suppose a farmer uses pesticides to improve the crop yield and to maximize profits. Today's pesticides break down naturally and lose their toxic properties (i.e. they are biodegradable), but this was not always the case. In the past, pesticides weren't biodegradable, and they had serious knock-on effects for ecosystems. Figure 2.5 shows the effect of the very effective non-biodegradable pesticide **DDT** on food chains. The producers, the algae and plants or grass (first accumulators) take in the DDT. The first trophic level (the primary consumers) eat the DDT-containing producers and retain the pesticide in their body tissue (mainly in fat) – this is called **bioaccumulation**. The process continues up the food chain with more and more DDT being accumulated at each level. The top carnivores (humans, at level 6 in the aquatic food chain or level 3 in the terrestrial chain) are the final destination of the pesticide (ultimate accumulators).

To watch animations and learn more about ecological pyramids, go to www.pearsonhotlinks.com, insert the express code 2630P and click on activity 2.3.

Figure 2.5 ▶
Simple food chains showing the accumulation of the non-biodegradable pesticide, DDT.

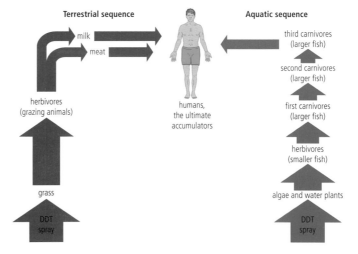

The pesticide accumulates in body fat and is not broken down. Each successive trophic level supports fewer organisms, so the pesticide becomes increasingly concentrated in the tissues (this is called **biomagnification**). Organisms higher in the food chain also have progressively longer life spans so they have more time to accumulate more of the toxin by eating many DDT-containing individuals from lower levels. Top carnivores are therefore at risk from DDT poisoning.

Species, populations, habitats and niches

Ecological terms are precisely defined and may vary from the everyday use of the same words. Definitions for key terms are given below.

Species

A species is defined as a group of organisms that interbreed and produce fertile offspring. If two species breed together to produce a hybrid, this may survive to adulthood but cannot produce viable gametes and so is sterile. An example of this is when a horse (*Equus caballus*) breeds with a donkey (*Equus asinus*) to produce a sterile mule.

The species concept cannot:
- identify whether geographically isolated populations belong to the same species
- classify species in extinct populations
- account for asexually reproducing organisms
- clearly define species when barriers to reproduction are incomplete (Figure 2.6).

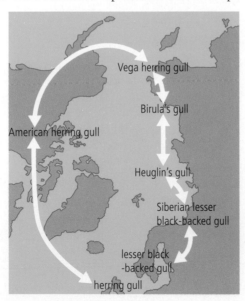

Population

A population is defined in ecology as a group of organisms of the same species living in the same area at the same time, and which are capable of interbreeding.

The species concept is sometimes difficult to apply: for example, can it be used accurately to describe extinct animals and fossils? The term is also sometimes loosely applied to what are, in reality, sub-species that can interbreed. This is an example of an apparently simple term that is difficult to apply in practical situations.

Figure 2.6
Gulls interbreeding in a ring around the Arctic are an example of ring species. Neighbouring species can interbreed to produce viable hybrids but herring gulls and lesser black-backed gulls, at the ends of the ring, cannot interbreed.

Habitat

Habitat refers to the environment in which a species normally lives. For example, the habitat of wildebeest is the savannah and temperate grasslands of eastern and south-eastern Africa.

Wildebeest in their habitat. ▶

- Species – A group of organisms that interbreed and produce fertile offspring.
- Population – A group of organisms of the same species living in the same area at the same time, and which are capable of interbreeding.
- Habitat – The environment in which a species normally lives.
- Niche – Where and how a species lives. A species' share of a habitat and the resources in it.
- Community – A group of populations living and interacting with each other in a common habitat.
- Ecosystem – A community of interdependent organisms and the physical environment they inhabit.

To access worksheet 2.1 on mini-ecosystems, please visit www. pearsonbacconline.com and follow the on-screen instructions.

Niche

An ecological niche is best be described as where, when and how an organism lives. An organism's niche depends not only on where it lives (its habitat) but also on what it does. For example, the niche of a zebra includes all the information about what defines this species: its habitat, courtship displays, grooming, alertness at water holes, when it is active, interactions between predators and similar activities. No two different species can have the same niche because the niche completely defines a species.

Community

A community is a group of populations living and interacting with each other in a common habitat. This contrasts with the term 'population' which refers to just *one* species. The grasslands of Africa contain wildebeest, lions, hyenas, giraffes and elephants as well as zebras. Communities include all biotic parts of the ecosystem, both plants and animals.

Ecosystem

An ecosystem is a community of interdependent organisms (the biotic component) and the physical environment (the abiotic component) they inhabit.

Population interactions

Ecosystems contain numerous populations with complex interactions between them. The nature of the interactions varies and can be broadly divided into four types (**competition**, **predation**, **parasitism** and **mutualism**), each of which is discussed below.

Competition

When resources are limiting, populations are bound to compete in order to survive. This competition can be either within a species (**intraspecific competition**) or between different species (**interspecific competition**). Interspecific competition exists when the niches of different species overlap (Figure 2.7). No two species can occupy the same niche, so the degree to which niches overlap determines the degree of interspecific competition. In this relationship, neither species benefit, although better competitors suffer less.

● **Examiner's hint:**
You must be able to define the terms *species, population, habitat, niche, community* and *ecosystem* and apply them to examples from your local area.

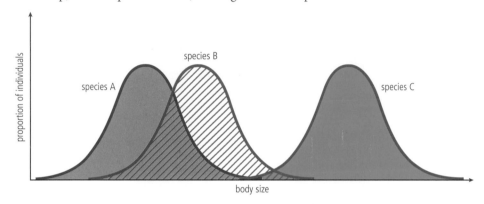

◀ **Figure 2.7**
The niches of species A and species B, based on body size, overlap with each other to a greater extent than with species C. Strong interspecific competition will exist between species A and B but not with species C.

Experiments with single-celled animals have demonstrated the principle of competitive exclusion: if two species occupying similar niches are grown together, the poorer competitor will be eliminated (Figure 2.8).

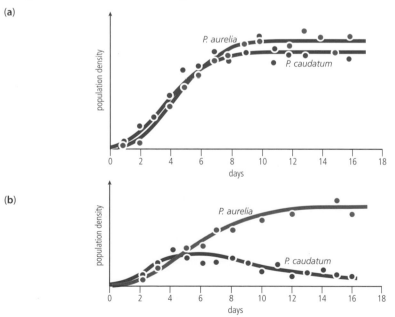

◀ **Figure 2.8**
Species of *Paramecium* can easily be gown in the laboratory. **(a)** If two species with very similar resource needs (i.e. similar niches) are grown separately, both can survive and flourish. **(b)** If the two species are grown in a mixed culture, the superior competitor – in this case *P. aurelia* – will eliminate the other.

Individuals within the same species occupy the same niche. Thus, if resources become limiting for a population, intraspecific competition becomes stronger.

Predation

Predation occurs when one animal (or, occasionally, a plant) hunts and eats another animal. These predator–prey interactions are often controlled by negative feedback mechanisms that control population densities (e.g. the snowshoe hare and lynx, page 8).

Nepenthes rajah, the largest pitcher plant, can hold up to 3.5 litres of water in the pitcher and has been known to trap and digest small mammals such as rats. *Nepenthes rajah* is endemic to Mount Kinabalu where it lives between 1500 and 2650 m above sea level (pages 66–67).

Not all predators are animals. Insectivorous plants, such as the Venus fly traps and pitcher plants trap insects and feed on them. Such plants often live in areas with nitrate-poor soils and obtain much of their nitrogen from animal protein.

Parasitism

In this relationship, one organism (the parasite) benefits at the expense of another (the host) from which it derives food. Ectoparasites live on the surface of their host (e.g. ticks and mites); endoparasites live inside their host (e.g. tapeworms). Some plant parasites draw food from the host via their roots.

Rafflesia have the largest flowers in the world but no leaves. Without leaves, they cannot photosynthesize, so they grow close by South-East Asian vines (*Tetrastigma* spp.) from which they draw the sugars they need for growth.

Mutualism

Symbiosis is a relationship in which two organisms live together (parasitism is a form of symbiosis where one of the organisms is harmed). Mutualism is a symbiotic relationship in which both species benefit. Examples include coral reefs and lichens. Coral reefs show a symbiotic relationship between the coral animal (polyp) and zooxanthellae (unicellular brown algae or dinoflagellates) that live within the coral polyp (Figure 2.9).

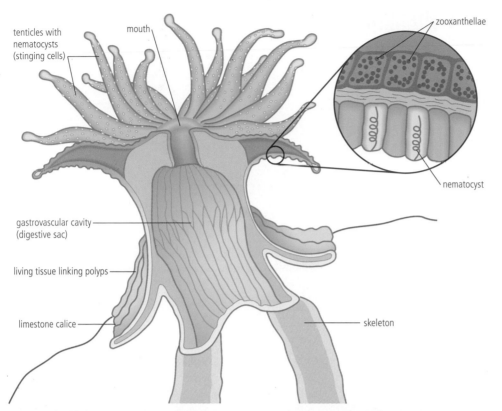

tenticles with nematocysts (stinging cells)

mouth

zooxanthellae

nematocyst

gastrovascular cavity (digestive sac)

living tissue linking polyps

limestone calice

skeleton

Figure 2.9
The zooxanthellae living within the polyp animal photosynthesize to produce food for themselves and the coral polyp, and in return are protected.

Mutualism is a symbiotic relationship in which both species benefit.

Parasitism is a symbiotic relationship in which one species benefits at the expense of the other.

Lichens consist of a fungus and alga in a symbiotic relationship. The fungus is efficient at absorbing water but cannot photosynthesize, whereas the alga contains photosynthetic pigments and so can use sunlight energy to convert carbon dioxide and water into glucose. The alga therefore obtains water and shelter, and the fungus obtains a source of sugar from the relationship. Lichens with different colours contain algae with different photosynthetic pigments.

EXERCISES

1   Define the terms *species*, *population*, *habitat*, *niche*, *community*, and *ecosystem*. What is the difference between a habitat and a niche? Can different species occupy the same niche?

2   What is the difference between mutualism and parasitism? Give examples of each.

3   The abundance of one species can affect the abundance of another. Give an ecological example of this, and explain how the predator affects the abundance of the prey, and vice versa. Are population numbers generally constant in nature? If not, what implications does this have for the measurement of wild population numbers?

2.2 Measuring abiotic components of the system

Measuring abiotic components

Ecosystems can be broadly divided into three types.
- Marine – The sea, estuaries, salt marshes and mangroves are all characterized by the high salt content of the water.
- Freshwater – Rivers, lakes and wetlands.
- Terrestrial – Land-based.

Each ecosystem has its own specific abiotic factors (listed below) as well as the ones they share.

Abiotic factors of a marine ecosystem:
- salinity
- pH
- temperature
- dissolved oxygen
- wave action.

Estuaries are classified as marine ecosystems because they have high salt content compared to freshwater. Mixing of freshwater and oceanic sea water leads to diluted salt content but it is still high enough to influence the distribution of organisms within it – salt-tolerant animals and plants have specific adaptations to help them cope with the osmotic demands of saltwater.

Only a small proportion of freshwater is found in ecosystems (Figure 2.10). Abiotic factors of a freshwater ecosystem:
- turbidity
- flow velocity
- pH.
- temperature
- dissolved oxygen

Figure 2.10
The majority of the Earth's freshwater is locked up in ice and snow, and is not directly available to support life. Groundwater is a store of water beneath ground and again is inaccessible for living organisms.

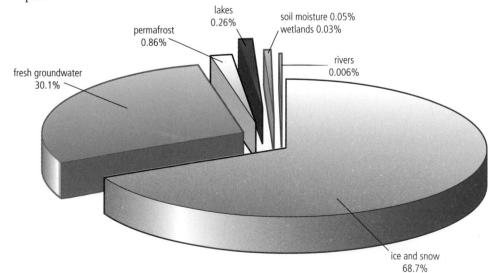

Abiotic factors of a terrestrial ecosystem:

- temperature
- light intensity
- wind speed
- particle size
- slope/aspect
- soil moisture
- drainage
- mineral content.

The Nevada desert, USA. Water supply in terrestrial ecosystems can be extremely limited, especially in desert areas, and is an important abiotic factor in controlling the distribution of organisms.

You must know methods for measuring each of the abiotic factors listed above and how they might vary in any given ecosystem with depth, time or distance. Abiotic factors are examined in conjunction with related biotic components (pages 29–34). This allows species distribution data to be linked to the environment in which they are found and explanations for the patterns to be proposed.

To learn more about sampling techniques, go to www.pearson.co.uk, insert the express code 2630P and click on activity 2.4.

Distribution of Earth's water

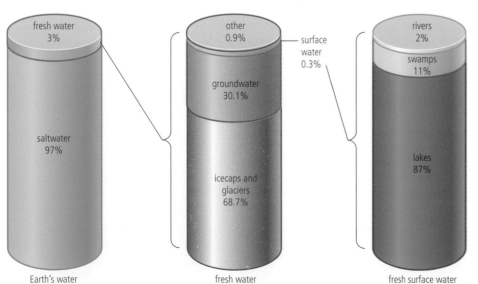

Earth's water
- fresh water 3%
- saltwater 97%

fresh water
- other 0.9%
- surface water 0.3%
- groundwater 30.1%
- icecaps and glaciers 68.7%

fresh surface water
- rivers 2%
- swamps 11%
- lakes 87%

The majority of the Earth's water is found in the oceans, with relatively little in lakes and rivers. Much of the freshwater that does exist is stored in ice at the poles (Figures 2.10 and 2.11).

Figure 2.11
The percentage of the planet containing freshwater ecosystems is extremely low compared to oceanic ones.

Evaluating measures for describing abiotic factors

This section examines the techniques used for measuring abiotic factors. An inaccurate picture of an environment may be obtained if errors are made in sampling: possible sources of error are examined below.

Light

A light-meter can be used to measure the light in an ecosystem. It should be held at a standard and fixed height above the ground and read when the value is fixed and not fluctuating. Cloud cover and changes in light intensity during the day mean that values must be taken at the same time of day and same atmospheric conditions: this can be difficult if several repeats are taken. The direction of the light-meter also needs to be standardized so it points in the same direction at the same angle each time it is used. Care must be taken not to shade the light-meter during a reading.

Temperature

Ordinary mercury thermometers are too fragile for fieldwork, and are hard to read. An electronic thermometer with probes (datalogger) allows temperature to be measured in air, water, and at different depths in soil. The temperature needs to be taken at a standard depth. Problems arise if the thermometer is not buried deeply enough: the depth needs to be checked each time it is used.

pH

This can be measured using a pH meter or datalogging pH probe. Values in freshwater range from slightly basic to slightly acidic depending on surrounding soil, rock and vegetation. Sea water usually has a pH above 7 (alkaline). The meter or probe must be cleaned between each reading and the reading taken from the same depth. Soil pH can be measured using a soil test kit – indicator solution is added and the colour compared to a chart.

Wind

Measurements can be taken by observing the effects of wind on objects – these are then related to the Beaufort scale. Precise measurements of wind speed can be made with a digital anemometer. The device can be mounted or hand-held. Some use cups to capture the wind whereas other smaller devices use a propeller. Care must be taken not to block the wind. Gusty conditions may lead to large variations in data.

Particle size

Soil can be made up of large, small or intermediate particles. Particle size determines drainage and water-holding capacity (page 125). Large particles (pebbles) can be measured individually and the average particle size calculated. Smaller particles can be measured by using a series of sieves with increasingly fine mesh size. The smallest particles can be separated by sedimentation. Optical techniques (examining the properties of light scattered by a suspension of soil in water) can also be used to study the smallest particles. The best techniques are expensive and the simpler ones time consuming.

An anemometer measuring wind speed. It works by converting the number of rotations made by three cups at the top of the apparatus into wind speed.

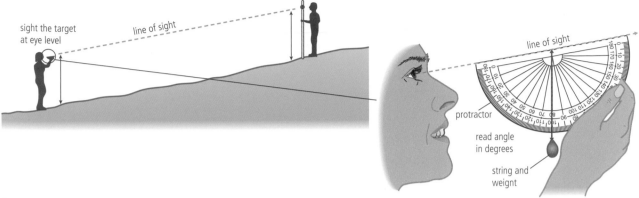

Slope

Surface run-off is determined by slope which can be calculated using a clinometer (Figure 2.12). Aspect can be determined using a compass.

If the slope is 10 degrees,

$$\text{percentage slope} = \tan(10) \times 100 = 0.176 \times 100 = 17.6\%$$

Soil moisture

Soils contain water and organic matter. Weighing samples before and after heating in an oven shows the amount of water evaporated and therefore moisture levels. Temperatures must not be hot enough to burn off organic content as this would further reduce soil weight and give inaccurate readings. Repeated readings should be taken until no further weight loss is recorded – the final reading should be used. Soil moisture probes are also available, which are simply pushed into the soil. These need to be cleaned between readings, and can be inaccurate.

Mineral content

The loss on ignition (LOI) test can determine mineral content. Soil samples are heated to high temperatures (500–1000 °C) for several hours to allow volatile substances to escape. Mass loss is equated to the quantity of minerals present. The temperature and duration of heating depend on the mineral composition of the soil, but there are no standard methods. The same conditions should be used when comparing samples.

Flow velocity

Surface flow velocity can be measured by timing how long it takes a floating object to travel a certain distance. More accurate measurements can be taken using a flow-meter (a calibrated propeller attached to a pole). The propeller is inserted into water just below the surface and a number of readings taken to ensure accuracy. As velocity varies with distance from the surface, readings must be taken at the same depth. Results can be misleading if only one part of a stream is measured. Water flows can vary over time because of rainfall or glacial melting events.

Salinity

Salinity can be measured using electrical conductivity (with a datalogger) or by the density of the water (water with a high salt content is much denser than low-salt water). Salinity is most often expressed as parts of salt per thousand parts of water (ppt). Sea water has an average salinity of 35 ppt, which is equivalent to $35\,g\,dm^{-3}$ or 35‰.

Figure 2.12
The slope angle is taken by sighting along the protractor's flat edge and reading the degree aligned with the string. Percentage slope can be calculated by determining the tangent of the slope using a scientific calculator and multiplying by 100.

A flow-meter allows water velocity to be recorded at any depth.

Dissolved oxygen

Oxygen-sensitive electrodes connected to a meter can be used to measure dissolved oxygen. Care must be taken when using an oxygen meter to avoid contamination from oxygen in the air. A more labour-intensive method is Winkler titration – this is based on the principle that oxygen in the water reacts with iodide ions, and acid can then added to release iodine that can be quantitatively measured.

Wave action

Areas with high wave action have high levels of dissolved oxygen due to mixing of air and water in the turbulence. Wave action is measured using a dynamometer, which measures the force in the waves. Changes in tide and wave strength during the day and over monthly periods mean that average results must be used to take this variability into account.

Turbidity

Cloudy water is said to have high turbidity and clear water low turbidity. Turbidity affects the penetration of sunlight into water and therefore rates of photosynthesis. Turbidity can be measured using a Secchi disc (Figure 2.13). Problems may be caused by the Sun's glare on the water, or the subjective nature of the measure with one person seeing the disc at one depth but another, with better eyesight, seeing it at a greater depth. Errors can be avoided by taking measures on the shady side of a boat.

More sophisticated optical devices can also be used (e.g. a nephelometer or turbidimeter) to measure the intensity of light scattered at 90° as a beam of light passes through a water sample.

▲
Figure 2.13
A Secchi disc is mounted on a pole or line and is lowered into water until it is just out of sight. The depth is measured using the scale of the line or pole. The disc is raised until it is just visible again and a second reading is taken. The average depth calculated is known as the Secchi depth.

Evaluation of techniques

Short-term and limited field sampling reduces the effectiveness of the above techniques because abiotic factors may vary from day to day and season to season. The majority of these abiotic factors can be measured using datalogging devices. The advantage of dataloggers is that they can provide continuous data over a long period of time, making results more representative of the area. As always, the results can be made more reliable by taking many samples.

 Abiotic data can be collected using instruments that avoid issues of objectivity as they directly record quantitative data. Instruments allow us to record data that would otherwise be beyond the limit of our perception.

EXERCISES

1. List as many abiotic factors as you can think of. Say how you would measure each of these factors in an ecological investigation.

2. Evaluate each of the methods you have listed in exercise 1. What are their limitations, and how may they affect the data you collect?

3. Which methods could you use in **(a)** marine ecosystems, **(b)** freshwater ecosystems and **(c)** terrestrial ecosystems?

2.3 Measuring biotic components of the system

Assessment statements
2.3.1 Construct simple keys and use published keys for the identification of organisms.
2.3.2 Describe and evaluate methods for estimating abundance of organisms.
2.3.3 Describe and evaluate methods for estimating the biomass of trophic levels in a community.
2.3.4 Define the term *diversity*.
2.3.5 Apply Simpson's diversity index and outline its significance.

Keys for species identification

Ecology is the study of living organisms in relation to their environment. We have examined the abiotic environmental factors that need to be studied, now we will look at the biotic or living factors. In any ecological study, it is important to correctly identify the organisms in question otherwise results and conclusions will be invalid. It is unlikely that you will be an expert in the animals or plants you are looking at, so you will need to use dichotomous keys.

Dichotomous means 'divided into two parts'. The key is written so that identification is done in steps. At each step, two options are given based on different possible characteristics of the organism you are looking at. The outcome of each choice leads to another pair of questions, and so on until the organism is identified.

For example, suppose you were asked to create a dichotomous key based on the following list of specimens: rat, shark, buttercup, spoon, amoeba, sycamore tree, pebble, pine tree, eagle, beetle, horse, and car. An example of a suitable key is given below.

1	**a** Organism is living	go to 4
	b Organism is non-living	go to 2
2	**a** Object is metallic	go to 3
	b Object is non-metallic	pebble
3	**a** Object has wheels	car
	b Object does not have wheels	spoon
4	**a** Organism is microscopic	amoeba
	b Organism is macroscopic	go to 5
5	**a** Organism is a plant	go to 6
	b Organism is an animal	go to 8
6	**a** Plant has a woody stem	go to 7
	b Plant has a herbaceous stem	buttercup
7	**a** Tree has leaves with small surface area	pine tree
	b Tree has leaves with large surface area	sycamore tree
8	**a** Organism is terrestrial	go to 9
	b Organism is aquatic	shark
9	**a** Organism has fewer than 6 legs	go to 10
	b Organism has 6 legs	beetle
10	**a** Organism has fur	go to 11
	b Organism has feathers	eagle
11	**a** Organism has hooves	horse
	b Organism has no hooves	rat

The key can also be shown graphically (Figure 2.14, overleaf).

Figure 2.14
A dichotomous key for a
random selection of animate
and inanimate objects.

To learn more about
using dichotomous
keys, go to www.
pearsonhotlinks.com,
insert the express code
2630P and click on
activity 2.5.

● **Examiner's hint:**
You need to be able to
construct your own keys for up
to eight species.

The measurement of the
biotic factors is often
subjective, relying on your
interpretation of different
measuring techniques
to provide data. It is
rare in environmental
investigations to be
able to provide ways of
measuring variables that
are as precise and reliable
as those in the physical
sciences. Will this affect
the value of the data
collected and the validity
of the knowledge?

Describe and evaluate methods for estimating abundance of organisms

It is not possible for you to study every organism in an ecosystem, so limitations must be put on how many plants and animals you study. Trapping methods enable limited samples to be taken. Examples of such methods include:

- pitfall traps (beakers or pots buried in the soil which animals walk into and cannot escape from)
- small mammal traps (often baited, with a door that falls down once an animal is inside)
- light traps (a UV bulb against a white sheet that attracts certain night-flying insects)
- tullgren funnels (paired cloth funnels, with a light source at one end, a sample pot the other and a wire mesh between: invertebrates in soil samples placed on the mesh move away from the heat of the lamp and fall into the collecting bottle at the bottom).

You can work out the number or abundance of organisms in various ways – either by directly counting the number or **percentage cover** of organisms in a selected area (for organisms that do not move or are limited in movement), or by indirectly calculating abundance using a formula (for animals that are mobile – see the Lincoln index).

The Lincoln index

This method allows you to estimate the total population size of an animal in your study area. In a sample using the methods outlined above, it is unlikely you will sample all the animals in a population so you need a mathematical method to calculate the total numbers. The Lincoln index involves collecting a sample from the population, marking them in some way (paint can be used on insects, or fur clipping on mammals), releasing them back into the wild, then resampling some time later and counting how many marked individuals you find in the second capture. It is essential that marking methods are ethically acceptable (non-harmful) and non-conspicuous (so that the animals are not easier to see and therefore easier prey).

Because of the procedures involved, this is called a 'capture–mark–release–recapture' technique. If all of the marked animals are recaptured then the number of marked animals is assumed to be the total population size, whereas if half the marked animals are recaptured then the total population size is assumed to be twice as big as the first sample. The formula used in calculating population size is shown below.

N = total population size of animals in the study site

$n1$ = number of animals captured on first day

$n2$ = number of animals recaptured

m = number of marked animals recaptured on the second day

$$N = \frac{n1 \times n2}{m}$$

To learn more about the Lincoln index, go to www. pearsonhotlinks.com, insert the express code 2630P and click on activity 2.6.

Movement of your animals into and out from your study area will lead to inaccurate results.

Quadrats

Quadrats are used to limit the sampling area when you want to measure the population size of non-mobile organisms (mobile ones can move from one quadrat to another and so be sampled more than once thus making results invalid). Quadrats vary in size from 0.25 m square to 1 m square. The size of quadrat should be optimal for the organisms you are studying. To select the correct quadrat size, count the number of different species in several differently sized quadrats. Plot the number of species against quadrat size: the point where the graph levels off, and no further species are added even when the quadrats gets larger, gives you the size of the quadrat you need to use.

If your sample area contains the same habitat throughout, quadrats should be located at **random** (use a random number generator, page 332 – these can be found in books or on the internet). First, you mark out an area of your habitat using two tape measures placed at right angles to each other. Then you use the random numbers to locate positions within the marked-out area . For example, if the grid is 10 m by 10 m, random numbers are generated between 0 and 1000. The random number 596 represents a point 5 metres 96 centimetres along one tape measure. The next random number is the coordinate for the second tape. The point where the coordinates cross is the location for the quadrat.

If your sample area covers habitats very different from each other (e.g. an undisturbed and a disturbed area), you need to use **stratified random sampling**, so you take sets of results from both areas. If the sample area is along an environmental gradient, you should place quadrats at set distances (e.g. every 5 m) along a **transect**: this is called **systematic sampling** (**continuous sampling** samples along the whole length of the transect).

Population density is the number of individuals of each species per unit area. It is calculated by dividing the number of organisms sampled by the total area covered by the quadrats.

Plant abundance is best estimated using percentage cover. This method is not suitable for mobile animals as they may move from the sample area while counting is taking place.

Percentage cover is the percentage of the area within the quadrat covered by one particular species. Percentage cover is worked out for each species present. Dividing the quadrat into a 10 × 10 grid (100 squares) helps to estimate percentage cover (each square is 1 per cent of the total area cover).

Percentage frequency is the percentage of the total quadrat number that the species was present in.

Sample methods must allow for the collection of data that is scientifically representative and appropriate, and allow the collection of data on all species present. Results can be used to compare ecosystems.

In the early 1980s, Terry Erwin, a scientist at the Smithsonian Institution collected insects from the canopy of tropical forest trees in Panama. He sampled 19 trees and collected 955 species of beetle. Using extrapolation methods, he estimated there could be 30 million species of arthropod worldwide. Although now believed to be an overestimate, this study started the race to calculate the total number of species on Earth before many of them become extinct.

Canopy fogging uses a harmless chemical to knock-down insects into collecting trays (usually on the forest floor) where they can be collected. Insects not collected can return to the canopy when they have recovered.

Describe and evaluate methods for estimating the biomass of trophic levels

We have seen how pyramids of biomass can be constructed to show total biomass at each trophic level of a food chain. Rather than weighing the total number of organisms at each level (clearly impractical) an extrapolation method is used: the mass of one organism, or the average mass of a few organisms, is multiplied by the total number of organisms present to estimate total biomass.

Biomass is calculated to indicate the total energy within in a living being or trophic level. Biological molecules are held together by bond energy, so the greater the mass of living material, the greater the amount of energy present. Biomass is taken as the mass of an organism minus water content (i.e. **dry weight biomass**). Water is not included in biomass measurements because the amount varies from organism to organism, it contains no energy and is not organic. Other inorganic material is usually insignificant in terms of mass, so dry weight biomass is a measure of organic content only.

Biomass is the mass of organic material in organisms or ecosystems, usually per unit area.

To obtain quantitative samples of biomass, biological material is dried to constant weight. The sample is weighed in a previously weighed container. The specimens are put in a hot oven (not hot enough to burn tissue) – around 80 °C – and left for a specific length of time. The specimen is reweighed and replaced in the oven. This is repeated until a similar mass is obtained on two subsequent weighings (i.e. no further loss in mass is recorded as no further water is present). Biomass is usually stated per unit area (i.e. per metre squared) so that comparisons can be made between trophic levels. Biomass productivity is given as mass per unit area per period of time (usually years).

To estimate the biomass of a primary producer within in a study area, you would collect all the vegetation (including roots, stems, and leaves) within a series of 1 m by 1 m quadrats and then carry out the dry-weight method outlined above. Average biomass can then be calculated.

> Variables can be measured but not controlled while working in the field. Fluctuations in environmental conditions can cause problems when recording data. Standards for acceptable margins of error are therefore different. Is this acceptable?

ENVIRONMENTAL PHILOSOPHIES

Ecological sampling can at times involve the killing of wild organisms. For example, to help assess species diversity of poorly understood organisms (identification involves taking dead specimens back to the lab for identification), or to assess biomass. An **ecocentric** worldview, which promotes the preservation of all life, may lead you to question the value of such approaches. Does the end justify the means, and what alternatives (if any) exist?

● **Examiner's hint:** Dry-weight measurements of quantitative samples can be extrapolated to estimate total biomass.

Diversity and Simpson's diversity index

Diversity is considered as a function of two components: the number of different species and the relative numbers of individuals of each species. It is different from simply counting the number of species (**species richness**) because the relative abundance of each species is also taken into account.

There are many ways of quantifying diversity. You must be able to calculate diversity using the Simpson's diversity index as shown below and in the example calculation on page 35.

D = diversity index

N = total number of organisms of all species found

n = number of individuals of a particular species

Σ = sum of

$$D = \frac{N(N - 1)}{\Sigma n(n - 1)}$$

● **Examiner's hint:** You are not required to memorize the Simpson's diversity formula but must know the meaning of the symbols.

You could examine the diversity of plants within a woodland ecosystem, for example, using multiple quadrats to establish number of individuals present or percentage cover and then using Simpson's diversity index to quantify the diversity. A high value of D suggests a stable and ancient site, and a low value of D could suggest pollution, recent colonization or agricultural management (Chapter 4). The index is normally used in studies of vegetation but can also be applied to comparisons of animal (or even all species) diversity.

Samples must be comprehensive to ensure all species are sampled (Figure 2.15, overleaf). However, it is always possible that certain habitats have not been sampled and some species missed. For example, canopy fogging does not knock down insects living within the bark of the tree so these species would not be sampled.

> **Diversity** is the function of two components: the number of different species and the relative numbers of individuals of each species. This is different from **species richness**, which refers only to the number of species in a sample or area.

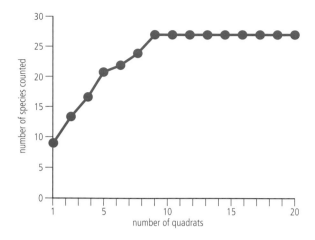

Figure 2.15
To make sure you have sampled all the species in your ecosytem, perform a cumulative species count: as more quadrats are added to sample size, any additional species are noted and added to species richness. The point at which the graph levels off gives you the best estimate of the number of species in your ecosystem.

Measures of diversity are relative, not absolute. They are relative to each other but not to anything else, unlike, say, measures of temperature, where values relate to an absolute scale. Comparisons can be made between communities containing the same type of organisms and in the same ecosystem, but not between different types of community and different ecosystems. Communities with individuals evenly distributed between different species are said to have high 'evenness' and have high diversity. This is because many species can co-exist in the many available niches within a complex ecosystem. Communities with one dominant species have low diversity which indicates a poorer ecosystem not able to support as many types of organism. Measures of diversity in communities with few species can be unreliable as relative abundance between species can misrepresent true patterns.

Only 1 per cent of described species are vertebrates (Figure 2.16), yet this is the group that conservation initiatives are often focussed on.

Figure 2.16
Of the total number of described species (about 1.8 million), excluding microbes, over three-quarters are invertebrates. Over half are insects. The most successful group are the beetles, which occupy all ecosystems apart from oceanic ones.

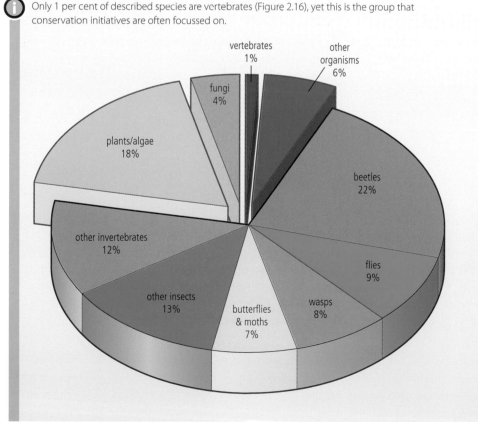

Example calculation of Simpson's diversity index

The data from several quadrats in woodland were pooled to obtain the table below.

Species	Number (*n*)	*n*(*n* − 1)
woodrush	2	2
holly (seedlings)	8	56
bramble	1	0
Yorkshire fog	1	0
sedge	3	6
total (*N*)	15	64

Putting the figures into the formula for Simpson's diversity index:

$$N = 15$$
$$N - 1 = 14$$
$$N(N - 1) = 210$$
$$\Sigma n(n - 1) = 64$$
$$D = \frac{210}{64} = 3.28$$

 To download a Simpson's diversity index calculator, go to www.pearsonhotlinks.com, insert the express code 2630P and click on activity 2.7.

 Applying the rigorous standards used in a physical science investigation would render most environmental studies unworkable. Whether this is acceptable or not is a matter of opinion, although it could be argued that by doing nothing we would miss out on gaining a useful understanding of the environment.

EXERCISES

1 Create a key for a selection of objects of your choice. Does your key allow you to accurately identify each object?

2 What ethical considerations must you bear in mind when carrying out mark–release–recapture exercises on wild animals?

3 Take a sheet of paper and divide it into 100 squares. Cut these squares out and put them into a tray. Select 20 of these squares and mark them with a cross. Put them back into the tray. Recapture 20 of the pieces of paper. Record how many are marked. Use the Lincoln index to estimate the population size of all pieces of paper. How closely does this agree with the actual number (100)? How could you improve the reliability of the method?

4 What is the difference between *species diversity* and *species richness*?

5 What does a high value for the Simpson's index tell you about the ecosystem from which the sample is taken? What does a low value tell you?

 **2.4 Biomes**

Assessment statements

2.4.1 Define the term *biome*.
2.4.2 Explain the distribution, structure and relative productivity of tropical rainforests, deserts, tundra, and any other biome.

Definition of *biome*

A biome is a collection of ecosystems sharing similar climatic conditions. A biome has distinctive abiotic factors and species which distinguish it from other biomes (Figure 2.17, overleaf). Water (rainfall), insolation (sunlight), and temperature are the climate controls important in understanding how biomes are structured, how they function and where they are found round the world.

Water is needed for **photosynthesis**, **transpiration**, and support (cell turgidity). Sunlight is also needed for photosynthesis. Photosynthesis is a chemical reaction, so temperature affects the rate at which it progresses. Rates of photosynthesis determine the productivity of

 To access worksheet 2.2 investigating different biomes, please visit www.pearsonbacconline.com and follow the on-screen instructions.

Net primary productivity (NPP) is the gain in energy or biomass per unit area per unit time remaining after allowing for losses of energy due to respiration. Climate is a limiting factor as it controls the amount of photosynthesis that can occur in a plant.

an ecosystem (net primary productivity, NPP, pages 52–54) – the more productive a biome, the higher its NPP. Rainfall, temperature and insolation are therefore key climate controls that determine the distribution, function and structure of biomes because they determine rates of photosynthesis.

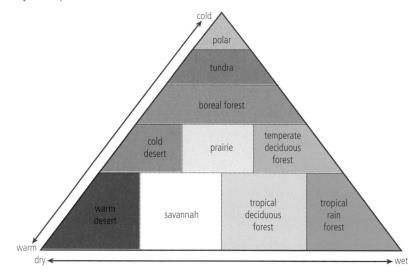

Figure 2.17
Temperature and precipitation determine biome distribution around the globe. Levels of insolation also play an important role, which correlates broadly with temperature (areas with higher levels of light tend to have higher temperatures).

Tri-cellular model of atmospheric circulation

As well as the differences in insolation and temperature found from the equator to more northern latitudes, the distribution of biomes can be understood by looking at patterns of atmospheric circulation. The 'tri-cellular model' helps explain differences in pressure belts, temperature and precipitation that exist across the globe (Figure 2.18).

Figure 2.18
The tri-cellular model of global atmospheric circulation is made up of the polar cell, the Ferrel cell in mid-latitudes and the Hadley cell in the tropics. The model suggests that the most significant movements in the atmosphere are north–south. Downward air movement creates high pressure. Upward movement creates low pressure and cooling air that leads to increased cloud formation and precipitation.

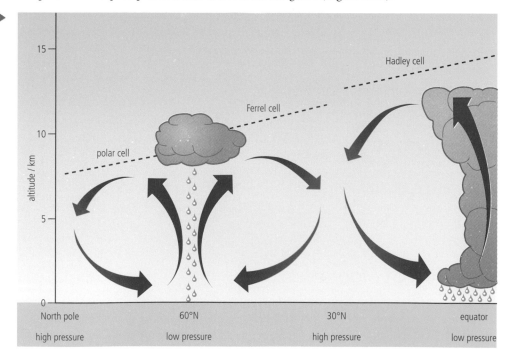

Atmospheric movement can be divided into three major cells: Hadley, Ferrel and polar, with boundaries coinciding with particular latitudes (although they shift with the Sun's movement). Hadley cells control weather over the tropics, where the air is warm and unstable, having crossed warm oceans. The equator receives most insolation per unit area of Earth: this heats up air which rises, creating the Hadley cells. As the air rises, it cools and condenses, forming large cumulonimbus clouds that create the thunderstorms characteristic of tropical rainforest. These conditions provide the highest rainfall per unit area on the planet. The pressure at the equator is low as air is rising. Eventually, the cooled air begins to spread out, and descends at approximately 30° north and south of the equator. Pressure here is therefore high (because air is descending). This air is dry, so it is in these locations that the desert biome is found. Air then either returns to the equator at ground level or travels towards the poles as warm winds (south-westerly in the northern hemisphere, north-easterly in the southern hemisphere). Where the warm air travelling north and south hits the colder polar winds, at approximately 60° N and S, the air rises as it is less dense, creating an area of low pressure. As the air rises, it condenses and falls as precipitation, so this is where temperate forest biomes are found. The model explains why rainfall is highest at the equator and 60° N and S.

 To learn more about biomes, go to www. pearsonhotlinks.com, insert the express code 2630P and click on activity 2.8.

 Biomes cross national boundaries and do not stop at borders. The Sahara, for example, stretches across northern Africa. Studying biomes requires studies to be carried out across national frontiers – this can sometimes be politically as well as logistically difficult.

Tropical rainforest

Tropical rainforests have constant high temperatures (typically 26 °C) and high rainfall (over 2500 mm yr^{-1}) throughout the year. Because tropical rainforests, as their name implies, lie in a band around the equator within the tropics of Cancer and Capricorn (23.5° N and S), they enjoy high light levels throughout the year (Figure 2.19). There is little seasonal variation in sunlight and temperature (although the monsoon period can reduce levels of insolation) providing an all-year growing season. Their position of low latitudes, with the Sun directly over head, therefore determines their climatic conditions, and enables high levels of photosynthesis and high rates of NPP throughout the year. Tropical rainforests are estimated to produce 40 per cent of NPP of terrestrial ecosystems.

● **Examiner's hint:**
You need to be able to explain the distribution, structure and relative productivity of tropical rainforests, deserts, tundra and one other biome (e.g. temperate grassland or a local example). Climate should be explained in terms of temperature, precipitation and insolation only.

◀ **Figure 2.19**
Tropical rainforest distribution around the globe.

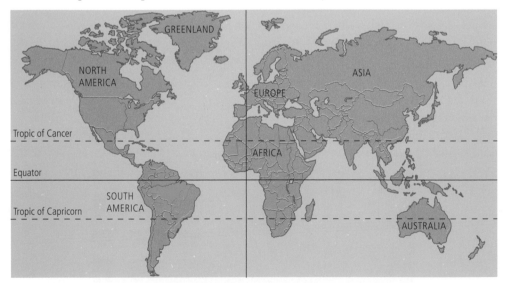

Rainforests are broad evergreen forests with a very high diversity of animals and plants. A rainforest may have up to 480 species of tree in a single hectare (2.5 acres), whereas temperate forest may only have six tree species making up the majority of the forest. The high diversity of plants is because of the high levels of productivity resulting from year-round high rainfall and insolation. The high diversity of animals follows from the complexity of the forests: they are multi-layered and provide many different niches allowing for an enormous variety of different organisms (Figure 2.20).

Figure 2.20
Rainforests show a highly layered, or stratified, structure. Emergent trees can be up to 80 m high, although overall structure depends on local conditions and varies from forest to forest. Only about 1 per cent of light hitting the canopy layer reaches the floor, so the highest levels of NPP are found in the canopy – one of the most productive areas of vegetation in the world. High productivity in the canopy results in high biodiversity, and it is believed that half of the world's species could be found in rainforest canopies.

emergent layer

canopy layer

understory layer

immature layer

herb layer

Although rainforests are highly productive, much of the inorganic nutrients needed for growth are locked up in the trees and are not found in the soil, which is low in nutrients. Trees obtain their nutrients from rapid recycling of detritus that occurs on the forest floor. If rates of decay are high enough, the forest can maintain levels of growth. However, heavy rainfall can cause nutrients to be washed from soils (leaching) resulting in an increased lack of inorganic nutrients that could limit primary production.

Because soils in rainforest are thin, trees have shallow root systems with one long tap root running from the centre of the trunk into the ground plus wide buttresses to help support the tree (as shown in the photograph). The forest canopy provided by the trees protects the soils from heavy rainfall – once areas have been cleared through logging, the soils are quickly washed away (eroded) making it difficult for forests to re-establish.

Buttressed roots grow out from the base of the trunk, sometimes as high as 5 m above the ground. These extended roots also increase the area over which nutrients can be absorbed from the soil. The urban setting of this ancient tree suggests it was left in place when rainforest was cleared to build Kuching, Sarawak (Malaysia).

Deserts

Deserts are found in bands at latitudes of approximately 30° N and S (Figure 2.21). They cover 20–30 per cent of the land surface. It is at these latitudes that dry air descends having lost water vapour over the tropics. Hot deserts are characterized by high temperatures at the warmest time of day (typically 45–49 °C) and low precipitation (typically under 250 mm yr^{-1}). Rainfall

The Sahara Desert in northern Africa is the world's largest desert. Covering more than 3.5 million square miles (9 million square kilometres), it is slightly smaller than the USA. However, it is not the site of the world's lowest rainfall – that occurs in Antarctica, which receives less than 50 mm of precipitation annually.

may be unevenly distributed. The lack of water limits rates of photosynthesis and so rates of NPP are very low. Organisms also have to overcome fluctuations in temperature (night temperatures, when skies are clear, can be as low as 10 °C, sometimes as low as 0 °C) which make survival difficult.

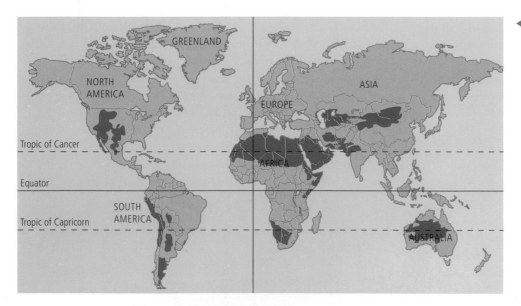

Figure 2.21
Distribution of deserts around the globe.

Low productivity means that vegetation is scarce. Soils can be rich in nutrients as they are not washed away; this helps to support the plant species that can survive there. Decomposition levels are low because of the dryness of the air and lack of water.

The species that can exist in deserts are highly adapted, showing many **xerophytic** adaptations (adaptations to reduce water loss in dry conditions). Cacti (a group restricted to the Americas) have reduced their surface area for transpiration by converting leaves into spines. They store water in their stems, which have the ability to expand, enabling more water to be stored and decreasing the surface area : volume ratio thus further reducing water loss from the surface. The spiney leaves deter animals from eating the plants and accessing the water. Xerophytes have a thick cuticle that also reduces water loss. Roots can be both deep (to access underground sources of water) and extensive near the surface (to quickly absorb precipitation before it evaporates).

Animals have also adapted to desert conditions. Snakes and reptiles are the commonest vertebrates – they are highly adapted to conserve water and their cold-blooded metabolism is ideally suited to desert conditions. Mammals have adapted to live underground and emerge at the coolest parts of day.

Tundra

Elk crossing frozen tundra.

Tundra is found at high latitudes, adjacent to ice margins, where insolation is low (Figure 2.22). Short day length also limits levels of sunlight. Water may be locked up in ice for months at a time and this combined with little rainfall means that water is also a limiting factor. Lack of light and rainfall mean that rates of photosynthesis and productivity are low. Temperatures are very low for most of the year; temperature is also a limiting factor because it affects the rate of photosynthesis, respiration and decomposition (these enzyme-driven chemical reactions are slower in colder conditions). Soil may be permanently frozen (permafrost) and nutrients are limiting. Low temperature means that the recycling of nutrients is low, leading to the formation of peat bogs where much carbon is stored. The vegetation consists of low scrubs and grasses.

Figure 2.22
Map showing the distribution of tundra around the globe.

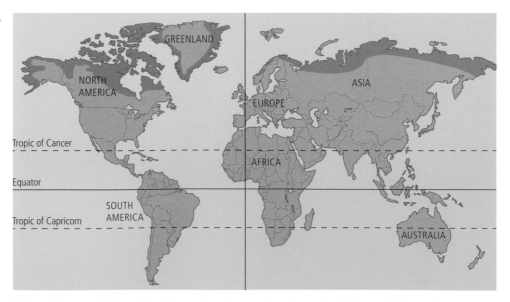

Most of the world's tundra is found in the north polar region (Figure 2.22), and so is known as Arctic tundra. There is a small amount of tundra in parts of Antarctica that are not covered with ice, and on high altitude mountains (alpine tundra).

During winter months, temperatures can reach −50 °C – all life activity is low in these harsh conditions. In summer, the tundra changes: the Sun is out almost 24 hours a day, so levels of insolation and temperature both increase leading to plant growth. Only small plants are found in this biome because there is not enough soil for trees to grow and, even in the summer, the permafrost drops to only a few centimetres below the surface.

In the summer, animal activity increases, due to increased temperatures and productivity. The growing period is limited to six weeks of the year, after which temperatures drop again and hours of sunlight decline. Plants are adapted with leathery leaves or underground storage organs, and animals with thick fur. Arctic animals are, on average, larger than their more southerly relations, which decreases their surface area relative to their size enabling them to reduce heat loss (e.g. the arctic fox is larger than the European fox).

Tundra is the youngest of all biomes as it was formed after the retreat of glaciers 10 000 years ago.

Temperate forest

Temperate forests are largely found between 40° and 60° N of the equator (Figure 2.23). They are found in seasonal areas where winters are cold and summers are warm, unlike tropical rainforests which enjoy similar conditions all year. Two different tree types are found in temperate forest – evergreen (which leaf all year round) and deciduous (which lose their leaves in winter). Evergreen trees have protection against the cold winters (thicker leaves or needles) unlike deciduous trees whose leaves would suffer frost damage and so shut down in winter. Forests might contain only deciduous trees, only evergreens, or a mixture of both. The amount of rainfall determines whether or not an area develops forest – if precipitation is sufficient, temperate forests form; if there is not enough rainfall, grasslands develop. Rainfall in these biomes is between 500 and 1500 mm yr^{-1}.

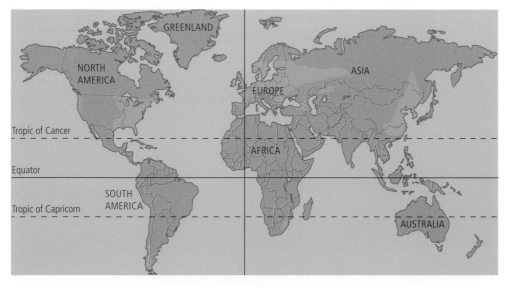

Figure 2.23
Distribution of temperate forest around the globe.

Variation in insolation during the year, caused by the tilt of the Earth and the corresponding changes in the distance of these latitudes from the Sun, means that productivity is lower than in tropical rainforests. The mild climate, with lower average temperatures and lower rainfall than that found at the equator, also reduces levels of photosynthesis and productivity, although temperate forests have the second highest NPP (after rainforests).

Diversity is lower than in rainforest and the structure of temperate forest is simpler. These forests are generally dominated by one species and 90 per cent of the forest may consist of

The loss of leaves from deciduous trees over winter allows increased insolation of the forest floor, enabling the seasonal appearance of species such as bluebells.

only six tree species. There is some layering of the forest, although the tallest trees generally do not grow more than 30 m, so vertical stratification is limited. The less complex structure of temperate forests compared to rainforest reduces the number of available niches and therefore species diversity is much less. The forest floor has a reasonably thick leaf layer that is rapidly broken down when temperatures are higher, and nutrient availability is in general not limiting. The lower and less dense canopy means that light levels on the forest floor are higher than in rainforest, so the shrub layer can contain many plants such as brambles, grasses, bracken and ferns.

Grassland

Bison roaming on mixed grass prairie.

Grasslands are found on every continent except Antarctica, and cover about 16 per cent of the Earth's surface (Figure 2.24). They develop where there is not enough precipitation to support forests, but enough to prevent deserts forming. There are several types of grassland: the Great Plains and the Russian Steppes are temperate grasslands; the savannas of east Africa are tropical grassland.

Figure 2.24
The distribution of grasslands around the globe.

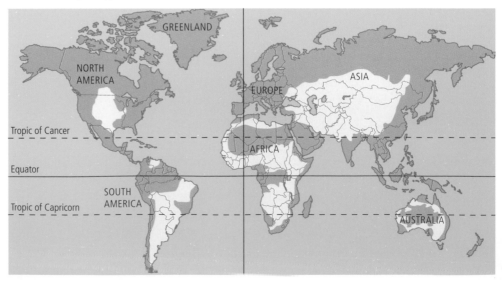

Grasses have a wide diversity but low levels of productivity. Grasslands away from the sea have wildly fluctuating temperatures which can limit the survival of animals and plants. They are found in the area where the polar and Ferrel cells meet (Figure 2.18, page 36), and the mixing of cold polar air with warmer southerly winds (in the northern hemisphere) causes increased precipitation compared to either polar and more tropical (e.g. 30° N) regions. Rainfall is approximately in balance with levels of evaporation. Decomposing vegetation forms a mat containing high levels of nutrients, but the rate of decomposition is not high because of the cool climate. Grasses grow beneath the surface and during cold periods (more northern grasslands suffer a harsh winter) can remain dormant until the ground warms.

To interactively explore biomes, go to www.pearsonhotlinks.com, insert the express code 2630P and click on activity 2.9.

EXERCISES

1   Define the term *biome*. How does this differ from the term *ecosystem*?

2   Draw up a table listing the following biomes: tropical rainforest, hot desert, tundra, and temperate forest. The table should include information about the levels of insolation (sunlight), rainfall (precipitation) and productivity for each biome.

3   Which biome has the highest productivity? Why? Which has the lowest? Why?

2.5 Function

Assessment statements

2.5.1 Explain the role of producers, consumers and decomposers in the ecosystem.

2.5.2 Describe photosynthesis and respiration in terms of inputs, outputs and energy transformations.

2.5.3 Describe and explain the transfer and transformation of energy as it flows through an ecosystem.

2.5.4 Describe and explain the transfer and transformation of materials as they cycle within an ecosystem.

2.5.5 Define the terms *gross productivity*, *net productivity*, *primary productivity* and *secondary productivity*.

2.5.6 Define the terms and calculate the values of both *gross primary productivity* (GPP) and *net primary productivity* (NPP) from given data.

2.5.7 Define the terms and calculate the values of both *gross secondary productivity* (GSP) and *net secondary productivity* (NSP) from given data.

The role of producers, consumers and decomposers

As we have already seen, the biotic components of ecosystems can be divided into those organisms that convert sunlight energy into chemical energy in the form of food (producers, or autotrophs), and those organisms that feed on other animals and plants in order to obtain the food they need (consumers, or heterotrophs). When organisms die, decomposition processes are carried out by decomposers (bacteria and fungi) thus recycling the chemical elements that bodies are made from.

Producers can make their own food, whereas consumers and decomposers feed on other organisms. Elements such as carbon cycle through ecosystems.

Producers

Plants, algae and some bacteria are autotrophs. Organisms that use sunlight energy to create food are called photoautotrophs; all green plants are photoautotrophs (Figure 2.25, overleaf). Producers are the basis of ecosystems, supporting them through constant input of energy and new biomass.

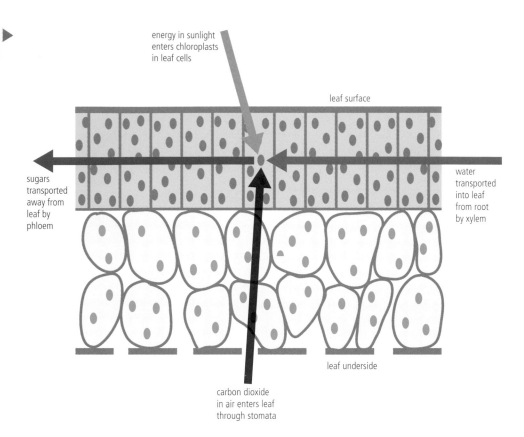

Figure 2.25
Plants absorb carbon dioxide from air and water from soil. Sunlight enters through the upper epidermis and strikes chlorophyll in chloroplasts of leaf cells. In the chloroplasts, the energy in sunlight is used to combine the water and carbon dioxide into glucose – a store of chemical energy.

energy in sunlight enters chloroplasts in leaf cells

leaf surface

sugars transported away from leaf by phloem

water transported into leaf from root by xylem

leaf underside

carbon dioxide in air enters leaf through stomata

Consumers

Consumers do not contain photosynthetic pigments such as chlorophyll so they cannot make their own food. They must obtain their energy, minerals and nutrients by eating other organisms – they are heterotrophs. Herbivores feed on autotrophs, carnivores feed on other heterotrophs, and omnivores feed on both. Whereas autotrophs convert inorganic compounds into organic ones, heterotrophs do the opposite.

Decomposers

Decomposers obtain their food and nutrients from the breakdown of dead organic matter. When they break down tissue, they release nutrients ready for reabsorption by producers. They form the basis of a decomposer food chain (which may be energetically more important in some ecosystems than grazing food chains). Decomposers also contribute to the build up of humus and improve nutrient retention capacity in soil through incomplete breakdown of organic material.

Some bacteria found in the soil are autotrophs, but rather than use sunlight to obtain the energy to create complex organic molecules, they use chemical energy from oxidation reactions. These bacteria are called chemoautotrophs – they are key players in the nitrogen cycle (page 49). They convert ammonia from decomposing organisms and excretory waste into nitrites and then nitrates. Plants can take in nitrates through their root systems. Chemoautotrophs can therefore form the basis of food chains.

Photosynthesis and respiration

Two processes control the flow of energy through ecosystems: photosynthesis and respiration. Photosynthesis stores energy in biomass and respiration releases this energy so that it can be used to support the organisms' life processes.

Photosynthesis

Photosynthesis is the process by which green plants convert light energy from the Sun into useable chemical energy stored in organic matter. It requires carbon dioxide, water, chlorophyll and light, and is controlled by enzymes. Oxygen is produced as a waste product in the reaction. In terms of inputs, outputs and energy transformations, photosynthesis can be summarized as follows.

- Inputs – Sunlight as energy source, carbon dioxide and water.
- Processes – Chlorophyll traps sunlight; the energy is used to split water molecules; hydrogen from water is combined with carbon dioxide to produce glucose.
- Outputs – Glucose used as an energy source for the plant and as a building block for other organic molecules (e.g. cellulose, starch); oxygen is released to the atmosphere through stomata.
- Transformations – Light energy is transformed to stored chemical energy.

Respiration

Respiration releases energy from glucose and other organic molecules inside all living cells. It begins as an anaerobic process in the cytoplasm of cells, and is completed inside mitochondria with aerobic chemical reactions occurring. The process is controlled by enzymes. The energy released is in a form available for use by living organisms, but is ultimately lost as heat (Chapter 1).

Respiration can be summarized as follows (Figure 2.26).

- Inputs – Glucose and oxygen.
- Processes – Oxidation processes inside cells.
- Outputs – Release of energy for work and heat.
- Transformations – Stored chemical energy to kinetic energy and heat.

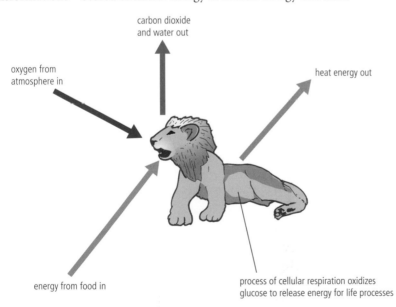

carbon dioxide and water out

oxygen from atmosphere in

heat energy out

energy from food in

process of cellular respiration oxidizes glucose to release energy for life processes

Transfer and transformation of energy

The pathway of sunlight entering the Earth's atmosphere is complex (Figure 2.27, overleaf). Sunlight contains a broad spectrum of wavelengths from X-rays to radio waves, though most exists as ultraviolet, visible light and infrared radiation. Almost half of the Sun's total radiation is visible light.

Photosynthesis combines carbon dioxide and water using sunlight energy to produce sugar (glucose). **Respiration** takes organic matter and oxygen to produce carbon dioxide, water and the release of energy.

- **Examiner's hint:**
Photosynthesis involves the transformation of light energy into the chemical energy of organic matter. Respiration is the transformation of chemical energy into kinetic energy, and ultimately heat lost from the system.

To learn more about energy transformations in ecosystems, go to www. pearsonhotlinks.com, insert the express code 2630P and click on activity 2.10.

Figure 2.26
The inputs, outputs and processes involved in respiration.

Figure 2.27
The Earth's energy budget. Mean vertical energy flows in the terrestrial system (atmosphere and surface), in watts per square metre. Most important are the 342 W m^{-2} of solar energy which enter the outer atmospheric layer and the approximately 390 W m^{-2} which emanate from the soil in the form of infrared waves.

To learn more about energy stores and flows in an ecosystem, go to www.pearsonhotlinks. com, insert the express code 2630P and click on activity 2.11.

Not all solar radiation ends up being stored as biomass. Losses include:
- reflection from leaves
- light not hitting chloroplasts
- light of the wrong wavelengths (not absorbed by chloroplast pigments)
- transmission of light through the leaf
- inefficiency of photosynthesis.

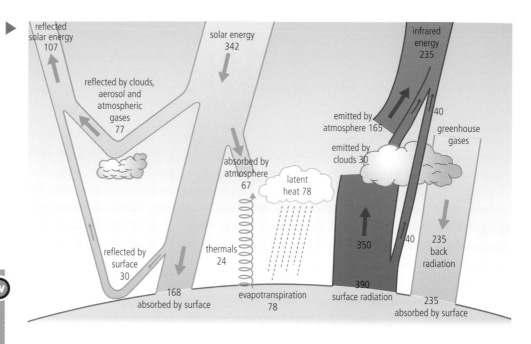

Very little of the sunlight available from the Sun ends up as biomass in ecosystems. First, much of the incoming solar radiation fails to enter the chloroplasts of leaves because it is reflected, transmitted or is the wrong wavelength to be absorbed (Figure 2.1, page 15). Of the radiation captured by leaves, only a small percentage ends up as biomass in growth compounds the conversion of light to chemical energy is inefficient. Overall, only around 0.06 per cent of all the solar radiation falling on the Earth is captured by plants.

Once converted into a chemical store, energy is available in useable form both to the producers and to organisms higher up the food chain. As we saw in Chapter 1, there is loss of chemical energy from one trophic level to another. The percentage of energy transferred from one trophic level to the next is called the ecological efficiency: these efficiencies of transfer are low and they account for the energy loss. Ecological efficiency varies between 5 and 20 per cent with an average of 10 per cent: on average, one tenth of the energy available to one trophic level becomes available to the next.

Ultimately all energy lost from an ecosystem is in the form of heat, through the inefficient energy conversions of respiration, so overall there is a conversion of light energy to heat energy by an ecosystem. Heat energy is re-radiated into the atmosphere.

Energy stores and flows

We have seen how diagrams can be used to show energy flow through ecosystems. Stores of energy are usually shown as boxes (other shapes may be used) which represent the various trophic levels. Flows of energy are usually shown as arrows (with the amount of energy in joules or biomass per unit area). Arrows can also show productivity (rates in J m^{-2} day^{-1}). Varying width of the arrows indicates proportionally how much energy or productivity is flowing at any point in the diagram.

Energy flow can be shown in the form of Sankey diagrams (Figure 2.28). The relative width of the bands (which can also be shown as arrows) represents the relative amount of energy flowing in joules. In Figure 2.28, mammals lose more energy to the environment as a result of the high levels of respiration needed to maintain body temperature and higher activity. Herbivores eat only plants so they take in contain large amounts of indigestible substances such as cellulose (in plant cell walls); the energy in indigestible substances is not absorbed, so is lost in faeces.

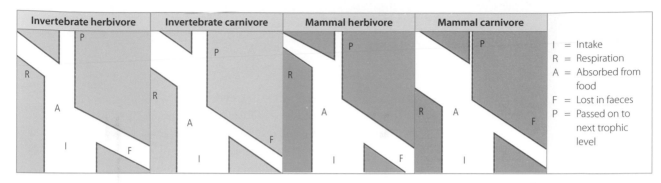

| Invertebrate herbivore | Invertebrate carnivore | Mammal herbivore | Mammal carnivore |

I	= Intake
R	= Respiration
A	= Absorbed from food
F	= Lost in faeces
P	= Passed on to next trophic level

▲ **Figure 2.28**
Energy flow in animals. Diagrams show energy flow through four types of animals. The diagrams are drawn to scale so that the width of the sections enables comparisons to be made.

Productivity diagrams were pioneered by American scientist Howard Odum in the 1950s. He carried out the first complete analysis of a natural ecosystem (a spring-fed stream) at Silver Spring in Florida. He mapped in detail all the flow routes to and from the stream, and measured the energy and organic matter inputs and outputs, and from these calculated productivity for each trophic level and the flows between them. Productivity was calculated in kcal m^{-2} yr^{-1}. From these figures he was able to draw the stream's energy budget (Figure 2.29). The main inputs are sunlight and other biomass, and energy leaves the system as heat from respiration in animals and as decomposed matter (not shown in the diagram). He also drew the diagram in the form of a river system which showed the same information but in a more naturalized way. The information from the Silver Spring study can be simplified still further (Figure 2.30). Productivity diagrams such as these are more useful than simple energy flow diagrams as they give an indication of turnover in ecosystems by measuring energy flows per unit time as well as area.

 To learn more about Howard Odum and his work, go to www.pearsonhotlinks.com, insert the express code 2630P and click on activity 2.12.

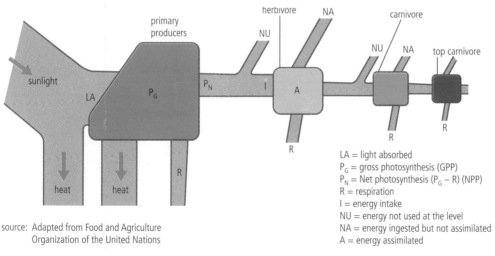

source: Adapted from Food and Agriculture Organization of the United Nations

LA = light absorbed
P_G = gross photosynthesis (GPP)
P_N = Net photosynthesis (P_G – R) (NPP)
R = respiration
I = energy intake
NU = energy not used at the level
NA = energy ingested but not assimilated
A = energy assimilated

◀ **Figure 2.29**
Productivity in a stream ecosystem at Silver Spring, Florida. Boxes show levels of productivity at each trophic level, from producers through to top carnivores, and linking bands (or arrows) show the flow of energy. (NPP and GPP are discussed later in this chapter.) Decomposers are not included in the diagram. Size relations in the diagram are approximate but not precisely to scale. Units are kcal m^{-2} yr^{-1} (1 kcal = 4.2 J).

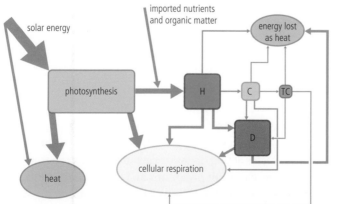

H = herbivores
C = carnivores
TC = top carnivores
D = decomposers

◀ **Figure 2.30**
Energy flows through an ecosystem simplified from Odum's Silver Springs model. Squares represent stores of biomass and ovals are movements of energy from the system. Arrows are approximately proportional to each other and indicate differences in energy flow between different parts of the system.

Transfer and transformation of materials within an ecosystem

Carbon cycle

Unlike energy, nutrients can be recycled and reused in ecosystems. Without this recycling, the Earth would be covered with detritus and the availability of nutrients would decline. Decomposition is at the centre of these nutrient cycles, but other processes play their part as well.

Carbon is an essential element in ecosystems as it forms the key component of biological molecules (e.g. carbohydrates, fats and protein). Although ecosystems form an important store of carbon (especially trees), it is also stored in fossil fuels (coal, gas, peat and oil) and in limestone, and can remain in these forms for very long periods of time (Figure 2.31).

Figure 2.31
Carbon stores and movement between them.

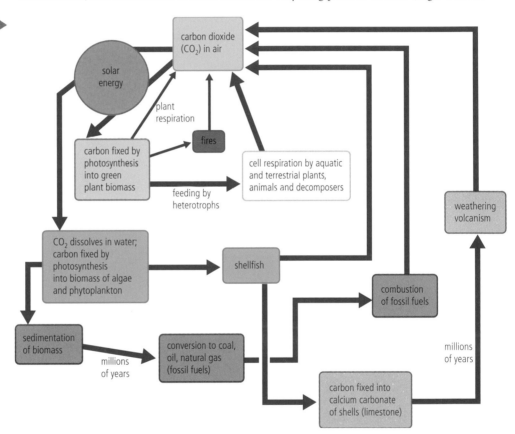

Carbon dioxide is fixed (i.e. converted from a simple inorganic molecule into a complex organic molecule – glucose) by autotrophs in either aquatic or terrestrial systems. These organisms respire and return some carbon into the atmosphere as carbon dioxide, or assimilate it into their bodies as biomass. When the organisms die, they are consumed by decomposers which use the dead tissue as a source of food, returning carbon to the atmosphere when they respire.

Oil and gas were formed millions of years ago when marine organisms died and fell to the bottom of the ocean, where anaerobic conditions halted the decay process. Burial of the organisms followed by pressure and heat over long periods of time created these fuels. Coal was formed largely by similar processes acting on land vegetation. Limestone (calcium carbonate) was formed by the shells of ancient organisms and corals being crushed and compressed into sedimentary rock. Weathering of limestone, **acid rain**, and the burning of fossil fuels, returns carbon to the atmosphere.

Nitrogen cycle

Nitrogen is an essential building block of amino acids (which link together to make proteins) and nucleic acids (which form the basis of DNA). It is a vital element for all organisms.

Nitrogen is the most abundant gas in the atmosphere (80 per cent) but because it is very stable (the two nitrogen atoms in a nitrogen molecule are triple-bonded) it is not directly accessible by animals or plants. Only certain species of bacteria (nitrogen-fixing bacteria) can generate the energy needed to split the triple bond to convert nitrogen gas into ammonia.

The nitrogen cycle (Figure 2.32) is driven by four types of bacteria:
- nitrogen-fixing bacteria
- decomposers
- nitrifying bacteria
- denitrifying bacteria.

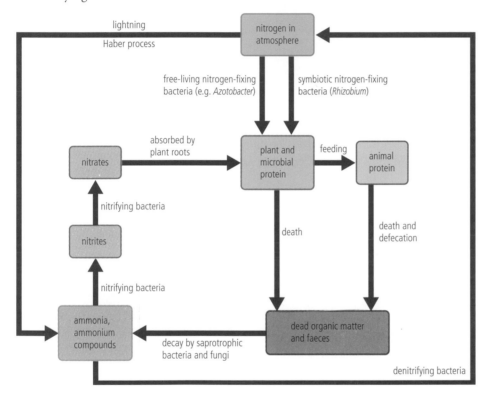

◀ **Figure 2.32**
Flows and storage of nitrogen in ecosystems.

Nitrogen-fixing bacteria are found either free-living in the soil (e.g. *Azotobacter*) or living within root nodules of leguminous plants (*Rhizobium*). Species in root nodules are symbiotic with the plant – they derive the sugars they need for respiration from the plant (a lot of energy is needed to split the nitrogen molecule) and the plants gain a useable form of nitrogen.

Lightning can fix atmospheric nitrogen into ammonia. Decomposers produce ammonia and ammonium compounds. Ammonia is also present in excretory products.

Nitrifying bacteria found in the soil oxidize the ammonia first into nitrites and then into nitrates. The bacteria gain energy from this reaction to form food (they are chemoautotrophs). Ammonia and nitrites are toxic to plants but the nitrates are taken up with water into plant roots and used to create amino acids and other organic chemicals.

Nitrogen is returned to the atmosphere by denitrifying bacteria, which remove oxygen from nitrates for use in respiration (they live in oxygen-poor soils where free oxygen is not readily available). Nitrogen gas is released as a by-product. The reason that water-logged soils are not good for farmers is that denitrifying bacteria enjoy these conditions and dramatically reduce the quantity of nitrates available for crop growth.

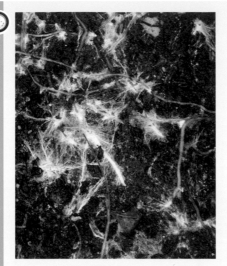

The breakdown of organic matter is higher in tropical forest than in temperate woodland because high temperatures and year-round availability of water in tropical forests allow for continuous breakdown of nitrogen-containing compounds. This results in very rapid turn-around and reabsorption. In temperate woodland, the breakdown of organic matter slows down significantly during winter months, causing nitrogen build up in soil.

Some tropical forest trees have specific species of mycorrhizal fungi associated with their roots that increase rate of organic matter breakdown leading to rapid reabsorption of nitrogen. Although soils are nutrient poor in tropical forests, the rapid recycling of nitrogen compared to temperate forests therefore allows for more rapid growth to occur.

Mycorrhizae attached to plant roots, form a thread-like network, extending beyond the roots. This extra network takes up additional water and nutrients and supplies them to the plant.

Nutrient cycles

Nutrient cycles can be shown in simple diagrams which show stores and transfers of nutrients (Figure 2.33).

Figure 2.33
Gersmehl's nutrient cycle.

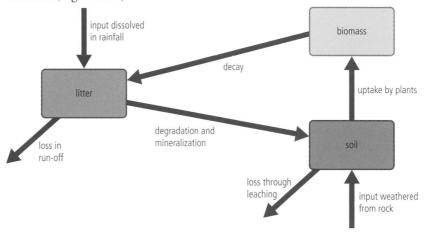

The factors that affect the store of nutrients and their transfer are those that affect:
- the amount and type of weathering
- overland run-off and soil erosion
- eluviations
- the amount of rainfall
- rates of decomposition
- the nature of vegetation (woody species hold onto nutrients for much longer than annuals)
- the age and health of plants
- plant density
- fire.

Hence, explaining the differences between nutrient cycles in different ecosystems involves a consideration of many processes.

Nutrients are circulated and re-used frequently. All natural elements are capable of being absorbed by plants, either as gases or as soluble salts. Only oxygen, carbon, hydrogen and nitrogen are needed in large quantities. These are known as macronutrients. The rest are trace elements or micronutrients and are needed only in small quantities (e.g. magnesium, sulfur and phosphorus). Nutrients are taken in by plants and built into new organic matter. When animals eat the plants, they take up the nutrients. The nutrients eventually return to the soil when the plants and animals die and are broken down by the decomposers.

All nutrient cycles involve interaction between soil and the atmosphere, and many food chains. Nevertheless, there is great variety between the cycles. Nutrient cycles can be sedimentary based, in which the source of the nutrient is from rocks, or they can be atmospheric based, as in the case of the nitrogen cycle. Generally, gaseous cycles are more complete than sedimentary ones, as the latter are more easily disturbed, especially by human activity.

Global water cycle

The hydrological cycle refers to the cycle of water between atmosphere, lithosphere and biosphere (Figure 2.34).

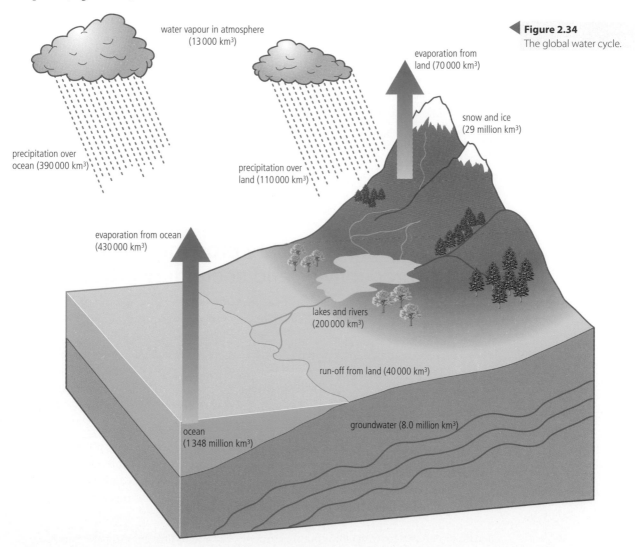

water vapour in atmosphere (13 000 km³)

evaporation from land (70 000 km³)

Figure 2.34
The global water cycle.

snow and ice (29 million km³)

precipitation over ocean (390 000 km³)

precipitation over land (110 000 km³)

evaporation from ocean (430 000 km³)

lakes and rivers (200 000 km³)

run-off from land (40 000 km³)

ocean (1 348 million km³)

groundwater (8.0 million km³)

At a local scale, the cycle has a single input (precipitation, PPT) and two major outputs (evapotranspiration, EVT, and run-off). A third output (leakage) may also occur from the deeper subsurface to other basins.

Throughput refers to the transfer of water through the system. Water can be stored at a number of stages or levels within the cycle. These stores include vegetation, surface, soil moisture, groundwater and water channels. The global hydrological cycle also includes the oceans and the atmosphere.

Human modifications are made at every scale. Good examples include large scale changes of channel flow and storage, irrigation and land drainage, and large-scale abstraction of groundwater and surface water for domestic and industrial use.

 To learn more about the water, carbon and nitrogen cycles, using a systems approach, go to www.pearsonhotlinks.com, insert the express code 2630P and click on activity 2.13.

EXERCISES

1 Explain the role of producers, consumers and decomposers in the ecosystem.

2 Summarize photosynthesis in terms of inputs, outputs and energy transformations. Now do the same for respiration.

3 **(a)** Why is not all available light energy transformed into chemical energy in biomass?
   (b) Why is not all of the energy in biomass made available to the next tropic level?

4 Construct a simple energy-flow diagram illustrating the movement of energy through ecosystems, including the productivity of the various trophic levels.

5 Draw systems diagrams for each of the following cycles:
   - the carbon cycle
   - the nitrogen cycle
   - the water cycle.

   Each should contain storages, flows, transfers and transformations.

Definitions: gross primary productivity, net primary productivity, and secondary productivity

We have already looked at productivity in ecosystems and described it as production per unit time. Productivity can be divided into primary and secondary productivity defined as follows.

- Primary productivity – The gain by producers (autotrophs) in energy or biomass per unit area per unit time.
- Secondary productivity – The biomass gained by heterotrophic organisms, through feeding and absorption, measured in units of mass or energy per unit area per unit time.

 Productivity is production per unit time.

Primary productivity is the conversion of solar energy whereas secondary productivity involves feeding or absorption. Primary productivity depends on the amount of sunlight, the ability of producers to use energy to synthesize organic compounds, and the availability of other factors needed for growth (e.g. minerals and nutrients) (Figure 2.35).

Secondary productivity depends on the amount of food present and the efficiency of consumers turning this into new biomass.

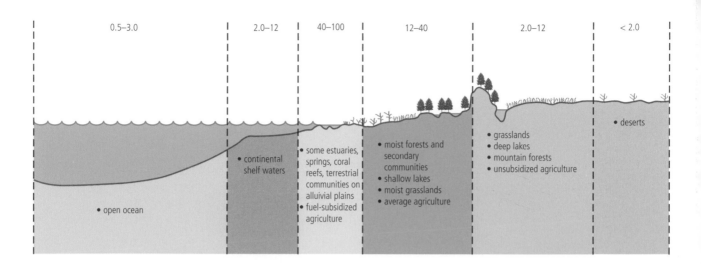

0.5–3.0		2.0–12	40–100	12–40		2.0–12	< 2.0

• open ocean

• continental shelf waters

• some estuaries, springs, coral reefs, terrestrial communities on alluvial plains
• fuel-subsidized agriculture

• moist forests and secondary communities
• shallow lakes
• moist grasslands
• average agriculture

• grasslands
• deep lakes
• mountain forests
• unsubsidized agriculture

• deserts

▲ **Figure 2.35**
Comparison of biomes in terms of primary production / 10^3 kJ m^{-2} yr^{-1}.

Primary production is highest where conditions for growth are optimal – where there are high levels of insolation, a good supply of water, warm temperatures, and high nutrient levels. For example, tropical rainforests have high rainfall and are warm throughout the year so they have a constant growing season and high productivity. Deserts have little rain which is limiting to plant growth. Estuaries receive sediment containing nutrients from rivers, they are shallow and therefore light and warm and so have high productivity. Deep oceans are dark below the surface and this limits productivity of plants.

Productivity can further be divided into gross and net productivity, in the same way that income can be divided into gross and net profits. Gross income is the total monetary income, and net income is gross income minus costs. Similarly, **gross productivity** (**GP**) is the total gain in energy or biomass per unit area per unit time; **gross primary productivity** (**GPP**) is gained through photosynthesis in primary producers, **gross secondary productivity** (**GSP**) is gained through absorption in consumers.

Net productivity (**NP**) is the gain in energy or biomass per unit area per unit time remaining after allowing for respiratory losses (R). NP represents the energy that is incorporated into biomass and is therefore available for the next trophic level. It is calculated by taking away from gross productivity the energy lost through respiration (other metabolic process may also lead to the loss of energy but these are minor and are discarded). As with gross productivity, NP can be divided into that made by producers (**net primary productivity, NPP**) and that made by consumers (**net secondary productivity, NSP**).

- NPP – The gain by producers in energy or biomass per unit area per unit time remaining after allowing for respiratory losses (R). This is potentially available to consumers in an ecosystem.
- NSP – The gain by consumers in energy or biomass per unit area per unit time remaining after allowing for respiratory losses (R).

• **Examiner's hint:**
The term 'assimilation' is sometimes used instead of 'secondary productivity'.

To learn more about primary and secondary productivity, go to www.pearsonhotlinks.com, insert the express code 2630P and click on activity 2.14.

Calculations of NPP, NSP and GSP

GPP is the total energy fixed by photosynthesis into new biomass. It is not easily calculable, NPP is usually calculated, as this can be easily measured by recording change in biomass.

Calculations of productivity can be summarized as follows:

Primary productivity (Figure 2.36):

where R = energy used in respiration

$$NPP = GPP - R$$

Figure 2.36
NPP is the rate at which plants accumulate dry mass in an ecosystem. It is a more useful value than GPP as it represents the actual store of energy contained in potential food for consumers rather than just the amount of energy fixed into sugar initially by the plant. The accumulation of dry mass is more usually termed biomass, and has a key part in determining the structure of an ecosystem.

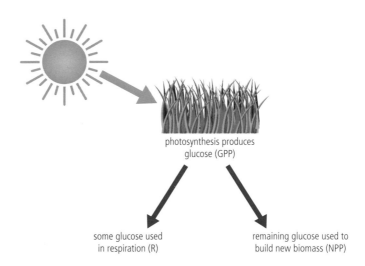

photosynthesis produces glucose (GPP)

some glucose used in respiration (R)

remaining glucose used to build new biomass (NPP)

Secondary productivity (Figures 2.37 and 2.38):

where GSP = food eaten – faecal loss

and R = respiratory loss

$$NSP = GSP - R$$

Figure 2.37
Animals do not use all the biomass they consume. Some of it passes out in faeces and excretion. Gross production in animals (GSP) is the amount of energy or biomass assimilated minus the energy or biomass of the faeces.

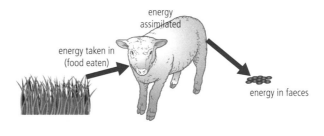

energy assimilated

energy taken in (food eaten)

energy in faeces

Figure 2.38
Some of the energy assimilated by animals is used in respiration, to support life processes, and the remainder is available to form new biomass (NSP). It is this new biomass that is then available to the next trophic level.

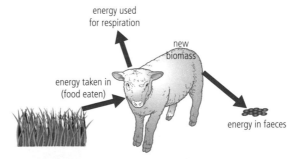

energy used for respiration

new biomass

energy taken in (food eaten)

energy in faeces

EXERCISES

1   Define the terms *gross productivity*, *net productivity*, *primary productivity* and *secondary productivity*.

2   How is NPP calculated from GPP? Which figure represents the biomass available to the next trophic level?

3   Define the terms *gross secondary productivity* (GSP) and *net secondary productivity* (NSP). Write the formula for each.

4 NPP, mean biomass, and NPP per kg biomass vary in different biomes, depending on levels of insolation, rainfall and temperature. Mean NPP for tropical rainforest is greater than tundra because rainforest is hot and wet, so there is more opportunity to develop large biomass than in tundra. However, NPP per kg biomass is far lower in rainforest than tundra because rainforest has a high rate of both photosynthesis and respiration, so NPP compared to total biomass is low. Tundra are cold and dry and have low rates of photosynthesis and respiration; plants are slow growing with a gradual accumulation of biomass but relatively large growth in biomass per year.

The table below shows values for these parameters for different biomes.

Biome	Mean net primary productivity (NPP) / $kg\,m^{-2}\,yr^{-1}$	Mean biomass / $kg\,m^{-2}$	NPP per kg biomass per year
desert	0.003	0.002	
tundra	0.14	0.60	0.233
temperate grassland	0.60	1.60	0.375
savannah (tropical) grassland	0.90	4.00	0.225
temperate forest	1.20	32.50	0.037
tropical rainforest	2.20	45.00	0.049

(a) Calculate the NPP per kg of biomass per year for the desert biome.

(b) How does this figure compare those for other biomes? Explain the figure you have calculated in terms of NPP, and NPP per kg biomass.

(c) Compare the figures for NPP in temperate and tropical grassland. Explain the difference.

 Changes

Limiting factors and carrying capacity

Populations are constrained by limiting factors. Carrying capacity is the maximum number of organisms that an area or ecosystem can sustainably support over a long period of time.

Limiting factors include temperature, water and nutrient availability. The main limiting climatic features are temperature and water availability. Every species has a tolerance range for any environmental factor; those with a wide range are described as stenoecious species, those with a narrow range are described as euryoecious species.

The concept of tolerance suggests that there are upper and lower levels of environmental factors beyond which a population cannot survive, and that there is an optimum range within which species can thrive (Figure 2.39, overleaf).

Figure 2.39
The concept of tolerance.

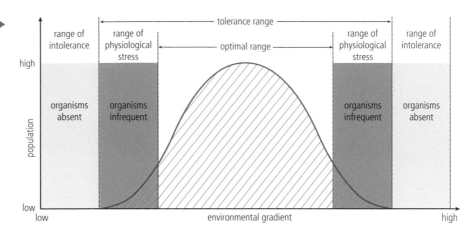

Species at the lower end of the tolerance curve are known as oligotypic, those at the higher end are known as polytypic, and those in the middle are known as mesotypic.

Limiting factors are the factors that limit the distribution or numbers of a particular population. Limiting factors are environmental factors which slow down population growth.

Carrying capacity refers to the number of organisms – or size of population – that an area or ecosystem can support sustainably over a long period of time.

The term limiting factor was first used by the German agricultural chemist Justus von Liebig (1803–1873) who noted that the growth of crops was limited by the shortage of certain minerals. Liebig established the 'law of minimum' – that the productivity, reproduction and growth of organisms will be limited if one or more environmental factors lies below its limiting level. Equally, there can be too much of a factor (e.g. there is an upper limit to how much of a particular nutrient plants can tolerate).

Temperature

Many aspects of temperature affect species. These include daily, monthly and annual extremes, and mean temperatures. Temperature may be limiting at different stages in the life cycle – for example, some seeds in savannah grasslands will germinate only after high temperatures caused by fires. These fires enrich the soil with nutrients and kill off competitors thereby helping the survival chances of the seeds.

In most animals, temperature is a vital limiting factor. Cold-blooded animals can take advantage of sunny areas or warm rocks to heat their bodies. In hot deserts, animals are limited by excessive heat. To cope, some animals avoid the heat by burrowing, while others have physiological adaptations to tolerate high body temperatures.

Plants vary enormously in their ability to tolerate extremes of temperature. Categories of cold-tolerance in plants include the following.
- Chill-sensitive – Plants are damaged below 10 °C (e.g. tropical plants).
- Frost-sensitive – Plants can survive below 10 °C but are damaged if ice forms in their tissues.
- Frost-resistant – Plants can survive temperatures as low as –15 °C.
- Frost-tolerant – Plants survive by withdrawing water from their cells, so preventing ice from forming.
- Cold-tolerant – Plants with needle-shaped leaves which can survive low temperatures.

Water

All plants and animals need water to survive. For plants, water stress (i.e. too little water) may cause germination to fail, seedlings to die, and seed yield to be reduced. Water and temperature conditions vary around the world (Figure 2.10).

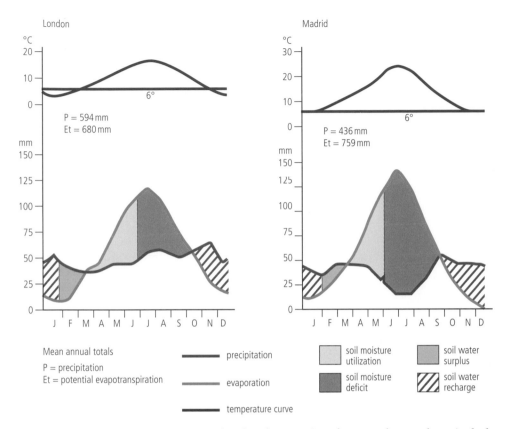

London
°C
P = 594 mm
Et = 680 mm
6°

Madrid
°C
P = 436 mm
Et = 759 mm
6°

Mean annual totals
P = precipitation
Et = potential evapotranspiration

— precipitation
— evaporation
— temperature curve

soil moisture utilization
soil moisture deficit
soil water surplus
soil water recharge

Figure 2.40
Climographs and soil moisture status.

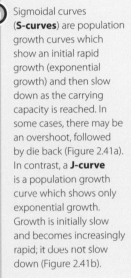

Sigmoidal curves (**S-curves**) are population growth curves which show an initial rapid growth (exponential growth) and then slow down as the carrying capacity is reached. In some cases, there may be an overshoot, followed by die back (Figure 2.41a). In contrast, a **J-curve** is a population growth curve which shows only exponential growth. Growth is initially slow and becomes increasingly rapid; it does not slow down (Figure 2.41b).

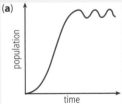
(a)
population
time

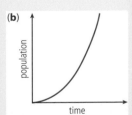
(b)
population
time

Figure 2.41
(a) S-curve.
(b) J-curve.

Plants are extremely sensitive to water level and categories of water-tolerant plants include the following.

- Hydrophytes – Water-tolerant plants which can root in standing water.
- Mesophytes – Plants that inhabit moist but not wet environments.
- Xerophytes – Plants that live in dry environments.

Xerophyte adaptations to avoid water shortages include remaining as seeds until rain prompts germination, and storing water in stems, leaves or roots. Plants that store water are called succulents. Many succulents have a crassulacean acid metabolism (CAM) which allows them to take in carbon dioxide at night when their stomata are open, and use it during the day when the stomata are closed. Other xerophytes have thick, waxy cuticles, sunken and smaller stomata, and drop their leaves in dry periods.

S- and J-curves

The **S-curve** has been recorded for the re-establishment of vegetation after the eruption of Krakatau in 1883 (Chapter 4, page 184) and the Mt St Helens eruption in 1980. The typical S-curve shows three stages:

- exponential growth stage – in which the population grows at an increasingly rapid rate
- transitional phase – where the population growth slows considerably – but it continues to grow
- plateau (or stationary) phase – in which the number of individuals stabilizes and population growth stabilizes.

Exponential growth phase

In this phase, if there are no limiting factors, a population can double in size on a regular basis. A population of rabbits, for example, can double every four months. A good example of exponential growth is that of cane toads in Australia. The reasons for the exponential growth include:

- plentiful resources such as light, space and food
- lack of competition from other species
- favourable abiotic factors such as temperature and rainfall
- lack of predators or disease.

Transitional phase

In this phase, unlimited growth declines as the factors listed above begin to change. The causes of the slowdown include:

- increase in competition for resources because there are too many individuals in the population
- increase in predators attracted by the large population (food supply)
- increase in rate of disease (and mortality) due to increased numbers of individuals living in a small area.

Plateau phase

Over time, as available space and resources decrease, birth rates decline. As the risk of disease increases, mortality rates rise. This slows population growth. The combination of fewer births and increased mortality reinforce the decline in population increase. The population plateaus.

There is a limit to the size of a population that can be supported by an environment. Exponential increase can only occur when the population size is small in relation to the carrying capacity. Once the population exceeds the carrying capacity, death rates increase and population crashes may occur.

Long- and short-lived species

Some populations have a cyclical explosion–crash cycle (Figure 2.42). Such a pattern characterizes fast-reproducing, short-lived species at lower trophic levels; examples include rodents, insects and annual plants. The numbers of these species are generally regulated by external factors such as climatic conditions, predators or nutrition (food supply).

Figure 2.42
Periodic population explosion and crash.

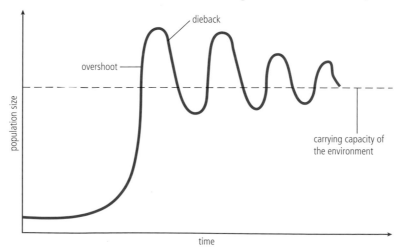

Longer-lived species with few predators tend to follow the S-curve. Exponential growth is followed by slower growth due to density-dependent and density-independent factors. The population adapts to the environmental carrying capacity (Figure 2.43).

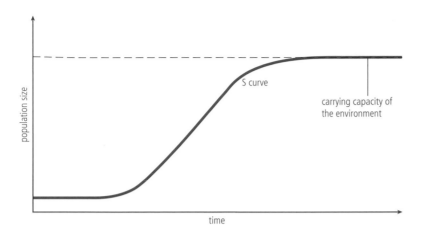

S curve

carrying capacity of the environment

population size

time

Figure 2.43
Population growth adapting to carrying capacity.

To learn more about population growth curves, go to www. pearsonhotlinks.com, insert the express code 2630P and click on activity 2.15.

EXERCISES

1   The data below show rates of growth in ticklegrass (as above ground biomass in g m⁻²) in soils with low or high nitrogen content and using high or low seed density.

Year	Low nitrogen, high seed density: above ground biomass / $g\,m^{-2}$	Low nitrogen, low seed density: above ground biomass / $g\,m^{-2}$	High nitrogen, high seed density: above ground biomass / $g\,m^{-2}$	High nitrogen, low seed density: above ground biomass / $g\,m^{-2}$
1	0	0	0	0
2	420	60	500	30
3	780	80	1050	100
4	0	70	0	90
5	50	100	160	80
6	180	110	600	70

(a) Plot the data showing the growth rates among ticklegrass depending on nitrogen availability and density of seeds.

(b) Describe the results you have produced.

(c) Suggest reasons for these results.

2   The table below shows population growth in a population with discrete generations, starting with a population of 1000 and increasing at a constant reproductive rate of 1.2 per cent per generation.

Generation number	Population (N)	Increase in population
N0	1000	–
N1	1200	200
N2	1440	240
N3	1728	288
N4	2074	346
N5	2488	414
N6	2986	498
N7	3583	597
N8		
N9		
N10		
N11		
N12		
N13		
N14		
N15		

(a) Complete the table by working out total population (Column 2) and working out the increase in population size from generation to generation (column 3).

(b) Plot the graph of total population size.

(c) Describe the graph and identify the type of population growth that it shows.

● **Examiner's hint:**
The figures in Column 2 have been rounded to a whole number, but the real number for each generation has been multiplied by 1.2 to get the answer for the next generation (e.g. N4 has a population of 2073.6. This has been rounded up to 2074. However, to find N5, 2037.6 has been multiplied by 1.2 to make 2488.32 which is rounded down to 2488).

Density-dependent and density-independent factors

Density-dependent factors

Some limiting factors are related to population density. Examples are competition for resources, space, disease, parasitism and predation. As a population grows in size, the availability of food per individual decreases and this can lead to a reduced birth rate and an increased death rate. Predators may be attracted to areas of high prey population density, hence the mortality rate may increase. Disease spreads more easily in dense populations. Other **density-dependent** factors include the size of the breeding population and size of territory. The larger the population size, and the larger the territory, the greater the potential chance that a species has for survival.

Density-dependent factors operate as negative feedback mechanisms (Figure 2.44) regulating the population and leading to stability.

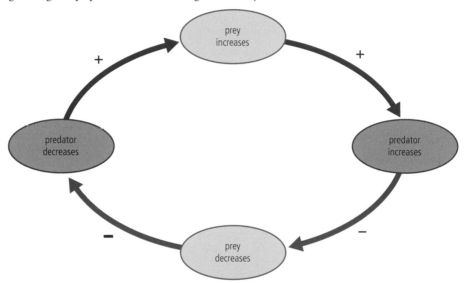

Figure 2.44
Predator–prey relationships show negative feedback.

Predator–prey relationships are a good example of density-dependent control. In a relative absence of predators (due to a limited prey population), the prey population may begin to increase in size. As the availability of prey increases, there is an increase in predator numbers, after a time-lag. As the number of predators increases, the population size of the prey begins to decrease. With fewer prey, the number of predators decreases, but with fewer predators the number of prey may begin to increase again and the cycle continues. This can be seen in the variations of the snowshoe hare and lynx populations in Canada (Figure 1.10, page 8) and also in the variations of the lemming and snowy owl populations in the northern circumpolar regions (Figure 2.45, opposite). Nevertheless, predation may be good for the prey: it removes old and sick individuals first as these are easier to catch. Those remaining are healthier and form a superior breeding pool.

Density-independent factors

Density-independent factors can operate alongside density-dependent factors. Density-independent factors are generally abiotic. The most important ones are extremes of weather (drought, fire, hurricanes) and long-term climate change. Others include geophysical events such as volcanic eruptions and tsunamis. Their impact is to increase the death rate and reduce the birth rate, especially of smaller individuals. The response depends, in part, on the frequency and severity of the event.

 Density-dependent factors are those that lower the birth rate or raise the death rate as a population grows in size. In contrast, **density-independent** factors are those which affect a population irrespective of population density, notably environmental change.

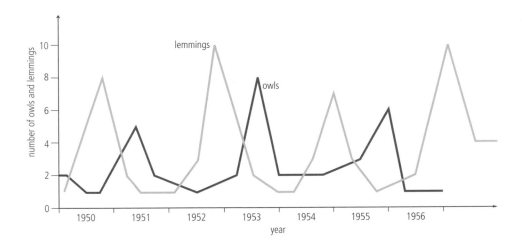

Figure 2.45
Variations in the populations of lemmings and snow owls.

Internal and external factors

Internal factors include density-dependent fertility or size of breeding territory, and external factors include predation or disease.

The ultimate causes of population regulation are found in the environment: factors external to the population limit the rate at which individuals can reproduce and survive. These factors can be divided into physical and biological classes. The physical class of environmental factors include water availability, nutrient availability, temperature, and so on. The biological factors include predation and competition. Competition can be between species (interspecific competition) or within the same species (intraspecific competition).

Increasingly, human activities have had an impact on natural populations. Farming, settlement, transport and industry have all disrupted natural populations. Humans may cause population growth by removing previous limitations, or cause population decline by creating new stresses.

Four ways that humans can cause population growth:
- increase available resources (e.g. by farming; by nutrient pollution in lakes)
- reduce competition (e.g. by poisoning insect pests)
- reduce pressure from predators (e.g. by over-hunting large carnivores)
- introduce animals to new areas (e.g. game releases).

Four ways that humans can cause population decline and extinction:
- change the physical environment and cause habitat disruption (e.g. by draining a swamp; by causing toxic pollution)
- change the biological environment by introducing new species (e.g. rabbits in Australia; rats on islands)
- overkill (e.g. big-game hunting)
- cause secondary extinctions (e.g. loss of food species).

 Human impact, both direct and indirect, on the world's rainforest is having a major effect on species survival. Uncontrolled hunting for bushmeat is removing large species and creating an 'empty forest syndrome' – the trees are there but the large species have disappeared. The replacement of natural tropical rainforest by oil palm plantations is replacing a diverse ecosystem with a monoculture ecosystem. In addition, the impact of climate change is a major threat to the rainforest. As many tropical species evolved in environments that had little temperature variation, they may be ill-equipped to deal with changes of more than 3 °C. By 2100, 75 per cent of tropical forests will be warmer than today.

 The environmental damage inflicted by hurricane Katrina in 2005 was widespread. About 85 000 barrels of crude oil escaped from an oil plant in Chalmette, Louisiana, and a further 68 000 barrels were spilled by a damaged storage tank in Venice. The oil pollution from Katrina is among the worst ever in US history. More than 6.5 million gallons of crude oil was spilt in seven major incidents. This figure does not include petrol and oil spilt from up to 250 000 cars that were submerged, or from petrol stations. In addition, more than 500 sewerage systems were damaged across Louisiana. Some 6600 petrol stations, each with an average of three underground storage tanks, as well as hundreds of industrial facilities, were damaged.

Damage to the oyster, crab and shrimp populations was extensive. The Gulf is home to more than 80 per cent of oysters grown in the United States and is the centre of the shrimp industry. In addition, the accumulated long-term industrial pollution held in the soil was released by the floodwaters. Much was pumped into Lake Pontchartrain. The ecology is definitely being changed.

A range of ecological impacts were caused by the Boxing Day 2004 tsunami. The force of the tsunami drove approximately 100 000 tonnes of water onto every 1.5 m of coastline and therefore caused considerable erosion in some parts and devastating deposition in others. The intrusion of salt water has polluted fresh water sources and farmland sometimes as far as several kilometres inland. Coral reefs were damaged, and large area of mangrove uprooted. Of particular concern are the endangered sea turtles of Sri Lanka and some of the Indian islands. On the east coast of Sri Lanka, almost all of the hatcheries were destroyed when the sandy beaches were washed away.

 The introduction of a few pairs of European rabbits into Australia (for hunting) resulted in a population explosion to around 600 million animals. In 1950, the government sanctioned the release of the myxomatosis virus – a density-independent factor – and cut the population to 100 million.

However, by 1991, genetic resistance had rebuilt the population to as many as 300 million, prompting a second virus, the calicivirus, to be released. Where there was a greater density of rabbits, the virus was more lethal than where the population was lighter – thus this viral disease illustrates density-dependent control.

Survivorship curves – *r*- and *K*-strategists

Slow growing organisms tend to be limited by the carrying capacity of an environment (K), and so are known as **K-strategists** or K-species. They inhabit stable environments. Species characterized by periods of rapid growth followed by decline, tend to inhabit unpredictable, rapidly changing environments and are termed opportunistic species. They have a fast rate of increase (r) and are called **r-strategists** or r-species. Many species lie in between these two extremes and are known as C-strategists or C-species.

A female cane toad spawns twice a year and produces up to 35 000 eggs each time!

Species characterized as r-strategists produce many, small offspring that mature rapidly. They receive little or no parental care. Species producing egg-sacs are a good example. In contrast, species that are K-strategists produce very few, often very large offspring that mature slowly and receive much parental support. Elephants and whales are good examples. As a result of the low birth rate, K-strategists are vulnerable to high death rates and extinction.

 K-strategists are slow growing and produce few, large offspring that mature slowly; **r-strategists** grow and mature quickly and produce many, small offspring.

r- and *K*- selection theory

This theory states that natural selection may favour individuals with a high reproductive rate and rapid development (r-strategists) over those with lower reproductive rates but better competitive ability (K-strategists). Characteristics of the classes are shown in Table 2.1.

TABLE 2.1 A COMPARISON OF *r*- AND *K*-SPECIES	
r-strategists	*K*-strategists
initial colonizers	dominant species
large numbers of a few species	diverse range of species
highly adaptable	generalists
rapid growth and development	slow development
early reproduction	delayed reproduction
short life	longer living
small size	larger size
very productive	less productive

In predictable environments – those in which resources do not fluctuate – there is little advantage to rapid growth. Instead, natural selection favours species that can maximize use of natural resources and which produce only a few young which have a high probability of survival. These *K*-strategists have long life spans, large body size and develop slowly.

In contrast, disturbed habitats with rapidly changing conditions favour *r*-strategists that can respond rapidly, develop quickly and have early reproduction. This leads to a high rate of productivity. Such colonizer species often have a high dispersal ability to reach areas of disturbance.

 Species can have traits of both *K*- and *r*-strategists. Studies of dandelions in a disturbed lawn had high reproduction rates whereas those on an undisturbed lawn produced fewer seeds but were better competitors.

Survivorship curves

Rates of mortality vary with age, size and sometimes gender. Survivorship curves shows changes in survivorship over the lifespan of the species (Figure 2.46).

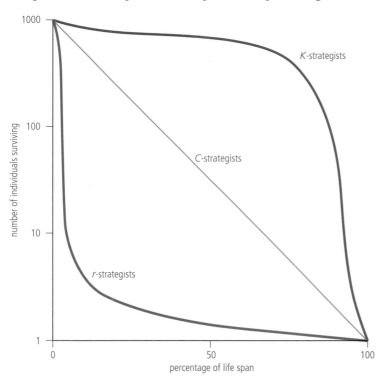

◀ **Figure 2.46**
Survivorship rates.

Factors that influence survivorship rates include:
- competition for resources
- adverse environmental conditions
- predator–prey relationships.

The two extreme examples of a survivorship curve (as shown in Figure 2.46) are:
- the curve for a species where almost all individuals survive for their potential life span, and then die almost simultaneously (*K*-strategists) – salmon and humans are excellent examples
- the curve for a species where most individuals die at a very young age but those that survive are likely to live for a very long time (*r*-strategists) – turtles and oysters are very good examples.

● **Examiner's hint:**
Note that the scale in Figure 2.47 is semi-logarithmic. This means that one axis – here, the horizontal or *x*-axis – is a normal scale and the gaps between each unit are regular: the distance between 0 and 50 is the same as between that between 50 and 100. In contrast, the vertical or *y*-axis is logarithmic.

Note that on the logarithmic scale:
● the scale does not start at 0 (in this example, it starts at 1)
● the scale goes up in logarithms (the first cycle goes up in 1s, the second cycle in 10s, the next in 100s).

The reason for using a logarithmic scale is that it enables us to show very large values on the same graph as very small values.

1 Explain the concepts of limiting factors and carrying capacity in the context of population growth.

2 **(a)** Describe and explain each of the following graphs:

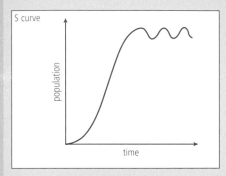

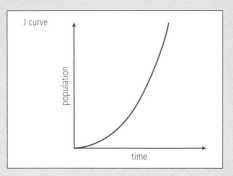

(b) Which species show the S-shaped population curve?
(c) Which species follow the J-shaped population curve?

3 Describe the role of density-dependent and density-independent factors, and internal and external factors, in the regulation of populations.

4 Draw survivorship curves for *K*-strategists, and for *r*-strategists. Describe and explain your graphs.

5 Draw a table with *r*-strategists in one column and *K*-strategists in the other. List the characteristics that apply to each.

Figure 2.47
A typical forest succession pattern. Left undisturbed, uncolonized land will grow from a meadow into a scrub community, then become populated by pines and small trees and ultimately by large hardwood trees.

Succession

Succession is the long-term change in the composition of a community (Figure 2.47). It explains how ecosystems develop from bare substrate over a period of time. The change in communities from the earliest (**pioneer**) community to the final community is called a **sere**. Successions can be divided into a series of stages, with each distinct community in the succession called a **seral stage**.

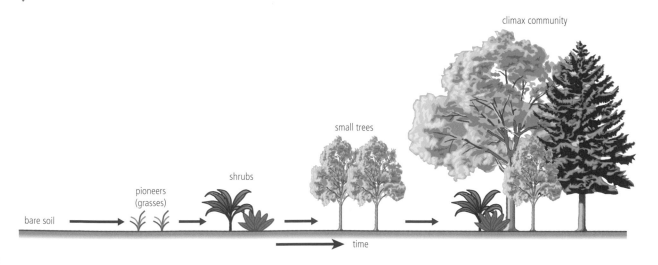

There are various types of succession, depending on the type of environment occupied:
- succession on bare rock is a **lithosere** (Figure 2.48)
- succession in a freshwater habitat is a **hydrosere**
- succession in a dry habitat (e.g. sand) is a **xerosere**.

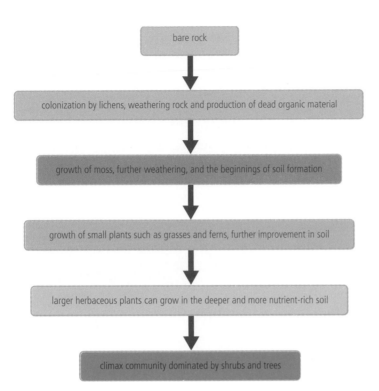

Figure 2.48
A model of succession on bare rock.

```
                    bare rock

colonization by lichens, weathering rock and production of dead organic material

     growth of moss, further weathering, and the beginnings of soil formation

    growth of small plants such as grasses and ferns, further improvement in soil

      larger herbaceous plants can grow in the deeper and more nutrient-rich soil

            climax community dominated by shrubs and trees
```

Succession occurring on a previously uncolonized substrate (e.g. rock) is called a **primary succession**. **Secondary succession** occurs in places where a previous community has been destroyed (e.g. after forest fires). Secondary succession is faster than a primary succession because of the presence of soil and a seed bank.

Succession happens when species change the habitat they have colonized and make it more suitable for new species. For example, lichens and mosses are typical pioneer species. Very few species can live on bare rock as it contains little water and has few available nutrients. Lichens can photosynthesize and are effective at absorbing water, so they need no soil to survive and are excellent pioneers. Once established, they trap particles blown by the wind; their growth reduces wind speed and increases temperature close to the ground. When they die and decompose they form a simple soil in which grasses can germinate. The growth of pioneers helps to weather parent rock adding still further to the soil. Other species, such as grasses and ferns that grow in thin soil, are now better able to colonize.

The new species are better competitors than the earlier species; for example, grasses grow taller than mosses and lichen, so they get more light for photosynthesis. Their roots trap substrate thereby halting erosion, and they have a larger photosynthetic area, so they grow faster. The next stage involves the growth of herbaceous plants (e.g. dandelion and goosegrass), which require more soil to grow but which out-compete the grasses – they have wind-dispersed seeds and rapid growth, so they become established before larger plants. Shrubs then appear (e.g. bramble, gorse, and rhododendron), which are larger plants that can grow in good soil, and which are better competitors than the slower-growing pioneers.

The final stage of a succession is the **climax** community. Here grown trees produce too much shade for the shrubs, which are replaced by shade-tolerant forest floor species. The amount of organic matter increases as succession progresses because as pioneer and subsequent species die out, their remains contribute to a build-up of litter from the biomass. Soil organisms move in and break down litter, leading to a build up of organic matter in the soil making it easier for other species to colonize. Soil also traps water, and so increasing amounts of moisture are available to plants in the later stages of the succession.

Succession and zonation

The concept of **succession** must be carefully distinguished from the concept of **zonation** (Figure 2.49). Succession refers to changes over time, and zonation to spatial patterns. Rocky shores can be divided into zones from lower to upper shore, with each zone defined by the spatial patterns of animals and plants. Seaweeds in particular show distinct zonation patterns, with species more resilient to water loss found on the upper shore (e.g. channel wrack) and those less resilient on the lower shore where they are not out of water for long (e.g. kelp).

Figure 2.49
Zonation: the arrangement or patterning of communities into parallel or sub-parallel bands in response to change, over a distance, in some environmental factor. For example, changes in ecosystems up a mountain with increasing altitude.

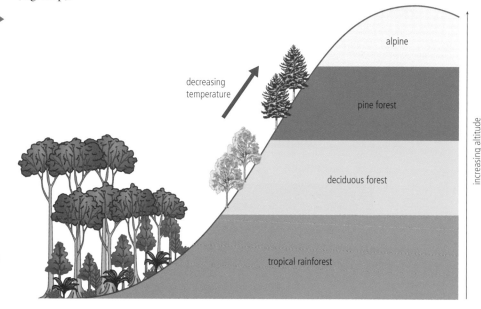

- **Succession** – The orderly process of change over time in a community. Changes in the community of organisms frequently cause changes in the physical environment that allow another community to become established and replace the former through competition. Often, but not inevitably, the later communities in such a sequence or sere are more complex than those that appear earlier.
- **Zonation** – The arrangement or patterning of plant communities or ecosystems into bands in response to change, over a distance, in some environmental factor. The main biomes display zonation in relation to latitude and climate. Plant communities may also display zonation with altitude on a mountain, or around the edge of a pond in relation to soil moisture.

CASE STUDY

Mt Kinabalu, Borneo

At 4100 m, Mount Kinabalu is the highest peak between the Himalayas and Papua New Guinea.

Mount Kinabalu shows classic altitudinal zonation, with tropical rainforest at its base, through tropical montane (containing mixed broad-leaved and coniferous evergreen trees) to alpine communities near the bare granite summit. Temperature in the rainforest at the base of the mountain is around 26 °C but at the summit can be as low as 0 °C, and it is this change in temperature that causes the zonation seen.

The large number of different ecosystems found on the mountain provides a huge variety of different habitats for species to live in, and Mount Kinabalu is well-known worldwide for its tremendous botanical and biological species diversity (Figure 2.50). It has one of the world's richest orchid flora with over 800 species. There are more species of fern (600 species) than in the whole of Africa (500 species). A recent botanical study estimated a colossal 5000 to 6000 plant species. Because some of the upper communities are isolated from similar communities elsewhere, the mountain has many endemic species (i.e. species found only on Mount Kinabalu). Five of its thirteen pitcher plants are not found anywhere else on Earth; for example, *Nepenthes rajah* (page 22).

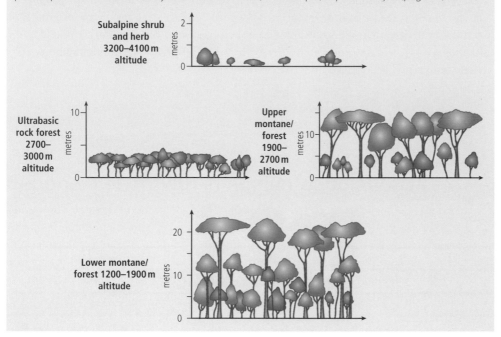

◀ **Figure 2.50**
Forest structure changes dramatically through the different zones on the mountain, from tall rainforest to short and sparse alpine shrub and herb communities near the summit.

W To learn more about Mount Kinabalu, go to www.pearsonhotlinks. com, insert the express code 2630P and click on activity 2.16.

Changes in succession

Table 2.2 shows some changes that are seen as a succession progresses.

● **Examiner's hint:**
Succession occurs over time, whereas **zonation** refers to a spatial pattern.

TABLE 2.2	FEATURES OF EARLY AND LATE SUCCESSION	
Feature	Early	Late
organic matter	small	large
nutrients	external	internal
nutrient cycles	open	closed
nutrient conservation	poor	good
role of detritus	small	large
niches	wide	narrow
size of organisms	small	large
life cycles	simple	complex
growth form	*r*-species	*K*-species
diversity	low	high
stability	poor	good

Source: Adapted from Briggs D, et al. *Fundamentals of the physical environment*, 1997, p. 380

Gross productivity, net productivity and diversity will change over time as an ecosystem goes through succession. In the early stages of succession, gross productivity is low due to the initial conditions and low density of producers. The proportion of energy lost through community respiration (i.e. respiration of all organisms present) is relatively low too, so net productivity is high (e.g. the system is growing and biomass is accumulating). As succession progresses, soils become better structured and more fertile, and can support a greater diversity of producers, as well as larger producers. Gross productivity by producers therefore increases. As plants grow, the number of niches increases, food webs become more complex, and diversity increases. As food webs become more complex, net productivity increases. Gross primary productivity, net primary productivity and diversity stabilize as the ecosystem reaches climax population.

Figure 2.51
Changes in biotic and abiotic factors along a sand-dune succession.

Further changes in a succession are shown in Figure 2.51.

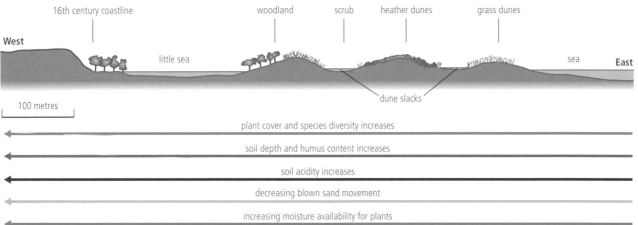

Production : respiration ratio

We have seen how early stages of a succession have low GPP but high NPP due to the low overall rates of respiration. This relationship can be described as a ratio (production : respiration or P/R). If production is equal to rate of respiration, the value is 1. Where P/R is greater than 1, biomass accumulates; where P/R is less than 1, biomass is depleted. Where P/R = 1 a steady-state community results. In the later stages of a succession, with an increased consumer community, rates of community respiration are high. Gross productivity may be high in a climax community but, as this is balanced by respiration, the net productivity approaches zero (NP = GP – respiration), and the P/R ratio approaches 1.

If the production : respiration ratios of a food production system are compared to a natural ecosystem with a climax community, clear differences can be seen (Figure 2.52). This diagram compares intensive crop production with deciduous woodland. Fields and woodland both have low initial productivity, which increases rapidly as biomass accumulates. Farmers do not want the P/R ratio to reach 1 because, at that point, community respiration negates the high rates of gross productivity, which means that yields are not increased. The wheat is therefore harvested before P/R = 1. Community respiration is also controlled in the food production system by isolating herbivores and thereby increasing net productivity and growth. In natural woodland, the consumer community increases, so naturally high productivity is balanced by consumption and respiration. The woodland reaches its climax community when P/R = 1 (i.e. all woodland productivity is balanced by respiration).

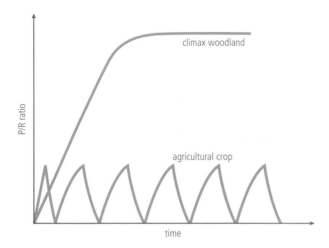

Climax communities

Ecosystem stability refers to how well an ecosystem is able to cope with changes. As we saw in Chapter 1, most ecosystems are negative feedback systems – they contain inbuilt checks and balances without which they would spiral out of control, and no ecosystem would be self-sustaining. Ecosystems with more feedback mechanisms are more stable than simple ecosystems. Thus, ecosystems in the later stages of succession are likely to be more stable because food webs are more complex (because of high species diversity). This means that a species can turn to alternative food sources if one species is reduced. By late succession, large amounts of organic matter are available to provide a good source of nutrients. Nutrient cycles are closed and self-sustaining; they are not dependent on external influences. This also contributes to stability.

The features of a climax community (compared to an early community) are:
- greater biomass
- higher levels of species diversity
- more favourable soil conditions (e.g. greater organic content)
- better soil structure (therefore, greater water retention)
- lower pH
- taller and longer-living plant species
- more *K*-strategists or fewer *r*-strategists
- greater community complexity and stability
- greater habitat diversity
- steady-state equilibrium.

Lowland tropical rainforest is a climax community in South-East Asia. Hardwood trees of the family Dipterocarpaceae are dominant. They are often very tall and provide a rich three-dimensional architecture to the forest.

Temperate forests are often dominated by a single tree species, such as the oak. ▶

Redwood forests along the Pacific coast of the USA contain some of the tallest trees in the world. The dominant species in terms of biomass is *Sequoia sempervirens*. Trees can reach up to 115.5 m (379.1 ft) in height and 8 m (26 ft) in diameter ▶

Plagioclimax

Climatic and edaphic factors determine the nature of a climax community. Human factors frequently affect this process through disturbance. The interference halts the process of succession so that the climax community is not reached. Interrupted succession is known as **plagioclimax**. An example is the effect of footpath erosion caused by continued trampling by feet. Or consider a sand dune ecosystem, where walkers might trample plants to the extent that they are eventually destroyed.

Human activity can affect the climax community through agriculture, hunting, clearance, burning, and grazing: all these activities create a plagioclimax by arresting succession.

Burning and deforestation of the Amazon forest to make grazing land leads to loss of large areas of rainforest. Continued burning and clearance, and the establishment of grasslands, prevents succession occurring. ▶

Large parts of the UK were once covered by deciduous woodland. Some heather would have been present in the north, but relatively little. From the Middle Ages onwards, forests were cleared to supply timber for fuel, housing, construction of ships (especially oak), and to clear land for agriculture. As a result, soil deteriorated and heather came to dominate the plant community. Sheep grazing has prevented the re-growth of woodland by destroying young saplings.

Controlled burning of heather also prevents the re-establishment of deciduous woodland. The heather is burnt after 15 years, before it becomes mature. If the heather matured, it would allow colonization of the area by other plants. The ash adds to the soil fertility and the new heather growth that results increases the productivity of the ecosystem.

Deforestation is having a major impact on one of the most diverse biomes, tropical rainforest (Figures 2.53, 2.54 and 2.55). An area of rainforest the size of a football pitch is destroyed every four seconds. As well as loss of habitat and destruction of a complex climax community, the carbon dioxide released when the trees are burnt returns to the atmosphere: this amount of carbon dioxide is more than that from the entire global transport sector (Chapter 6).

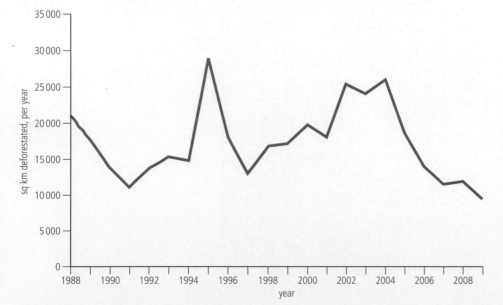

Figure 2.53
Deforestation in the Brazilian Amazon basin fluctuates but remains high despite warnings about the consequences for the planet. The loss of the highly diverse climax community and its replacement by agricultural or grazing ecosystems affects global biodiversity, regional weather, the water cycle and sedimentation patterns.

Figure 2.54
Deforestation in the Brazilian Amazon basin, 2000–05 – the reasons land is deforested. The high percentage of meat in western diet, and the increasing consumption of beef in the developing world, demand land for cattle ranching. This is the main driver of human impact on the ecology of the Amazon.

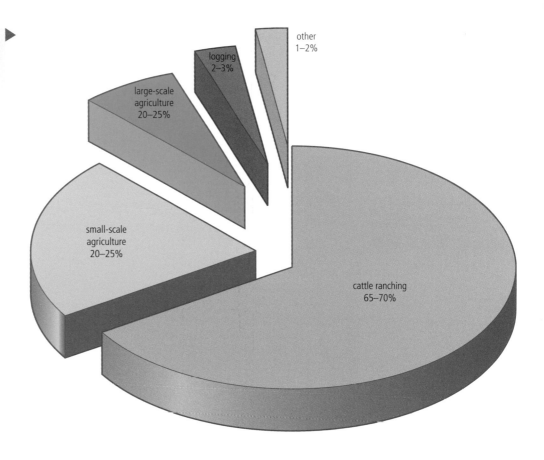

Figure 2.55
Deforestation in Borneo affects people, animals and the environment. A recent assessment by the United Nations Environment Program (UNEP) predicts that the Bornean orang-utan (endemic to the island) will be extinct in the wild by 2025 if current trends continue. Rapid forest loss and degradation threaten many other species, including the Sumatran rhinoceros and clouded leopard. The main cause of forest loss in Borneo is logging and the clearance of land for oil palm plantations.

2.7 Measuring changes in the system

Assessment statements

2.7.1 Describe and evaluate methods for measuring changes in abiotic and biotic components of an ecosystem along an environmental gradient.

2.7.2 Describe and evaluate methods for measuring changes in abiotic and biotic components of an ecosystem due to a specific human activity.

2.7.3 Describe and evaluate the use of Environmental Impact Assessments (EIAs).

Describe and evaluate methods for measuring change along an environmental gradient

Ecological gradients are often found where two ecosystems meet (e.g. on beaches or on lake shores) or where an ecosystem suddenly ends (e.g. at forest edges). In these situations, both biotic and abiotic factors vary with distance and form gradients in which trends can be recorded. The techniques used in sampling ecological gradients are based on the quadrat method and, as such, are more easily done on vegetation and immobile or slow-moving animals.

Because environmental variables change along the gradient, random quadrat sampling is not appropriate. All parts of the gradient need to be sampled, so a **transect** is used. The simplest transect is a line transect – a tape measure laid out in the direction of the gradient (e.g. on a beach this would be at 90° to the sea). All organisms touching the tape are recorded. Many line transects need to be taken to obtain valid quantitative data. Larger samples can be taken from a transect by using a **belt transect**. This is a band of chosen width (usually between 0.5 and 1 m) laid along the gradient (Figure 2.56).

Figure 2.56
Belt transects sample a strip through the sample area. Replication of transects is needed to obtain valid quantitative data.

start

finish

 species 1   species 2   ⬭ species 3

In both line and belt transects, the whole transect can be sampled (a **continuous transect**) or samples are taken at points of equal distance along the gradient (an **interrupted transect**). If there is no discernable vertical change in the transect, horizontal distances are used (e.g. along a shingle ridge succession), whereas if there is a climb or descent then vertical distances are normally used (e.g. on a rocky shore).

It is important that transects are carried out, as far as possible, at the same time of day, so abiotic variables are comparable. Seasonal fluctuations also mean that samples should be taken either as close together in time as possible or throughout the whole year: datalogging equipment allows the latter to take place, although this may be impractical in school studies.

So that data are reliable, and quantitatively valid, transects should be repeated – at least three times is recommended. To avoid bias in placing the transects, a random number generator can be used (page 332). A tape measure is laid at right angles to the environmental gradient: transects are located at random intervals along the tape (Figure 2.57).

Figure 2.57
All transects can be located randomly or, they can be systematically located following the random location of the first. So, for example, subsequent transects might be located every 10 metres along a line perpendicular to the ecological gradient.

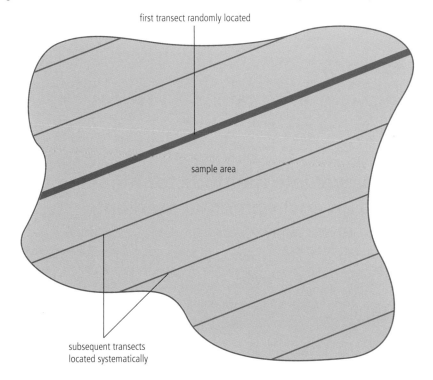

first transect randomly located

sample area

subsequent transects located systematically

Describe and evaluate methods for measuring changes in abiotic and biotic components of an ecosystem due to a specific human activity
Nuclear contamination following the Chernobyl disaster

Table 2.3 shows how nuclear accidents are rated worldwide.

ENVIRONMENTAL PHILOSOPHIES

Greater awareness of environmental issues has caused environmental philosophies to alter over time. What would not have been seen as a problem in the past (e.g. mining activity) is now understood to produce toxins and to lead to environmental damage. Greater understanding of scientific issues has influenced public perception of human effects on the environment, and has changed worldviews.

Level	Description	Criteria	Example
TABLE 2.3 THE INTERNATIONAL NUCLEAR EVENT SCALE			
7	major accident	• External release of a large amount of radioactive material. Such an event would have acute health affects, delayed health effects over a large area, and long-term environmental consequences.	Chernobyl 1986
6	serious accident	• External release of radioactive material requiring emergency countermeasures.	Kyshtym (Russian Federation) 1957
5	accident with off-site risk	• External release of radioactive material requiring partial emergency measures. • Severe damage to the nuclear facility – fire or explosion releasing nuclear material within the facility.	Windscale, UK 1957 Three Mile Island, USA 1979
4	accident without significant off-site risk	• External release of radioactivity resulting in the need for local food control. • Significant damage to the nuclear facility. • Overexposure to one or more workers causing a high probability of an early death.	Windscale, UK 1973
3	serious incident	• External release of radioactive material. • On-site events causing a health risk. • Incidents which could lead to further accidents.	
2	incident	• A failure in safety procedure but no external risk. • A worker is placed at risk; precautions need to be taken.	
1	anomaly	• Outside normal operating levels.	

Chernobyl is located on the Pripyat River, about 100 km north of Kiev (Ukraine) and 140 km south of Gomel (Belarus). Four nuclear reactors were located there, one of which exploded in April 1986. A combination of factors and circumstances contributed to the disaster. First, there were design drawbacks with the reactor. Second, human error, as a result of poor supervision, led to unstable operations.

The result was an increase in thermal power on 26 April 1986 which led to two non-nuclear explosions in quick successions. These penetrated the nuclear reactor and blew the roof off the reactor building. Concrete, graphite and other debris heated to very high temperatures then escaped to the atmosphere.

Radionuclides, normally contained within the reactor core, were released into the atmosphere for nearly 10 days. Widespread distribution of airborne radionuclides resulted across western Europe. This resulted in the contamination of soil, plants and animals, leading to contamination of foodstuffs.

Responding to the hazard

The first response to the incident was the arrival of firefighters from the nearby town of Pripyat. Firefighters fought the fire at very close quarters and all received serious radiation doses. It took over three hours to extinguish all the main fire sites, with the exception of the fire in the core of the reactor. This was achieved by dumping 5000 tonnes of sand, lead and clay by helicopter onto the reactor.

There were 31 deaths and over 200 cases of radiation burns. The health effects of the disaster are still emerging. For example, a sharp increase in throat cancers has been recorded.

In order to isolate the exposed reactor, a sarcophagus (coffin) was built around it. However, due to the difficult working conditions, there are gaps in the container, although these are regularly monitored for radiation. More than a decade later, in September 1997, the EU pledged £75 million to make the sarcophagus safe. An international team had found it in dire need of repairs to prevent radiation leakage.

The nearby town of Pripyat was closed and the residents were advised to stay indoors. It was later decided to evacuate everybody living within 30 km of the reactor. After the evacuation, decontamination work began. All soil to a depth of 15 cm was removed, and all buildings had to be cleaned. These measures were later found to be of limited effectiveness.

To prevent the contaminated land being washed away, and to prevent radionuclides seeping into rivers and the Kiev reservoir, 140 dykes and dams were built. A large concrete wall was constructed around the plant to prevent radionuclides passing into the soil water and groundwater. In addition, a channel was created to prevent contaminated water getting into the River Dnepr and downstream into drinking sources.

Further afield, the deposition of radioactive material varied. Many places had less than 1 kBq m^{-2} whereas others had in excess of 100 kBq m^{-2}. This lead to wide variations in the contamination of foods.

The Russian authorities at first denied internationally that there had been a problem at Chernobyl. They were reluctant to admit observers or release information. Scientists in Finland and Sweden used satellites to track the cloud of radioactive isotopes, notably caesium and iodine. Rainfall caused the caesium and iodine to be flushed out of the atmosphere and onto pastureland; it was monitored by scientists in countries affected by the radioactive fall-out. Dosimeters are used to measure radiation and measurements were provided at microroentgens per hour at ground level. Satellites are still used to monitor flooding in the Pripyat river because floodwaters release radon from the groundwater.

To learn more about how to manage radiation, go to www.pearsonhotlinks. com, insert the express code 2630P and click on activity 2.17.

Satellite images

Another way of measuring change is by using satellite images as shown in the photos below. This method is very reliable, covers a large area and allows us to see change over time. Its visual nature is useful for motivating action.

These images show deforestation and the development of settlement and farming areas.

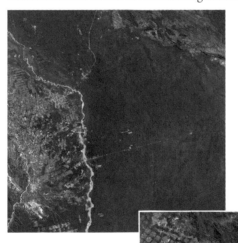

To learn more about measuring change with satellite images, go to www.pearsonhotlinks. com, insert the express code 2630P and click on activity 2.18

Excavations and mining

The size of the landforms created or destroyed can be measured by estimating rates of erosion. This can be done by measuring either the lowering of the surface (in millimetres per year or centimetres per century), or the volume carried away be rivers (in tonnes per m³ per year), or the volume of material removed.

Excavation and dumping involve the mining of sediments, the tipping of waste material, and the subsidence such activities create. Construction and dumping can create important landforms, such the Stone Age (megalithic) passage-tomb at Newgrange in County Meath, Ireland, and the Iron Age hill fort at Maiden Castle in Dorset. In addition, transport developments have required the creation of new landforms.

However, the most important effect has been the dumping of waste material. In Britain alone, there are over 2000 million tonnes of spoil heaps. Rates of sedimentation associated with mining activities are very high. After mining activities cease, rates decrease rapidly. In addition, some of the features excavated in one era are filled in by later generations. For example, many of the depressions caused by marl (lime) diggers in south-west Lancashire and north-west Cheshire have been filled in. Less than 40 per cent of the 5000 depressions formed in the mid-nineteenth century still exist.

The environmental destruction caused by strip mining, for example, far exceeds any other direct form of impact that humans have on landforms. As early as 1922, Sherlock estimated that as much as 31 billion tonnes of rock had been removed from Britain as a result of human activity (Table 2.4). This is likely to be a severe underestimate. Even then, he stated that 'man is many times more powerful, as an agent of denudation, than all the atmospheric forces combined' (quoted in Goudie, 1993).

TABLE 2.4 TOTAL EXCAVATION OF MATERIAL IN BRITAIN PRE-1922	
Activity	Approximate volume of material removed/m³
mines	15 147 000 000
quarries and pits	11 920 000 000
railways	2 331 000 000
road cuttings	480 000 000
foundations of buildings and street excavations	385 000 000
other canals	153 800 000
docks and harbours	77 000 000
Manchester Ship Canal	41 154 000
total	30 534 954 000

Source: Adapted from Goudie A. *The human impact on the natural environment,* **Blackwell, 1993**

The demand for mineral resources continues to increase. The production of aggregates for concrete includes the extraction of sand and gravel, crushed limestone, artificial and manufactured aggregates, and crushed sandstone. Demand for these materials increased from 20 million tonnes in 1900 to 300 million tonnes in 1989.

The largest single engineering project in the UK was the Channel Tunnel. The material excavated for this project allowed new landforms to be created. Samphire Hoe, formerly the Samphire Cliff construction site, is an artificially created 35 ha piece of land between Folkestone and Dover. It was created from over 5 million cubic metres of the 8.75 million cubic metres of the material excavated when digging the tunnel. The Hoe reaches 28 m at its highest point, and is fully landscaped to provide a variety of habitats, including three ponds. The Hoe is protected from wave erosion by a sea wall of almost $225\,000\,\text{m}^3$ of concrete. Access to the Hoe is through a 130 m tunnel, itself created as part of the 1974 Channel Tunnel project.

Environmental Impact Assessments

Demand for resources, for new housing, for new energy supplies and for new transport links are inevitable, but before any development project gets permission to begin, an Environmental Impact Assessment (EIA) must be carried out. The purpose of an EIA is to establish the impact of the project on the environment. It predicts possible impacts on habitats, species and ecosystems, and helps decision makers decide if the development should go ahead. An EIA also addresses the mitigation of potential environmental impacts associated with the development. The report should provide a non-technical summary at the conclusion so that lay-people and the media can understand the implications of the study.

Some countries incorporate EIAs within their legal framework, with penalties and measures that can be taken if the conditions of the EIA are broken, whereas other countries simply use the assessment to inform policy decisions. In some countries, the information and suggestions of the EIA are often ignored, or take second place to economic concerns.

The first stage of an EIA is to carry out a baseline study. This study is undertaken because it is important to know what the physical and biological environment is like before the project starts so that it can be monitored during and after the development. Variables measured as part of a baseline study should include:

- habitat type and abundance – record total area of each habitat type
- species list – record number of species (faunal and flora) present
- species diversity – estimate the abundance of each species and calculate diversity of the community
- list of endangered species
- land use – assess land use type and use coverage
- hydrology – assess hydrological conditions in terms of volume, discharge, flows, and water quality
- human population – assess present population
- soil – quality, fertility, and pH.

To learn more about how EIAs are applied in the UK, go to www.pearsonhotlinks.com, insert the express code 2630P and click on activity 2.19.

ENVIRONMENTAL PHILOSOPHIES

EIAs offer advice to governments, but whether or not they are adopted depends on the environmental philosophy of the government involved. In China, for example, the EIA for the Three Gorges Dam showed the damage that would be done to the environment, but the government chose to focus on the benefits to the country.

It is often difficult to put together a complete baseline study due to lack of data, and sometimes not all of the impacts are identified. An EIA may be limited by the quality of the baseline study. The value of EIAs in the environmental decision-making process can be compromised in other ways. Environmental impact prediction is speculative due to the complexity of natural systems and the uncertainty of feedback mechanisms thus making environmental decisions more difficult: the predictions of the EIA may, therefore, prove to be inaccurate in the long term. On the other hand, at their best, EIAs can lead to changes in the development plans, avoiding negative environmental impact. It could be argued that any improvement to a development outweighs any negative aspects.

Three Gorges Dam, Yangtze River

The Three Gorges Dam is one and a half miles wide and more than 600 feet high. On completion, it created a reservoir hundreds of feet deep and nearly 400 miles long.

The Three Gorges Dam is the largest hydroelectric dam development in the world. Located on the Yangtze River in the People's Republic of China (Figure 2.58), construction began in 1993 and the dam was fully operational by the end of 2009. Project engineers have estimated that the dam could generate an eighth of the country's electricity. This energy will be produced without the release of harmful greenhouse gases. The Chinese government cite other improvements that the development produces: reduced seasonal flooding and increased economic development along the edges of the new reservoir.

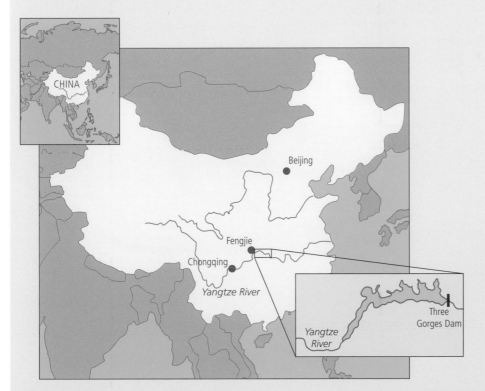

Figure 2.58
Location of the Three Gorges Dam. As well as affecting the immediate area of the reservoir formed, the river is affected upstream by changes in the flow of the Yangtze, and downstream by changes in siltation.

An EIA was required to look at potential ecosystem disruption; relocation of people in areas to be flooded, and the social consequences of resettlement; the effects of sedimentation in areas behind the dam which would have reduced water speed; the effects of landslides from the increase in geological pressure from rising water; and earthquake potential.

Case study continued

To learn more about the Three Gorges Dam, go to www.pearsonhotlinks. com, insert the express code 2630P and click on activity 2.20.

The EIA determined that there are 47 endangered species in the Three Gorges Dam area, including the Chinese river dolphin and the Chinese sturgeon. The report identified economic problems as well as the environmental problems that disruption of the ecosystem would cause. For example, the physical barrier of the dam would interfere with fish spawning and, in combination with pollution, that would have a serious impact on the fishing economy of the Yangtze River. In terms of social costs, the dam would flood 13 cities, 140 towns, 1352 villages, and 100 000 acres of China's most fertile land. Two million people would have had to be resettled by 2012, and 4 million by 2020. Geological problems included the growing risk of new landslides and increased chance of earthquakes (due to the mass of water in a reservoir altering the pressure in the rock below), and a reduction in sedimentation reaching the East China Sea (reducing the fertility of the land in this area).

The overall view of the people responsible for the development was that the environmental and social problems did not reduce the feasibility of the project, and that the positive impact on the environment and national economy outweighed any negative impact.

EXERCISES

1 Describe methods for measuring changes along an environmental gradient. Divide these into abiotic and biotic factors. Evaluate each – what are the limitations of each and how will they affect the data you collect?

2 Find your own example of an EIA. What were the conclusions of the study? Were the recommendations followed?

PRACTICE QUESTIONS

1 The figure below shows a food web for a small-scale ecosystem.

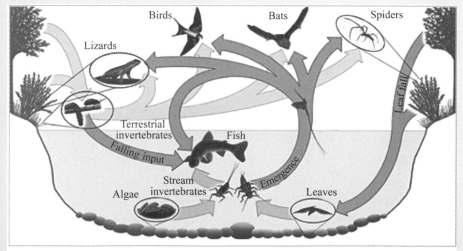

[Source: www.isu.edu/departments/strmecol/images/Baxteretal_FWBiol_2005_Fig1b.jpg]

(a) State which trophic level is occupied by the bats.   [1]

(b) Describe **two** impacts of a reduction in stream invertebrates on the food web of the ecosystem.   [2]

© International Baccalaureate Organization [2008]

2 (a) State **two** functions of producers in an ecosystem.   [2]

(b) For a named ecosystem, draw a food chain with named species showing **three** appropriately labelled trophic levels.   [3]

(c) Distinguish between a pyramid of biomass and a pyramid of productivity.   [2]

© International Baccalaureate Organization [2008]

3 Simpson's diversity index states that: $D = \dfrac{N(N-1)}{\Sigma n(n-1)}$ where N = the total number of individuals of all species found and n = the number of individuals of a particular species.

A garden pond contains the following organisms

Animal type	Number of individuals
goldfish	24
carp	5
frogs	6
water boatmen	1500
water snail	1200
water flea	2500

Using the Simpson diversity index formula above, calculate the diversity of this pond. [3]

© International Baccalaureate Organization [2004]

4 The table and graphs below show population data for the mayfly (*Ephemerella subvaria*) in two similar streams, A and B, in Minnesota, USA. Data were collected on population size (number of mayfly m^{-2}) and mean mass of mayfly between September 1970 and June 1971.

POPULATION DYNAMICS OF MAYFLY IN STREAMS A AND B						
	Stream A			Stream B		
Month	No. of mayfly / m^{-2}	Mean biomass / $g\,m^{-2}$	Mean mass of mayfly / mg	No. of mayfly / m^{-2}	Mean biomass / $g\,m^{-2}$	Mean mass of mayfly / mg
Sept	6530	1.4	0,2	5251	1.2	0.2
Oct	4432	4.6	1.0	2001	1.3	0.6
Nov	4082	6.6	1.6	905	0.7	0.8
Dec	4053	10.8	2.6	400	0,4	1.1
Jan	3660	13.0	3.5	123	0.2	1.7
Feb	2007	12.8	6.3	99	0.2	2.4
Mar	1587	18.4	11.6	98	0.3	3.2
Apr	230	4.9	21.5	80	0.9	11.4
May	84	1.8	22.4	34	0.3	10.6
June	44	1.0	23.6	24	0.4	20.0

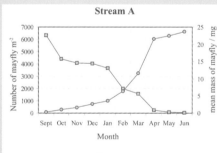

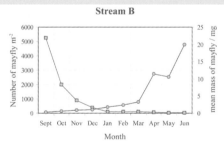

Key: —□— Number of mayfly m^{-2} —○— Mean mass of mayfly / mg

[Source: Adapted from Waters and Crawford, *Limnology and Oceanography*, (1973), **18**, pages 286-296]

(a) **(i)** Using the data from the table and graphs, describe the relationship between population size and mean mass for mayfly in stream A. [2]

(ii) Outline **two** differences in the populations of stream A and stream B during the study period. [2]

(iii) Calculate the percentage change in the population of mayfly in stream A from September to June. [1]

(**b**) Define the term *biomass*.   *[1]*

(**c**) (**i**) Scientists wish to assess the abundance of a brown trout (*Salmo trutta*) population within a chalk stream using the Lincoln index. Describe a possible method for this.   *[3]*

Brown trout

[Source: Alberta Government - Sustainable Resource Development, Fish and Wildlife
www.gov.ab.ca/srd/fw/fishing/FishID/brown_t.html]

   (**ii**) It is suspected that a number of abiotic factors may influence the biology of the chalk stream. Outline **three** abiotic factors that may be important in the stream.   *[3]*

© International Baccalaureate Organization [2004]

5   The figure below shows succession in a sand dune ecosystem.

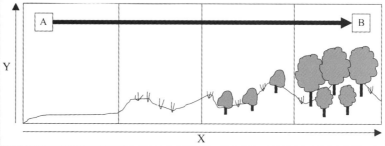

(**a**) (**i**) Define the term succession.   *[2]*

   (**ii**) State what variable may be appropriate for the *x*-axis in the figure above.   *[1]*

   (**iii**) Outline what will happen to soils as the ecosystem in the figure above changes from A to B.   *[2]*

(**b**) State what is happening within a system when a decrease in variable P leads to a decrease in variable Q which in turn leads to a further decrease in variable P.   *[1]*

(**c**) Discuss how gross productivity, net productivity and diversity change over time as a habitat goes through succession. Illustrate your answer with a **named** case study.   *[5]*

© International Baccalaureate Organization [2007, 2008]

● **Note:**
There are additional practice questions relating to this chapter on pages 352–354.

To access worksheet 2.3 with more practice questions relating to Chapter 2, please visit www.pearsonbacconline.com and follow the on-screen instructions.

3 HUMAN POPULATION, CARRYING CAPACITY AND RESOURCE USE

3.1 Population dynamics

Assessment statements

3.1.1 Describe the nature and explain the implications of exponential growth in human populations.
3.1.2 Calculate and explain, from given data, the values of crude birth rate, crude death rate, fertility, doubling time and natural increase rate.
3.1.3 Analyse age/sex pyramids and diagrams showing demographic transition models.
3.1.4 Discuss the use of models in predicting the growth of human populations.

Exponential growth in human populations

The world's population is growing very rapidly. Most of this growth is quite recent. The world's population doubled between 1804 and 1922, 1922 and 1959, 1959 and 1974. It is thus taking less and less time for the population to double, although growth has slowed down since 1999 (Figure 3.1). Up to 95 per cent of population growth is taking place in less economically developed countries (LEDCs). However, the world's population is expected to stabilize at about 8.5 billion following a peak at 9 billion.

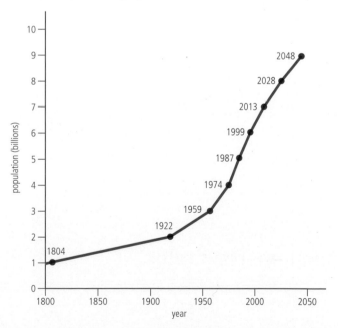

In 1990, the world's women were, on average, giving birth to 3.3 children in their lifetime. By 2002, the figure had dropped to 2.6 children – slightly above the level needed to ensure replacement of the population. If these trends continue, the level of fertility for the world as a whole will drop below replacement level before 2050. The projections also suggest that AIDS, which has killed more than 20 million people in the past 20 years, will lower the average life expectancy at birth in some countries to around 30 years by 2010. AIDS

Figure 3.1
Exponential growth in world population.

Exponential growth refers to a growth rate which is increasingly rapid or an accelerating rate of growth.

In 2002, the world's population increased by 74 million people – the population of Egypt – but that is well below the peak of 87 million added in 1989–90. At 1.2 per cent a year, the increase is also well below the 2.2 per cent annual growth seen 40 years ago. The slowdown in global population growth is linked primarily to declines in fertility.

To learn more about
global demographic
(population) trends, go
to www.pearsonhotlinks.
com, insert the express
code 2630P and click on
activity 3.1.

continues to have its greatest impact in the developing countries of Asia, Latin America and especially sub-Saharan Africa. Botswana and South Africa are among the countries that may see population decline because of AIDS deaths.

The impact of exponential growth is that a huge amount of extra resources are needed to feed, house, clothe, and look after the increasing number of people. However, it can be argued that the resource consumption of much of the world's poor population (i.e. those in less economically developed countries, LEDCs) is much less than the resource consumption of populations in more economically developed countries (MEDCs) where population growth rates are much lower.

The price to be paid for a shrinking world population is an increase in the number of elderly people in the world. **Life expectancy** is increasing but social security systems are not. The forecast divides the world into 13 regions. In all but two – North and Latin America – the population is predicted to fall.

To learn more about
world population
highlights from the
2007 World Population
Data Sheet, go to www.
pearsonhotlinks.com,
insert the express code
2630P and click on
activity 3.2.

The biggest predicted falls are in the China region (China and Hong Kong and five smaller neighbouring nations), down from 1.4 billion (now) to 1.25 billion in 2100, and in Europe, from 813 million to 607 million. The population in the European part of the Former Soviet Union (FSU) is falling sharply already; it is predicted to shrink by 18 million to 218 million in 2025, and to slump to 141 million, a 40 per cent depopulation, by 2100.

Other regions will have shrinking populations by 2100, but will still have many more people than they do today. Sub-Saharan Africa will have a population of 1.5 billion in 2100, compared to 611 million now. South Asia – including India and Pakistan – will, by 2100, have a population of almost 2 billion rather than the current 1.4 billion.

Key predictions from the Global Population Forecast

- The world's population is likely to peak at 9 billion in 2070. By 2100, it will be 8.4 billion.
- North America (USA and Canada) will be one of only two regions in the world with a population still growing in 2100. It will have increased from 314 million today to 454 million, partly because first-generation immigrant families tend to have more children. The other expanding region is Latin America where the population is forecast to increase from 515 million to 934 million.
- Despite disease, war and hunger, the population of Africa will grow from 784m today to 1.6 billion in 2050. By 2100, it will be 1.8 billion, although it will have begun to decline. By the end of the century, more than a fifth of Africans will be over 60, a higher proportion than in western Europe today.
- The China region will see its population shrink significantly by 2100, from 1.4 billion to 1.25 billion. When China is reaching its population peak of about 1.6 billion (by 2020), it will have more well-educated people than Europe and North America combined. This is because of its education programme.
- India will overtake China as the world's most populous nation by 2020.
- Europe – including Turkey and the FSU west of the Urals – will see its population fall from 813m now to 607m in 2100: from 13 per cent of the world's population to just 7 per cent. Eastern countries such as Russia have already seen their populations fall; western Europe's population is likely to peak in the next few decades.
- A tenth of the world's population is over 60. By 2100, that proportion will have risen to one-third.
- In 1950, there were thought to be three times as many Europeans as Africans. By 2100, the proportions will be reversed.

Calculating important rates

You need to be able to calculate and explain, from given data, the values of crude birth rate, fertility, doubling time, crude death rate, and natural increase rate.

Birth rates

Should we predict
changes in population
growth when many
people are free to choose
how many children
they have while in other
countries, the government
tries to control how many
children people have?

In the USA in 2005, there were 4 138 349 births out of a total population of 295 895 897; this gives a **crude birth rate** (**CBR**) of 13.98 per thousand. In Mauritius in 2001, there were 19 600 births out of a population of 1 189 000; this gives a crude birth rate of 16.5 per thousand. Globally, there are major variations in the crude birth rate, with the highest rates in poorer countries and lower rates in rich countries (Figure 3.2).

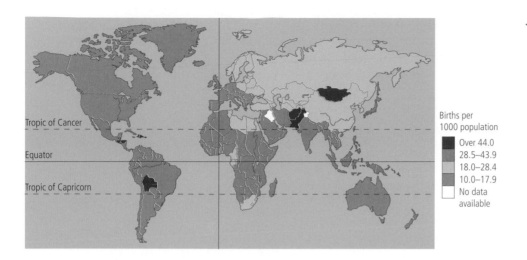

Figure 3.2
Global variations in the birth rate.

Births per 1000 population

- Over 44.0
- 28.5–43.9
- 18.0–28.4
- 10.0–17.9
- No data available

Tropic of Cancer

Equator

Tropic of Capricorn

CBR is defined as the number of live births per thousand people in a population. CBR is easy to calculate and the data are readily available. For example:

$$CBR = \frac{\text{total number of births}}{\text{total population}} \times 1000$$

However, the crude birth rate does not take into account the age and sex structure of the population. The **standardized birth rate** gives a birth rate for a region on the basis that its age composition is the same as the whole country.

Fertility

The **total fertility rate** (**TFR**) is the average number of births per women of child-bearing age (Table 3.1). It is the completed family size if fertility rates remain constant. The **general fertility rate** (**GFR**) is the number of births per thousand women aged 15–49 years. The **age-specific birth rate** (**ASBR**) is the number of births per 1000 women of any specified year groups.

TABLE 3.1 ASBR AND TFR FOR WOMEN OF DIFFERENT AGES IN SELECTED COUNTRIES								
Country	ASBR							TFR
Age groups	15–19	20–24	25–29	30–34	35–39	40–44	45–49	
France	9.3	71.0	137.0	91.0	36.6	7.3	0.5	1.76
Germany	12.4	57.3	108.8	81.1	28.2	5.1	0.3	1.47
Belarus	45.2	168.0	88.1	39.5	14.4	3.2	0.2	1.79
Russia	55.6	156.8	93.2	48.2	19.4	4.2	0.2	1.89

$$\text{Age-specific birth rate} = \frac{\text{total number of births}}{\text{1000 women of any specified year group(s)}}$$

In general, highest fertility rates are found among the poorest countries, and very few LEDCs have made the transition from high birth rates to low birth rates. Most MEDCs have brought the birth rate down. In MEDCs, fertility rates have fallen as well – the decline in population growth is not, therefore, due to changing population structure.

Changes in fertility are a combination of both socio-cultural and economic factors. While there may be strong correlations between these sets of factors and changes in fertility, it is impossible to prove the linkages or to prove that one set of factors is more important than the other.

Level of education and material ambition

In general, the higher the level of parental education, the fewer the children (Table 3.2). Poor people with limited resources or ambition often have large families. Affluent parents can afford large families. In general, middle-income families with high aspirations but limited means tend to have the smallest families. They wish to improve their standard of living, and limit their family size to achieve this.

TABLE 3.2 WOMEN'S EDUCATIONAL LEVEL AND BIRTHS – EVIDENCE FROM CHINA		
Education level	Fertility rate per 1000	Average no. of births per 1000
university	42.18	1.15
senior middle school	63.88	1.23
junior middle school	67.43	1.44
primary school	86.25	2.02
illiterate	94.50	2.44

Political factors and family planning

Most governments in LEDCs have introduced some programmes aimed at reducing birth rates. Their effectiveness is dependent on:

- a focus on general family planning not specifically birth control
- investing sufficient finance in the schemes
- working in consultation with the local population

Where birth controls have been imposed by government, they are less successful (except in the case of China). In the MEDCs, financial and social support for children is often available to encourage a pro-natalist approach. However, in countries where there are fears of negative population growth (as in Singapore), more active and direct measures are taken by the government to increase birth rates.

Economic prosperity

The correlation between economic prosperity and the birth rate is not total, but there are links. As gross domestic income (GDI) increases, the total fertility rate generally decreases, and as gross national product (GNP) per capita (per head) increases, so the birth rate decreases (Figure 3.3).

Figure 3.3
GNP per capita and the crude birth rate.

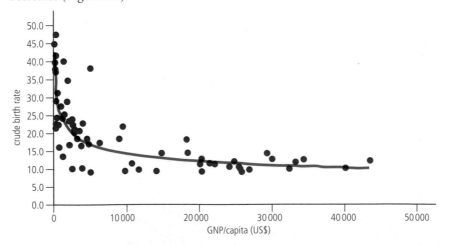

Economic prosperity favours an increase in the birth rate, while increasing costs lead to a decline in the birth rate. Recession and unemployment are also linked with a decline in the birth rate. This is related to the cost of bringing up children. Surveys have shown that the cost of bringing up children in the UK can be over £200 000, partly through lost earnings on the mother's part. Whether the cost is real or perceived (imagined) does not matter. If parents believe they cannot afford to bring up children, or that having more children will reduce their standard of living, they are less likely to have children.

At the global scale, a strong link exists between fertility and the level of economic development; the United Nations (UN) and many non-governmental organizations (NGOs) believe that a reduction in the high birth rates in LEDCs can only be achieved by improving the standard of living in those countries.

The need for children

High infant mortality rates increase the pressure on women to have more children. Such births offset the high mortality losses and are termed replacement births or compensatory births. In some agricultural societies, parents have larger families to provide labour for the farm and as security for the parents in old age. This is much less important now as fewer families are engaged in farming, and many farmers are labourers not farm owners.

Doubling times

The doubling time refers to the length of time it takes for a population to double in size, assuming its natural growth rate remains constant.

Approximate values for doubling time can be obtained by the formula:

$$\text{doubling time (years)} = \frac{70}{\text{percentage growth rate}}$$

Death rates

In the USA in 2005, there were 2 448 017 deaths among a population of 295 895 897; this gives a **crude death rate (CDR)** of 8.27 per thousand. However, the CDR is a poor indicator of mortality trends – populations with a large number of aged (as in most MEDCs) have a higher CDR than countries with more youthful populations (Denmark 11 per thousand and Mexico 5 per thousand). To compare mortality rates, we use the **standardized mortality rate (SMR)** or **age-specific mortality rates (ASMR)**, such as the **infant mortality rate (IMR)**.

The pattern of mortality in MEDCs differs from that in LEDCs (Figure 3.4). In the former, as a consequence of better nutrition, healthcare and environmental conditions, the death rate falls steadily to a level of about 9 per thousand, with very high life expectancies (over 75 years). In many very poor countries, high death rates and low life expectancies are still common although both have shown steady improvement over the past few decades because improvements in food supply, water, sanitation and housing. This trend, unfortunately, has been reversed as a consequence of AIDS.

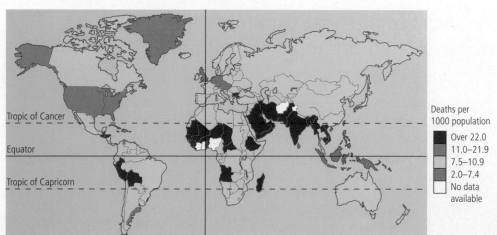

CDR is the number of deaths per thousand people in a population.

IMR is the total number of deaths of children aged under 1 year per 1000 live births.

Life expectancy (E_o) is the average number of years that a person can be expected to live, given that demographic factors remain unchanged.

To access worksheet 3.1 on death rates, please visit www.pearsonbacconline.com and follow the on-screen instructions.

Figure 3.4
Global variations in the death rate.

Deaths per 1000 population

- Over 22.0
- 11.0–21.9
- 7.5–10.9
- 2.0–7.4
- No data available

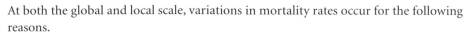

As a country develops, the major forms of illness and death change. LEDCs are characterized by a high proportion of infectious and contagious diseases such as cholera, TB, gastroenteritis, diarrhoea and vomiting. These are often fatal. In MEDCs, fatal diseases are more likely to be degenerative diseases such as cancer, strokes, or heart disease. The change in disease pattern from infectious to degenerative is known as the epidemiological transition model. (epidemiology is the study of diseases). Such a change generally took about a century in MEDCs but is taking place faster in LEDCs.

At both the global and local scale, variations in mortality rates occur for the following reasons.

- Age structure – Some populations (e.g. those in retirement towns and especially in the older industrialized countries) have very high life expectancies and this results in a rise in the CDR. Countries with a large proportion of young people, have much lower death rates (e.g. Mexico has 34 per cent of its population under the age of 15 years and has a CBR of 5 per thousand).
- Social class – Poorer people within any population have higher mortality rates than the more affluent. In some countries (e.g. South Africa) this is also reflected in racial groups.
- Occupation – Certain occupations are hazardous (e.g. the military, farming, oil extraction and mining). Some diseases are linked to specific occupations (e.g. mining and respiratory disease).
- Place of residence – In urban areas, mortality rates are higher in areas of relative poverty and deprivation, such as inner cities and shanty towns. This is due to overcrowding, pollution, high population densities and stress. In rural areas where there is widespread poverty and limited farm productivity, mortality rates are high (e.g. in rural north-east Brazil, life expectancy is 27 years shorter than in the richer south-east region).
- Child mortality and IMR – While the CBR shows small fluctuations over time, the IMR can show greater fluctuations and is one of the most sensitive indicators of the level of development. This is due to:
  – high IMRs are only found in the poorest countries
  – the causes of infant deaths are often preventable
  – IMRs are low where there is safe water supply and adequate sanitation, housing, healthcare and nutrition.

In South Africa, for example, the IMR varies with race. Whites have a higher income and a better standard of living; they have a lower IMR (10–15 per thousand) than the other racial groups (blacks 50–100 per thousand, coloureds 45–55 per thousand).

Crude death rate is calculated as follows:

$$CDR = \frac{\text{total number of deaths}}{\text{total population}} \times 1000$$

The cause and age of infant death also varies with race:
  – for whites, **neonatal deaths** (0–7 days) and **perinatal deaths** (7–28 days) are more likely to be due to congenital (birth) deformities
  – for blacks, such deaths are more likely to be due to low birth weight, gastroenteritis, pneumonia, and jaundice, occurring between 7 and 365 days, the **post-neonatal period**.

Natural increase

Natural increase is calculated by subtracting CDR from the CBR.

Analysis of age/sex pyramids and diagrams showing demographic transition models

Population pyramids

To access worksheet 3.2 on changing population structure, please visit www.pearsonbacconline.com and follow the on-screen instructions.

Population structure or composition refers to any *measurable* characteristic of the population. This includes the age, sex, ethnicity, language, religion and occupation of the population. These are usually shown by population pyramids.

Population pyramids tell us a great deal of information about the age and sex *structure* of a population:
- a wide base indicates a high birth rate
- narrowing base suggests falling birth rate
- straight or near vertical sides reveal a low death rate
- concave slopes characterize high death rates

- bulges in the slope suggest high rates of immigration or in-migration (for instance, excess males 20–35 years will be economic migrants looking for work; excess elderly, usually female, will indicate retirement resorts)
- deficits in the slope indicate emigration or out-migration or age-specific or sex-specific deaths (epidemics, war).

Population pyramids for the USA and Swaziland are shown in Figures 3.5 and 3.6.

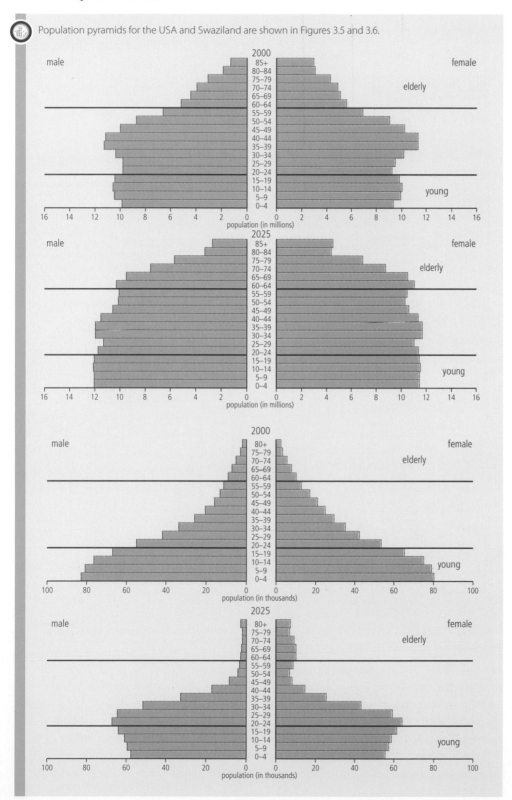

Figure 3.5
Population pyramids for USA showing changes between 2005 and 2025.

Figure 3.6
Population pyramids for Swaziland showing changes between 2005 and 2025.

The general demographic transition model (DTM) shows the change in population structure from LEDCs to MEDCs (Figure 3.7).

Stage 2
Early expanding:
- birth rate remains high but the death rate comes down rapidly
- population growth is rapid
- Afghanistan, Sudan and Libya are at this stage
- UK passed through this stage by 1850

Stage 3
Late expanding:
- birth rate drops and the death rate remains low
- population growth continues but at a smaller rate
- Brazil and Argentina are at this stage
- UK passed through this stage in about 1950

Stage 4
Low and variable:
- birth rates and death rates are low and variable
- population growth fluctuates
- UK and most developed countries are at this stage

Stage 1
High and variable:
- birth rates and death rates are high and variable
- population growth fluctuates
- no countries, only some indigenous (primitive) tribes still at this stage
- UK at this stage until about 1750

High birth and death rates
Parents want children:
- for labour
- to look after them in old age
- to continue the family name
- prestige
- to replace other children who have died

People die from:
- lack of clean water
- lack of food
- poor hygiene and sanitation
- overcrowding
- contagious diseases
- poverty

Stage 5
Low declining:
- the birth rate is lower than the death rate
- the population declines

Low birth and death rates
Birth rates decline because:
- children are very costly
- the government looks after people through pensions and health services
- more women want their own career
- there is more widespread use of family planning
- as the infant mortality rate comes down there is less need for replacement children

Death rates decline because:
- clean water
- reliable food supply
- good hygiene and sanitation
- lower population densities
- better vacations and healthcare
- rising standards of living

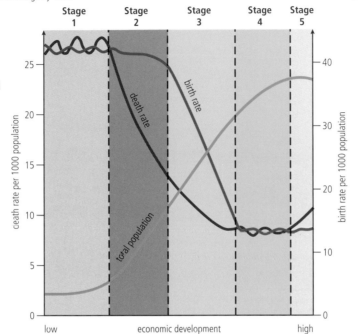

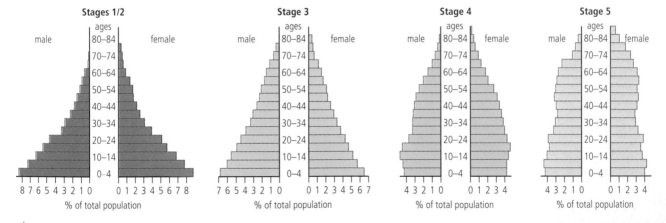

▲
Figure 3.7
The demographic transition model.

The DTM suggests that death rates fall before birth rates, and that the total population expands.

However, the DTM is based on the data from just three countries – England, Wales and Sweden. Not only is the time-scale for the DTM in these countries longer than in many LEDCs, there are other types of DTM (Figure 3.8). For example, Ireland's DTM was based on falling birth rates and rising death rates as a result of emigration following the 1845–49 famine. The DTM in Japan shows a period of population expansion before World War II, followed by population contraction once the country's expansionist plans could not be fulfilled. Other nations have experienced a similar drop in birth rates and death rates (e.g. former Yugoslavia).

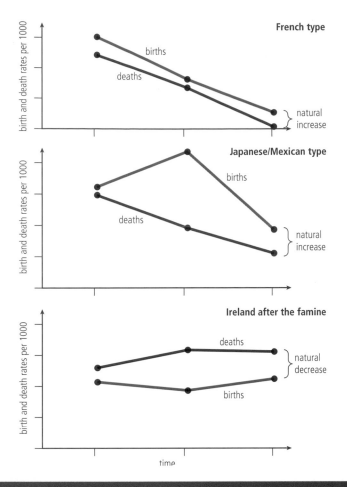

French type

Japanese/Mexican type

Ireland after the famine

time

Figure 3.8
Alternative demographic transitions.

 The DTM suggests that countries progress through recognized stages in the transition from LEDC to MEDC.

To learn more about data from the CIA World Factbook, go to www.pearsonhotlinks.com, insert the express code 2630P and click on activity 3.3.

To learn more about national population pyramids, go to www.pearsonhotlinks.com, insert the express code 2630P and click on activity 3.4.

EXERCISES

1 Study the table below, then fill in the gaps.

Natural increase = crude birth rate – crude death rate.

Doubling time = 70/ growth rate

SELECTED POPULATION DATA							
	World	USA	UK	China	India	Highest	Lowest
Crude birth rate/per thousand (‰)	20.18	14.18	10.65	13.71	22.22	Niger 49.62	Hong Kong 7.37
Crude death rate/per thousand (‰)	8.23	8.27	10.05	7.03	6.40	Swaziland 30.70	United Arab Emirates 2.13
Natural increase/per thousand (‰)						Niger 29.36	Singapore 4.46
Fertility rate	2.61	2.10	1.66	1.77	2.76	Mali 7.34	Macau 0.90
Infant mortality rate/per thousand (‰)	42.09	6.30	4.93	21.16	32.31	Angola 182.31	Singapore 2.30
Life expectancy/years	66.26	78.14	78.85	73.18	69.25	Macau 84.33	Swaziland 31.99
Growth rate/%	1.89	0.88	0.28	0.63	1.58	Maldives 5.57	Montenegro −0.93
Doubling time/years							

2 Copy this grid then use it to plot the changes in China's birth rates, death rates and total population between 1950 ad 1990 using the information in the table.

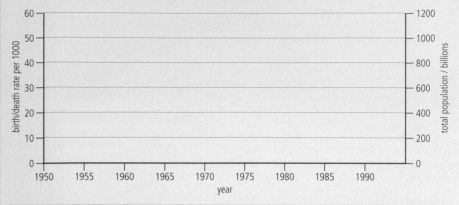

KEY POPULATION DATA FOR CHINA			
Year	Birth rate / ‰	Death rate / ‰	Total population/ millions
1950	44	38	570
1955	44	25	600
1960	29	22	670
1965	40	12	750
1970	38	10	825
1975	25	9	950
1980	20	8	1000
1985	18	8	1050
1990	16	9	1160

Note: In 1961 the death rate suddenly soared to 45 per thousand due to famine and starvation.

3 Use the CIA World Factbook (hotlinks box, page 91) to find out the current birth rate, death rate and population size for China.

4 The figure below shows China's population pyramid for 1990.

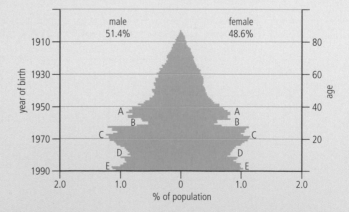

Match each of the letters A to E with one of the following explanations (i–v):
(i) Famine and starvation cause millions to die (population declines steeply).
(ii) Effect of the one-child policy (population declines).
(iii) Relaxation of the one-child policy (population expands).
(iv) Baby boom following the creation of the People's Republic of China in 1949 (increase in population).
(v) Large-scale population growth prompts a need for population control.

5   The table below shows demographic data for China in the years 2000 and 2025.

POPULATION DATA FOR CHINA, 2000 AND 2025					
2000			2025		
Age	% male	% female	Age	% male	% female
0–4	7.7	7.2	0–4	5.7	5.5
5–9	8.3	8.0	5–9	6.3	6.1
10–14	10.0	9.8	10–14	6.7	6.4
15–19	8.1	8.1	15–19	6.2	5.8
20–24	7.5	7.6	20–24	5.8	5.3
25–29	9.3	9.4	25–29	6.5	6.0
30–34	9.8	9.9	30–34	7.0	6.7
35–39	8.0	8.1	35–39	8.4	8.2
40–44	6.5	6.4	40–44	6.8	6.7
45–49	6.6	6.6	45–49	6.2	6.3
50–54	4.8	4.8	50–54	7.7	7.7
55–59	3.7	3.6	55–59	7.9	8.0
60–64	3.2	3.2	60–64	6.1	6.4
65–69	2.7	2.8	65–69	4.5	4.7
70–74	1.9	2.1	70–74	4.0	4.5
75–79	1.1	1.4	75–79	2.3	2.7
80+	0.7	1.2	80+	1.8	2.9

(a) Draw the two population pyramids for China in 2000 and 2025.

(b) Compare the two pyramids in terms of:

  (i) percentage population under the age of 19 years

  (ii) percentage population over the age of 60 years

  (iii) gender imbalances.

Suggest reasons for the differences that you have noted.

Use of models in predicting growth

The range of factors which affect population growth is varied and differs with different scales. For example, national or regional change in population takes into account in-migration and out-migration whereas global population change does not take migration into account at all.

Factors influencing the birth rate include population age-structure, status of women, type of economy, wealth, religion, social pressure, educational status, availability of contraceptives, desire for children, need for government policies such as child benefit, provision of child-care measures, and provision of pensions. To accurately predict changes in all these factors is difficult.

Similarly, the death rate is affected by many factors. These include the age-structure of the population, availability of clean water, sanitation, adequate housing, reliable food supply, prevalence of disease, provision of healthcare facilities, type of occupation, natural hazards, civil conflict and war, and chance factors. To predict how these factors will change over time is also difficult. The sheer number as well as the complexity of factors affecting birth and death rates make it extremely diifficult to predict how populations will change over time.

A model is a simplified structuring of reality.

Figure 3.9 shows that predictions for the world's population vary between 7.5 billion and 11 billion people. Planning for 7.5 billion people is very different from planning for 11 billion people – in terms of houses, jobs, schools, hospitals, reservoirs, food resources, energy resources and so on.

Figure 3.9
Range of UN population predictions 1950–2050.

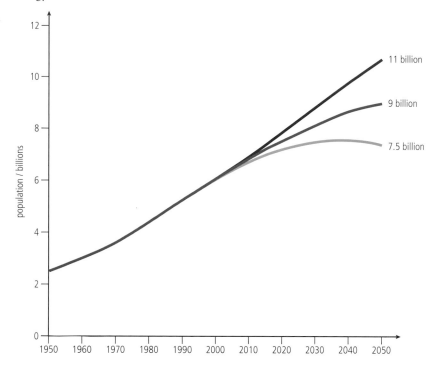

Predictions for population growth in China depend on how many children each Chinese couple are allowed to have. The one-child policy in China has reduced the number of live births since 1979 by over 300 million – however, the eventual size of China's population depends on what size the government wants the country to be.

Figure 3.10 shows options for family size and projected total population for China

Figure 3.10
Options for family size and projected total population for China.

Source: based on Chinese population census 1982

1   What is the difference in the population of China between options 1 and 5?
2   Suggest some of the positive aspects for China of having a low level of population growth.
3   Should families be forced to have no more than one child? Give reasons for your views.

Changing projections

In 1798, when the world's population was about 1 billion, Thomas Malthus published his *Essay on the Principle of Population Growth*, predicting that by the middle of the nineteenth century there would no longer be enough food to go round. In the event, population growth continued but there was enough food to go round.

However, in the early 1990s, the World Bank and others began to issue dire warnings about an entirely new 'demographic time bomb'. A combination of growing longevity and falling birth rates, has led to a rise in the average age of populations, first in MEDCs and later in LEDCs. By 2050, the world will have about 2 billion people aged over 60, three times as many as in 2010. In some MEDCs (mainly Japan and western Europe) that age group already makes up nearly 25 per cent of the population. By 2050, their share will rise to 30–40 per cent, and even in LEDCs it will rise to 25–30 per cent.

Consequently, those of working age will have to support an increased number of dependants. In MEDCs there are now approximately four workers for every pensioner. By 2050, that will have reduced to just over two, who will have to work harder to keep the elderly supplied with retirement benefits and healthcare unless something is done very soon. In western Europe, the working population may start shrinking from 2010. The same is true for China which, largely because of its one-child policy, will grow old before it becomes very rich.

There is no doubt that global greying will happen (i.e. there will be an increase in the proportion of the population over working age). What remedies should be adopted is harder to say. Academics and politicians who have spoken on this topic fall into three main camps:

- those who claim that this is just another Malthusian scare story and can be sorted out with a few changes to retirement ages and pension policies
- those who preach gloom and doom (e.g. meltdown in asset prices, poverty in old age, healthcare rationing and intergenerational warfare as young and the old compete for scarce resources)
- those in the middle, who try to come up with sensible ideas to reduce the impact of global greying.

The biggest part of the solution lies in:

- expanding the shrinking population of workers, mainly by increasing retirement age and persuading more women to take up paid employment
- increasing productivity of the labour force
- persuading people to save more for their retirement.

None of this will be easy, particularly in poor countries or in wealthy ones in a time of recession. One of the biggest problems is timing. In order to head off the worst problems a few decades hence, action needs to be taken straight away. Yet politicians are elected for just a few years at a time. Will they have the nerve to antagonize voters by introducing tough measures that will take decades to pay off?

In the early twentieth century, when the world's population was about 2 billion, there were fears that people were having too few children and the human race was in danger of dying out. The baby-boomer generation after World War II put paid to that scare story. By 1972, fears had come full circle. The Club of Rome, a global think-tank, produced a report called *The Limits to Growth* in which they claimed that, within a century, a mixture of man-made pollution and resource depletion would cause widespread population decline. However, due to the intervention of the green revolution (the use and application of science and technology in farming) by 2000, world population had reached 6 billion. It is predicted to rise to nearly 9 billion by 2050.

EXERCISES
1   Describe the nature and explain the implications of exponential growth in human populations.
2   Outline the factors that affect birth and death rates.
3   Discuss the use of models in predicting the growth of human populations.

- **Examiner's hint:**
- Describe – Give a detailed account.
- Outline – Give a brief account.
- Discuss – Give a considered and balanced account.

3.2 Resources – natural capital

Natural capital (resources) and natural income

The Earth contains many resources that support its natural systems: the core and crust of the planet; the biosphere (the living part) containing forests, grassland, deserts, tundra and other biomes, and the upper layers of the atmosphere. These resources are all extensively used by humans to provide food, water, shelter and life-support systems. We tend to have an **anthropocentric** (human-centred) view of these resources and their use. In this section, we examine the way in which resources are discussed in terms of their use by and relationship to human populations.

Ecologically minded economists describe resources as **natural capital**. This is equivalent to the store of the planet (or stock) – the present accumulated quantity of natural capital. If properly managed, **renewable** and **replenishable** resources are forms of wealth that can produce **natural income** indefinitely in the form of valuable goods and services (Figure 3.11).

Figure 3.11
Natural capital and natural income. Raw materials from the environment (natural capital) are harvested and used by producers to generate products and services (natural income) that are then used by consumers. A renewable resource is a natural resource that the environment continues to supply or replace as it is used, and whose emissions and waste are recycled in a sustainable way.

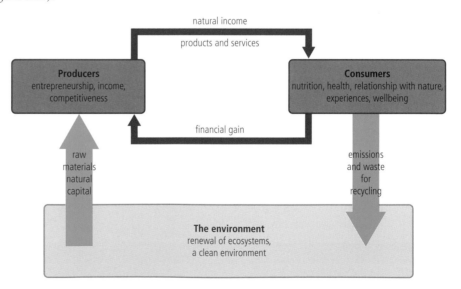

Renewable resources can be used over and over again. In order to provide income indefinitely, the products and services used should not reduce the original resource (or capital). For example, if a forest is to provide ongoing income in the form of timber, the amount of original capital (the forest) must remain the same while income is generated from new growth. This is the same idea as living on the interest from a bank account – the original money is not used and only the interest is removed and spent.

The income from natural capital may be in the form of **goods** or **services**:
- goods are marketable commodities such as timber and grain
- ecological services might be flood and erosion protection, climate stabilization, maintenance of soil fertility (Table 3.3).

Ecosystem	Service provided										
	Fresh water	Food	Timber and fibre	New products	Regulate diversity	Cycle nutrients	Quality air and climate	Human health	Detox	Regulate hazards	Cultural
cultivated		✔	✔	✔	✔	✔	✔				✔
dryland		✔		✔	✔	✔	✔	✔	✔		✔
forest	✔	✔	✔	✔	✔	✔	✔	✔	✔	✔	✔
urban		✔			✔		✔	✔	✔		✔
lakes and rivers	✔	✔		✔	✔	✔	✔	✔	✔	✔	✔
coastal	✔	✔	✔		✔	✔	✔	✔	✔	✔	✔
marine		✔		✔	✔	✔	✔		✔		✔
polar	✔	✔			✔		✔				✔
mountain	✔	✔			✔		✔			✔	✔
island		✔			✔		✔				✔

TABLE 3.3 ECOSYSTEM TYPES AND SERVICES THEY PROVIDE

Source: Adapted from Pagiola S, von Ritter K, Bishop J. *How much is an ecosystem worth? Assessing the economic value of conservation.* The International Bank for Reconstruction and Development (World Bank), 2004

Other resources may not be replenished or renewed following removal of natural capital. These **non-renewable** resources will eventually run out if they are not replaced. Using economic terms, these resources can be considered as parallel to those forms of economic capital that cannot generate wealth (i.e. income) without liquidation of the estate. In other words, the capital in the bank account is spent.

Predictions about how long many of Earth's minerals and metals will last before they run out are usually rudimentary. They may not take into account any increase in demand due to new technologies, and they may assume that production equals consumption. Accurate estimates of global reserves and precise figures for consumption are needed for more exact predictions. However, it is clear that key non-renewable natural resources are limited and that there is a need to minimize waste, recycle, reuse and, where possible, replace rare elements with more abundant ones.

To learn more about non-renewable resources, go to www.pearsonhotlinks.com, insert the express code 2630P and click on activity 3.5.

A resource is only a resource when it becomes useful to people – uranium only became a resource in the twentieth century despite existing for millions of years.

This oil rig is Norwegian. Oil is a non-renewable resource the use of which has been a key feature of the twentieth century.

Renewable, replenishable and non-renewable natural capital (resources)

There are three categories of natural capital.

- Renewable – Living species and ecosystems which can be replaced by natural productivity (photosynthesis – a biotic process) as fast as they are used (e.g. food crops, timber). They have a sustainable yield or harvest equal to or less than their natural productivity so the natural capital is not diminished.
- Replenishable – Non-living resources which are continuously restored by natural processes (e.g. rivers and streams, the ozone layer) as fast as they are used up. They provide sustainable natural income as the natural capital is not diminished They depend on abiotic processes for their replenishment (in contrast to renewable resources which depend on biotic processes).
- Non-renewable – Natural resources which cannot be replenished within a timescale of the same order as that at which they are taken from the environment (i.e. cannot be replenished at the same rate at which they are used). Any use of these resources results in depletion of the stock. These resources include:
  – fossil fuels
  – minerals.

  If these resources are being depleted then we must improve their efficiency of use, develop substitutes, or recycle (Figure 3.12).

Figure 3.12
Examples of renewable and non-renewable sources of energy.

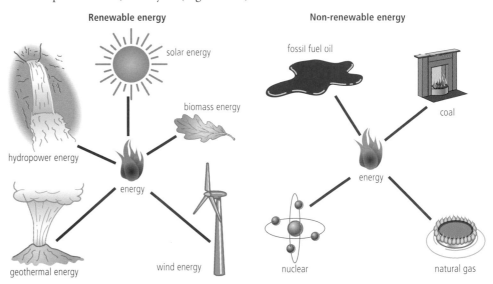

In many cases, renewable and replenishable natural capital are being damaged by human action. For example, ozone-depleting substances such as chlorofluorocarbons (CFCs) are found in refrigerants and propellants. These pollutants enhance the rate of destruction of ozone in the stratosphere and remain active for long periods of time. There has been a decline in the amount of ozone in the stratosphere by 4 per cent every 10 years. Ozone depletion has led to 'holes' in the ozone layer over areas such as Antarctica.

Ozone prevents the most harmful wavelengths of ultraviolet light (UV-B, wavelength 270–315 nm) from passing through the Earth's atmosphere. A thinning of the ozone layer therefore allows more UV-B wavelengths through, which has consequences such as increased DNA mutations in humans resulting in increased incidence of skin cancer. UV-B also causes damage to plant tissue and reduction in plankton populations, which has knock-on effects for their consumers (zooplankton) and for food chains and webs (Chapter 5, page 245).

Another example of irresponsible use of a resource concerns groundwater. Pollutants from agricultural products and run-off from storage tanks, landfills and septic tanks are reducing the water quality. Excessive extraction from groundwater mining means that water tables are lowered, which can lead to the intrusion of salt water in coastal areas and further contamination of the supply. Excessive use of surface water, often for agriculture, means that groundwater supplies are not replenished. The effect of groundwater pollution and reduction is decreased availability of water resources. This has a knock-on impact on agriculture – less water is available for irrigation, so yields decline. At the same time, the cost of water for industry and agriculture increases, which has serious implications for the economy. Water shortages can lead to tensions and conflict over the limited resource (water resources are discussed in detail starting on page 146).

ENVIRONMENTAL PHILOSOPHIES

People with a **technocentric** worldview see humanity as being ultimately able to solve shortages of natural capital by finding alternative technological solutions. Such people tend to be from MEDCs, where continuation of the lifestyle enjoyed in these countries depends on such solutions being found. People from cultures in closer contact with the environment would seek to find solutions by limiting our use of non-renewable natural capital and replacing them with renewable and sustainable sources (an **ecocentric** approach). This is discussed further starting on page 287.

Dynamic nature and concept of a resource

The value of a resource should be seen as dynamic, with the possibility that its status may change over time. As humans advance culturally and technologically, and our resource base changes, the importance of a resource may be transformed. Resources become more valuable as new technologies need them. For example, flint – once an important resource – is now redundant; it was superseded by the development of metal extraction from ores (i.e. technological progress).

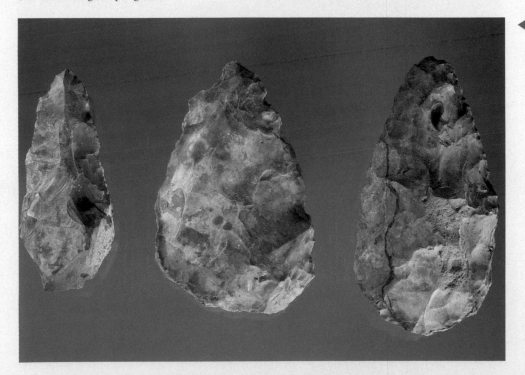

Stone Age tools were made from a variety of stones such as flint. Stones were shaped by chipping to provide a sharp edge. The tools could be attached to arrows or hand-held to skin animals and cut meat.

The advent of metalworking in the Bronze Age made stone tools redundant – in effect technological progress and cultural change devalued a once valuable resource. Many Bronze Age weapons were still in use in the Iron Age.

Uranium, in contrast, was of little value before the advent of the nuclear age. Nuclear fission involves the bombardment of uranium atoms with neutrons. A neutron splits a uranium atom, releasing a great amount of energy as heat and radiation. A different process, nuclear fusion, powers the Sun. In nuclear fusion, the nuclei of atoms (e.g. deuterium and tritium, both isotopes of hydrogen) fuse together, causing a much greater release of energy than in nuclear fission. If we ever learn to generate power by harnessing the energy from nuclear fusion, uranium, like flint before it, will lose its value.

The Diablo Canyon nuclear power plant in San Luis Obispo County, California, USA. The advent of nuclear power made uranium a more valuable commodity than it had previously been. Technological change led to a change in the status of uranium as a resource.

Intrinsic value of the environment

Natural capital has various values. We usually, rightly or wrongly, assess worth in monetary terms. **Economic value** can be determined from the market price of the goods and services a resource produces. **Ecological values**, however, have no formal market price: soil erosion control, nitrogen fixation and photosynthesis are all essential for human existence but have no direct monetary value. Similarly, **aesthetic values** (e.g. the appreciation of a landscape for its visual attraction) have no market price. Ecological and aesthetic values do not provide easily identifiable commodities, so it is difficult to assess the economic contributions of these values using traditional methods of accounting. They are usually undervalued from an economic viewpoint (Figure 3.13).

Ethical, spiritual and philosophical perspectives tend to give organisms and ecosystems **intrinsic value** (i.e. value in their own right, irrespective of economic value). They are valued regardless of their potential use to humans. The evaluation of natural capital therefore requires many diverse perspectives that lie outside the remit of conventional economics.

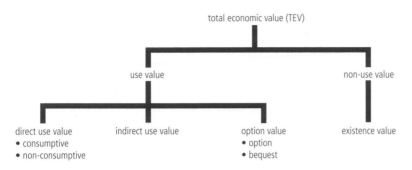

Figure 3.13

Ways of assessing the value of natural capital.

Direct use values are ecosystem goods and service that are directly used by humans, most often by people visiting or residing in the ecosystem. **Consumptive use** includes harvesting food products, timber for fuel or housing, medicinal products and hunting animals for food and clothing. **Non-consumptive use** includes recreational and cultural activities that do not require harvesting of products. **Indirect use** values are derived from ecosystem services that provide benefits outside the ecosystem itself (e.g. natural water filtration which may benefit people downstream). **Optional values** are derived from potential future use of ecosystem goods and services not currently used – either by yourself (**option value**) or your future offspring (**bequest value**). **Non-use values** include aesthetic and intrinsic values, and are sometimes called **existence values**.

Other ways of measuring the value of a resource (besides calculating the direct price of its products) include calculating or estimating:

- the cost of replacing it with something else
- the cost of mitigating its loss
- the cost of averting the cost of its degradation
- its contribution to other income or production
- how much people are prepared to pay for it.

There are attempts to acknowledge these diverse valuations of nature. For example, scientists are examining the importance of biodiversity for ecosystem functioning by looking at connections between species diversity and the integrity of ecosystem processes (e.g. the role of pollinators such as wasps and bees in maintaining flowering and fruiting in rainforest). Biodiversity also has value in its contribution to ongoing evolution and speciation, and as a genetic resource. We need to find ways to value nature more rigorously against common economic values (e.g. GNP). However, some argue that these valuations are impossible to quantify and price realistically (Figure 3.14). Not surprisingly, much of the sustainability debate (page 104) centres on the problem of how to weigh conflicting values in our treatment of natural capital.

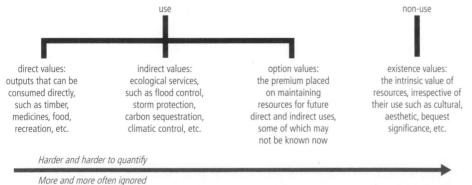

Figure 3.14

Levels of difficulty in assessing the economic value of natural capital.

Natural resources can have **recreational value**, as holiday destinations and places for people to relax. Ecotourism is a growing source of revenue for countries with natural resources

To learn more about the economic value of biodiversity, go to www.pearsonhotlinks. com, insert the express code 2630P and click on activity 3.6.

How can we quantify values such as aesthetic value, which are inherently qualitative?

that are attractive to tourists, and can provide an alternative income that is sustainable and does not deplete the source of natural capital. For example, rainforests are under threat from logging which is non-sustainable and damages the original stock; however, ecotourism provides income at the same time as requiring the resource to remain intact so as to attract tourists. The income is therefore sustainable.

ENVIRONMENTAL PHILOSOPHIES

The value that different cultures place on natural capital ultimately depends on the environmental philosophies through which they see the world.

Sustainability

Sustainability means using global resources at a rate that allows natural regeneration and minimizes damage to the environment. If human well-being is dependent on the goods and services provided by certain forms of natural capital, then long-term harvest (or pollution) rates should not exceed rates of capital renewal. For example, a system harvesting renewable resources at a rate that enables replacement by natural growth shows sustainability. Sustainability is living within the means of nature (i.e. on the 'interest' or sustainable income generated by natural capital) and ensuring resources are not degraded (i.e. natural capital is not used up) so that future generations can continue to use the resource. The concept can be applied in our everyday lives.

When processing a natural resource to create income, sustainability needs to be applied at every level of the supply chain (Figure 3.15).

Figure 3.15
Sustainability applies to harvesting natural capital, to the generation of energy to process the product, and to how the product is packaged and marketed.

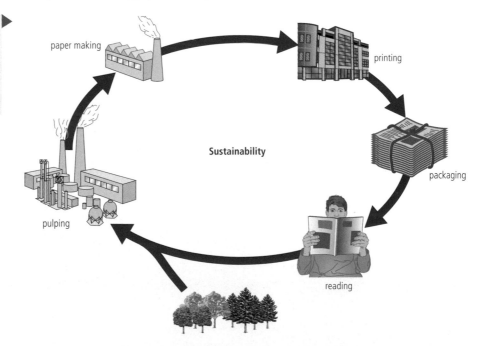

Sustainability can be encouraged though careful application of:
- ecological land-use to maintain habitat quality and connectivity for all species
- sustainable material cycles (e.g. carbon, nitrogen and water cycles) to prevent the contamination of living systems
- social systems that contribute to a culture of sufficiency that eases the consumption pressures on natural capital.

Humans can be driven to use resources beyond sustainable limits through over-population (unrealistic demand for limited resources), financial motives (exploitation of resources for short-term financial gain), or ignorance (lack of knowledge of the resource's sustainable level). For example, unsustainable practice with regard to soils includes:

- overgrazing (trampling and feeding of livestock leads to loss of vegetation and exposure of the underlying soil)
- over-cultivation (loss of soil fertility and structure leave top soil vulnerable to erosion by wind and water).

Local or global?

A global perspective for managing resources sustainably is desirable because many problems have worldwide impact (e.g. global warming, Chapter 6, page 269). Such a perspective allows for understanding the knock-on effects of environmental problems beyond national boundaries and helps governments to be more responsible. Ecosystems are affected by global processes, so sustainability needs to be understood as a global issue (e.g. the atmospheric system with regard to climate change). A global perspective also helps us to understand that our actions have an impact on others, which is useful for getting societies to think about impacts on different generations, as well as different countries. A world-view stresses the inter-relationships between systems so knock-on effects are reduced.

But because ecosystems exist on many scales, a more local perspective is sometimes appropriate. Human actions are often culturally specific (e.g. traditional farming methods) and so global solutions to sustainable development may not be locally applicable. Often local methods have evolved to be more sustainable and appropriate for the local environment. It is also often the case that individual and small-scale community action can be very effective for managing resources sustainably (e.g. local recycling schemes). Sometimes environmental problems are local in nature, such as point source pollution (page 217), so a global approach is not appropriate.

 The term 'sustainability' has a precise meaning in this course. It means the use of global resources at a rate that allows natural regeneration and minimizes damage to the environment. For example, a system of harvesting renewable resources at a rate that allows replacement by natural growth demonstrates sustainability.

Sustainable development

The term 'sustainable development' was first clearly defined in 1987 in the Brundtland Report, *Our Common Future*, produced by the United Nations World Commission on Environment and Development (WCED). The definition is: *development that meets the needs of the present without compromising the ability of future generations to meet their own needs*. The concept also incorporates economic and social factors (Figure 3.16).

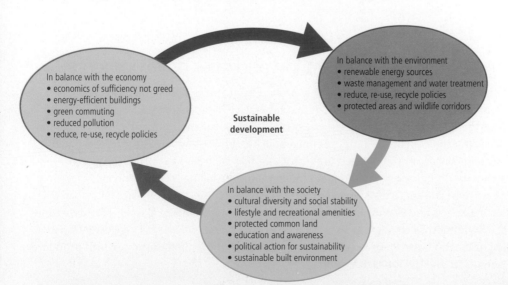

Figure 3.16
Sustainable development focuses on the quality of environmental, economic, and social and cultural development. The concept encompasses ideas and values that inspire individuals and organizations to become better stewards of the environment and promote positive economic growth and social objectives.

However, the definition of sustainable development varies depending on viewpoint, which makes it a problematic term. For example, some economists view sustainable development in purely commercial terms as a stable annual return on investment regardless of the environmental impact, whereas some environmentalists may view it as a stable return without environmental degradation. In the minds of many economists, development and sustainability are contradictory positions. Environmentalists hold the concept of sustainable development to be the best way forward for society and the planet. Some people believe that development (particularly development designed to allow LEDCs to compete with MEDCs) can never be sustainable within a free market as the relationship is unequal. The value of this approach is therefore a matter of considerable debate.

Is sustainable development possible in the long term?

You might think this is not possible, since we have finite resources which may not be enough for everyone to use as they want. If people are not prepared to reduce their standards of living, this may well be true. In LEDCs, people are using increasing amounts of resources, and as these countries contain 80 per cent of all people, sustainable development will be difficult. If we cannot find new technologies fast enough to replace fossil fuels, and do not increase our use of renewable resources, non-renewable resources will run out. Population growth is a key factor in sustainable development. If we prove incapable of stopping this growth, or at least slowing it down, there will be more and more pressure on natural resources and increased likelihood of many being used unsustainably.

On the other hand, you may see sustainable development as being possible, given certain precautions. We should be able to develop the technology to use renewable resources for all our needs – micro-generation using wind turbines and solar power, for example (pages 115–16). Renewable resources could provide energy for domestic homes and factories. Transport could use hydrogen-powered engines replacing the need for fossil fuels. We could use less energy in general by insulating our homes and places of work. Personal choices backed up by legislation could make us reuse and recycle more. Technological developments in crop growing could mean more production. Given all these factors, it is possible and certainly desirable for sustainable development to be possible in the long term.

ENVIRONMENTAL PHILOSOPHIES

Ultimately, the choices people make depend on their environmental philosophy. People with a technocentric worldview see the technological possibilities as central to solving environmental problems. An ecocentric worldview leads to greater caution and a drive to use Earth's natural resources in a sustainable way rather than rely on technology to solve the problems. These ideas are discussed further in Chapter 7.

The Stockholm Declaration and later developments

Global summits can play a leading role in shaping attitudes to sustainability. The UN Conference on Human Environment that took place in Stockholm in 1972 was the first time the international community met to consider global environment and development needs (Chapter 7, page 292). It examined how human activity was affecting the global environment. Countries needed to think about how they could improve the living standards of their people without adding to pollution, habitat destruction and species extinction. The conference led to the Stockholm Declaration, which played a pivotal role in setting targets and shaping action at both an international and local level. The ideas from the Stockholm Declaration were developed in *Our Common Future*. These early initiatives led to the Rio Earth Summit in 1992, coordinated by the United Nations, which produced **Agenda 21** and the Rio Declaration.

The Earth Summit changed attitudes to sustainability on a global scale, and changed the way in which people perceived economic growth (i.e. that sometimes this was at the expense of the environment). It encouraged people to think of the indirect values of ecosystems rather than just the purely economic ones.

Agenda 21 is a comprehensive plan of action to be taken globally, nationally and locally by organizations of the UN, governments, and environmental groups in every area in which humans impact on the environment. It was adopted by more than 178 governments at the Rio Summit in June 1992.

Some national and state governments have legislated or advised that local authorities take steps to implement Agenda 21. Known as 'Local Agenda 21' (LA21), these strategies apply the philosophy of the Earth Summit at the local level. Each country is urged to develop an LA21 policy, with the agenda set by the community itself rather than by central or local government, as ownership of any initiatives by society at large is most likely to be successful.

The effect of climate change, both in terms of sustainable development and its affect on the planet in general, was discussed at a UN conference in Kyoto in 1997. Agreements were made to reduce emissions of greenhouse gases, including reversing carbon dioxide emissions, to their 1990 levels. The Kyoto Protocol stipulated that these targets should be reached by the year 2012 (Chapter 6, page 273).

The 1992 Earth Summit was followed up ten years later by the Johannesburg World Summit on Sustainable Development (Figure 3.17). The Johannesburg meeting looked mainly at social issues, and targets were set to reduce poverty and increase people's access to safe drinking water and sanitation (problems that cause death and disease in many LEDCs).

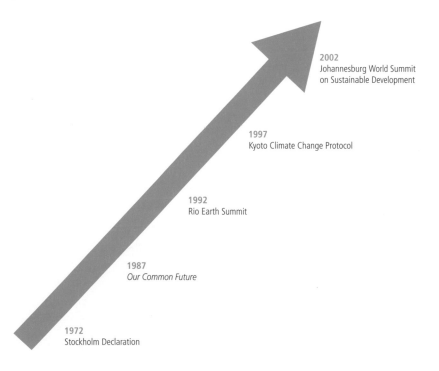

Figure 3.17
Important milestones in the sustainable development movement.

2002
Johannesburg World Summit
on Sustainable Development

1997
Kyoto Climate Change Protocol

1992
Rio Earth Summit

1987
Our Common Future

1972
Stockholm Declaration

It is true that countries can break these agreements and there is little the international community can do about this. Moreover, summits may not achieve their initial goals, but they do act as important catalysts in changing the attitudes of governments, organizations and individuals.

International summits on sustainable development have highlighted the issues involved in economic development across the globe, yet the viewpoints of environmentalists and economists may be very different.

Calculating sustainable yield

Sustainable yield (**SY**) is calculated as the rate of increase in natural capital (i.e. natural income) that can be exploited without depleting the original stock or its potential for replenishment. Exploitation must not affect long-term productivity. So, the annual sustainable yield for a given crop may be estimated as the annual gain in biomass or energy through growth and recruitment.

Where t = the time of the original natural capital

$t + 1$ = the time of the original capital plus yield,

SY = (total biomass at $t + 1$) − (total biomass at t)

or

SY = (total energy at $t + 1$) − (total energy at t)

Because it is the amount of increase per unit time, the measurement is the rate of increase. The two equations above can be summarized:

$$SY = \left[\frac{\text{total biomass at } t + 1}{\text{total energy}}\right] - \left[\frac{\text{total biomass at } t}{\text{total energy}}\right]$$

The relationship can be simplified as:

SY = (annual growth and recruitment) − (annual death and emigration)

Maximum sustainable yield (**MSY**) is the largest yield (or catch) that can be taken from the stock of a species over an indefinite period. MSY aims to maintain the population size at the point of maximum growth rate by harvesting the individuals that would normally be added to the population, allowing the population to continue to be productive indefinitely (Figure 3.18). MSY is the point where the highest rate of recruitment can occur (this is often difficult to determine). It is used extensively by fisheries management (Figure 3.19).

Figure 3.18

Maximum sustainable yield occurs at maximum rate of increase in population. Near the carrying capacity, the yield reduces.

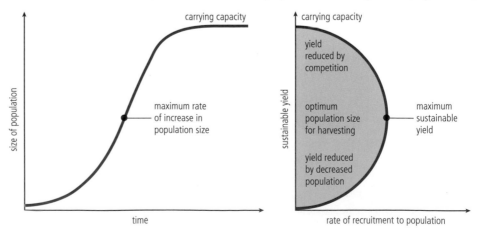

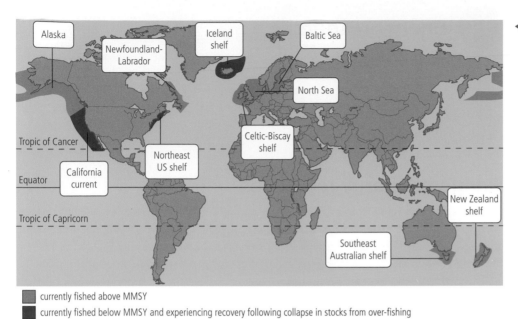

Figure 3.19
Multi-species maximum
sustainable yield (MMSY):
MSY values for whole fish
communities worldwide.

■ currently fished above MMSY

■ currently fished below MMSY and experiencing recovery following collapse in stocks from over-fishing

■ currently fished below MMSY

Populations of cod have been particularly affected by over-fishing in the North Atlantic
(Figures 3.20 and 3.21).

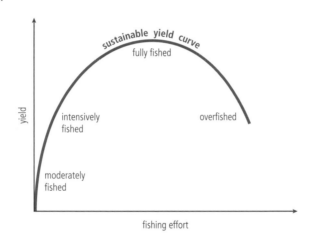

Figure 3.20
In the 1960s and 1970s,
poor understanding of what
constituted the MSY for cod
led to over-fishing of cod
in the North Atlantic. This
resulted in serious decreases
in yield.

Figure 3.21
North-west Atlantic cod
populations, off the coasts
of the USA and Canada,
were particularly affected by
over-fishing. By 1992, cod
populations were only
1 per cent of their 1960 levels.

To access worksheet 3.3 on
sustainability, please visit
www.pearsonbacconline.
com and follow the on-
screen instructions.

3.3 Energy resources

Range of energy resources

Energy can be generated from both renewable and non-renewable resources. Renewable energy resources are sustainable because there is no depletion of natural capital. Renewable energy sources include solar, hydroelectric, geothermal, biomass, and tidal schemes. They can be large scale (e.g. country-wide schemes of energy generation) or small scale (micro-generation) within houses or communities. Non-renewable energy supplies cannot be replenished at the same rate as they are used; this results in depletion of the stock. Such supplies include fossil fuels (e.g. coal, gas and oil). Nuclear power can be considered non-renewable because the source of the fission process is uranium, which in a non-renewable form of natural capital.

In 2004, total worldwide energy consumption was 500 exajoules (1 exajoule = 10^{18} J). Most of this energy is derived from the combustion of fossil fuels (Figure 3.22, Figure 3.23).

Figure 3.22
Energy sources worldwide (2004). Only 9 per cent of energy is from supplies that are renewable (biomass, hydroelectric, solar, wind, geothermal, biofuels and photovoltaic). Data from MEDCs

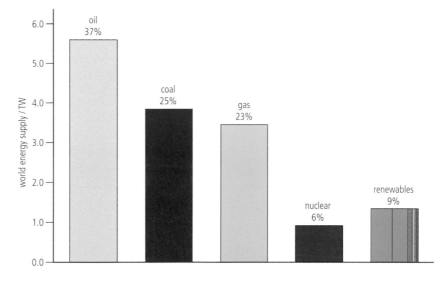

Figure 3.23
Bar charts showing relative contributions to total energy generation (TW = terawatt, 1 terawatt = 1012 watts; GW = gigawatt, 1 GW = 109 watts).

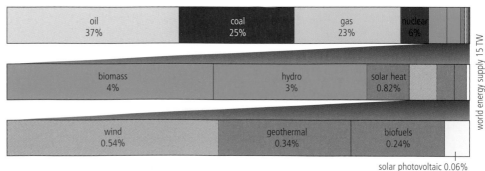

From the industrial revolution onwards, transport and energy generation have been founded on fossil fuel technology. Ready sources of coal led to early forms of transport being based on this fuel. Processing of fossil fuels to produce petroleum led to the advent of the combustion engine, and this technology has continued to dominate until the present day. Growth of fossil fuel technology has been accompanied by a general unawareness of the effects on the environment. Pollution and global warming were not factors that were considered when fossil fuels were adopted as the primary source of energy generation. More recently, our growing awareness of environmental problems linked to fossil fuel use (Chapters 5 and 6) has put more emphasis on renewable forms of energy.

Energy consumption is much higher in MEDCs than LEDCs (Figure 3.24). The economies of MEDCs have been based on high energy generation built on fossil fuel use, whereas energy demands in LEDCs have traditionally been much lower due to less available technology and reliance on natural resources (wood burning or other biomass sources).

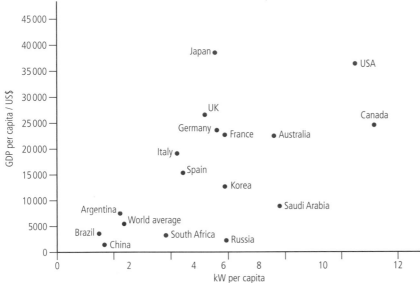

Figure 3.24
Energy consumption (kilowatts per capita) vs. GDP per capita by country.

Renewable sources of energy have been slow to grow globally (Figure 3.25). There are several reasons for this. Non-renewable sources of energy (e.g. gas) are generally cheaper than renewables (although government grants are often available to help with set-up costs). Gas is cheap because it is relatively plentiful, can be burned directly without the need for refining, and the technology is already in place to access the gas and burn it in existing gas-fired power stations. Renewables such as wind power often require high set-up costs (e.g. the installation of new wind turbines) and may still be in the experimental stage (e.g. offshore wind technology, which can also be disrupted by rough seas).

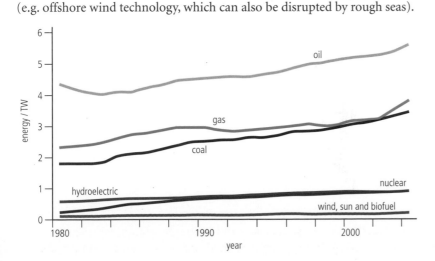

Figure 3.25
Global energy use between 1980 and 2004.

In future, the cost of non-renewable energy is likely to be much higher. This is because stocks will become depleted and the easiest and most accessible resources will have already been mined. Only resources which are difficult to access (and therefore more costly to reach) will remain. The increasing scarcity of non-renewable resources will push costs up, and environmental taxes to compensate for global warming will also make fossil fuels more expensive. Therefore, in the future, renewable sources of energy will become more attractive and increased use is likely. Adoption of sustainable energy will have a significant beneficial effect on the planet.

CASE STUDY

Energy use in the USA

In the USA, energy sources are varied. States are being encouraged to adopt a renewable electricity 'standard': this mechanism requires electricity suppliers to gradually increase the amount of renewable energy resources they use. Twenty-eight states, plus Washington DC, have adopted renewable electricity standards three of which have also adopted a goal. In addition, five states have a voluntary renewable energy goal, with no specific enforcement mechanisms (Figure 3.26). Adoption of these standards should have a very significant future effect on the environment (Figure 3.27) – scientists project an annual carbon dioxide reduction of 183 million metric tonnes (equivalent to 30 million fewer cars on the road).

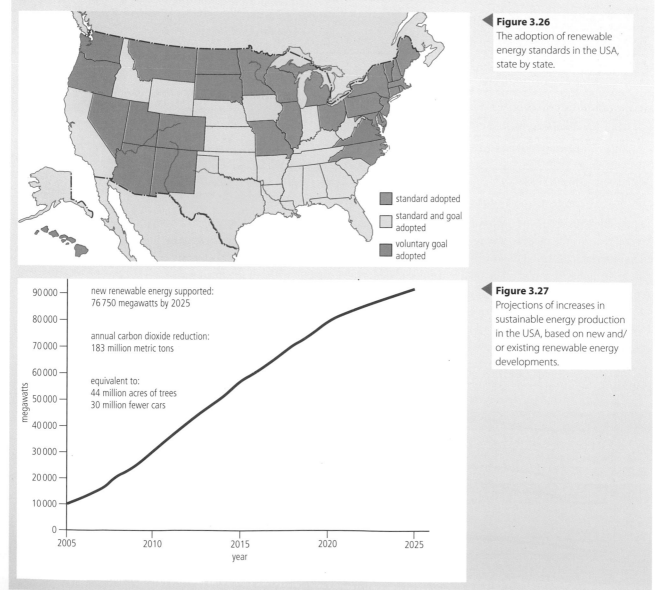

Figure 3.26
The adoption of renewable energy standards in the USA, state by state.

standard adopted

standard and goal adopted

voluntary goal adopted

Figure 3.27
Projections of increases in sustainable energy production in the USA, based on new and/ or existing renewable energy developments.

new renewable energy supported:
76 750 megawatts by 2025

annual carbon dioxide reduction:
183 million metric tons

equivalent to:
44 million acres of trees
30 million fewer cars

Advantages and disadvantages of energy sources

Advantages and disadvantages of fossil fuels

Fossil fuels are formed when dead animals and plants decompose in anoxic conditions (where oxygen is absent), are covered by silt and mud, and are subjected to heat and pressure over tens of thousands of years. The term 'fossil' refers to the fact that the fuels are made from preserved dead organisms. Gas and oil are largely made from oceanic organisms (e.g. plankton) and coal from land plants (mainly from trees growing during the Carboniferous Period – carboniferous means coal-bearing).

All fossil fuels generate energy in the same way (Figure 3.28). The original source of energy contained within fossil fuels is the Sun. Photosynthesis traps the energy in plant matter, converting it to chemical energy. This store of energy can remain below ground for millions of years, until humans mine and drill for it.

Coal-fired power stations turn chemical energy in the coal into (about) 40 per cent electricity and 60 per cent waste heat. The clouds emitted from their cooling chimneys are formed by condensed water vapour created by this method of energy generation.

Because the fuels are made from dead organisms, they contain much carbon – they lock-up extensive amounts of carbon beneath the ground (burning fossil fuels releases the carbon in the form of carbon dioxide).

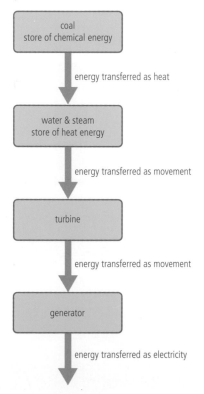

Figure 3.28
Energy transfer for the generation of electricity from a fossil fuel such as coal.

coal
store of chemical energy

↓ energy transferred as heat

water & steam
store of heat energy

↓ energy transferred as movement

turbine

↓ energy transferred as movement

generator

↓ energy transferred as electricity

The advantages of fossil fuels are that they are relatively cheap and plentiful. At the same time, advanced technologies have been developed to allow safe extraction and the technology already exists for their use (e.g. the combustion engine). The technology for controlling pollution from these fuels also exists. At present, no other energy source is close to replacing the amount of energy generated by fossil fuels. Oil has a particular advantage in that it can be delivered over long distances by pipeline.

The two main disadvantages of fossil fuels are their contribution to climate change, and their unsustainability. They are the most important contributor to the build-up of carbon dioxide in the atmosphere and consequently global warming. Use of fossil fuels is unsustainable because it implies liquidation of a limited stock of the resource: we can extend the lifetime of this resource, but it is ultimately unsustainable. Other disadvantages are that these fuels will become increasingly difficult to extract, and extraction may become more and more potentially dangerous as mines get deeper and oil-rigs are placed further out to sea. Oil spillages from tankers and burst pipelines can severely damage natural ecosystems, and it is very expensive to clear up this sort of pollution. While coal from underground (extraction techniques using tunnelling) causes minimal disturbance at the surface, open-cast mining clears habitat from the surface and can cause extensive environmental damage.

Fossil fuel consumption is largest in MEDCs (Figure 3.29). However, fossil fuel consumption in LEDCs is expected to increase in future because of increasing population and technological development. Coal is not easily transported over long distances, it is mainly consumed where it is locally available (Figure 3.29). Oil and gas can be consumed far from their source of extraction because they can be piped.

Figure 3.29
Global fossil fuel use, 2004. The availability of energy still relies extensively on fossil fuels, which account for around 80 per cent of global energy consumption. Consumption varies country by country. The biggest consumers are the USA, China, and Europe (together accounting for more than half of all fossil fuel consumption).

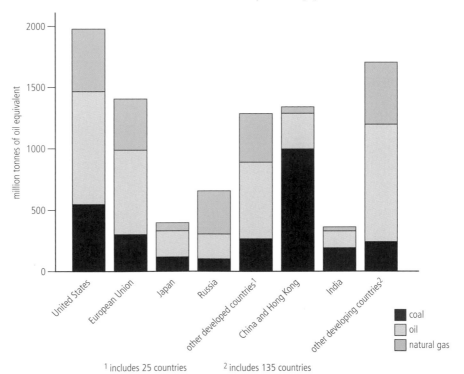

¹ includes 25 countries   ² includes 135 countries

In the US town of Centralia, Pennsylvania, an exposed coal seam caught fire in 1962. It burned for 17 years before a petrol station dealer found the ground temperature was 77.8 °C and other residents found their cellar floors too hot to touch. Smoke began to seep from the ground. The town was abandoned, residents relocated, and buildings bulldozed in 2002. The coal is still burning and may do so for 250 years.

Advantages and disadvantages of nuclear power

The equations of Albert Einstein first alerted scientists to the possibility of generating huge amounts of energy from splitting atoms. Fission technology was first developed in 1945 and used in atomic bombs at the end of World War II. It was then used in generating atomic energy (Figure 3.30). When enough fissionable material (e.g. uranium or plutonium) is brought together, and the process initiated, a chain reaction occurs that splits atoms releasing a tremendous amount of energy.

Nuclear power plants produce radioactive wastes, including some that can remain dangerous for tens of thousands of years. Radioactivity is the result of nuclear changes in which unstable (radioactive) isotopes emit particles and energy continuously until the original isotope is changed into a stable one. When people are exposed to radiation, the DNA in their cells can be damaged by mutation. If mutation occurs in body (somatic cells), cancers, miscarriages and burns can be caused. If the mutation occurs in reproductive cells (eggs and sperm), genetic defects can appear in subsequent generations.

Einstein's equation $E = mc^2$ related energy and matter, where the amount of energy in matter (E) was calculated by multiplying mass (m) by the speed of light squared (c^2), generating enormous numbers for E from even small quantities of matter.

Figure 3.30
When a fission reaction takes place, a large amount of heat is given off. This heats water around the nuclear core and turns it to steam. The steam passes over the turbine causing it to spin, which turns a large generator, creating electricity. The steam is then cooled by cold water from the cooling tower travelling through the condenser below the turbine. The drop in temperature condenses the steam back into water, which is pumped back to the reactor to be reheated and continue the process.

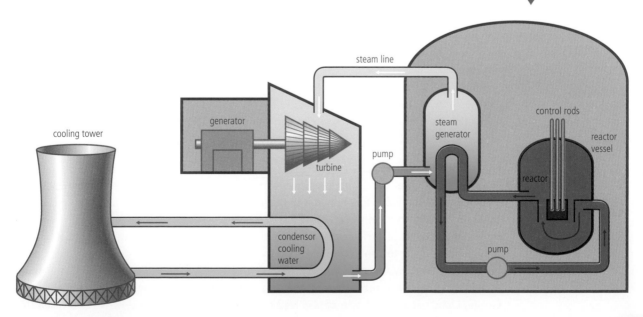

The advantages of nuclear power generation are as follows.
- It does not emit carbon dioxide and so does not contribute to global warming.
- The technology is readily available.
- A large amount of electrical energy is generated in a single plant.
- It is very efficient, especially in comparison to fossil fuels: 1 kg uranium contains 20 000 times more energy than 1 kg coal.

Nuclear power generation has the following disadvantages.
- The waste from nuclear power stations is extremely dangerous and remains so for thousands of years. How best to dispose of this is still an unresolved problem.
- The associated risks are high. It is impossible to build a plant with 100 per cent reliability, and there will always be a small probability of failure – as we have already seen with the Chernobyl disaster (Chapter 2, page 75; Chapter 7, page 291). The more nuclear power plants (and nuclear waste storage shelters) are built, the higher is the probability of a disastrous failure somewhere in the world. The potential of nuclear power plants to become targets for terrorist attack has been pointed out by opponents of this type of power generation.
- The energy source for nuclear energy is uranium, which is a scarce and non-renewable resource. Its supply is estimated to last for only the next 30–60 years depending on actual demand.
- The time frame needed to plan and build a new nuclear power plant is 20–30 years: uptake of nuclear power will therefore take time.

In 1996, there were 435 nuclear power stations operating worldwide, with 30 under construction. In the USA, nuclear energy is 20 per cent of the total energy generated (second to coal); in France, 78 per cent of the total energy is from nuclear sources.

Advantages and disadvantages of renewables

General advantages of renewable sources of energy are that they do not release pollutants such as greenhouse gases or chemicals that contribute to acid rain. Because they are renewable, they will not run out. Ecological footprint is calculated as the amount of land required to absorb waste carbon dioxide from fossil fuel (page 161). As renewable energy produces fewer emissions than fossil fuels, it has a smaller ecological footprint.

There are several restrictions that currently limit large-scale use of renewable energy sources. Fossil fuel resources are still economically cheaper to exploit, and the technologies to harness renewable sources are not available on a large scale. Inertia within the culture and traditions of both MEDCs and LEDCs means that non-renewable resources are favoured (although certain renewable energy supplies have always been widely used in LEDCs). The locations available for renewable energy sources are often limited by politics – for example, sites for wind turbines are often not exploited because people living nearby do want their environment 'spoilt' by the presence of wind turbines. All these factors mean that renewable resources are not able to meet current demand.

Hydroelectric power

Hydroelectric power (HEP) uses turbines which can be switched on whenever energy is needed, so it is a reliable form of energy generation (Figure 3.31). Dams are used to block the flow of water so forming large artificial lakes which can be used for leisure purposes and irrigation as well as electricity generation. Once the construction is completed, HEP schemes are relatively cheap to run. However, there are several disadvantages to HEP. Vast areas may be flooded involving loss of habitats, farmland and displacement of people, and dams may restrict the flow of sediment thereby affecting ecosystems or farming downstream (the Three Gorges Dam, page 79). They may also lead to increased erosion rates downstream when the flow of natural river systems are disrupted. The cost of building dams is high, and dams may eventually silt-up rendering them unusable.

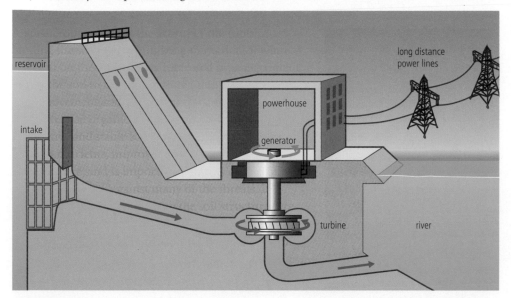

Figure 3.31
Hydroelectric energy is generated when water contained in an artificially made reservoir (created by damming a river) is allowed to flow though a turbine under immense pressure. The water turns the propellers which cause rotation in the turbine shaft, which generates electricity in the turbine's motor.

Tidal power

Tidal power produces energy by using the ebbing or flooding tide to turn turbines which produce energy (Figure 3.32). The major limitations of this method are that a good tidal range is required to generate sufficient energy, and the right shape of coastline to channel water through the turbines. Such installations may interfere with navigation and can have impact on wildlife. They are expensive to set up.

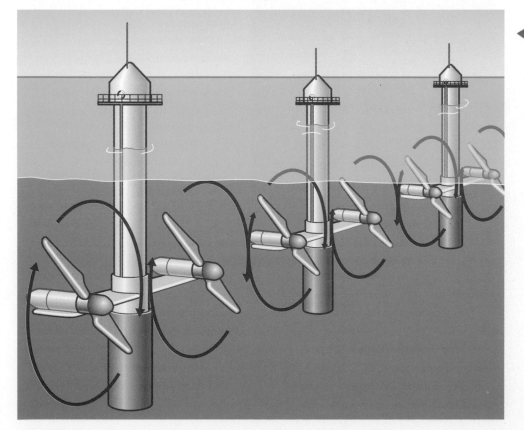

Figure 3.32
The turbines generate power as the tide comes in and again as it goes out.

Solar energy

At present, it is very expensive to turn solar energy into high-quality energy needed for manufacturing (compared to using fossil fuels). However, passive solar energy (combined with insulation) is much cheaper for heating homes than fossil fuels. Solar energy has the disadvantage that its usefulness is limited in northern countries during winter months.

Solar panels are large flat panels made up of many individual solar cells. ▶

A wind turbine. ▶

Wind power

Wind power is produced by wind turbines driven by available wind energy – the wind turns the rotor blades which rotate a metal shaft which transfers the rotational energy into a generator. The generator generates electricity using electromagnetism. The energy is then supplied to an electrical grid. The major limitations of wind turbines are that if there is no wind, no energy is generated. Thus, placement of the turbines is critical: they need to be in areas of consistent high wind.

Biofuel

Biofuel energy is produced by burning plant material to produce heat (Figure 3.33). Other forms of biofuel transform plant matter into ethanol which is then used as a fuel, or use methane digestion methods to convert biomass to methane which is then burnt to generate electricity. The disadvantages of these techniques are that they produce emissions and require large amounts of land to grow the biofuel crop (page 118). Biofuel crops may take up land once used for growing food crops, thus pushing up the price of food, and disadvantaging local people who cannot get enough food to live (page 136). Biofuel crops are often planted at the expense of natural ecosystems, where new land clearance to create space for the biofuel crop has destroyed the natural ecosystem.

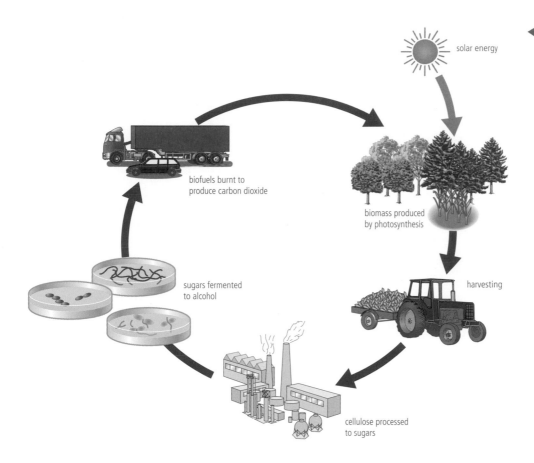

Figure 3.33
Biofuels are seen as a green form of power generation because, although they produce carbon dioxide, the gas is recycled (biofuel crops absorb carbon dioxide when they photosynthesize).

solar energy

biomass produced by photosynthesis

harvesting

cellulose processed to sugars

sugars fermented to alcohol

biofuels burnt to produce carbon dioxide

Wastes

Energy can be obtained from wastes. Organic waste decomposes and gives off methane gas which can be burned. Waste can also be burned directly to generate energy, for example burning straw. Advantages are that the resource used is readily available and its use does not deplete natural capital. At the same time, a useful purpose is being served by waste that would otherwise have to be disposed of in some other way. Disadvantages are that the burning adds to global warming gases in the atmosphere (although it could be argued that decomposition of the waste would do this in any case).

Geothermal energy

Energy can be obtained from residual heat in the ground. Water is pumped into pipes beneath the ground and the geothermal heat from the ground heats the water which can then be used to heat buildings. The pipes do not have to be buried at great depth to be effective, although deeper burial allows greater heat capture. This method of heat transfer is low impact and does not release any form of pollution. The pipes can be arranged in various formations (Figure 3.34).

Figure 3.34
Designs for pipe layout to supply geothermal energy to the home.

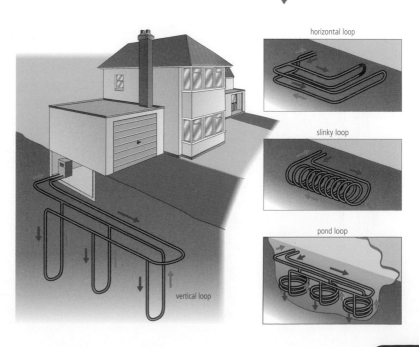

horizontal loop

slinky loop

pond loop

vertical loop

In *Renewable energy – a global perspective*, Mohamed El-Ashry – Senior Fellow, UN Foundation – argues that 2008, seemingly the peak of the global financial crisis, was the best year for renewables. In just one year, all forms of grid-connected solar power grew by 70 per cent. Wind power grew by 29 per cent, and solar hot water increased by 15 per cent. According to the *Financial Times*, more than 50 per cent of total added power capacity in 2008 in both the USA and Europe was renewable – more than new capacity for oil, gas, coal, and nuclear combined.

National investments in renewable energy also changed. In 2006, Germany and China were the global leaders in new capacity investment, with the USA far behind. But a massive increase in wind power investment in the USA allowed it to become the global leader in 2008. Spain, China, and Germany were not far behind. Spain moved up to second place thanks to its large investments in solar power. Brazil was fifth, due to large investments in biofuels. The global recession might turn out to be a blessing in disguise for renewable energy, because governments of the world's largest economies have, for the first time, provided direct financial support. Governments did not invest just for energy security and climate change. They recognized the economic benefits of clean energy. At the end of 2008 and in early 2009, a number of national governments announced plans to greatly increase public finance of renewables and other low-carbon technologies. Many of these announcements were directed at economic stimulus and job creation, with millions of new 'green jobs' targeted.

CASE STUDY

Oil palm and habitat destruction

By 2020, Indonesia's oil palm plantations are projected to triple in size to 16.5 million hectares. Many conservationists believe that this, in Indonesia and other countries, will lead directly and indirectly to the further clearance of a huge area of rainforest.

To learn more about palm oil as a biofuel, go to www.pearsonhotlinks. com, insert the express code 2630P and click on activity 3.7.

Oil palm is the second most traded vegetable oil crop after soy. Over 90 per cent of the world's oil palm exports are produced in Malaysia and Indonesia, in areas once covered by rainforest and peat forest. Palm oil is traditionally used in the manufacture of food products, but is now increasingly used as an ingredient in bio-diesel. It is also used as biofuel burnt at power stations to produce electricity. This new market has the potential to dramatically increase the global demand for oil palm. In the UK, the conversion of just one oil-fired power station to palm oil could double UK imports. The 6.5 million hectares of oil palm plantation across Sumatra and Borneo is estimated to have caused the destruction of 10 million hectares of rainforest – an increase in demand for palm oil as a biofuel would further increase the threat to natural ecosystems unless checks and balances are put in place.

Factors which affect the choice of energy generation

Energy usage varies around the globe, and so do the ways in which energy is generated. In general, MEDCs have higher energy demands than LEDCs (Figure 3.35, 1Btu = 1054 joules), as people in these countries depend on energy for transport, heating, air-conditioning, cooking and all aspects of their lives. Global carbon dioxide emissions closely match figures for total energy use per country, reflecting the fact that the majority of energy is currently generated from fossil fuels, which emit high levels of carbon dioxide (page 111).

Figure 3.35
Worldwide energy consumption (1989–98). Besides high consumption in MEDCs, countries such as India and China have increasing energy demands to support their growing populations, increasing technological base, and aspirations to high-energy dependent lifestyles.

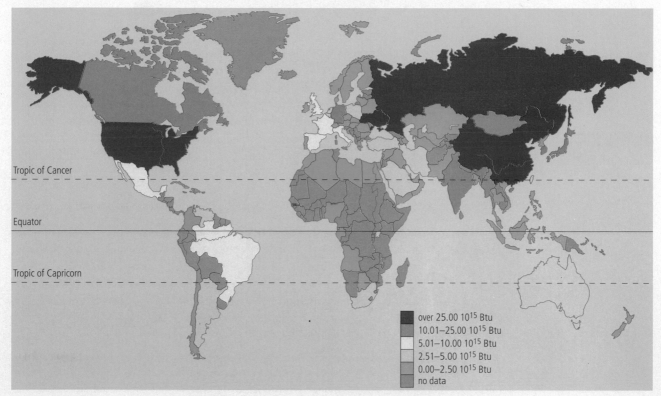

Tropic of Cancer

Equator

Tropic of Capricorn

over 25.00 10^{15} Btu
10.01–25.00 10^{15} Btu
5.01–10.00 10^{15} Btu
2.51–5.00 10^{15} Btu
0.00–2.50 10^{15} Btu
no data

The choice of energy sources adopted by different countries often has an historical basis (page 109). Large oil, coal and gas reserves in certain countries (e.g. the UK) made fossil fuels an obvious choice for exploitation in those countries. Energy generation may also depend on economic, cultural, environmental and technological factors.

Figure 3.36 (overleaf) shows that oil use in MEDCs is almost 50 per cent greater than in LEDCs, and fossil fuels in MEDCs account for 85 per cent of energy use as opposed to 58 per cent in LEDCs. The use of nuclear power is five times more important in MEDCs than in LEDCs. Biomass use in LEDCs is more than ten times that in MEDCs. In some instances, both LEDCs and MEDCs have similar levels of usage of a resource; examples are coal (25 per cent), HEP, geothermal and solar power (6 per cent in LEDCs and 7 per cent in MEDCs).

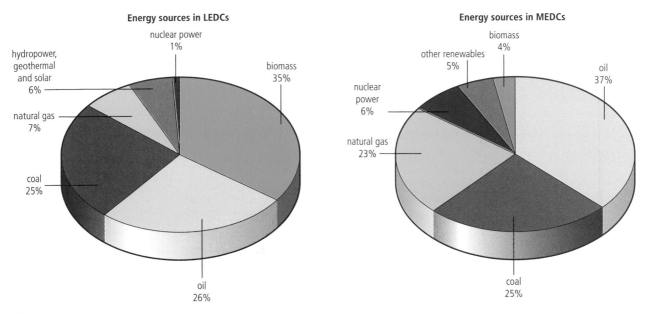

Figure 3.36
Relative contributions of different sources of commercial energy for LEDCs and MEDCs.

There are various explanations for these observed patterns. Oil is used extensively to produce petroleum products, and difference in oil use between LEDCs and MEDCs can be explained by the more prevalent use of cars in MEDCs. Biomass is very important in LEDCs as fuel for cooking, whereas MEDCs use gas or electricity (i.e. fossil fuels). The relatively small contribution of nuclear power may be due to the problems of disposing of nuclear fuel and the cost of nuclear technology. The relatively small proportion of nuclear power generation in MEDCs may also be affected by the general distrust of the industry in certain countries (e.g. fear of potential environmental impacts, page 114). Cultural fears, based on perception of nuclear accidents and waste, have made this a politically unpopular choice in many countries.

There are various factors that are currently restricting the use of renewable energy sources. Fossil fuel resources are still economically cheaper to exploit, and the technology to harness renewable sources is currently not available on a large scale. Culture and tradition means that non-renewable resources are favoured, and the locations for renewable energy sources are often limited by available sites and local political issues. The low uptake of renewables globally means that they are not able to meet current demand. However, recession can change things (Global perspectives, page 118).

ENVIRONMENTAL PHILOSOPHIES

Environmental philosophies are important in determining energy usage. A technocentric worldview may lead to continued use of fossil fuels in the belief that pollution can be minimized through technological solutions. A more ecocentric philosophy would see humanity living more within its means, and making better use of renewable sources of energy. These ideas are discussed further in Chapter 7.

Changes in methods of energy generation employed can result from changing costs of production and from changes in social perspectives on established fuel supplies, which in turn may lead to shifts in environmental philosophy. In countries that rely on fossil fuels, the costs of exploitation have increased as the most easily accessible reserves have been used up, thus alternative sources been sought. Increasing cost of fossil fuels will change peoples' views of them.

At the same time, changing awareness of the environmental implications of fossil fuel exploitation (e.g. global warming) has led to a shift in attitude towards renewable energy sources (e.g. wind power), despite aesthetic and environmental implications, and increased demand for renewable, non-polluting sources. This has led to greater investment and research into alternatives (e.g. wind and tidal power).

CASE STUDY

Narmada Dam, India

In India, biomass is a traditional source of energy. A huge proportion of the population relies on local sources of firewood for energy because it is the most readily available source and is inexpensive. Technology such as solar-powered stoves is neither available nor affordable.

The Indian government, in a drive to develop economically, has sought to harness other sources of cheap energy to stimulate industrial development. In particular, the government is promoting hydroelectric power, which historically has sometimes been extremely controversial for social and environmental reasons.

The most controversial dam development in India is the Narmada River Dam project. Plans were initiated in the 1940s by the country's first prime minister Jawaharlal Nehru. Legal and logistical problems delayed the start of the project until 1979. The plan involves the construction of some 3200 dams of varying sizes on the Narmada River (Figure 3.37).

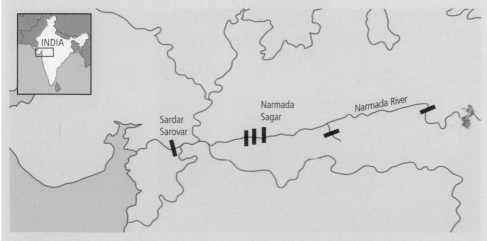

Figure 3.37
The location of dams in the Narmada River, India.

The Sardar Sarovar is the biggest dam on the river and its construction has been fiercely opposed. 200 000 people could be displaced by the project, and major damage caused to the ecosystems of the region. Those in favour of the project say that it will supply water to 30 million people and irrigate crops to feed another 20 million people. In October 2000, the Indian Supreme Court gave a go-ahead for the construction of the Sardar Sarovar Dam, saying that the benefits of the project outweigh negative environmental and social impacts. The project is expected to be completed by 2025.

EXERCISES

1   Outline the range of energy resources available to society.

2   Evaluate the advantages and disadvantages of two contrasting energy sources.

3   Discuss the factors that affect the choice of energy sources adopted by different societies.

3.4 The soil system

Assessment statements

3.4.1 Outline how soil systems integrate aspects of living systems.
3.4.2 Compare and contrast the structure and properties of sand, clay and loam soils, including their effect on primary productivity.
3.4.3 Outline the processes and consequences of soil degradation.
3.4.4 Outline soil conservation measures.
3.4.5 Evaluate soil management strategies in a named commercial farming system and in a named subsistence farming system.

Soil systems

Soils are a major component of the world's ecosystems (Figure 3.38). They form at the interface of the Earth's atmosphere, lithosphere (rocks), biosphere (living matter) and hydrosphere (water). Soils form the outermost layer of the Earth's surface, and comprise weathered bedrock (regolith), organic matter (both dead and alive), air and water.

Figure 3.38
Soils in the environment.

Soils perform a number of vital functions for humans.

- Soils are the medium for plant growth – most foodstuffs for humans are grown in soil.
- Soils act as a major store of relatively accessible freshwater – approximately 70 000 km³ or 0.005 per cent of the global freshwater total.
- Soils filter materials added to the soil thereby maintaining water quality.
- Some recycling of nutrients takes place in the soil through the breakdown of dead organic matter.
- Soil acts as a habitat for billions of microorganisms as well as for some larger animals.
- Soils provide raw materials in the form of peat, clays, sands, gravels and minerals.

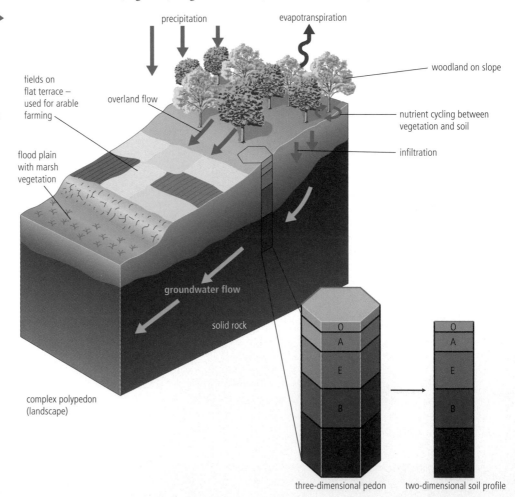

Soil has matter in all three states:
- organic and inorganic matter form the solid state
- soil water (from precipitation, groundwater and seepage) form the liquid state
- soil atmosphere forms the gaseous state.

Soils are a vital resource for humans but they take a long time to develop. Thus, they should be considered as a non-renewable resource.

◀ Peat cutting; peat can be burnt to provide heat.

Soil profiles

A soil profile is a two-dimensional vertical section through a soil, and is divided into horizons (distinguishable layers) as shown in Table 3.4 and Figure 3.38. These layers have distinct physical and chemical characteristics, although the boundaries between horizons may be blurred by earthworm activity.

TABLE 3.4 SOIL HORIZONS		
Horizon	**Labels**	
O organic horizon	l f h	undecomposed litter partly decomposed (fermenting) litter well-decomposed humus
A mixed mineral–organic horizon	h p g	humus ploughed, as in a field or a garden gleyed or waterlogged
E eluvial or leached horizon	a b	strongly leached, ash-coloured horizon weakly bleached, light brown horizon, as in a brown earth
B illuvial or deposited horizon	Fe t h	iron deposited clay deposited humus deposited
C bedrock or parent material	r u	rock unconsolidated loose deposits

The top layer of vegetation is referred to as the organic (O) horizon. Beneath this is the mixed mineral–organic layer (A horizon). It is generally a dark colour due to the presence of organic matter. An Ap horizon is one that has been mixed by ploughing.

In some soils, leaching takes place. This removes material from the horizon. Consequently, the layer is much lighter in colour. Where leaching is intense, an ash-coloured Ea horizon is formed. By contrast, in a brown earth, where leaching is less intense, a light brown Eb horizon is found.

The B horizon is the deposited or illuvial horizon. It contains material that has been moved from the E horizon, such as iron (Fe) humus (h) and clay (t).

At the base of the horizon is the parent material or bedrock. Sometimes labels are given to distinguish rock (r) from unconsolidated loose deposits (u).

Soil forming processes

Soil forming processes involve:

- gains and losses of material to and from the profile
- movement of water between the horizons
- chemical transformations within each horizon.

Therefore, soils must be considered as open systems in a steady-state equilibrium, varying constantly as the factors and processes that influence them change.

The principal processes include weathering, translocation, organic changes and gleying (waterlogging). The weathering of bedrock gives the soil its C horizon and also its initial bases and nutrients (fertility), structure and texture (drainage).

Translocation includes many processes, mostly by water, and mostly downwards. Leaching refers to the downward movement of soluble material, while eluviation is the physical downwashing of small particles such as clay and humus. The parallel between these processes and solution and suspension in a river is clear. Such movements produce eluvial (removal) and illuvial (deposited) horizons.

In arid and semi-arid environments, evapotranspiration (EVT) is greater than precipitation, so the movement of soil solution is upwards through the soil. Water is drawn to the drying surface by capillary action and leaching is generally ineffective apart from during occasional storms. Calcium carbonates and other solutes remain in the soil. This process is known as calcification. In grasslands, calcification is enhanced because grasses require calcium; they draw it up from the lower layers and return it to the upper layers when they die down.

In extreme cases where EVT is intense, sodium or calcium may form a crust on the surface. This may be toxic to plant growth. Excessive sodium concentrations may occur due to capillary rise of water from a water table that is saline and close to the surface as in the case of the Punjab irrigation scheme in India. Such a process is known as salinization or alkalization.

Organic changes occur mostly at or near the surface. Plant litter is decomposed (humified) into a dark amorphous mass. It is also degraded gradually by fungi, algae, small insects, bacteria and worms. Under very wet conditions, humification forms peat. Over a long periods of time, humus decomposes due to mineralization, which releases nitrogenous compounds. Degradation, humification and mineralization are not separable processes and always accompany each other. At the other end of the scale, human activity seriously alters soils.

Is soil a renewable resource or a non-renewable resource? How does the length of time that it takes a soil to form affect its renewable or non-renewable status?

To learn more about soils online, go to www.pearsonhotlinks.com, insert the express code 2630P and click on activity 3.8.

To watch a soils animation, go to www.pearsonhotlinks.com, insert the express code 2630P and click on activity 3.9.

Soil structures and properties

The ideal soil for cultivation is a loam in which there is a balance between water-holding ability and freely draining, aerated conditions. This is influenced by a number of factors, especially soil texture. Soil texture refers to the proportion of differently sized materials, usually sand, silt and clay (Figure 3.39) present in a soil. A loam is a well-balanced soil with significant proportions of sand, silt and clay. The agricultural potential of a soil depends on:

- the porosity and permeability of the soil
- the surface area of the soil particles (peds).

type of particle	diameter (mm)
clay	<0.002
silt	<0.02
sand	<0.2
gravel	<2
coarse gravel	>2

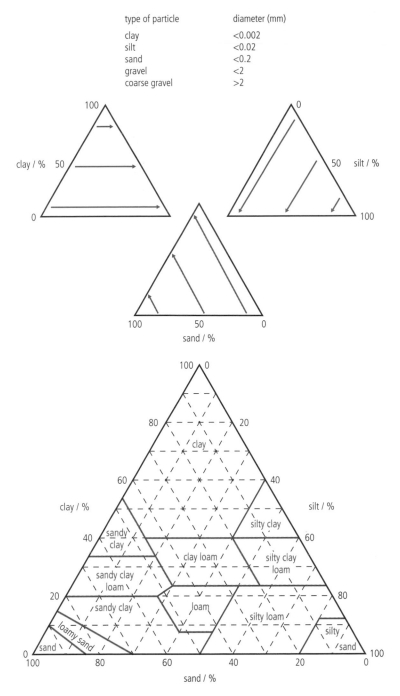

Figure 3.39
Soil textural groups.

The pore spaces determine the rate at which water drains through a soil. The surface area determines the amount of water and nutrients in solution that can be retained against the force of gravity. For example, a heavy clay soil can hold twice as much water as a light soil.

The terms 'light', 'medium' and 'heavy' refer to the workability of a soil. Light soils (over 80 per cent sand) are coarse-textured and are easily drained of water and nutrients. They do, however, warm up more quickly than heavy clay soils and so allow early growth in spring. Heavy soils contain more than 25 per cent clay and are fine-textured. Many of their pores are <0.001 mm and the very large chemically active surface area means that these soils are water- and nutrient-retentive. Clay absorbs water, so that the soil swells when wet and shrinks when dry. Because clay is so chemically active, it tends to dominate other soil constituents.

 Different soil types have different levels of primary productivity. These can be summarized as follows:

- sandy soil – low
- clay soil – quite low
- loam soil – high.

A brown earth. This soil has an Eb horizon (page 123).

Soil structure refers to the shape and arrangement of individual soil peds. The ideal structure is a crumb structure in which peds are small and porous. The soil structural condition can also be measured by its porosity – this determines its air capacity and water availability (Table 3.5).

TABLE 3.5 SOIL QUALITY, AIR CAPACITY AND WATER AVAILABILITY		
Soil quality	Air capacity / %	Available water / %
very good	>15	>20
good	10–15	15–20
moderate	5–<10	10–<15
poor	<5	<10

For optimum structure, a variety of pore sizes is required to allow root penetration, free drainage and water storage. This is because pore spaces of over 0.1 mm allow root growth, oxygen diffusion and water movement, whereas pore spaces below 0.05 mm help store water.

Soil structure depends on:
- soil texture (i.e. the amount of sand, silt and clay)
- dead organic matter
- earthworm activity.

Nevertheless, there are important differences between the same soil type in different parts of the world. Clay soils are often fertile in temperate locations but in tropical areas, clay soils are permeable and easily penetrated by roots. Thus, in the tropics, they tend to be nutrient deficient and easily leached.

The workability of a soil depends on the amount of clay present. As Table 3.6 shows, the force needed to pull a plough increases with clay content.

TABLE 3.6 FORCE NEEDED TO PULL A PLOUGH AND CLAY CONTENT OF SOIL				
Clay content / %	23.6	30.0	31.1	34.3
Force needed to pull a plough / N	580	635	680	703

EXERCISES

1   For each of the following soils, suggest its likely relative position on Table 3.5 above: clay, sand, loam.

2   Describe the relationship between clay content and force needed to pull a plough.

3   Suggest reasons to explain the relationship you have described in Exercise 2

The **shrinking limit** is the state at which the soil passes from having a moist to a dry appearance. There is just enough moisture to fill micro-pores. The **plastic limit** occurs where each ped is surrounded by a film of water sufficient to act as a lubricant. The **liquid limit** occurs when there is sufficient water to reduce cohesion between the peds. **Field capacity** is the maximum amount of water that a particular soil can hold.

Heavy soils in which the clay content is over 28 per cent are the most difficult for arable cultivation. They are highly water retentive, have low permeability and field drainage is slow. Drying out is slow. Heavy soils become plastic when too wet and hard when too dry. The number of days in which they can be worked is small in comparison with other soils (Table 3.7). The main limiting factor for light soils is drought during the growing season because these soils have a poor nutrient-holding capacity.

Primary productivity of soil depends on:

- mineral content
- drainage
- water-holding capacity
- air spaces
- biota
- potential to hold organic matter.

TABLE 3.7 INFLUENCE OF RAINFALL AND SOIL TEXTURE ON THE AVERAGE NUMBER OF DAYS IN WHICH CULTIVATION WOULD BE SATISFACTORY

Month	Feb			Mar			Apr		
Soil type	Light	Medium	Heavy	Light	Medium	Heavy	Light	Medium	Heavy
Higher than average rainfall	3	2	0	16	14	9	21	19	16
Average rainfall	8	5	3	25	24	20	26	23	16
Lower than average rainfall	11	9	8	29	29	27	28	26	25

Source: Adapted from Tivy J. *Agricultural ecology*, 1990, Table 4.8, p. 55

Moisture content at the plastic limit and field capacity are shown in Table 3.8.

TABLE 3.8 MOISTURE CONTENT AT THE PLASTIC LIMIT AND FIELD CAPACITY

Soil texture	Moisture content / %		Clay content / %	Organic matter / %
	Plastic limit	Field capacity		
sandy loam	19.7	26.0	17.0	2.8
clay loam (1)	35.9	42.0	39.0	6.4
clay loam (2)	48.8	55.2	58.0	8.8

Source: Adapted from Tivy J. *Agricultural ecology*, 1990, Table 4.6 p. 54

EXERCISES

1   Describe the variations in the number of workdays for light soils:
    (a) by month
    (b) by rainfall.

2   Suggest reasons for your answers to 1(a) and (b).

3   Comment on the variations in the number of days in which cultivation would be satisfactory for light, medium and heavy soils.

4   What is meant by a loam soil? Describe the differences between a sandy loam and a clay loam.

5   Describe the relationship between moisture content and the percentage of clay and organic matter.

6   Suggest why there is a difference between the sandy loam and the clay loam in terms of moisture content.

Soil degradation

Soil degradation is the decline in quantity and quality of soil. It includes erosion by wind and water, biological degradation (e.g. the loss of humus and plant or animal life), physical degradation (loss of structure, changes in permeability), and chemical degradation (acidification, declining fertility, changes in pH, salinity).

Soil degradation in Sicily.

Causes of degradation

The universal soil loss equation (USLE) is an attempt to predict the amount of erosion that will take place in an area on the basis of certain factors which increase susceptibility to erosion. The equation takes the form:

$$A = RKLSCP$$

In this equation:

A = the predicted soil loss

R = the climatic erosivity or the rainfall erosivity index

K = soil erodibility

L = slope length

S = slope gradient

C = cover and management

P = erosion control practice.

These factors are explained in Table 3.9.

- Rill erosion – Small channels (maximum extent of a few centimetres) that change location with every run-off event (overland flow or run-off can occur during each storm event).
- Tunnel erosion – Water erosion that forms clearly defined tunnels or pipes (sometimes called pipe flow). Some tunnel flow may cause the surface to collapse thus forming steep gullies.
- Surface erosion – Erosion of the soil surface by water when rainfall intensity (mm per hour) exceeds infiltration capacity (the rate at which water can enter the soil) to produce overland flow.
- Gully erosion – Pronounced erosion by ephemeral streams (streams that occur only after storms) producing steep-sided channels. May be formed by the merging of many rills

TABLE 3.9 FACTORS RELATING TO THE UNIVERSAL SOIL LOSS EQUATION	
Factor	**Description**
erosivity, R	Rainfall totals, intensity and seasonal distribution. Maximum erosivity occurs when rainfall occurs as high-intensity storms. If this happens when land has just been ploughed, or full crop cover is not yet established, erosion is greater than when rain falls on an established crop. Minimum erosion occurs when gentle rain falls onto frozen soil, land with natural vegetation, or land with full crop cover.
erodibility, K	The susceptibility of a soil to erosion. Erodibility depends on infiltration capacity and the structural stability of soil. Soil with high infiltration capacity and high structural stability that resists the impact of rain splash, has the lowest erodibility.
slope length and gradient, LS	Slope length and gradient influence the movement and speed of water down the slope, and thus its ability to transport particles. The greater the slope, the greater the erosivity; the longer the slope, the more water is received on the surface.
cover and management, C	This factor relates to the type of crop and cultivation practice. Established grass and forest provide the best protection against erosion; of agricultural crops, those with the greatest foliage and thus greatest ground cover are optimal. Fallow land or land with crops that expose the soil for long periods after planting or harvesting has little protection.
erosion control practice, P	Soil conservation measures such as contour ploughing and terracing can reduce erosion or slow runoff water.

Source: Adapted by Huggett, et al. *Physical geography – a human perspective*. Arnold, 2004, p. 298

Soil degradation is a complex process with a range of underlying causes. There are several issues operating at different times and places.

- Water erosion accounts for about 60 per cent of soil degradation. Erosion takes several forms: surface-, gully-, rill- and tunnel-erosion.
- Wind erosion
- Acidification (toxification) is change in the chemical composition of the soil, which may trigger the circulation of toxic metals.

- Eutrophication (nutrient enrichment) may degrade the quality of groundwater. Groundwater over-abstraction may lead to dry soils.
- Salt-affected soils are typically found in marine-derived sediments, coastal locations and hot arid areas where capillary action brings salts to the upper part of the soil (salinization). Soil salinity has been a major problem in Australia following the removal of vegetation for dryland farming.
- Atmospheric deposition of heavy metals and persistent organic pollutants may render soils less suitable to sustain the original land cover and use.
- In extreme cases, soil degradation can be a cause and a consequence of desertification (spread of desert conditions into previously productive areas).
- Climate change will probably intensify the problem because it is likely to affect hydrology and hence land use.

Climate change

Climate change – higher than average temperature and changing precipitation patterns – may have three direct impacts on soil conditions. Higher temperatures cause higher decomposition rates of organic matter. Soil organic matter is important as a source of nutrients and it improves moisture storage. More precipitation and flooding cause more water erosion; more droughts cause more wind erosion.

Besides these direct effects, climate change may:
- create a need for more agricultural land to compensate the loss of degraded land
- lead to higher yields for the major European grain crops due to the carbon dioxide fertilization effect (Chapter 6, page 271).

These two indirect effects seem to balance out.

Human activity

Human activity has often led to degradation of the world's land resources (Table 3.10).

TABLE 3.10 HUMAN ACTIVITY AND ITS IMPACT ON SOIL EROSION	
Action	Effect
removal of woodland or ploughing established pasture	When vegetation cover is removed, roots binding the soil die and the soil is exposed to wind and water. The land becomes particularly susceptible to erosion if on slopes.
cultivation	Exposure of bare soil surface before planting and after harvesting. Cultivation on slopes can generate large amounts of runoff and create rills and gullies. Irrigation in hot areas can lead to salinization.
grazing	Overgrazing can severely reduce the vegetation cover and leave the surface vulnerable to erosion. Grouping of animals can lead to over-trampling and the creation of bare patches. Dry regions are particularly susceptible to wind erosion.
roads or tracks	Roads and tracks can collect water due to reduced infiltration that can cause rills and gullies to form.
mining	Mining leads to exposure of bare soil.

The global assessment of human-induced soil degradation has shown that damage is widespread (Table 3.11, overleaf) and that it has occurred on 15 per cent of the world's total land area (13 per cent light and moderate, 2 per cent severe and very severe). These impacts frequently lead to reductions in yields. Land conservation and rehabilitation are essential parts of sustainable agricultural development. While severely degraded soil is found in most regions of the world, the negative economic impact of degraded soil may be most severe in the countries most dependent on agriculture for their incomes.

TABLE 3.11 HUMAN-INDUCED LAND DEGRADATION			
Region	Land area / 000s km²	Total affected by severe or very severe land degradation / 000s km²	Amount of severe or very severe land degradation due to agricultural activities / 000s km²
Sub-Saharan Africa	23 772	5 931	1 996
North Africa and Near East	12 379	4 260	759
North Asia, east of Urals	21 033	4 421	1 180
Asia and Pacific	28 989	8 407	3 506
South and Central America	20 498	5 552	1 795
North America	19 237	3 158	2 427
Europe	6 843	3 274	727
World	134 907	35 003	12 390

EXERCISES

1 Choose an appropriate method to show the following data:

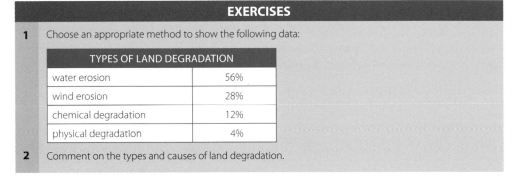

TYPES OF LAND DEGRADATION	
water erosion	56%
wind erosion	28%
chemical degradation	12%
physical degradation	4%

2 Comment on the types and causes of land degradation.

To learn more about soil degradation around the world, go to www. pearsonhotlinks.com, insert the express code 2630P and click on activity 3.10.

Soil conservation measures

Managing soil degradation

Strategies for combating accelerated soil degradation are lacking in many areas. To reduce the risk, farmers are encouraged towards more extensive management practices such as organic farming, afforestation, pasture extension, and benign crop production. Nevertheless, there is a need for policy makers and the public to combat the pressures and risks to the soil resource.

Methods to reduce or prevent erosion can be mechanical (e.g. physical barriers such as embankments and wind breaks), or they may focus on vegetation cover and soil husbandry. Overland flow can be reduced by increasing infiltration.

Mechanical methods to reduce water flow

Mechanical methods include bunding, terracing and contour ploughing. The key is to prevent or slow down the movement of rain water down slope. Contour ploughing takes advantage of the ridges formed at right angles to the slope to act to prevent or slow the downward accretion of soil and water. On steep slopes and those with heavy rainfall (e.g. the monsoon in South-East Asia) contour ploughing is insufficient and terracing is undertaken. The slope is broken up into a series of flat steps (terraces) with bunds (raised levées) at the edge. The use of terracing allows areas to be cultivated that would not otherwise be suitable.

Land around gullies and ravines can be fenced off, and planted with small trees and grass. Check dams can be built across gullies to reduce the flow of water and trap soil.

Cropping and soil husbandry methods against water and wind damage

Preventing erosion by different cropping techniques largely focuses on:

- maintaining a crop cover for as long as possible
- keeping in place the stubble and root structure of the crop after harvesting
- planting a grass crop.

A grass crop maintains the action of the roots in binding the soil, and minimizing the action of wind and rain on the soil surface. Increased organic content allows the soil to hold more water, thus reducing mass movement and erosion, and stabilizing the soil structure. Soil organic matter is a vital component of productive and stable soils. It is an important source of plant nutrients, improves water retention and soil structure, and is important in terms of the soil's buffering capacity against many of the threats. In addition, to prevent damage to the soil structure care should be taken to reduce use of heavy machinery on wet soils, and ploughing on soils sensitive to erosion.

In areas where wind erosion is a problem shelterbelts of trees or hedgerows are used. The trees act as a barrier to the wind and disturb its flow. Wind speeds are reduced which therefore reduce its ability to disturb the topsoil and erode particles.

Multi-cropping is also useful if it maintains a cover crop throughout the year. On the steepest slopes, cultivation is not recommended and the land should be forested or vegetated to maintain a soil cover and reduce run-off.

Check dam in the Eastern Cape Province, South Africa.

CASE STUDY

Common measures to minimize wind erosion on light agricultural soils of Northern Europe

Table 3.12 comments on some measures to curb wind erosion.

TABLE 3.12 MOST COMMON MEASURES TO MINIMIZE WIND EROSION ON LIGHT AGRICULTURAL SOILS OF NORTHERN EUROPE	
Measure	Comment
Measures that minimize actual risk (short-term effect)	
autumn sown varieties	need to be sown before the end of October to develop a sufficient cover
mixed cropping	after the main crop is harvested, second crop remains on the field
nursing or cover crop	more herbicides needed
straw planting	unsuitable on light sandy soils
organic protection layer (e.g. liquid manure; sewage sludge; sugar beet factory lime)	depends on availability, and regulations on the use of these products
synthetic stabilizers	unsuitable on peat soils
time of cultivation	depends on availability of labour and equipment
cultivation practice (e.g. minimum tillage; plough and press)	not suitable for all crop or soil types
Measures that lower the potential risk (long-term effect)	
smaller fields	increase in operational time and costs
change of arable land to permanent pasture or woodland	loss of agricultural production and farm income
marling (increasing the clay content to 8–10%)	suitable material should be available close by
wind barriers	high investment cost, and loss of productive land; takes several years before providing full protection; level of protection reduces with distance from the shelter

Management of salt-affected soils

There are three **m**ain approaches in the management of salt-affected soils:
- flushing the soil with water and leaching the salt away
- application of chemicals (e.g. gypsum – calcium sulfate – to replace the sodium ions on the clay and colloids with calcium ions)
- reduction in evaporation losses to reduce the upward movement of water in the soil.

Summary of soil conservation methods

Socio-economic and ecological factors have been ignored for too long. An integrated approach to soil conservation is required in which non-technological factors such as population pressure, social structures, economy and ecological factors can determine the most appropriate technical solutions. A wide variety of possible solutions include: strip and ally cropping, rotation farming, contour planning, agroforestry, adjusted stocking levels, mulching, use of cover crops, construction of mechanical barriers such as terraces, banks and ditches (Figure 3.40).

Figure 3.40
Soil conservation methods.

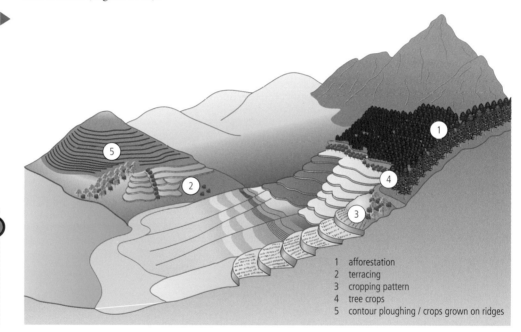

1   afforestation
2   terracing
3   cropping pattern
4   tree crops
5   contour ploughing / crops grown on ridges

To learn more about conservation in Tennessee, go to www.pearsonhotlinks.com, insert the express code 2630P and click on activity 3.11.

Evaluation of soil conservation measures

CASE STUDY

Soil conservation on the Great Plains of the USA

The opening-up of the American drylands coincided with a period of high demand for food, when rainfall was above average. With the droughts of the 1930s, the soils suffered severe wind erosion creating the Dust Bowl in the southern Great Plains.

Soil conservation methods were eventually imposed by the Soil and Conservation Act of 1935.

Soil conservation techniques included:

- contour ploughing
- strip cultivation with an alternation of cultivated and fallow (crop-free) land aligned across the direction of the prevailing wind
- temporary cover crops such as a fast-growing millet
- shallow ploughing to eliminate weeds and conserve crop residues on the surface
- a stubble mulch with a cloddy compacted soil surface.

In addition, the summer fallow was used to regenerate soil nitrogen as well as conserving moisture. However, nitrogen levels continued to decline, and many soils in the USA still contain less than half of their original store.

To tackle this:

- some areas were converted to permanent grazing
- use of a 'grass-break' was introduced to help stabilize soils by the accumulation of organic matter and development of a crumb structure.

However, since the end of World War II, the introduction of herbicides has:

- made weed control possible
- reduced the risk of soil erosion
- reduced nitrogen loss
- increased salinity problems due to increased soil water evaporation.

A more recent change in dry-farming methods in North America has been the change from traditional cropping with summer fallow to methods using no ploughing. This was helped by the introduction, in 1961, of paraquat, a herbicide that leaves no active soil residues. Crop yields under zero tillage have been comparable, if not better, than under conventional methods. The stubble left on the surface retains twice as much snow, which also melts more slowly, than on the ordinary fallow. Other advantages include:

- a reduction of the soil salinity and of annual weeds
- greater conservation of organic matter.

On the other hand, perennial weeds can become more difficult to control. Fertilizer placement is less easy and soil temperatures at the time of seeding are lower than in tilled land.

There is clear evidence that soil conservation measures are practised on the Great Plains, and that they are evolving over time. New techniques can generate new problems although they can also lead to higher yields.

CASE STUDY

Soil degradation at Texizapan watershed, Sierra de Santa Marta, Veracruz, Mexico

The Sierra de Santa Marta is a remote, mountainous region in the humid tropical state of Veracruz, Mexico. Soil erosion and soil fertility loss are major problems and result in:

- reduced agricultural productivity
- decreased availability of drinking water in nearby urban centres
- increased road maintenance
- falling hydroelectric potential
- a decline in the fishing industry in coastal lagoons.

The effects of shifting cultivation on soil.

Soil degradation can be severe when annual crops are grown on steep hillsides using practices that do not include cover crops or surface mulch. This is especially serious when fallow periods are reduced. In traditional shifting cultivation systems, the soil degradation occurring during the years of cultivation is offset by a fallow period long enough to rebuild the soil's productive capacity. Such a system generally collapses with increasing land pressure, as fallow periods are reduced.

In Texizapan, the erosive ability of the natural environment, the high erodibility of the soil, and the limited soil cover provided by the annual crop leads to high rates of soil degradation. Perennial crops such as coffee, especially when grown under shade trees, generally provide better soil protection. However in Veracruz, as in other areas in Central America, annual crops such as maize and beans provide most of the food and cash needs of the population. Resource-poor farmers are generally reluctant to stop growing these crops, even when others appear economically more attractive or environmentally less degrading.

CASE STUDY

Subsistence farming – sustainable agroforestry

The Popoluca Indians of Santa Rosa, Mexico practise a form of agriculture that resembles shifting cultivation, known as the milpa system. This is a labour-intensive form of agriculture, using fallow. It is a diverse form of **polyculture** with over 200 species cultivated, including maize, beans, cucubits, papaya, squash, water melon, tomatoes, oregano, coffee and chilli. The variety of a natural rainforest is reflected by the variety of shifting cultivation. For example, lemon trees, peppervine and spearmint are light seeking, and prefer open conditions not shade. Coffee, by contrast, prefers shade. The mango tree requires damp conditions.

The close associations that are found in natural conditions are also seen in the Popolucas' farming system. For example, maize and beans go well together, as maize extracts nutrients from the soil whereas beans return them. Tree trunks and small trees are left because they are useful for many purposes such as returning nutrients to the soil and preventing soil erosion.

As in a rainforest the crops are multi-layered, with tree-, shrub- and herb-layers. This increases NPP per unit area, because photosynthesis is taking place on at least three levels (with the highest NPP in the forest canopy), and soil erosion is reduced because no soil or space is left bare. Animals include chickens, pigs and turkeys. These are used as a source of food, and their waste is used as manure.

Thus, whereas there is widespread degradation in Veracruz, the Popolucas are able to maintain soil quality by working with nature.

● **Examiner's hint:**
Compare and contrast – Give
an account of similarities and
differences between two (or
more) items or situations,
referring to both (or all) of
them throughout.

EXERCISES

1   Outline how soil systems integrate aspects of living systems.
2   Compare and contrast the structure and properties of sand, clay and loam soils, including
    their effect on primary productivity.
3   Outline the processes and consequences of soil degradation.
4   Outline soil conservation measures.
5   Evaluate soil management strategies in a named commercial farming system and in a named
    subsistence farming system.

3.5 Food resources

Assessment statements

3.5.1 Outline the issues involved in the imbalance in global food supply.
3.5.2 Compare and contrast the efficiency of terrestrial and aquatic food production
       systems.
3.5.3 Compare and contrast the inputs and outputs of materials and energy (energy
       efficiency), the system characteristics, and evaluate the relative environmental
       impacts for two named food production systems.
3.5.4 Discuss the links that exist between social systems and food production systems.

Food production and distribution – imbalances in global food supply

Although on average there is enough food in the world, there is an imbalance in the food
supply. Many people in LEDCs are suffering from under-nourishment (food intake not
containing enough energy) or malnutrition (food intake lacking essential nutrients such
as protein and minerals). Three-quarters of the world population is inadequately fed and
around 1 billion are going hungry (about a sixth of the global population); the majority of
these live in LEDCs. It is estimated that a child dies from hunger every six seconds. Food
prices play a crucial role: a 10 per cent increase in food prices can lead to 40 million more
people in food poverty. Yet in MEDCs there is a surplus of food, with overgrown markets
producing too much food for the population to consume.

There has been an increased demand for food production in many societies around
the world. Lowering of death rate due to better medical care has led to increases in
population growth. The increased wealth in MEDCs enables people to consume more;
in many cases, more than they need. In Europe, the economics of food production
systems mean that food production is a business, and Common Agricultural Policy
(CAP) subsidies guarantee the prices of crops no matter how much is produced.
There are concerns in MEDCs about food availability, stability of supply and access
to supplies, causing these countries to take protectionist measures to protect supplies.
Import tariffs imposed by MEDCs make the import of food more expensive, which can
have knock-on effects for exporting countries.

In LEDCs food production is used as a way to generate foreign currency, from cash crops
such as sugar cane and tobacco, so there is often an emphasis on export in these countries.
The current food crisis is partly a result of long-standing imbalances between rich and poor
countries in international agricultural trade. Countries that rely more on export are more
affected than those that are self-sufficient.

Huge domestic support and **export subsidies** provided by MEDCs to their farmers make farm products from LEDCs uncompetitive. For example, rice subsidies for farmers in the USA have affected rice farmers in the Asia–Pacific region (in Thailand, Vietnam, and India). Corn subsidies have also driven prices down, affecting farmers in the Philippines and China.

Rapid increase in food prices occurred between 2006 and 2007 (Figure 3.41). The price rises may have been due to increased demands to use land for biofuel, leaving less land available for food-crops. High meat consumption in MEDCs and increased meat and dairy consumption in LEDCs has meant a higher proportion of corn crops going to cattle feed than directly to feed human populations; this leads to higher corn prices. Increased oil prices also contributed to higher food costs. Despite the increase in prices recently, overall, in MEDCs the cost of food is fairly inexpensive. Seasonal foods have generally disappeared as imports fill gaps. Modern technology and transport ensure that food-stuffs can be imported from all-round the globe.

Figure 3.41
Percentage increase in food prices between June 2006 and June 2007.

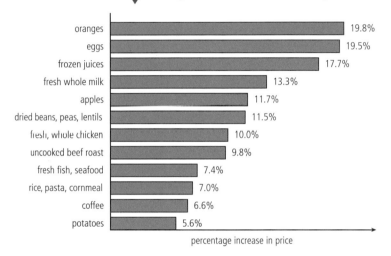

percentage increase in price

In LEDCs, however, many populations struggle to produce enough food, and generally food prices remain high (Figure 3.42). Political, economic and environmental issues may all limit food production. The export-driven economies of many LEDCs may lead to crops being generated for cash (cash crops) rather than to feed the local population (e.g. in Kenya many vegetable crops end up in MEDC supermarkets rather than feeding the local population, many of whom remain hungry). More recently, increased demands for biofuel by MEDCs (page 116) means that LEDCs are increasingly allocating fertile land for the growth of biofuel crops, at the expense of using this land to grow food for their indigenous population. In India, for example, the *Jatropha* plant is grown as a biofuel as the plant produces seeds that are up to 40 per cent oil. The plant is grown on land once used for growing crops, pushing up the cost of food as land for edible crops becomes more limited.

Figure 3.42
Imbalances in global food supply combined with increases in food prices will affect LEDCs more than MEDCs.

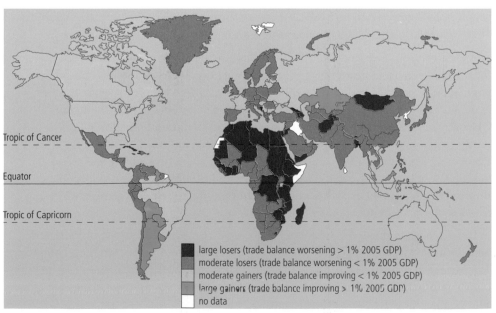

Climate change has had more impact on LEDCs (e.g. increased incident of drought has reduced the amount of growing land, impacting food production). Global warming could lead to tropical and sub-tropical countries like India facing short periods of super-high temperatures – into the high 40s Celsius. These temperatures could completely destroy crops if they coincide with the crop's flowering period.

As more and more land is used for settlement and industry, there is an increasing need to intensify production on existing farm land. In MEDCs, food production is a complex process, involving high levels of technology, low labour and high fuel costs; fertilizers and pesticides are factory produced and the product processing and packaging is on a grand scale. In MEDCs, the advent of technological approaches has enabled yield and production to be maximized. During the nineteenth century and early in the twentieth, agricultural production in Europe and the USA involved large numbers of labourers. As tractor use increased in the twentieth century, farm labour decreased and agriculture became more mechanized and intensive, with many small fields combined into fewer large ones. Pesticide use (to protect crops and livestock), and the use of high-yielding species, increased yields. More recently the introduction of GM crops have increased yields further. Overall in MEDCs, agriculture has become more technocentric.

Agriculture in LEDCs, in contrast, suffers from low levels of technology, lack of capital, and high levels of labour. Rice farming is typical of LEDCs, where rice is often the staple crop: there is a dependence on working animals rather than machinery, making it a labour-intensive process (labour often comes from within families). Whereas MEDCs have large monocultures, mixed cropping on a small scale is common in LEDCs.

Efficiency of terrestrial and aquatic food production systems

Food production systems can be compared and contrasted in terms of their trophic levels and efficiency of energy conversion. We have already seen that the second law of thermodynamics (page 5) means that energy conversion through food chains is inefficient (page 46 and Figure 3.43) and that energy is lost by respiration and waste production at each level within a food web.

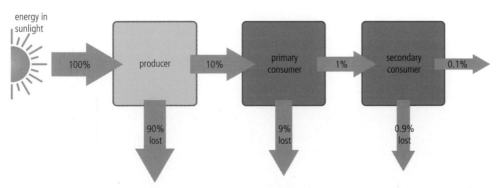

Figure 3.43
Energy loss through food chains.

In terrestrial systems, most food is harvested from relatively low trophic levels (producers and herbivores). Systems that produce crops (arable) are more energy efficient that those that produce livestock. This is because in the former, producers are at the start of the food chain and contain a greater proportion of the Sun's energy than subsequent trophic levels (Figure 3.44, overleaf).

In parts of the developing world, increased income has led to more meat and milk consumption. People earning around $2 a day do not consume much meat or milk, but those earning around $5 a day increase their intake of these products. In India, over the past 30–40 years there has been a six-fold increase, due to population growth and a two-fold per capita increase in meat consumption. More meat and dairy consumption in LEDCs will put further pressures on food production (i.e. corn to feed the animals) and lead to increases in grain prices.

It is estimated that for people in LEDCs to enjoy the same level of meat and dairy consumption as people in MEDCs, the latter will have to halve their meat and dairy intake. Is this something MEDC populations should be morally expected to do? Should legal agreements be put in place to force MEDCs to adopt this strategy? Can we all expect to continue to eat as much meat if it puts global food production at risk?

Figure 3.44
One hectare of land can produce a greater biomass of food in an arable system than in livestock.

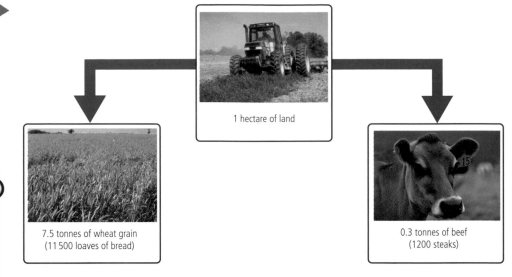

1 hectare of land

7.5 tonnes of wheat grain
(11 500 loaves of bread)

0.3 tonnes of beef
(1200 steaks)

Around 15 kg of grain and 100 000 dm³ of water goes into producing 1 kg of beef. The energy necessary to produce one steak can feed around 40 people in **grain-equivalents**. Around 10 per cent of global water consumed annually is used for cattle (in the USA, about half of total water consumption goes to cattle, including water used to grow the crops to feed them). A vegetarian diet makes better use of the Earth's resources (land, solar input, water) and can support more people than a meat-eating and dairy-based diet.

Despite the more efficient land-use of arable systems, many cultures continue to use livestock as a part of their farming system. Taste and cultural demand play a role in this, and the animals provide a source of protein (essential for the human diet). Animals can convert vegetation to food that would not be available to humans directly. Additionally, the products from livestock can be diverse (e.g. milk, meat, blood, wool, hide). And in many cultures the livestock are used as working animals.

In aquatic systems, perhaps largely due to human tastes, most food is harvested from higher trophic levels where the total storages are much smaller (Figure 3.45). This is less energy efficient than crop production (i.e. crops capture energy directly from the primary source; fish are several steps away from primary production). Although energy conversions along an aquatic food chain may be more efficient than in a terrestrial chain, the initial fixing of available solar energy by aquatic primary producers tends to be less efficient due to the absorption and reflection of light by water.

Figure 3.45
The fishing industry takes organisms from high in the food chain as humans prefer the taste of top predators.

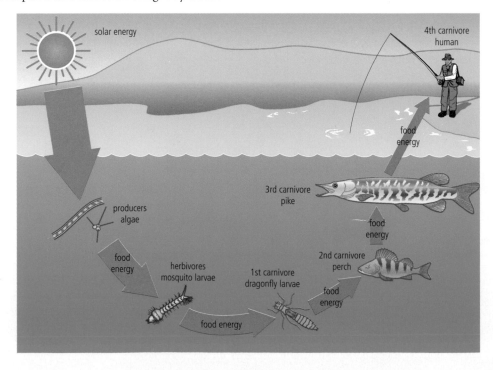

● **Examiner's hint:**
When comparing the efficiency of terrestrial and aquatic food production systems, you do not need to consider individual production systems in detail.

Inputs, outputs and environmental impacts of terrestrial food production systems

Terrestrial farming systems can be divided into several types. **Commercial farming** is farming for profit – often of a single crop. A **subsistence farmer** produces only enough to feed their family, with none to sell for profit. Both commercial and subsistence farming can be either intensive or extensive: **intensive farms** generally take up a small area of land but aim to have very high output (through large inputs of capital and labour) per unit area of land, whereas **extensive farms** are large in comparison to the money and labour put into them (e.g. the cattle ranches of central Australia, where only a few workers are responsible for thousands of acres of land). The efficiency of the system can be calculated by comparing outputs (e.g. marketable product) to inputs (fuel, labour, transport, fertilizer, dealing with waste products) per unit area of land.

CASE STUDY

North American cereal farming and subsistence farming in South-East Asia

Cereal growing in North America and the Canadian prairies is an extensive commercial farming system. In terms of inputs, this system has high use of technology and fertilizers. Labour can be low per unit area as few workers are needed. Because large flat areas are farmed, mechanization is particularly effective. Outputs are low per hectare, due to the large areas of land in production and to yields being lower than when using intensive methods. On the other hand, outputs are high per farmer (because each owns a lot of land). Efficiency is medium, but environmental impact can be high as the farms require the clearance of natural ecosystems. This limits the habitat of wild native species and leads to loss of biodiversity; it may also result in soil erosion. In the future, genetic modification (GM) technology may be used to improve crop yield.

Subsistence farms in South-East Asia produce only enough food to feed the family or small community working each farm. Farmers typically use no machines: instead they use draft animals which can be fed and raised on the farm. This farming system uses a polyculture (many crops) approach rather than the monocultures grown on extensive farms. No artificial fertilizers are used: subsistence farmers rely on crop rotation to maintain the fertility of the ground, along with animal manure and compost to restore nutrients in the soil. Inputs are therefore low (hand tools and labour), as are outputs (enough food to feed the family). In areas which are sparsely populated, subsistence agriculture is sustainable for long periods of time, and has a low impact on the environment. In more densely populated areas, subsistence agriculture may deplete the soil of nutrients, and damage the environment. Efficiency is high: subsistence farming can yield food energy up to 20 times the human energy invested. It is estimated that current world food production is still mainly produced from the subsistence multi-cropping system, and small farmers provide as much as 70 per cent of the food production in many tropical countries.

CASE STUDY

Intensive beef production in MEDCs and the Maasai tribal use of livestock

In intensive beef production, cattle are housed all year round and fed a diet of rolled barley mixed with a protein concentrate (often beans, soya or rapeseed meal), fortified with vitamins and minerals. In the USA cattle are put into pens containing up to 10 000 or 100 000 cows and fed corn for the last weeks of their lives, which can double their biomass before slaughter. Their movement within the pens is restricted. Intensive beef production is an energy inefficient form of farming, with can yield as low as one tenth as much food energy as is invested in energy inputs. In terms of costs, however, it is very efficient, and significantly increases yield per acre, per person, per input, relative to extensive farming.

There is not much space for the animals to move about, so they use less energy. This means less food is required, which leads to cheaper product. On the other hand, the animals are fed

Case study continued

● **Examiner's hint:**
Exam questions will ask you to compare and contrast either two terrestrial or two aquatic systems – the systems you select to write about should therefore be both terrestrial or both aquatic. The inputs and outputs of the two systems should differ qualitatively and quantitatively (not all systems will be different in all aspects). The case-study examples selected here fit these criteria, although other local or global examples are equally valid.

continuously for maximum growth and selective breeding has produced cows with high yield and good quality meat, which adds to overall costs. Inputs are therefore high (technology, heating, food) but so are the outputs (cost-effective production), although there may be hidden costs, such as transport. Environmental impact is high – energy usage releases greenhouse gases, and cows produce waste. Restraining animals in this way also has ethical implications.

The Maasai are an indigenous group living semi-nomadically in Kenya and parts of Tanzania. Their livestock are able to wander freely, herded by their owners (i.e. this is a nomadic form of farming). The Maasai diet is traditionally meat, milk, and blood supplied by their cattle. Once a month, blood is taken from living animals by shooting a small arrow into the jugular vein in the neck. The blood is mixed with milk for consumption. Virtually all social roles and status derive from the relationship of individuals to their cattle. This is an example of extensive subsistence farming – inputs are low (the animals are allowed to roam freely so fences and pens are not required, only human labour is used) and so are outputs (enough food to feed the community). As with other subsistence methods, efficiency is high and environmental impact is low (the Maasai use their natural environment to raise their animals). Socio-cultural factors can, however, lead to problems: for the Maasai: cattle equal wealth and quantity is more important than quality, and this has lead to overgrazing and desertification.

Nomadic herding is practised by 2.7 billion people (44 per cent of world population) and provides 20 per cent of the world's food supply.

Maasai herding cattle in Tanzania.

Inputs, outputs and environmental impacts of aquatic food production systems

CASE STUDY

Open-net fish farming was introduced in Norway in the 1960s. Since then, the industry has expanded to Scotland, Ireland, Canada, the USA, and Chile, and is dominated by a handful of multinational corporations.

Commercial salmon farming in Norway and Scotland

The term 'fishing' refers to all commercial fishing for fish, molluscs and crustaceans in the sea. 'Fish farming' is the commercial farming of fish and other aquaculture, and involves the feeding of bred or wild fish in open nets. One species is raised (i.e. it is a monoculture). Today, salmon makes up 85 per cent of the total sale of Norwegian fish farming. Farming was introduced when populations of wild Atlantic salmon in the North Atlantic and Baltic seas crashed due to over-fishing. Similar programmes have been set up in Scotland for the same reasons.

Technological costs are high and include the cost of antibiotics to keep fish healthy, and steroids to improve growth. Breeding programmes to generate brood-stock (a group of sexually mature individuals of a cultured species that is kept separate for breeding purposes) are expensive. Outputs are high per hectare and per farmer, and efficiency is also high.

Environmental effects can be high and damaging. Salmon are carnivores so they need to be fed pellets made from other fish. It is possible that farmed salmon represent a net loss of protein in the global food supply as it takes from two to five kilograms of wild fish to grow one kilogram of salmon. In contrast, most global aquaculture production (about 85 per cent) uses non-carnivorous fish species, such as tilapia and catfish, for domestic markets. Fish like herring, mackerel, sardines, and anchovy are used to produce the feed for farmed salmon, and so the production of salmon leads to the depletion of other fish species on a global scale. Other environmental costs include the sea lice and disease that spread from farmed salmon into wild stocks, and pollution (created by uneaten food, faeces, and chemicals) contaminating surrounding waters. Organic debris of this type, with steroids and other chemical waste, can contaminate coastal waters. Accidental escape of fish can affect local wild fish gene pools, when escaped fish interbreed with wild populations, reducing their genetic diversity, and potentially introducing non-natural genetic variation. In some parts of the world, escapes from farmed fish threaten native wild fish (e.g. the British Columbia salmon farming industry has inadvertently introduced a non-native species – Atlantic salmon – into the Pacific Ocean).

The positive environmental benefits of not removing fish from wild stocks, but growing them in farms, are great. Wild populations are allowed to breed and maintain stocks, while the farmed variety provides food.

CASE STUDY

Rice–fish farming in Thailand

Rice–fish farming in Thailand. Once the newly planted rice is established, fish are released into the flooded fields from holding pens.

Cultivating rice and fish together has been a tradition for over 2000 years in South-East Asia. This polyculture system (padi rice field stocked with fish) was gradually abandoned due to population pressures and decreasing stocks of wild fish. The fall in fish stocks was due to the toxic effects of the pesticides and herbicides used in high-yield rice monoculture. However, this farming method experienced a revival in the early 1990s, as concerns over the widespread use of pesticides emerged. Implementation is relatively inexpensive and low-risk.

The system requires farmers to dig small ponds or trenches in low-lying areas of rice, which become refuges for fish during rice planting and harvesting, or when water is scarce. The

Case study continued

excavated soil is used to raise banks around the field to grow other crops on (e.g. vegetables and fruit trees). Once the padi fields are flooded, young fish (fingerlings) are introduced to the trenches: carp, tilapia, catfish, or other species. After three weeks, when the rice is well established, the fish are let into the rice fields. They obtain their food from the fields, but carnivorous species can be fed if necessary. The fish contribute to a decrease of disease and pest incidence in the rice, and rice yields are higher. Because rice productivity increases, farmers do no need to use fertilizers (the fish produce faeces and excreta which naturally fertilize the soil). Rice–fish culture may increase rice yields by up to 10 per cent, and increase income by 50–100 per cent over rice alone, while providing farmers with an important source of protein.

The process counters the decrease in available wild fish in many countries. The most common and widespread fish species used in rice–fish farming are the common carp (*Cyprinus carpio*) and the Nile tilapia (*Oreochromis niloticus*). Both are happy to feed on the vegetation and plankton available and do not attack other fish, so they are preferred species in the culture systems. Other species such as catfish (*Clarias* spp.) are well adapted to the swamp-like conditions of rice fields, but are carnivorous and will feed on other introduced fish.

This food production system is an example of intensive subsistence farming. The cost of feeding the fish is low but demands on labour are high. Technology is low. Other inputs include water for irrigation, and the cost of the breeding stock. The outputs are high per hectare but low per farmer, but overall efficiency is high, and yields of rice improve significantly with this system compared to standard rice agriculture. Environmental impacts are low, but include change in the nutrient balance, and the introduction of alien species, which may have impacts for local biodiversity – both plant and animal.

There are several cultural issues regarding the system: other sources of animal protein may be preferred (e.g. poultry, beef, and pork), and the commonly cultured fish species (e.g. tilapia and carp) are not highly valued by people who have access to marine species and wild species. Fish predators such as snakes can lower the fish yield. The system may only be appropriate if there is a reliable water supply, a source of young fish, and fields located close to the family house so they can be monitored.

Links between social systems and food production systems

There are many links between social systems and food production systems – we will examine here **shifting cultivation**, wet rice agriculture (South-East Asia) and **agribusiness**.

Shifting cultivation

Shifting cultivation supports small communities and sometimes individual families. ▶

Shifting cultivation is also known as 'slash and burn' agriculture because new land is cleared by cutting down small areas of forest and setting fire to them: the ash fertilizes the soil for a while and the clearing produced enables crops to be grown. Once the land in one area has been exhausted (e.g. minerals in the soil depleted) the farmer moves on to a new area (Figure 3.46). Old land can be returned to once the fertility has recovered. It is an example of extensive subsistence farming.

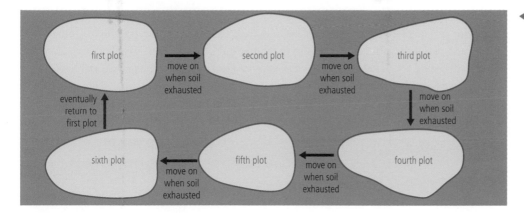

◀ **Figure 3.46**
Shifting cultivation follows a cycle where a sequence of forest clearings is used. Recognition that soil has become infertile leads farmers to shift and thus allow small pockets of forest to regenerate before returning to the plot often some 50 years later. This allows soil fertility to be restored.

Slash-and-burn is practised in many tropical forest areas, such as the Amazon region, where yams, cassava, and sweet potatoes can be grown. This system is possible because low population densities (typical of these societies) can be supported by the food produced. If population densities increase too much, old land is returned too soon, before soil fertility has been restored. The conditions of the forest encouraged shifting cultivation. It would be possible to clear only small areas of forest with the labour available (often from one family or small community), and hilly terrain meant that clearings often had to be on plains or along rivers (where fertility was better also).

The socio-cultural features of people who use this method have developed in response to the farming system as well as shaping it. Shifting cultivation practice is bound to cultural practices and beliefs – traditions and rituals linked to choosing the site and carrying out the clearance. The plot cycle is used to recall past history by connecting events with the plots cleared at particular times. The people tend to be animists – believing that everything contains a spirit (or soul), including animals, plants and trees. The spiritual role of forest is therefore a central feature of cultural life, leading to respect for trees and other species. Understanding how the forest works has led some shifting cultivators to adapt their practices to mimic the layering of the forest, where ground crops are protected from harsh sunlight and heavy downpours. As well as cultivation, land use includes forest materials for construction of homes and canoes, and for medicines.

 People who live in close connection with nature, such as shifting cultivators in the Brazilian Amazon, show a closer connection between social systems and ecological systems (i.e. an ecocentric approach) than societies living away from natural systems, such as city dwellers. Urban capitalist elites in Brazil are more likely to view the interior of the country as a new frontier, and rainforest as a resource for development and cash (i.e. a technocentric approach). The lack of understanding of people disconnected from nature makes them more likely to underestimate the true value of natural resources (e.g. that a rainforest is worth more standing than cut down). They are also more likely to make decisions that produce wasteful and damaging actions (e.g. the construction of dams and whole-scale clearance of forest for timber or cattle ranching). Urban shanty dwellers who migrate to use deforested land are less likely to succeed than indigenous people as the areas they select are likely to have infertile soils. These issues are repeated globally, in different ecosystems and societies, but the underlying message remains the same.

Wet rice ecosystems of South-East Asia

Rice can be grown in dry-fields, but padi field (wet rice) agriculture has become the dominant form of growing rice in South-East Asia. It is an example of intensive subsistence farming, using high labour inputs but low technology. The high population densities in these countries lead to a high demand for food. Rice is in particular demand because it is a staple part of the diet and a central part of Asian culture. Soil fertility is good and supports the intensive nature of the agriculture.

Padi fields can be placed adjacent to rivers and areas that flood naturally, where annual inundation causes new deposits of silt in the fields and increased fertility. They can also be put on hills using terracing. The heavy clay soils created by river deposits are ideal for padi fields – sandy and light-textured soils are not suitable as water drains away. High rainfall in these regions facilitates this type of agriculture, allowing extensive field irrigation to be maintained throughout the year. Warm weather allows high productivity year-round.

Terracing is used to grow rice in hills areas of South-East Asia. ▶

Recently, less land has been available for new expansion of rice farming in South-East Asia. Declining soil fertility has also been a problem, and rice yields have been reaching their maximum. In the next 30 years, as populations grow, the security of smaller farms may depend on increasing diversification into higher value crops (e.g. vegetables and citrus), and into small livestock production and aquaculture (e.g. fish farming, pages 140–41).

Agribusiness

After World War II there was concern in the UK about self-sufficiency: this led to significant changes in farming practice. Before the war, farming was done within a patchwork of small farms. Afterwards, demands for increased production capacity led to these small farms being combined into bigger farms, with fields combined to provide large uniform areas for agriculture. Greater intensification of products was achieved through increased fertilizer use. Other countries followed suit and introduced this method of agriculture.

Throughout the second half of the twentieth century, there was a shift from producing food for people's needs to producing food for commercial profit – a cultural factor within the capitalist societies where these intensive farming methods were introduced. Agribusiness is the name of the game when regulation of food production is not to satisfy the community's needs but is to ensure profitable return for capital investment.

The foundation of agribusiness is the desire to maximize productivity and profit in order to compete in a global market. It can be distinguished from traditional forms of food production, although the latter may assume either a subsistence or agribusiness form. The distinguishing methods of agribusiness are large-scale monoculture, intensive use of fertilizers and pesticides, mechanized ploughing and harvesting, and food production geared to mass markets including export.

Loss of crop rotation and natural ways of maintaining field fertility, has led to substantial increase in fertilizer use. This form of agriculture has a large impact on the environment, with loss of biodiversity, and increased run-off pollution. Genetically modified crops are currently used in some counties to increase yield. This may have a knock-on effect on wild populations should modified species cross-pollinate with wild ones. National political economies encourage agribusiness as a means to support gross national income, and the lifestyles that their populations have come to expect.

Agribusiness supplies most of the products found in supermarkets. Many have travelled long distances from locations around the globe. Agribusiness in non-seasonal climates (e.g. parts of Africa) supply food throughout the year, so once-seasonal crops are available year-round in MEDCs.

To what extent is it possible to assess the environmental impact of food production – are the costs of food miles higher than the cost of fertilizer use or habitat destruction?

Culturally, the effect of agribusiness has been significant. The small farms common before World War II supported large numbers of workers and maintained local communities in rural locations. With the advent of large farms, much of this labour was no longer needed, which led to local migration of people into towns and cities as they sought new work.

General points about social systems and food production systems

Socio-cultural factors influence tastes and the development of different food production systems. For example, the desire for more organic food in Europe has led to the growth of organic farming. Also, in MEDCs there has been a growing trend for concern about animal welfare, which has affected the farming methods adopted by some farms (e.g. free-range pigs and chickens rather than intensive battery farming).

Educational levels determine the degree of exchange of ideas about new farming practices and the extent to which new technologies are applied. In Singapore, for example, the government has invested large amounts of time and money in promoting new technologies (e.g. hydroponics – growing plants in mineral solutions without soil): shortage of available land on the island had led to pressure to find alternative ways of growing food.

Indirectly, socio-cultural factors such as land ownership, migration patterns and attitudes to land in general have an impact on how land is used. Native American Indians did not believe that people could own land – they saw land as a communal commodity, so development was limited (Chapter 7). Environmental constraints (e.g. rainfall, growing seasons, natural disasters and soil fertility) also influence choice of farming practices. Fertile soil and plenty of rainfall favour intensive crop production, and economic factors determine input costs (e.g. seeds, technology, and access to credit, page 139).

Economic and technological factors are interconnected with socio-cultural features – they develop in response to farming systems as well as shape such systems.

EXERCISES

1 Outline the issues involved in the imbalance in global food supply.

2 Compare and contrast the efficiency of terrestrial and aquatic food production systems.

3 Compare and contrast the inputs and outputs of materials and energy (energy efficiency), the system characteristics, and evaluate the relative environmental impacts for two named food production systems.

4 Discuss the links that exist between social systems and food production systems.

3.6 Water resources

Earth's water budget

Assessment statements

3.6.1 Describe the Earth's water budget.

3.6.2 Describe and evaluate the sustainability of freshwater resource usage with reference to a case study.

To access worksheet 3.4 on water resources please visit www. pearsonbacconline.com and follow the on-screen instructions.

Only a small fraction (2.5 per cent by volume) of the Earth's water supply is fresh water (Figure 3.47). Of this, around 70 per cent is in the form of ice caps and glaciers, around 30 per cent is groundwater, and the rest is made up of lakes, soil water, atmospheric water vapour, rivers and biota. Water on the surface of the Earth to which we have direct access (freshwater lakes and rivers) is around 0.3 per cent of the total. Atmospheric water vapour contains about 0.001 per cent of the Earth's total water volume. Taken together, all the forms in which the Earth's water can exist are called the hydrosphere.

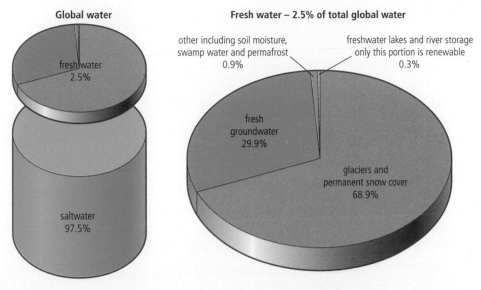

Global water

fresh water 2.5%

saltwater 97.5%

Fresh water – 2.5% of total global water

other including soil moisture, swamp water and permafrost 0.9%

freshwater lakes and river storage only this portion is renewable 0.3%

fresh groundwater 29.9%

glaciers and permanent snow cover 68.9%

Figure 3.47
The Earth's water budget. Most water is not directly accessible by human populations. Fresh water is therefore an extremely limited resource.

The different forms of water in the Earth's water budget are fully replenished during the hydrological cycle but at very different rates. The time for a water molecule to enter and leave a part of the system (i.e. the time taken for water to completely replace itself in part of the system) is called **turnover time**. Turnover time varies enormously between different parts of the system (Table 3.13).

TABLE 3.13 TURNOVER TIMES FOR DIFFERENT PARTS OF THE HYDROSPHERE	
Water location	Turnover time
polar ice caps	10 000 years
ice in the permafrost	10 000 years
oceans	2 500 years
groundwater	1 500 years
mountain glaciers	1 500 years
large lakes	17 years
bogs	5 years
upper soil moisture	1 year
atmospheric moisture	12 days
rivers	16 days
biological water	a few hours

Source: based on table from www.itg.be

The degree to which water can be seen as a renewable (i.e. replenishable) or non-renewable resource depends on where it is found in the hydrological cycle. Renewable water resources are waters that are replenished yearly or more frequently in the Earth's water turnover processes. Thus, groundwater is a non-renewable resource. An aquifer is an underground formation of permeable rock or loose material which stores groundwater. Aquifers can produce useful quantities of water when tapped by wells. Aquifers come in all sizes, from small (a few hectares in area) to very large (covering thousands of square kilometres). They may be only a few metres thick, or they may measure hundreds of metres from top to bottom. Intensive use of aquifers unavoidably results in depleting the storage and has unfavourable consequences: it depletes the natural resource and disturbs the natural equilibrium established over centuries. Restoration requires tens to hundreds of years.

● **Examiner's hint:**
Precise figures for describing
the Earth's water budget are
not required.

The Earth's water resources contain many different ecosystems, some of which are extremely biodiverse (e.g. coral reefs). Parts of the Earth's water budget therefore have great value in the support of life on Earth, as well as acting as a vital resource for humans. Human populations use this resource both sustainably and unsustainably.

The sustainability of freshwater resource usage
Managing supply and demand – sustainable use

Human populations require water for home use (drinking, washing and cooking), agriculture (irrigation and livestock), industry (manufacturing and mining), and hydroelectric power. Given the scarcity of freshwater, the pressure on this resource is great and likely to increase, particularly in certain parts of the world (Figure 3.48). Without sustainable use, humans are likely to face many problems. Already, there are a billion people living without clean drinking water, and 2.6 billion who lack adequate sanitation.

Figure 3.48
Projected global water
scarcity by 2025 (based on
data from International Water
Management Institute).

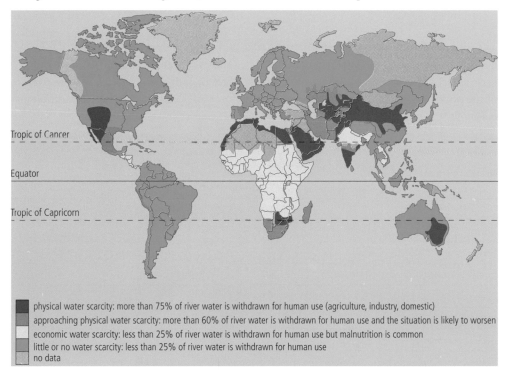

physical water scarcity: more than 75% of river water is withdrawn for human use (agriculture, industry, domestic)
approaching physical water scarcity: more than 60% of river water is withdrawn for human use and the situation is likely to worsen
economic water scarcity: less than 25% of river water is withdrawn for human use but malnutrition is common
little or no water scarcity: less than 25% of river water is withdrawn for human use
no data

The demand for water has continued to grow throughout the industrial period, and is still expanding in both MEDCs and LEDCs. Increased demand in LEDCs is due to expanding populations, changing agricultural practice and expanding (often heavy) industry. In MEDCs, people require more and more water as they wash more frequently, water their gardens and wash their cars. Overall, a general increase in water use per person is making the demands heavier. Water is a finite resource and countries are reaching their resource availability limits – existing water resources need to be managed and controlled more carefully, and new water resources found.

Water resources can be managed sustainably if individuals and communities make changes locally, and this is supported by national government. Water usage needs to be coordinated within natural processes, and ensure that non-renewable sources of freshwater (e.g. aquifers) are not used at an unsustainable rate. Use can be reduced by self-imposed restraint; for example when people use only water that is essential, do not cause waste, and reuse supplies such as bath water. Education campaigns can increase local awareness of issues and encourage water conservation.

Sustainable use in cities and populated areas could be reached by:

- making new buildings more water-efficient (e.g. recycle rainwater for sanitation and showers)
- offsetting new demand by fitting homes and other buildings with more water-efficient devices and appliances (e.g. dishwashers and toilets)
- expanding metering to encourage households to use water more efficiently.

In rural areas, solutions for sustainable water use could include selecting drought-resistant crops to reduce the need for irrigation (which uses up fresh water – much of it wasted through evaporation – and causes soil degradation). Contamination of water supplies through fertilizer and pesticide can be addressed by reducing their use: organic fertilizers cause less pollution and biocontrol measures (i.e. using natural predators of pests) can be used to reduce crop pests. Industries can be forced to remove pollutants from their waste water through legislation.

The responses of individuals and governments to make their use of fresh water more sustainable depend on the level of development of their country. Competing calls on fresh water vary between countries (Figure 3.49). Domestic water consumption is the minority water use in all countries, so the biggest impacts in terms of sustainable water use will be within the agricultural sector in LEDCs, and within the industrial sector in MEDCs.

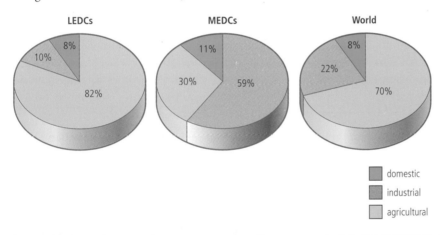

Figure 3.49
Water use is different in LEDCs and MEDCs.

Managing supply and demand – unsustainable use

Irrigation, industrialization and population increase all make demands on the supply of fresh water. Global warming may disrupt rainfall patterns and water supplies. The hydrological cycle supplies humans with fresh water but we are withdrawing water from underground aquifers and degrading it with wastes at a greater rate than it can be replenished.

While some uses of river resources can be unsustainable (e.g. because of the siltation caused by dams), rivers can generally be replenished over a short period of time. Unsustainable use of fresh water largely concerns the overuse of aquifers. These non-renewable sources of water cannot be replenished at a rate fast enough to make current usage sustainable. The USA is one of the world's largest agricultural producers. In certain areas, irrigation has been depleting groundwater resources beyond natural recharge rates for several years. For example, the High Plains (Ogallala) aquifer, which irrigates more than 20 per cent of US cropland, is close to depletion in parts of Kansas because the water level has fallen so much. In some regions, water depletion now poses a serious threat to the sustainability of the agricultural and rural economy. The USA is not the only country that faces these problems. France is one of the world's leading agricultural exporters: farming's share in groundwater use rose from 10 per cent in the mid-1980s to 17 per cent by mid-1990s.

Projections over the next decade suggest that demand for water from irrigators will continue to rise, notably in countries where irrigated farming provides the major share of agricultural production (e.g. Australia, Mexico, Spain and the USA). Groundwater pumping in Saudi Arabia exceeds replenishment by five times. This will lead to stiffer competition for water among other users (e.g. domestic use). Pressure on irrigated farming in many drier and semiarid areas is being caused by the growing incidence and severity of droughts over the past decade, perhaps related to the impact of climate change.

Groundwater pollution from fertilizer run-off is adding to depletion of the stock. Over a fifth of groundwater monitoring sites in agricultural areas of Denmark, the Netherlands and the USA have recorded nitrate levels that exceed drinking water standards: a particular concern where groundwater provides the main source of drinking water for both people and livestock. The situation is likely to deteriorate as phosphates (also widely used in agriculture) can take many years to seep into groundwater from the soil.

Examiner's hint:
You must be able to use a case study to demonstrate either sustainable or unsustainable water use.

Over-exploitation of water resources by agriculture has damaged some aquatic ecosystems, and has harmed recreational and commercial fishing (page 107).

CASE STUDY

Water shortage in the Middle East

Oil is the traditional cause of conflict in the Middle East. In the future, water shortage is more likely to be a major problem here. Although the region contains 5 per cent of world population, it holds only 0.5 per cent of the planet's fresh water resources. The annual rate of renewable water use is currently around 60 per cent of supplies, compared to a global average of 8 per cent. It is predicted that the region's per capita renewable water supply will fall from the 1960 consumption level of 3430 cubic metres per year to 667 cubic metres by 2025. Stress on renewable water has led to a depletion of local aquifers, which is proceeding at a rapid rate.

In 2008, Israel suffered a major drought and had to stop pumping from its principal source of fresh water (the Sea of Galilee – one of the world biggest freshwater lakes) and switch to underground aquifers. Population growth, improvement in quality of life, and agriculture (which consumes a large proportion of fresh water under a heavily subsidized government scheme) had already led to water shortages, and the drought made this situation worse. Despite the shortages, Israel did not seek to restrict water to neighbouring Jordan, with which it has a treaty regarding water supply. Israel has two desalination plants that supply a third of water needed by households and municipalities, and three new plants (scheduled for completion by 2013) could double this amount. Jordan relies on supplies from Israel to meet its water needs, as it does not have direct access to Israel's aquifers (Figure 3.50). Future water shortages could lead to conflict between countries in the region, and also between Israel and the Palestinian territories – access to the River Jordan and Israel's aquifers are likely to be flash-points.

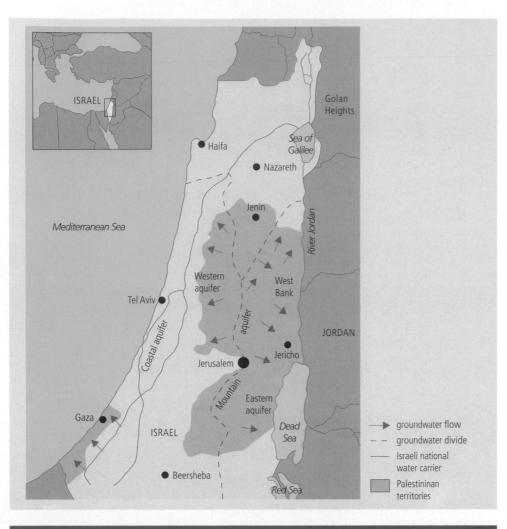

Figure 3.50
Water resources in the Middle East.

CASE STUDY

Water shortage in India

Harvesting wheat in Madhya Pradesh, central India. This region is predominantly agricultural, with a relatively small population. Almost 75 per cent of the wheat harvested here depends on rain for watering, rather than on the irrigation techniques used in the Punjab, Haryana and Rajasthan. The best quality Durum wheat is grown in this state. Madhya Pradesh is also the largest producer of soybean in India. The state contains several important rivers, including the Narmada (page 121). The state capital is Bhopal (page 290).

The Punjab region is known as the breadbasket of India because it is where most of the country's wheat is grown. It is an area now severely short of water and wheat production has been in decline

Case study continued

151

As populations grow, greater demands are made on water resources. Water resources are now becoming a limiting factor in many societies, and the availability of water for drinking, industry and agriculture needs to be considered. Many societies are now dependent primarily on groundwater which is non-renewable. As societies develop, water needs increase. The increased demand for fresh water can lead to inequity of use and political consequences. When water supplies fail, populations will be forced to take drastic steps, such as mass migration. Water shortages may also lead to civil unrest and wars.

for a over a decade. Although the area has five rivers flowing through it, much of the intensive agricultural land (used to grow wheat) relies on groundwater for irrigation. The water table is dropping by 1 metre a year, so sources of water in some areas now have to be reached using deep underground aquifers (up to 500 feet deep).

The north-western states of Haryana, Punjab, and Rajasthan lost about 109 km^3 of groundwater between 2002 and 2008 – that's about three times the capacity of the largest reservoir in the USA (Lake Mead). Almost half the water used in irrigation is groundwater (from the Indus River plain aquifer and smaller neighbouring stores of groundwater). Groundwater also accounts for the majority of water consumed domestically in these three Indian states. Data indicate that between August 2002 and October 2008, 17.7 km^3 of water were withdrawn each year, far exceeding the natural rate at which water replenishes the aquifers. Whether the increased usage is due to increased populations or the intensive agriculture is unclear. What is clear is that this level of usage is unsustainable.

Global water consumption is predicted to double every 20 years, and the problems faced in India may be a glimpse of problems people will face elsewhere. Water shortages may lead to a reduction in food crops equivalent to the entire US grain crop within 15 years.

EXERCISES

1   Describe the Earth's water budget.

2   Describe and evaluate the sustainability of freshwater resource usage with reference to a case study.

3.7 Limits to growth

Assessment statements

3.7.1 Explain the difficulties in applying the concept of carrying capacity to local human populations.

3.7.2 Explain how absolute reductions in energy and material use, reuse and recycling can affect human carrying capacity.

Explain the difficulties in applying the concept of carrying capacity to local human populations

The limits-to-growth model

The limits-to-growth study by the Club of Rome (1970) examined the five basic factors that determine and, therefore, ultimately limit growth on the planet:

- population
- natural resources
- pollution.
- agricultural production
- industrial production

Many of these factors were observed to grow at exponential rate. A given quality exhibits exponential growth when it increases by a constant percentage of the whole in a constant time period. The authors of the model illustrated exponential growth by considering the growth of lilies on a pond. The lily patch doubles in area every day. When the pond is half covered by lilies, it will only be another day for the pond to be covered totally. This emphasized the apparent suddenness with which the exponential growth of a phenomenon approaches a fixed limit. It also demonstrates the short period of time within which corrective action can be taken. If the predicted growth of world population is correct then there is an alarmingly short space of time for preventive action.

The team then examined:

- physical necessities that support all physiological and industrial activity (e.g. food, raw materials and fuels)
- social necessities (e.g. peace, stability and education).

The team assumed that there would be no great changes in human values in the future and produced the graph in Figure 3.51.

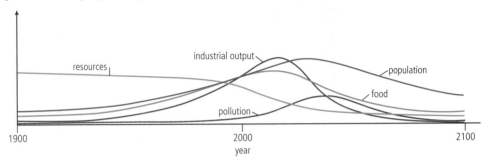

Figure 3.51
The original limits-to-growth model.

Food induced output and population grow exponentially until the rapidly diminishing resource base forces a slowdown in industrial growth. Because of natural delays in the system, both population and pollution continue to increase for some time after the peak of industrialization. Population growth is finally halted by a rise in the death rate due to decreased food and medical services.

The team concluded that:

- if present trends continue, the limits to growth will be reached in the next 100 years – the result will probably be a sudden and uncontrollable decline in population and industrial capabilities
- it is possible to alter these growth trends and to establish a condition of ecological and economic stability that is sustainable into the future.

There are a number of criticisms about the limits-to-growth model. First, it is a world model and does not distinguish between different parts of the world. It ignores the spatial distribution of population, resources, agriculture, industry and pollution. People and resources do not always coincide with space. Their distribution and size are part of the world's problem. The model emphasizes exponential growth and not the rate of discovery of new resources or of new users of resources.

An alternative sustainable model has since been produced taking into account factors including resource substitution, recycling and conservation of resources (Figure 3.52).

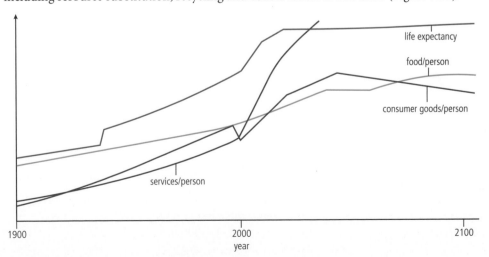

Figure 3.52
The sustainable limits-to-growth model.

Carrying capacity

The concept of a population ceiling is one of a saturation level where population equals the carrying capacity of the local environment. Figure 3.53 shows three models of a population growing exponentially and approaching carrying capacity.

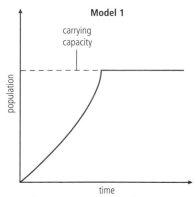

Model 1

There is no reduction in the rate of increase until the ceiling is reached at which point the increase drops to zero. This highly unlikely situation is unsupported by evidence from either human or animal populations.

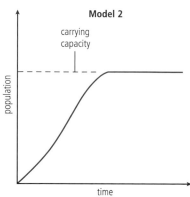

Model 2

The population increase begins to taper off as the carrying capacity is approached and levels off when the ceiling is reached. It is claimed that populations which are large in size, have long lives, and low fertility rates conform to this S-curve pattern.

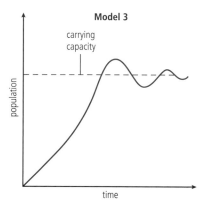

Model 3

The rapid rise in population overshoots the carrying capacity resulting in a sudden check (e.g. by famine, birth control, etc.). The population then recovers and fluctuates eventually settling at the carrying capacity. This J-shaped curve appears more applicable to populations which are small in number, have short lives and high fertility rates.

Figure 3.53
Population growth and carrying capacity.

Optimum-, over-, and under-population

Optimum population is the number of people which, when working with all the available resources, will produce the highest per capita economic return (Figure 3.54). It represents the point at which the population has the highest standard of living and quality of life. If the size of the population increases or decreases from the optimum, the standard of living will fall. This concept is dynamic and changes with time as techniques improve, as population totals and structures change and as new materials are discovered.

Figure 3.54
Over- and under-population.

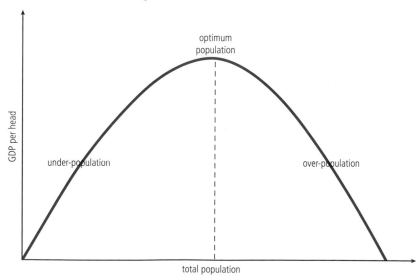

Standard of living is the result of the interaction between physical and human resources and can be expressed as:

$$\text{standard of living} = \frac{\text{natural resources} \times \text{technology}}{\text{population}}$$

Over-population occurs when there are too many people relative to the resources and technology locally available to maintain an adequate standard of living. Bangladesh (population density of 132/km²), Somalia and parts of Brazil and India are over-populated as they have insufficient food and materials. They suffer from natural disasters such as drought and famine and are characterized by low incomes, poverty, poor living conditions and a high level of emigration.

Under-population occurs when there are far more resources in an area (e.g. food production, energy and minerals) than can be used by the people living there. Canada could theoretically double its population and still maintain its standard of living. Countries like Canada and Australia can export their surplus food, energy and mineral resources. It is possible that the standard of living would increase through increased production if population were to increase.

Carrying capacities and local populations

Malthus

In 1798, the Reverend Thomas Malthus produced his *Essays on the Principle of Population Growth*. He believed that there was finite optimum population size in relation to food supply and that any increase in population beyond this point would lead to a decline in the standard of living and to war, famine and disease. His theory was based on two principles:

- in the absence of checks, population would grow at a geometric or exponential rate and could double every 25 years
- food supply at best increases at an arithmetic rate (Figure 3.55).

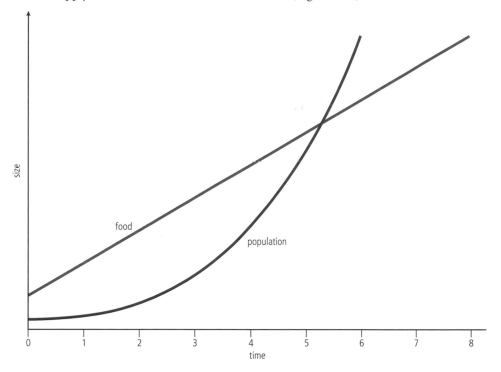

Figure 3.55
Malthus's views on population growth and growth of food resources.

In 100 years. the ratio of population:food would be 16:5. Lack of food is, therefore, argued to be the ultimate check on population growth.

These principles state *potential* and not the *actual* growth of population and food production. Thus, the limit of food production creates a block or ceiling to the population growth in a given country. Malthus suggested preventive and positive checks as two main ways by which population would be curbed once this ceiling had been reached.

It is difficult to reliably estimate the carrying capacity for human populations because:
- the range of resources used is great
- humans can substitute one resource for another when the first becomes limiting
- lifestyle affects resource requirement
- technological developments change resources required and available for consumption
- resources can be imported.

- Preventive checks include abstinence from marriage, a delay in the timing of marriage, and abstinence from sex within marriage. All these would reduce fertility rate.
- Positive checks such as lack of food, disease and war directly affect mortality rates.

Malthus suggested that optimum population is related to resources and the level of technology. We now consider the concepts of over-population and under-population rather than the optimum-population. Optimum population is difficult to identify and may vary as technology improves and attitudes change.

During the industrial revolution, the rate of growth in production was very rapid – greater than arithmetic rate and exceeding the rate of population growth. Malthus's ceiling was always ahead of and moving away from the population. Industrial development also had a positive effect on agricultural production through both intensification (labour and capital) and extension (more land). Nevertheless, as population increased and standard of living rose, so consumption of resources increased and diet changed from grain-and-vegetable based to dairy-and-fish based. The latter cannot sustain as many people as the former.

Unsustainable fishing – tuna landed at the Tokyo fish market.

Boserup

Esther Boserup had a different view. She believed that people have the resources to increase food production. The greatest resource is knowledge and technology. When a need arises, someone will find a solution.

Whereas Malthus thought that food supply limited population size, Boserup suggested that in a pre-industrial society, an increase in population stimulated a change in agricultural techniques so that more food could be produced. Population growth has thus enabled agricultural development to occur.

She examined different land-use systems according to their intensity of production (measured by the frequency of cropping). At one extreme was shifting cultivation: at its least intensive, any one plot would be used less than once every 100 years. At the other extreme was multi-cropping with more than one harvest per year. Boserup suggested that there was a close connection between agricultural techniques and the type of land use system. The most primitive was shifting cultivation, and the most advanced was ploughing with multiple cropping. She considered that any increase in the intensity of productivity by the adoption of new techniques would be unlikely unless population increased. Thus, population growth leads to agricultural development and the growth of the food supply.

Boserup's theory was based on the idea that people knew of the techniques required by more intensive systems, but adopted them only when the population grew. If knowledge was not available, the local agricultural system would regulate the population size in a given area.

Since Malthus's time, people have increased food production in many ways:

- draining marshlands
- reclaiming land from the sea
- cross-breeding cattle
- developing high-yield varieties of plants
- terracing on steep slopes
- growing crops in greenhouses
- using more sophisticated irrigation techniques
- utilizing new foods such as soya
- making artificial fertilizers
- farming native species of crops and animals
- fish farming.

Re-use and recycling – changing carrying capacities

Recycling refers to the processing of industrial and household waste (e.g. paper, glass, some metals, some plastics) so that materials can be reused. This saves scarce raw materials and helps reduce pollution. The UK has lagged behind other EU countries in recycling, mainly because there are many more landfill sites which are cheaper to use. The UK has a recycling target of 33 per cent by 2015.

Recycling.

Re-use refers to the multiple use of a product by returning it to the manufacturer or processor each time. Re-use is usually both more energy-efficient and more resource-efficient than recycling.

Reduce refers to using less energy; for example, turn off lights when not needed, use only the amount of water required when boiling a kettle.

Substitution refers to using one resource rather than another – the use of renewable resources rather than non-renewable resources would be a major benefit to the environment.

 Human carrying capacity is determined by:

- rate of energy and material consumption
- level of pollution
- interference with life-support systems.

157

CASE STUDY

Recycling and re-use at the Casuarina Beach Club, Barbados

The Casuarina Beach Club was one of the best examples of how sustainable tourism can operate. The hotel showed considerable environmental awareness and responsibility by:

- meeting the internationally recognized Green Globe 21 criteria for sound environmental practices
- forging partnerships with national and local governments, NGOs and the local community
- conserving natural resources
- environmental awareness training for the staff, fellow hoteliers, learning institutes and schools
- making massive reductions in waste by composting and other re-use and recycling initiatives
- preferring natural alternatives to chemical use
- promoting local culture, history, music and furniture
- protecting turtle nesting habitats
- undertaking revegetation projects
- conserving coastal forest strip to act as a hurricane defence.

Recycling, Casuarina. ▶

Re-use of plastic bottles. ▶

 Re-use and recycling can increase human carrying capacity.

The Casuarina adopted the policy of 'reduce, re-use and recycle'.

To reduce, the hotel contacted suppliers and requested less packaging. Individual portions of ketchup and butter, for example, were not provided in the restaurants. Instead hard, reusable bottles and containers were used. Paper towels were replaced by hand driers. Large shampoo and conditioner dispensers replaced individual sachets.

Water loss was reduced by installing low-flow devices on showers and taps. Beach and poolside showers were fitted with 'pull chain flush valve' systems. Waste water from the beach showers was used to irrigate the gardens. The well water on the property was used to irrigate the grounds. There were signs in the hotel's rooms regarding the choice of frequency with which towels may be changed, which also reduces the consumption of water.

Reduction of waste. This metal drum was used to compost vegetable waste.

The biggest re-use initiative was the collection and modification of 320 plastic containers in which the cooking oil was delivered. After modification, the containers were used for the garbage collection in the guest rooms. Composting of food was facilitated by means of four compostumblers.

Recycling initiatives include the manufacture of pot pourri from cut flowers, and recycled paper from waste generated on the property. Separation of garbage for recycling was apparent throughout the property.

Other initiatives included:

- purchasing local produce as much as possible
- using only degradable plastic bags in the hotel
- employing local handicapped people in the hotel.

Sadly, in 2005, the Casuarina Beach Club was bought by the Almond Beach hotel and converted into an all-inclusive hotel, where the focus on recycling and re-use was not continued. However, sustainable tourism is still being advocated across many parts of the Caribbean. The Caribbean Alliance for Sustainable Tourism aims to enhance the practices of the region's hotel and tourism operators by providing high-quality education and training related to sustainable tourism; promoting the industry's efforts and successes to the travelling public and other stakeholders; and serving as a vital link to all stakeholders with sustainable tourism interests in the Caribbean region.

EXERCISES

1   Study Figure 3.1 on page 83. Describe the growth of the world's population. To what extent is population growth occurring in developing countries? Suggest reasons for this.

2   Explain the difficulties in applying the concept of carrying capacity to local human populations.

3   Explain how absolute reductions in energy and material use, reuse and recycling can affect human carrying capacity.

3.8 Environmental demands of human populations

Assessment statements

3.8.1 Explain the concept of an ecological footprint as a model for assessing the demands that human populations make on their environment.

3.8.2 Calculate from appropriate data the ecological footprint of a given population, stating the approximations and assumptions involved.

3.8.3 Describe and explain the differences between the ecological footprints of two human populations, one from an LEDC and one from an MEDC.

3.8.4 Discuss how national and international development policies and cultural influences can affect human population dynamics and growth.

3.8.5 Describe and explain the relationship between population, resource consumption and technological development, and their influence on carrying capacity and material economic growth.

Ecological footprints

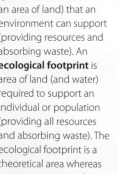

Carrying capacity is the number of individuals or species (i.e. the load of an area of land) that an environment can support (providing resources and absorbing waste). An **ecological footprint** is area of land (and water) required to support an individual or population (providing all resources and absorbing waste). The ecological footprint is a theoretical area whereas carrying capacity refers to a real area. These concepts are therefore the inverse of each other. Carrying capacity involves sustainable support of a population, whereas ecological footprints are not necessarily sustainable.

An **ecological footprint** is the hypothetical area of land required by a society, group or individual to fulfil all their resource needs and assimilate all wastes. The term was initially coined by William Rees in 1992, and further developed with Mathis Wackernagel in *Our ecological footprint: reducing human impact on the Earth*. A country described as having an ecological footprint of 2.4 times its own geographical area is consuming resources and assimilating its wastes on a scale that would require a land area 2.4 times larger than the actual size of the country. Ecological footprint can act as a model for monitoring environmental impact. It can also allow for direct comparisons between groups and individuals, such as comparing LEDCs and MEDCs (page 163). It can highlight sustainable and unsustainable lifestyles: for example, populations with a larger footprint than actual land area are living beyond sustainable limits. Wackernagel and Rees originally estimated that the available biological capacity for the population of the Earth (around 6 billion people at that time but nearer 6.8 billion now) was about 1.3 hectares of land per person (or 1.8 global hectares if marine areas are included as a source of productivity).

Ecological footprint can be increased by:
- greater reliance on fossil fuels (page 112)
- increased use of technology and, therefore, energy (but technology can also reduce the footprint, page 161).
- high levels of imported resources (which have high transport costs)
- large per capita production of carbon waste (i.e. high energy use, high fossil fuel use)
- large per capita consumption of food
- a meat-rich diet (pages 138, 164).

Local biomes with high productivity produce a lower footprint as they absorb carbon dioxide (net emission of carbon dioxide is used in the calculation of footprint size).

Ecological footprint can be reduced by:
- reducing amounts of resources used
- recycling resources
- reusing resources
- improving efficiency of resource use
- reducing amount of pollution produced
- transporting waste to other countries to deal with

- improving technology to increase carrying capacity
- importing more resources from other countries
- reducing population to reduce resource use
- using technology to increase carrying capacity (e.g. use GM crops to increase yield on the same amount of land)
- using technology to intensify land use.

Many innovations are still in the early stages (e.g. renewable technologies, page 114) but these could have a huge impact on ecological footprints in the future. The funding to support technological change exists in MEDCs, which currently face the biggest problem with their ecological footprints (Figure 3.56). There is a real incentive to address the issue.

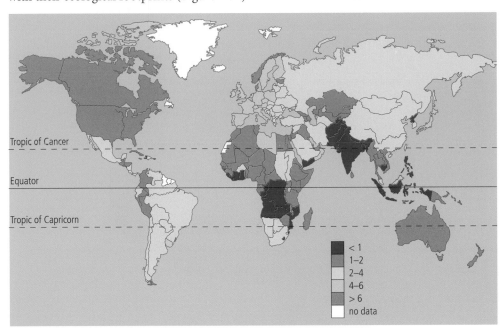

Figure 3.56
The ecological footprints (in hectares) of countries around the world.

Calculating ecological footprint

Ideally, all resource consumption and land uses are included in an ecological footprint calculation (full calculation). But this would make the calculation very complex. Ecological footprints are usually simplified and an approximation achieved, by using only net carbon dioxide emissions (Chapter 6, pages 265 and 275) and food production (page 135).

To calculate the ecological footprint of a country the following data are used:

per capita land requirement for food production (ha) =

$$\frac{\text{per capita food consumption (kg yr}^{-1})}{\text{mean food production of local arable land (kg ha}^{-1}\text{ yr}^{-1})} \qquad \text{Equation (1)}$$

per capita land requirement for absorbing waste carbon dioxide from fossil fuels (ha) =

$$\frac{\text{per capita carbon dioxide emission (kg C yr}^{-1})}{\text{net carbon fixation of local natural vegetation (kg C ha}^{-1}\text{ yr}^{-1})} \qquad \text{Equation (2)}$$

Food production is usually calculated as kilogram of **grain equivalents**. Counties with high meat diets have high food consumption because large amounts of grain are needed to support a high meat diet (pages 46, 138 and 164).

The total land requirement (ecological footprint) is calculated as the sum of these two per capita requirements (equation 1 + equation 2), multiplied by the total population.

Factors used in a full ecological footprint calculation would include those in the following list (Figure 3.57).

- Bioproductive (currently used) land – Land used for food and materials such as farmland, gardens, pasture and managed forest.
- Bioproductive sea – Sea area used for human consumption (often limited to coastal areas).
- Energy land – An equivalent amount of land that would be required to support renewable energy instead of non-renewable energy. The amount of energy land depends on the method of energy generation (large in the case of fossil fuel use) and is difficult to estimate for the planet.
- Built (consumed) land – Land that is used for development such as roads and buildings.
- Biodiversity land – Land required to support all of the non-human species.
- Non-productive land – Land such as deserts is subtracted from the total land available.

Figure 3.57
Some of the factors used to calculate a full ecological footprint (pie chart represents averages for the planet but doesn't include figures for energy land or bioproductive sea).

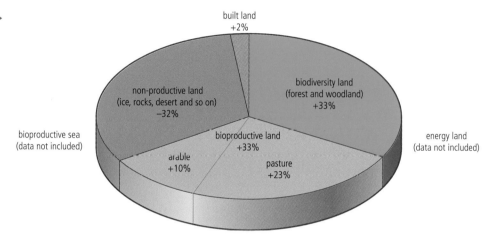

Thus, the simplified calculation of ecological footprint clearly ignores the following factors that influence the amount of land a population needs to support itself:

- the land or water required to provide any aquatic and atmospheric resources
- land or water needed to assimilate wastes other than carbon dioxide
- land used to produce materials imported into the country to subsidize arable land and increase yields
- replacement of productive land lost through urbanization.

In North America, a high per capita grain consumption relates to the meat-rich diet of MEDCs, where high grain production supports intensive cattle farming. Grain productivity is high in Africa reflecting the warmer conditions and high incident solar radiation, which increase NPP. The same conditions are also reflected by the high net carbon dioxide fixation by local vegetation. Carbon dioxide emissions are much higher in North America, reflecting an industrialized society reliant on fossil fuels (Table 3.14).

TABLE 3.14 GRAIN CONSUMPTION AND PRODUCTION, AND CARBON DIOXIDE EMISSIONS AND ABSORPTION IN AFRICA AND NORTH AMERICA				
Country	Per capita grain consumption / $kg\,yr^{-1}$	Local grain productivity / $kg\,ha^{-1}\,yr^{-1}$	Per capita carbon dioxide emission from fossil fuels / $kg\,C\,yr^{-1}$	Net carbon dioxide fixation by local vegetation / $kg\,C\,ha^{-1}\,yr^{-1}$
Africa	300	6000	200	6000
North America	600	300	1500	3000

The per capita ecological footprints (food land and carbon dioxide absorption land only) of North America and Africa are calculated by using the figures from Table 3.14 in equations (1) and (2) on page 161. So:

$$\text{per capita ecological footprint for Africa} = \left(\frac{300}{6000}\right) + \left(\frac{200}{6000}\right) = 0.05 + 0.033 = 0.083 \text{ hectares}$$

$$\text{per capita ecological footprint for North America} = \left(\frac{600}{300}\right) + \left(\frac{1500}{3000}\right) = 2.0 + 0.5 = 2.5 \text{ hectares}$$

You cannot calculate the ecological footprint for either Africa or North America as a whole because you do not have a figure for the total population in either case.

North America clearly has a much higher per capita ecological footprint than Africa. Remember, these figures are only for food land and carbon dioxide absorption land, so they are lower than full footprint calculations (Africa is about 1.1 ha per person, and North America about 8.4 ha per person).

If everyone on Earth adopted the same lifestyle as people in MEDCs, many Earths would be needed to support the global population.

To learn more about calculating your ecological footprint, go to www.pearsonhotlinks.com, insert the express code 2630P and click on activity 3.12.

Ecological footprints – MEDCs and LEDCs

As we have seen, an ecological footprint is the hypothetical area of land required to support a defined human population at a given standard of living: the measure takes account of the area required to provide all the resources needed by the population and the assimilation of all wastes. Given the different standards of living between LEDCs and MEDCs, differences in resource consumption, energy usage and waste production, disparities should be expected between the ecological footprints of LEDCs and MEDCs.

LEDCs tend to have smaller ecological footprints than MEDCs (Table 3.15). MEDCs generally have much greater rates of resource consumption than LEDCs. This is partly because people have more disposable income, which means demand for energy resources is high. Consumption is also high because resource use is often wasteful. MEDCs produce far more waste and pollution as by-products of production. LEDCs, in contrast, are often characterized by lower consumption as people have less to spend. The informal economy in LEDCs is responsible for recycling many resources. However, as LEDCs develop their ecological footprint size increases.

TABLE 3.15 ECOLOGICAL FOOTPRINTS FOR SELECTED COUNTRIES						
Country	Population 1997	Footprint / ha per capita	Available capacity / ha per capita	Deficit / ha per capita	Total footprint / km^2	total capacity / km^2
China	1 247 315 000	1.2	0.8	−0.4	14 967 780	9 978 520
India	970 230 000	0.8	0.5	−0.3	7 761 840	4 851 150
USA	268 198 000	10.3	6.7	−3.6	27 623 467	17 968 663
Germany	81 845 000	5.3	1.9	−3.4	4 337 785	1 555 055
France	58 433 000	4.1	4.2	0.1	2 395 763	2 454 186
Canada	30 101 000	7.7	9.6	1.9	2 317 777	2 889 696
Peru	24 691 000	1.6	7.7	6.1	395 056	1 901 207
World	5 892 480 000	2.8	2.1	−0.7		

Source: Adapted from Wackernagel M, Larry O, et al. *Ecological Footprints of Nations: How Much Nature Do They Use? How Much Nature Do They Have?* Rio+5 Forum Study, 1997

A meat-eating diet, prevalent in MEDCs where 30 per cent of diet may be based on animal protein, requires the use of much more land than a vegetarian diet. This is because animals do not use up to 90 per cent of the available energy from crops; only a small quantity goes into new biomass (Chapter 2). More of the energy from the crop goes to humans if the crop is eaten directly (as in LEDCs, where little meat features in the diet – about 12 per cent). Data for food consumption are often given in grain equivalents. So a population with a meat-rich diet consumes a higher grain equivalent than a population feeding directly on grain (Table 3.16).

TABLE 3.16 PROJECTIONS FOR FOOD GRAIN REQUIREMENTS IN DIFFERENT REGIONS OF THE WORLD IN 2025

Country	Population / billions	Average per capita consumption / kg	Food grains requirement / Mt
Asia	4.54	300	1362
Africa	1.62	257	416
South America	0.78	296	231
Europe	0.53	700	364
FSU	0.37	983	364
North America	0.35	885	310
Oceania	0.04	578	23
World	8.22	373	3070

Source: data based on a UN study which projected the population size and growth rates up to 2025 (figures assume no significant changes in per capita grain consumption)

In MEDCs, about twice as much energy in the diet is provided by animal products than in LEDCs. Grain production is therefore higher, using high-yield farming strategies. Greenhouse gas emissions from agriculture also affect footprint totals. According to the International Panel on Climate Change (IPCC), the agricultural sector emits between 5.1 and 6.1 billion tonnes of greenhouse gases annually, about 10–12 per cent of the total greenhouse gas emissions. The main sources of these gases are nitrous oxides from fertilizer, methane emissions from cows, and biomass burning.

Populations more dependent on fossil fuels have higher carbon dioxide emissions. Fixation of carbon dioxide is clearly dependent on climatic region and vegetation type, with countries nearer the equator containing vegetation with higher rates of net primary production (Chapter 2, page 53).

Lower rates of carbon dioxide uptake in MEDCs compared to LEDCs, and higher rates of emissions, contribute to the higher ecological footprints in MEDCs.

ENVIRONMENTAL PHILOSOPHIES

People in MEDCs generally have a technocentric worldview, which encourages continued high consumption of resources, in the expectation that technology will provide solutions to minimize the environmental impact. LEDCs have not only had an historically low consumption of non-renewable resources, but have also embraced environmental philosophies that have encouraged working in balance with nature, particularly where failure to do so would result in direct negative impact on the community (e.g. cutting down a forest on which you directly depend for food and shelter).

Peru versus Canada

Table 3.17 shows the breakdown of the ecological footprint (in hectares) for an average Canadian.

TABLE 3.17 PER CAPITA ECOLOGICAL FOOTPRINT OF CANADA					
Part of footprint	Energy	Agricultural land	Forest	Built environment	Total
housing	0.5	0.0	1.0	0.1	1.6
food	0.4	0.9	0.0	0.0	1.3
transport	1.0	0.0	0.0	0.1	1.1
consumer goods	0.6	0.2	0.2	0.0	1.0
resources in services	0.4	0.0	0.0	0.0	0.4
total	2.9	1.1	1.2	0.2	5.4

Source: Adapted from *Sustainable Consumption and Production.* www.iisd.ca

The per capita ecological footprint of Canada is 5.4, for Peru it is 0.9 (in 2001). Peru, a less economically developed country (LEDC), has an energy component of 16.0 per cent within its ecological footprint, whereas Canada has an energy component of 53.7 per cent. Canada has a larger consumer-driven economy, a greater car culture, uses more energy for heating, and has higher consumer spending per capita than Peru, all of which contribute to the high percentage of energy within the Canadian ecological footprint. Non-renewable energy generation in Canada, using fossil fuels, adds to the carbon dioxide emission component of the footprint. The higher rates of photosynthesis and NPP in Peruvian vegetation, due to its location nearer the equator, contribute to Peru's lower net contributions to atmospheric carbon dioxide levels.

 To learn more about the ecological footprints for individual countries, go to www.pearsonhotlinks. com, insert the express code 2630P and click on activity 3.13.

Population policies – national and international – and population dynamics and growth

Population policies refer to official government actions to control the population in some way.

Key terms

- **Pronatalist** policies are in favour of increasing the birth rate.
- **Anti-natalist policies** attempt to limit the birth rate.

National level anti-natalist policies: China

Almost a quarter of the world's population lives in China. Although the government used to believe that a large population made the country strong both economically and politically, it now realizes that the larger the population, the more people there are to feed, clothe and house. This prompted the government to think about family planning – that is, methods of reducing the number of children being born.

To control its population growth, the Chinese government introduced its one-child policy in 1979. The policy rewarded families that had only one child and penalized those that had more than one. For example, families that had two or more children paid higher taxes, and the parents were prevented from reaching high-level positions in their jobs. Other measures included forced sterilizations and abortions so that families were limited to one child.

But the policy has been relaxed somewhat since October 1999. In most rural areas, couples can now have two children without penalties. Increasingly, rich farmers are able and willing to pay fines or bribes in order to get permission to have more children; poor families simply take the view that they have nothing much to lose.

Case study continued

One of the results of the policy has been gender imbalance. In 2003, in China, 117 boys were born for every 100 girls, whereas the global average is 105 boys to every 100 girls. The disparity is greater in rural areas: 130 to 100. There is a resurgence of female infanticide. Girls are hidden from the authorities, or die at a young age through neglect. China is offering to pay couples a premium for producing baby girls to counter this imbalance.

Most Chinese families in urban areas have only one child, and the growing urban middle classes do not discriminate against daughters as much. However, the rural populations remain traditionally focussed on male heirs. But even in urban areas, boys are generally preferred because they are regarded as more able than girls to provide for their families, care for elderly relatives and continue the family line. The preference for a son makes simple economic sense as sons are less likely to leave the family home after marrying and, as higher earners than women, are more able to provide for the extended family.

China now offers welfare incentives to couples with two daughters and has tightened the prohibition on sex-selective abortions. In some areas, couples with two daughters and no sons have been promised an annual payment of 600 yuan (£38) once they reach 60 years of age. The money will also be given to families with only one child to discourage couples with a daughter from trying again for a boy.

Statistically, the one-child policy has had success. The government says it has prevented well over 300 million births since it was introduced and is fulfilling its initial aim of ensuring that China can combat rural poverty and improve standards of living across the board. China's population stood at 1.3 billion in 2003. As the country's economy continues to grow and transform at an unprecedented rate, pressure to relax the policy looks likely to intensify.

It is forecast that there will be a shortage of potential marriage mates which will lead to some social instability.

CASE STUDY

Fertility in the Arab world

The Arab performance in improving women's health is unmatched. Female life expectancy is up from 52 years in 1970 to more than 70 years in 2004. The number of children borne by the average Arab woman has fallen by half in the past 20 years, to a level scarcely higher than world norms. In Oman, fertility has plummeted from ten births per woman to fewer than four. A main reason for this is a dramatic rise in the age at which girls marry. A generation ago, three-quarters of Arab women were married by the time they were 20. That proportion has dropped by half. In large Arab cities, the high cost of housing, added to the need for women to pursue degrees or start careers, is prompting many to delay marriage until they are in their 30s.

CASE STUDY

Government policy in France

There has been a long-term decline in the French population since the eighteenth century. The government of France now generally encourages large families.

Maternity leave, on nearly full pay, ranges from 20 weeks for the first child to 40 or more for a third. A range of grants, allowances and tax breaks is available, increasing substantially once a family has three children: all French *familles nombreuses* get some 300 euros in monthly allowances and can travel almost freely on public transport. At the same time, there is a nationwide network of state-run or state-approved creches for children aged over two months. Depending on income, childcare costs from almost nothing to around 500 euros a month for the most well-off. Nursery school from 8.30 a.m. to 4.30 p.m. is free for every child aged three and over.

In 2006, the French statistical office announced that France's population would grow by 5 million between 2005 and 2050, and would level off at 70 million. At this point, France would become the most populous country in Europe – assuming Germany's population continues to fall. Such a change would mark a historic recovery. At the time of Napoleon, France was the largest country in Europe, and the third largest in the world. It accounted for about 20% of Europe's population.

International development policy – Millennium Development Goals

Millennium Development Goals were formulated by the UN in 2000. The goals and their links to the environment are summarized in Tables 3.18 and 3.19.

TABLE 3.18 UN MILLENNIUM DEVELOPMENT GOALS	
Goal	**Target**
1 Eradicate extreme poverty and hunger	• Reduce by 50 per cent the proportion of people living on less than $1 a day • Reduce by 50 per cent the proportion of people suffering from hunger
2 Achieve universal primary education	• Ensure all children complete a full course of primary schooling
3 Promote gender equality and empower women	• Eliminate gender disparity in primary and secondary education by 2005 (all levels by 2025) • Ensure literacy parity between young men and women • Women's equal representation in national parliaments
4 Reduce child mortality	• Reduce by two-thirds the under-five mortality rate • Universal child immunization against measles
5 Improve maternal health	• Reduce the maternal mortality ratio by 75 per cent
6 Combat HIV/AIDS, malaria and other diseases	• Halt and begin to reverse the spread of HIV/AIDS • Halt and begin to reverse the incidence of malaria • Halt and begin to reverse the incidence of tuberculosis
7 Ensure environmental sustainability	• Reverse loss of forests • Halve proportion without improved drinking water in urban areas • Halve proportion without improved drinking water in rural areas • Halve proportion without sanitation in urban areas • Halve proportion without sanitation in rural areas • Improve the lives of at least 100 million slum dwellers by 2020
8 Develop global partnership for development	• Reduce youth unemployment

To learn more about the Millennium Development Goals, go to www.pearsonhotlinks.com, insert the express code 2630P and click on activity 3.14.

TABLE 3.19 LINKS BETWEEN THE ENVIRONMENT AND THE MILLENNIUM DEVELOPMENT GOALS	
Goal	**Links to the environment**
1 Eradicate extreme poverty and hunger	• Poor people's livelihoods and food security often depend on ecosystem goods and services. • Poor people tend to have insecure rights to environmental resources and inadequate access to markets, decision-making and environmental information – limiting their capability to protect the environment and improve their livelihoods and well-being. • Lack of access to energy services also limits productive opportunities, especially in rural areas.
2 Achieve universal primary education	• Time spent collecting water and fuel wood reduces time available for schooling. • In addition, the lack of energy, water and sanitation services in rural areas discourages qualified teachers from working in poor villages.
3 Promote gender equality and empower women	• Women and girls are especially burdened by water and fuel collection, reducing their time and opportunities for education, literacy and income-generating activities. • Women often have unequal rights and insecure access to land and other natural resources, limiting their opportunities and ability to access other productive assets.

table continued

To learn more about the progress of any country in achieving the Millennium Development Goals, go to www.pearsonhotlinks.com, insert the express code 2630P and click on activity 3.15.

4 Reduce child mortality	• Diseases (such as diarrhoea) tied to unclean water and inadequate sanitation, and respiratory infections related to pollution are among the leading killers of children under five. • Lack of fuel for boiling water also contributes to preventable waterborne diseases.
5 Improve maternal health	• Inhaling polluted indoor air and carrying heavy loads of water and fuel wood hurt women's health and can make them less fit to bear children, with greater risks of complications during pregnancy. • Lack of energy for illumination and refrigeration, as well as inadequate sanitation, undermine healthcare, especially in rural areas.
6 Combat HIV/AIDS, malaria and other diseases	• Up to 20 per cent of the disease burden in developing countries may be due to environmental risk factors (as with malaria and parasitic infections). • Preventive measures to reduce such hazards are as important as treatment – and often more cost-effective. • New biodiversity-derived medicines hold promise for fighting major diseases.
7 Ensure environmental sustainability	• Reverse the loss of forests. • Halve the proportion of people without drinking water or sanitation.
8 Develop global partnership for development	• Improve the lives of at least 100 million slum dwellers by 2010.

To see interactive maps for the Millennium Development Goals, go to www.pearsonhotlinks.com, insert the express code 2630P and click on activity 3.16.

National development policies

Declining birth rates in East Asia

According to the *New York Times* (18 May 2007), East Asia has seen a collapse in birth rates far more sudden than in the West. Japan, with a fertility rate stuck at 1.3 births per woman, is on track to lose half its population by 2105. Hong Kong, at 0.9 births per woman, is at the bottom of the world fertility league. Singapore, Taiwan and South Korea all have rates marginally lower than Japan.

China continues to pursue its one-child policy, despite a fertility rate of only 1.7 and in the face of a gender imbalance that has produced close to 10 per cent more boys than girls in the 5–14 age group.

In some countries, notably Japan and Korea, the low birth rate may be partly attributable to rising job opportunities and earning power for women. There is a reluctance to marry, particularly among the better educated women, as well as a preference for few, if any, children.

So what is different in the West?

Immigrants not only add to the population, they tend to have more children. The fertility rate for the Hispanic population in the USA, for example, is 2.9, while that for the established ethnic groups is no higher than the European average.

It is now generally accepted that urbanization is as much a social process as it is an economic process. It transforms social organizations, the role of the family, demographic structures, the nature of work, and the way we choose to live and with whom.

Initially, the shift from rural living to urban living changes the rate of natural population increase. It first reduces the death rate, despite the often appalling living conditions in many cities. Only later does urbanization reduce the birth rate (i.e. the fertility rate). The time lag between declining death and birth rates is often two generations and this means rapid urban population growth. Subsequently, fertility rates drop sharply and the rate of growth of urban populations declines.

As a result, families become smaller relatively quickly, not only because parents have fewer children on average, but also because the extended family typical of rural settings is much less common in urban areas. In urban settlements, children are less useful as units of labour and producers, than in rural settings. They are also more expensive to house and feed. In fact, fertility levels in developed countries have dropped so low that cities are seldom capable of reproducing their own populations. They grow, if at all, largely through in-migration from other countries, but also from other national cities or from rural areas – the latter is now a largely depleted source of population in Western countries.

Evolution to an urban society often involves a decline in the status of the family, with a proliferation of non-traditional family forms and new types of household.

CASE STUDY

Birth rate in Japan

A study was undertaken to determine whether regional differences existed for the decline in the total fertility rate in Japan between 1970 and 1990. Age-stratified data for 20–39-year-old females were examined. The factors included birth rate, percentage of married women, rates of birth by married women, and percentage of the work force in the service industry. The results were as follows:

- average marriage age for females shifted from 20–24 to 25–29, causing the birth rates for females aged of 25–29 years to decline
- urbanization had a significant effect on the declining birth rate for females grouped by age – the extent of urbanization in each region was inversely related to the rate of birth by married women.

The trend toward delaying marriage and childbirth in the urbanized regions appeared to be a major factor leading to the decline in the total fertility rate.

Is there a relationship between urbanization and the demographic transition?

An urban area can be defined as an area with increased density of human-created structures in comparison to the areas surrounding it. The definition is rather vague and does not provide a clear border between what is an urban area and what is not, and this will certainly have an impact on the data.

The impact of urbanization on the demographic transition is mainly through decline in mortality. Prior to the demographic transition, all populations are overwhelmingly rural, and migration tends to take place between rural areas. At this stage, migration is mostly short-distance and short-term, so permanent movement happens on a minimal scale. Urban death rates are extremely high prior to entering the demographic transition. This is mainly because the dense living conditions and the large-scale human contact in urban areas is an excellent environment for infectious and parasitic diseases to spread. For example, in Bombay in India at the start of the twentieth century, half of all births died before reaching their first birthday.

The high urban death rate limits the degree to which any population can become urban. As a country starts moving further into the demographic transition, death rates start to fall. The point where the urban death rate falls below the urban birth rate is where urban areas cease to be demographic sinks and experience a positive natural increase for the first time. The urban sector eventually grows without the rural-to-urban migration, but early in the process, the rural-to-urban migration is the main engine of urban population growth (and urbanization).

As a country continues to move into the demographic transition, the natural increase of the urban population overtakes rural-to-urban migration and becomes the main driver of urban population growth.

The volume of rural-to-urban migration declines in the final stages of the demographic transition, as does the absolute size of the rural population due to falling fertility (a consequence of the demographic transition). After the demographic transition is complete, populations are predominantly urban. At this level, the level of urbanization is high and virtually all migration is now urban-to-urban.

CASE STUDY

Pronatalist policies in Romania

In Romania, long-range planning was a cornerstone of economic growth. Demographic trends took on significant impact. In the 1960s, the country was approaching zero population growth, which carried alarming implications for future labour supplies and industrialization. In 1966, the government responded with a decree that prohibited abortion on demand and introduced other pronatalist policies to increase birth rates. The decree stipulated that abortion would be allowed only when:

- pregnancy endangered the life of a woman
- pregnancy was the result of rape or incest
- the child was likely to have a congenital disease or deformity
- the woman was over 45 years of age or had given birth to at least four children who remained under her care.

Abortion performed for any other reason became a criminal offence with penalties for those who sought or performed such operations.

There were other punitive policies. People who remained childless after the age of 25 were liable for a special tax amounting to between 10 and 20 per cent of their income. The government also made divorce much more difficult. The rule was rigidly enforced – in 1967 there were only 28 divorces compared with 26 000 in 1966.

There were some positive pronatalist policies. Family allowances were raised. Monetary awards were given to mothers with the birth of the third child. Moreover, the income tax rate for parents of three or more children was reduced by 30 per cent.

As contraceptives were not manufactured in Romania, and importation of them had stopped, the sudden unavailability of abortion made birth control extremely difficult. The pronatalist policies had an immediate impact. The number of live births rose from 273 687 in 1966 to 527 764 in 1967 – an increase of 92.8 per cent. Legal abortions fell from 1 million in 1965 to 52 000 in 1967. This success was due in part to the presence of police in hospitals to ensure that no illegal abortions were performed. However, the policy's initial success was marred by rising maternal and infant mortality rates associated with the restrictions on abortion.

Nevertheless, the increase in live births was short-lived. After the police returned to more normal duties, the number of abortions increased. The incentives provided by the state were not enough to sustain an increase in birth rate, which again began to decline. In 1974, the government granted special allowances for pregnant women and nursing mothers, giving them a lighter workload that excluded overtime and hazardous work and allowed time off to care for children without loss of benefits.

By 1983 the birth rate had fallen to 14.3 per 1000, the rate of annual increase in population had dipped to 3.7 per 1000, and the number of abortions (421 386) again exceeded the number of live births (321 489). In 1984, the legal age for marriage was lowered to 15 years for women, and additional taxes were levied on childless individuals over 25. Monthly gynaecological examinations for all women of childbearing age were instituted.

Case study continued

By 1985, a woman had to have five children, all still under her care, or be more than 45 years old to qualify for an abortion. Other steps to increase material incentives to have children included again raising taxes for childless individuals, increasing monthly allowances to families with children by 27 per cent, and giving bonuses for the birth of the second and third child.

The measures were not very effective. Although government expenditures on material incentives rose by 470 per cent between 1967 and 1983, the birth rate actually decreased during that time by 40 per cent. After 1983, despite the extreme measures taken by the regime to combat the decline, there was only a slight increase in birth rate, from 14.3 to 15.5 per 1000 in 1984 and 16 per 1000 in 1985.

Romanian demographic policies continued to be unsuccessful largely because they ignored the relationship of socio-economic development and demographics. Thus the woman's double burden of childcare and full-time work was not eased by consumer durables that save time and labour in the home.

In 1989, abortion remained the only means of fertility control available to an increasingly desperate population. The number of quasi-legal abortions continued to rise, as women resorted to whatever means necessary to secure permission for the procedure.

Despite the obvious reluctance of women to bear children because of socio-economic conditions, the Ceausescu regime continued its crusade to raise birth rates. In 1986, mass media campaigns were launched, extolling the virtues of the large families of the past and of family life in general. The new approach, like previous attempts, met with little success. Currently, Romania's birth rate is 10.3 per 1000 (185th in the world) and its total fertility rate is 1.39 children per woman (198th in the world).

The relationship between population, resource consumption and technological development

The relationship between population and resources can be described in relation to population density, resources and technology. Regions of the world can be classified according to population–resource ratios. According to Ackerman's classification (Table 3.20) there are four main types of region: USA type, India–China type, Brazil type and European type. His classification is based on economic development and there is little recognition of social or regional inequalities within a country. Moreover, population structure is not considered.

TABLE 3.20 ACKERMAN'S CLASSIFICATION OF POPULATION, RESOURCES AND TECHNOLOGY		
Type	Characteristics	Examples
USA type	• technologically innovative • low population–resource ratio	• USA • parts of Canada • parts of Russia • parts of S Africa • parts of Australia
European type	• technologically innovative • high population–resource ratio	• NW Europe
Indo–China type	• technologically deficient • high population–resource ratio	• India • China • northern Africa • central America
Brazil type	• technologically deficient • low population–resource ratio	• Brazil • sub-Saharan Africa

The geographer Earl Parker-Hanson argued that, in general:

culture (C) =

(society (S) + technology (T)) × (environmental resources (R) + anti-resources (AR))

Countries could be great or small, weak or poor with respect to society, technology, resources and anti-resources. Thus, using capital letters to represent great amounts, and small letters to represent small amounts, Parker believed that Russia was characterized:

C = (S + t) × (R + AR)

whereas the USA was characterized:

C = (s + T) × (r + ar)

According to the Soviet view, humans were a distinct but integral part of the environment. Socialist philosophy was that humans should master the environment. In contrast, the US capitalist view was that the environment was there to be exploited and to create wealth. The two views were not so very different in practice.

Global perspectives

Some societies (e.g. the USA and USSR from the 1930s to 1970s) have attempted to massively triumph over nature. Both states acted in highly anti-environmentalist ways. Stalin's 1948 'Plan for the transformation of nature' argued that a vigorously controlled society could conquer the physical environment. Large-scale schemes, such as the diversion of the Syr Darya and the Amu Darya, were designed to use nature to benefit mankind. The same could be said of the damming of the Colorado River by the US government.

Through the early and mid-twentieth century, most societies did to the environment what they thought they had to. Environmentalists were seen as denying the role of technology. But the environmentalists' case was helped by pictures sent back by the space programmes of the 1960s and 1970s. The images increased awareness of the fragility of the Earth and its finite resources; they caused many organizations and nations to think again. People were now seen part of a physical environment as well as a cultural one. Society gained an understanding of the geographical basis of human affairs. In many countries (e.g. Germany and New Zealand), the Green Party gained significant representation in government. Today, the anti-environmentalists are isolated.

Industrialization in the West accelerated the consumption of natural resources. When resources became scarce, the West turned to its colonies and trading partners. Agricultural development in the colonies led to widespread deforestation for the development of plantations. Similarly, industrialization in Russia and China led to massive environmental degradation, first at home then abroad.

Emerging superpowers (e.g. Brazil, India and China) wish to use natural resources to further their economic development. Countries that are already rich (e.g. the UK and Germany) argue for the conservation of resources – even though they did not do so in their pursuit of wealth and development.

Arguably it is the indigenous hunter–gatherers and subsistence farmers (e.g. the Penan of Borneo and the Kalahari bushmen) who manage the environment sustainably. Nevertheless, even among hunter–gatherers, anthropologists suggest that infanticide rates may be high, so as to permit the survival of the tribe. And infanticide may still occur elsewhere in parts of the world today. In South-East Asia it is estimated that there are about 100 million more men than women. The reason for this is largely due to sex-selective abortion, but there are also allegations of female infanticide and neglect of girls. Boys may be seen as potential money-earners whereas girls may be a drain on financial resources if a dowry payment has to be made to the family they marry into.

1 Explain the concept of an ecological footprint as a model for assessing the demands that human populations make on their environment.

2 Describe and explain the differences between the ecological footprints of two human populations, one from an LEDC and one from an MEDC.

3 Discuss how national and international development policies and cultural influences can affect human population dynamics and growth.

4 Describe and explain the relationship between population, resource consumption and technological development, and their influence on carrying capacity and material economic growth.

PRACTICE QUESTIONS

1 Study the population pyramids below.

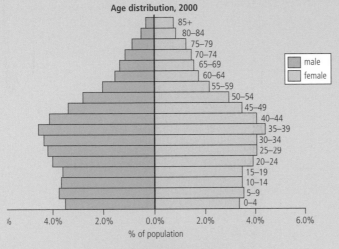

Area A: Population pyramid showing age distribution

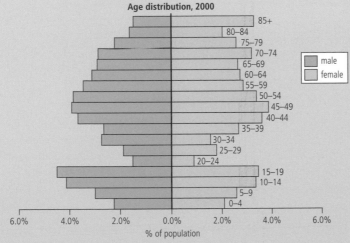

Area B: Population pyramid showing age distribution

(a) Label the two population pyramids to describe the main characteristics of the population. [6]

(b) Identify which of the pyramids is likely to be drawn from an urban area and which is likely to be from a rural location. [2]

(c) Give reasons for your answer to (b). [4]

(d) What are the demographic issues likely to be faced in the two contrasting areas? [8]

2   Using the table below, answer the following questions.

Energy source	Cost / pence per kilowatt hour at 1991 prices
coal	low 3.5, high 4.0
gas	low 2.3, high 2.8
nuclear	low 5.0, high 7.5
wind onshore	low 2.9, high 5.2
wind offshore	approx. 8.0
hydro-power	6.0
waste to energy	6.5
landfill gas	5.7

Source: based on: Byrne. *Environmental Science*. Nelson, 1997, page 167

(a) **(i)** Identify which energy type provides the cheapest electricity and which provides the most expensive. *[1]*

      (ii) Suggest reasons for your answers to (a) (i). *[2]*

(b) Explain how energy can be obtained from waste. *[2]*

(c) **(i)** Predict how the costs of production for fossil fuels might be different 50 years from now. *[1]*

      (ii) Justify your prediction in (c) (i). *[2]*

(d) Outline some of the advantages and disadvantages of hydro-power (hydroelectric power). *[4]*

(e) Explain the link between increasing use of renewable energy sources and the ecological footprint of a population. *[2]*

© International Baccalaureate Organization [2003]

3   The table below shows the impact of intensive farming on soil profiles.

Soil characteristic	Natural state	Intensive agriculture
organic content	A horizon – high (7%) B horizon – low (0%)	uniform (3–5%) in ploughed horizon
carbonates	A horizon – low/zero B/C horizon – maximum	uniform if limed and tilled
nitrogen	medium/low	high (nitrate fertilizers)
biological activity	high	medium
exchangeable cation balance	Ca – 80% K – 5% P – 3% H – 7%	Ca – 70% K – 10% P – 12% H – 4%

(a) Describe the main differences in organic content in natural soils and farmed soils. *[2]*

(b) Comment on the changes in nitrogen (nitrate) levels between natural soils and farmed soils. *[1]*

(c) Briefly explain why the level of carbonates in a natural soil varies between horizons whereas in an intensively farmed soil, the levels are uniform throughout the horizons. *[2]*

(d) Describe and suggest reasons for, the differences in calcium (Ca), potassium (K), phosphorus (P) and hydrogen (H) in natural and farmed soils. *[4]*

4   The table below shows population change and water consumption for 1971 and 2001 in an MEDC.

	1971	2001	Growth rate per year / %
Population / 10^6	48.6	57.0	0.53
Total water consumption / $10^6 \, m^3 day^{-1}$	42.7	83.3	2.3

(a) Compare relative growth rates for population and water consumption between 1971 and 2001. *[1]*

(b) Suggest two factors which may explain the difference you have identified in (a). *[2]*

© International Baccalaureate Organization [2007]

Note:
There are additional questions relating to this chapter on pages 354–359.

To access worksheet 3.5 with more practice questions relating to Chapter 3, please visit www.pearsonbacconline.com and follow the on-screen instructions.

4 CONSERVATION AND BIODIVERSITY

4.1 Biodiversity in ecosystems

Assessment statements

4.1.1 Define the terms *biodiversity*, *genetic diversity*, *species diversity* and *habitat diversity*.
4.1.2 Outline the mechanism of natural selection as a possible driving force for speciation.
4.1.3 State that isolation can lead to different species being produced that are unable to interbreed to yield fertile offspring.
4.1.4 Explain how plate activity has influenced evolution and biodiversity.
4.1.5 Explain the relationships among ecosystem stability, diversity, succession and habitat.

Terminology
Biodiversity

The word 'biodiversity' is a conflation of 'biological diversity' and was first made popular by ecologist E. O. Wilson in the 1980s. It is now widely used to represent the variety of life on Earth. 'Bio' makes it clear we are interested in the biological parts of an ecosystem, and 'diversity' is a measure of both the number of species in an area and their relative abundance (Chapter 2, pages 33–34). The term can be used to evaluate both the complexity of an area and its health.

Biodiversity can be measured in three different ways: species diversity, habitat diversity, and genetic diversity.

Rainforests have high diversity. They are rich in resources (e.g. food, space) with many different niches available, so many species can co-exist.

- Biodiversity refers to the amount of biological or living diversity per unit area. It includes the concepts of species diversity, habitat diversity and genetic diversity.
- Conservation of habitat diversity usually leads to the conservation of species and genetic diversity.

A niche is both the habitat where a species lives and how it lives there.

To learn more about the diversity of life on Earth, go to www.pearsonhotlinks. com, insert the express code 2630P and click on activity 4.1.

Ecosystems such as deserts have low biodiversity as there are fewer opportunities for species to coexist.

Early definitions of diversity have become limited as scientific knowledge has increased. Species diversity depends on the correct identification of different organisms and their distribution around the Earth. In the past, this was based on physical characteristics, which we now know can prove unreliable. Genetic diversity allows a more accurate way to describe species, although variation within the gene pool of individual species may cause problems.

Species diversity

This refers to the variety of species per unit area; it includes both the number of species present and their relative abundance. The higher the species diversity of a community or ecosystem, the greater the complexity. Areas of high species diversity are also more likely to be undisturbed (e.g. primary rainforest).

Habitat diversity

This means the range of different habitats in an ecosystem. It is often associated with the variety of ecological niches. For example, a woodland may contain many different habitats (e.g. river, soil, trees) and so have a high habitat diversity, whereas a desert has few habitats (e.g. sand, occasional vegetation) and so has a low habitat diversity.

Genetic diversity

This means the range of genetic material present in a gene pool or population of a species. Genes are sections of DNA found in the nucleus of all cells. They are essentially the instructions from which a species is produced. Gene pool refers to all the different types of gene found within every individual of a species. A large gene pool leads to high genetic diversity and a small gene pool to low genetic diversity. Although the term normally refers to the diversity within one species, it can also be used to refer to the diversity of genes in all species within an area.

Overview of diversity

The term '**diversity**' is often used as a way of referring to the heterogeneity (variability) of a community, ecosystem or biome, at the species, habitat or genetic level. The scientific meaning of diversity can become clear from the context in which it is used and may refer to any of the meanings explained above. For the meaning to be obvious, the level should be spelled out by using the correct term (i.e. species diversity, habitat diversity or genetic diversity).

Of the three types of diversity, the increase of habitat diversity is most likely to lead to an increase in the other two. This is because different habitats tend to have different species, and so more habitats will generally have a greater variety of species. Similarly, different species tend to have different genes and so more species will generally include a greater variety of genes. The conservation of habitat diversity will therefore usually lead to the conservation of species and genetic diversity.

The Simpson Index (*D*) is a method for measuring diversity (Chapter 2, page 33). Areas with a high *D* value suggest a stable and ancient site. A low value of *D* could suggest pollution, recent colonization or agricultural management.

Biodiversity refers to the variety of life on Earth. The word was first used by conservation biologists to highlight the threat to species and ecosystems, and is now widely used in international agreements concerning the sustainable use and protection of natural resources.

Species with low genetic diversity, such as cheetahs, are more prone to extinction. This is because if the environment changes, such a species is less likely to have the genes to help it survive.

Mechanism of natural selection (evolution) and speciation

A species is defined as 'a group of organisms that interbreed and produce fertile offspring'. So, donkeys and horses are different species: although they can mate to produce offspring (mules), mules cannot reproduce themselves. Speciation is the process by which new species form.

Evolution, or the development of new species over very long periods of geological time (millions of years), has been accepted by scientists for many years. Evidence is found by examination of the fossil record: older rocks contain simpler forms of life, more recent rocks contain more complex life forms. However, the explanation of how evolution actually occurred took longer to work out, and was finally described by Charles Darwin in his book *On the Origin of Species* in 1859. This is one of several theories of evolution but is the only one that is now widely recognized within the scientific community, and has survived the test of time.

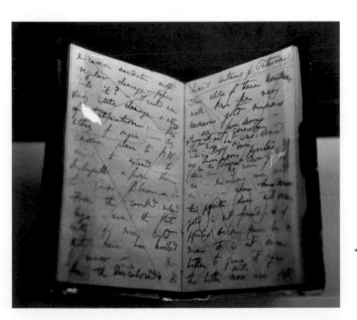

● **Examiner's hint:**
Diversity refers to the heterogeneity, or variability, of a species, community, or ecosystem. The meaning of diversity becomes clear from the context in which it is used: to describe the heterogeneity of a community, use **species diversity**; in relation to variability within a species, use **genetic diversity**; to describe the range of habitats within an ecosystem, use **habitat diversity**.

Charles Darwin about 20 years after the voyage of the *Beagle*, when he was in his forties and accumulating evidence in support of his theory of evolution.

To learn more about the full works of Charles Darwin, go to www.pearsonhotlinks.com, insert the express code 2630P and click on activity 4.2.

Pages from one of Darwin's notebooks, in which he first outlined his ideas on evolution by natural selection.

Darwin made a five-year trip on HMS *Beagle* between 1831 and 1836. The aim of the expedition was to map the coasts and waters of South America and Australia. Darwin was on board as a companion to the captain, but Darwin was also a talented and curious naturalist. During the trip, he was exposed to some of the most diverse ecosystems on Earth (the rainforests of South America), and the Galapagos Islands of the west coast of South America. It was essentially the interrelationship between species and environment on the Galapagos that stimulated Darwin to produce his theory of evolution. Darwin noted that:

- all species tend to over-reproduce
- this leads to competition for limited resources (a 'struggle for existence')
- species show variation (all individuals are not alike, they have subtle differences in appearance or behaviour).

From this Darwin concluded that:
- those best adapted to their surroundings survive
- these can then go on to reproduce.

We now know that variation is caused by genetic diversity, and that survival has a genetic basis –nature selects individuals with what it takes to survive, so successful genes are selected and passed on to the next generation. Over time, a change in the species' gene pool takes place, such changes ultimately lead to new species.

Darwin compared this process to artificial selection (selective breeding), a common practice in which humans choose animals to breed together based on desirable characteristics. It is selective breeding that has lead to all the varieties of domestic and agricultural animals we see today. Darwin called his theory 'natural selection', because nature 'does the choosing'. The result, over millennia, is not just new varieties, as in artificial selection, but new species.

Darwin collected huge numbers of animals, plants and fossils during his trip on the *Beagle*. Many of these are now in the Natural History Museum, London. It was after his return to the UK when he had examined his specimens, that Darwin began to develop his theory. He was particularly influenced by specimens of three species of mockingbird from the Galapagos Islands. He noticed that each species was from a different island and each was specifically adapted to conditions of its island (in body size and beak shape). This led him to start to think that, rather than each species being created separately (as was widely thought at the time), perhaps all were related to a common ancestor from the South American mainland. Moreover, perhaps each had evolved through the process of natural selection to become adapted to different niches on different islands. The mockingbirds are believed to have had a more important role in the development of Darwin's initial ideas than the famous Galapagos finches. In *The Voyage of the Beagle* (1839), Darwin wrote: 'My attention was first thoroughly aroused by comparing together the various specimens ... of the mocking-thrush.'

In other books you will find accounts referring to Darwin's finches. The Galapagos Islands are home to 12 species of finch, each clearly adapted to its specific island's type of vegetation. Although Darwin collected specimens of the finches, he did not label them with the locations where they were found. So, he paid them little attention until he was certain that his three mockingbirds were indeed different species. Fortunately, other finches, which had collected by members of the *Beagle's* crew, had been labelled with the islands on which they were found. So, the finches were after all able to play a useful back-up role in leading Darwin to his conclusion that new species can develop.

Different species of giant tortoise are found on different islands of the Galapagos, each adapted to local conditions. (**a**) On islands with tall vegetation, saddle-shaped shell fronts enable the animals to stretch up and reach the plants. (**b**) Animals with domed-shaped shell fronts are found on islands where vegetation is common on the ground.

The first publication of the theory of evolution by natural selection was not in Darwin's *On the Origin of Species*, but in 1858 in a joint publication between Darwin and Wallace (see ToK box, opposite) in the *Proceedings of the Linnean Society of London*, following a presentation of their findings at the Society earlier that year.

ENVIRONMENTAL PHILOSOPHIES

The evidence for Darwin's theory is overwhelming. Despite this, some people (creationists) do not believe it to be true,. These people believe that the Genesis story in the Bible is literally true, with all life on Earth being created within 6 days. Scientific evidence strongly contradicts this version of events. Most religions accept Darwin's theory while maintaining a belief in a creator God. What do you think? Ultimately you must weigh your worldview with the scientific evidence and draw your own conclusions

 To learn more about advocates of Darwin's theory (for example, Richard Dawkins), go to www. pearsonhotlinks.com, insert the express code 2630P and click on activity 4.3.

The role of isolation in forming new species
Geographical isolation

The islands of the Galapagos are quite widely separated and very different from each other. This caused animal and plant populations which arrived from mainland South America (ancestral populations) to become geographically isolated from each other. For example, in the case of the mockingbirds, an ancestral population arriving from the mainland would have spread onto several different islands of the Galapagos. As local environmental and biological conditions were different on each island, different species evolved to fulfil different ecological niches. Because the islands are some 600 miles from the mainland and the distances between them sufficiently large, the geographically isolated populations on different islands would have found it difficult to interbreed, limiting 'gene flow' (the exchange of genetic material through interbreeding). Geographical isolation is essential in the formation of new species. Without it, interbreeding would cause the genes from two populations to continue to mix (Figure 4.1) and characteristics of the ancestral species to remain.

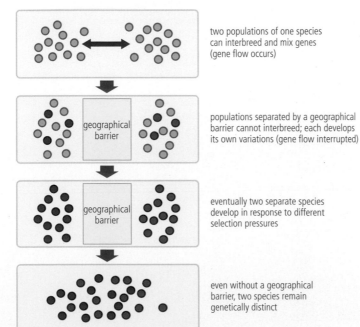

two populations of one species can interbreed and mix genes (gene flow occurs)

populations separated by a geographical barrier cannot interbreed; each develops its own variations (gene flow interrupted)

eventually two separate species develop in response to different selection pressures

even without a geographical barrier, two species remain genetically distinct

 In 1858, Charles Darwin unexpectedly received a letter from a young naturalist, Alfred Russel Wallace. Wallace outlined a remarkably similar theory of natural selection to Darwin's own. Wallace had come up with the idea while travelling in South-East Asia. The men had developed the same theory independently. Why was this possible? Common experiences seem to have been crucial, and both had read similar books. For two individuals to arrive at one of the most important theories in science independently and at the same time is remarkable.

● **Examiner's hint:**
There have been many theories of evolution. The accepted explanation is Darwin's theory of evolution by natural selection.

- Species show variation.
- All species over-produce.
- Despite over-production, population levels remain the same.
- Over-production leads to competition for resources.
- The fittest, or best adapted organisms, survive.
- The survivors reproduce and pass on their adaptive genes to the next generation.
- Over time, the population's gene pool changes and new species emerge.

◀ **Figure 4.1**
Geographical barriers include mountains, water (sea, river or lake), or hostile environment.

Reproductive isolation

Reproductive isolation can also lead to speciation. Evolutionary changes to the appearance or behaviour of populations may result in males and females of those populations no longer being attracted to each other and therefore not breeding together. If the females of one population are decreasingly attracted to the males of the other population, or vice versa, the exchange of genes through reproduction may slow, eventually stop, and different species may arise.

Isolation is the process by which two populations become separated by geographical, behavioural, genetic or reproductive factors. If gene flow between the two sub-populations is prevented, new species may evolve.

Bowerbirds

Bowerbirds are found in Australia and New Guinea. Male bowerbirds make elaborate bowers from twigs and in many cases decorate them with shells, leaves, flowers, feathers, stones, and berries. The bowers are designed to attract females, and different species of bowerbird design different bowers. For example, the satin bowerbird builds a channel between upright sticks and decorates the bower with bright blue objects. The MacGregor's bowerbird builds a tall tower of sticks and decorates it with pieces of charcoal. The females of one species are not attracted to the bowers (or, therefore, the males) of other species. Evolutionary changes to mating rituals, such as bower construction, can lead to the isolation of populations and cause speciation.

Figure 4.2
Male reproductive organs from four different species of damselfly – females can mate only with the appropriate male.

Reproductive isolation may also occur if two populations can no longer physically breed together, due to changes in reproductive organs (Figure 4.2) or other physical differences such as size (e.g. a great Dane cannot breed with a poodle).

Speciation in progress

Before different species are formed from ancestral populations, sub-species (or varieties) occur; these can still interbreed but show physical, behavioural, and genetic differences.

Different species cannot interbreed to produce fertile offspring – this is the biologists' definition of species.

Spotted owls

Populations of the spotted owl in Northern America have become geographically separated over time, forming two varieties: the northern spotted owl and the Mexican spotted owl (Figure 4.3). Given enough time and continued isolation, these will eventually be unable to interbreed and produce fertile offspring. They will then be two separate species.

Figure 4.3
The ranges of these two varieties of spotted owl do not overlap and they occupy different niches – geographical isolation means there is little gene flow between the two varieties.

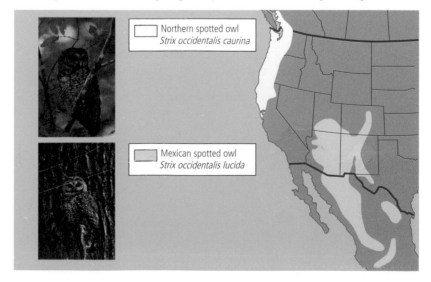

Northern spotted owl
Strix occidentalis caurina

Mexican spotted owl
Strix occidentalis lucida

Male birds of paradise have bright and colourful feathers which they use to attract females. Different species have different patterns. Dancing displays also vary. Alfred Russel Wallace was one of the first naturalists to observe these species in the wild.

◀ Male Raggiana bird of paradise (left) displaying his plumage to a female. The male bird is brightly coloured but the female is plain.

Plate tectonics

The outer layer of the Earth, the crust (lithosphere), is divided into eight major and many minor plates. These plates vary in size and shape but can move relative to each other. They are carried on the mantle (asthenosphere) beneath them, which can flow like a liquid on geological time scales. The edges of adjacent plates can move parallel to each other, be pushed one under the other, or collide. Earthquakes, volcanoes, and mountain-building occur at these junctions.

During the Paleozoic and Mesozoic eras (about 250 million years ago) all land mass on Earth existed as one supercontinent, Pangaea. This name is derived from the Greek for 'entire'. About 175 million years ago, the land mass split into two separate supercontinents, Laurasia and Gondwana. Laurasia contained land that became North America, Eurasia (Europe and Asia) and Greenland, and Gondwana contained the land that became South America, Africa, Australia, Antarctica and India. The distribution of all extinct and extant (still living) species found in these geographical areas today can be explained in terms of these ancient land masses.

Movement of the tectonic plates can produce barriers such as mountain ranges, oceans and rift valleys that can lead to isolation of gene pools and then speciation. Movement apart of the plates can also lead to isolation and the development or preservation of unique species. For example, the separation of Australia led to the preservation of its distinctive flora and fauna (e.g. eucalypts, monotremes and marsupials). Similarly, Madagascar is the only place where lemurs are found today.

Formation of land bridges between previously separated plates can provide opportunities for species to spread from one area to another. For example, species from Australia spread onto new islands in the East Indies, and the similarity between caribou and reindeer (in Alaska and Siberia) suggests a common ancestry.

The movement of plates through different climatic zones allows new habitats to present themselves. For example, the northward movement of the Australian plate, and the subsequent drying of much of the continent, has provided changes in the selective forces on species leading to the evolution of drought-tolerant species.

Plate movement can generate new and diverse habitats, thus promoting biodiversity (Figures 4.4–4.8, overleaf).

It is rare for a continental plate to be pushed (subducted) beneath an oceanic plate. However, an example can be found in north-western Australia, where the Australian plate is being subducted beneath the oceanic island of Timor. Loss of land in this way will eventually lead to loss of habitats and biodiversity from the region.

Plate tectonics refers to the movement of the eight major and several minor internally rigid plates of the Earth's lithosphere in relation to each other and to the partially mobile asthenosphere below.

To learn more about plate tectonics, species diversity and distribution of organisms, go to www.pearsonhotlinks.com, insert the express code 2630P and click on activity 4.4.

During the Pleistocene ice ages, a land bridge connected Alaska with eastern Siberia. It is possible that the earliest human colonizers of the Americas entered from Asia via this route. At the same period, the islands of South-East Asia (Borneo, Java and Sumatra) were connected to the mainland of Asia forming one land mass (Sundaland). Land bridges were caused by a drop in lea level due to climate change – these bridges are called Beringia. As sea levels rose again, the land bridges were lost and areas became isolated once more.

Figure 4.4
Subduction of heavier oceanic crust beneath the lighter continental crust. This can lead to new island arcs (e.g. New Zealand, where the Pacific plate is being subducted under the Indian/Australian plate), and mountain areas where magma rises up from under the subduction area causing volcanic action and thickening of the crust (e.g. the Andes of South America and the Cascade Range of north-western USA).

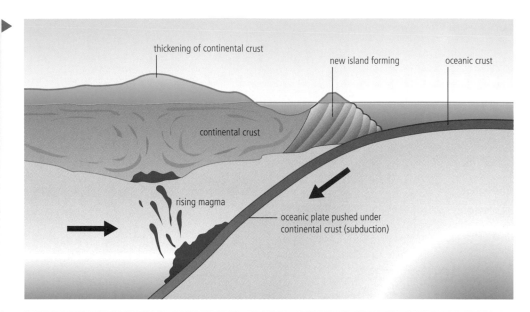

Figure 4.5
Oceanic crust is subducted beneath oceanic crust – as both are the same density, the effect is different from that in Figure 4.4. Resulting volcanic activity from rising magma causes new islands to form, with new habitats providing possibilities for speciation. Japan, the Philippines, the Aleutians of Alaska, and the Leeward Islands of the Caribbean were all created in this way.

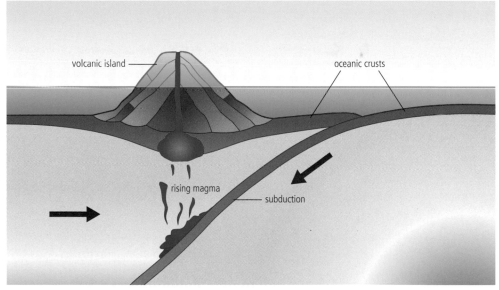

Figure 4.6
Continental plates colliding. This leads to an increase in continental plate thickness and eventually to new mountain ranges (e.g. the Himalayas, where the Indian plate is being pushed against the large Asian plate). Creation of new habitats at different altitudes adds to the biodiversity of the region.

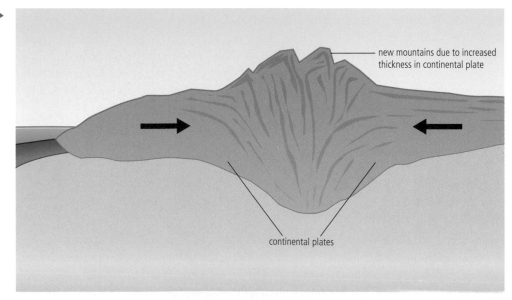

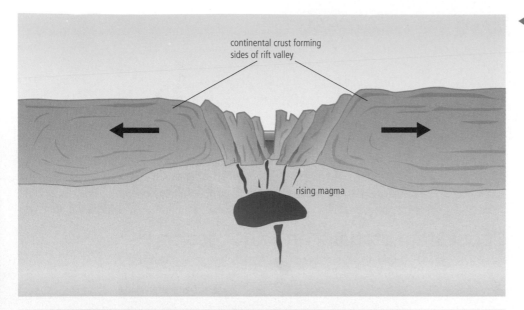

continental crust forming
sides of rift valley

rising magma

Figure 4.7
Continental plates moving
apart cause rift valleys. Deep
lakes may form in these
valleys (e.g. Lake Tanganyika
and Lake Victoria in the East
African rift valley and the
world's deepest lake, Baikal,
in Siberia). Given time, new
seas may form – The Red Sea,
which separates Africa and
Saudi Arabia, is an example
here. The creation of new
aquatic habitats drives
speciation in these rift areas.
Magma rising from the rift
can stick to the separating
plates creating new land (e.g.
Iceland, Ascension Island, the
Azores, and Tristan de Cunha
in the Atlantic) again creating
new opportunities for species
evolution.

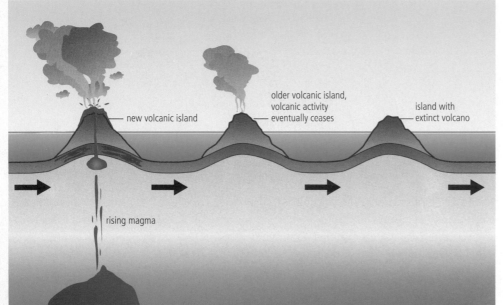

new volcanic island

older volcanic island,
volcanic activity
eventually ceases

island with
extinct volcano

rising magma

Figure 4.8
In some areas, hot rock rises
from deep in the mantle and
breaks through the oceanic
crust. These 'hot spots' are
not actually caused by plate
tectonics but the movement
of plates over the hot spots
can create chains of islands
(e.g. Galapagos Islands and
Hawaii). As Darwin found,
the creation of volcanic
islands and their colonization
by animals and plants that
become adapted to local
conditions can lead to
increased regional diversity.

Mount Everest, the world's tallest
mountain at nearly 9000 metres,
has been created over 40 million
years by the collision between the
Indian and Eurasian plates. The rocks
on the summit are 50-million-year-
old limestones that formed in the
shallow waters of an ocean that
once lay between India and Asia.
The Himalayas are a physical barrier
that has led to the separation of
populations and the evolution of
new species: this is true of mountain-
building in general.

Mount Everest.

Evidence for the role
of plate tectonics in
contributing to speciation
can be interpreted
from the fossil record,
and from the current
distribution of organisms
around the planet. Before
the continental drift
hypothesis, there was no
satisfactory explanation
of the distribution of life
forms. Why, therefore,
didn't scientists establish
such a hypothesis earlier?

● **Examiner's hint:**
The movement of the Earth's plates have led to the separation of gene pools through the creation of physical barriers (e.g. islands, seas, mountain ranges). Isolated gene pools cannot interbreed, and over long periods of time the different gene pools adapt organisms to local surroundings until the different populations become genetically distinct, forming new species.

EXERCISES

1   Define the terms *genetic diversity*, *species diversity* and *habitat diversity*.

2   Darwin's theory of evolution is explained in terms of natural selection. What is natural selection, and how does it lead to the generation of new species?

3   Isolation mechanisms are essential for the generation of new species. List three isolating mechanisms. How does the isolation of populations lead to speciation?

4   Name three different ways that the Earth's plates interact. How does each lead to speciation events?

5   Outline how land bridges have contributed to the current distribution of species. Give one example and say how and when this affected species distribution patterns.

Ecosystem stability and succession

To access worksheet 4.1 on succession on Krakatau, please visit www.pearsonbacconline.com and follow the on-screen instructions.

Figure 4.9
Krakatau is part of Indonesia, a band of islands on the equator.

Krakatau erupted with a force ten times the magnitude of Mt St Helens and 2000 times the force of a nuclear explosion. The sound of the explosion was heard 2700 miles away.

To learn more about succession on Krakatau, go to www.pearsonhotlinks.com, insert the express code 2630P and click on activity 4.5.

Studies of colonization of the volcanic island of Krakatau (Figure 4.9), after the massive eruption in 1883, show that tropical rainforest ecosystems are capable of recovery from even extreme damage, given sufficient time. After the initial eruption, no living thing remained on what was left of the island, whereas today Krakatau is covered by tropical forest. On the islands left after the eruption, there are now over 400 species of vascular plants, thousands of species of arthropods, over 30 species of birds, 18 species of land molluscs, 17 species of bats and 9 reptiles.

Organisms can colonize isolated land using several mechanisms.
- Air – By flying (birds, insects) or by passive transportation (lightweight seeds or spores).
- Sea – By swimming or floating on a log.
- Animal – By travelling (or hitchhiking) inside or attached to animals that swim or fly (plant seeds and animal larvae).

Specific types of dispersal

- **Jump dispersal** – Long-distance dispersal to remote areas by one or a few individuals. This dispersal mechanism explains widely distributed species in geographically isolated areas. It can be used to explain the aerial spread of plants, insects and microbial organisms over huge distances. The colonization of the Galapagos Islands by finches from mainland South America is an example of this type of dispersal.
- **Diffusion** – Slower than jump dispersal and involves populations, rather than individuals. It describes the spread of species at the edge of their ranges into new areas. Diffusion often follows jump dispersal events.

- **Secular migration** –Dispersal over geological timescales (thousands to millions of years). This is diffusion taking place so slowly that the diffusing species undergoes evolutionary change during the process. It includes the diversification and spread of flowering plants, and the evolution of South American llamas and vicunas that are descended from the now extinct North American members of the camel family that migrated during the Pliocene.

The process of succession

The formation of an ecosystem from bare rock (as on Krakatau) is called a **primary succession**. The succession always follows the same sequence with the arrival of different organisms in turn (Figure 4.10).

- Pioneer species arrive (e.g. lichens, algae, bacteria) and colonize a bare or disturbed site. As these organisms die, soil is created.
- Growth in plants causes changes in the physical environment (e.g. light, moisture).
- New species of plants arrive that need soil to survive. They displace existing pioneer plants because their seedlings are better able to become established in the changed environment.
- The growth of roots enables soil to be retained and not washed away.
- Newly arriving species alter the physical conditions (e.g. increased shade; more minerals and nutrients in the soil as plants die and decay, and nitrogen-fixing plants arrive), allowing other species to become established.
- Animals come in with or after the plants they need for food.
- Eventually, a climax community that is more or less stable is established.
- Disturbances start the process of succession again.

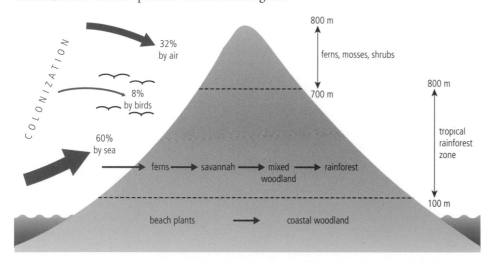

Soil depth, moisture and species diversity increase through the succession, reaching their maximum in the climax community (the last stage of the succession). Greater habitat diversity leads to greater species and genetic diversity.

When succession occurs in an area that already has soil it is called a **secondary succession**. Human activities, such as forest clearance (logging or burning), can cause this type of succession, providing no further disturbance occurs. Succession can be modified (i.e. halted at an early stage) through activities such as grazing, where climax species (e.g. trees) are not allowed to become established.

The set of communities that succeed one another over the course of succession at a given location is called a **sere**.

 A **sere** is the set of communities that succeed one another over the course of succession at a given location.

Disturbance

Three factors determine the ability of ecosystems to recover following disturbance:

- **inertia** (persistence) – resistance to being altered
- **resilience** – ability of a system to recover after a disturbance
- **diversity** – the number and proportions of species present.

Tropical rainforest has high diversity and inertia, but if it undergoes catastrophic disturbance through logging or fires it has low resilience (i.e. takes a long time to recover), whereas grasslands have low diversity and low inertia (i.e. they burn very easily) but are very resilient, because a lot of nutrients are stored below ground in root systems. So, after fire sweeps through, they can recover quickly.

Complex ecosystems such as rainforests have complex food webs which allow animals and plants many ways to respond to disturbance of the ecosystem and thus provide high inertia. They also contain long-lived species and dormant seeds and seedlings that promote inertia. Rainforests have low resilience because they have thin, low-nutrient soils. Nutrients are locked-up in decomposing plant matter on the surface and in rapidly-growing plants within the forest, so when the forest is disturbed, nutrients are quickly lost (the leaf layer and top soil is washed away). Ecosystems with high resilience have nutrient-rich soils which can promote new growth.

CASE STUDY

Disturbance of tall grass prairie

Tall grass prairie.

Tall grass prairie is a native ecosystem to central USA. High diversity, complex food webs and nutrient cycles in this ecosystem maintain stability. The grasses are between 1.5 and 2 m in height, with occasional stalks as high as 2.5 or 3 m. Due to the build up of organic matter, they have deep soils and recover quickly following periodic fires which sweep through them.

Prairie wheat farming.

North America wheat farming has replaced native ecosystems (e.g. tall grass prairie) with a monoculture (a one-species system). Such systems are prone to the outbreak of crop pests and damage by fire – low diversity and low inertia combined with soils that need to be maintained artificially with added nutrients lead to poor recovery following disturbance.

4.2 Evaluating biodiversity and vulnerability

Assessment statements

4.2.1 Identify factors that lead to loss of diversity.

4.2.2 Discuss the perceived vulnerability of tropical rainforests and their relative value in contributing to global biodiversity.

4.2.3 Discuss current estimates of numbers of species and past and present rates of species extinction.

4.2.4 Describe and explain the factors that may make species more or less prone to extinction.

4.2.5 Outline the factors used to determine a species' Red List conservation status.

4.2.6 Describe the case histories of three different species: one that has become extinct, another that is critically endangered, and a third species whose conservation status has been improved by intervention.

4.2.7 Describe the case history of a natural area of biological significance that is threatened by human activities.

Loss of diversity

Throughout the history of the Earth, diversity has never remained constant; there have been a number of natural periods of extinction and loss of diversity. More recently, humans have played an increasing role in diversity loss, especially in biodiverse ecosystems such as rainforests and coral reef.

Natural hazard events such as volcanoes, drought, ice ages, and meteor impact have lead to periods of loss of diversity. The eruption of Krakatau caused a dust plume that reduced sunlight over large areas of the globe, reducing surface temperatures. Changes in the Australian climate through tectonic movement and global warming have caused increased frequency of fires and a general drying of the continent that have lead to the prevalence of drought-tolerant species and the extinction of other species.

Changes in the orbit of the Earth and its tilt, plus tectonic movement, have lead to repeated long-term cold periods (Figure 4.11, overleaf), which have resulted in the selection of species adapted to the colder conditions and extinction of less-adapted species. One reason for the success of mammals is their ability to generate their own heat and control their temperature, which has enabled them to survive in colder environments.

● **Examiner's hint:**
Species and genetic diversity increase through a succession. This is the result of increased habitat diversity. Early succession establishes soils with increased nutrients, which can then be colonized by larger plants. When these die, the soils increase in depth and water content is retained. Competition between plants leads to the elimination of pioneer communities. Successful competitors tend to be larger, creating greater habitat complexity. The greater range of habitats lead to higher plant and animal diversity, as the number of niches increases.

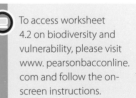

To access worksheet 4.2 on biodiversity and vulnerability, please visit www. pearsonbacconline. com and follow the on-screen instructions.

Figure 4.11

Variation in the temperature of the Earth taken using data from ice in the Antarctic. Major ice ages have occurred about every 100 000 years.

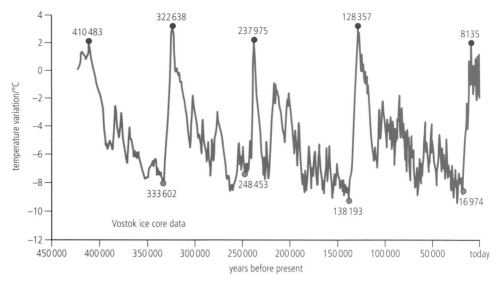

Vostok ice core data

Factors that lead to the loss of diversity include:

- natural hazards (e.g. volcanoes, drought, ice ages, meteor impact)
- habitat degradation, fragmentation and loss
- agricultural practices (e.g. monoculture, pesticide use, use of genetically modified (GM) species)
- introduction of non-native species
- pollution
- hunting, collecting and harvesting.

The rate of loss of biodiversity may vary from country to country depending on the ecosystems present, protection policies and monitoring, environmental viewpoints and the stage of economic development.

To learn more about preserving biodiversity for the future, go to www.pearsonhotlinks.com, insert the express code 2630P and click on activity 4.6.

Human-caused losses to diversity include habitat degradation, fragmentation and loss. Agricultural practices (e.g. introduction of monocultures, the use of pesticides and GM species) threaten native species, which are less able to compete with the introduced species. Monocultures represent a large loss of diversity compared to the native ecosystems they replace. However, increasing awareness of this has lead to the re-establishment of hedgerows and undisturbed corridors that encourage more natural communities to return. Non-specific pesticides can wipe out native as well as imported pest species, which again leads to an overall loss of diversity. If GM species are allowed to escape and reproduce in the wild, they might eventually eliminate less competitive native species.

Tropical rainforests

Tropical rainforests are characterized by long wet seasons and tall trees and plants that grow year-round. These forests presently cover 5.9 per cent of the Earth's land surface (around 1.5 per cent of the entire Earth's surface). In the tropics, the Sun shines at its brightest and for nearly the same number of hours every day of the year: this makes the climate warm and stable. Temperatures vary between 20 °C at night and 35 °C (maximum) during the day. Rainfall is high (sometimes 50 mm per hour, and up to 2500 mm a year). About 33 per cent of all rainforest is in the Amazon Basin, 20 per cent is found in Africa and a further 20 per cent in Indonesia. The remainder is scattered around the world. High levels of light and water make rainforests very productive. This explains why they can support such high biomass and wide diversity of life.

Rainforests are complex ecosystems with many layers: the tops of the tallest trees (up to 80 m) form the emergent layer; the canopy layer (45 m) contains the tops of most trees and gets about 80 per cent of the light; the next layer is the understory which gets 2–5 per cent of the light; the ground layer receives around 1 per cent of available solar energy. Most photosynthesis occurs in the upper layers, which have high levels of NPP (pages 52–54). The complex layered structure of rainforests enables them to support many different niches (i.e. many different ways of living). They are one of the two most species-rich and biodiverse ecosystems on Earth (coral reefs being the other). Despite their limited distribution, scientists believe that rainforests may contain half of all species on Earth, with many existing only in the canopy. Many are termed 'biodiversity hotspots' as they contain large numbers of species, often endemic to the area (not found anywhere else). Over 50 per cent of the world's plant species and 42 per cent of all terrestrial vertebrate species are endemic to 34 identified biodiversity hotspots (the majority of which are rainforests).

Tropical rainforests are under constant threat, and large areas are being lost: an average of 1.5 hectares (the size of a football pitch) are lost every four seconds. Deforestation and forest degradation are driven by external demands for timber, beef, soya and bio fuels – these demands lead to the destruction of trees for land. Developing 'carbon markets' – which value ecosystems as stores of carbon (in vegetation) – could provide the means to give sufficient monetary value to rainforests to help protect them. But many current programmes encourage continued conversion and degradation of forests and discourage their restoration and capacity to contribute to sustainable development.

Rainforests have thin, nutrient-poor soils – this has implications when forests are cleared (Chapter 2, page 38). Because there are not many nutrients in the soil, it is difficult for rainforests to re-grow once they have been cleared. Studies in Brazilian Atlantic forest have shown that certain aspects can return surprisingly quickly – within 65 years – but for the landscape to truly regain its native identity takes a lot longer – up to 4000 years. Recovery depends on the level of disturbance – a large area of cleared land will take a lot longer to grow back (if at all) than small areas which have been subject to shifting cultivation (Chapter 3, pages 143–44). Forest which has been selectively harvested for timber (only large trees have been removed) can grow back if not too much timber has been removed – a larger amount of timber removal may mean that the forest never fully recovers because fast-growing, light-loving species (such as vines and creepers) block out the light for slow growers so the forest remains at a sub-climax level.

Rainforest showing layered structure near Kuranda, Queensland, Australia.

Green politics

Green politics is a political ideology which places an importance on ecological and environmental goals, and on achieving these goals through broad-based, grassroots, participatory democracy. Green politics is advocated by supporters of the Green movement, which has been active through Green parties in many nations since the early 1980s. The Green movement was in part stimulated by the threats to rainforests. One of the principal aims is to obtain sustainable development by reducing deforestation and encouraging reforestation. Many politicians get involved because they know it is an important and popular topic for many voters; they hope to gain votes by working on improving the country's environmental impact. Anti-capitalism is a prominent feature of Green politics: it focuses on the way in which people are destroying nature for personal gain.

 Some species, such as tree frogs, spend all their time in the rainforest canopy; they never reach the forest floor, so are not commonly seen. *Rhacophorus gadingensis* was recently discovered in a remote forest reserve in the centre of the island of Borneo.

The newly discovered rainforest tree frog, *Rhacophorus gadingensis*.

Terry Erwin, a scientist from the Smithsonian Institute, collected beetles from the canopy in Panamanian rainforest and used these collections to estimate that there may be up to 30 million arthropod species on Earth – much higher than had previously been thought and now thought to be an overstimate. He used a harmless chemical fog to knock down insects in the canopy and collected them in large funnels on the ground.

 To learn more about loss of rainforest, go to www.pearsonhotlinks.com, insert the express code 2630P and click activities 4.7 and 4.8.

Present and past extinctions

The fossil record shows that over millions of years, there have been five **mass extinctions**, caused by natural physical (abiotic) phenomena. A mass extinction means that a large proportion of the total number of species on the Earth at the time are wiped out The Earth is currently undergoing a sixth mass extinction, caused by human activities (biotic factors).

Extinctions caused by abiotic phenomena

- The **Cretaceous–Tertiary** extinction occurred about 65 million years ago and was probably caused by the impact of a several-mile-wide asteroid that created a huge crater now hidden beneath the Gulf of Mexico. Other possible causes are gradual climate change and flood-like volcanic eruptions of basalt lava from India's Deccan Traps. The extinction killed 16 per cent of marine families, 47 per cent of marine genera and 18 per cent of land vertebrate families, including the dinosaurs.
- The **End Triassic** extinction occurred roughly 199 million to 214 million years ago and was most likely caused by massive floods of lava erupting from an opening in the Atlantic Ocean. 23 per cent of all families and 48 per cent of all genera went extinct.
- The **Permian–Triassic** extinction was the largest of these events, and occurred about 251 million years ago. It is suspected to have been caused by a comet or asteroid impact, although direct evidence has not been found. Others believe the cause was flood volcanism (as with the End Triassic extinction) from the Siberian Traps, which destroyed algae and plants, reducing oxygen levels in the sea. It wiped out 95 per cent of all species, 53 per cent of marine families, 84 per cent of marine genera and an estimated 70 per cent of land species such as plants, insects and vertebrate animals. In total, 57 per cent of all families and 83 per cent of all genera went extinct.
- The **Late Devonian** extinction occurred about 364 million years ago from an unknown cause. 19 per cent of all families and 50 per cent of all genera went extinct.
- The **Ordovician–Silurian** extinction, which occurred about 439 million years ago, was caused by a drop in sea levels as glaciers formed, then by rising sea levels as glaciers melted. 27 per cent of all families and 57 per cent of all genera became extinct.

The average time between these mass extinctions is around 100 million years. The exception is the gap between the Permian–Triassic and the End Triassic extinctions, which were approximately 50 million years apart.

The total number of species on Earth today remains poorly understood. The USA National Science Foundation estimates that there could be anywhere from 5 million to 100 million species on the planet, but science has only identified about 1.8 million. It is impossible to get an accurate count on the number of species, because the majority of the species that have yet to be discovered and described are in the realm of the very small: insects, and bacteria and other microbes.

Our current situation

In contrast to these abiotic causes for extinction, most scientists consider that the Earth is currently going a sixth mass extinction related to human (or biotic) causes. If this is the case, it is the first extinction event to have biotic, rather than abiotic causes. The difference between abiotic and biotic factors is important, and represents a significant shift in the cause of extinction (Figure 4.12).

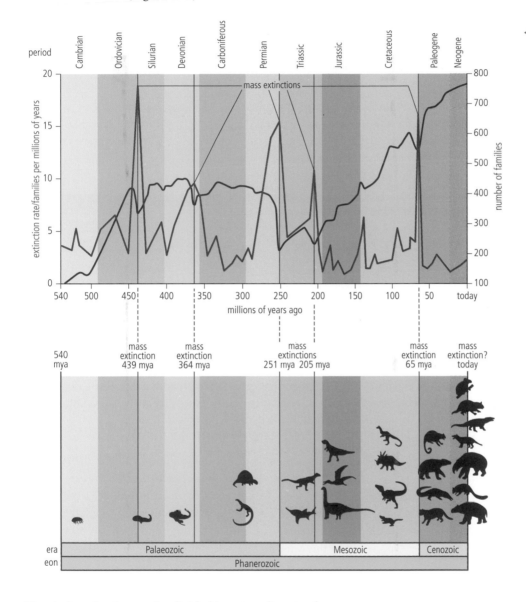

Figure 4.12
The evolution of life – and the six mass extinctions that have wiped out 99 per cent of all species that have ever existed on Earth.

● **Examiner's hint:**
Past extinctions occurred suddenly over relatively short time periods, caused by environmental catastrophes (e.g. meteorite strike, volcanic eruption and earthquakes). Animals and plants died from both the initial event and the short-term environmental turmoil that followed (e.g. climate change and planetary cooling that occurred following a meteor strike or massive volcanic eruption). The current mass extinction is happening at an even faster rate, which does not give species time to adapt to changing conditions.

The sixth extinction can be divided into two discrete phases:
● phase 1 began when the first modern humans began to disperse to different parts of the world about 100 000 years ago
● phase 2 began about 10 000 years ago when humans turned to agriculture.

The development of agriculture and the clearance of native ecosystems accelerated the pace of extinction. Over-population, invasive species, and over-exploitation are fuelling the extinction. Pollution and the advent of global warming (Chapter 6) are also accelerating changes to the planet and increasing extinction rates in species that cannot adapt to the changing conditions or migrate to new areas.

The background (natural) level of extinction known from the fossil record is between 10 and 100 species per year. Human activities have increased this rate. Estimates from tropical rainforest suggest the Earth is losing 27 000 species per year from those habitats alone. The rate of extinction differs for different groups of organisms, but examining the figures for one group (mammals) gives an indication of the extent of the problem.

Mammal species have an average species lifespan, from origin to extinction, of about 1 million years. There are about 5000 known mammalian species alive at present. Given the average mammalian species lifespan, the background extinction rate for this group should be approximately one species lost every 200 years. Yet the past 400 years have seen 89 mammalian extinctions, almost 45 times the predicted rate, and another 169 mammal species are listed as critically endangered.

Extinctions of the past took place over geological time (i.e. thousands or millions of years), thus allowing time for new species to evolve to fill the gaps left by the extinct species. Current changes to the planet are occurring much faster, over the period of human lifetimes. This does not allow time for species to adapt and change. Some scientists have predicted that 50 per cent of all species could be extinct by the end of the twenty-first century.

> We can never know for sure what has caused past extinctions. Scientists can only look at the fossil record and the geology of the Earth and draw conclusions from them. Does this lack of experimental evidence limit the validity of the conclusions drawn?

EXERCISES
1   List five factors that lead to the loss of diversity. How does each result in biodiversity loss?
2   Why is rainforest vulnerable to disturbance?
3   How many mass extinctions have there been in the past? What was the cause of these extinctions? How do they differ from the current mass extinction?
4   Why can scientists not be confident about the current estimations of species extinction?

Factors that make species prone to extinction

Not all species are equally prone to extinction. Certain animals and plants, through their ecology or behaviour, place themselves more at risk. Risk factors are discussed below.

> Certain factors make species more prone to extinction. These include:
> - small population size
> - limited distribution
> - high degree of specialization
> - low reproductive potential
> - non-competitive behaviour
> - high trophic level.

Small population size and limited distribution

This is especially true for island species – any change in habitat or a small dip in their population can eliminate them. Widespread and common species are less likely to be wiped out. For example, the slender-billed grackle (*Cassidix palustris*), a bird which once occupied a single marsh near Mexico City, was driven to extinction. Species with small populations also tend to have low genetic diversity – inability to adapt to changing conditions can prove fatal. Many of the large cat species are in this category (e.g. cheetah, snow leopard, and tiger).

Habitat specialists

These include organisms with a specific diet or habitat requirements: if their specific resource or habitat is put under threat, so are they. Some animals can live on only certain tree species, such as the palila bird (an Hawaiian honeycreeper), which is dependent on the mamane tree (*Sophora chrysophylla*) for its food and is therefore losing habitat as the mamane tree is cut down. Other examples include the giant panda (dependent on bamboo) and the koala (dependent on a particular eucalypt).

Low reproductive capacity

Species that live for a long time tend to have a low reproductive rate, which makes them vulnerable to extinction. If a change in habitat or the introduction of a predator occurs, the population drops and there are too few reproductive adults to support and maintain the population. Because they are slow-reproducing, any loss in numbers means a fast decline. The Steller's sea cow was heavily hunted and unable to replace its numbers fast enough.

Animals with long gestation times, for example elephants and rhinos, are also prone to low rates of reproduction, and it can take many years to recover from any reduction in population number.

Poor competitors

Flightless and slow-moving birds, such as the great auk, great elephant bird, and the dodo, are helpless under the pressures of hunting and predation. Lack of mobility and poor defensive instincts make them sitting targets. Animals that have evolved in the absence of predators (e.g. the dodo on Mauritius) are prone to extinction once a predator is introduced.

Large mammals

Because of they are a ready and significant source of meat, large animals are vulnerable to over-hunting (e.g. whales hunted with harpoons). Animals of large size also require large amounts of habitat and food: if their habitat is reduced or fragmented, these animals find it difficult to find sufficient food or space to survive. Most of the largest mammals on Earth are now endangered, including elephants, rhinoceros, many antelope species, and the large cats.

Most described species belong to groups that have been studied extensively in the past – these tend to be the larger organisms (e.g. mammals, birds, flowering plants). Scientists have also focussed on what they see as more appealing groups (e.g. those with fur or feathers). Smaller species which may be more difficult to identify and study are less well represented, including some of the most species-diverse groups on the planet (insects, spiders, bacteria, fungi, etc.). Estimations of current extinction rates are therefore based on very tenuous data. Does this matter?

Large mammals are prone to hunting practices and some species are threatened with extinction.

Valuable products

Wild animals and plants which have a value as food, pets, ceremonial objects or marketable products are at risk from humans. This includes animals valued as bushmeat (e.g. monkeys, forest antelope, chimpanzees, and gorillas) and hunted for markets in west and central Africa. Many bird species with elaborate and colourful plumage, such as the birds of paradise (page 181) and the Huia bird of New Zealand are hunted for their feathers.

Altruistic species

The passenger pigeon, dodo, Carolina parakeet and Steller's sea cow all developed **altruistic** tendencies that helped preserve bonds between animals and frightened off predators. However, when confronted with hunters with guns, animals which come to the aid of hunted mates are easily killed. Wolves, gorillas, whales and elephants, all refuse to leave their wounded companions and are often killed themselves.

Clumping

Species that require large numbers of their own kind for protection or to locate food are vulnerable to extinction. The passenger pigeon is an example; these birds could only survive among large numbers of their own species, flocking and seeking food sources. When numbers in the flocks reduced, they split up and the separated populations declined even further, eventually dying out.

Position in food chain

Top predators are sensitive to any disturbance in the food chain and any reduction in numbers of species at lower trophic levels can have disastrous consequence. Also, due to the '10 per cent rule' of energy loss through ecosystems (Chapter 2, pages 46–47), large fierce animals tend to be rare and are therefore particularly sensitive to hunters and reductions in population size.

Irrespective of human interference, any animal or plant which is rare, has a restricted distribution, has a highly specialized habitat or niche, or a low reproductive potential, or is at the top of the food chain, is prone to extinction

Determining conservation status

For more than four decades, the International Union for the Conservation of Nature (IUCN) has published documents called the *Red Data Books*. They assess the conservation status of a particular species in order to highlight species threatened with extinction, and to promote their conservation. The Red List is an inventory of all threatened species. The genetic diversity represented by the plants and animals in the Red List is an irreplaceable resource which the IUCN is looking to conserve through increased awareness. These species also represent key building blocks of ecosystems, and information on their conservation status provides the basis for making informed decisions about conserving biodiversity from local to global levels.

A range of factors are used to determine conservation status:
- population size
- reduction in population size
- numbers of mature individuals
- geographic range and degree of fragmentation
- quality of habitat
- area of occupancy
- probability of extinction.

The main purpose of the IUCN Red List is to highlight plants and animals facing a higher risk of global extinction than others. Various factors are used to determine the conservation status of a species, and a sliding scale operates (from severe threat to low risk). The range of factors used to determine conservation status includes:

- population size
- reduction in population size
- numbers of mature individuals
- geographic range and degree of fragmentation
- quality of habitat
- area of occupancy
- probability of extinction.

The photographs opposite show a range of species that are included on the Red List, and reasons for their inclusion.

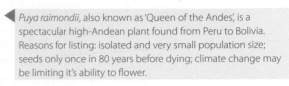

Puya raimondii, also known as 'Queen of the Andes', is a spectacular high-Andean plant found from Peru to Bolivia. Reasons for listing: isolated and very small population size; seeds only once in 80 years before dying; climate change may be limiting it's ability to flower.

The peacock parachute tarantula (*Poecilotheria metallica*) is known from a single location in the Eastern Ghats of Andhra Pradesh in India. Reasons for listing: restricted-range and habitat loss caused by logging for firewood and timber.

The European eel (*Anguilla anguilla*) is at an historical low in most of its range and it continues to decline. Reasons for listing: low population number caused by over-fishing; the introduction of a parasitic nematode which may affect the ability of eels to reach their spawning grounds; dam construction for hydropower has blocked migration routes.

The Indri (*Indri indri*) is a primate from Madagascar. Reasons for listing: loss of its rainforest habitat (to supply fuel and timber and to make way for slash-and-burn agriculture); greatly reduced population numbers (estimated to be a 50 per cent reduction over the last 36 years).

The fishing cat (*Prionailurus viverrinus*) is found in South-East Asian wetland areas where it is a skilful swimmer. Reasons for listing: loss of habitat (due to human settlement, draining of wetlands for agriculture, pollution, excessive hunting, wood-cutting); over-fishing leading to a reduction in fish stocks is likely to be a significant threat to this species as it relies heavily on fish for its survival.

Sometimes conservation actions come too late. Below are listed some extinct species and reasons for their extinction.

- Small habitat area (not enough area for species to survive) – Holdridge's toad, St Helena olive, Percy Island flying fox.
- Narrow geographic area – Golden toad.
- Poor competitor – Holdridge's toad (deaf and mute), dodo (cannot fly).
- Human intervention – Dodo (introduction of rats), thylacine (introduction of non-native species to Tasmania, e.g. dogs), desert rat kangaroo.
- Disease (the introduction of a non-native disease so no local immunity) – Darwin's Galapagos mouse.
- Hunting (over-hunting of species to extinction) – Bali tiger, passenger pigeon, thylacine, western black rhino, Queen of Sheba's gazelle, Madagascan pygmy hippo, Steller's sea cow.
- Shallow gene pool (little or no genetic variation so little chance to adapt to changing environment) – North elephant seal, saiga antelope.
- Coextinction (loss of one species causes extinction of another) – The bird lice found on passenger pigeons went extinct when their hosts did; the Hawaiian tree of the genus *Hibiscadelphus* went extinct as a consequence of the disappearance of the pollinator, the Hawaiian honeycreeper.

To learn more about the Encyclopaedia of Life, go to www.pearsonhotlinks. com, insert the express code 2630P and click on activity 4.9.

To learn more about the Red List, go to www. pearsonhotlinks.com, insert the express code 2630P and click on activity 4.10.

This topic raises some engaging issues of debate concerning the moral justification for exploiting species and the moral imperative for conserving them. Think carefully about the following questions (there are no correct answers).
- Do some organisms have more of a right to conservation than others? How can this be justified?
- Do pandas have a greater right to conservation than lichens?
- Do 'pests' or pathogenic organisms have a right to be conserved?
- To what extent are these arguments based on emotion and to what extent on reason? And how does this affect their validity?

Extinct, critical, and back from the brink

The Falkland Islands wolf. ▶

Extinct: Falkland Islands wolf

Description

The Falkland Islands wolf was the only native land mammal of the Falkland Islands. The islands were first sighted in 1692. In 1833, Charles Darwin visited the islands and described the wolf as 'common and tame'.

The genus name, *Dusicyon*, means 'foolish dog' in Greek (Dusi = foolish, cyon = dog).

Ecological role

The Falkland Islands wolf is said to have lived in burrows. As there were no native rodents on the islands (the usual prey), it is probable that its diet consisted of ground-nesting birds (such as geese and penguins), grubs, insects and some seashore scavenging.

Pressures

The many settlers of the Islands (mainly the Scottish inhabitants, but also the French and some English) considered the Falkland Islands wolf a threat to their sheep. A huge-scale operation of poisoning and shooting the dog began with the aim of pushing it into extinction. The operation was successful very rapidly, assisted by the lack of forests and the tameness of the animal (due to the absence of predators, the animal trusted humans who would lure it with a piece of meat and then kill it).

Consequences of disappearance

The Falkland Islands wolf was not particularly threatening nor was it a significant predator, although the removal of a top predator would have had an impact on the rest of the food chain.

● **Examiner's hint:**
You need to know the case histories of three different species: one that has become extinct, one that is critically endangered, and a third whose conservation status has been improved. You need to know:

● the ecological, socio-political and economic pressures that caused or are causing the species' extinction

● the species' ecological roles and the possible consequences of their disappearance.

CASE STUDY

Critically endangered: Iberian lynx

The Iberian lynx.

Description

The Iberian lynx (*Lynx pardinus*) is also known as the Spanish lynx and is native to the Iberian peninsula. It has distinctive, leopard-like spots with a coat that is often light grey or various shades of light brownish-yellow. It is smaller than its northern relatives such as the Eurasian lynx, and so typically hunts smaller-sized animals, usually no larger than hares. It also differs in habitat choice, inhabiting open scrub whereas the Eurasian lynx inhabits forests.

Ecological role

The Iberian lynx is a specialized feeder, and rabbits account for 80–100 per cent of its diet. Lynx often kill other carnivore species, including those regarded as pests by humans, such as feral cats and foxes, but do not eat them.

Pressures

The lynx's highly specialized diet makes it a naturally vulnerable species and the rapid decline in rabbit populations since the 1950s has had a direct impact on lynx numbers. The Iberian lynx occurs only in isolated pockets of Spain and possibly Portugal. Habitat destruction, deterioration and alteration have impacted negatively on the lynx for centuries. The Iberian lynx were protected against hunting in the early 1970s since when hunting has declined. Some lynxes are still shot and killed in traps and snares set for smaller predators, particularly on commercial hunting and shooting estates.

case study continued

Methods of restoring population

The Iberian lynx is fully protected under national law in Spain and Portugal, and public awareness and education programmes have helped to change attitudes towards the animal, particularly among private landowners. Two international seminars have been held (2002 and 2004) to establish a coordinated strategy to save the Iberian lynx from extinction. A captive breeding programme has been started in Spain. In Portugal, the National Action Plan foresees a re-introduction programme. The construction of facilities for breeding and reintroduction have been prepared. Further protection stems from the fact that one lynx's endemic areas has been turned into the Doñana National Park.

CASE STUDY

Improved by intervention: American bald eagle

The American bald eagle.

Description

The bald eagle (*Haliaeetus leucocephalus*), also known as the American eagle, was officially declared the National Emblem of the United States in 1782. It was selected by the USA's Founding Fathers because it is a species unique to North America and has since become the living symbol of the USA's spirit and freedom.

Bald eagles are one of the largest birds in North America with a wing span of 6–8 feet. Females tend to be larger than males. They live for up to 40 years in the wild, and longer in captivity. Bald eagles are monogamous and have one life partner.

Ecological role

Bald eagles live near large bodies of open water such as lakes, marshes, seacoasts and rivers. They nest and roost in tall trees. The eagles live in every US state except Hawaii. They use a specific territory for nesting, winter feeding or a year-round residence. Their natural domain is from Alaska to California, and from Maine to Florida. Bald eagles that reside in the northern USA and Canada migrate to the warmer southern areas during the winter to obtain easier access to food. Some bald eagles that reside in the southern states migrate slightly north during the hot summer months. They feed primarily on fish, but also eat small animals (ducks, coots, muskrats, turtles, rabbits, snakes, etc.) and occasional carrion.

Pressures

Bald eagle population numbers have been estimated to be 300 000 to 500 000 birds in the early 1700s. Their population fell to less than 10 000 nesting pairs by the 1950s, and to less than 500 pairs by the early 1960s. This population decline was caused by the mass shooting of eagles, the use of pesticides on crops, the destruction of habitat, and the contamination of waterways and food sources by a wide range of poisons and pollutants. For many years, the use of DTT pesticide on crops caused thinning of eagle egg shells, which often broke during incubation.

Methods of restoring population

The use of DDT pesticide was outlawed in the USA in 1972 and in Canada in 1973. This action contributed greatly to the return of the bald eagle.

The bald eagle was listed as endangered in most of the USA from 1967 to 1995, when it was slighted upgraded to threatened in the lower 48 states. The number of nesting pairs of bald eagles in the lower 48 states increased from less than 500 in the early 1960s to over 10 000 in 2007. That was enough to de-list them from threatened status on June 28, 2007.

Since de-listing, the primary law protecting bald eagles has shifted from the Endangered Species Act to the Bald and Golden Eagle Act. Although bald eagles have made an encouraging comeback throughout the USA since the early 1960s, they continue to be face hazards that must be closely monitored and controlled. Even though it is illegal, bald eagles are still harassed, injured and killed by guns, traps, power lines, windmills, poisons, contaminants and destruction of habitat.

A species first discovered in 1966 was recorded as extinct by the IUCN in 2004. The golden toad (*Incilius periglenes*) was a small, shiny, bright toad that was once common in a small region of high-altitude, cloud-covered tropical forests, about 30 square kilometres in area, above the city of Monteverde in Costa Rica. The last recorded sighting of the toad was in 1989. Possible reasons for its extinction include a restricted range, global warming, airborne pollution, increase in UV radiation, fungus or parasites, or lowered pH levels.

The golden toad.

A natural area of biological significance that is threatened

CASE STUDY

The Great Barrier Reef

Coral reef, like rainforest, is amazingly diverse (and for similar reasons – such as its location, complexity, and high productivity). The Great Barrier Reef stretches 2300 kilometres along the Queensland coastline of northern Australia. It is home to 1500 species of fish, 359 types of hard coral, a third of the world's soft corals, 6 of the world's 7 species of threatened marine turtle and more than 30 species of marine mammals including vulnerable dugongs (sea cows). In addition, there are 5000 to 8000 molluscs and thousands of different sponges, worms and crustaceans, 800 species of echinoderms (starfish, sea urchins) and 215 bird species, of which 29 are seabirds (e.g. reef herons, ospreys, pelicans, frigate birds and shearwaters).

There are many and varied threats to this ecosystem.

Human threats

Ecological, socio-political and economic pressures are causing the degradation of the coral reef, and as a consequence are threatening the biodiversity of the area. Tourism is now a major contributor to the local economy, but tourism can have negative impacts: coral is very fragile and is easily damaged by divers' fins. Although it is illegal to take pieces of coral from the country of origin, tourism inevitably leads to coral being damaged as tourists break bits off for souvenirs. As the sea is rich in fish, over-fishing can disrupt the balance of species in the food chain and there may also be inadvertent damage from anchors and pollution from boats. Seafloor trawling for prawns is still permitted in over half of the marine park, resulting in the unintentional capture of other species and also the destruction of the seafloor.

Case study continued

Land-use in Australia has shifted from low-level subsistence agriculture to large-scale farming. Queensland has extensive sugar plantations where once forests stood. The plantations need heavy input of fertilizers and pesticides, so now, run-off from the soils into the sea has caused inorganic nitrogen pollution to increase by 3000 per cent. Combined with sewage and pollution from coastal settlements such as Cairns, this means there are excessive nutrients in the water and algal blooms occur.

In addition, sedimentation (leading to mud pollution) has increased by 800 per cent due to deforestation of mangroves to make space for tourist developments, housing and farming. Traditionally, coastal wetland ecosystems provided a natural filter to sediment run-off. Extensive mangrove forests along the coast chiefly fulfilled this function, but clearance has caused serious mud pollution issues. Mud pollution makes the water cloudy and reduces coral reef productivity thus disrupting the interdependence of the coral ecosystem with sea-grass beds and mangrove ecosystems.

Socially, there is pressure to raise important revenues for the country through agriculture, which is backed-up politically at the national level. Increasing awareness of the effect of this agriculture on the environment is causing people to rethink their priorities.

Global warming (Chapter 6, page 269) is also affecting the reef. Increases in sea temperature have caused two mass coral bleaching events (plant and algal life on the reef dies, so the reef loses colour) in 1998 and 2002. Bleaching was more severe in 2002, when aerial surveys showed that almost 60 per cent of reefs were bleached to some degree. Increases in sea level and changes to sea temperatures may have a permanent effect on the Great Barrier Reef causing loss in biodiversity and ecological value of the area.

In addition, climate change may be causing some fish species to move away from the reef to seek waters which have their preferred temperature. This leads to increased mortality in seabirds that prey on the fish. The available habitat for sea turtles will also be affected, causing reduction in population numbers.

Natural threats

All the human impacts have knock-on effects and thereby make the coral even more vulnerable to natural threats such as disease and natural predators. One such predator is the crown-of-thorns starfish which preys on the animals (coral polyps – Figure 2.9, page 23) that form the coral reef. The starfish climbs onto the reef and extrudes its stomach over the coral, releasing digestive enzymes that digest the polyps so they can be absorbed. One adult starfish can destroy six metres of coral in a year. Outbreaks of these starfish are thought to be natural, but the frequency and size of outbreaks has increased due to human activity. Reduction in water quality enables the starfish larvae to thrive, and unintentional over-fishing of natural predators (e.g. the giant triton, a large aquatic snail) is believed to have caused increase in starfish numbers.

Crown-of-thorns starfish – one of the threats to the Great Barrier Reef.

Structural damage can be done to the coral by storms and cyclones. Another key atmospheric effect, linked to changes in sea water temperature, is El Niño. In this regular event, fluctuations in the surface waters of the tropical eastern Pacific Ocean lead to increases in sea temperature across the east–central and eastern Pacific Ocean area, including Australia. Increased sea temperature, as we have already seen, can lead to coral bleaching – this has knock-on effects on the fish species that depend on the reef for food and protection, and for nurseries for their young.

Consequences

Coral reefs are able to withstand some threats, but the current combined effect of human and natural processes can lead to irreversible damage to the reef, and the species that depend on it. In turn, these effects can lead to the breakdown of the reef ecosystem. When a 'critical threshold' is reached, the problems may well become irreversible and the ecosystem will not recover even if the threats stop. Loss of biodiversity and the valuable role that the ecosystem provides (e.g. in conjunction with mangroves and sea-grass beds as a line of coastal defence against erosion and sediment run-off) will inevitably lead to a reduction in its value as an economic resource.

The Great Barrier Reef Marine Park is 345 000 km^2: larger than the entire area of the UK and Ireland combined. The reef is the world's biggest single structure made by living organisms and is large enough to be seen from space.

The Great Barrier Reef is an important part of the Aboriginal Australian culture and spirituality. It is also a very popular destination for tourists, especially in the Cairns region, where it is economically significant. Fishing also occurs in the region, generating AU\$ 1 billion per year.

The Great Barrier Reef.

The United Nations Educational, Scientific and Cultural Organization (UNESCO) encourages the protection and preservation of cultural and natural heritage sites considered to be of outstanding value to humanity. There are 679 cultural and 174 natural World Heritage sites so far listed, including the Great Barrier Reef, Yosemite National Park and the Galapagos Islands.

EXERCISES

1   List five factors that make some species more prone to extinction.

2   What factors are used to determine a species' Red List status? List five.

3   Which types of species are common in the Red List, and which are less common? What implication does this have for the conservation of biodiversity?

4   Summarize the case history of three different species: one that is extinct, one that is critically endangered, and a third species whose conservation status has been improved by intervention. For each, list the ecological, socio-political and economic pressures that are involved, and outline the possible consequences of their disappearance on the ecosystem.

5   Describe a local example of a natural area of biological significance that is threatened by human activities. List the ecological, socio-political and economic pressures that caused or are causing the degradation of the area, and outline the possible impacts on biodiversity.

● **Examiner's hint:**
You need to know the case history of a natural area of biological significance that is threatened by human activities. You need to know:
● the ecological, socio-political and economic pressures that caused or are causing the degradation of the chosen area
● the consequent threat to biodiversity.

4.3   Conservation of biodiversity

Assessment statements
4.3.1   State the arguments for preserving species and habitats.
4.3.2   Compare and contrast the role and activities of intergovernmental and non-governmental organizations in preserving and restoring ecosystems and biodiversity.
4.3.3   State and explain the criteria used to design protected areas.
4.3.4   Evaluate the success of a named protected area.
4.3.5   Discuss and evaluate the strengths and weaknesses of the species-based approach to conservation.

Rainforest canopy near Kuranda, Queensland, Australia.

Figure 4.13
The biological significance of a forest.

Forest people are found in rainforests in Brazil, Colombia, Paraguay, Canada, Peru, Argentina, Botswana, Kenya, Ethiopia, Sudan, Central Africa, Australia, Indonesia, the Philippines, India, Bangladesh, Russia, Malaysia and Sri Lanka. The majority are under threat from logging and rainforest loss, for example the Awá tribe in Brazil. The Awá's territory has been invaded and destroyed. Cattle ranchers illegally occupy Awá land and, in another part of their territory, groups of heavily armed loggers have destroyed much of the forest.

Arguments for preserving species and habitats

Valuing rainforest

The value of biodiversity can be difficult to quantify. Goods harvested from an ecosystem are easier to evaluate than indirect values such as the aesthetic or cultural aspects of an ecosystem. For example, it is easy to value rainforest in terms of amount of timber present because this has direct monetary value. But intact rainforests also provide invaluable ecosystem services for the local, national and global communities (Figure 4.13). Rainforests are vital to the hydrologic (water) cycle, stabilize some of the world's most fragile soils by preventing soil erosion, and are responsible for regulating temperature and weather patterns in the areas surrounding the forest. In addition, they sequester (isolate) and store huge amounts of carbon from the atmosphere. They cool and clean the world's atmosphere. They are a huge source of the world's biodiversity, and they provide fresh water (the Amazon provides 20 per cent of the world's fresh water).

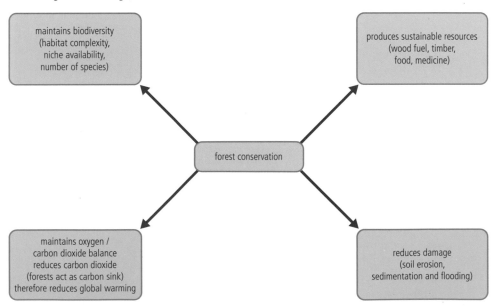

- maintains biodiversity (habitat complexity, niche availability, number of species)
- produces sustainable resources (wood fuel, timber, food, medicine)
- forest conservation
- maintains oxygen / carbon dioxide balance reduces carbon dioxide (forests act as carbon sink) therefore reduces global warming
- reduces damage (soil erosion, sedimentation and flooding)

Most of these benefits are difficult to give monetary value to: every person on the planet benefits from these services, but none of us pay for them. Intact rainforests are aesthetically pleasing and this makes people want to visit them, which gives rainforest value from an eco-tourism point of view. As rainforests house such a high percentage of the existing global biodiversity, it can also be argued that we have an ethical responsibility to conserve them.

The value of ecosystems depend on cultural background as well as economic status. The value of a rainforest to someone who lives in and relies on it for their livelihood is very different from an outsider who does not have these concerns.

Economic values of biodiversity

As we have already seen, biodiversity can be valued on ethical, aesthetic, genetic resource and commercial considerations, as well as in terms of life-support and ecosystem-support functions. Some aspects of biodiversity are easy to give monetary value to; but for others, this is less easy.

It is easy to give economic value to the following.
- Natural products such as timber and medicines.
- Food such as wheat, rice and maize – all are derived from wild plants. Preservation of biodiversity within key ecosystems should retain sufficient genetic and species diversity for each of these staple foods (basic dietary components). This may prove invaluable in the future if pests and diseases overcome present agricultural strains.

It is difficult to give economic value to a larger range of features.
- Ecosystem productivity – The function of ecosystems depends on many different interacting biological components. Insects are needed for pollination, decomposers and detritivores (e.g. bacteria, fungi and worms) for soil aeration and fertility, and mammals and birds for seed dispersal. Ecosystems contain plants which remove carbon dioxide from the air, provide oxygen and to help regulate the climate. Ecosystems are at their most stable, and least prone to disturbance from external factors, when they contain the largest number of native species.
- Environmental indicators – Changes to certain indicator species may show effects of disturbance or other changes to an ecosystem.
- Scientific reasons – The number of species on Earth and their interactions are still poorly understood. When areas of biodiversity are lost before they can be studied, irreversible damage is done to scientific knowledge.
- Education – Naturally occurring biodiversity represents a huge wealth of information that can be incorporated into educational programmes.
- Genetic diversity – All species on Earth are a potential source of valuable genes for genetic engineering and genetic enhancement. Once a species is lost, so is its genetic inheritance.
- Recreation and ecotourism – Areas such as the Great Barrier Reef provide significant revenue for the local economy.
- Aesthetic value – The pleasure derived from an undisturbed ecosystem.
- Human rights – Preservation of rainforests means that indigenous people can continue to live in them.
- Ethical reasons – Each species on Earth has a right to exist. Humans, as the dominant form of life, have a responsibility to protect the widest range of biodiversity as possible.

▲ Iban woman with baby near her home.

The Iban are an indigenous people of Sarawak (Malaysia), Brunei and western Kalimantan (Indonesian Borneo). Traditionally, they live in communal longhouses, hunting and fishing in rainforest areas, and growing crops using shifting cultivation. Pulp and paper companies have cleared Iban land and planted acacia trees, and other areas have been cleared for oil palm. The Iban have appealed against the loss of their traditional lands, although these rights have so far been denied as courts decided that land-ownership based on continuous occupation should 'not be extended to areas where the natives used to roam to forage for their livelihood in accordance with their tradition'.

To learn more about Survival International, go to www.pearsonhotlinks.com, insert the express code 2630P and click on activity 4.11.

To learn more about Forests Now, go to www.pearsonhotlinks.com, insert the express code 2630P and click on activity 4.12.

To access worksheet 4.3 on the future of rainforests, please visit www.pearsonbacconline.com and follow the on-screen instructions.

ENVIRONMENTAL PHILOSOPHIES

▲ Nomadic Penan hunting with blowpipe.

The Penan of Borneo are nomadic hunter–gatherers who have historically relied on the rainforests for their survival. They have a comprehensive knowledge of the forest and are highly skilled in surviving there (e.g. a poison-headed dart from a blowpipe can strike an animal high in the upper canopy 40 m above them).

Forest peoples' views of rainforest differ from the views of people from developed countries. To forest people, the forest is their home, from which they derive food, medicine and their cultural values. Economically developed countries see the rainforest as an opportunity to cash in on natural resources and land on which to build. To forest people, losing the forest is losing their home, their source of food, and the destruction of their culture which has developed through generations of forest living.

EXERCISES

1   In which countries are indigenous rainforest peoples found?

2   Are there tribes which have not yet been contacted?

3   What are the threats to these people?

4   Do these peoples' views of rainforest differ from ours?

5   Do these peoples' views of the value of the rainforest differ from ours?

6   What environmental services do rainforests provide?

7   What other reasons may there be for conserving rainforest?

Conservation organizations

As individuals, we all have concerns about the state of the world in which we live, although it is often difficult to make your voice heard by those who influence global policies (e.g. national governments). Combined voices are more effective and conservation organizations that work at both local and global levels are good at campaigning on key environmental issues such as climate change and the preservation of biodiversity.

Non-governmental organizations (**NGOs**) are not run by, funded by, or influenced by governments of any country (e.g. Greenpeace and the World Wide Fund for Nature, WWF). **Intergovernmental Organizations** (**GOs**) are bodies established through international agreements to protect the environment and bring together governments to work together on an international scale (e.g. United Nations Environment Programme (UNEP), International Union for Conservation of Nature (IUCN), and European Environment Agency (EEA)).

Each type of organization has its own strengths and weaknesses (Table 4.1). GOs tend to be more conservative (i.e. have a more conventional approach to conservation and are not likely to be controversial) whereas NGOs tend to be more radical (and often have to be to get their message across and to be heard). NGOs also tend to be field-based, gathering information to back up their arguments, whereas GOs tend to gather information from scientific research which they pay for (Figure 4.14).

TABLE 4.1 COMPARISON OF THE STRENGTHS AND WEAKNESSES OF GOs AND NGOs		
	GOs (e.g. UNEP)	NGOs (e.g. WWF, Greenpeace)
Use of media	• Professional media liaison officers prepare statements. • International news clips and informative videos released.	• Advertise on popular channels, using footage of own protest activities. • Leaflets and events such as 'Earth Hour'. • Produce press packs.
Speed of response	• Fairly slow – many counties are involved in reaching a consensus. • Must meet legal requirements in many countries.	• Can be rapid and regular. Organizations are independent and can make own decisions.
Diplomatic constraints	• Cannot give opinion without consulting lawyers and other countries because they represent many nations. • International disagreements can cause serious constraints.	• Relations are with international non-profit-making companies and generally unaffected by politics. • Activities may be illegal although this is generally discouraged.
Political influence	• Great – direct access to the governments of many countries.	• No direct political influence but Green politics may establish environmental concerns as part of the political process.
Enforceability	• Through international agreements and laws (e.g. UNEP can pass laws within Europe to address environmental issues).	• Rely on public pressure rather than legal power to influence governments; no power to enforce laws.

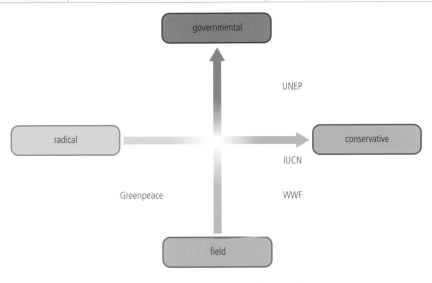

Figure 4.14
Different niches for different conservation organizations: GOs and NGOs.

International conventions on biodiversity

The IUCN (aka World Conservation Union) was founded in 1948. It is concerned with the importance of conservation of resources for sustainable economic development. The IUCN has three agenda:

- maintaining ecological processes
- preserving genetic diversity
- using species and ecosystems in a sustainable fashion.

In 1980, the IUCN established the World Conservation Strategy (WCS) along with UNEP and WWF. The WCS outlined a series of global priorities for action and recommended that each country prepare its own national strategy as a developing plan that would take into account the conservation of natural resources for long-term human welfare. The strategy also drew attention to a fundamental issue: the importance of making the users of natural resources become their guardians. It stressed that without the support and understanding of the local community, whose lives are most closely dependent on the careful management of natural resources, the strategies cannot succeed.

To access worksheet 4.4 on the roles of conservation organizations, please visit www.pearsonbacconline.com and follow the on-screen instructions.

History of the IUCN

- **1948** – Foundation of the organization, named International Union for the Protection of Nature (IUPN).
- **1949** – Main focus on protecting habitats and species from the exploitative tendencies of humans.
- **1956** – IUPN seen as too preservationist; changed its name to the International Union for the Conservation of Nature and Natural Resources.
- **1961** – Lack of funds led to the establishment of an independent fund-raising organization, WWF, to raise funds and support IUCN.
- **1966** – Species Survival Commission published Red Data Lists to provide detailed information on status, distribution, breeding rate, causes of decline, and proposed protective measures for all endangered species.
- **1967** – UN List of National Parks and Equivalent Reserves produced (gives definitions and classification of types of protected areas; regularly updated and revised).
- **1973** – Convention on the International Trade of Endangered Species of Wild Fauna and Flora (CITES) established.
- **1980** – World Conservation Strategy (WCS) published.
- **1991** – Update of the WCS *Caring for the Earth: A Strategy for Sustainable Living* launched in 65 countries. Stated the benefits of sustainable use of natural resources, and the benefits of a sharing resources more equally among the world population.
- **1992** – Global Biodiversity Strategy. The aim of the strategy was to aid countries integrate biodiversity into their national planning. Three main objectives:
  – conservation of biological variation
  – sustainable use of its components
  – equitable sharing of the benefits arising out of the utilization of genetic resources.

World Conservation Strategy (WCS) has as its main objectives:
- maintain ecological processes or life-support systems
- preserve genetic diversity
- ensure sustainable utilization of species and ecosystems.

Global and local approaches to environmental problem-solving

Some environmental problems are global, so it makes sense that international cooperation is used in addressing them. For example, global warming will have far-reaching global impacts so a united response to monitoring and mitigation is more likely to be effective. International agreements can help to motivate governments to take action and honour their commitments (e.g. to cut carbon dioxide emissions – such action was taken at the Montreal protocol). As an international organization, UNEP has the resources to mobilize and coordinate action (e.g. environmental research) when individual nations, especially LEDCs, might not have access to funds or expertise. When problems cross borders (e.g. smuggling endangered species), international cooperation is vital; this is what led to establishment of CITES.

When planning conservation strategies, certain arguments are likely to be more influential than others. The more important arguments concern socio-economics, genetic resources, and ecology because these factors are more easily quantified. They are more universally agreed by people with different environmental paradigms, and different ethical or aesthetic arguments. Most influential nations, including those involved in drawing up the WCS, attach more value to scientific validity than to other forms of argument.

On the other hand, problems are often local, so local people should be involved in providing a local solution. This is recognized by the WCS. The motivation for addressing problems often starts at local level, when individuals feel passionately about an issue. Issues such as recycling and landfill are local ones, so a global strategy would be cumbersome, bureaucratic and inappropriate.

Global summits have shaped attitudes towards sustainability. The UN Conference on Human Environment (Stockholm, 1972) was the first meeting of the international community to consider global environment and development needs (Chapter 3, page 104). Summits play a pivotal role in setting targets and shaping action at both an international and local level. In 1992, the UN Rio Earth summit led to **Agenda 21** and the Rio declaration (Chapter 3, page 105). The 2000 UN Millennium Summit agreed a set of Millennium Development Goals (MDGs) (Chapter 3, page 167). The subsequent World Summit in New

York, USA, recommended that each country developed its own strategy for fulfilling the MDGs. Other summits have led to legally binding conventions on climate change such as those agreed in Montreal (1987). However, should countries break these agreements, there is little the international community can do about it.

Even when summits do not achieve their initial goals, they may act as a catalyst in changing the attitudes of governments, organizations and individuals.

Media are also important in shaping public opinion. In 1963, an American environmentalist, Rachel Carson, published *Silent Spring* – a book that was pivotal in changing people's attitudes to the use of pesticides in agriculture (Chapter 5, page 228; Chapter 7, pages 289–90). In 1987, the UN commissioned the Brundtland Report, *Our Common Future*, which established the initial definition for sustainable development (Chapter 3, page 103).

Designing a protected area

Conservation areas are often isolated and in danger of becoming islands within a sea of disturbance (often cleared habitat). 'Island Biogeography' theory was developed in the 1960s by Robert MacArthur and Edward Wilson. They showed that smaller conservation areas contain comparatively fewer species and lower diversity than larger areas. Ever since, reserve designers have been using these ideas to ensure maximum preservation of species within conservation areas. Size, shape, impact of changed environmental conditions at the edge of the reserves (**edge effects**), and whether or not reserves are linked by corridors, are all taken into account when designing reserves (Figure 4.15).

To learn more about the IUCN, WWF, Greenpeace and Friends of the Earth International, go to www.pearsonhotlinks.com, insert the express code 2630P and click on activities 4.13, 4.14, 4.15 and 4.16.

To learn more about halting extinctions among birds, go to www.pearsonhotlinks.com, insert the express code 2630P and click on activity 4.17.

To access worksheet 4.5 on designing a conservation area, please visit www.pearsonbacconline.com and follow the on-screen instructions.

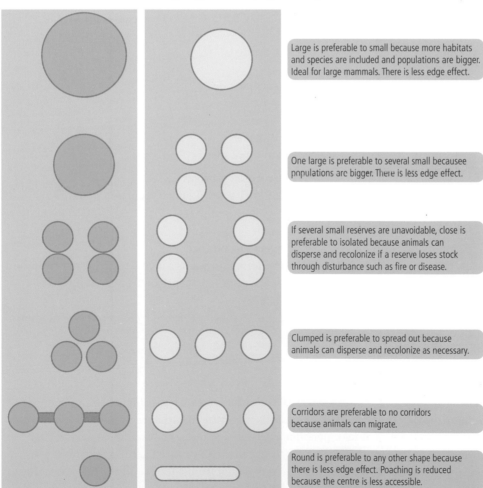

Large is preferable to small because more habitats and species are included and populations are bigger. Ideal for large mammals. There is less edge effect.

One large is preferable to several small because populations are bigger. There is less edge effect.

If several small reserves are unavoidable, close is preferable to isolated because animals can disperse and recolonize if a reserve loses stock through disturbance such as fire or disease.

Clumped is preferable to spread out because animals can disperse and recolonize as necessary.

Corridors are preferable to no corridors because animals can migrate.

Round is preferable to any other shape because there is less edge effect. Poaching is reduced because the centre is less accessible.

Figure 4.15
The shape, size and connectivity of reserves are important in the design of protected areas.

Area

One of the great debates in reserve design is known as SLOSS (single large or several small): Is it better to have one large reserve (say, 10 000 ha) or several smaller ones (say, four at 2500 ha)? Much depends on location of the habitats – if habitats to be preserved are not all found reasonably close together, then several small reserves may be necessary. But overall, bigger is better because one large area can support more species than several smaller areas (they have more habitats and can support more top carnivores). The best indicator of species survival and success of the reserve's size is the population size of individual species. In an ideal situation, several large reserves would allow the protected habitats to be replicated thus guarding against the possible effects of fire or a disease which could lead to the extinction of species contained within the affected reserve.

Edge effects

At the edge of a protected area, there is a change in abiotic factors (e.g. more wind, or warmer and less humid conditions compared to the interior of the reserve). These edge effects will attract species that are not found deeper in the reserve, and may also attract exotic species from outside the reserve.

Shape

The best shape for a reserve is a circle because this has the lowest edge effects. Long thin reserves have large edge effects. In practice, the shape is determined by what is available and where the habitats to be conserved are located. Parks tend to be irregular shapes.

Corridors

The benefits of linking reserves by corridors include:
- allowing gene flow – immigration/emigration
- allowing seasonal movements
- reducing collisions between cars and animals
- reducing roads which act as a barrier to some species.

The disadvantages of linking reserves by corridors include:
- some species breeding outside the protected area leading to reduction in numbers (out-breeding depression)
- invasion of exotic pests or disease
- poachers can easily move from one reserve to another
- corridors may be narrow (30–200 m wide) – this means a big increase in edge conditions rendering the corridors unsuitable for the dispersal of species from the centre of reserves, which normally avoid edge habitat
- corridors becoming barriers to some species when protected by fences or obstructions (designed, for example, to deter poachers).

● **Examiner's hint:**
Well-designed conservation areas:

- large size promotes large population sizes and high biodiversity; enables protection of large vertebrates/top carnivores; has smaller perimeter relative to size, so edge effects and disturbance are minimized
- unfragmented and connected to other reserves (by corridors) to allow movement and migration between reserves; not have roads that act as a barrier to migration and increase disturbance and edge effects.

Buffer zone

Areas around conservation areas are called **buffer zones**. They contain habitats and may be either managed or undisturbed. These areas minimize disturbance from outside influences such as people, agriculture or invasion by diseases or pests. For example, a nearby large town or extensive disturbance (e.g. logging) can directly impact a protected area if it is not surrounded by an area that buffers (protects) it from effects of the disturbance. Most successful protected areas are surrounded by buffer zones.

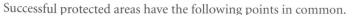

Successful protected areas have the following points in common.

- They are all currently being partially or completely funded and run by the government.
- They all have education programmes to inform the local people of the situation and of possible solutions.
- They all attract many visitors (but numbers are controlled to stop disturbance).
- They all have management programmes (are actively looked after and not just left to develop).
- They often have high profile animals (e.g. royal Bengal tigers in Nepal, giant pandas in China, black bears in the USA, orang-utans in Borneo, marsupials in Australia).

Why is it easier to protect an area if there is a well-known mammal in it?

- People want to see animals (usually mammals) that are familiar and spectacular (e.g. lions, bears, pandas, tigers as shown on TV and in the media)
- The behaviour and appearance of these animals are interesting to watch and study.
- The size and risk factors of these animals are attractive aspects.
- Mammals are closer relatives to humans than other animals, so we relate more to them.
- People are brought up learning about big mammals but rarely get to see them.

▲ Orang-utans are found on the islands of Borneo and Sumatra. They are high-profile animals and are used to promote the conservation of rainforest.

ENVIRONMENTAL PHILOSOPHIES

Some people see GOs as offering the best way to preserve and restore biodiversity, because solid agreements can be reached and laws passed. Others see governmental processes as taking too long to reach concrete results, and prefer to act within NGOs which offer greater freedom to promote individual agendas and produce direct results. Individual worldviews influence which path is taken.

Evaluating the success of a protected area

CASE STUDY

Danum Valley Conservation Area, Malaysian Borneo

Granting protected status to a species or ecosystem is no guarantee of protection without community support, adequate funding and proper research. In north eastern Borneo, the third largest island in the world, a large area of commercial forest owned by the Sabah Foundation (also known as Yayasan Sabah) is a model of how effective conservation can be matched with local economic needs.

The Yayasan Sabah Forest Management Area (YSFMA) is an extensive area of commercial hardwood forest containing within it protected areas of undisturbed forest, areas that are being rehabilitated with 'enrichment planting' (adding seedlings to heavily disturbed logged forest), and areas of commercial softwood forestry. Research of the primary rainforest within the Danum Valley Conservation Area (DVCA) has established the biological importance of the native forest and acted as a beacon for conservation in the region. DVCA covers 43 800 hectares, comprising almost entirely lowland dipterocarp forest (dipterocarps are valuable hardwood trees). The DVCA is the largest expanse of pristine forest of this type remaining in Sabah.

Until the late 1980s, the area was under threat from commercial logging. The establishment of a long-term research programme between Yayasan Sabah and the Royal Society in the UK (the oldest scientific body in the world) has created local awareness of the conservation value of the area and provided important scientific information about the forest and what happens to it when it is disturbed through logging. Danum Valley is controlled by a management committee containing all the relevant local institutions – wildlife, forestry and commercial sectors are all represented.

Case study continued

Two other conservation areas, the Maliau Basin and Imbak Canyon, are linked by commercial forest which form corridors between all areas. To the east of DVCA is the 30 000 hectare Innoprise-FACE Foundation Rainforest Rehabilitation Project (INFAPRO), one of the largest forest rehabilitation projects in South-East Asia, which is replanting areas of heavily disturbed logged forest. The Innoprise-IKEA project (INIKEA) to the west of DVCA, is a similar rehabilitation project (Figure 4.16).

Figure 4.16
Location of conservation areas, rehabilitation projects and commercial softwood forestry within YSFMA. The combined network of different types of forest has enabled effective conservation of animals and plants important to the region.

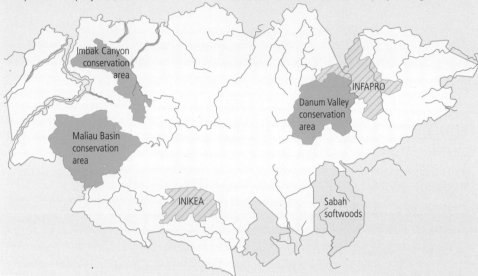

Because all areas of conservation and replantation are embedded within the larger commercial forest, the value of the whole area is greatly enhanced. Movement of animals between forest areas is enabled and allows the continued survival of some important and endangered Borneo animals such as the Sumatran rhino, the orang-utan and the Borneo elephant.

In the late 1990s, a hotel was established on the north-eastern edge of the DVCA. It has established flourishing ecotourism in the area and exposed the unique forest to a wider range of visitors than was previously possible. As well as raising revenue for the local area, it has raised the international profile of the area as an important centre for conservation and research.

Such projects require significant funding which has come from Yayasan Sabah (a state foundation funded by the Sabah Government and Federal Government of Malaysia) and companies such as Malaysia's Petra Foundation, Shell, BP, the Royal Society and others. The now high international profile of the Danum Valley, and key research over a long period of time (the programme is now the longest running in South-East Asia), have helped to establish the area as one of the most important conservation areas in region if not the world. Support from the local community in running the various facilities on site and in local towns, and much interest from nature groups in schools, have also been important to the success of the project.

Danum Valley Field Centre. Research at the centre focuses on local primary forest ecology as well as the effect of logging on rainforest structure and communities.

The DVCA contains more than 120 mammal species including 10 species of primate. The DVCA and surrounding forest is an important reservation for orang-utan, due in part to minimal hunting pressure. These forests are particularly rich in other large mammals including the Asian elephant, Malayan sun bear, clouded leopard, bearded pig and several species of deer. The area also provides one of the last refuges in Sabah for the critically endangered Sumatran rhino. Over 340 species of bird have been recorded at Danum, including the argus pheasant, Bulwer's pheasant, and seven species of pitta bird. Higher plants include more than 1300 species in 562 genera of 139 families, representing 15 per cent of the species recorded for Sabah.

● **Examiner's hint:**
Successful protected areas have:
- partial or complete funding by the government
- involvement of governmental agencies
- educational programmes
- local support
- management programmes
- high-profile animals to attract visitors
- scientific research programmes.

ENVIRONMENTAL PHILOSOPHIES

The value of protected areas varies according to the viewpoint of the people who use it. An area of rainforest, to people from MEDCs, may be appreciated as a tourist destination for its aesthetic and intrinsic value. Locals see it as a source of revenue.

Strengths and weaknesses of the species-based approach to conservation

The Convention on International Trade in Endangered Species of Wild Fauna and Flora (**CITES**) is an international agreement between governments that aims to ensure international trade in wild animals and plants does not threaten their survival. This trade is worth billions of dollars every year and involves hundreds of millions of plant and animal specimens. Trade in animal and plant specimens and parts plus factors such as habitat loss can seriously reduce their wild populations and bring some species close to extinction. CITES came into force on 1 July 1975 and is voluntary in membership. Each member country must adopt legislation to implement CITES at the national level.

All import, export, re-export or introduction of specimens or parts and derivatives of any species covered by CITES has to be authorized through a licensing system. Permits must be obtained. International trade in species listed by CITES and threatened with extinction is only permitted in exceptional circumstances. The scheme has its limitations: it is voluntary and countries can opt out; penalties may not necessarily match the gravity of the crime or be sufficient deterrent to wildlife smugglers. However, taken overall, CITES has been responsible for deterring the international trade in endangered animals and plants.

 To evaluate the strengths and weaknesses of the species-based approach to conservation, consider the relative strengths and weaknesses of:
- CITES
- captive breeding and reintroduction programmes
- zoos
- aesthetic versus ecological values.

The role of zoos in conservation

Zoos have become increasingly focussed on conservation and many now lead the way in the preservation of species threatened with extinction. In prioritizing areas for conservation, zoos have to answer many crucial questions discussed below.

How to select what to conserve?
- What is the level of threat? It is better to conserve endangered animals than ones that are not endangered.
- What to focus on? Different zoos have different expertise and areas of influence; they focus on their particular strengths.
- Can the zoo afford to financially support the project in the long term?
- If the zoo is helping to save a species where it is found, the location is important – zoos tend to focus on developing countries rather than developed countries (which can help themselves).
- How involved are other organizations? If large organizations are already involved, it may be better to focus on projects struggling for funds.

 Threats to species include:
- trade in souvenirs (body parts, fragments of coral reef, etc.)
- fashion (furs for coats, hats, etc.)
- bush-meat (eating animals, trading meat)
- habitat loss (land clearance, pollution, fragmentation)
- exotic pet trade
- medicine (traditional therapies using body parts)
- competition (with introduced species).

In situ conservation involves preserving the local habitat where the animal is found.

Ex situ conservation is preserving the species in a zoo.

In situ or ex situ conservation?

- How big is the animal? Smaller ones are easier to keep in zoos.
- Avoid species that are threatened for natural reasons (natural ecology) such as those threatened by natural predation.
- Species facing habitat loss need to be conserved ex situ (e.g. Livingstone fruit bat – where 90 per cent of the habitat was lost due to cyclone damage).
- Animals threatened by diseases need to be kept ex situ (e.g. amphibian species are currently under threat globally from a fungus which is wiping them out in the wild).
- Which projects are undertaken will be influenced by staff expertise and whether or not the zoo vet has the knowledge to look after the species.
- If local people are willing to help, in situ conservation may be appropriate. If there are local political problems, ex situ may be preferred.
- Zoos often use species that are attractive to the public (e.g. lemurs and meerkats) to bring in visitors to provide funds for conservation. Ex situ conservation is therefore used, even if the species is not especially threatened.

Is intervention helping?

Research to see if intervention is helping can be carried out by studying whether or not numbers are improving in the wild. Local expertise can assess whether the conservation effort is effective.

How to manage zoo populations?

When keeping animals in zoos, the welfare of the species must be taken into account. Behavioural studies can indicate whether or not animals are under stress. These studies may look at male and female social interactions, and how the animal uses their enclosures.

The zoo would also consider whether the five freedoms are being met. The five freedoms were established in 1965 and were important in establishing modern zoo standards.

1 Freedom from thirst, hunger, malnutrition through ready access to fresh water and a diet to maintain full health and vigour.
2 Freedom from thermal and physical discomfort by providing an appropriate shelter and a comfortable resting area.
3 Freedom from pain, injury and disease by prevention or rapid diagnosis and treatment.
4 Freedom to express normal behaviour by providing sufficient space, proper facilities and company of the animal's own kind.
5 Freedom from fear and distress by ensuring conditions and treatment avoid mental suffering.

How to manage breeding programmes?

For effective conservation and re-establishment of species in the wild, breeding programmes can be used. To be effective, details of the species' natural breeding behaviour must be known.

- Is it acceptable to choose the mate? Do you allow mate choice?
- The zoo may want to look at genes and the genetic compatibility of mates. Leaving it to chance may lead to an animal choosing an unsuitable partner.
- Stud books can be used to establish genetic compatibility.
- Is artificial insemination a possibility? This will get round the problem of shipping in a mate.
- Birth control may be needed as the zoo may not want to have animals breeding (if zoo capacity is full).
- Keeper intervention may be needed – females sometimes reject young.
- Latest knowledge of reproductive biology and genetics is needed. Research is used (e.g. DNA testing by establishing parentage within a population).
- Correct enclosure design and enrichment schemes mean that a species is more likely to breed.

There are many benefits of modern zoos:

- education of the public
- increased knowledge of species
- the ability to keep species in a controlled environment which protects individual organisms
- genetic monitoring
- captive breeding improves reproductive success
- a higher chance of offspring surviving to adulthood
- the ability to hold species while habitats are restored.

The benefits more than outweigh disadvantages

- narrowed gene pool for the species
- captive animals may be unable to adapt to being back in the wild
- some people object to animals being kept in captivity for profit.

How do we justify the species we choose to protect? Is there a focus on animals we find attractive (the ones with fur and feathers) and is there a natural bias within the system? Do tigers have a greater right to exist than endangered and endemic species of rat?

 Coordination of efforts between zoos helps in the effective conservation of species. The European Association for Zoos and Aquaria (EAZA) works out where specific zoos can help in specific areas. They have a number of Regional Collection Plans (RCPs). One of the RCPs is for the Callitrichid group of monkeys. The golden lion tamarin is a member of this group and has been brought back from the brink of extinction.

The golden lion tamarin is one of the great success stories of zoo conservation. This small primate has been saved from extinction through captive breeding programmes.

ENVIRONMENTAL PHILOSOPHIES

Although most modern zoos take great care of their animals, it could be argued from an ecocentric point of view that all animals belong in the wild and not in captivity. Is this a valid viewpoint?

EXERCISES

1. Draw up a table contrasting governmental organizations and NGOs in terms of use of the media, speed of response, diplomatic constraints and political influence.

2. State the criteria used to design protected areas. Your answer should address size, shape, edge effects, corridors and proximity to other reserves.

3. What makes a protected area a success? List at least five essential factors that are required.

4. What are the advantages of the species-based approach to conservation? What are the disadvantages?

● **Examiner's hint:**

The species-based approach to conservation involves the conservation of high profile, charismatic species catch public attention both nationally and internationally (e.g. tigers).

Advantages of this approach: saving a named species means preserving the animal's habitat and this benefits all other organisms in that habitat.

Disadvantages: it favours charismatic organisms and is less successful in saving small undistinguished species. A species can be preserved in a zoo, while its natural habitat is destroyed (e.g. giant panda).

PRACTICE QUESTIONS

1   '... loss of biological diversity around the world, from a multitude of causes, is correlated with decreasing productivity, increasing fragility in systems and increasing exposure of farming families to uncertainty, poverty and hunger. Reversing these trends will require a huge effort to understand the ecological, economic and social problems, while at the same time educating people from all walks of life – producer, consumer, scientist, policy maker and farmer.'

Source: Food and Agriculture Organization (FAO).

(a) With reference to examples of specific ecosystems you have studied, outline the factors which can lead to a loss in biodiversity.   [6]

(b) Describe and explain the relationship between biodiversity and 'increasing fragility' in ecosystems.   [5]

(c) Evaluate the importance of educating "people from all walks of life" in reversing the loss of biodiversity.   [7]

© International Baccalaureate Organization [2005]

2   The table below shows the bird biomass per square km, the total number of birds per square km, the number of species of birds, and the diversity for three types of habitat in the same country.

	City	Farmland	Forest
Bird biomass / kg km^{-2}	213	30	22
Number of birds km^{-2}	1089	371	2927
Number of bird species	21	80	54
Diversity index	1.13	3.40	3.19

Source: Data slightly modified from A Goudie, *The Human Impact on the Natural Environment*, 5th edition, Blackwell, 2000

(a) Define the terms *species diversity* and *habitat diversity*.   [2]

(b) Describe and explain the data in the table above.   [4]

(c) (i) Define the term *speciation*.   [1]

(ii) Outline how natural selection may influence speciation.   [2]

(iii) Explain how the isolation of a population of an organism (i.e. on an island) could alter the characteristics of the species over time.   [2]

© International Baccalaureate Organization [2005]

3   (a) Discuss the causes and timing of past extinction episodes within the fossil record.   [4]

(b) What is the main difference between the current mass extinction (the sixth mass extinction) and the previous five?   [2]

(c) Describe the case histories of **one** species that is in danger of going extinct and **one** species that was endangered but has now been successfully been brought back from the point of extinction.   [7]

© International Baccalaureate Organization [2003]

4   (a) Outline the factors that make some organisms less prone to extinction and the factors that make others more prone to extinction. Use named examples to support your answer   [5]

(b) Outline **two** historic causes of mass extinction.   [2]

(c) Outline the factors used to determine a species' conservation status (e.g. level of threat). Illustrate your answer with named examples.   [6]

(d) The table at the top of the next page shows reasons why some plant species have become endangered.

Threat	Number of endangered species
Collecting by gardeners or tourists	35
Overgrazing	33
Populations critically low for breeding	31
Clearance for agriculture	22
Industrial and urban growth	16
Logging in forests	12
Dams and flooding	8
Changes in farming practice	6

Source: Adapted from Chapman and Reiss. *Ecology principles and application*, page 279, CUP, 1999

Select **two** threats from the table and suggest a conservation strategy for reducing each threat.   [4]

Expression of ideas   [3]

© International Baccalaureate Organization [2004 and 2007]

5 **(a)** With reference to the figures below and on page 216, suggest why biodiversity within the Albufera marsh is so high.   [3]

(b) Outline **four** threats to the wildlife or habitats within the Albufera marsh.   [2]

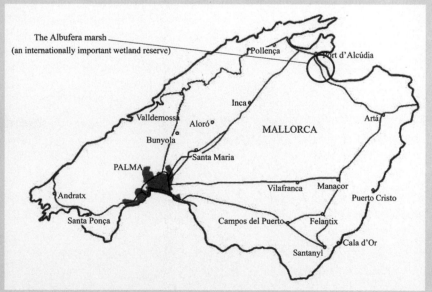

(c) (i) With reference to the figure below, describe how you might expect plant species at site 1 and site 5 to differ. [2]

    (ii) Suggest reasons for the differences you have described in (c) (i). [2]

(d) With reference to the figure below suggest, giving a reason, what results you might expect to find if Simpson's Diversity Index was applied to insect data collected from site 2 and site 4. [2]

Key:

freshwater marsh ecosystem	Site 1 – mature sand dune
saltwater marsh ecosystem	Site 2 – freshwater marsh
sand dune ecosystem	Site 3 – saltwater marsh
river	Site 4 – agricultural land
road	Site 5 – developed sand dune
building	
agricultural land	

(e) The Albufera marsh represents an important reserve in the Mediterranean. Discuss the criteria used to design reserves. Support your answer with evidence from Albufera and other case studies you have studied. [4]

(f) Discuss the strengths and weaknesses of a species-based approach to conservation. [3]

© International Baccalaureate Organization [2006, 2007]

5 POLLUTION MANAGEMENT

5.1 Nature of pollution

Assessment statements
5.1.1 Define the term *pollution*.
5.1.2 Distinguish between the terms *point source pollution* and *non-point source pollution*, and outline the challenges they present for management.
5.1.3 State the major sources of pollutants.

Define the term *pollution*

Pollution is defined as the contamination of the Earth and atmosphere to such an extent that normal environmental processes are adversely affected. Polluted elements are disagreeable, toxic, harmful and/or objectionable.

- Pollution can be natural, such as from volcanic eruptions, as well as human in origin.
- It can be deliberate or it may be accidental.
- It includes the release of substances which harm the sustainable quality of air, water and soil, and which reduces human quality of life.

It is difficult to define the levels which constitute pollution. Much depends on the nature of the environment. For example, decomposition is much slower in cold environments – so oil slicks pose a greater threat in Arctic areas than in tropical ones. Similarly, levels of air quality which do not threaten healthy adults may affect young children, the elderly or asthmatics.

Point source pollution and non-point source pollution

Point source pollution refers to discrete sources of contaminants that can be represented by single points on a map and the source of the pollution can be tracked. The nuclear explosion at Chernobyl, Ukraine (Chapter 2, pages 74–75; Chapter 7, page 291) and the industrial pollution at Bhopal, India (Chapter 7, page 290) are good examples of point-source pollution.

Point-source pollution – sediment is coming from a single identifiable source, a drain mid-way along a stream.

Many rich countries have polluted the environment on purpose, in return for the economic benefits they gain (e.g. energy production). Much of the cost of this pollution is borne by other countries – is this moral?

Non-point source pollution refers to more dispersed sources from which pollutants originate and enter the natural environment. A good example is the release of air pollutants from numerous, widely dispersed origins (e.g. vehicles and industries).

Point-source pollution is generally the more easily managed. Its point source is localized, making it easier to control emissions, apportion responsibility, and take legal action, if necessary. The localized impact is also easier to manage.

Major sources of pollution

The major sources of pollution include the combustion of fossil fuel, domestic and industrial waste, manufacturing and agricultural systems (Figure 5.1).

Figure 5.1
Sources of pollution.

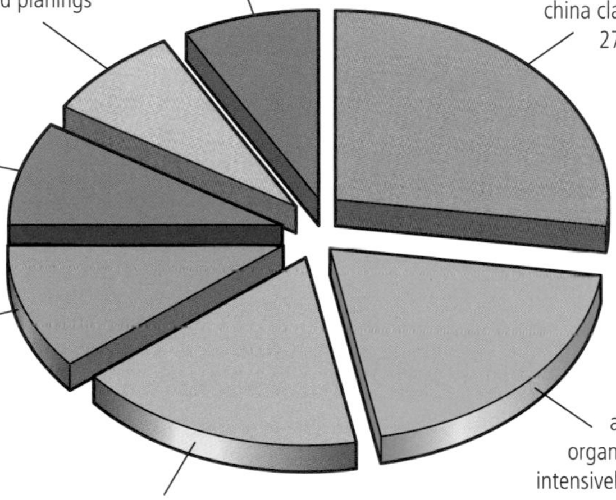

sewage sludge
8%

demolition and construction
e.g. rubble, road planings
8%

mining and quarrying
e.g. colliery shale, slate,
china clay wastes
27%

domestic and commercial
e.g. paper, food, glass,
metals, plastics
9%

dredging
sand and mud
11%

agriculture
organic wastes from
intensively farmed livestock
20%

industry
e.g. furnace slag and ash,
many hazardous wastes
17%

To learn more about pollution, go to www. pearsonhotlinks.com, insert the express code 2630P and click on activities 5.1 and 5.2.

Pollution costs

The costs of pollution are widespread: death, decreased levels of health, declining water resources, reduced soil quality, and poor air quality. It is vital to control and manage pollution. To be effective, pollution treatment must be applied at source. However, unless point sources can be targeted, this may be impossible. There is no point treating symptoms (e.g. treating acidified lakes with lime) if the cause is not tackled (e.g. emission of acid materials).

ENVIRONMENTAL PHILOSOPHIES

Most industrial nations adopt a Cornucopian approach to the environment, believing that people can find a solution to the problems created by human (mis-)use of the environment.

EXERCISES

1 Define the term *pollution*.

2 Distinguish between the terms *point source pollution* and *non-point source pollution*, and outline the challenges they present for management.

3 State the major sources of pollutants.

● **Examiner's hint:**
Distinguish – Make clear the differences between two or more concepts/items.

Detection and monitoring of pollution

Monitoring pollution

Soil pollution

Soil quality indicators include physical, chemical and biological properties, processes, and characteristics that can be measured to monitor changes in soil quality. No single soil characteristic can be used to measure soil quality, a group of soil attributes is used. These include soil texture, density, infiltration, water retention characteristics, soil organic matter, extractable nitrogen, phosphorus and potassium, microbial biomass, and soil respiration.

Water quality

Standard water quality tests on drinking water, rivers and other sites can be performed with portable equipment that enables detection of nitrate, nitrite, free chlorine, chloride, fluoride, hardness and heavy metals such as lead. River water-quality tests include biochemical oxygen demand (BOD), chemical oxygen demand (COD), turbidity, ammonia and dissolved oxygen.

There are two main ways of measuring water quality. One is to take samples of the water and measure the concentrations of different chemicals that it contains. If the chemicals are dangerous or the concentrations are too great, we can regard the water as polluted. Measurements like this are known as chemical indicators of water quality (Table 5.1). The second method involves examining the fish, insects, and other invertebrates that the water will support. If many different types of creatures can live in a river, the quality is likely to be very good; if the river supports no fish life at all, the quality is obviously much poorer. Measurements like this are called biological indicators of water quality.

 To access additional text 5.1 on using lichens to monitor air pollution, please visit www.pearsonbacconline.com and follow the on-screen instructions.

● **Examiner's hint:**

Soil pH can be measured using a universal indicator as follows.

1 Take a small soil sample from a known depth (horizon) of soil.

2 Place about 1–2 cm of soil in the bottom of a test tube.

3 Add 1–2 cm of barium sulfate (this causes the clay to settle leaving a clear solution).

4 Fill the tube with distilled water and shake.

5 Add a few drops of universal indicator to clear the solution. Compare the colour of the liquid to the colour of the chart provided. The pH can be read off to the nearest 0.5.

TABLE 5.1 CHEMICAL INDICATORS OF WATER QUALITY		
Indicator	**Methods**	**What the results show**
dissolved oxygen	Use a test kit or meter or sensor for dissolved oxygen. Follow instructions to measure the amount of oxygen saturation in a sample of water. Oxygen is usually measured in percentage saturation.	• healthy clean water shows >75% oxygen saturation • polluted water shows between 10–50% oxygen saturation • raw sewage contains 10% saturation of oxygen or less
pH	Dip pH or universal indicator paper into a sample of water. Compare the colour of the pH paper with the pH colour chart. Record the pH number (e.g. pH 8).	• pH 1–6 indicates that the water is acidic, pH 1 is very acidic • pH 7 indicates a neutral solution • pH 8–11 indicates that the water is alkaline, pH 11 is very alkaline
phosphate	Use a test kit. Follow instructions to measure the amount of phosphate in a sample of water. Phosphate is measured in $mg\,dm^{-3}$.	• clean water contains >5 $mg\,dm^{-3}$ • polluted water contains 15–20 $mg\,dm^{-3}$ phosphate
nitrate	Use a test kit. Follow instructions to measure the amount of nitrate in a sample of water. Nitrate is measured in $mg\,dm^{-3}$.	• clean water contains 4–5 $mg\,dm^{-3}$ • polluted water contains 5–15 $mg\,dm^{-3}$ nitrate
salt (as chloride)	Use a test kit or meter or sensor. Follow instructions to measure the amount of chloride in a sample of water. Salinity is measured in $mg\,dm^{-3}$.	• seawater contains 20 000 $mg\,dm^{-3}$ • tidal or brackish water contains 100–20 000 $mg\,dm^{-3}$ chloride
ammonia	Use a test kit. Follow instructions to measure the amount of ammonia in a sample of water. Ammonia is measured in $mg\,dm^{-3}$.	• clean water contains 0.05–1.00 $mg\,dm^{-3}$ • polluted water contains 1–10 $mg\,dm^{-3}$ • raw sewage contains 40 $mg\,dm^{-3}$ ammonia

Monitoring air pollution

There are a number of ways of monitoring air pollution and there are many organizations that do so on a regular basis. It is, therefore, relatively easy to get secondary data (data collected and published by someone else), especially for large urban areas. Pollutants that are regularly monitored include sulfur dioxide, oxides of nitrogen, ozone, volatile organic compounds, and particulate matter.

Biochemical oxygen demand (BOD)

Aerobic organisms use oxygen in respiration. The more organisms there are at a particular site (e.g. in a river) and the faster their rate of respiration, the more oxygen they will use. So, the BOD at any particular point in the river is determined by:
- the number of aerobic organisms at that point
- their rate of respiration.

BOD can indicate whether a particular part of a river is polluted with organic matter (e.g. sewage, silage). This is because the presence of an organic pollutant stimulates an increase in the population of organisms that feed on and break down the pollutant. In doing so, they respire and use up a lot of oxygen. In other words, organic pollutants cause a high BOD.

BOD is measured in the following way.
1 Take a sample of water of measured volume.
2 Measure the oxygen level.
3 Place the sample in a dark place at 20 °C for five days (lack of light prevents photosynthesis which would release oxygen and give an artificially low BOD).
4 After five days, re-measure the oxygen level.
5 BOD is the difference between the two measurements.

Certain species are tolerant of organic pollution and the low oxygen levels associated with it. They are found in high population densities where an organic pollution incident occurs. Other species cannot tolerate low oxygen levels and, if organic pollution enters the river where they live, they move away (Figure 5.2). We can use these groups as indicator species (i.e. indicators of organic pollution).

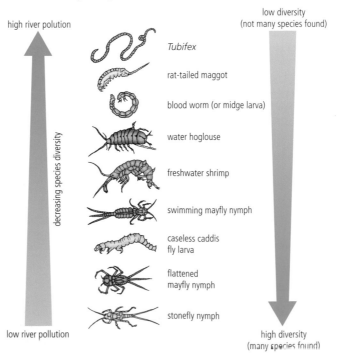

high river polution · low diversity (not many species found)

decreasing species diversity

- Tubifex
- rat-tailed maggot
- blood worm (or midge larva)
- water hoglouse
- freshwater shrimp
- swimming mayfly nymph
- caseless caddis fly larva
- flattened mayfly nymph
- stonefly nymph

low river pollution · high diversity (many species found)

Figure 5.2
Indicator species.

Organic pollutants in water can be more dangerous in summer. This is because the solubility of oxygen decreases as the water temperature increases. So on warm days there is less available oxygen in the water. Aquatic invertebrates and fish can do little to regulate their body temperature; as water temperature increases, so does their internal temperature and so does their rate of respiration. This means they need more oxygen – but the amount of oxygen dissolved in the water is going down. If warm organic pollutants are released into rivers, the effect can be even more devastating.

Figure 5.3 illustrates how *Tubifex* worms and mayfly nymphs can be used as indicator species. The *Tubifex* worms feed on and tunnel into the effluent; their populations increase rapidly immediately downstream of any effluent entry. A high population of these organisms in any river could indicate that organic pollution has recently occurred. In contrast, the population of mayfly nymphs crashes as soon as the effluent enters. They need clean water and, at the point of entry, either die or move away. Thus, the absence of mayfly nymphs in a particular river might indicate organic pollution has occurred and large populations might indicate clean, unpolluted water.

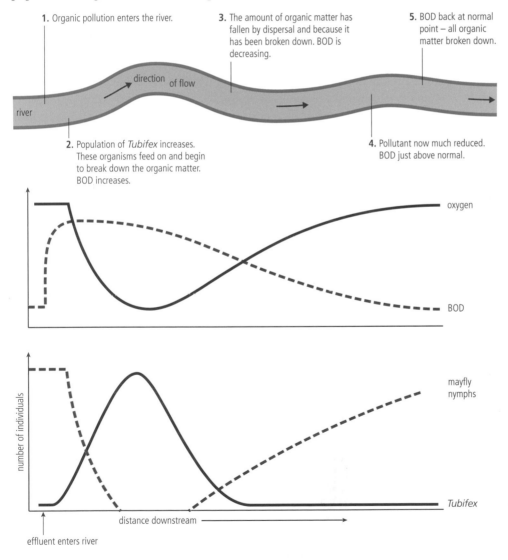

To learn more about air pollution monitoring in the USA, go to www.pearsonhotlinks.com, insert the express code 2630P and click on activity 5.3.

To learn more about investigating air pollution in Cambridge, UK, go to www.pearsonhotlinks.com, insert the express code 2630P and click on activity 5.4.

BOD5 (the amount of oxygen consumed in a sample of water over a period of five days in the dark at 20 °C) is compared to dissolved oxygen content measured in the field – the difference is the BOD.

An indicator species is one whose presence, absence or abundance can be used as an indicator of pollution. It doesn't have to be water pollution – some species can be used to indicate air pollution, soil nutrient levels and abiotic water characteristics:

- lichen (*Usnea alliculata*) indicates very low levels of sulfur dioxide in air
- nettles (*Ullica dioica*) indicate high phosphate levels in soil
- red alga (*Corauina officinalis*) indicate saline rock pools (absent from brackish ones).

Figure 5.3
Using indicator species to estimate river pollution.

It is often faster and cheaper to measure organisms such as *Tubifex* or mayfly nymphs than it is to try to measure the concentration of specific pollutants – this is one of the advantages of using indicator species. Table 5.2 relates type of fauna present in a waterway to levels of BOD.

Class of waterway	Fauna present	BOD / mg O₂ absorbed per dm³ of water at 20 °C in 5 days	Waterway used for
	TABLE 5.2 BOD AND TYPE OF FAUNA PRESENT		
I	salmon, trout, grayling, stonefly and mayfly nymphs, caddis larvae, *Gammarus*	0–3	• domestic supply
II	trout rarely dominant; chub, dace, caddis larvae, *Gammarus*	4–10 (increased in summer in times of low flow)	• agriculture • industrial processes
III	roach, gudgeon, *Asellus*, mayfly nymphs and caddis larvae rare	11–15	• irrigation
IV	fish absent, red chironomid larvae (bloodworms) and *Tubifex* worms present	16–30 (completely deoxygenated from time to time)	• unsuitable for amenity use
V	barren or with fungus or small *Tubifex* worms	>30	• none

To learn more about BOD, go to www.pearsonhotlinks.com, insert the express code 2630P and click on activity 5.5.

Trent Biotic Index

The **Trent Biotic Index** is based on the disappearance of indicator species as the level of organic pollution increases in a river. This occurs because the species are unable to tolerate changes in their environment such as decreased oxygen levels or lower light levels. Those species best able to tolerate the prevailing conditions become abundant – which can lead to a change in diversity. In extreme environments (e.g. a highly polluted river) diversity is low, although numbers of individuals may be high. Diversity decreases as pollution increases.

The Trent Biotic Index has a maximum value of ten. The indices are in the form of marks out of ten and give a sensitive assessment of pollution levels.

Here is how it works.
1 Sort your sample, separating the animals according to group.
2 Count the number of groups.
3 Note which indicator species are present, starting from the top of the list in Table 5.3.
4 Take the highest indicator species on the list and read across the row, stopping at the column with the appropriate number of groups for your sample.

So, if your highest indicator animal belongs to the Trichoptera, you have more than one species and a total of 7 groups, the Trent Biotic Index for your sample is 6.

Indicator groups present	Number of species	0–1	2–5	6–10	11–15	16+
		Total number of groups present				
		Trent Biotic Index				
stonefly nymph (Plecoptera)	>1	–	7	8	9	10
	1	–	6	7	8	9
mayfly nymph (Ephemeroptera)	>1	–	6	7	8	9
	1	–	5	6	7	8
caddis fly larvae (Trichoptera)	>1	–	5	6	7	8
	1	4	4	5	6	7
Gammarus	all above groups absent	3	4	5	6	7
shrimps, crustaceans (*Aseilus*)	all above groups absent	2	3	4	5	6
Tubifex and/or chironomid larvae	all above groups absent	1	2	3	4	–
all above groups absent	organisms not requiring dissolved oxygen may be present	0	1	2	–	–

TABLE 5.3 INDICATOR SPECIES FOR THE TRENT BIOTIC INDEX

To learn more about Trent Biotic Index for Chesapeake Bay 2006–08, go to www.pearsonhotlinks.com, insert the express code 2630P and click on activity 5.6.

EXERCISES

1 Describe two direct methods of monitoring pollution.

2 Define the term *biochemical oxygen demand* (*BOD*) and explain how this indirect method is used to assess pollution levels in water.

3 Describe and explain an indirect method of measuring pollution levels using a biotic index.

4 Figure 5.3 (page 221) shows changes in characteristics below an outlet.
(a) Describe the relative changes in *Tubifex* and mayfly larvae along the course of the river.
(b) Suggest reasons for these changes.
(c) Compare and contrast the presence and abundance of mayfly nymphs and *Tubifex* worms.
(d) Explain the variations in BOD and dissolved oxygen.

Indirect methods (surrogate measures) such as using lichens to monitor air pollution, assume that the species is a reliable indicator of change in the environment. Will all members of the population react in a similar way or may some adapt to the new environment?

5.3 Approaches to pollution management

Assessment statements

5.3.1 Outline approaches to pollution management with respect to the process of pollution and strategies for reducing impacts.

5.3.2 Discuss the human factors that affect the approaches to pollution management.

5.3.3 Evaluate the costs and benefits to society of the World Health Organization's ban on the use of the pesticide DDT.

Pollution management: the process of pollution and strategies for reducing impacts

An example of natural pollution is the on-going eruption of the Soufrière volcano on Montserrat in the Caribbean. This has led to widespread pollution of land, water and sea.

Human causes of pollution are widespread and include farming and industrial practices, urbanization, development of transport, and the transport and burning of energy sources. The result depends on the amount of material released into the environment.

Natural pollution: pyroclastic flows and lahars at Montserrat. A pyroclastic flow is a very hot, very fast flow of fragmented rock, cinders and ash blown into the air by volcanic activity. A lahar is a volcanic mudflow formed by ash mixing with water.

To access worksheet 5.1 on pollution management, please visit www.pearsonbacconline.com and follow the on-screen instructions.

Pollutants result from
natural and human
processes which
result in too much of a
substance released into an
environment.

There are a number of ways in which the impacts of pollution can be managed (Figure 5.4).
These include:
- changing human activities
- regulating and reducing quantities of pollutants released at the point of emission
- cleaning up the pollutant and restoring the ecosystem after pollution has occurred.

Each of these strategies has advantages and limitations.

Figure 5.4
Processes of pollution and
management strategies.

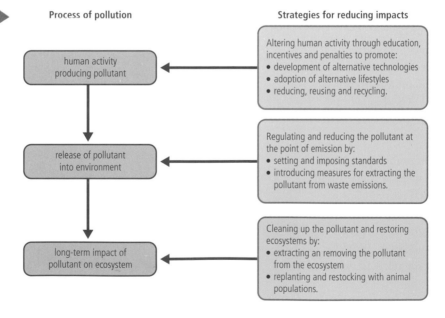

Changing human activities

The main advantage of changing human activities is that it may prevent pollution from
happening. For example, if more societies were to use solar, hydro- or wind power there
would be reduced emissions of greenhouse gases, and less risk of global warming. However,
there are major limitations. Alternative technologies are expensive to develop and may only
work in certain environments (Chapter 3, pages 114–16). Solar power is most effective in

areas which have reliable hours of sunshine. Wind energy requires relatively high wind speeds and is best suited to coastal areas and high ground.

Reusing and recycling materials has reduced consumption of resources. Many items can be recycled such as newspapers, cans, glass, aluminium and plastics. However, there are certain goods which can only be recycled under special conditions. The increasing volume of electronic waste (e-waste) is creating major problems for its disposal and recycling.

Computer equipment contains toxic substances and is effectively hazardous waste. Much e-waste ends up in the developing world, and there is increasing concern about the pollution caused by hazardous chemicals and heavy metals there. A single computer can contain up to 2 kilograms of lead, and the complex mixture of materials make PCs very difficult to recycle. New legislation came into force in 2007 to cover waste electrical and electronic equipment (WEEE).

Increasingly, manufacturers of electronic goods incorporate e-waste management into their environmental policies and operate consumer recycling schemes. Dell, for example, cover the cost of home pick-up, shipping to the recycling centre, and recycling of any obsolete equipment. Hewlett–Packard (HP) recycled over 74 million kilograms of electronics in 2005. HP has recycling operations in 40 world regions. These schemes help to:

- reduce the volume of waste which ends up in landfill sites
- cut down on the amount of raw materials needed for the manufacture of new products
- make recycling convenient for the consumer.

The management of pollution is easiest when human activities do not pollute. However, this is unlikely to occur in most places.

Regulating activities

The next easiest way of reducing pollution is to reduce the amount of pollution at the point of emission. This may be done by having measures for extracting the pollutant from the waste emissions. A good example is the use of flue gas desulfurization (FGD). FGD is widely used to control the emissions of sulfur dioxide (SO_2) from coal- and oil-fired power stations and refineries. There are a variety of FGD processes available; most use an alkali to extract the acidic sulfur compounds from the flue gas. Flue gas treatment (FGT) is the process used for removing pollutants from waste incinerators. Such treatments are expensive and it is difficult to enforce such measures in the unregulated part of the economy (the informal sector) and to every potential source of pollution.

Levels of pollution can also be controlled by setting standards for air or water quality. For example, in 2008 the Environmental Protection Agency (EPA) in the USA improved air quality standards in an effort to help improve public health. It lowered the amount of ground-level ozone permitted in the atmosphere from 80 parts per billion (ppb) to 75 ppb. The EPA claimed the change could save 4000 lives each year. However, standards are not imposed to the same levels in all countries. Many developing countries need to develop their industries in order to improve their wealth and are anxious not to be regulated by strict controls. Indeed, some companies from rich countries locate in poor countries as the environmental legislation there is weaker or not enforced. US companies locating across the border in Mexico, the *maquiladora* industries, are a good example of this practice.

Cleaning up afterwards

The most expensive option (in terms of both time and money) is to clean up the environment after it has been polluted. Under natural conditions, bacteria take time to break down pollutants before the ecosystem recovers through secondary succession. In cold conditions, bacterial activity is reduced so pollutants in colder environments persist for

It may be possible for people to adopt alternative, less-polluting lifestyles. During the period of high oil prices in 2008, more people than usual travelled by public transport, cycled or walked to work or school. Since the 1990s, the Living Streets Walk to School Campaign has encouraged over one million primary school children to walk to school in the UK.

In the USA, up to 20 million 'obsolete' PCs are discarded annually.

To see how green you are, go to www. pearsonhotlinks.com, insert the express code 2630P and click on activity 5.7.

Countries at different stages of development place different sets of values on the natural environment. Many developing countries wish to use their resources for economic development. They argue that they are only doing the same as the rich countries, albeit many decades later. Are they justified in this argument?

PM_{10} are small enough to enter deep into the lungs; $PM_{2.5}$ are thought to be able to pass through alveoli. Increased morbidity and mortality follow increased levels of these pollutants. Even quite low concentrations lead to decreased lung capacity and increased heart and respiratory disease, including asthma.

longer than in warm environments. When people are employed in the clean-up process, it is often labour-intensive and, therefore, expensive.

Integration of policies

It is increasingly likely that integrated pollution-management schemes will employ aspects of each of the three approaches. It is unrealistic to expect human activities to cease to pollute the environment. However, any reduction will be beneficial. If the pollutants can be captured at the source of pollution, it will be cheaper in the long term because they will not have polluted the environment at that stage, so no clean-up will be required. Cleaning up widespread pollution is necessary, but it is the least effective option.

Human factors and approaches to pollution management

There are a number of factors which influence the choice and implementation of pollution management strategy. These include economic systems, cultural values and political systems. The case study below is an excellent example as it deals with one of the world's most polluted cities and one of the world's most authoritarian governments.

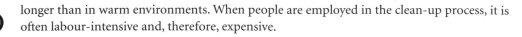

CASE STUDY

Air quality and the Beijing Olympics

China has been trying to improve the air quality and environment of its large cities such as Beijing.

In 2005, the European Space Agency released satellite data that showed that Beijing and surrounding areas in northern China had the worst levels of nitrogen dioxide (NO_2) in the world. The city is often cloaked in haze, which occasionally hits such noxious levels that the authorities warn children and elderly people to stay indoors.

Beijing is full of potential sources of pollution. Over 5700 industrial enterprises operate in the city, including power plants, non-ferrous and ferrous metal smelters, coking plants, chemical plants, and metal products factories. Nevertheless, not all the ozone and particulates (PM) come from within the city. Particulates are measured according to their size: PM_{10} refers to particulates of up to 10 micrometres (10 μm); $PM_{2.5}$ refers to particulates of up to 2.5 micrometres (2.5 μm). About 34 per cent of $PM_{2.5}$ on average and 35–60 per cent of ozone during high ozone episodes at the Olympic Stadium site can be attributed to sources outside Beijing.

Neighbouring Hebei and Shandong Provinces and the Tianjin Municipality (Figure 5.5) all have significant influence on Beijing's air quality. During sustained wind flow from the south, Hebei Province can contribute 50–70 per cent of Beijing's $PM_{2.5}$ concentrations and 20–30 per cent of ozone. Controlling only local sources in Beijing is not sufficient to improve air quality. The city government has attempted to control industrial pollution by relocating certain industries (e.g. electroplating), away from the central area, and new enterprises are actively discouraged from entering the city.

Figure 5.5
Location of Beijing.

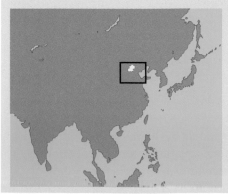
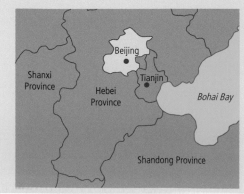

The air pollution index (API), published by China's Ministry of Environmental Protection, is derived from measurements of five pollutants: sulfur dioxide, nitrogen dioxide, PM_{10} (includes $PM_{2.5}$), carbon monoxide and ozone. The average concentration for each pollutant is calculated daily. In Beijing, PM_{10} is the major pollutant most days; of this, a significant proportion is $PM_{2.5}$ (Figure 5.6). The Chinese government terms all days with an API of 100 or less as 'blue-sky days' or 'slightly polluted'. In 1998, Beijing recorded 100 blue-sky days; in 2007, 246 were recorded.

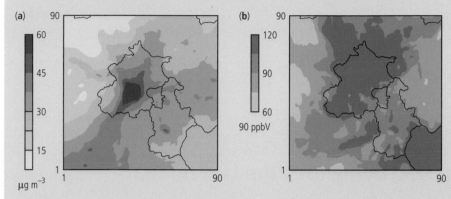

Figure 5.6
Concentrations of (**a**) $PM_{2.5}$ and (**b**) ozone in Beijing.

In 1988, the Beijing Municipal Government passed regulations to implement the 1987 Air Pollution Prevention Act, which requires industries to monitor and report their own emissions. At the same time, stricter emission standards than the national ones were set.

Recent emission control programmes put into effect include:

- increase the supply of coal gas and natural gas for industrial use
- convert urban residential fuel from coal to liquefied petroleum gas and natural gas
- require residential sources still using coal to burn briquettes and shaped-coal to reduce emissions
- develop central heating plants to replace smaller boilers with a single large installation with emission controls
- modify existing boilers (where the location of industry makes central heating impractical) to reduce emissions by automatic feeding and ash removal (all boilers with a capacity greater than one tonne must install scrubbers)
- pave dirt roads and plant trees, flowers, and grass to reduce wind-blown dust.

Official readings just before the 2008 Olympic Games gave an API of 91 for Beijing as a whole, and 87 at the Olympic stadium. The World Health Organization (WHO) regards an API of more than 50 as high, and a reading of 100 or more is considered unsafe. The authorities monitor air quality hourly, including levels of particulates, carbon monoxide and nitrogen dioxide, and take limited readings for ozone.

Further attempts to reduce pollution
Beijing's biggest single source of pollution, the vast Shougang steel complex, was closed down ahead of the Olympics in an attempt to improve air quality. Normally, the factory emits 10 per cent of Beijing's particulate matter. In addition:

- four of Shougang's five blast furnaces were shut down in a pre-Olympic environmental clean-up
- hundreds of construction sites and factories were closed during the Games
- millions of coal-burning homes have been converted to gas
- more than 2000 buses and 5000 taxis were upgraded or replaced with cleaner models
- five new urban railways have been added to the public transport system
- the city's 3 million cars were allowed on the roads only on alternate days depending on whether their licence plates are odd or even numbered.

Case study continued

Such measures reflect the powers of China's authoritarian government and the scale of the pollution problems the city faces.

The scaling down of production at Shougang was the key environmental project to cut air pollution. By the start of the Olympic Games, the factory, also known as Capital Steel, had cut production by 73 per cent and spent 140 billion yuan (£10.3 billion) on reducing pollution and improving energy efficiency. About 60 000 of the 134 000 workers were laid off in a phased relocation to a plant outside the city. By 2010, production of steel and iron at Shougang's complex in Beijing will cease for good. Production will take place at a new plant in Caofeidian, north-eastern China. This is part of China's campaign to make its industry more environmentally friendly.

Despite these measures, air quality failed to reach national standards for four of the first seven days after the city took more than 1 million cars off the roads and shut hundreds of factories.

Compared to the past, the situation is much better. But set against international standards, the country is lagging by some distance. Environmental groups applauded the measures, but said they were unlikely to satisfy global expectations.

W To learn more about pollution in China, go to www.pearsonhotlinks.com, insert the express code 2630P and click on activity 5.8.

Costs and benefits of the ban on DDT

DDT (dichlorodiphenyl-trichloroethane) is a synthetic pesticide with a controversial history. Commercial DDT is actually a mixture of several closely related compounds, including DDE (dichlorodiphenyl-dichloroethylene) and DDD (dichlorodiphenyl-dichloroethane). DDE and DDD are also the major products of the breakdown of DDT in the environment.

DDT was used extensively during World War II to control the lice that spread typhus and the mosquitoes that spread malaria. Its use led to a huge decrease in both diseases. After the war, DDT was used as an insecticide in farming, and its production soared.

In 1955, the WHO began a programme to eradicate malaria worldwide. This relied heavily on DDT. The programme was initially successful, but resistance evolved in many insect populations after only six years, largely because of the widespread agricultural use of DDT. In many parts of the world including Sri Lanka, Pakistan, Turkey and central America, DDT has lost much of its effectiveness.

ⓘ In 1962, the American biologist Rachel Carson published her hugely influential book *Silent Spring* in which she claimed that the large-scale spraying of pesticides, including DDT, was killing wildlife. Top carnivores such as birds of prey were declining in numbers and, moreover, DDT could cause cancer in humans. Public opinion turned against DDT (Chapter 7, pages 289–90).

Rachel Carson

'. . . what we have to face is not an occasional dose of poison, which has accidentally got into some article of food, but a persistent and continuous poisoning of the whole human environment . . .'

Silent Spring

Rachel Carson's famous book became a *cause célèbre* and marked a turning point in attitudes to DDT. ▶

Between 1950 and 1980 DDT was used extensively in farming, and over 40 000 tonnes were used each year worldwide. Up to 1.8 million tonnes of DDT have been produced globally since the 1940s. About 4000–5000 tonnes of DDT are still produced and used each year for the control of malaria and other diseases. DDT is applied to the inside walls of homes (a process known as indoor residual spraying – IRS) to kill or repel mosquitoes entering the home. India is the largest consumer. The main producers are India, China and North Korea.

Restrictions on the use of DDT

In the 1970s and 1980s, agricultural use of DDT was banned in most developed countries. DDT was first banned in Hungary (1968) followed by Norway and Sweden (1970), USA in 1972, and the UK in 1984. The use of DDT in vector control has not been banned, but it has been largely replaced by less persistent alternative insecticides.

The Stockholm Convention banned several persistent organic pollutants (POPs), and restricted the use of DDT to disease control. The Convention was signed by 98 countries and is endorsed by most environmental groups. Despite the worldwide ban on agricultural use of DDT, its use in this context continues in India and North Korea.

Environmental impacts of DDT

DDT is a POP that is extremely hydrophobic and strongly absorbed by soils. DDT is not very soluble in water but is very soluble in lipids (fats). This means it can build up in fatty tissue. Its soil half-life can range from 22 days to 30 years. Loss and degradation occur through run-off, volatilization, photolysis and biodegradation.

Bioaccumulation is the retention or build-up of non-biodegradable or slowly biodegradable chemicals in the body. This produces a body-burden of the substance. **Biomagnification** or biological amplification is the process whereby the concentration of a chemical increases at each trophic level. The end result is that top predators may have in their bodies concentrations of a chemical several million times higher than the same chemical's concentration in water and primary producers (Chapter 2, page 18).

DDT, and its breakdown products DDE and DDD, all biomagnify through the food chain (Figure 5.7). DDT is believed to be a major reason for the decline of the bald eagle in North America in the 1950s and 1960s. Other species affected included the brown pelican and peregrine falcon. Recent studies have linked the thinning of birds' eggs with high levels of DDE in particular.

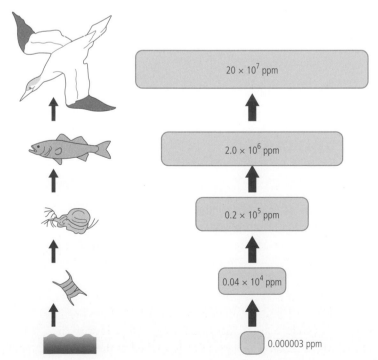

Figure 5.7
Biomagnification of DDT along a food chain.

20×10^7 ppm

2.0×10^6 ppm

0.2×10^5 ppm

0.04×10^4 ppm

0.000003 ppm

Effects on human health

The effects of DDT on human health are disputed and conflicting. For example, some studies have shown that:

- farmers exposed to DDT occupationally had an increased incidence of asthma and/or diabetes;
- some people exposed to DDT had a higher risk of liver-, breast-, and/or pancreatic-cancer;
- DDT exposure is a risk factor for early pregnancy loss, premature birth and/or low birth weight;
- a 2007 study found increased infertility among South African men from communities where DDT is used to combat malaria.

Use of DDT against malaria

Malaria remains a major public health challenge in many parts of the world. The WHO estimates that there are 250 million cases every year, resulting in almost 1 million deaths. About 90 per cent of these deaths occur in Africa. In 2006, only 13 countries were still using DDT.

To learn more about the use and impacts of DDT, go to www.pearsonhotlinks.com, insert the express code 2630P and click on activity 5.9.

Nevertheless, the WHO is 'very much concerned with health consequences from use of DDT' and it has reaffirmed its commitment to eventually phase it out. In South America, malaria cases increased after countries stopped using DDT. In Ecuador between 1993 and 1995, the use of DDT increased and there was a 61 per cent reduction in malaria rates.

Some donor governments and agencies have refused to fund DDT spraying, or made aid contingent on not using DDT. Use of DDT in Mozambique was stopped because 80 per cent of the country's health budget came from donor funds, and donors refused to allow the use of DDT.

● Examiner's hint:
Discuss – Make a considered and balanced review that includes a range of arguments, factors or hypotheses. Opinions or conclusions should be presented clearly and supported by appropriate evidence.

EXERCISES

1 Outline the processes of pollution.
2 Outline strategies for reducing the impacts of pollution.
3 Discuss the human factors that affect the approaches to pollution management.
4 Describe the variations in the level of DDT along a food chain.
5 Outline the main uses (past and present) of DDT.
6 Comment on the risks of using DDT.

5.4 Eutrophication

Assessment statements
5.4.1 Outline the processes of eutrophication.
5.4.2 Evaluate the impacts of eutrophication.
5.4.3 Describe and evaluate pollution management strategies with respect to eutrophication.

Eutrophication refers to the nutrient enrichment of streams, pond and groundwater. It is caused when increased levels of nitrogen or phosphorus are carried into water bodies. It can cause algal blooms, oxygen starvation and eventually the decline of biodiversity in aquatic ecosystems.

Processes of eutrophication

In eutrophication, increased amounts of nitrogen and/or phosphorus are carried in streams, lakes and groundwater causing nutrient enrichment. This leads to an increase in algal blooms as plants respond to the increased nutrient availability. This is an example of positive feedback (Chapter 1, page 7).

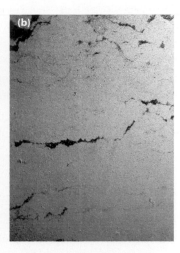

(a) Overgrowth of algae due to eutrophication, Cambridgeshire, UK. (b) Close-up of surface algal bloom due to eutrophication.

However, the increase in algae and plankton shade the water below, cutting off the light supply for submerged plants. The prolific growth of algae and cyanobacteria, especially in autumn as a result of increased levels of nutrients in the water and higher temperatures, results in **anoxia** (oxygen starvation in the water). The increased plant biomass and decomposition – which lead to a build up of dead organic matter – also lead to changes in species composition.

Some of these changes are the direct result of eutrophication (e.g. stimulation of algal growth in water bodies) while others are indirect (e.g. changes in the diversity of fish species due to reduced oxygen concentration). Eutrophication is very much a dynamic system – as levels of nitrates and phosphorus in streams and groundwater change, there is a corresponding change in species composition.

A number of changes may occur as a result of eutrophication.

- Turbidity (murkiness) increases, reducing the amount of light reaching submerged plants.
- Rate of deposition of sediment increases, due to increased vegetation cover reducing the speed of water, decreasing the lifespan of lakes.
- Net primary productivity is usually higher compared with unpolluted water and may be seen by extensive algal or bacterial blooms.
- Dissolved oxygen in water decreases, as organisms decomposing the increased biomass consume oxygen.
- Diversity of primary producers changes and finally decreases; the dominant species change. Initially, the number of primary producers increases and may become more diverse. However, as eutrophication proceeds, early algal blooms give way to cyanobacteria.
- Fish populations are adversely affected by reduced oxygen availability, and the fish community becomes dominated by surface-dwelling coarse fish, such as pike and perch.

In freshwater aquatic systems, a major effect of eutrophication is the loss of the submerged **macrophytes** (aquatic plants). Macrophytes are thought to disappear because they lose their energy supply (sunlight penetrating the water). Due to eutrophication, sunlight is intercepted by the increased biomass of phytoplankton exploiting the high nutrient conditions. In principle, the submerged macrophytes could also benefit from increased nutrient availability, but they have no opportunity to do so because they are shaded by the free-floating microscopic organisms.

Algae and cyanobacteria are tiny organisms occurring in fresh water and saltwater. Algae belong to the eukaryotes – single celled or multi-cell organisms whose cells contain a nucleus. The cyanobacteria belong to the prokaryotes – single-cell organisms without a membrane-bound nucleus. The cyanobacteria used to be called 'blue–green algae' (a term you may still come across) but they have been reclassified as bacteria. The first members of the cyanobacteria to be discovered were indeed blue–green in colour, but since then, new members of the group have been found that are not this distinctive colour.

Natural eutrophication

The process of primary succession (Chapter 2, page 65; Chapter 4, page 185) is associated with gradual eutrophication as nutrients are trapped and stored by vegetation, both as living tissue and organic matter in soil or lake sediments. Nutrient enrichment occurs through addition of sediment, rainfall and the decay of organic matter and waste products. Starting from an oligotrophic (nutrient-poor) state with low productivity, a typical temperate lake increases in productivity fairly quickly as nutrients accumulate.

Anthropogenic eutrophication

Human activities worldwide have caused the nitrogen and phosphorus content of many rivers to double and, in some countries, local increases of up to 50 times have been recorded.

Phosphorus

Phosphorus is a rare element in the Earth's crust. Unlike nitrogen, there is no reservoir of gaseous phosphorus compounds available in the atmosphere. In natural systems, phosphorus is more likely to be a growth-limiting nutrient than nitrogen.

In addition, domestic detergents are a major source of phosphates in sewage effluents. Estimates of the relative contribution of domestic detergents to phosphorus build-up in Britain's watercourses vary between 20 per cent and 60 per cent. As phosphorus increases in a freshwater ecosystem, the amount of plankton increases and the amount of freshwater plants decreases.

About three-quarters of the world's production of phosphorus (167 Mt in 2008) comes from the USA, China, Morocco and Russia.

The mining of phosphate-rich rocks has increased the mobilization of phosphorus. A total of 12×10^{12} g P yr^{-1} are mined from rock deposits. This is six times the rate at which phosphorus is locked up in ocean sediments from which the rocks are formed.

Nitrogen

Nearly 80 per cent of the atmosphere is nitrogen. In addition, air pollution has increased rates of nitrogen deposition. The main anthropogenic source is a mix of nitrogen oxides (NO_x), mainly nitrogen monoxide (NO), released during the combustion of fossil fuels in vehicles and power plants. Despite its abundance, nitrogen is more likely to be the limiting nutrient in terrestrial ecosystems (as opposed to aquatic ones), where soils can typically retain phosphorus while nitrogen is leached away.

Nutrients applied to farmland through fertilizers may spread to the wider environment by:

- drainage water percolating through the soil, leaching soluble plant nutrients
- washing of excreta, applied to the land as fertilizer, into watercourses
- erosion of surface soils or the movement of fine soil particles into subsoil drainage systems.

To learn more about the World Resources Institute assessment of eutrophication in coastal areas, go to www.pearsonhotlinks.com, insert the express code 2630P and click on activity 5.10.

In Europe, large quantities of slurry from intensively reared and housed livestock is spread on the fields. Animal excreta are very rich in both nitrogen and phosphorus and, therefore, their application to land can contribute to problems from polluted run-off.

Evaluating the impact of eutrophication

There are three main reasons why the high concentrations of nitrogen in rivers and groundwater are a problem. First, nitrogen compounds can cause undesirable effects in the aquatic ecosystems, especially excessive growth of algae. Second, the loss of fertilizer is an economic loss to the farmer. Third, high nitrate concentrations in drinking water may affect human health.

Eutrophication of Lake Erie

Natural eutrophication normally takes thousands of years to progress. In contrast, anthropogenic or cultural eutrophication is very rapid. During the 1960s, Lake Erie (on the USA–Canada border) was experiencing rapid anthropogenic eutrophication and was the subject of much concern and research.

Eutrophication of Lake Erie caused algal and cyanobacterial blooms which caused changes in water quality. The increase in cyanobacteria at the expense of water plants led to a decline in biodiversity. With fewer types of primary producer, there were fewer types of consumer, and so the overall ecosystem biodiversity decreased. Cyanobacteria are unpalatable to zooplankton, thus their expansion proceeds rapidly. The cyanobacterial blooms led to oxygen depletion and the death of fish. In addition, algal and bacterial species can cause the death of fish by clogging their gills and causing asphyxiation. Many indigenous fish disappeared and were replaced by species that could tolerate the eutrophic conditions. Low oxygen levels caused by the respiration of the increased lake phytomass killed invertebrates and fish. Increased levels of bacteria reduced water velocity and light levels, causing increased turbidity in the water and increased sedimentation. The death of macrophytes on the lake floor increased the build up of dead organic matter in the thickening lake sediments. Rotting, bacterial masses covered beaches and shorelines.

Researchers at the University of Manitoba set up the Experimental Lakes Area (ELA) in 1968 to investigate the causes and impacts of eutrophication in Lake Erie. Between June 1969 and May 1976, it was the main focus of experimental studies at the ELA.

Aerial view of lake 227 in 1994. The bright green colour is caused by cyanobacteria stimulated by the experimental addition of phosphorus for the 26th consecutive year. Lake 305 in the background is unfertilized with phosphorus.

Over a number of years, seven different lakes (ELA lakes 227, 304, 302, 261, 226, 303, and 230) were treated in different ways. Lakes 227 and 226 were especially important in showing the effect of phosphorus in eutrophication. Studies of gas exchange and internal mixing in lake 227 during the early 1970s clearly demonstrated that algae in lakes were able to obtain sufficient carbon dioxide, via diffusion from the atmosphere to the lake water, to support eutrophic blooms. 'Blue–green algae' (now called cyanobacteria) were found to be able to fix nitrogen that had diffused naturally into the lake from the air, making nitrogen available for supporting growth.

Algae may be a nuisance but they do not produce substances toxic to humans or animals. Cyanobacteria, on the other hand, produce substances that are extremely toxic causing serious illness and death if ingested. This is why cyanobacteria are a very worrying problem in water sources or reservoirs used for leisure facilities.

ELA lake 226 was the site of a very successful experiment. The lake was divided into two relatively equal parts using a plastic divider curtain. Carbon and nitrogen were added to one half of the lake, while carbon, nitrogen and phosphorus were added to the other half of the lake. For eight years, the side receiving phosphorus developed eutrophic cyanobacterial blooms, while the side receiving only carbon and nitrogen did not. The experiment suggested that in this case phosphorus was the key nutrient. A multi-billion dollar phosphate control programme was soon instituted within the St. Lawrence Great Lakes Basin. Legislation to control phosphates in sewage, and to remove phosphates from laundry detergents, was part of this programme.

Case study continued

View from above lake 226 divider curtain in August 1973. The bright green colour results from cyanobacteria which are growing on phosphorus added to the near side of the curtain.

By the mid-1970s, north American interest in eutrophication had waned. Nevertheless, the nutrient-pollution problem remains the number one water-quality problem worldwide.

Loss to farmers

Eutrophication can result in an economic loss for farmers. Farmers are keen to use NPK (nitrogen, phosphorus and potassium) fertilizers because these products increase crop growth, improve farmers' income and may help increase crop self-sufficiency in a country. However, the removal of these nutrients from the soil reduces these benefits. Even when fertilizer is not applied in autumn, arable soils often contain much inorganic nitrogen. Some of this is from fertilizer unused by the previous crop but most is from the mineralization of organic matter caused by autumn ploughing – ploughing releases vast quantities of nitrogen. However, unless a new crop is planted quickly, much of this is lost by leaching. Another influence is climate – there is normally much mineralization in the autumn when warm soils begin to get wet. In still-growing grass pasture, the nitrate is absorbed but when fields are bare soil, the nitrate is liable to leaching. This problem is especially severe where a wet autumn follows a dry summer. Much soil organic matter may be mineralized and leached at such a time.

Health concerns

The concern for health relates to increased rates of stomach cancer (caused by nitrates in the digestive tract) and to blue baby syndrome (methaemoglobinaemia), caused by insufficient oxygen in the mother's blood for the developing baby. However, critics argue that the case against nitrates is not clear – stomach cancer could be caused by a variety of factors and the number of cases of blue baby syndrome is statistically small.

CASE STUDY

Eutrophication in England and Wales

The amount of nitrates in tap water is a matter of general concern. The pattern of nitrates in rivers and groundwater shows marked regional and temporal characteristics. In the UK, it is concentrated towards the arable areas of the east, and concentrations are increasing. In England and Wales over 35 per cent of the population derive their water from the aquifers of lowland England and over 5 million people live in areas where there is too much nitrate in the water. The problem is that nitrates applied on the surface slowly make their way down to the groundwater zone – this may take up to 40 years. Thus, increasing levels of nitrate in drinking water will continue to be a problem well into the twenty-first century. The cost of cleaning nitrate-rich groundwater is estimated at between £50–300 million a year.

Management strategies for eutrophication

 It is difficult to control eutrophication because of the varied sources of the contaminants. In developing countries, many cities have a limited or absent sewage system.

In the UK, a major problem occurs when nitrates from agricultural areas percolate into the groundwater. In east Suffolk, for example, over 40 per cent of wells have nitrate concentrations over 88 mg dm^{-3}, more than twice the safe limit.

In parts of Nigeria, where nitrate concentrations have exceeded 90 mg dm^{-3} the death rate from gastric cancer is abnormally high. Table 5.4 shows global variations in eutrophication compiled from research by the United Nations Environment Programme (UNEP) and the International Lake Environment Committee (ILEC).

TABLE 5.4 GLOBAL VARIATION IN EUTROPHICATION (BASED ON UNEP/ILEC SURVEYS)	
Area	Percentage of lakes and reservoirs suffering eutrophication / %
Asia and the Pacific	54
Europe	53
Africa	28
North America	48
South America	41

CASE STUDY

Eutrophication in Kunming City, China

Dianchi Lake, near Kunming City in the Yannan Province of China, has huge problems with eutrophication. Untreated sewage has been drained into the lake since before the 1980s. Cyanobacteria (*Microcystis* spp.), have killed over 90 per cent of native water weed, fish and molluscs, so destroying the fish industry. The lake is largely green slime but because water supplies have run short, lake water from Dianchi Lake has been used since 1992 to supply Kunming's 1.2 million residents.

The city opened its first sewage treatment plant in 1993, but this copes with only 10 per cent of the city's sewage. Billions of dollars have been spent since the 1980s in attempts to clean up the lake, but with no real success.

There are three main ways of dealing with eutrophication:
- altering the human activities that produce pollution by using alternative types of fertilizer, detergent, and so on
- regulating and reducing pollutants at the point of emission (e.g. sewage treatment plants that remove nitrates and phosphates from the waste)
- clean-up and restoration of polluted water by pumping mud from eutrophic lakes.

Changing human activities

Possible measures to reduce nitrate loss (based on the northern hemisphere) include the following.
- Avoid using nitrogen fertilizers between mid-September and mid-February when soils are wet and fertilizer is most likely to be washed through the soil.
- Give preference to autumn-sown crops – their roots conserve nitrogen in the soil and use up nitrogen left from the previous year.
- Sow autumn-sown crops as early as possible and maintain crop cover through autumn and winter to conserve nitrogen.

- Use split applications to obtain the best match of nitrogen supply and demand by the crop and to reduce risk of nitrogen loss by leaching.
  - For cereals: main application in March–April, after a small early application in February.
  - For grass: small applications monthly throughout the growing season to match the requirement of plants, and especially after cutting, reduces risk of loss.
- Do not apply nitrogen next to headlands (areas at the edges of fields where tractors turn round) when the field is by a stream or lake.
- Do not apply nitrogen just before heavy rain is forecast (assuming that forecasts are accurate).
- Use less nitrogen if the previous year was dry because less will have been less lost. This is difficult to assess precisely.
- Do not plough up grass as this releases nitrogen.
- Use steep slopes for permanent pasture grass or woodland; use flat land above slopes for arable crops. This minimizes the greater risk of wash from steep land.
- Incorporate straw – straw decay uses nitrogen, with up to 13 per cent less nitrogen lost – it also locks up phosphorus.
- Direct drilling and minimal cultivation reduces nitrogen loss by up to a half. Less disturbance means less conversion of nitrogen to nitrate but straw has to be burnt.

Regulating and reducing the nutrient source

CASE STUDY

Effluent diversion at Lake Washington, USA
In some circumstances it may be possible to divert sewage effluent away from a water body. This was achieved at Lake Washington, near Seattle, USA. In 1955, Lake Washington was affected by cyanobacteria. The lake was receiving sewage effluent from about 70 000 people. The sewerage system was redesigned to divert effluent away from the lake to the nearby sea inlet of Puget Sound.

ENVIRONMENTAL PHILOSOPHIES

Different users and organizations view eutrophication in different ways – farmers claim to need to use fertilizers to improve food supply; chemical companies argue they produce fertilizers to meet demand from farmers; water companies seek money from the government and the consumer to make eutrophic water safe to drink; the consumers see rising water bills and potential health impacts of eutrophication.

Phosphate stripping
Up to 45 per cent of total phosphorus loadings to freshwater in the UK comes from sewage treatment works. This input can be reduced by 90 per cent or more by carrying out phosphate stripping. The effluent is run into a tank and dosed with a precipitant, which combines with phosphate in solution to create a solid, which then settles out and can be removed.

Domestic campaigns
Public campaigns in Australia have encouraged people to:
- use zero- or low-phosphorus detergents
- wash only full loads in washing machines
- wash vehicles on porous surfaces away from drains or gutters
- reduce use of fertilizers on lawns and gardens
- compost garden and food waste
- collect and bury pet faeces.

Clean-up strategies

Once nutrients are in an ecosystem, it is much harder and more expensive to remove them than it would have been to tackle the eutrophication at source.

The main clean-up methods available are:
- precipitation (e.g. treatment with a solution of aluminium or ferrous salt to precipitate phosphates)
- removal of nutrient-enriched sediments, for example by mud pumping
- removal of biomass (e.g. harvesting of common reed) and using it for thatching or fuel.

Removal of fish can allow primary consumer species to recover and control algal growth. Once water quality has improved, fish can be re-introduced.

Mechanical removal of plants from aquatic systems is a common method for mitigating the effects of eutrophication. Efforts may be focussed on removal of unwanted aquatic plants (e.g. water hyacinth) that tend to colonize eutrophic water. Each tonne of wet biomass harvested removes about 3 kilograms of nitrogen and 0.2 kilograms of phosphorus from the system. Alternatively, plants may be introduced deliberately to mop-up excess nutrients.

Managing eutrophication using barley bales. The bales of barley straw are just visible (brown) beneath the water surface at the right-hand edge of the lake.

Prevention of eutrophication at source compared with treating its effects (or reversing the process) has the following advantages.
- Technical feasibility – In some situations prevention at source may be achieved by diverting a polluted watercourse away from the sensitive ecosystem, while removal of nutrients from a system by techniques such as mud-pumping is more of a technical challenge.
- Cost – Nutrient stripping at source using a precipitant is relatively cheap and simple to implement. Biomass stripping of affected water is labour-intensive and therefore expensive.
- Products – Constructed wetlands may be managed to provide economic products such as fuel, compost or thatching material more easily than trying to use the biomass stripped from a less managed system.

 To learn more about experiments related to eutrophication, go to www.pearsonhotlinks.com, insert the express code 2630P and click on activity 5.11.

To learn more about experiments related to eutrophication, go to www.pearsonhotlinks.com, insert the express code 2630P and click on activity 5.11.

● **Examiner's hint:**
Evaluate – make an appraisal by weighing up the strengths and limitations.

EXERCISES

1 Outline the processes of eutrophication.

2 Evaluate the impacts of eutrophication.

3 Describe and evaluate pollution management strategies with respect to eutrophication.

4 Outline the effects of eutrophication on natural and human environments.

5 'It is easier and more cost-effective to control the causes of eutrophication rather than to deal with the symptoms (results) of eutrophication.' Critically examine this statement.

5.5 Solid domestic waste

Assessment statements
5.5.1 Outline the types of solid domestic waste.
5.5.2 Describe and evaluate pollution management strategies for solid domestic (municipal) waste.

Types of solid domestic waste

The amount of waste produced by the global population is steadily increasing. The world faces an on-going problem in how and where to dispose of this waste.

The WEEE man: a robotic figure 7 metres tall, weighing 3.3 tonnes and made from **w**aste **e**lectrical and **e**lectronic **e**quipment.

To access worksheet 5.2 on solid domestic waste, please visit www.pearsonbacconline.com and follow the on-screen instructions.

Solid domestic waste in the UK

- The UK population produces approximately 28 million tonnes of municipal (household) waste per year.
- This is almost 500 kilograms per person per year.
- The figure is growing by about 3 per cent per year.
- The disposal of this waste has local, natural and global consequences for the environment

Household waste is composed of a wide variety of materials. There is limited compositional data available, but the best overall estimates currently available are shown in Figure 5.8.

Figure 5.8
Composition of household waste.

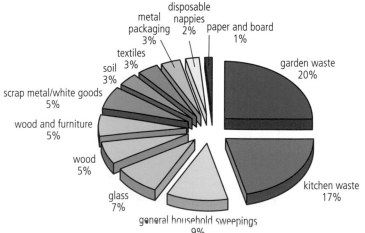

disposable
metal nappies
packaging 2% paper and board
3% 1%
textiles 3%
soil 3%
scrap metal/white goods 5%
wood and furniture 5%
wood 5%
glass 7%
general household sweepings 9%
garden waste 20%
kitchen waste 17%

1 Monitor your waste for a week and keep a waste diary. After the week, complete the table below.

Activity	Is waste produced?	Type of waste produced	What happens to the waste?
At home			
cooking			
eating			
drinking			
washing/cleaning			
watching TV			
homework			
play in garden			
In the community			
meeting friends			
going to films, etc.			
sport			
part-time work			
At school			
lessons			
break time			
other			

Nappies

Some waste material is more problematic than others. Nappies are a particular problem. Nappy waste is harmful, unnecessary and expensive. It costs £40 million a year to dispose of an estimated 1 million tonnes of nappy waste, which 75 per cent is urine and faeces. Most nappy waste is taken to landfill sites, where nappies can take an estimated 500 years to break down, and add to the build-up of methane gas. Environmentalists say that using washable nappies would represent a £500 saving per baby.

Solid domestic waste in Europe

The percentage make-up of waste in Europe other than the UK is shown in Table 5.5.

TABLE 5.5 THE PERCENTAGE COMPOSITION OF EUROPE'S WASTE							
Country	Organics	Paper/ Board	Glass	Metals	Plastics	Textiles	Other
Belgium	43	28	9	4	7	9	none
Denmark	37	30	6	3	7	18	none
Germany	32	24	8	5	9	none	22
France	21	27	7	4	11	2	28
Greece	49	20	5	4	9	13	none
Ireland	42	15	6	4	11	8	14
Italy	32	27	8	4	7	3	19
Luxembourg	41	16	4	3	8	3	25
Netherlands	39	25	8	5	8	15	none
Portugal	39	20	4	2	9	5	21
Spain	44	21	7	4	11	5	8

 To learn more about the composition of household waste in England, go to www.pearsonhotlinks.com, insert the express code 2630P and click on activity 5.12.

To learn more about the sources of domestic waste in a Japanese household, go to www.pearsonhotlinks.com, insert the express code 2630P and click on activity 5.13.

 Solid domestic waste is one of the world's major development issues. Over 25 per cent of the world's population do not have proper sanitation. The link between contaminated water and disease is very strong. Can we afford to ignore solid domestic waste?

Pollution management strategies

There are a number of methods of dealing with solid domestic waste. The most common ones include recycling, composting, landfill, and incineration. In addition, it is possible to reduce the amount of waste generated, and reuse goods to extend their lifespan (Table 5.6).

TABLE 5.6 WASTE MANAGEMENT OPTIONS FOR SOLID DOMESTIC WASTE	
Waste management options	How it works
reduce the amount of waste	• producers think more about the lifespan of goods and reduce packaging • consumers consider packaging and lifespan when buying goods
reuse goods to extent their lifespan	• bring-back schemes where containers are refilled (e.g. milk bottles) • refurbish/recondition goods to extend their useful life • used goods put to another use rather than thrown out (e.g. plastic bags used as bin liners; old clothes used as cleaning cloths) • charity shops pass on goods to new owners
recover value	• recycle goods such as glass bottles and paper • compost biodegradable waste for use as fertilizer • incinerate (burn) waste – collect electricity and heat from it
dispose of waste in landfill sites	• put waste into a hole (natural or the result of quarrying) or use to make artificial hills

Recycling

The UK has a poor record of recycling, which is much more common in other countries of the EU (Figure 5.9). The UK has long lagged behind with recycling mainly because there are many more landfill sites which are cheaper to use. Nevertheless, the UK has set a recycling target of 33 per cent by 2015. In 2005, 410 000 tonnes of plastic were collected, 43 per cent of which was recycled in the UK and almost 57 per cent was exported for recycling, mainly to Asia. However, there is growing concern that exported plastic never reaches recycling plants.

Figure 5.9
Waste management in Europe.

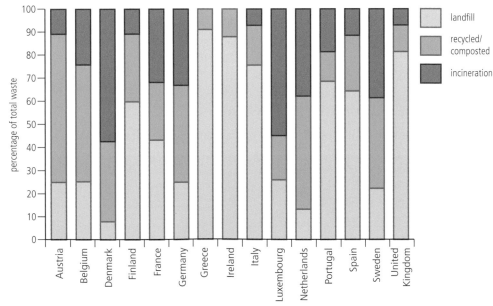

Up to 60 per cent of household waste in the USA is recyclable or compostable. But Americans compost only 8 per cent of their waste. Surveys suggest that the main reason Americans don't compost is because they think it is a complicated process.

Composting

Composting is the aerobic decomposition of biodegradable material. It recycles organic household waste into a humus-like soil. It returns valuable nutrients to the soil.

Landfill

Landfill may be cheap but it is not always healthy – and will eventually run out. Recent research and surveys show that living near to landfill sites increases the risk of health problems including heart problems and birth defects. Landfills need to be located relatively close to the source of waste, so they tend be found near areas of high population density. Landfill can give off gases such as methane and may contaminate water supplies. However, landfills are generally designed to prevent leaching. Many landfills are sited in old quarries which could be turned into lakes or nature reserves instead.

Currently, most domestic waste ends up in landfill sites. However, the reliance on landfill is unsustainable for a number of reasons:.

- There are already areas struggling to find suitable new landfill sites. This shortage of space will become more acute as the amount of waste continues to grow.
- When biodegradable waste, such as food, decomposes it releases methane which, as a greenhouse gas, contributes to global warming. It is also explosive.
- Chemicals and heavy metals can pollute the soil and groundwater. Leachate, produced from organic waste, breaks down causing the same problem.
- Communities are often violently opposed to the creation of any new sites (not-in-my-back-yard (NIMBY) principle).

Incineration

Incineration means burning. It converts the waste into ash, gas particulates and heat which can, in turn, be used to generate electricity.

Incinerators can reduce the volume of the original waste by as much as 80–90%. Thus the technology could significantly reduce the volume of waste for which for landfill disposal is necessary.

Incineration has particularly strong benefits for the treatment of certain types of waste, notably clinical waste and hazardous waste.

To learn more about landfill, go to www.pearsonhotlinks.com, insert the express code 2630P and click on activity 5.14.

ENVIRONMENTAL PHILOSOPHIES

Development organizations frequently provide aid for conservation, clean water and housing developments. Rarely do they provide funding for solid domestic waste projects. Why should sanitation be the 'Cinderella option' in the development process?

Problems with landfill and incineration

Landfill is considered the cheapest approach only because the economics of waste disposal do not yet fully take environmental costs into account. The major environmental problems associated with landfill are as follows.

- When biodegradable matter (paper, food waste and garden waste) decomposes in anaerobic conditions (without oxygen), as is the case in a landfill site, methane (a greenhouse gas) is given off.
- Some parts of any landfill site are not anaerobic, so carbon dioxide is also given off – another greenhouse gas.
- Leachates from the landfill can contaminate aquifers (underground water stores). Unfortunately, the measures used to try to reduce the escape of gases and leachates (liner systems, waste compaction and capping) also stop oxygen entering and this increases the generation of methane.
- There are local problems with noise, smell and vermin.

The major environmental problems associated with incineration are as follows.

- Air pollution – carbon dioxide, sulfur dioxide, nitrogen dioxide, nitrous oxide, chlorine, dioxin and particulates all result from incineration. In turn, these lead to a host of other environmental problems – acid rain, smogs, lung disease etc.
- The volume of traffic generated is increased – again leading to greater air pollution, noise, vibration and accidents.

In 2005, incineration produced 4.8 per cent of the electricity consumed and 13.7 per cent of the total domestic heat consumption in Denmark. A number of other European countries including Germany, the Netherlands, France and Luxemburg rely heavily on incineration for handling municipal waste.

Methane is 21 times more powerful as a greenhouse gas than carbon dioxide. Methane can seep into buildings where it represents a fire and explosive risk, or into sewers where it may suffocate workers.

- The ash which results (usually equal to 10–20 per cent of the mass of the original waste) is often toxic and still needs to be disposed of in landfill.
- Building incinerators represents a high initial capital outlay.

EXERCISES

1   Outline the types of solid domestic waste.

2   Describe and evaluate pollution management strategies for solid domestic (municipal) waste.

3   Describe how landfill works as a type of waste disposal.

4   What are the advantages of landfill?

5   What are the disadvantages of landfill?

6   In what ways is incineration a better option than landfill?

7   What are the disadvantages of incineration?

5.6   Depletion of stratospheric ozone

Assessment statements

5.6.1   Outline the overall structure and composition of the atmosphere.

5.6.2   Describe the role of ozone in the absorption of ultraviolet radiation.

5.6.3   Explain the interaction between ozone and halogenated organic gases.

5.6.4   State the effects of ultraviolet radiation on living tissues and biological productivity.

5.6.5   Describe three methods of reducing the manufacture and release of ozone-depleting substances.

5.6.6   Describe and evaluate the role of national and international organizations in reducing the emissions of ozone-depleting substances.

Structure and composition of the atmosphere

The atmosphere contains a mix of gases, liquids and solids. Atmospheric gases are held close to the Earth by gravity. These gases are relatively constant in the lower atmosphere. Nevertheless, there are important spatial and temporal variations in atmospheric composition, and this causes variations in temperature, humidity and pressure over time and between places.

Most water vapour in the atmosphere is held in the lower 10–15 kilometres. Above this, it is too cold and there is not enough turbulence or mixing to carry vapour upwards.

Solids such as dust, ash, soot and salt allow condensation to occur causing cloud formation and precipitation (rain). Locally, large concentrations of solid particles cause increases in fog, smog, haze and/or precipitation.

Variations in composition with altitude

Turbulence and mixing in the lower 15 kilometres of the atmosphere produces fairly similar 'air' throughout this section. At higher altitudes, by contrast, concentrations of certain gases occur at particular altitudes. For example, at 10–50 kilometres above the Earth there is a concentration of ozone (Figure 5.10). This concentration is significant enough to lead to an increase in atmospheric temperature in this region and, moreover, the ozone has an important screening function.

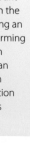

The normal components of dry air include nitrogen (78.1 per cent), oxygen (20.9 per cent), argon (0.93 per cent) and carbon dioxide (0.038 per cent). In addition, there are other important gases such as helium, ozone, hydrogen and methane. These gases are crucial. For example, changes in the amount of carbon dioxide in the atmosphere is having an effect on global warming and the destruction of ozone is having an important effect on the quality of radiation reaching the Earth's surface.

The most significant concentrations of gases at higher altitudes are:

- ozone at 10–50 kilometres
- nitrogen at 100–200 kilometres
- oxygen at 200–1100 kilometres
- helium at 1100–3500 kilometres
- hydrogen above 3500 kilometres

These concentrations of gases have an important effect on changes in temperature through the atmosphere. Above the tropopause, the temperature starts to rise. This is related to the presence of ozone and the band of warmer gases acts as a ceiling to weather systems. Its height varies seasonally and latitudinally: it is higher in summer and towards the equator. Temperatures fall in the mesosphere but increase again in the thermosphere.

Increasing lightness and decreasing density occur with increasing altitude. As air is compressible, it is denser at ground level than at altitude, since there is more air above it.

The role of ozone in the absorption of ultraviolet radiation

The amount of ozone in the atmosphere is a small but it is a vital component. Ozone occurs because oxygen rising up from the top of the troposphere reacts under the influence of sunlight to form ozone. Most ozone is created over the equator and between the tropics because this is where solar radiation is strongest. However, winds within the stratosphere transport the ozone towards the polar regions where it tends to concentrate.

Ozone has the vital role of absorbing ultraviolet (UV) radiation (wavelength 0.1–0.4 μm). It also absorbs some outgoing terrestrial radiation (wavelength 10–12 μm) – so it is a greenhouse gas. Ozone is constantly being produced and destroyed in the stratosphere in a natural dynamic balance produced by sunlight and destroyed by nitrogen oxides).

The short-wave UV radiation breaks down oxygen molecules into two single oxygen atoms. The free oxygen atoms (O) combine with oxygen molecules (O_2) to form ozone (O_3). However, other mechanisms are at work to destroy the ozone. These include photochemical interactions with molecular oxygen, the oxides of nitrogen, chlorine and bromine.

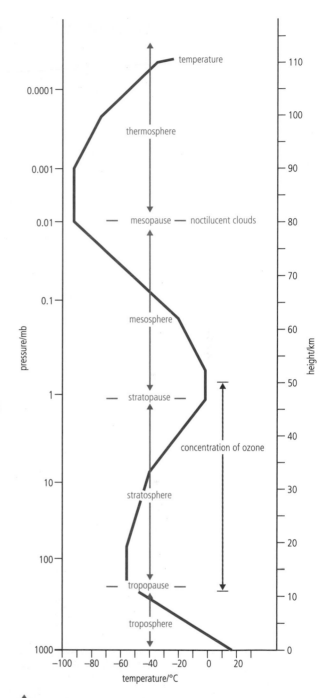

Figure 5.10
Changes in atmospheric temperature and pressure with altitude.

 To learn more about stratospheric and ground level ozone, go to www.pearsonhotlinks.com, insert the express code 2630P and click on activity 5.15.

The interaction between ozone and halogenated organic gases

Halogen – Any of a group of five non-metallic elements with a similar chemical bonding: fluorine, chlorine, bromine, iodine and astatine. They react with metals to produce a salt. Halogenated means a halogen atom has been added.

To discover the Ozone Tour, go to www.pearsonhotlinks.com, insert the express code 2630P and click on activity 5.16.

Although ozone is constantly produced and destroyed, human activities may tilt the balance. There is now clear evidence that human activities have led to the creation of a 'hole' in the ozone layer over Antarctica. Levels of ozone have been falling since 1965. Between 1970 and 1974, Crutzen and Johnson, and Stolarski and Ciceone, identified ozone destruction mechanisms involving the oxides of nitrogen and chlorine respectively. In 1974, Molina and Rowland discovered the role of chlorofluorocarbons (CFCs) in destroying stratospheric ozone. In 1985, the British Antarctic Survey reported dramatic decreases in springtime atmospheric ozone compared with the previous 30 years – they had discovered the ozone hole.

Increasing measurements of CFCs correlate with declining ozone levels. Although there are important natural sources of chlorine (e.g. volcanoes and forest fires) which affect the ozone layer, the increases recorded are probably too large to be entirely natural. There are now ozone holes at both poles, the one over Antarctica stretching as far as Argentina.

The balance of formation and destruction of stratospheric ozone is seriously affected by ozone-depleting substances (ODSs), notably those containing the halogens chlorine, fluorine and bromine. Most of ODSs do not occur naturally; they are industrial products or by-products and include CFCs, hydrochlorofluorocarbons (HCFCs), halons, and methyl bromide (bromomethane). These are usually very stable compounds – they persist in the atmosphere for decades as they travel upwards to the stratosphere. But once in the stratosphere and under the influence of UV radiation, they break down and release halogen atoms. The halogen atoms act as catalysts for the reactions that destroy ozone molecules. Thus, ODSs greatly accelerate the rate of ozone destruction.

The ozone hole is an area of reduced concentration of ozone in the stratosphere, which varies from place to place and over the course of a year. There is a very clear seasonal pattern – each springtime in Antarctica (between September and October) there is a huge reduction in the amount of ozone in the stratosphere (Figure 5.11). The ozone layer above the whole of Antarctica now thins to between 40 per cent and 55 per cent of its pre-1980 levels, with up to a 70 per cent deficiency for short periods. As the summer develops, the concentration of ozone recovers. So what causes the springtime depletion in ozone?

Figure 5.11
October ozone levels over Antarctica 1955–2005. The red line shows the trend in ozone levels whereas the blue line plots the actual concentrations measured.

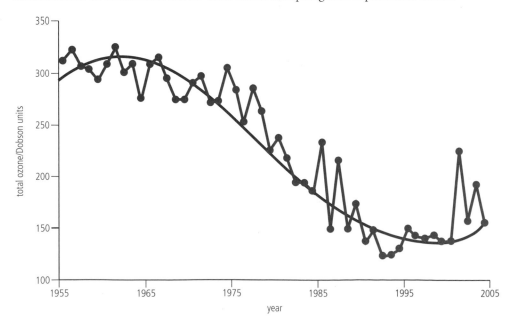

During winter in the southern hemisphere, the air over Antarctica is cut off from the rest of the atmosphere by circumpolar winds – these winds block warm air from entering Antarctica. Therefore, the temperature over Antarctica becomes very cold, often down as far as –90°C in the stratosphere. This allows the formation of clouds of ice particles. The ice particles offer surfaces on which chemical reactions can take place, involving chlorine compounds present in the stratosphere as a result of human activities. The reactions release chlorine atoms. In the presence of sunlight in the spring, the chlorine atoms destroy the ozone in a series of chemical reactions. Hence the hole in the ozone layer enlarges very rapidly in the spring.

By summer, the ice clouds have evaporated and the chlorine is converted to other compounds such as chlorine nitrate. Thus the ozone hole diminishes, although it returns the following spring.

The size of the ozone hole is impressive as well as variable. As early as 1987, it covered an area the size of continental USA and was as deep as Mount Everest.

To learn more about the development of the ozone hole, go to www.pearsonhotlinks.com, insert the express code 2630P and click on activity 5.17.

Effects of ultraviolet radiation

Effects on humans

Even though the southern hemisphere ozone hole is no longer increasing, its recurrence each year exposes humans to the most harmful wavelengths of ultraviolet radiation (UV-B). In humans, exposure to UV-B is associated with eye damage and cataracts, sunburn and skin cancers.

The effects of UV-B radiation on the eye may be acute (occurring after a short, intense exposure) or chronic (occurring after long-term exposure). The commonest acute effect, snow blindness, leaves no permanent or limited effects. In contrast, the effects of chronic exposure are irreversible and can cause the development of cataracts on the eye and eventually blindness.

Monitoring of ozone concentrations suggests an annual loss of 1 per cent. As a result, there is a rise in the rate of skin cancers, estimated at 4 per cent.

Acute exposure of the skin to solar UV-B radiation causes sunburn and, in the long term, skin cancers. The amount of UV-B radiation required to produce sunburn depends on latitude, time of day, and skin colour. Chronic exposure of the skin to UV-B radiation causes wrinkling, thinning, and loss of elasticity. Skin cancers occur most often and with high frequency in fair-skinned individuals living in sunny climates.

The immune system can be damaged by UV-B irradiation, leading to decreased immune responses to infectious agents and skin cancers. It is thought that UV-B radiation at a critical time during infection can increase the severity and duration of the disease. It is also believed that UV-B exposure during immunization can reduce the effectiveness of vaccinations. However, the full implications of the immunological effects are not well understood.

Effects on plants

Some crops and wild plants may suffer detrimental effects from increased UV-B radiation. Some varieties of crops are UV-B-sensitive and produce reduced yield following an increase in UV-B. On the other hand, commercial forests, tree breeding and genetic engineering may be used to improve UV-B tolerant plants. The spread of the ozone hole over South America is believed to have had an impact on plant productivity there – herbaceous plants native to the southern tip of South America and the Antarctic Peninsula have been affected by the current high levels of UV-B irradiation.

In aquatic ecosystems, organisms such as phytoplankton live in the upper layer of the water where there is sufficient light to support photosynthetic life. It is here that exposure to UV-B can occur. UV-B radiation may damage, in particular, those organisms that live at the surface of the water during their early life stages. The effects of UV-B radiation are particularly significant on phytoplankton, fish eggs and larvae, zooplankton and other primary and secondary consumers. Most adult fish are protected from UV-B radiation since they inhabit deep waters. Some shallow-water fish have been found to develop skin cancer.

Stratospheric ozone depletion over mid-latitudes means that UV-B levels in southern Australia are likely to have risen by 10–15 per cent over the past 20 years. There is also a clear correlation between declining ozone levels and rising UV radiation on clear-sky days in the South Island of New Zealand. Melanoma incidence has risen 15 per cent in men and 12 per cent in women over the past decade. The Cancer Institute estimates that by 2011, there will be 4184 new cases of melanoma each year for New South Wales.

Animals suffer similar effects to humans from high UV-B levels. Aquatic fauna (e.g. frogs) and aquatic flora (e.g. phytoplankton) are particularly vulnerable to UV-B radiation. Recent studies of the effects of UV-B on phytoplankton have confirmed adverse effects on growth, photosynthesis, protein and pigment content, and reproduction.

Reducing ozone-depleting substances (ODSs)

Sources of ODSs traditionally include the production of refrigerants, gas-blown plastics and the use of CFCs as propellants in aerosol cans.

In the past, huge quantities of CFCs were used as propellants in aerosol sprays but most of this demand is now met by hydrocarbons and other technologies. After aerosols, refrigeration was the next most important use for CFCs; today it seems likely that a combination of HFCs, ammonia, carbon dioxide and hydrocarbon refrigerants will replace the CFCs. Nitrogen oxides also deplete the ozone layer and can be reduced through reduced use of fossil fuels, less polluting combustion engines and cleaner plane engines.

Besides these replacement compounds, a whole raft of alternative procedures have been implemented (e.g. trigger sprays have replaced aerosol propellants, leaking CFCs have been collected, some CFC waste has been incinerated and old fridges have been locally or centrally collected).

The recovery of ODSs from products that are already in use (e.g. old refrigerators and air conditioning units) is another important part of the response to stratospheric ozone depletion. Since 1993, Australia has collected more than 3000 tonnes of ODSs which have either been recycled, stored or destroyed. Nonetheless, significant amounts remain to be collected.

In the USA, the Clean Air Act of 1990 aims to maximize recovery and recycling of ODSs (CFCs and HCFCs and their blends) during the servicing and disposal of air-conditioning and refrigeration equipment. US operations release some 111 000 metric tons of ozone-depleting refrigerants annually.

In 1992, German scientists successfully manufactured hydrocarbons for use as alternatives to CFCs in fridges. However, the development of fridges that used hydrocarbons was initially slow. The environmental campaigner, Greenpeace, commissioned *greenfreeze* fridges that used hydrocarbons from a factory in east Germany. Now most of the east German fridge market uses *greenfreeze* fridges and the first UK *greenfreeze* factory opened in 1996.

The phase-out of methyl bromide

Methyl bromide (MeBr) is an odourless, colourless gas that has been used as a soil fumigant to control pests across a wide range of agricultural sectors. Because MeBr depletes the stratospheric ozone layer, its production and import in the USA and Europe was **phased out** in 2005. Allowable exemptions to the phase-out include:
- the Quarantine and Preshipment (QPS) exemption, to eliminate quarantine pests
- the Critical Use Exemption (CUE), designed for agricultural users with no technically or economically feasible alternatives.

Among chemical alternatives, the combination of 1,3-dichloropropene (1,3-D) plus chloropicrin, dazomet, or reduced doses of metam-sodium are as effective as MeBr when applied with solarization – the UV radiation in sunlight may also have a germicidal effect. Among the non-chemical alternatives, biofumigation and solarization can be outstanding; soil-less cultivation, crop rotation, resistant varieties, and grafting are effective means of control.

National and international organizations and the reduction of ODSs

International cooperation between governments has been successful. Much of this has been organized by the UNEP. In 1985, UNEP implemented the Vienna Convention for the Protection of the Ozone Layer. This aimed to protect human health and the environment against adverse effects resulting from human activities which modified or were likely to modify the ozone layer

The 1987 Montreal Protocol on Substances that Deplete the Ozone Layer has reduced the consumption of ODSs by more than 90 per cent. By the end of 2002, industrialized countries had reduced their ODS consumption by more than 99 per cent and developing countries had reduced their consumption by slightly more than 50 per cent. A total phasing out is due by 2030. Total phase out in Europe occurred by 2000. Nevertheless, CFCs are persistent and long-lasting so their impact will continue for many decades.

Production and consumption of CFCs, halons and other ODSs have been almost completely phased out in industrialized countries and the timetable for banning the use of methyl bromide, a pesticide and agricultural fumigant, has been agreed.

Developing countries have been given a longer time period over which to phase out their release of ODSs. Many developing countries have complained that there are many valuable CFCs which would help them develop. Although there has been a fund to help industry in developing countries switch from CFCs to ozone-friendly technologies, the funds are somewhat limited hence reduction of CFC-use in some developing countries has been limited.

The most widely used ODSs (CFC-11 and CFC-12) have often been replaced with HCFCs. Although these are greenhouse gases, their global warming potential (GWP) is less than that of CFCs. However, even greater GWP reductions can be achieved by replacing CFCs with substances such as hydrocarbons (e.g. *n*-pentane, cyclopentane and isobutane), ammonia, carbon dioxide, water and air. These substances contribute only minimally (or not at all) to GWP (Table 5.7).

To learn more about the ozone secretariat, go to www.pearsonhotlinks.com, insert the express code 2630P and click on activity 5.18.

ODP stands for ozone depleting potential. ODP figures are relative to CFC-11, which has a nominal ODP of 1.

TABLE 5.7 CFCs, HCFCs AND THEIR REPLACEMENTS					
Compound	Use	Atmospheric lifetime / years	ODP relative to CFC-11	GWP relative to CO_2 at 100 years	Current main substitute
Compounds already phased out in developed countries					
CFC-11	foam expander	50	1	4000	HCFC-141
CFC-12	refrigerant	102	1	8500	HCFC-134a
CFC-113	solvent	85	0.8	5000	other technology
CFC-114	propellant	300	1.0	9300	hydrocarbon
halon-1211	fire extinguishant	20	3.0	No data	dry powder
carbon tetrachloride	raw material	42	1.1	1400	none
Compounds due to be phased out by the Montreal Protocol					
HCFC-22	refrigerant	13.3	0.06	1700	HFC blends
HCFC-123	refrigerant	1.5	0.02	93	HFC blends
HCFC-124	refrigerant	5.9	0.02	480	HFC-134a
Potential replacements, emissions controlled under Kyoto Protocol					
HFC-32	refrigerant	5.6	0	650	
HFC-125	refrigerant	32.6	0	2800	
HFC-134a	refrigerant	14.6	0	1300	
HFC-152a	propellant	1.5	0	140	
HFC-236	foam expander	20	0	6300	

CASE STUDY

Australia

Australia's obligations under the Montreal Protocol have been implemented at the national level. State legislation for ozone protection has been replaced by national legislation. For example, the New South Wales Ozone Protection Regulation 1997 was repealed in 2006.

The manufacture, import and export of all major ODSs has been completely phased out in Australia, with the exception of HCFCs, which will be phased out by 2015. In addition, methyl bromide is used for quarantine and feedstock purposes. National regulations allow for limited categories of essential or critical use for halons, CFCs and methyl bromide where no feasible alternatives are available.

Transition substances, such as hydrofluorocarbons and perfluorocarbons (which were used in place of CFCs and halons as refrigerants, solvents, cleaning solutions and fire extinguishers), are strong greenhouse gases and contribute to climate change. Their concentrations are rising rapidly in the atmosphere, albeit from currently low concentrations. Australia is the first country to implement integrated control measures to manage both ODSs and their synthetic replacements that can also act as greenhouse gases.

Future directions

Australia's response to phasing out the use of ODSs under the Montreal Protocol has been swift and effective. However, Australia accounts for less than 1 per cent of these global emissions. To assist this process, Australia participates in the Multilateral Fund for the Implementation of the Montreal Protocol (which provides funds to help developing countries phase out their usage of ODSs).

The Montreal Protocol now covers all CFCs, carbon tetrachloride and most halons. Consumption of these compounds is banned in developed countries. There is, however, some use of CFCs and halons in developing countries. A small volume of these chemicals is therefore manufactured for essential uses and developing countries.

Because they are highly stable, ODSs will persist in the atmosphere for decades to come despite action to reduce their usage. There is, therefore, a lag between action addressing ODSs and recovery of the ozone layer. Based on projections of future levels of ODSs in the stratosphere, the recovery of the ozone layer over much of Australia is likely by 2049, and over Antarctica by 2065. However, the continued accumulation of greenhouse gases is changing the temperature and thus the rate of chemical reactions in this region of the atmosphere, which may push full recovery beyond 2050, and possibly to 2100.

EXERCISES

1. Outline the overall structure and composition of the atmosphere.
2. Describe the role of ozone in the absorption of ultraviolet radiation.
3. Explain the interaction between ozone and halogenated organic gases.
4. State the effects of ultraviolet radiation on living tissues and biological productivity.
5. Describe three methods of reducing the manufacture and release of ODSs.
6. Describe and evaluate the role of national and international organizations in reducing the emissions of ODSs.
7. What was the international treaty that led to a decline in the production of CFCs?
8. Outline the difficulties in implementing and enforcing international agreements.
9. Evaluate the effectiveness of international policies to reduce ODSs.

5.7 Urban air pollution

Assessment statements
5.7.1 State the source and outline the effect of tropospheric ozone.
5.7.2 Outline the formation of photochemical smog.
5.7.3 Describe and evaluate pollution management strategies for urban air pollution.

Source and impact of tropospheric ozone

In the troposphere (lower atmosphere), ozone is considered a pollutant. It is different from the protective layer of ozone in the upper atmosphere or stratosphere (refer back to Figure 5.10, page 243). In the upper atmosphere, ozone is formed by sunlight splitting oxygen molecules into atoms which regroup to form ozone. In the lower atmosphere, ozone is formed as the result of pollution by volatile organic compounds (VOCs), hydrocarbons and oxides of nitrogen (NO_x).

VOCs are organic chemical compounds able to evaporate into gases and take part in photochemical reactions. There are many of them, including methane, ethane and alcohol.

Hydrocarbons (from unburned fuel) and nitrogen monoxide (NO) are given off when fossil fuels are burned. Nitrogen monoxide (nitric oxide) reacts with oxygen to form nitrogen dioxide (NO_2), a brown gas that contributes to urban haze and smogs (see below).

The main sources of VOCs and nitrogen oxides are road transport, solvent release from drying paints, glues or inks, and petrol handling and distribution. Nitric oxide and nitrogen dioxide are formed in combustion processes from the nitrogen present in fuels and the oxidation of nitrogen in air. At the high temperature of the internal combustion engine, atmospheric nitrogen is oxidized to nitric oxide and some nitrogen dioxide. Once the exhaust gases leave the engine, nitric oxide is oxidized to nitrogen dioxide. Nitrogen dioxide can absorb sunlight and break up to release oxygen atoms that combine with oxygen in the air to form ozone.

The photochemical reactions between the nitrogen oxides and VOCs in sunlight may take hours or days to produce ozone. Because the reactions are photochemical, ozone concentrations are greatest during the day, especially during warm, sunny, stable conditions. Above 20 °C reactions are accelerated.

Unlike other pollutants, ozone is not directly emitted from human-made sources in large quantities. Ozone occurs naturally in the upper atmosphere, but the chemical reactions between volatile organic compounds (VOCs), nitrogen oxides and sunlight can produce ground-level ozone.

To learn more about trends in ground-level ozone in the twenty-first century, go to www. pearsonhotlinks.com, insert the express code 2630P and click on activity 5.19.

Impacts

Ozone damages crops and forests; in humans it irritates eyes, causes breathing difficulties and may increase susceptibility to infection. It is highly reactive and can attack fabrics and rubber materials.

Effects on forests and crops

Ozone concentrations are generally lower in major urban areas. This is because ozone reacts with nitric oxide from exhaust emissions to form nitrogen dioxide (the most likely pollutant of city centres – see below).

Tropospheric ozone pollution has been suggested as a cause of the dieback of German forests (which had previously been linked with acid rain). Tropospheric ozone is a cause of poor air quality in the UK.

The relatively high temperature and sunshine level in the southern UK, combined with additional VOCs and nitrogen oxides blown over from Europe, mean that ozone concentrations are higher there than elsewhere in the UK. Ground level ozone affects plant photosynthesis and growth and so may significantly reduce crop yields. Crop exposure to ozone levels above a 40 ppb (the threshold used by the United Nations Economic Commission for Europe to measure crop damage) tends to be higher in the southern UK and to affect extensive areas of arable farming.

Effects on humans

Ozone can harm lung tissues, impair the body's defence mechanism, increase respiratory tract infections, and aggravate asthma, bronchitis and pneumonia. Even at relatively low levels, coughing, choking and sickness increase. The long-term effects include premature ageing of the lungs. Children born and raised in areas where there are high levels of ozone can experience up to a 15 per cent reduction in their lung capacity.

CASE STUDY

Ozone and risk of death in the USA

A new study in the USA has found that exposure to ground-level ozone is associated with an increased risk of death. Increases in the ozone level contribute to thousands of deaths every year. The risk of death is similar for adults of all ages but slightly higher for people with respiratory or cardiovascular problems. The increase in deaths occur at ozone levels below the clean air standards of the Environmental Protection Agency (EPA).

National air quality and mortality data from 95 large urban areas in the USA for years 1987–2000 were used to investigate whether daily and weekly exposure to ground-level ozone was associated with mortality. The researchers adjusted for particulate matter, weather, seasonality, and long-term trends. An increase of 10 ppb in the daily ozone levels for the previous week was associated with a 0.52 per cent increase in daily mortality. This corresponds to 3767 additional deaths annually in the 95 urban areas studied. According to the study, if ozone levels in the USA were reduced by about a third, about 4000 lives each year would be saved.

To learn more about ozone and its impact on health, go to www.pearsonhotlinks.com, insert the express code 2630P and click on activity 5.20.

The formation of photochemical smog

Photochemical smog refers to poor air quality caused by a mixture of nitrogen oxides and VOCs. Photochemical smog is associated with high air pressure. This is because winds in a high pressure system are usually weak. Hence pollutants remain in the area and are not dispersed. Poor air quality often persists for many days because stable high pressure conditions generally prevail for a few days. In some climates, notably Mediterranean climates, stable high pressure conditions persist all season, hence poor air quality can remain for months. In monsoonal areas, smog occurs in the dry season.

Photochemical smog over Mexico City (page 252).

Summer smog

Summer smog occurs on calm sunny days when photochemical activity leads to ozone formation. Ozone is formed when nitrogen oxides and VOCs react in the sunlight. Other compounds are also formed including acid aerosols (sulfates, sulfuric acid, nitrates and nitric acid), aldehydes, hydrogen peroxide and peroxacetyl nitrate (PAN). Ozone formation may take a number of hours, by which time the polluted air has drifted into surrounding suburban and rural areas. Hence ozone pollution may be greater outside the city centre.

In city centres, nitrogen dioxide is more likely to be the main pollutant. Vehicles emit two forms of nitrogen oxide – nitric oxide and nitrogen dioxide. The nitric oxide is converted (oxidized) into nitrogen dioxide by reactions with oxygen and ozone. This is turn reduces the ozone concentration over city centres.

To learn more about smog levels in Los Angeles on 4 July 2008, go to www.pearsonhotlinks.com, insert the express code 2630P and click on activity 5.21.

Winter smog

Winter smogs are associated with temperature inversions (Figure 5.12) and high levels of sulfur dioxide and other pollutants, due to increased heating of homes, offices and industries. Under cold conditions, vehicles operate less efficiently until they have warmed up. This inefficient operation releases larger amounts of carbon monoxide and hydrocarbons. Urban areas surrounded by high ground are especially at risk from winter smog. This is because cold air sinks in from the surrounding hills, reinforcing the inversion. This occurs on a range of scales from relatively minor (e.g. Oxford, UK) to major (e.g. Mexico City).

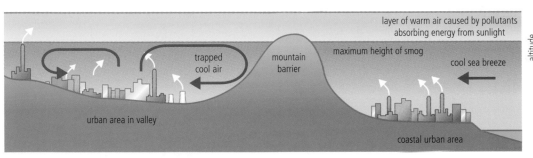

Figure 5.12
Temperature inversion and winter smog.

Trends

Background levels of ground-level ozone have risen substantially over the last century. There is evidence that the pre-industrial near ground-level concentrations of ozone were typically 10–15 ppb. The current annual mean concentrations are approximately 30 ppb over the UK. The number of hours of high ozone concentrations tends to increase from north to the south across the country. Concentrations can rise substantially above background levels in summer heat waves when there are continuous periods of bright sunlight with temperatures above 20 °C, and light winds. Once formed, ozone can persist for several days and can be transported long distances. Thus, pollution transported with continental air masses plays a significant role in UK ozone episodes.

ENVIRONMENTAL PHILOSOPHIES

Environmental philosophies (and policies) may change when certain administrations are under the spotlight. In order to clean up Beijing for the 2008 summer Olympics, the Chinese government enacted a series of policies (banning cars, closing factories, relocating a steel works) so that air quality was above average for the duration of the Games when the world's gaze was firmly fixed on Beijing (pages 226–28).

CASE STUDY

Air pollution in Mexico City

In Mexico City, the average visibility has decreased from 100 kilometres in the 1940s to about 1.5 kilometres in the 2000s. Levels of nitrogen dioxide regularly exceed international standards by two to three times, and levels of ozone are twice as high as the maximum allowed limit for one hour a year. This occurs several times every day.

The average altitude of Mexico City is 2240 metres above sea level. Consequently, average atmospheric pressure is roughly 25 per cent lower than at sea level. The lowered partial pressure of oxygen (pO_2) has significant effects:

- people living at this altitude require more red blood cells
- fuel combustion in vehicle engines is incomplete and results in higher emissions of carbon monoxide and other compounds such as hydrocarbons and VOCs.

The most important air pollutants in Mexico City are PM_{10}, ozone (O_3), sulfur dioxide (SO_2), nitrogen oxides (NO_x), hydrocarbons, and carbon monoxide (CO). Intense sunlight turns these into photochemical smog. In turn, the smog prevents the Sun from heating the atmosphere enough to penetrate the inversion layer blanketing the city.

The most serious pollutants are PM_{10} and ozone (Figure 5.13). In the late 1990s, ozone levels exceeded standards on almost 90 per cent of days and PM_{10} exceeded standards on 30–50 per cent of days. Research suggests that reducing PM_{10} would yield the greatest health and financial benefits. Reducing both ozone and PM_{10} by 10 per cent would save US$760 million a year. In human terms, this would result in over 33 000 fewer emergency visits and over 4000 fewer hospital admissions for respiratory distress in 2010. In addition, it would lead to more than 260 fewer infant deaths a year.

Figure 5.13
Air quality in Mexico City.

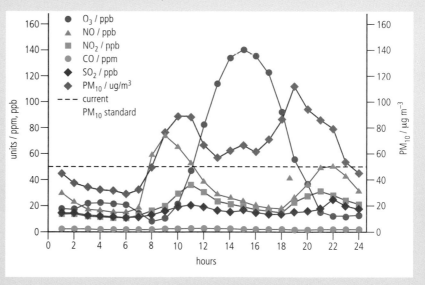

The main programmes to combat air pollution in the Mexico City Metropolitan Area are as follows.
- Reduce the use of private vehicles: the government has implemented a one-day-stop programme called *Hoy no curcula* (today my car doesn't move).
- Stopping days are randomly distributed to encourage car owners to use public transport and/or adopt car-pooling.
- Control of vehicle conditions: the enforcement of engine maintenance standards.
- Change of fuels: only small changes in gasoline quality have been accepted so far.
- Two major programmes already working within the Mexico City Metropolitan Area:
  – reduction of lead and sulfur in fuels
  – compulsory implementation of catalytic converters.

Most people travel around Mexico City using public transport (74 per cent). Although private transport only accounts for about a quarter of the population, it uses about three-quarters of the total energy. More than 3 million vehicles – 30 per cent of them more than 20 years old – use Mexico City's roads.

However, despite the measures taken so far, the combination of Mexico City's size (20 million), the number of cars, industries and its altitude mean that photochemical smog is likely to remain a problem. The national debt and the poverty experienced by so many of its population mean that a number of more costly policies to improve the environment cannot be implemented.

To access worksheet 5.3 on urban air pollution, please visit www. pearsonbacconline.com and follow the on-screen instructions.

5.8 Acid deposition

Assessment statements

5.8.1   Outline the chemistry leading to the formation of acidified precipitations.

5.8.2   Describe three possible effects of acid deposition on soil, water and living organisms.

5.8.3   Explain why the effect of acid deposition is regional rather than global.

5.8.4   Describe and evaluate pollution management strategies for acid deposition.

Acid rain and its effects

Sulfur dioxide (SO_2) and nitrogen oxides (NO_x) are emitted from industrial complexes, vehicles and urban areas. Some of these oxides fall directly to the ground as **dry deposition** (dry particles, aerosols and gases) close to the source (Figure 5.14).

Formation of acid rain

The longer the SO_2 and NO_x remain in the air, the greater the chance they will be oxidized to sulfuric acid (H_2SO_4) and nitric acid (HNO_3). These acids dissolve in cloud droplets (rain, snow, mist, hail) and reach the ground as **wet deposition**. Wet deposition can be carried thousands of kilometres downwind from the source.

Rainwater is normally a weak carbonic acid with a pH of about 5.5. Acid rain is a more acidic substance, due to the addition of sulfur dioxide and the oxides of nitrogen. Any rain with a pH below 5.5 is termed 'acid rain'.

Figure 5.14
Formation of acid deposition.

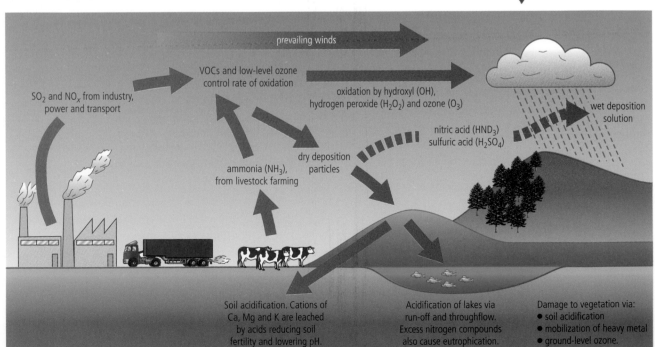

prevailing winds

VOCs and low-level ozone control rate of oxidation

oxidation by hydroxyl (OH), hydrogen peroxide (H_2O_2) and ozone (O_3)

wet deposition solution

SO_2 and NO_x from industry, power and transport

nitric acid (HND_3) sulfuric acid (H_2SO_4)

dry deposition particles

ammonia (NH_3), from livestock farming

Soil acidification. Cations of Ca, Mg and K are leached by acids reducing soil fertility and lowering pH.

Acidification of lakes via run-off and throughflow. Excess nitrogen compounds also cause eutrophication.

Damage to vegetation via:
● soil acidification
● mobilization of heavy metal
● ground-level ozone.

The dissolved acids consist of sulfate ions (SO_4^{2-}), nitrate ions (NO_3^-) and hydrogen ions (H^+). These ions form **acid rain**. Transport of pollutants over 500 kilometres is most likely to produce strong acid rain. Until about the 1960s, acid rain was a local phenomenon. However, the construction of tall smokestacks (e.g. the 381 metre superstack at Sudbury, Ontario) forced the pollutants higher in the atmosphere and resulted in acid rain falling at greater distances from the original source.

Effects of acid rain

Acidified lakes

Acidified lakes are characterized by:
- an impoverished species structure
- visibility several times greater than normal
- white moss spreading across the bottom of the lake
- increased levels of dissolved metals such as cadmium, copper, aluminium, zinc and lead (so these metals become more easily available to plants and animals).

The most important health effect of acid water is the result of its ability to flush trace metals from soil and pipes. Some wells in Sweden have aluminium levels of up to 1.7 mg dm^{-3}, the World Health Organization safe limit is 0.2 mg dm^{-3}. High levels of mercury accumulated in fish can cause serious health problems when the fish are eaten by people.

The first effects of acid rain were noted in Scandinavian lakes in the 1960s. Over 18 000 lakes in Sweden are acidified, 4000 of them are seriously affected. Fish stocks in about 9000 Swedish lakes, mostly in the south and the centre of the country, are badly affected. In the Eastern USA and Canada, over 48 000 lakes are too acidic to support fish.

Trees and forests

Acid rain severely affects trees and forests. It breaks down lipids in the foliage and damages membranes which can lead to plant death. Sulfur dioxide interferes with the process of photosynthesis. Coniferous trees seem to be most at risk from acid rain. These trees do not shed their needles at the end of every year: on a healthy conifer, needles can be up to seven years old, but trees affected by acid rain often have needles from only the last two or three years. This means the tree has far fewer needles than normal. If a conifer loses over 65 per cent of its needles, it will probably die. Besides this, where soil pH is below 4.2, aluminium is released – this damages root systems and decreases tree growth, as well as increasing development of abnormal cells and premature loss of needles.

Young trees in soils affected by acid rain often show abnormally rapid growth. This is because the nitrogen in the pollutants acts as a fertilizer. However, the root systems do not develop as well as in trees that have to collect their nutrients from a larger area and the trees are more easily blown over. Also, they are short of other vital nutrients and the wood is likely to be very soft making the trees more prone to attacks from insects.

Damaged conifers are easily recognizable. The extremities of the trees die, especially the crown which is most exposed. Needles drop, so the tree looks very thin. Branches on some trees droop. In most cases, acid rain does not kill the tree. But it is an added pressure on the tree which is more likely to suffer damage from stresses such as insects, fungi, frost, wind and drought. Although deciduous trees generally do not suffer as much, research is showing that their growth is also affected.

The low pH of soil and the presence of metals may cause damage to root hairs (used by the tree to absorb nutrients). The tree loses vitality, growth is retarded, there is an inability to cope with stress (such as frost, drought and pests); the tree becomes susceptible to injury. Needles turn brown, fall off, and finally the whole branches snap away. In parts of Germany, more than 50 per cent of the spruce trees are dead or damaged.

It is the extreme pH values which cause most damage to plants and animals. Very often organisms are exposed to extremely low levels of pH during the most sensitive part of their life cycle (for fish this may be the fry stage). These short periods coincide with snow melt and the accompanying acid surge. At these times the water also has a high metal content.

To learn more about acid rain in general, go to www. pearsonhotlinks.com, insert the express code 2630P and click on activity 5.23.

Distribution of acid deposition and management strategies

Acidification is largely related to human activity. Many countries produce the pollutants and they may be deposited many hundreds of kilometres from their point of origin. However, there are variations within areas receiving acid rain. Some storms produce more acid rain than usual; lime-rich soils and rocks are better able to absorb and neutralize the acidity.

In the 1980s and 1990s, the areas most affected by acid rain included Sweden, Norway, eastern North America, Germany, Belgium, the Netherlands, Scotland, countries of the former Yugoslavia, Austria and Denmark (Figure 5.15).

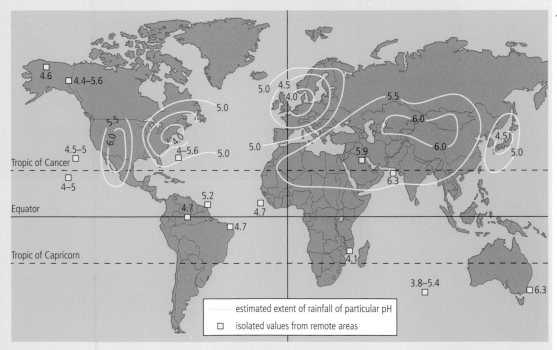

Figure 5.15
Global locations of acidified deposition.

These areas have a number of features in common.
- They are industrialized belts.
- They are downwind of dense concentrations of fossil-fuel power stations, smelters and large cities.
- Some of them are in different climate zones from the source areas – coniferous forests in cooler areas are more affected than temperate deciduous forests because carbon dioxide is more soluble at lower temperatures, so colder areas have more acidic precipitation.
- They are upland areas with high rainfall.
- They contain lots of forest, streams and lakes.
- They have thin soils.

The main trends in the distribution of acid deposition in the last 20 years have been due to increased sulfur emissions in newly industrializing countries (NICs) and in developing countries. In China, the worst affected areas have been in the south – the Pearl River delta and central and eastern areas of Guangxi. In South Africa, coal-burning power stations and large metal-working industries are concentrated in the Eastern Transvaal Highveld; rainfall in the area has, on average, a pH of 4.2 and has been recorded at pH 3.7. Brazil and Nigeria have also been affected.

In contrast, there has been a dramatic decrease in sulfur dioxide emissions in 1990–2000, especially in the EU (decreased 52 per cent) and North America (by 17 per cent).

There are also natural causes of acidification: bog moss secretes acid, heathers increase soil acidity and conifer plantations acidify soils. Litter from conifers is acidic and not easily broken down – the sitka spruce is not native to Britain and specialized decomposing bacteria are absent. This leads to the accumulation of an acid humus layer in the soil.

Volcanoes are also important sources of sulfur dioxide and nitrogen dioxide. For example, before the eruption of the Soufrière volcano in 1995, Montserrat had some of the finest cloud forest in the Caribbean. By 1996, vegetation loss from acid rain, gases, heat, and dust was severe and the lake at the top of Chances Peak was recorded at pH 2.0 (1000 times more acidic than a pH 5.0).

Acidified forests near Plymouth, capital of Montserrat.

Some environments are able to neutralize the effects of acid rain. This is referred to as buffering capacity. Chalk and limestone areas are very alkaline and can neutralize acids effectively. The underlying rocks over much of Scandinavia, Scotland and northern Canada are granite. They are naturally acid, and have a very low buffering capacity. It is in these areas that there is the worst damage from acid rain.

Management of acid deposition: prevention or cure?

Given the causes of acid deposition – industrial and transport emissions – it is not easy to target all potential polluters. But it is expensive and time-consuming to treat extensive areas already affected by acid deposition.

Repairing the damage may include liming acid waters; however, this is not really sustainable.

Prevention has a number of options:
- burn less fossil fuel (this requires a government initiative in order to switch to nuclear or hydro-power)
- reduce the number of private cars on the road and increase the number of people using public transport or park-and-ride schemes
- switch to low sulfur fuel (oil/gas plus high-grade coal)
- remove sulfur before combustion (expensive for coal, cheaper for oil)
- reduce sulfur oxides released on combustion (fluidized bed technology, FBT)
- burn coal in presence of crushed limestone in order to reduce the acidification process
- remove sulfur from waste gases after combustion (flue-gas desulfurization, FGD)
- allow decomposition of plants to return nutrients to the soil and offset the acidification process.

Both FBT and FGD are well developed and effective but they are very expensive. FBT brings the flue gases into contact with a sulfur-absorbing chemical, such as limestone, which can capture up to 95 per cent of the sulfur pollutants in power stations. FGD removes sulphur dioxide from exhaust flue gases in power stations.

There are different methods of FGD:
- wet scrubbing – uses alkaline sorbents such as limestone to absorb the sulfur dioxide
- spray dry scrubbing – uses hydrated lime to form a mix of calcium sulfate/sulfite
- scrubbing with a sodium sulfite solution
- dry scrubbing – uses a dry absorbent of coal ash and lime to collect the sulfur dioxide.

In the UK, 46 per cent of nitrogen oxides come from power stations, 28 per cent comes from vehicle exhausts. Emission from power stations can be reduced by FGD and special boilers which reduce the amount of air present at combustion. Car exhaust emissions can be reduced by different types of engine or exhaust, lower speed limits and more public transport.

To learn more about acid rain and its management, go to www.pearsonhotlinks.com, insert the express code 2630P and click on activity 5.24.

Legislation

As acid deposition is often a transboundary issue, legislation has to involve many countries. The 1979 *Convention on Long-Range Transboundary Air Pollution* was crucial in the clean-up of acidification in Europe.
- It brought together polluter and polluted.
- It set clear targets for pollution reduction.
- It made polluters recognize their international environmental responsibilities.

The 1999 Gothenburg Protocol to abate acidification, eutrophication and ground level ozone commits countries to reduce their emissions of sulfur dioxide, oxides of nitrogen, VOCs and ammonia.

To learn more about the *Convention on Long-Range Transboundary Air Pollution*, go to www.pearsonhotlinks.com, insert the express code 2630P and click on activity 5.25.

EXERCISES

1 Outline the chemistry leading to the formation of acidified precipitation.
2 Describe three possible effects of acid deposition on soil, water and living organisms.
3 Explain why the effect of acid deposition is regional rather than global.
4 Describe and evaluate pollution management strategies for acid deposition.
5 This photo shows a natural cause of acidification.

   (a) Identify and explain the cause of acidification.
   (b) Identify and explain two other natural causes of acidification.
   (c) Distinguish between wet and dry deposition.
   (d) Outline the impacts of acidification of vegetation.

PRACTICE QUESTIONS

1 Study the table below which shows the results of a survey of a stream above and below an outlet from a sewage works. The figure below is a sketch map of the stream and the outlet.

Site	CSA* / m²	Velocity / m sec⁻¹	Temp / °C	Oxygen / %	pH	No. of caddis fly	No. of bloodworms
1	2.1	0.2	18	0.1	6.0	12	0
2	2.3	0.2	17	0.2	6.0	15	0
3	2.2	0.3	18	0.1	7.0	11	0
4	3.8	0.3	23	0.3	6.5	0	16
5	3.9	0.6	22	1.8	7.0	0	1
6	4.1	0.8	22	1.7	7.5	1	0
7	3.9	0.7	20	1.6	6.5	2	0
8	4.0	0.7	22	1.5	7.0	7	0

* Cross sectional area

Map of the surveyed stream. ▶

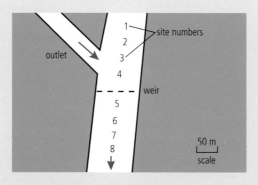

(a) Define the terms *water quality*, *pollution* and *discharge*. *[3]*

(b) Plot the results for variations in oxygen content along the course of the stream. How does the oxygen content change at sites 4 and 5? Explain why. *[6]*

(c) What is the trend in temperature levels between site 1 and site 8? *[3]*

(d) **(i)** What does pH measure?
    (ii) What type of scale is it measured on?
    (iii) How do you account for the relatively small linear variations in the stream's pH? *[3]*

(e) Choose a river or stream that you have studied in detail. How easy is it to:
    (i) monitor water quality along the length of the stream?
    (ii) trace the source of the 'pollution'? *[3]*

2 The figure below shows the monthly average air pollution index in Beijing between August 2003 and January 2009.

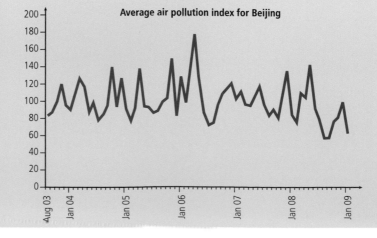

(a) What is meant by the term *blue sky days*? [1]

(b) Describe the trend in blue sky days between August 2003 and January 2009. [4]

(c) What evidence is there to suggest a seasonal pattern in the number of blue sky days? [3]

(d) Suggest reasons to explain the variations or lack of variations in the seasonal frequency of blue sky days. [4]

3 Evaluate the costs and benefits to society of the World Health Organization's ban on the use of the pesticide DDT. [5]

Sources of cultural eutrophication.
▼

4 Study the figure below which shows sources of cultural eutrophication.

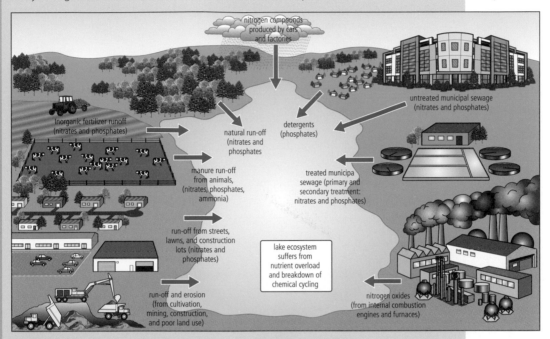

Source: http:///library.thinkquest.org/04oct/01590/pollution/culturaleutroph.jpg

(a) What is meant by the term *cultural eutrophication*? [1]

(b) Suggest **two** ways in which urban areas may contribute to eutrophication. [2]

(c) What are the natural sources of nutrients as suggested by the figure above? [1]

(d) Briefly explain the process of eutrophication. [5]

5 The table below shows the main methods of waste disposal in selected European countries.

Country	Landfill	Incineration	Composting	Recycling	Other
Belgium	39	52	2	7	–
Denmark	18	58	1	22	1
France	45	45	6	4	–
Germany	42	25	10	22	1
Greece	94	–	–	6	–
Ireland	99	–	–	1	–
Italy	85	7	–	4	4
Luxembourg	24	47	1	28	–
Netherlands	40	28	15	17	–
Portugal	35	–	10	1	54
Spain	83	6	10	1	–
UK	85	10	–	5	–
Total	58	22	5	10	5

(a) Choose a suitable method to show this data. [5]

(b) Compare the variations in the proportion of landfill between the countries. [4]

(c) Suggest reasons why there is such a large variation in the proportion of waste that is recycled. [4]

(d) Comment on the amount of composting that occurs in European countries. [5]

6 The figure below shows how human activity can destroy ozone in the atmosphere.

How ozone is destroyed by CFCs. ▶

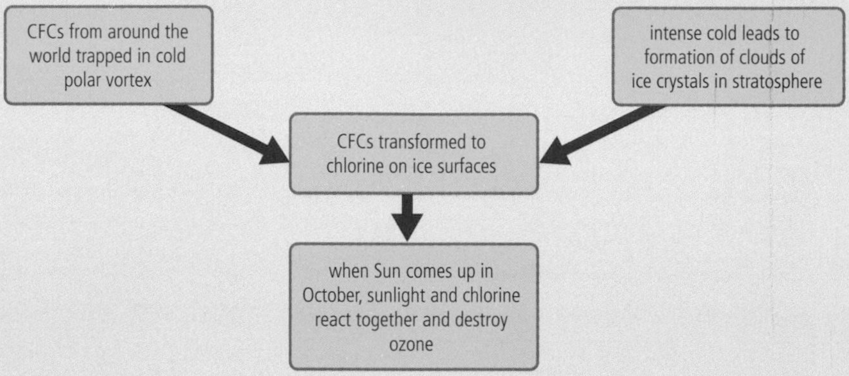

CFCs from around the world trapped in cold polar vortex

intense cold leads to formation of clouds of ice crystals in stratosphere

CFCs transformed to chlorine on ice surfaces

when Sun comes up in October, sunlight and chlorine react together and destroy ozone

(a) State **one** advantage of stratospheric ozone. [1]

(b) Identify **two** sources of CFCs. [2]

(c) Explain how CFCs can lead to a decline in ozone. [3]

7 The figure below shows the ozone hole over the southern hemisphere in 1980 and 1991.

Ozone hole over the Antarctic (1980 and 1991). ▶

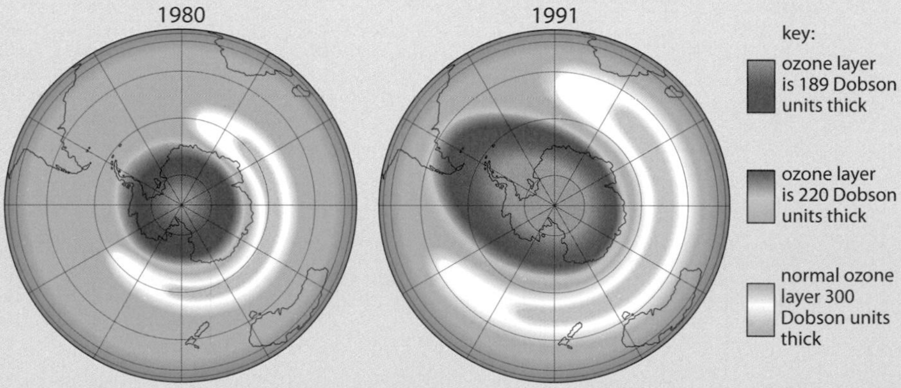

1980

1991

key:

ozone layer is 189 Dobson units thick

ozone layer is 220 Dobson units thick

normal ozone layer 300 Dobson units thick

To access worksheet 5.4 with more practice questions relating to Chapter 5, please visit www.pearsonbacconline.com and follow the on-screen instructions.

(a) What is meant by the term *ozone hole*? [1]

(b) Describe the changes in the ozone hole over the southern hemisphere between 1980 and 1991. [3]

(c) Outline the potential impacts of UV radiation on ecosystems and human health. [4]

Assessment statements
6.1.1 Describe the role of greenhouse gases in maintaining mean global temperature.
6.1.2 Describe how human activities add to greenhouse gases.
6.1.3 Discuss qualitatively the potential effects of increased mean global temperature.
6.1.4 Discuss the feedback mechanisms that would be associated with an increase in mean global temperature.
6.1.5 Describe and evaluate pollution management strategies to address the issue of global warming.
6.1.6 Outline the arguments surrounding global warming.
6.1.7 Evaluate contrasting human perceptions of the issue of global warming.

Role of greenhouse gases in maintaining mean global temperature

The preconditions for life to exist are a source of energy, water, nutrients, and warmth. The chemical reactions that support life-processes work at optimal temperatures. Colder conditions mean that enzyme reactions do not operate at fast enough rates to support life. The average temperature on the Earth is 15 °C, and without this warmth, life could not exist on the planet. The temperature of the Earth is maintained by the atmosphere that surrounds the planet. Within the atmosphere, certain gases trap radiation that heats the surface (Figure 2.27, page 46).

Short-wave ultraviolet (UV) light from the Sun is reflected from the surface of the Earth as infrared (IR) light (which has a longer wavelength). Atmospheric gases are transparent to incoming short-wave radiation but either trap or reflect back to Earth outgoing long-wave radiation. The process is sometimes known as 'radiation trapping'. This effect is caused mainly by water vapour and carbon dioxide. Other gases involved are methane (CH_4), nitrous oxide (N_2O), and ozone (O_3). The gases create a 'thermal blanket' that maintains an average Earth temperature that can support life.

Because these gases act in the same way that glass acts in a greenhouse, they are called **greenhouse gases** and the effect they have is called the **greenhouse effect** (Figure 6.1).

To access worksheet 6.1 on greenhouse gas emissions, please visit www.pearsonbacconline.com and follow the on-screen instructions.

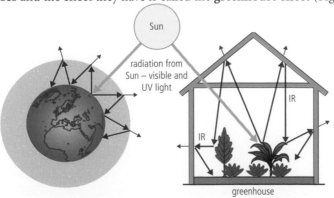

radiation from Sun – visible and UV light

Figure 6 1
Greenhouse gases let through short-wave UV radiation but trap longer wavelength IR radiation, which warms the planet. Glass in greenhouses performs the same function to keep the interior of the greenhouse warm.

Water vapour is the largest single greenhouse gas – it accounts for about 95 per cent by volume of all greenhouse gases.

Although greenhouse gases make up only about 1 per cent of the atmosphere, they regulate our climate and make life possible. The term 'greenhouse effect' tends to be viewed negatively today, but greenhouse gases enable world temperatures to be warmer than they would otherwise be. Without them, the average temperature on Earth would be colder by approximately 30 °C (54 °F) – far too cold to sustain our current ecosystems.

Greenhouse gases in geological time

There has been considerable fluctuation of carbon dioxide level and temperature throughout the history of the Earth (Figure 6.2).

Figure 6.2
(**a**) Carbon dioxide and temperature change throughout the Quaternary Period (the Pleistocene and Holocene Epochs make up the Quaternary Period).
(**b**) Carbon dioxide levels and average global temperature over Phanerozoic time (the span of geological periods from the Precambrian to the present Quaternary when animal life became abundant on the Earth – up to 542 million years ago).

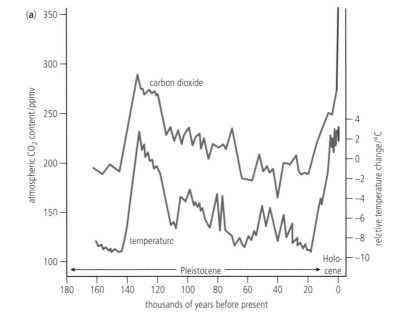

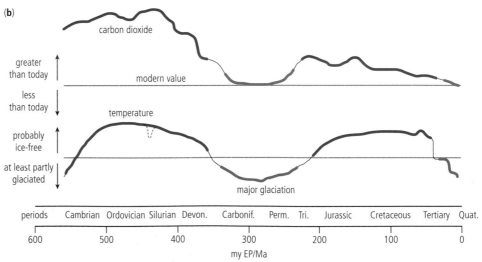

Earth's atmosphere today contains about 380 ppm (parts per million) carbon dioxide (CO_2) – 0.038 per cent of the atmosphere. Atmospheric concentrations of carbon dioxide in the Early Carboniferous Period were very high at around 1500 ppm, but by the Middle Carboniferous had declined to about 350 ppm – comparable to today's figure.

Average global temperatures in the Early Carboniferous Period were approximately 20 °C, corresponding to the high carbon dioxide levels. Cooling during the Middle Carboniferous reduced average global temperatures to about 12 °C (which is also comparable to today's levels).

So, in the last 600 million years of Earth's history, only the Carboniferous Period and our present age (the Quaternary Period) have had carbon dioxide levels of less than 400 ppm. However, levels of carbon dioxide are currently rising and the increase is thought to be entirely due to human activities. Humans have added up to 2.7 gigatonnes (Gt) of carbon to the atmosphere every year, increasing carbon dioxide levels from 280 ppm in 1850 to 379 ppm today (although this is still far less carbon dioxide than has been usual over geological time, it is still a significant rise in 160 years). Temperatures have been rising over this same period (Figure 6.3).

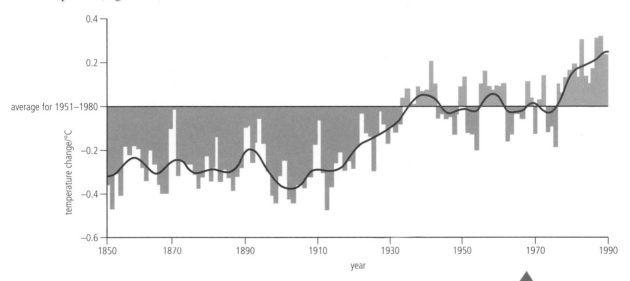

There are various explanations for the trend seen in the graph in Figure 6.3:
- the onset of global industrialization and the subsequent production of pollution derived from fossil fuels
- deforestation, particularly of rainforest
- volcanic activity
- sunspot activity.

The first two bullet points above assume a link between carbon dioxide emissions and temperature increase. The last two suggest possible natural phenomena that may have increased temperatures. Bearing in mind the large increase in carbon dioxide concentrations since the Industrial Revolution, most scientists make the assumption that the increase in temperature is caused by human activities, although as with comparisons between any two variables, correlation does not prove causation, especially when complex systems such as the atmosphere and biosphere are involved.

▲
Figure 6.3
Mean global climate change from 1850 to 1990. The graph shows smoothed curve of annual average temperature. There is an overall upward trend, accelerating in the last quarter of the graph. Before about 1935, temperatures were all below the average for 1951–1980, from about 1980 they have all been above the average.

 Global warming challenges views of certainty within the sciences. In the popular perception, global warming is having a negative impact on the world. There is, moreover, some confusion between the public perception of global warming and the greenhouse effect. The greenhouse effect is a natural process, without which there would be no life on Earth. The *enhanced* or *accelerated* greenhouse effect is synonymous with global warming. The enhanced greenhouse effect is largely due to human (anthropogenic) forces, although feedback mechanisms may trigger some natural forces, too. Lobby groups and politicians will take views which suit their own economic and political ends. In the USA, the strength of the oil companies during the Bush Administration was seen by many as an example of economic groups, and the politicians they supported, choosing a stance which was not in the long-term environmental, social or economic interest of the world. But it did benefit the oil companies and the politicians they supported.

Human activity and the greenhouse effect

Human activities have increased levels of greenhouse gases in the atmosphere. The best known example is the increase in carbon dioxide release by burning fossil fuels. But increases in levels of other gases (e.g. methane and nitrous oxide) are also linked to human activity.

There is much concern that the increases in these gases in the atmosphere is causing an increase in average temperature of the Earth's atmosphere (Figure 6.4).

Figure 6.4
The increase in greenhouse gases in the atmosphere due to human activity (human-enhanced greenhouse effect) may be causing global warming.

To learn more about current trends in carbon dioxide levels, go to www.pearsonhotlinks.com, insert the express code 2630P and click on activity 6.1.

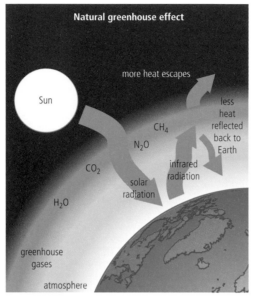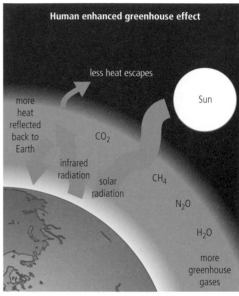

The main human activities releasing greenhouse gases are as follows (Figures 6.5 and 6.6).
- Burning fossil fuels (coal, oil, gas) and releasing carbon dioxide.
- Deforestation affects carbon dioxide levels in a number of ways. Carbon dioxide is released through the breakdown of forest biomass and the increased rate of breakdown in organic content in soils (due to exposure to heat and water). Reduction in forest cover reduces the amount of carbon dioxide taken out of the atmosphere by photosynthesis. Deforestation is largely driven by pressures to free-up land for housing and agriculture and to generate income from timber exports.
- Increased cattle ranching has led to increased methane levels: cows digest grass via fermentation and anaerobic bacteria in their gut. This releases methane as a waste product. Cattle ranching increases as the demands for beef increases.
- Rice farming in padi fields creates waterlogged fields where anoxic conditions (low oxygen levels) enable anaerobic bacteria to thrive, also leading to increased methane release.
- Using fertilizers in agricultural systems has led to higher nitrous oxide (N_2O) concentrations when the fertilizers break down.

Figure 6.5
Deforestation, mainly in the tropics, and use of fossil fuels account for the vast bulk of carbon dioxide emissions.

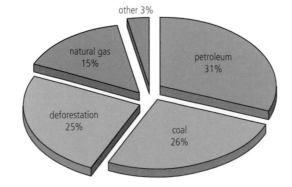

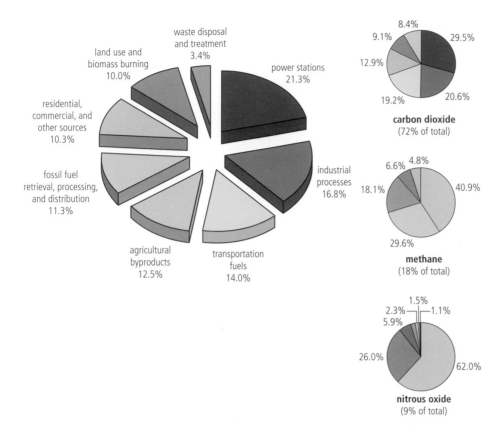

Annual greenhouse gas emissions by sector

waste disposal and treatment 3.4%

land use and biomass burning 10.0%

power stations 21.3%

residential, commercial, and other sources 10.3%

industrial processes 16.8%

fossil fuel retrieval, processing, and distribution 11.3%

agricultural byproducts 12.5%

transportation fuels 14.0%

8.4%
9.1%
29.5%
12.9%
20.6%
19.2%

carbon dioxide
(72% of total)

6.6% 4.8%
18.1%
40.9%
29.6%

methane
(18% of total)

1.5%
2.3% 1.1%
5.9%
26.0%
62.0%

nitrous oxide
(9% of total)

Figure 6.6
Primary industrial sources of greenhouse gases and relative contribution of each source.

The quantity of greenhouse gases emitted by any individual country depends on its economy, level of development and societal expectations. Figures 6.7 and 6.8 show that greenhouse gas emissions in the USA follow the global trend (carbon dioxide emissions relating to energy dominate) but the larger percentage of this sector in the USA reflects the high-energy demands of this country. Transport, a lifestyle with expectations of air-conditioning and other high-energy demands at home and work all lead to the high fuel economy seen there. On the other hand, other emissions such as methane are lower, due to an absence of rice growing and large-scale cattle ranching, reflecting again the culture and environment of the USA.

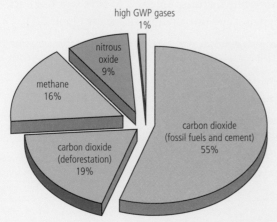

high GWP gases 1%

nitrous oxide 9%

methane 16%

carbon dioxide (fossil fuels and cement) 55%

carbon dioxide (deforestation) 19%

Figure 6.7
Global greenhouse emissions in 2000.

Figure 6.8
US greenhouse gas emissions in 2005.

Studies of cores taken from ice packs in Antarctica and Greenland show that the level of carbon dioxide remained stable at about 270 ppm from around 10 000 years ago until the mid-nineteenth century. By 1957, the concentration of carbon dioxide in the atmosphere was 315 ppm and it has since risen to about 380 ppm. Most of the extra carbon dioxide has come from burning fossil fuels, especially coal, although some of the increase may be due to the disruption of the rainforests. Much of the evidence for the greenhouse effect comes from ice cores dating back 160 000 years. These show that the Earth's temperature closely parallels the amount of carbon dioxide and methane in the atmosphere.

For every tonne of carbon burned, four tonnes of carbon dioxide are released. By the early 1980s, 5 Gt (5000 million tonnes) of fuel were burned every year. Roughly half the carbon dioxide produced is absorbed by natural sinks, such as vegetation and plankton.

To learn more about long-term trends in carbon dioxide levels, go to www.pearsonhotlinks.com, insert the express code 2630P and click on activity 6.2.

To learn more about scepticism and carbon dioxide levels, go to www.pearsonhotlinks.com, insert the express code 2630P and click on activity 6.3

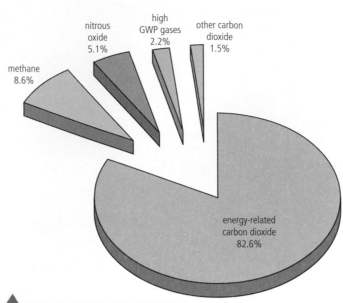

US greenhouse gas emissions in 2005.

All greenhouse gases have global warming potential (GWP). The GWP of carbon dioxide is defined as 1. Thus the GWP of all other gases is a measure of how much more a greenhouse gas contributes to global warming than carbon dioxide (Chapter 5, page 147). Gases with very high GWPs are known as high GWP gases. They are hydrofluorocarbons (HFCs), perfluorocarbons (PFCs) and sulfur hexafluoride (SF_6), all of which are released by human activities. Over the past 100 years, atmospheric concentrations of these gases have risen from zero to the parts-per-trillion level. They are emitted from a variety of sources, including air conditioning and refrigeration equipment, where they were introduced as a replacement for chlorofluorocarbons (CFCs). In the 1990s, CFCs were phased out of use when their ozone-depleting character was recognized. They caused thinning of the ozone layer, allowing an increased amount of UV radiation to reach the Earth and increasing cancer risks. Unfortunately the replacement of CFCs has traded one problem for another.

The effects of global warming

We have already seen how biome distribution is influenced by temperature patterns (Chapter 2, page 36), so any change in those patterns is likely to be followed by new global distribution of biomes. Temperature increases are likely to have serious knock-on effects on the Earth's climate and ecosystems, and thus on human society (Table 6.1).

TABLE 6.1 IMPACT OF TEMPERATURE INCREASE ON ASPECTS OF THE ENVIRONMENT AND SOCIETY	
Feature	Effect or impact
Environmental features	
ice and snow	retreat of polar ice caps and glaciers
coastlines	increase in sea level causing coastal flooding
water cycle	increased flooding
ecosystems	change in biome distribution and species composition
Societal features	
water resources	severe water shortages and possibly wars over supply
agriculture	may shift towards poles (away from drought areas)
coastal occupation	relocation due to flooding and storms
human health	increased disease

Climate change in the geological past can show how we might expect biomes to move with changes in global temperature in the future (Figure 6.9). Models suggest a north/south shift in biomes relative to the equator (a latitudinal shift). Biomes will also move up slopes (altitudinal shift) such as on mountains (Figure 6.10). Low-lying biomes such as mangroves may be lost due to changes in sea level.

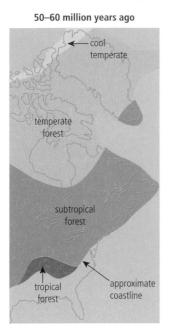

50–60 million years ago

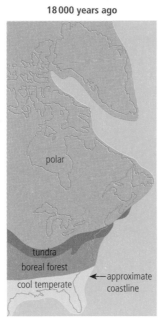

18 000 years ago

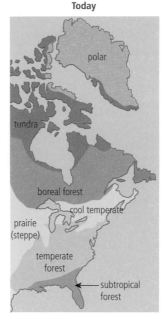

Today

Figure 6.9
In the most recent globally warm period 50–60 Ma, the Arctic was free of ice and sub-tropical forests extended northwards to Greenland. During the Pleistocene glaciations (18 000 years ago) these areas were covered by ice sheets. In the last 18 000 years, temperatures have increased and tundra and temperate forest biomes have shifted north. With further increases, all biomes are likely to move further northwards, with the probable disappearance of tundra and boreal forests.

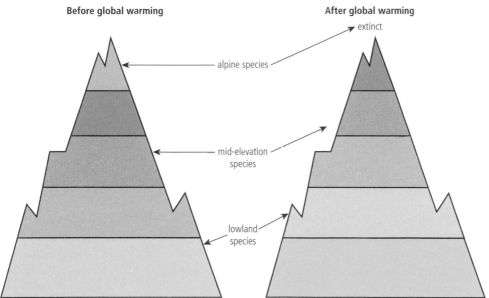

Figure 6.10
Alpine (mountain) species are particularly at risk, because zonation will move up the mountain.

Species composition in ecosystems is also likely to change. Climate change in the past has happened over long periods of time, allowing adaptation of animals to new conditions. Current increases in temperature are happening very rapidly so there is little time for organisms to adapt. Some organisms will be able to migrate to new areas where the conditions they need are found, but many face insurmountable obstacles to migration (e.g. rivers and oceans) or even no suitable habitat, and will become extinct (Figure 6.10). Tropical diseases can be expected to spread as warmer conditions are found in more northern latitudes.

Change in climate can lead to changes in weather patterns and rainfall (in both quantity and distribution). Climates may become stormier and more unpredictable. An increase in more extreme weather conditions (e.g. hurricanes) can be expected as atmospheric patterns are disturbed.

Agriculture will be affected. Drought reduces crop yield, and the reduction in water resources will make it increasingly difficult for farmers in many areas to irrigate fields. Changes in the location of crop-growing areas can be expected, with movements north and south from the equator: recent models predict dramatic changes to the wheat-growing regions of the USA, with many becoming unviable by 2050 (Figure 6.11). This would have serious knock-on effects on the economy. Crop types may need to change and changing water resources will either limit or expand crop production depending on the region and local weather patterns.

Figure 6.11
Scientists project a northward shift of wheat-growing in North America (map is simplified because existing boundaries are highly complex).

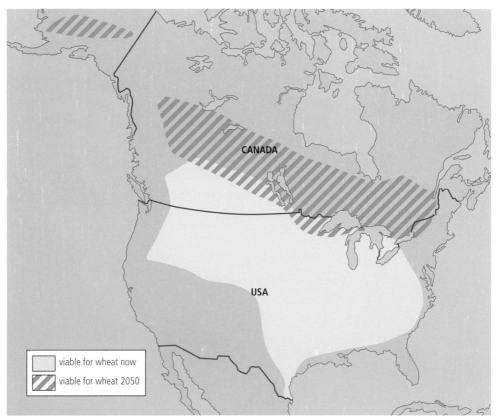

Tourism is also likely to change as global warming changes weather patterns. Summer seasons may be extended and coastal resorts selling Sun, sea and sand may develop further north. Winter sports holidays, however, may be curtailed by lack of snow and ice. Reduced precipitation in some areas may make some currently popular resorts untenable due to lack of water resources.

The impacts outlined above will indirectly lead to social problems such as conflict and hunger, which will have implications for levels of economic development (Figure 6.12). National resource bases will change, which will drive economic, social and cultural change. These issues are more likely to affect less economically developed countries (LEDCs) than more economically developed countries (MEDCs) because LEDCs are technologically and economically less able to cope. On top of which, a greater percentage of the population in LEDCs is already vulnerable to the effects of climate change (e.g. in Bangladesh 20 per cent of gross domestic product (GDP) and 65 per cent of the labour force is involved in agriculture which would be threatened by floods in low-lying areas). Coastal flooding, caused by the melting of the polar ice caps and the thermal expansion of the oceans, will particularly affect countries that have land below sea level, and may lead to economic and social stress due to loss of land and resources. LEDCs are also more likely to have weak infrastructure, communications and emergency services, which will also make them less able to respond to the effects of climate change.

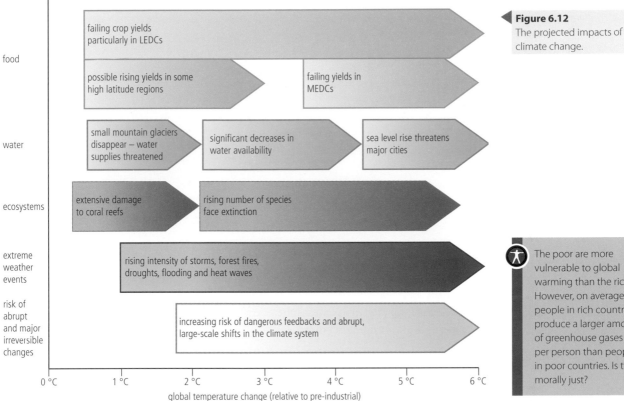

◀ **Figure 6.12**
The projected impacts of climate change.

The poor are more vulnerable to global warming than the rich. However, on average, people in rich countries produce a larger amount of greenhouse gases per person than people in poor countries. Is this morally just?

The effects of global warming are very varied. Much depends on the scale of the changes. Impacts could include the following.

- A rise in sea levels, causing flooding in low-lying areas such as the Netherlands, Egypt and Bangladesh – up to 200 million people could be displaced.
- 200 million people are at risk of being driven from their homes by flood or drought by 2050.
- 4 million square kilometres of land, home to one-twentieth of the world's population, is threatened by floods from melting glaciers.
- An increase in storm activity such as more frequent and intense hurricanes (because of more atmospheric energy).
- Changes in agricultural patterns (e.g. a decline in the USA's grain belt, but an increase in Canada's growing season).
- Reduced rainfall over the USA, southern Europe and the Commonwealth of Independent States (CIS).
- 4 billion people could suffer from water shortage if temperatures rise by 2 °C.
- A 35 per cent drop in crop yields across Africa and the Middle East is expected if temperatures rise by 3 °C.
- 200 million more people could be exposed to hunger if world temperatures rise by 2 °C, 550 million if temperatures rise by 3 °C.
- 60 million more Africans could be exposed to malaria if world temperatures rise by 2 °C.
- Extinction of up to 40 per cent of species of wildlife if temperatures rise by 2 °C.

To access worksheet 6.2 on the effects of a 4 °C rise in temperature, please visit www.pearsonbacconline. com and follow the on-screen instructions.

Up to 4 billion people could be affected by water shortages if temperatures increase by 2 °C.

CASE STUDY

Changes in the UK

These are the likely impacts of climate change on the UK for the 2020s.

- Temperatures are expected to increase at a rate of about 0.2 °C per decade; higher rates of increase will occur in the south east, especially in summer. It will be about 0.9 °C warmer than the average of 1961–90 by the 2020s and about 1.5 °C warmer by the 2050s.
- This temperature change is equivalent to about a 200 km northward shift of the UK climate along a south-east to north-west gradient in the UK (i.e. the difference in the current temperature between Oxford and Manchester).
- Annual precipitation over the UK as a whole is expected to increase by about 5 per cent by the 2020s and by nearly 10 per cent by the 2050s; winter precipitation increases everywhere but more substantially over the southern UK.
- The contrast in the UK's climate is likely to become exaggerated: the currently dry south-east will tend to become drier and the moist north-west will get wetter. Drought in the south-east and flooding in the north-west will both become more common.
- Sea level is expected to rise at a rate of about 5 cm per decade. This is likely to be increased in southern and eastern England by the sinking land, whereas in the north it will be offset by rising land (as a result of glacial melt).
- Extreme tidal levels will be experienced more frequently. For some east coast locations, extreme tides could occur 10 to 20 times more frequently by the 2080s than they do now.

By the 2050s, the UK climate will be about 1.5 °C warmer and 8 per cent wetter than during the period of 1961–90. Average sea levels will be about 35 cm higher and the probability of storm surges will have increased. By 2050, the UK will be subject to more intense rainfall events and extreme wind speeds, especially in the north. Gale frequencies will increase by about 30 per cent.

To learn more about the potential impacts of global warming, go to www.pearsonhotlinks.com, insert the express code 2630P and click on activities 6.4 and 6.5.

Feedback and global warming

We have already examined how feedback mechanisms play a pivotal role in creating equilibrium in ecosystems (Chapter 1, pages 7–8). Feedback mechanisms also play a key role in controlling the Earth's atmosphere, and any changes to these mechanisms are likely to have implications for the climate.

Both positive and negative feedback mechanisms are associated with changes in mean global temperature.

Positive feedback

- Some people believe that the impacts of global warming may be greatest in periglacial environments. These are the regions of seasonal ice cover at the edges of otherwise permanent glaciers and ice sheets. Moreover, it is believed that the effects will be most noticeable in terms of winter warming. Melting of the polar ice caps results in less ice and lowers planetary **albedo**. Albedo is the amount of incoming solar energy reflected back into the atmosphere by the Earth's surface. Since ice is more reflective than water in this respect, less ice means less reflection. Lowering albedo increases the amount solar energy absorbed at the Earth's surface, and leads to increase in temperature (Figure 6.13).

Figure 6.13
Melting ice reduces the planet's albedo.

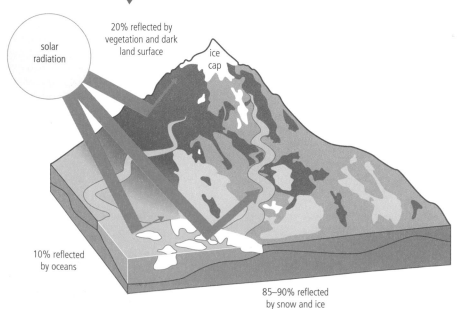

solar radiation

20% reflected by vegetation and dark land surface

ice cap

10% reflected by oceans

85–90% reflected by snow and ice

- Rotting vegetation trapped under permafrost in northern tundra releases methane that is unable to escape because of the ice covering. Increased thawing of permafrost will lead to an increase in methane levels as the gas escapes, adding to global warming gases in the atmosphere and thereby increasing mean global temperature.

Bubbles of methane in ice in a frozen pool. The methane comes from the rotting vegetation trapped at the bottom of the pool.

Other mechanisms of positive feedback include:
- increased carbon dioxide released from increased biomass decomposition, especially in forest regions leads to further increase in temperature
- tropical deforestation increases warming and drying, causing a decline in the amount of rainforest
- increased forest cover in high latitudes decreases albedo and increases warming
- warming increases the decomposition of gas hydrates leading to a release of methane and a further increase in warming.

Snow and ice increase reflectivity. As large sea ice masses melt at the poles, warming intensifies.

Feedback mechanisms associated with global warming tend to involve very long time lags. By the time effects appear, the mechanisms responsible may have already gone past the tipping point (the point of no return), and attempts to alleviate the problem may be doomed to fail.

Negative feedback

- Increased evaporation in tropical latitudes due to higher levels of precipitation will lead to increased snowfall on the polar ice caps, reducing the mean global temperature.
- Increase in carbon dioxide in the atmosphere leads to increased plant growth by allowing increased levels of photosynthesis (carbon dioxide fertilization effect). Increased plant biomass and productivity would reduce atmospheric concentrations of carbon dioxide.

CASE STUDY

Negative feedback – changes in Greenland

Increased evaporation in tropical and temperate latitudes leading to increased snowfalls in polar areas would be an example of negative feedback. There is some evidence to suggest this has happened in parts of Norway. Growth of glaciers and ice caps, albeit localized, can reduce mean temperatures.

In addition, the amount of ice melting from the surface of the Greenland ice sheet in 2002 threatened a rise in sea levels and a return of very cold winters to Britain. Increased melting of the Greenland ice could shut off the currents of the Gulf Stream, allowing depressions to dump snow rather than rain on Britain and thus leading to a much colder continental climate. This would be comparable to the situation on the eastern seaboard of Canada, which is at the same latitude as Britain but without the mitigating effects of a warm ocean current like the Gulf Stream. Were this to happen, the sea could freeze and snow lie for weeks or months instead of a day of two. Thus, there is uncertainty as to whether global warming will lead to an increase or decrease in temperatures over Britain.

Since 2002, large areas of the Greenland ice shelf, previously too high and too cold to melt, have begun pouring billions of gallons of fresh water into the northern Atlantic. The Greenland ice sheet's maximum melt area increased on average by 16 per cent from 1979 to 2002. In particular, the northern and north-eastern part of the ice sheet experienced melting reaching up to an elevation of 2000 metres.

To learn more about climate change in Greenland, changes in the Arctic sea ice and changes to Greenland's ice sheet, go to www.pearsonhotlinks.com, insert the express code 2630P and click on activity 6.6.

To learn more about feedback, go to www.pearsonhotlinks.com, insert the express code 2630P and click on activity 6.7.

To access worksheet 6.3 on the management of greenhouse gases, please visit www.pearsonbacconline.com and follow the on-screen instructions.

Warm water from the tropics currently travels north past British shores and warms the western coastlines of Europe as far north as Norway before sinking to the bottom of the ocean and returning south. This deep water convection in the north Atlantic has already been noted to be slowing down. In other studies, changes in the north Atlantic circulation have been implicated in starting and stopping northern hemisphere glacial phases.

Both sea ice and glacier ice cool the Earth, reflecting back into space about 80 per cent of springtime sunshine and 40–50 per cent during the summer melt. But winter sea-ice cover slows heat loss from the relatively warm ocean to the cold atmosphere. Without large sea ice masses at the poles to moderate the energy balance, warming escalates.

Other mechanisms of negative feedback include:
- deforestation leads to increased aerosols and thus reduced solar radiation at the surface thereby causing cooling
- increased evaporation increases cooling.

Pollution management strategies for global warming

National and international methods to prevent further increases in mean global temperature include:
- controlling the amount of atmospheric pollution
- reducing atmospheric pollution
- stopping forest clearance
- increasing forest cover
- developing alternative renewable energy sources
- improving public transport
- setting national limits on carbon emissions
- developing carbon dioxide capture methods.

There are ways in which individuals can contribute to the reduction of greenhouse gas emissions:
- grow your own food
- eat locally produced foods
- use energy-efficient products (e.g. light bulbs) rather than traditional ones
- reduce your heating – weather-proof your home
- unplug appliances when not in use
- turn off lights
- reduce the use of air conditioning and refrigerants
- use a manual lawnmower rather than an electric or diesel one
- turn off taps
- take a shower rather than a bath
- walk more
- ride a bike
- use public transport
- use biofuels
- eat lower down the food chain (vegetables rather than meat)
- buy organic food
- get involved in local political action.

ENVIRONMENTAL PHILOSOPHIES

Technocentrists would argue that humankind can continue to emit greenhouse gases because technological solutions will be found to solve the problem. People with an ecocentric point of view would put the counter-argument that reducing emissions is the first essential step to combating climate change.

The Kyoto Protocol

The Toronto Conference of 1988 called for the reduction of carbon dioxide emissions by 20 per cent of 1988 levels by 2005. Also in 1988, the United Nations Environment Programme and the World Meteorological Organization established the Intergovernmental Panel on Climate Change (IPCC). In 1997, at an international and intergovernmental meeting in Kyoto, Japan, 183 countries around the world signed up to an agreement that called for the stabilization of greenhouse gas emissions at safe levels that would avoid serious climate change. The agreement is known as the Kyoto Protocol and aims to cut greenhouse gas emissions by 5 per cent of their 1990 levels by 2012. It is currently the only legally binding international agreement that seeks to tackle the challenges of global warming.

The Kyoto Protocol came into force in 2005 and is due to expire in 2012. Within the agreement, countries were allocated amounts of carbon dioxide they were allowed to emit. These permitted levels were divided into units – and countries with emission units to spare are allowed to sell them to countries that have gone or would otherwise go over their permitted allowance – this carbon trading now works like any other commodities market and is known as the carbon market (see below).

To learn more about the UN Framework Convention on Climate Change, go to www.pearsonhotlinks.com, insert the express code 2630P and click on activity 6.8.

A Maiko girl from Kyoto in front of a Greenpeace sign marking the implementation of the Kyoto Protocol in February 2005.

The coordinating body of the Kyoto Protocol is the Conference of Parties (COP); it meets every year to discuss progress in dealing with climate change. Several of these recent climate conferences have focussed on working out a framework for climate change negotiations after 2012, when the protocol has expired. The COP meeting in 2008 agreed on the principles of financing a fund to help the poorest nations cope with the effects of climate change, and also approved a mechanism to incorporate forest protection into efforts. In 2009, a meeting in Copenhagen (the fifteenth COP meeting) failed to reach global climate agreement for the period from 2012, as a follow-up and successor to the Kyoto Protocol.

The use of alternative energy sources is also encouraged by the Kyoto Protocol. Avoidance of fossil fuels and the greater use of hydroelectric, solar and wind power are actively encouraged, as these do no emit greenhouse gases. Nuclear power has been adopted by some countries (e.g. France) as a method of 'clean energy' generation, although the problems of disposal of the radioactive waste means this method of energy generation remains controversial.

The success of international solutions to climate change depends on:
- the extent to which governments wish to sign up to international agreements
- whether governments are preventive (i.e. act before climate change gets out of hand) or reactive (i.e. respond once the problem becomes obvious).

Ultimately, individuals within a society are free to explore their own lifestyle in the context of local greenhouse gas emissions. All countries can ultimately adopt measures in response to the threat of climate change.

Carbon taxes

Some countries are introducing carbon taxes to encourage producers to reduce emissions of carbon dioxide. These environmental taxes can be implemented by taxing the burning of fossil fuel (coal, petroleum products such as gasoline and aviation fuel, and natural gas) in proportion to their carbon content. These taxes are most effective if they are applied internationally, but are also valuable nationally. Britain has a tax on emissions. It is one of the few EU countries where carbon emissions have fallen and the country should meet its target of a 20 per cent cut in emissions.

Carbon trading

Carbon trading is an attempt to create a market in which permits issued by governments to emit carbon dioxide can be traded. In Europe, carbon permits are traded through the Emissions Trading System (ETS). Governments set targets for the amount of carbon dioxide that can be emitted by industries; they are divided between individual plants or companies. Plants that exceed that limit are forced to buy permits from others that do not. Targets are set to reduce pollution but through a market system. It is working but not very well. Critics argue that targets are too generous.

Carbon offset schemes

To learn more about investigating carbon offsets, go to www.pearsonhotlinks.com, insert the express code 2630P and click on activities 6.9 and 6.10.

Carbon offset schemes are designed to neutralize the effects of the carbon dioxide human activities produce by investing in projects that cut emissions elsewhere. Offset companies typically buy carbon credits from projects that plant trees or encourage a switch from fossil fuels to renewable energy. They sell credits to individuals and companies who want to go 'carbon neutral'. Some climate experts say offsets are dangerous because they dissuade people from changing their behaviour.

Bangladeshi woman pumping water from a tube well but surrounded by rising floodwater.

CASE STUDY

Bangladesh

Bangladesh is a country at the forefront of the battle against climate change. Much of the country is low-lying and prone to flooding, and it lies within the cyclone belt. Cyclones will become more likely in the Bay of Bengal.

Although many of the causes of sea-level rise remain outside its control, there are measures that Bangladesh can take to alleviate its problems. Improvements for monitoring and predicting cyclones will allow greater preparation before they hit. Temporary shelters could be set up ready to house people evacuated during cyclones, and stocks of blankets and food set up ready for these situations. Appeals could be made to fund these emergency measures. As coastal flooding is likely, flood protection schemes could be put in place. Investment in basic health-care and education would help to combat the increase in tropical diseases that is likely. Small-scale micro-credit schemes (local banks that lend small amounts of money and do not charge interest on the loan) could be put in place to help people improve their housing to withstand higher water flows. Lobbying of wealthier nations and international bodies could also be done, to ratify international agreements to stick to reduction in emissions.

The effectiveness of reducing carbon dioxide emissions and the implications for economic growth and national development, vary depending on the level of development of the country in question. MEDCs have greater economic resources to apply to solving the problem (e.g. in developing alternative sources of energy).

To what extent can countries give up their self-interests (e.g. a thriving car industry, manufacturing industry, etc.) and pursue international treaties (e.g. the Kyoto Protocol) and allow other less developed countries to overtake them in terms of economic growth and development?

ENVIRONMENTAL PHILOSOPHIES

It may be difficult to change the expectations of those who live in MEDCs: a comfortable home, one's own transport, access to cheap flights around the globe, and general high-energy culture. People in LEDCs think it is unreasonable to expect their countries to curb emissions until they have caught up with standards in MEDCs. But ultimately, solutions must be found if irreversible climate change is to be avoided.

The majority of carbon emission targets in the Kyoto Protocol relate to MEDCs. In the future, it will be essential that LEDCs are brought into the agreement as they will be responsible for an increasing proportion of carbon dioxide emissions (Figure 6.14). Economic and social considerations make this a difficult area to negotiate – LEDCs rightly say that development in the MEDCs occurred on the back of an unenvironmental use of resources (largely, energy generation through burning fossil fuels). Allowing for development while capping greenhouse gas emissions calls for a new approach to energy generation (i.e. renewable rather than fossil fuel) and it is only through fresh thinking that solutions will be found.
The complexity of these issues was one of the reasons why the Copenhagen Summit failed to reach an agreement between all the parties.

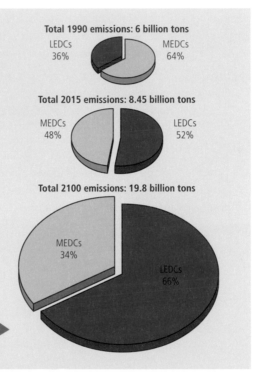

Figure 6.14
Changing patterns in carbon emissions.

Arguments about global warming

The arguments for the human influence on global climate change seem very persuasive, but there are also other non-human-related factors which can affect global climate. These include:

- greenhouse gases produced by a range of natural phenomena
  - volcanic activity can produce greenhouse gases
  - methane can be released by animals and peat bogs
  - sunspot activity (variations in the Sun's radiation)
- volcanic ash and dust blocking out solar radiation
- Earth's tilt and variation in orbit around the Sun leads to seasonal and regional changes in temperature
- reduced albedo due to position and extent of ice sheets
- changes in albedo due to variations in cloud cover
- ocean currents can lead to warming or cooling
- natural fluctuations in atmospheric circulation (e.g. El Niño and La Niña)
- bush fires can release carbon into the atmosphere.

Complexity of the problem

Climate change is a very complex issue for a number of reasons:

- it is an issue on a huge scale, which includes the atmosphere, the oceans, and the land mass of the whole planet
- the interactions between these three factors are many and varied
- it includes natural as well as anthropogenic forces
- not all the feedback mechanisms are fully understood
- many of the processes are long-term and the impact of changes may not yet have occurred.

Global warming could be entirely natural – or it could be anthropogenic – or it could be a combination of the two.

Uncertainty of climate models

There is considerable uncertainty with climate models. Not only are there high and low estimates, there are still some who question whether global warming actually exists, and whether current changes are just are normal variation in the Earth's climate.

For those who accept that global warming is occurring, there are two main questions.

- By how much is the planet warming?
- Where will the impacts of global warming be felt most acutely?

Global dimming

After the 9/11 attacks on the World Trade Center, the US air fleet was grounded for three days in the interests of national security. In the three-day absence of vapour trails, the temperature rose by an average of 1.1 °C.

Three dispersing vapour trails from high-flying aircraft. Vapour trails form small droplets (aerosols), which have high reflectivity and reflect solar energy. The aerosols therefore block solar radiation from entering the lower atmosphere. This has a cooling effect.

Air pollution from a car exhaust. Ironically, by cleaning up air pollution, climate change may be accelerated.

Air pollution also has a cooling effect. Scientists who discovered the phenomenon called it **global dimming**. It is possible that global dimming has been masking what would be even faster global warming than is currently occurring.

Scientists showed that from the 1950s to the early 1990s, the level of solar energy reaching the Earth's surface had dropped 9 per cent in Antarctica, 10 per cent in the USA, 16 per cent in parts of the UK, and almost 30 per cent in Russia. This was all due to high levels of pollution at that time.

Natural particles in clean air provide points of attachment for water. Polluted air contains far more particles than clean air (e.g. ash, soot, sulfur dioxide etc.) and therefore provides many more sites for water to bind to. The droplets formed tend to be smaller than natural droplets. Therefore, polluted clouds contain many more smaller water droplets than naturally occurring clouds. Many small water droplets reflect more sunlight than a fewer larger ones (Figure 6.15), so polluted clouds reflect far more light back into space, so preventing the Sun's heat from getting through to the Earth's surface.

To learn more about global dimming, go to www.pearsonhotlinks.com, insert the express code 2630P and click on activities 6.11 and 6.12.

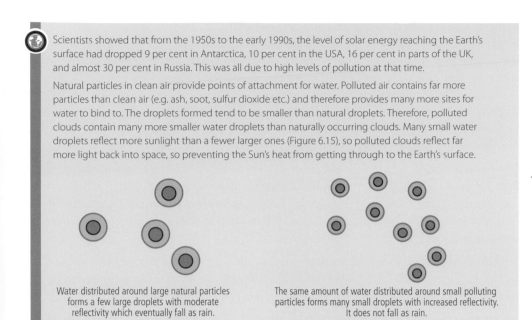

Water distributed around large natural particles forms a few large droplets with moderate reflectivity which eventually fall as rain.

The same amount of water distributed around small polluting particles forms many small droplets with increased reflectivity. It does not fall as rain.

Figure 6.15
A few large droplets in the atmosphere hold the same amount of water as more smaller ones. However, the total surface area is less for the larger particles so they reflect less sunlight than the smaller ones.

Personal viewpoint and global warming

There are many different perceptions of the global warming issues. Your response to climate change depends on your personal viewpoint. For example, you may focus on the positive benefits associated with the predicted changes in world climate. You could argue that some parts of the world will experience more rainfall, thus improving farming; and that the present very cold areas will become warmer meaning that habitat extensions further north and south could occur. You could further argue that climate change will provide new niches and opportunities for many species, and could push evolution in new and exciting directions. Humans may become more responsible and take greater care of the environment as they realize the impact they can have. There may be economic benefits from higher crop yields due to increased productivity as a result of more carbon dioxide in the air. Trade may benefit from new routes opened up as ice sheets melt (e.g. the north-west passage between the Atlantic and Pacific Oceans). Tourist revenue from warmer locations may increase. There may be new resources and land to exploit as the polar ice caps melt. Whether or not these benefits outweigh the environmental problems is a matter of personal viewpoint.

Most scientists are now convinced that there is a causal link between carbon dioxide levels and global temperature change, although some still argue that relationships are more complex and that the effects of global warming remain unclear. Some claim that current changes are part of wider patterns of natural fluctuation; their case is based on the idea that data has been collected over a very short time compared to geological time scales, so the full picture is not yet known. The complexity of the problem means that global climate models will always have an element of uncertainty about them.

Opinions of ordinary citizens depend on what scientific evidence they find most convincing, which depends on their overall awareness, level of education and specialized knowledge of the issues. The growth of the environmental movement (exponential in terms of both profile and influence in recent years) has played a large role in raising awareness of the issue, and has informed many peoples' opinions.

The hugely varied response to global warming is because personal viewpoints are so varied. Views are influenced by environmental **paradigms** (models or templates based on evidence or experience) which shape how you read scientific literature. These paradigms stem from your cultural context and ethical standpoint (e.g. whether or not you believe we have a moral obligation to future generations). Attitudes towards your relationship with the environment are also important, such as whether you think we should live in harmony with it or control it using technology. Your cultural or religious group may play a role in your views towards climate change and where you live may affect your views (e.g. near the sea, you are at risk from flooding). Socio-economic status plays a role (e.g. extreme poverty leads to short-term views and wealth leads to faith that money will solve the problem). Age may also be important (young people tend to be more concerned than the old).

Some citizens feel they have a responsibility to change the way in which they live to reduce their personal contribution to the problem, whereas others do not believe that actions at an individual level can make much difference. Some people do not prioritize environmental issues, including global warming, or think that the response should be from organizations rather than people.

In general, because science is an inductive process and can never be 100 per cent certain in its claims, judgment about the role of human activity in global warming must depend on personal attitudes, and priorities based on your own environmental paradigms.

ENVIRONMENTAL PHILOSOPHIES

Your worldview affects the way in which you consume resources and thus your ecological footprint. Technocentrists may be less willing to cut their carbon dioxide emissions because they believe in scientific solutions to problems. Ecocentrists would be more willing to change the way they live in order to lower greenhouse gas emissions. Your worldview depends on your culture, education, geographical location, age, society and economic status.

Contrasting perceptions of global warming

Al Gore, *An inconvenient truth*

The former US Vice president Al Gore, won the 2007 Nobel Peace Prize 'for efforts to build up and disseminate greater knowledge about man-made climate change, and to lay the foundations for the measures that are needed to counteract such change'. In his book, *An inconvenient truth*, he states:

> *Our climate crisis may at times appear to be happening slowly, but in fact it is happening very quickly – and has become a true planetary emergency. The Chinese expression for crisis consists of two characters. The first is a symbol for danger; the second is a symbol for opportunity. In order to face down the danger that is stalking us and move through it, we first have to recognize that we are facing a crisis. So why is it that our leaders seem not to hear such clarion warnings? Are they resisting the truth because they know that the moment they acknowledge it, they face a moral imperative to act? Is it simply more convenient to ignore the warnings?*

> *Perhaps, but inconvenient truths do not go away just because they are not seen. Indeed, when they are not responded to, their significance doesn't diminish; it grows.*

To learn more about *An inconvenient truth*, go to www.pearsonhotlinks. com, insert the express code 2630P and click on activity 6.13.

ENVIRONMENTAL PHILOSOPHIES

Campaigns such as Al Gore's book and film actively promote the environmental movement and reach a global audience. The science and evidence about climate change would have reached people not previously exposed to this information due to their background or education. Such publicity can influence personal viewpoints in a way not possible prior to the advent of mass communication.

Bjorn Lomborg, *The sceptical environmentalist*

The sceptical environmentalist: measuring the real state of the world was written by the Danish environmentalist Bjorn Lomborg. In this book, he argues that many global problems such as aspects of global warming, over-population, biodiversity loss and water shortages are unsupported by statistical analysis. He argues that many of the problems are localized and are generally related to poverty, rather than being of global proportions.

Regarding global warming, he accepts that human activity has added to global temperature increases. However, he outlines a number of uncertainties (e.g. the simulation of future climate trends) and some weaknesses in the collection of data worldwide. Nevertheless, he finds issues relating to the politics and policy responses to global warming. For example, he concludes that the cost of combating global warming will be disproportionately borne by poor countries. He also believes that the Kyoto Protocol and various carbon taxes are among the least efficient ways of dealing with global warming. Instead he argues that a global cost–benefit analysis should be carried out before deciding on how to deal with global warming.

To learn more about Bjorn Lomborg's book and criticism of it, go to www.pearsonhotlinks.com, insert the express code 2630P and click on activity 6.14.

Martin Durkin, *The great global warming swindle*

The great global warming swindle by Martin Durkin is a documentary that argues against the consensus scientific view that global warming is likely to be due to an increase in anthropogenic emissions of greenhouse gases. The film was very sceptical about the accepted scientific community and called global warming 'the biggest scam of modern times'.

The film was broadcast in 2007 and, although welcomed by global warming sceptics, it was heavily criticized by scientific organizations, individual scientists and even two of the scientists who had appeared in it. The film claimed that there were numerous scientific flaws, vested monetary interests and a 'global warming activist industry'. For example, it made the claim that carbon dioxide levels change as a result of temperature change rather than the other way round. The film also highlighted the impact of variations in solar activity (sunspot theory), suggesting that recently increased sunspot activity is responsible for increases in temperature. Finally, the film claimed that global warming is nothing unusual and that, during the Middle Ages, there were very warm conditions that allowed farmers to prosper.

To learn more about the *Great global warming swindle* and criticism of it, go to www.pearsonhotlinks.com, insert the express code 2630P and click on activities 6.15 and 6.16.

The Stern Report

The report by Sir Nicholas Stern analysing the financial implications of climate change has a simple message:

- climate change is fundamentally altering the planet
- the risks incurred by inaction are high
- time is running out.

The report states that climate change poses a threat to the world economy and it will be cheaper to address the problem than to deal with the consequences. The global warming argument had seemed to be a straight dispute between the scientific case to act and the economic case not to. Now, economists are urging action.

The Stern Report says doing nothing about climate change – the business-as-usual (BAU) approach – would lead to a reduction in global per capita consumption of at least 5 per cent, now and forever. In other words, global warming could deliver an economic blow of between 5 per cent and 20 per cent of GDP to world economies because of natural disasters and the creation of hundreds of millions of climate refugees displaced by sea-level rise. Dealing with the problem, by comparison, will cost just 1 per cent of GDP, equivalent to £184 billion.

 To learn more about the Stern Report, go to www.pearsonhotlinks.com, insert the express code 2630P and click on activity 6.17.

Main points of the Stern Report
- Carbon emissions have already increased global temperatures by more than 0.5 °C.
- With no action to cut greenhouse gases, we will warm the planet another 2–3 °C within 50 years.
- Temperature rise will transform the physical geography of the planet and the way humans live.
- Floods, disease, storms and water shortages will become more frequent.
- The poorest countries will suffer earliest and most.
- The effects of climate change could cost the world between 5 per cent and 20 per cent of GDP.
- Action to reduce greenhouse gas emissions and the worst of global warming would cost 1 per cent of GDP.
- With no action, each tonne of carbon dioxide we emit will cause damage costing at least US$85 (£45).
- Levels of carbon dioxide in the atmosphere should be limited to the equivalent of 450–550 ppm.
- Action should include carbon pricing, new technology and robust international agreements.

EXERCISES

- **Examiner's hint:**
- State – Give a specific name, value or other brief answer without explanation or calculation.
- Outline – Give a brief account or summary.
- Justify – Give valid reasons or evidence for an answer or conclusion.

1 State the main greenhouse gases.

2 Describe the role of greenhouse gases in maintaining mean global temperature.

3 Describe how human activities add to greenhouse gases.

4 Discuss the potential effects of increased mean global temperature.

5 Discuss the feedback mechanisms that would be associated with an increase in mean global temperature.

6 Describe and evaluate pollution management strategies to address the issue of global warming.

7 Outline the arguments surrounding global warming.

8 Evaluate contrasting human perceptions of the issue of global warming.

9 Justify your personal viewpoint on global warming.

PRACTICE QUESTIONS

1 The figure below shows a model of the climatic system.

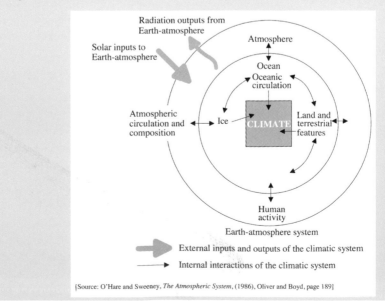

[Source: O'Hare and Sweeney, *The Atmospheric System*, (1986), Oliver and Boyd, page 189]

(a) Define the term *model*. [2]

(b) Identify **two** internal interactions in the figure which affect the climate. [1]

(c) List **four** gases which are part of the atmosphere. [2]

(d) State how solar inputs and Earth outputs differ in their radiation wavelengths. [1]

(e) Outline the ways in which human activity can have an impact on climate. [3]

(f) Evaluate the strengths and limitations of the model in the figure above for describing the atmospheric system. [4]

© International Baccalaureate Organization [2003]

2 (a) Describe the role of greenhouse gases in maintaining mean global temperature. [4]

(b) Discuss the impact of global warming. Consider the potential effect on biomes, global agriculture and human society. [7]

(c) Predictive models of climate change may give very different results. Explain this statement with reference to the limitations of models and the contrasting arguments about global warming. [6]

Expression of ideas [3]

© International Baccalaureate Organization [2004]

3 The graph below shows the mean concentrations of carbon doixide in the atmosphere between 1960 and 2000.

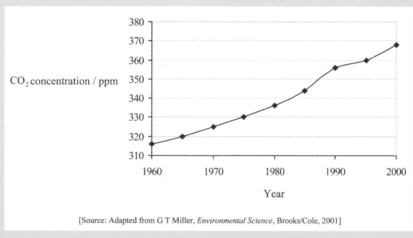

[Source: Adapted from G T Miller, *Environmental Science*, Brooks/Cole, 2001]

(a) Describe and explain these data. [6]

(b) Discuss the effect that increases in CO_2 levels might have on the environment. [6]

(c) Outline ways by which emissions of CO_2 may be reduced. [5]

Expression of ideas [3]

© International Baccalaureate Organization [2003]

4 (a) List **three** greenhouse gases. [1]

(b) Outline **one** way in which human activities are changing the proportion of one of these greenhouse gases in the atmosphere. [1]

(c) State **two** possible effects of the changes in the total proportion of greenhouse gases in the atmosphere. [2]

© International Baccalaureate Organization [2004]

5 Describe your personal viewpoint on the global warming issue and justify your position based on the evidence. [4]

(Ecosystems and Societies May 2007, paper 2, question 3d)

© International Baccalaureate Organization [2007]

6 (**a**) Define the term *feedback*. [1]

(**b**) With the use of examples associated with global warming, explain the meaning of the term *positive feedback*. [3]

(**c**) Outline the causes and consequences of global dimming. [6]

(**d**) Briefly explain why there are uncertainties with global warming. [3]

7 (**a**) (**i**) Identify **one** international policy to combat global warming. [1]

(**ii**) Briefly describe the main features of the policy. [3]

(**b**) Suggest reasons why international agreements on global warming are difficult to enforce. [3]

(**c**) Suggest how carbon trading and carbon taxes can reduce the rise of global temperatures. [3]

8 (**d**) Outline the ways it is possible for an individual to reduce their carbon impact. [6]

(**a**) Outline the link between greenhouse gases and global temperatures. [2]

(**b**) Explain why the effects of global environmental problems, such as global warming and ozone depletion, will not have an impact on every society to the same extent. [6]

(**c**) Human responses to global warming can be divided into strategies to prevent global warming from happening (preventive) and strategies to reduce the impacts that global warming might have (reactive). Outline preventive and reactive management strategies to address global warming. Evaluate the strengths and weaknesses of preventive versus reactive approaches. [10]

Expression of ideas [2]

© International Baccalaureate Organization [2009]

9 (**a**) Describe how **one** cause of climate change may be attributed to human activity. [1]

(**b**) Draw a sketch graph of temperature change against time over the last 2000 years. Using arrows and brief notes, annotate significant historical events that illustrate interesting trends or changes along the time–temperature graph. [3]

(**c**) Outline **two** causes of climate change that are natural. [2]

(**d**) (**i**) Outline how global warming may change the climate for a **named** country. [1]

(**ii**) Discuss how this new climate may lead to a change in the ecological footprint of the country named in (d) (i). [2]

© International Baccalaureate Organization [2008]

7 ENVIRONMENTAL VALUE SYSTEMS

7.1 Environmental value systems and philosophies

Assessment statements

7.1.1 State what is meant by an environmental value system.

7.1.2 Outline the range of environmental philosophies with reference to the evolution of environmentalist objectives and strategies in the seventies.

7.1.3 Discuss how these philosophies influence the decision-making process with respect to environmental issues covered in this course.

7.1.4 Outline key historical influences on the development of the modern environmental movement.

7.1.5 Compare and contrast the environmental value systems of two named societies.

7.1.6 Justify your personal viewpoint on environmental issues.

Definitions

An **environmental value system** (**EVS**) is a particular worldview or set of **paradigms** that shapes the way an individual, or group of people, perceive and evaluate environmental issues. As with perceptions of global warming, a person's or group's EVS is shaped and influenced by cultural factors (including religion), economic and socio-political context (e.g. whether from a LEDC or MEDC, democratic or authoritarian society).

EVSs, like all systems, are assemblages of parts and the relationships between them, which together constitute a whole. As with the other systems we have examined, an EVS has inputs and outputs; the outputs are determined by the processing of inputs.

EVS inputs are:
- education
- cultural influences
- religious texts and doctrine
- the media.

EVS outputs are:
- perspectives
- decisions on how to act regarding environmental issues
- courses of action.

Flows of information into individuals within societies are processed or transformed into changed perceptions of the environment and altered decisions about how best to act on environmental matters. At their strongest, such information flows cause people to take direct action to alleviate environmental concerns. It is possible that inputs will transfer through the individual or group without processing, although it is unlikely that the input will have no effect at all.

EVSs act within social systems. In contrast to ecosystems, social systems are more general: there are lots of different types, for example class-based; democratic or authoritarian; patriarchal (male dominance) or matriarchal (female dominance); religion-based;

An environmental value system is a particular worldview or set of paradigms that shapes the way an individual or group of people perceive and evaluate environmental issues.

industrial (technology-based) or agrarian (agriculture-based); capitalist or communist. Rather than the flows of energy and matter we see in ecosystems (Chapter 2, pages 45–51), social systems have flows of information, ideas and people. Both ecosystems and social systems exist at different scales, and have common features such as feedback and equilibrium. Trophic levels exist in ecosystems and in social systems there are social levels within society, and both contain consumers and producers. Producers in social systems are responsible for new input (e.g. ideas, films books, documentaries) and consumers absorb and process this information.

EVSs can broadly be divided into technocentrist and ecocentrist with anthropocentrists in the middle. Technocentrists believe that technology will keep pace with and provide solutions to environmental problems. At the other end of the spectrum, ecocentrists are nature-centred and distrust modern large-scale technology; they prefer to work with natural environmental systems to solve problems, and to do this before problems get out of control. The anthropocentrists include both technocentric and ecocentric viewpoints (Figure 7.1, opposite).

The technocentrist approach is sometimes termed a cornucopian view: a belief in the unending resourcefulness of humans and their ability to control their environment, leading to an optimistic view about the state of the world. Ecocentrists, in contrast, see themselves as subject to nature rather than in control of it. Ecocentrists see a world with limited resources where growth needs to be to be controlled so that only beneficial forms occur. At one end of the ecocentrist worldview are the self-reliance soft ecologists – those who reject materialism and tend to a conservative view on environmental problem-solving. At the other end are the deep ecologists – those who put more value on nature than humanity.

To learn more about summarizing the range of ecological values, go to www.pearsonhotlinks. com, insert the express code 2630P and click on activity 7.1.

CASE STUDY

A technocentrist approach to reducing carbon dioxide emissions

Energy and gasoline companies have been developing technological solutions to carbon dioxide emissions in order to alleviate global warming. Carbon-capture-and-storage (CCS) techniques involve taking the carbon dioxide produced from industrial processes and storing it in various ways (Figure 7.2). This means it is not released into the atmosphere and does not contribute to global warming. A BP project at In Salah in Algeria aims to store 17 million tonnes of carbon dioxide – an emission reduction equivalent to removing four million cars from the road. Such projects have yet to be made available on a large-scale commercial basis because of the costs involved.

Figure 7.2
Options for carbon capture and storage.

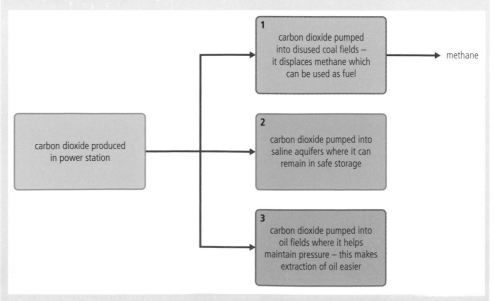

Environmental

| Ecocentrism (nature centred) | Anthropocentrism (people centred) | Technocentrism (technology centred) |

Ecocentrism
(nature centred)

Anthropocentrism
(people centred)

Technocentrism
(technology centred)

Holistic world view. Minimum disturbance of natural processes. Integration of spiritual, social and environmental dimensions. Sustainability for the whole Earth. Self-reliant communities within a framework of global citizenship. Self-imposed restraint on resource use.

People as environmental managers of sustainable global systems. Population control given equal weight to resource use. Strong regulation by independent authorities required.

Technology can keep pace with and provide solutions to environmental problems. Resource replacement saves resource depletion. Need to understand natural processes in order to control them. Strong emphasis on scientific analysis and prediction prior to policy-making. Importance of market and economic growth.

Deep ecologists

1 Intrinsic importance of nature for the humanity of man.

2 Ecological (and other natural) laws dictate human morality.

3 Biorights – the right of endangered species or unique landscapes to remain unmolested.

Self-reliance soft ecologists

1 Emphasis on smallness of scale and hence community identity in settlement, work and leisure.

2 Integration of concepts of work and leisure through a process of personal and communal improvement.

3 Importance of participation in community affairs, and of guarantees of the rights of minority interests. Participation seen as both a continuing education and a political function.

Environmental managers

1 Belief that economic growth and resource exploitation can continue assuming:
 a suitable economic adjustments to taxes, fees, etc.
 b improvements in the legal rights to a minimum level of environmental quality
 c compensation arrangements satisfactory to those who experience adverse environmental and/or social effects.

2 Acceptance of new project appraisal techniques and decision review arrangements to allow for wider discussion or genuine search for consensus among representative groups of interested parties.

Cornucopians

1 Belief that people can always find a way out of any difficulties, whether political, scientific or technological.

2 Acceptance that pro-growth goals define the rationality of project appraisal and policy formulation.

3 Optimism about the ability of humans to improve the lot of the world's people.

4 Faith that scientific and technological expertise provides the basic foundation for advice on matters pertaining to economic growth, public health and safety.

5 Suspicion of attempts to widen basis for participation and lengthy discussion in project appraisal and policy review.

6 Belief that all impediments can be overcome given a will, ingenuity and sufficient resources arising out of growth.

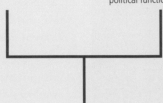

4 Lack of faith in modern large-scale technology and its associated demands on elitist expertise, central state authority and inherently anti-democratic institutions.

5 Implication that materalism for its own sake is wrong and that economic growth can be geared to providing for the basic needs of those below subsistence levels.

Adapted from Figure 10.1: The evolution of environmentalist objectives and strategies in the seventies, page 372. First published in O'Riordan, T. 1981. *Environmentalism* London, UK. Pion Limited.

Figure 7.1
The range of environmental philosophies.

To learn more about how BP is addressing environmental issues, go to www.pearsonhotlinks. com, insert the express code 2630P and click on activity 7.2.

Ecosystems often cross national boundaries and this may lead to conflict arising from the international clash of different value systems about how the resources can be best exploited or protected (e.g. ocean fishing and whaling).

The systems approach allows EVSs to be discussed in the same way as ecological systems (e.g. as having inputs (cultural influences), outputs (courses of action), storages (value systems of individuals) and flows (promotion of environmental issues in the media).

Norwegian philosopher Arne Næss pioneered and first named the ecocentric environmental philosophy known as deep ecology.

ENVIRONMENTAL PHILOSOPHIES

EVSs depend on education, cultural influences, religious beliefs, and the media. EVSs determine your global perspective, what decisions you make and the courses of action you take regarding environmental issues.

Range of environmental philosophies

An ecocentrist worldview sees nature as having an inherent value. This means that the natural world has integral worth independent of its value to anyone or anything else. The Endangered Species Act in the USA protects many species that are not economically valuable to humans, but these species are protected on the basis that they have an inherent right to exist. The biocentric view taken by the deep ecology movement (page 285) holds that all species have an intrinsic value and that humans are no more important than other species. This philosophy rejects the concept of natural resources because it implies that organisms and ecosystems are only important as economic commodities for humans.

The concept of ecosystems has contributed to the idea of holism in the environmental movement. This is the idea that a system cannot be understood just by looking at its components; it is necessary look at their interrelationships and the functioning of the whole system (Chapter 1, pages 1–6). This philosophy is at the centre of ecocentrism – humans need to work within natural systems to conserve the ecological processes on which all life depends.

Technocentrism, in contrast, states that technology will provide solutions to environmental problems even when human effects are pushing natural systems beyond their normal boundaries. At the more optimistic end the technocentric spectrum are the cornucopians, while the environmental managers see progress happening within closely defined frameworks to prevent over-exploitation of the Earth's resources.

Anthropocentrism is a human-centred worldview that spans the range of the environmental value system and includes both ecocentrists and technocentrists. Deep ecology supporters argue that anthropocentrism, where nature exists and is used for human benefit, is at the root of our environmental crisis. However, the self-reliance soft ecologists hold a people-centred (anthropocentric) view that is essentially ecocentric in nature. These environmentalists see humans as having a key role in managing sustainable global systems.

There are a range
of environmental
philosophies,
from ecocentric to
technocentric.

Decision-making and environmentalism

Environmental philosophies influence our decision-making processes. In this section, we will apply the contrasting perspectives of ecocentrism and technocentrism to four specific cases.

To learn more about environmental value systems, go to www.pearsonhotlinks.com, insert the express code 2630P and click on activity 7.3.

Environmental challenges posed by the extensive use of fossil fuels

Fossil fuels have problems associated with their use (i.e. global warming). The cornucopian belief in the resourcefulness of humans and their ability to control their environment would lead to an technocentric solution, where science is used to find a useful alternative (e.g. hydrogen fuel cells). As technocentrists, cornucopians would see this as a good example of resource replacement: an environmentally damaging industry can be replaced by an alternative one. Rather than seeing it necessary to change their lifestyles to reduce the use of fuel, cornucopians would look to develop technology to reduce the output of carbon dioxide from fuel use. A cornucopian would say that economic systems have a vested interest in being efficient so the existing problems will self-correct given enough time, and that development (which requires energy) will increase standards of living thus increasing demands for healthy environment. Scientific efforts should be devoted to removing carbon dioxide from atmosphere rather than curtailing economic growth, as a technocentrist would predict that market pressure would eventually result in lowering of carbon dioxide emission levels.

An ecocentrist approach to the same problem would call for the reduction of greenhouse gases thorough curtailing existing gas-emitting industry, even if this restricts economic growth.

The course helps you to appreciate and evaluate your own environmental philosophy. Such understanding will enable you to appreciate how worldviews influence the way in which you perceive and act regarding environmental issues. The issues contained within this chapter require you to evaluate your personal standpoint about the environment and the issues raised throughout the course.

Approaches of resource managers to increasing demand for water resources

The technocentric manager would suggest that future needs can be met by technology, innovation and the ability to use untapped reserves. They would support such measures as removal of freshwater from sea water (desalination) if they were near an ocean, iceberg capture and transport, wastewater purification, synthetic water production (water made through chemical reactions, or hydrogen fuel cell technology), cloud seeding (Figure 7.3), and extracting water from deep aquifers. They would also look at innovative ways to reduce water use per se, both in industry and at a domestic level.

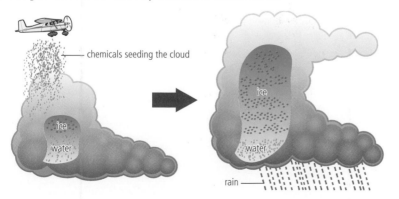

Figure 7.3

Chemicals such as silver iodide or frozen carbon dioxide are seeded into clouds. They offer surfaces around which ice crystals form. When they are large enough, they fall out of the cloud and become rain.

The ecocentric manager would highlight the overuse and misuse of water. They would encourage the conservation of water and greater recycling, and say that water use should be within sustainable levels. Monitoring would be recommended to ensure that water use remained within sustainable limits. An ecocentrist would encourage water use that had few detrimental impacts on habitat, wildlife and the environment.

Methods for reducing acid rain

The ecocentrist point of view will generally argue for a change in lifestyle that reduces the need for either the energy produced by coal, or the products that are made with that energy. This could be achieved through a reduction of heat in the home by dressing appropriately instead of raising indoor temperatures. Changes in transport use would reduce reliance on fossil fuels, and could be achieved by walking or bicycling to work or when doing the shopping. Avoiding the use of cars would reduce the release of acid deposition precursors. Ecocentrists would also encourage the 'reuse, reduce, recycle' philosophy (Chapter 3, page 157). Central to their worldview would be the idea that life should cherish spiritual well-being, as opposed to satisfaction of material desires, thereby curbing desires for continuously changing consumer goods.

Technocentrists would again argue for use of alternative technology and encouraging continued economic growth irrespective of the effect of greenhouse gas emissions because they see humanity as able to reign-in the problem as and when necessary.

The 'Reuse, Reduce, Recycle' campaign encourages people to care for goods (making them last as opposed to frequently replacing them with new ones), reduce consumption, and recycle waste.

ENVIRONMENTAL PHILOSOPHIES

EVSs determine the decision-making processes regarding environmental issues, such as choice of energy usage, reaction to limited natural resources such as water, responses to pollution, and attitudes towards ecological deficit.

Attitudes towards ecological deficit

The concept of **ecological deficit** relates to the available capacity of a country (the total amount of biologically productive space in a country). If the ecological footprint (Chapter 3, pages 160–65) of the country exceeds the biologically productive area, then the country has an ecological deficit. An ecocentrist sees the deficit as evidence that we are not living sustainably, with economic growth as a cause of the problem. The emphasis is on humans to change their behaviour and lifestyles, and ecocentrists stress the need to strive for greater social equality between people in LEDCs and MEDCs.

The technocentrist stresses the importance of technology for addressing the deficit, and economic growth is seen as a solution to the problem. The technocentrist believes in human ability to find technological solutions for all present and future deficits.

There are assumptions, values and beliefs, and worldviews that affect the way in which we view the world. These are influenced by the way we are brought up, by education, by our friends and by the society we live in.

EXERCISES

1   What is meant by an environmental value system? List three inputs and three outputs to these systems.

2   Environmental philosophies range between ecocentric and technocentric perspectives. What do these terms mean?

3   Choose three environmental issues covered by this course (e.g. food shortages, ecological footprint and climate change). Discuss how environmental philosophies influence the decision-making process with respect to each of these issues. Contrast ecocentric and technocentric responses.

4   Summarize the differences between ecocentric and technocentric philosophies with regard to the following issues:
   • environmental challenges posed by fossil fuels
   • the response of resource managers to increasing demands for water
   • methods for reducing acid rain
   • attitudes towards ecological deficit.

Developments of the modern environmental movement

The environmental movement advocates sustainable development through changes in public policy and individual behaviour. The modern movement owes much to developments in the latter part of the twentieth century, although its history stretches back for as long as humans have been faced with environmental issues. In this section, we examine significant moments in the environmental movement.

Major landmarks

• In 1956, a new disease was discovered in Minamata City in Japan. It was named Minamata disease and was found to be linked to the release of methyl mercury into the waste-water produced by the Chisso Corporation's chemical factory. The mercury accumulated in shellfish and fish along the coast; the contaminated fish and shellfish were eaten by the local population and caused mercury poisoning. The symptoms were neurological – numbness of the hands, damage to hearing, speech and vision, and muscle weakness. In extreme cases, Minamata disease led to insanity, paralysis and death.

• In 1962, American biologist Rachel Carson's influential book *Silent Spring* was published (Chapter 5, page 228). It remains one of the most influential books of the environmental movement. The case against chemical pollution was strongly made by documenting the harmful effects of pesticides, and the book led to widespread concerns about the use of pesticides and the pollution of the environment.

Rachel Carson, a well-known biologist who wrote many popular natural history magazine articles and books. ▶

- At midnight on 3 December 1984, the Union Carbide pesticide plant in the Indian city of Bhopal released 42 tonnes of toxic methyl isocyanate gas. The release was caused by one of the tanks involved with processing the gas overheating and bursting. Some 500 000 people were exposed to the gas. It has been estimated that between 8000 and 10 000 people died within the first 72 hours following the exposure, and that up to 25 000 have died since from gas-related disease.

The Bhopal disaster made headlines around the world. Despite protests, little has been done for families of the victims. ▶

- Protest about environmental disasters, and concern about the unsustainable use of the Earth's resources, have led to the formation of pressure groups, both local and international. All these groups have at their centre the concept of stewardship (the belief that every person has a responsibility to look after the planet, for themselves and for future generations, through wise management of natural resources). Such groups have resulted in increased media coverage that has raised public awareness about these issues. One of the most influential of these groups is Greenpeace, founded in the early 1970s, and which made its name in 1975 by mounting an anti-whaling campaign. The campaign encountered Soviet whalers in the Pacific Ocean off the Californian coast. It eventually developed into the 'Save the Whale' campaign, which made the news headlines around the world, and set the blueprint for future environmental campaigns. In the 1980s, Greenpeace made even bigger headlines with its anti-nuclear testing campaign.

The sinking of Greenpeace's flagship *Rainbow Warrior* in the port of Auckland, New Zealand, in July 1985, raised an international protest. The sinking was coordinated by French intelligence services to prevent the ship interfering with nuclear tests in the Polynesian island of Moruroa. For France, it was a public relations disaster that did much to promote Greenpeace's environmental campaign against nuclear testing.

- On 26 April 26 1986, early in the morning, reactor number four at the Chernobyl plant in the Ukraine (then part of the Soviet Union) exploded (Chapter 2, pages 75–76). A plume of highly radioactive dust (fallout) was sent into the atmosphere and fell over an extensive area. Large areas of the Ukraine, Belarus and Russia were badly contaminated. The disaster resulted in the evacuation and resettlement of over 336 000 people. The fallout caused increased incidence of cancers in the most exposed areas. An area around the plant still remains under exclusion due to radiation. The incident raised issues concerning the safety of Soviet nuclear power stations in particular, but also concerning the general safety of nuclear power – worries that remain to this day.

Damage to the Chernobyl nuclear reactor.

Major landmarks in the modern environmental movement include: Minamata, Rachel Carson's *Silent Spring*, the Save the Whale campaign, Bhopal, and the Chernobyl disaster. These led to:

- environmental pressure groups, both local and global
- the concept of stewardship
- increased media coverage raising public awareness.

Other significant milestones

- Many significant publications have contributed to the environmental movement. In 1972, the Club of Rome – a global think tank of academics, civil servants, diplomats and industrialists that first met in Rome – published *The Limits to Growth*. The report examined the consequences of rapidly growing world population on finite natural resources. It has sold 30 million copies in more than 30 translations and has become the best-selling environmental book in history.

- Also in 1972, the United Nations held its first major conference on international environmental issues in Stockholm, Sweden – the UN Conference on the Human Environment, also known as the Stockholm Conference.

- James Lovelock's book *Gaia* (1979) proposed the hypothesis that the Earth is a living organism, with self-regulatory mechanisms that maintain the climatic and biological conditions (Chapter 1, page 5). He saw the actions of humanity upsetting this balance with potentially catastrophic outcomes. Subsequent books, up to the present day, have developed these ideas.

- In 1987, a report by the UN World Commission on Environment and Development (WCED) was published, intended as a follow-up to the Stockholm Conference. The report was called *Our Common Future* (Chapter 3, pages 104–05). It linked environmental concerns to development and sought to promote sustainable development through international collaboration. It also placed environmental issues firmly on the political agenda. *Our Common Future* is also known as The Brundtland Report after the Chair of the WCED, former Norwegian Prime Minister Gro Harlem Brundtland.

- The publication of *Our Common Future* and the work of the WCED provided the groundwork for UN's Earth Summit at Rio in 1992. The conference was unprecedented for a UN conference, in terms of both its size and scope. It was attended by 172 nations: the wide uptake and international focus mean that its impact was likely to be felt across the world. The summit's radical message was that nothing less than a transformation of our attitudes and behaviour towards environmental issues would bring about the necessary changes. The conference led to the adoption of Agenda 21: a blueprint for action to achieve sustainable development worldwide (21 refers to the twenty-first century). The summit was important for emphasizing the relationships between human rights, population, social development, women and human settlements, and the need for environmentally sustainable development. Its emphasis was on change in attitudes affecting all economic activities, ensuring that its impact could be extensive. The conference ensured that environmental issues came to be seen as mainstream rather than the preserve of environmental activists.

- In 2006, the film *An inconvenient truth* examined the issues surrounding climate change, and increased awareness of environmental concerns (Chapter 6, page 278). The publicity surrounding the film meant that many more people heard about global warming, and its message was spread widely and rapidly through modern media, such as the Internet. The film made the arguments about global warming very accessible to a wider audience, and raised the profile of the environmental movement worldwide. The film was supported by a book that recorded hard scientific evidence to support its claims.

To learn more about the environmental movement, go to www.pearsonhotlinks.com, insert the express code 2630P and click on activities 7.4, 7.5 and 7.6.

To access worksheet 7.1 on major events in the environmental movement, please visit www.pearsonbacconline.com and follow the on-screen instructions.

An inconvenient truth, a documentary of Al Gore (former US Vice President) giving a lecture on climate change, marked a sea-change in public opinion in the USA. It was the first time a mainstream political figure had championed environmental issues.

ENVIRONMENTAL PHILOSOPHIES

Environmental disasters have affected the way people view human impacts on the planet. Realization of the negative influences people have had has led to the development of the environmental movement, which in turn has impacted on the worldviews of people around the globe.

EXERCISE

1 Draw a timeline from the 1950s to the present day to summarize development of the modern environmental movement.

Environmental value systems

Different types of society have different environmental perspectives, based on their individual philosophies and worldview. This section examines three pairs of contrasting societies:

CASE STUDY

Judaeo-Christian and Buddhist societies

The view of the environment in Judaeo-Christian religions is one of stewardship, where humans have a role of responsibility towards the Earth. The Genesis story suggests that God gave the planet to humans as a gift. Other biblical stories indicate that humanity should make the most of this gift as stewards.

An example of such a story is the parable of the talents told by Jesus. A rich employer sets off on a journey. He leaves his money in the care of his three employees. On his return, he calls his employees together to give an account of their activities in his absence.

- The first employee invested the money, and increased it ten times.
- The second also invested the money, and managed to increase it five times.
- The third, fearing his employer's reaction if he lost the money, buried it.

The employer fires the third man, and praises the other two for being good stewards and making something of the monies they were responsible for.

This contrasts with the Buddhist approach to the environment, which sees the human being as an intrinsic part of nature, rather than a steward. Buddhism is sometimes seen as an ecological philosophy (because of its worldview rather than anything that appears in its writings, which are not explicitly environmental). Buddhism emphasizes human interrelationships with all other parts of nature, and supports the belief that to think of ourselves as isolated from the rest of nature is unrealistic. The Buddhist approach can be summarized as:

- compassion is the basis for a balanced view of the whole world and of the environment
- a 'save and not waste' approach means that nothing in nature is spoiled or wasted; wanton destruction upsets the vital balance of life
- ecology is rebuilt through the philosophy 'uplift of all', which is based on people acting compassionately and working together altruistically.

Vegetarianism is part of the Buddhist tradition; it is a reflection of Buddhist respect for all life. Reincarnation, the belief that human consciousness (or spirit) is immortal and can be reborn after death in either human or animal form, also emphasizes humanity's interconnectedness with nature. Buddhists believe that nothing has a fixed and independent existence; all things are without self-existence and are impermanent. From this perspective, humans are intimately related to their environment and cannot exist separately from the rest of the world. Recognizing this principle of interdependence inspires an attitude of humility and responsibility towards the environment.

Popular books such as *Silent Spring*, and films such as Al Gore's *An inconvenient truth*, can provide knowledge about environmental issues on a global scale. People who previously had limited understanding of the environment are enabled to make their own minds up about global issues. But do they have enough information? A good education would put these arguments in a wider context. Is it a problem that many people only received one side of the argument?

A society is an arbitrary group of individuals who share some common characteristic such as geographical location, cultural background, historical timeframe, religious perspective, and value system.

CASE STUDY

Native Americans and European pioneers

Prior to the colonization of North America by Europeans from the late sixteenth century onwards, the country was occupied solely by native American Indian tribes. Native Americans, in general, saw their environment as communal, and had a subsistence economy based on barter. Their low-impact technologies meant that they lived in harmony with the environment – something supported by their animistic religion where all things have a soul – animals, plants, rocks, mountains, rivers, and stars.

The incoming European pioneers operated frontier economics, which involved the exploitation of what they saw as seemingly unlimited resources. This inevitably led to environmental degradation through over-population, lack of connectivity with the environment, heavy and technologically advanced industry, and unchecked exploitation of natural resources.

CASE STUDY

Communist and capitalist societies

Communist societies have been criticized for their poor environmental record. For example, the Buna chemical works in East Germany (prior to German reunification) dumped ten times more mercury into its neighbouring river than counterparts in the West. Cars in the East emitted 100 times as much carbon monoxide than those in the West, because they did not have catalytic converters. East German sulfur dioxide concentrations were the highest in the world. Some people argue that the economic principles of communism inevitably lead to environmental disaster: a world where free natural resources have no intrinsic value other than to serve (rather than constrain) the state cannot but be ruthlessly exploited. The communist ideal of equal distribution of resources with no profit motive meant that energy, materials and natural resources could be squandered without care.

In contrast, the capitalism model is seen by some as being environmentally friendly: the free market imposes checks-and-balances to ensure sound use of resources in order to maximize profits.

The actual story is, of course, more complex. Many of the criticisms of the communist environmental record stem from the period of the Cold War (a political battle of wills between the communist and capitalist systems). Such criticism was used as ammunition by the West against the communist states. Capitalism itself has a mixed record with regard to the environment. In Germany, before reunification, the communist state had protected the interests of farmers, foresters and fishermen, and thereby unintentionally benefited certain sectors of the environment. The rise of capitalism in the former communist state led to polluters organizing into powerful lobbies to protect their own interests at the expense to the environment.

In reality, a state's response to environmental concerns is not just a matter of political doctrine; many causes contribute (e.g. technology, affluence, geography, economic decision-making and democratic structures). In capitalist societies, civil liberties and the role of democracy may have played a more significant role in combating environmental problems than the economic basis of the system (i.e. the free market and profit motives).

 Different societies have different environmental perspectives, based on individual philosophies and worldviews. Individual and societal understanding and interpretation of data regarding environmental issues is influenced by these perspectives. Is there therefore such a thing as an unbiased view of the environment? Can we ever expect to establish a balanced view of global environmental issues?

● **Examiner's hint:**
You need to be able to compare and contrast the environmental value systems of two named societies that demonstrate significant differences. The hotlinks box on page 292 leads to useful information about contrasting societies.

Buddhist monks in Thailand are part of a growing environmental movement. They are involved in ecological conservation projects, and teach ecologically sound practices among Thai farmers. Unsustainable development based on rapid economic development is seen to be one of the primary causes of Thailand's environmental crisis. The respect in which Buddhist monks are held means that their views are listened to and can have a profound effect on the population.

The youngest daughter of the King of Thailand, Princess Chulabhorn, also plays a key role in environmentalism in Thailand. She founded The Chulabhorn Research Institute, which focuses on solving Thailand's urgent problems in areas such as health, the environment, and agriculture. She is greatly respected in Thai culture and, like the monks, is playing a significant role in promoting sustainable development in the country. Their actions are based on the Buddhist philosophy they follow.

Buddhist monks are frequently active in a range of campaigns including forest conservation in Thailand.

Her Royal Highness Princess Chulabhorn Mahidol, Princess of the Kingdom of Thailand.

Personal value systems

In this course, you are encouraged to reflect on where you stand on the continuum of environmental philosophies. These philosophies, or worldviews, relate to specific issues that arise throughout the syllabus, such as population control, resource exploitation, and sustainable development.

Your personal value system determines how you respond to environmental issues. For example, facing the problem of climate change will determine how you feel about the potential for humans to act: hopeful or fearful, enthused or frustrated, motivated or unmotivated, negative or positive (and all possibilities in-between). Questionnaires are often used to determine a person's environmental values (Table 7.1).

Low scores may indicate a technocentrist personal value system and high scores an ecocentrist one (at the deep ecology end of the spectrum), assuming a good level of understanding of the issues. Scores of over 40 on the 70-point total scale may alternatively suggest unacknowledged levels of alarm that might be turned into motivation for action in less-well-informed people.

TABLE 7.1 A QUESTIONNAIRE DESIGN TO DISCOVER ATTITUDES TOWARDS CLIMATE CHANGE											
I am optimistic about the future of children born today.	1	2	3	4	5	6	7	8	9	10	I am not optimistic about the future of children born today
Human civilization will survive the twenty-first century.	1	2	3	4	5	6	7	8	9	10	Human civilization will not survive the twenty-first century.
Global human population levels can be managed and reduced.	1	2	3	4	5	6	7	8	9	10	Global human population levels can not be managed and reduced.
I am optimistic that international agreements can limit climate change to less than 2 °C increase.	1	2	3	4	5	6	7	8	9	10	I am not optimistic that international agreements can limit climate change to less than 2 °C increase.
Runaway climate change can be prevented	1	2	3	4	5	6	7	8	9	10	Runaway climate change can not be prevented
A sixth mass species extinction can be prevented.	1	2	3	4	5	6	7	8	9	10	A sixth mass species extinction can not be prevented.
I believe I can make a difference through personal action.	1	2	3	4	5	6	7	8	9	10	I do not believe I can make a difference through personal action.
Total score											

As shown in Figure 7.4, your personal value system depends on:

- social influences – demographic characteristics (age, sex and social class); exposure to environmental issues via the media; options available to you to act in response to global issues; how you have been brought up (education; values of your parents and others around you);
- personal characteristics – knowledge about the issues; your values or ideology; demographics.

Your behaviour or actions you take on environmental issues are caused by interaction of your values with other factors.

Figure 7.4

Social influences and personal characteristics influence personal value systems.

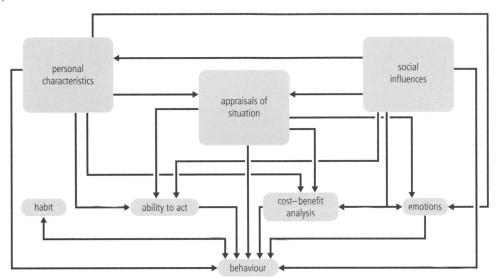

Your personal value system (which depends on social influences and personal characteristics) enables you to appraise a situation (judge how serious it is, what the possibilities for action are, who you think is responsible, who should act and your own role in the matter). But this appraisal is also influenced by your emotions (e.g. concern, anger, shame), by what you perceive as the benefits and costs of particular actions, and the ability of you or others to take specific actions.

So, for example, if you are strong willed, and have people around you who are environmentally proactive, then you are likely to take responsibility for solving environmental problems in an active way and try to make a real difference. If your city provides a convenient recycling procedure and your neighbours express their approval of this programme, then you are more likely to recycle than someone for whom recycling is inconvenient and whose neighbours ignore the matter.

But the habits you have become used to in response to daily issues will modify these responses. For example, if you live on the coast you may be fearful that climate change will bring flooding to your city: appraising the situation from the perspective of your environmental value system may cause you to sell your car and use public transport (reducing carbon dioxide emissions). But the habits you have become used to (i.e. making extensive use of your car) may ultimately modify this behaviour (e.g. you buy a hybrid car as a compromise). Your responses will be affected in turn by how serious you think a particular environmental problem is, what others are doing, and the effectiveness of alternative actions

The more knowledge you have about environmental issues, the greater your depth of understanding is likely to be. Thus, the more likely you are to engage with environmental issues and have this as part of your personal value system (Figure 7.5).

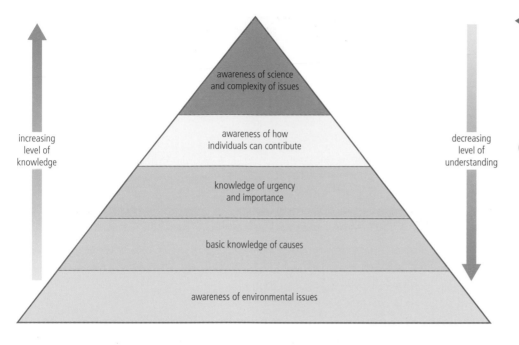

awareness of science
and complexity of issues

awareness of how
individuals can contribute

knowledge of urgency
and importance

basic knowledge of causes

awareness of environmental issues

increasing
level of
knowledge

decreasing
level of
understanding

Figure 7.5
A good level of knowledge about environmental problems provides a greater depth of understanding of the issues.

This part of the course particularly directs you to evaluate your own personal viewpoints. Any knowledge, including all that gained from this course, once it is put to use in either intellectual argument or practical application, tends to carry with it a value-laden context. Even where the data itself is highly objective, the selection of the data is rarely value-free.

ENVIRONMENTAL PHILOSOPHIES

Personal value systems determine your standing on a range of environmental issues, such as population control, resource exploitation, and sustainable development.

An online survey of homeowners in the USA divides environmental attitudes into different shades of green (Figure 7.6). The survey shows that green concerns are limited and not yet a compelling driver of green choices (those people in the darker shades of green make up a minority of the total population). Dividing personal value systems into shades of green provides a visual way of summarizing the views of society in relation to the environment.

Green consumers by age

21–29: 28%, 24%, 24%, 12%, 12%

30–43: 22%, 21%, 20%, 19%, 18%

44–62: 22%, 21%, 20%, 19%, 18%

63+: 27%, 21%, 19%, 18%, 15%

Green consumers by income

under $50,000: 21%, 21%, 20%, 19%, 19%

$50,000–$74,900: 24%, 21%, 19%, 19%, 17%

$75,000–$99,900: 22%, 22%, 22%, 17%, 17%

$100,000 or more: 23%, 22%, 21%, 17%, 17%

☐ no awareness / non-active   ☐ good awareness / slighty active   ■ excellent awareness /enthusiastic promotion
☐ slight awareness / neutral   ■ very good awareness / active promotion

Figure 7.6
Shades of green in response to environment.

To access worksheet 7.2 on environmental attitudes, please visit www.pearsonbacconline.com and follow the on-screen instructions.

To learn more about ideas for changing the world, go to www.pearsonhotlinks.com, insert the express code 2630P and click on activity 7.7.

EXERCISES

1 Compare and contrast the environmental value systems of two named societies.

2 What factors influence your personal viewpoint on environmental issues?

3 How does your worldview affect how you respond to environmental issues?

4 The environmental philosophy of an individual, as with that of a community will inevitably be shaped by cultural, economic and socio-political context. Explain why others may have equally valid viewpoints.

5 Design a questionnaire to assess the environmental viewpoints of members of your family, class, and community.

PRACTICE QUESTIONS

1 'Protecting the environment is a luxury that only the most economically developed countries of the world can afford.'

(**a**) State whether an ecocentrist or a technocentrist is more likely to agree with the statement above. Justify your answer. [2]

(**b**) Discuss the arguments for and against the statement above. In your answer you should refer to examples from both more economically developed and less economically developed countries. [10]

(**c**) Explain, using a named farming system, how

(**i**) a technocentric approach can aid soil conservation. [3]

(**ii**) an ecocentric approach can aid soil conservation. [3]

© International Baccalaureate Organization [2003, 2004]

2 Here is an ancient Chinese proverb.

If you are thinking a year ahead, sow seed.
If you are thinking ten years ahead, plant a tree.
If you are thinking a hundred years ahead, educate the people.

Kuan Tzu, 500 BC

(**a**) The poet Kuan Tzu could be seen as an ecocentrist or a technocentrist. Justify whether you think his views are ecocentric or technocentric. [4]

(**b**) Outline **two** factors which may affect someone's environmental philosophy. [2]

(**c**) Suggest what message the cartoonist is trying to depict about attitudes to environmental problems in the figure below. [2]

● **Examiner's hint:**
Personal value systems depend on social influences; demographic characteristics (age, sex, class); exposure to environmental issues in the media; education; the options available to you to act on global issues; and personal characteristics. The way in which you respond to specific problems depends on your emotions, perceived benefits and costs, and your ability to take specific actions.

[Source: *Thin Black Lines rides again*, Regan, Sinclair, Turner, development education centre, in association with Cartoonists and Writers Syndicate (67 Riverside Drive, New York 10024, fax. no. 010 1 212 595 4218), (1994), page 47]

© International Baccalaureate Organization [2005, 2006]

3   'While much attention has been focussed in the impending planet-wide oil shortage, a far greater problem awaits us. Already the next world war will be fought over water resources not oil reserves.'

[Source: adapted from www.waterconserve.org]

(a) Compare the approaches of technocentric and ecocentric resource managers to the issue of an increasing demand for water resources. *[8]*

(b) Discuss how ecocentric solutions to water resource needs can be applied on a local scale. *[5]*

(c) Describe and evaluate the role of technocentric solutions in meeting the demand for food. *[6]*

© International Baccalaureate Organization [2008]

4   Compare the attitudes towards the natural environment of **two** named contrasting societies, and discuss the consequences of these attitudes to the way in which natural resources are used. *[10]*

© International Baccalaureate Organization [2006]

5   (a) A view of Yosemite National Park, California, USA

Explain why the value of a view may be hard to measure. *[2]*

(b) Compare the environmental value systems of **two** named societies and describe how these societies might differ in the way they exploit their resources. *[10]*

© International Baccalaureate Organization [2009]

Chapter Eight

Theory of Knowledge and ESS

◀ Green thinking.

> If all mankind were to disappear, the world would regenerate back to the rich state of equilibrium that existed ten thousand years ago. If insects were to vanish, the environment would collapse into chaos.
>
> Edward O. Wilson

There are plenty of opportunities to explore the theory of knowledge within ESS. The systems approach used throughout ESS is different from traditional models of scientific exploration. This allows us to compare the two approaches to understanding.

Conventional science uses a reductionist approach to looking at scientific issues, whereas the systems approach requires a holistic understanding. While the systems approach is frequently quantitative in its representation of data, it also addresses the challenge of handling a wide range of qualitative data. This leads to questions about the value of qualitative versus quantitative data. There are many checks and guidelines to ensure objectivity in quantitative data collection and handling in the purely physical sciences, but these standards of objectivity are more difficult to rigorously control in ecological and biological sciences. In addition, ESS is a transdisciplinary subject, the material addressed often crosses what may seem to be clear subject boundaries (e.g. geography, economics, politics).

Thus, the systems approach allows comparisons to be made across disciplines, and the value and issues regarding this are discussed throughout the course and in this book. In exploring and understanding an environmental issue, you must be able to integrate the hard, scientific, quantitative facts with the qualitative value-judgments of politics, sociology and ethics. All this makes particularly fertile ground for discussions related to theory of knowledge.

> Whoever undertakes to set himself up as a judge in the field of Truth and Knowledge is shipwrecked by the laughter of the gods.
>
> Albert Einstein

Genius is 1% inspiration and 99% perspiration.
Thomas Edison

Trust yourself. You know more than you think you do.
Benjamin Spock

Care for the planet – it's the only one we have.

Throughout this book, ToK boxes contain advice and information relating to this aspect of the course. This chapter looks in more detail at ways in which ToK can be applied in specific parts of the syllabus.

▲ Is knowledge all you need?

▲ Can too much knowledge be a bad thing?

Chance favours the prepared mind.
Louis Pasteur

We see only what we know.
Johann Wolfgang von Goethe

1 Systems and models

Case study

Holism versus reductionism

The emphasis in this course is on understanding the sum of the parts of a system (i.e. a holistic approach) rather than considering the components separately. This contrasts with the reductionist approach of conventional science. Data collection is involved with measuring the inputs and outputs of a system, and processing the data reveals understanding of the processes within the system. The main difference between the systems approach and conventional science is that the former describes patterns and models of the whole system, whereas the latter aims at explaining cause and effect relationships within it. Is one approach better than the other, or is it a matter of perspective as to which approach brings real benefits in understanding?

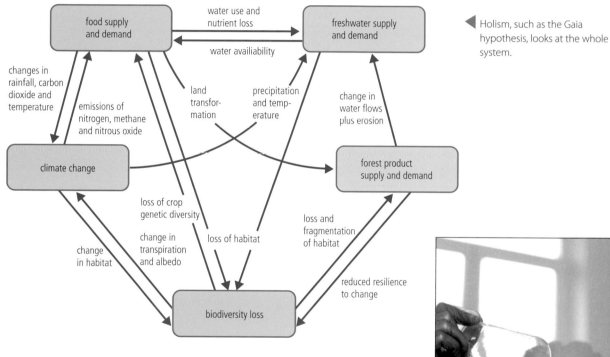

◀ Holism, such as the Gaia hypothesis, looks at the whole system.

All models are wrong, but some are useful.
George Box (innovator in statistical analysis)

A reductionist approach ▶

Advantage of holism

The advantage of the holistic approach in environmental science is that it is used extensively in other disciplines, such as economics and sociology, and so allows integration of these different subjects in a way that would not be possible (or at least not so easy) in conventional science.

Shall I refuse my dinner because I do not fully understand the process of digestion?
Oliver Heaviside

As systems are hierarchical, what may be seen as the whole system in one investigation may be seen as only part of another system in a different study (e.g. a human can be seen as a whole system with inputs of food and water and outputs of waste, or as part of a larger system such as an ecosystem or a social system). Difficulties may arise at where the boundaries are placed, and how this choice is made.

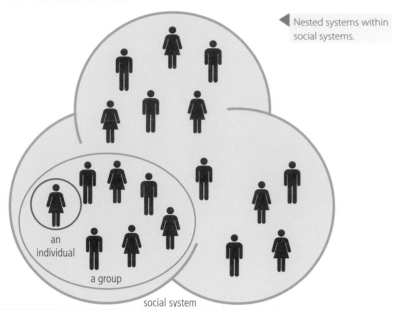

◀ Nested systems within social systems.

an individual

a group

social system

Holism and science

Does the holistic approach really differ from conventional science, or is it just a matter of using different terminology?

2 The ecosystem

Ecology provides many opportunities to explore issues regarding the reliability and validity of data and how it is collected. It also addresses the pros and cons of subjective as opposed to objective data. Nevertheless, the interpretation of data – even of objective data – is open to widely different viewpoints. See case study 'A matter of interpretation' (overleaf).

Ecology relies on the collection of both biotic and abiotic data. Abiotic data can be collected using instruments that avoid issues of objectivity as they directly record quantitative data. The measurement of the biotic (or living) component is often more subjective, relying on your interpretation of different measuring techniques to provide data. It is rare in environmental investigations to be able to provide ways of measuring variables that are as precise and reliable as those in the physical sciences. Working in the field means that variables cannot be controlled, only measured, and fluctuations in environmental conditions can cause problems when recording data. Standards of acceptable margins of error are therefore different. Will this affect the value of the data collected and the validity of the knowledge? Applying the rigorous standards used in a physics investigation would render most environmental studies unworkable, and we would miss out on gaining a useful understanding of the environment. A pragmatic approach is called for in ecological studies, but this leaves the subject open to criticism from physical scientists regarding the rigour with which studies are done. Is some understanding better than no understanding at all?

Succession

Can we substitute space for time? Is space (and spatial change) a surrogate for time (and temporal change)? In studying succession, we use spatial changes to make inferences about temporal changes. Should this be allowed? Succession may be affected by external factors, such as global warming.

Case study

A matter of interpretation

Ecosystem	Mean NPP / kg m^{-2} yr^{-1}	Mean biomass / kg m^{-2}	NPP / biomass
tropical rainforest	2.2	45	
tropical deciduous forest	1.6	35	
tropical scrub	0.37	3	
savannah	0.9	4	
Mediterranean sclerophyll	0.5	6	
desert	0.003	0.002	
temperate grassland	0.6	1.6	
temperate forest	1.2	32.5	
boreal forest	0.8	20	
tundra and mountain	0.14	0.6	
open ocean	0.12	0.003	
continental shelf	0.36	0.001	
estuaries	1.5	1	

Questions

1 Which are the three most productive ecosystems in terms of NPP?
   - tropical rainforest   2.2
   - tropical deciduous forest   1.6
   - estuaries   1.5

2 Which are the three most productive ecosystems in terms of NPP per unit of biomass?
   - continental shelf   360 kg m^{-2} yr^{-1} per kg m^{-2}
   - open oceans   40 kg m^{-2} yr^{-1} per kg m^{-2}
   - estuaries   1.5 kg m^{-2} yr^{-1} per kg m^{-2}
   - deserts   1.5 kg m^{-2} yr^{-1} per kg m^{-2}

3 How do you explain the differences between your two answers?

   Much of the biomass of a forest is woody, non-photosynthesizing material. This means it is non-productive, thus the NPP per unit of biomass is low.

Now there is one outstandingly important fact regarding Spaceship Earth, and that is that no instruction book came with it.

Buckminster Fuller

Case study

Plant knowledge

Tropical rainforest.

Carnivorous pitcher plant.

Meadow vegetation.

Water lilies, Eden Project, Cornwall, UK.

Salt marsh vegetation.

Xerophytic vegetation – adapted to dry conditions.

Questions

What can we conclude about plants from these images?

Which of the following are true?

- Some plants are carnivorous.
- Some plants are extremely tall.
- Some are woody.
- Some plants live in very dry conditions.
- Some plants live in very wet conditions.
- Some plants needs lots of water.

3 Human population, carrying capacity and resource use

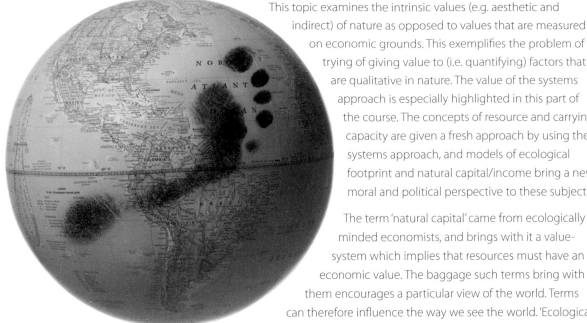

This topic examines the intrinsic values (e.g. aesthetic and indirect) of nature as opposed to values that are measured on economic grounds. This exemplifies the problem of trying of giving value to (i.e. quantifying) factors that are qualitative in nature. The value of the systems approach is especially highlighted in this part of the course. The concepts of resource and carrying capacity are given a fresh approach by using the systems approach, and models of ecological footprint and natural capital/income bring a new moral and political perspective to these subjects.

The term 'natural capital' came from ecologically minded economists, and brings with it a value-system which implies that resources must have an economic value. The baggage such terms bring with them encourages a particular view of the world. Terms can therefore influence the way we see the world. 'Ecological footprint' considers the environmental threat of a growing population, whereas 'carrying capacity' makes us see the same issues in terms of the maximum a population can reach sustainably. Does such use of language affect our understanding of concepts and environmental issues?

▲ Humans are leaving a massive footprint on the planet. Is this damage reversible?

Your descendants shall gather your fruits.
Virgil

Population and resources

'Population growth is going to use up the world's resources'. 'Population growth will stimulate the development of new resources'. Both of these views are valid. Which one do you believe?

It may depend on the time-scale and spatial scale that you use. On a small time scale, there is evidence that population growth can lead to famine (e.g. in Ethiopia in 1984). However, during the 1984 famine, Ethiopia was exporting crops – not everyone had access to food and that is why there was famine. In addition, there was long-term drought. Human populations have so far managed to survive on Earth, despite massive increases in the size of the human population. However, population decline in Easter Island suggests that environmental mis-management could lead to population creases. Maybe we just haven't been there on a global scale yet.

Case study

Population crash on Easter Island

Easter Island was discovered by Europeans in 1722. The island is about 117 km² and situated about 3700 km west of the Chilean coast. It is one of the most remote inhabited islands in the world. It was colonized by Polynesian people in 700 AD and the population peaked at 12 000 around 1600 AD. The population is now about 4000.

Pre-1600, the islanders had a diet of birds and fish. But after about 1600, palm forests disappeared and also the supply of birds and fish ran out. There was social disintegration, starvation, hardship, and conflict (Malthusian crisis) in the post-1600 period. The cause of the crisis appears to be total deforestation related to the cult of statue building. Trees were used to move the statues. Removal of the trees led to soil erosion, landslides, crop failures and famine. Thus it was a human-made ecological disaster – namely over-use of resources.

However, by 1722 when the island was discovered, there was no sign of crisis. The islanders had reorganized their society to regulate their use of resources and control their distribution (Boserup: 'necessity is the mother of invention'). Nevertheless, between 1722 and 1822, the arrival of Europeans led to a spread of disease and the death rate increased. In 1862, slave traders from Peru took 1500 slaves (a third of the population). Only 15 returned home, and these brought with them smallpox. By 1877, the population was down to just 111. The population has now risen to over 4000 largely as a result of migration. Easter Island is now struggling to cope with a new distinction: it was recently named by UNESCO as a World Heritage Site and the pressure caused by tourism is having a negative impact on resource availability for some of the islanders.

Easter Island is famous for its statues of heads.

- Is Easter Island an example of a Malthusian population–resource disaster?
- Is it an example of human ingenuity coping with a crisis?
- What do you think?

There is a sufficiency in the world for man's need but not for man's greed.
Mohandas K Gandhi

Moral issues

In 1997, an author wrote an article on agricultural issues in the UK. In a section entitled 'BSE (blame someone else)', the author wrote:

Why did it affect the UK? A number of theories can be put forward.

1 It could be just bad luck.
2 Few places outside the UK suffer from scrapie and also raise large numbers of cattle.
3 Cattle carcases in the UK are burnt at relatively low temperatures.
4 Cattle in the UK derive up to 5% of their cattle ration from meat and bone meal.

Consumers are worried about whether eating beef is safe. Steak almost certainly is. Muscle (meat) does not seem to carry BSE. The danger lies in eating pies, burgers and sausages which might have bits of infectious brain or spinal cord in them.

The publishers received an irate letter from the National Farmers Union (NFU) in which it was claimed that there was no scientific evidence to suggest that BSE was due to farming practices in the UK, that the author was scare-mongering and just trying to be sensationalist in order to get noticed.

As a result, the publishers sent a letter out with the article highlighting the views of the NFU. Should they have done so? Should the author offer an apology? Should the author and publisher publish what they believe to be right? One of the issues here is where do you draw the line – if an oil company were to say there is no link between burning fossil fuels and global warming, would you believe them? What interests does the NFU have? What interests do the author and the publisher have?

4 Conservation and biodiversity

Evolution versus creationism

What constitutes 'good science' and what makes a 'good theory'? Can we have confidence in scientific theories that rely on indirect evidence and that happen over such long periods of time as to make testability a problem?

In 1859, Charles Darwin's book *On the Origin of Species* revolutionized biology and the way it is studied. Despite this, some people still refute its claims: one such group are the creationists, who believe in the literal truth of the biblical Genesis story. Can their views be reconciled with the scientific evidence? What do their views say about the scientific method and what constitutes good science?

- Science concerns testable ideas.
- Science therefore focuses on recurrent, repeatable events.

Is this true for all science?

Is evolution by natural selection a testable theory? Are there organisms that are suitable for experimentation to see natural selection in operation?

Mark on the grid towards where your opinions lie in terms of the truth of creationism and evolution.

Creation | | | | | Evolution

Creationist claims

1 Is evolution scientific?

- Evolution within a species can be tested and is well established, but doesn't explain the creation of species.
- If evolution occurs over millions of years, it is untestable and therefore unscientific.

> **Facts do not cease to exist because they are ignored.**
> Aldous Huxley

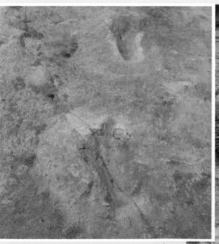

These tracks in the cretaceous limestone of the Paluxy River, near Glen Rose, Texas, were once considered by many creationists to be human tracks together with a trail of typical dinosaur tracks. It was thought that this was evidence for humans and dinosaurs living together in Texas before Noah's flood.

2 Evolution contradicts physics

- Physics, second law of thermodynamics: The entropy (disorder) in a system will always increase over time.
- Evolution: Life appears from disorder, becoming increasing ordered and complex over time.

3 Counter-evidence

- Fossilized allegedly human tracks with a trail of typical dinosaur tracks, in the same rock layer.
- Radio-isotope dating is the basis for almost all estimates of evolutionary time. It was applied in 1986 to lava from Mt St Helens, which erupted in 1980, and produced dates of millions of years ago. Since the dating is almost a million times too old, dating of fossils must likewise be a million times too old.
- The key 'missing link' fossils – intermediates between major groups – are still missing.
- *Archaeopteryx* – the famously feathered reptile – has been debunked as a fake, along with 'Piltdown man' and many others.

4 Key creationists in science

- Physics – Newton, Maxwell, Kelvin
- Chemistry – Boyle, Dalton, Ramsay
- Biology – Linnaeus, Mendel, Pasteur
- Astronomy – Copernicus, Galileo, Kepler, Herschel
- Mathematics – Pascal, Leibnitz.

5 Common sense

- The idea that we were created via a purely random process of mutation ...
  - ... is statistically absurd
  - ... contradicts the obvious signs of design all around us
  - ... denies humanity: it allows no meaning for creativity, love, or purpose
  - ... just gives selfish people the justification to act without regard for morality.

If you were to re-assess your view of which was true, creationism or evolution, based on belief in the arguments expressed above, where would you mark the grid?

Creation   Evolution

> **Darwinism is not a testable scientific theory, but a metaphysical research program.**
> Karl Popper

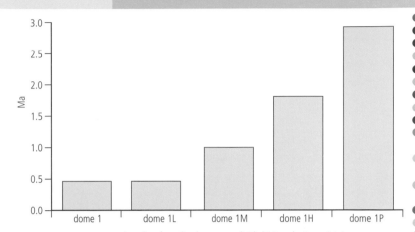

samples taken from the dome were divided into subsets containing different minerals and each tested for radioisotopes

Potassium/argon dating of the volcanic dome formed by lava at Mt St Helens

> **Ignorance more frequently begets confidence than does knowledge: it is those who know little, not those who know much, who so positively assert that this or that problem will never be solved by science.**
> Charles Darwin

> **Neither science nor maths can ever be complete.**
> Kurt Gödel

Re-assessing the creationist argument

1 Distortion

- The second law of thermodynamics is true as quoted but it only applies to isolated systems. Life is part of a system in which entropy does increase overall.
- Mutation is indeed random, but natural selection is not, so it can work cumulatively to bring about apparent design.
- Evolution by natural selection can be demonstrated in organisms with short generations (MRSA bacteria is an example).

2 Highly selective use of data

- For every creationist scientist mentioned, hundreds even thousands of others are not. Moreover, scientists who pre-date evolutionary theory cannot be called creationists since there was no creationist/evolutionist argument at that time.
- Huge areas of evolutionary data are completely ignored:
  - homologous structures
  - biogeographical evidence
  - molecular evidence (e.g. DNA)
  - embryological evidence.

> **Nothing in biology makes sense except in the light of evolution.**
> Theodosius Dobzhansky

3 Disinformation and misinterpretation

- *Archaeopteryx* is widely accepted as authentic by the scientific community; there is no basis for its 'debunking'.
- We now understand, from dedicated work in the 80s, how the tracks at Paluxy River were formed. Dinosaur footprints normally recognized as such were created by dinosaurs walking or running on their toes (these are the deep three-toed tracks, called digitigrade tracks). Dinosaurs walking on their soles or heels (metatarsal bones) create different impressions called metatarsal tracks which are longer than the digitigrade ones. Unlike digitigrade tracks, metatarsal tracks may look superficially like human tracks after erosion or if mud-movements followed formation of the track.

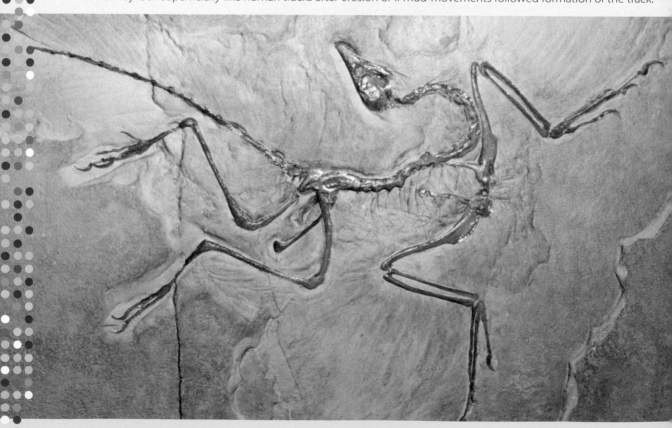

Archaeopteryx – a link between reptiles and birds.

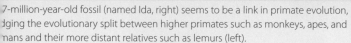
7-million-year-old fossil (named Ida, right) seems to be a link in primate evolution, bridging the evolutionary split between higher primates such as monkeys, apes, and humans and their more distant relatives such as lemurs (left).

- Many species living today are intermediates between other groups (see Richard Dawkins' book *The greatest show on Earth* for extensive evidence). It is not true that evidence for missing links is absent (see photo opposite).

4 Hype and spin

- Some real concerns about isotope dating voiced by scientists are hyped up to make the whole process appear void.
- Sensible explanations of anomalous results (e.g. for Mt St Helens) are spun as 'desperate evolutionists patching up a defunct theory'.

5 Learn to live with uncertainty

- There is much uncertainty in both science and faith.
- Doubt and questioning are creative.
- In science, uncertainty leads to new ideas.
- In faith, too, doubt can lead us to ask new questions and find new meaning.
- At the same time, you need to know what your core values are.

6 Learn to spot 'pseudo-science'

Pseudo-science	Good science
• shows fixed ideas (dogma)	• shows willingness to change
• selects favourable findings	• accepts and attempts to explain all findings
• does not have peer-review	• has ruthless peer-review
• is unable to predict	• has predictive power
• has unverifiable claims	• is experimentally verifiable
• has a hidden agenda	• makes few assumptions
• lacks consistency	• is usually consistent

 Metatarsal impressions are not the only reasons for creationists misinterpreting the tracks at Paluxy River. Several other phenomena have also been mistaken for human tracks including erosional features and some carvings on loose stone blocks. To learn more about the Paluxy River site, go to www.pearsonhotlinks.com, insert the express code 2630P and click on activity 8.1

Archbishop James Ussher (1581–1656), Church of Ireland (protestant) Bishop of Armagh, claimed to have established the date the Earth was formed as Sunday 23 October, 4004 BC whereas the evolutionist approach now puts the Earth as at least 4.5 billion years old.

Extraordinary claims require extraordinary evidence
Carl Sagan

Case study

How should we decide what to protect?

Humans make judgments about the natural world, and the ways in which it can be protected. Do species have an intrinsic right to exist even if they are of no economic value at the moment? Should as much as possible of the environment be protected, or do we need more pragmatic approaches based on realistic expectations?

How do we justify the species we choose to protect?

Is there a focus on animals we find attractive? Is there a natural bias within the system? Sometimes the choices we make are based on emotion rather than reason: does this affect their validity?

People are not going to care about animal conservation unless they think that animals are worthwhile.
David Attenborough

Do tigers have a greater right to exist than endangered and endemic species of rat?

Cheetahs have a very small gene pool with little genetic variation. They are especially prone to changes in their environment or the outbreak of disease. Should we focus conservation on species which are more resilient and more likely to survive into the future?

The nation behaves well if it treats the natural resources as assets which it must turn over to the next generation increased, and not impaired, in value.
Theodore Roosevelt

Describing species

Historically, taxonomists (scientists who describe new species) focussed on groups that interested them. These tend to be the larger more attractive groups (e.g. mammals, birds, flowering plants). Is there a bias in the way in which species are described? What about small and more obscure groups (e.g. nematodes) or smaller organisms that are difficult to collect and identify, or which have not attracted scientific attention? What impact does this have on estimations of the total number of species on the Earth? Can we reliably comment on species' extinction rates?

Most of the species of animals on the planet are beetles. Do you think the number of described species reflect this? What type of organisms have scientists historically focussed attention on?.

Like the resource it seeks to protect, wildlife conservation must be dynamic, changing as conditions change, seeking always to become more effective.
Rachel Carson

A little knowledge that acts is worth infinitely more than much knowledge that is idle.
Kahlil Gabran

5 Pollution

This part of the syllabus allows exploration of the concept of 'the tragedy of the commons'. There may be little control over the way common resources are used, and the selfish acts of a few individuals can destroy the resource for others. The 'prisoners' dilemma' model (aka Nash equilibrium, after the mathematician who developed it) can be used to explore the ethical issues involved, and the ways in which these problems can be resolved. Non-point source pollution may mean that an individual polluting a common resource suffers little, indeed may benefit from their disposal of pollutants, but the non-polluting users of the resource are not only affected by the pollution, they do not benefit in any way. There is, therefore, a benefit for those who continue to pollute.

This conundrum underlies many issues regarding the managing non-point pollution, from local (e.g. a lake) to global (e.g. the atmosphere). Pollution leading to global warming and acid rain are affected by the dilemma of making the polluter pay for the damage caused. The course explores ways in which solutions to the prisoners' dilemma can be found to solve both local and international issues of pollution. The ways in which legislation and public opinion can be used to address these problems is rich territory for ToK – is a system of rules better than a programme that educates and informs the public?

> **For the first time in the history of the world, every human being is now subjected to contact with dangerous chemicals, from the moment of conception until death.**
> Rachel Carson, *Silent Spring*, 1962

Vegetation destroyed by a combination of acid rain, sulfur emissions and lahars (mudflows) from the Soufrière volcano, Montserrat.

Case study

Natural pollution?

Are all forms of pollution necessarily human in origin? No. Many are natural. Some, like acidification, may be completely natural in some areas and anthropogenic in others. However, it is the case that acidification is largely related to human activity. It is an 'industrial form of ruination, which pays little heed to international boundaries'. Many countries produce acid pollutants and some export them.

Nevertheless, there are natural causes of acidification – bog moss secretes acid, heather increases acidity, and conifer plantations acidify soils. Volcanoes are also important sources of atmospheric pollution – especially by sulfur dioxide and hydrogen dioxide. For example, before the eruption of the Soufrière volcano, Montserrat had some of the finest cloud forest in the Caribbean, but by 1996 vegetation loss from acid rain, gases, heat, and dust was severe. In 1996, the pH of the lake at the top of Chances Peak was 2.0 (i.e. 1000 times more acidic than a pH of 5.0).

6 The issue of global warming

This topic addresses the way in which science can sometimes not be 100 per cent certain about certain issues, especially ones as complex as climate change. Is there correlation between temperature rise and carbon dioxide emissions, or is the evidence effectively circumstantial? To what extent do politicians and environmentalists take advantage of the lack of consensus on the issue and use this to their own advantage? Are there parallels between the influence of religious communities in the past and the influence of the political community today on science and how it is interpreted? Regardless of the lack of hard scientific certainly regarding the evidence, should we nevertheless take preventive measures to avoid potential future catastrophe?

> **If you don't read the newspaper, you are uninformed; if you do read the newspaper, you are misinformed.**
> Mark Twain

> **Some of the scientists, I believe, haven't they been changing their opinion a little bit on global warming? There's a lot of differing opinions and before we react I think it's best to have the full accounting, full understanding of what's taking place.**
> George W Bush

Case study

Bias and spin

Global warming challenges views of certainty within the sciences. In the popular perception, global warming is having a negative impact on the world. There is, moreover, some confusion in the public mind between global warming and the greenhouse effect. The greenhouse effect is a natural process, without which there would be no life on Earth. There is, however, an enhanced or accelerated greenhouse effect which is implicated in global warming. The enhanced greenhouse effect is largely due to human (anthropogenic) forces, although feedback mechanisms may trigger some natural forces, too. Lobby groups and politicians may take views which suit their own economic and political ends – it is possible to hide other agendas behind the uncertainties around global warming (causes, consequences and potential solutions). In the USA, the strength of the oil companies during the Bush administration was seen by many as an example of an economically powerful group, and the politicians it supported, choosing a stance which was not in the long-term environmental, social or economic interest of the world. However, there were short-term benefits for both the oil companies and the politicians they supported.

> **The warnings about global warming have been extremely clear for a long time. We are facing a global climate crisis. It is deepening. We are entering a period of consequences.**
> Al Gore

7 Environmental value systems

There are assumptions, values and beliefs, and worldviews that affect the way in which we view the world. These are influenced by the way we are brought up by our parents, education, the friends we have and the society we live in.

This course should have helped you to appreciate what your personal value system is, where it lies in a spectrum of other worldviews, and enabled you to justify and evaluate your position on a range of environmental issues

The great end of life is not knowledge but action.
Thomas Huxley

We know what we are, but know not what we may be.
William Shakespeare

How would you evaluate your personal standpoint about the environment and the issues raised throughout the course?

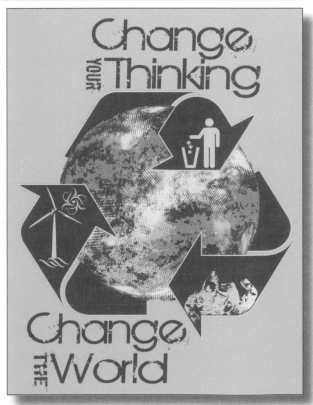

We *can* change the world.

If facts are the seeds that later produce knowledge and wisdom, then the emotions and the impressions of the senses are the fertile soil in which the seeds must grow.

Rachel Carson

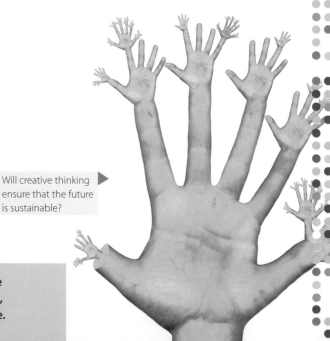

Will creative thinking ensure that the future is sustainable?

Imagination is more important than knowledge. For while knowledge defines all we currently know and understand, imagination points to all we might yet discover and create.
Albert Einstein

OVERALL ASSESSMENT

Grade descriptors

Grade 7: Excellent achievement

The work shows comprehensive understanding of factual material, subject vocabulary, ideas, skills and methods. The candidate has shown detailed understanding and synthesis of a wide range of ideas and information; thorough analysis (either quantitative and/or qualitative) and evaluation of information; assessed and balanced a wide range of opinions and views; provided a clear, well-reasoned and justified view, while considering alternative views and perceptions of others, and cultural determinants of such views; a high level of communication skills using appropriate language and symbols; scholarly and inventive.

The candidate shows personal skills, persistence and responsibility in a wide range of investigative studies in a very regular way. Works well individually and in a team, and is fully aware of environmental impacts. Shows a thorough ability in a wide variety of practical activities, and pays considerable attention to health and safety issues.

Grade 6: Very good achievement

The work shows a broad, detailed understanding of factual material, subject vocabulary, ideas, skills and methods. The candidate has shown good understanding and synthesis of a wide range of ideas and information; very good analysis (either quantitative and/ or qualitative) and evaluation of information; assessed and balanced a range of opinions and views; provided a reasoned and justified view, while considering alternative views and perceptions of others, and cultural determinants of such views; a good level of communication skills using appropriate language and symbols; sometimes scholarly and inventive.

The candidate shows personal skills, persistence and responsibility in a wide range of investigative studies in a regular way. Works well individually and in a team, and is aware of environmental impacts. Shows good ability in a wide variety of practical activities, and pays attention to health and safety issues.

Grade 5: Good achievement

The work shows a sound understanding of factual material, subject vocabulary, ideas, skills and methods. The candidate has shown competent understanding and synthesis of a range of ideas and information; good analysis (either quantitative and/or qualitative) and evaluation of information; assessed and balanced opinions and views; provided a reasoned view, while considering alternative views and perceptions of others, and cultural determinants of such views; a basic level of communication skills using appropriate language and symbols.

The candidate shows personal skills, persistence and responsibility in a wide range of investigative studies in a fairly regular way. Can work well individually but is better in a team, and is aware of environmental impacts. Shows competent ability in a variety of practical activities, and pays attention to health and safety issues.

Grade 4: Satisfactory achievement

The work shows secure understanding of factual material, subject vocabulary, ideas, skills and methods but with gaps. The candidate has shown some understanding and synthesis of a range of ideas and information; limited analysis (either quantitative and/or qualitative) and basic evaluation of information; some awareness of opinions and views of others; a limited level of communication skills using appropriate language and symbols.

The candidate shows personal skills, persistence and responsibility in a range of investigative studies in a slightly inconsistent way. Works well in a team, and is aware of environmental impacts. Shows competent ability in a variety of practical activities, and sometimes pays attention to health and safety issues. Needs supervision.

Grade 3: Mediocre achievement

The work shows limited understanding of factual material, subject vocabulary, ideas, skills and methods but with gaps. The candidate has shown a basic ability in the understanding and synthesis of a range of ideas and information; descriptive analysis (either quantitative and/or qualitative) and basic evaluation of information; vague awareness of opinions and views of others; a weak level of communication skills, characterized by some repetition and/ or irrelevant material.

The candidate shows personal skills, persistence and responsibility in a range of investigative studies in an inconsistent way. Works well in a team, and sometimes is aware of environmental impacts. Shows competent ability in some practical activities, and occasionally pays attention to health and safety issues. Needs detailed supervision.

Grade 2: Poor achievement

The work shows partial understanding of factual material, subject vocabulary, ideas, skills and methods but with major gaps. The candidate has limited ability in the understanding and synthesis of a range of ideas and information; limited descriptive analysis (either quantitative and/or qualitative); no awareness of opinions and views of others; a weak level of communication skills, characterized by frequent repetition, irrelevant material and/or incomplete nature.

The candidate shows little personal skills, persistence and responsibility in investigative studies. Works well in a team but contributes little; shows little awareness of environmental impacts. Shows competent ability in very few practical activities, and pays little attention to health and safety issues. Needs close supervision.

Grade 1: Very poor achievement

The work shows very little understanding of factual material, subject vocabulary, ideas, skills and methods and with major gaps. The candidate has very poor ability in the understanding and synthesis of a range of ideas and information; very poor or no descriptive analysis (either quantitative and/or qualitative); no awareness of opinions and views of others; a weak level of communication skills, characterized by frequent repetition, irrelevant material and/or incomplete nature.

The candidate rarely shows personal skills, persistence and responsibility in investigative studies. Does not work well in a team; shows very little awareness of environmental impacts. Rarely shows any competence in practical activities, and generally pays no attention to health and safety issues. Needs constant close supervision.

Assessment objectives

The objectives reflect those parts of the aims that will be assessed. It is the intention of the Environmental Systems and Societies course that students should achieve the following objectives.

1 Demonstrate an understanding of information, terminology, concepts, methodologies and skills with regard to environmental issues.

2 Apply and use information, terminology, concepts, methodologies and skills with regard to environmental issues.

3 Synthesize, analyse and evaluate research questions, hypotheses, methods and scientific explanations with regard to environmental issues.

4 Using a holistic approach, make reasoned and balanced judgments using appropriate economic, historical, cultural, socio-political and scientific sources.

5 Articulate and justify a personal viewpoint on environmental issues with reasoned argument while appreciating alternative viewpoints, including the perceptions of different cultures.

6 Demonstrate the personal skills of cooperation and responsibility appropriate for effective investigation and problem-solving.

7 Select and demonstrate the appropriate practical and research skills necessary to carry out investigations with due regard to precision.

Assessment objectives	Which components test these objectives?	How is the assessment objective tested?
1–3	• Paper 1 (1 hour, 45 marks) 30% of the marks	Short-answer and data-response questions
1–5	• Paper 2 (2 hours, 65 marks) 50% of the marks	Section A: case study Section B: two structured essay questions (from a choice of four)
1–7	• Internal assessment (30 hours, 42 marks) 20% of the marks	Practical work with some activities selected and marked against the internal assessment criteria

Mark bands for longer replies – guidance for bands

Mark band	Mark range	Descriptor
A	0	No relevant knowledge; neither examples nor case studies; no evidence of application; the question has been completely misinterpreted or omitted; no evaluation; no appropriate skills.
B	1–2	Little knowledge and/or understanding; largely superficial, marginal or irrelevant examples and case studies; very little application; important aspects of the question are ignored; no evaluation; very low level skills; little attempt at organization of material; no relevant terminology.
C	3–4	Some relevant knowledge and understanding, but with some omissions; examples and case studies included, but limited in detail; little attempt at application; answer partially addresses question; no evaluation; few or no maps or diagrams; little evidence of skills or organization of material; poor terminology.
D	5–6	Relevant knowledge and understanding, but with some omissions; examples and case studies are included, occasionally generalized; some attempt at application; competent answer although not fully developed, and tends to be descriptive; no evaluation or unsubstantiated evaluation; basic maps or diagrams, but evidence of some skills; some indication of structure and organization of material; acceptable terminology.
E	7–8	Generally accurate knowledge and understanding, but with some minor omissions; examples and case studies are well chosen, occasionally generalized; appropriate application; developed answer covers most aspects of the question; beginning to show some attempt at evaluation of the issue, which may be unbalanced; acceptable maps and diagrams; appropriate structure and terminology.
F	9–10	Accurate, specific, well-detailed knowledge and understanding; examples and case studies are well chosen and developed; detailed application; well-developed answer covers most or all aspects of the question; good and well-balanced attempt at evaluation; appropriate and sound maps and diagrams; well-structured and organized responses; terminology sound.

Source: Adapted from the Environmental Systems and Societies Subject Guide 2010, IBO 2008

INTERNAL ASSESSMENT

Assessment criteria for internal assessment

There are four assessment criteria for internal assessment. Each one has level descriptors describing different levels of achievement with appropriate marks.

Teachers judge the internally assessed work using the descriptors.

- The aim is to find the criteria descriptors that convey most accurately the levels attained by the student, using a best-fit model. The mark awarded is the one that most fairly reflects the overall achievement against the criterion. It is not necessary for the work to meet every descriptor in the level awarded.
- Where there are two or more marks available within a level, the higher mark should be given if the student's work demonstrates the qualities described to a great extent. The lower mark should be awarded if the work illustrates the qualities described to a lesser extent.
- The highest level descriptors do not imply perfect performance but should be achievable by a student. Teachers should use the full range of marks if they are appropriate descriptions to the work being assessed.
- A student who attains a high level of achievement in one criterion will not necessarily attain high levels in others. Similarly, a student who attains a low level of achievement for a criterion will not necessarily attain low levels for the others.

Criteria and aspects

These are the four assessment criteria used to assess the work of students.
- Planning (Pl)
- Data collection and processing (DCP)
- Discussion, evaluation and conclusion (DEC)
- Personal skills (PS)

The first three (i.e. planning, data collection and processing, and discussion, evaluation and conclusion) are each assessed twice. Personal skills, however, is assessed once only, summatively, at the end of the course. It should reflect any sustained improvement in performance.

Each of the assessment criteria is separated into three **aspects** as shown in Tables 10.1–10.4 below. The tables also show descriptions provided to indicate what is expected in order to meet the requirements of a given aspect **completely** (2 marks), **partially** (1 mark) or **not at all** (0 marks).

The maximum mark for each criterion is 6 (three 'completes').
- Pl $6 \times 2 = 12$
- DCP $6 \times 2 = 12$
- DEC $6 \times 2 = 12$
- PS $6 \times 1 = 6$

Marks gained are added together to give a final mark out of 42. This is then scaled by the IB to give a total out of 20%.

TABLE 10.1 PLANNING

Level/marks	Aspect 1	Aspect 2	Aspect 3
	Defining the problem and selecting variables	Controlling variables	Developing a method for collection of data
complete/2	State a focussed problem/research question and identify the relevant variables.	Design a method for the effective control of variables.	Describe a method that allows the collection of sufficient relevant data.
partial/1	State a problem/research question that is incomplete or identify only some relevant variables.	Design a method that makes some attempt to control the variables.	Describe a method that does not allow for the collection of sufficient relevant data.
not at all/0	Does not state a problem/research question and does not identify any relevant variables.	Designs a method that does not allow for the control of the variables.	Describes a method that does not allow for the collection of any relevant data.

TABLE 10.2 DATA COLLECTION AND PROCESSING

Level/marks	Aspect 1	Aspect 2	Aspect 3
	Recording data	Processing data	Presenting processed data
complete/2	Record systematically appropriate quantitative and/or qualitative data (primary and/or secondary), including units.	Correct processing of primary and/or secondary data.	Presents processed data appropriately and effectively.
partial/1	Record appropriate quantitative and/or qualitative data (primary and/or secondary) but with some mistakes and/or omissions (e.g. units).	Processing of primary and/or secondary data but with some mistakes and/or omissions.	Presents processed data appropriately but lacks clarity **or** with some mistakes and/or omissions.
not at all/0	Data is not recorded **or** is recorded incomprehensibly.	No processing of data **or** major mistakes in processing.	Data presented data inappropriately **or** incomprehensibly.

TABLE 10.3 DISCUSSION, EVALUATION AND CONCLUSION

Levels/marks	Aspect 1	Aspect 2	Aspect 3
	Discussing and reviewing	Evaluating procedure(s) and suggesting improvements	Concluding
complete/2	Clear and well reasoned discussion, showing a broad understanding of context and the implications of results.	Identifies weaknesses and limitations and suggests realistic improvements.	Reasonable conclusion stated, with a correct explanation, based on the data.
partial/1	Adequate discussion, showing some understanding of context and implications of results.	Identifies weaknesses and limitations but misses some obvious faults. Suggests superficial improvements.	States a reasonable conclusion **or** gives a correct explanation, based on the data.
not at all/0	Inadequate discussion, showing little understanding of context and implications of results.	The weaknesses and limitations are irrelevant **or** missing. Suggests unrealistic improvements.	States an unreasonable conclusion **or** no conclusion at all.

TABLE 10.4 PERSONAL SKILLS (ASSESSED SUMMATIVELY)

Levels/mark	Aspect 1	Aspect 2	Aspect 3
	Carrying out techniques	Working in a team	Working safely and ethically
complete/2	Fully competent and methodical in the use of a range of techniques and equipment.	Consistently collaborates well and communicates in a group situation and integrates the views of others.	Always pays attention to safety issues and shows due regard for the environmental consequences and academic integrity.
partial/1	Generally competent and methodical in the use of a range of techniques and equipment.	Occasionally collaborates and communicates in a group situation.	Usually pays attention to safety issues and shows some regard for the environmental consequences and academic integrity.
not at all/0	Rarely competent and methodical in the use of a range of techniques and equipment.	Little or no attempt to collaborate in a group situation.	Pays little attention to safety issues and shows little regard for the environmental consequences and academic integrity.

Guidance on the criteria

It is essential that teachers do not provide too much guidance because that may result in a reduction of students' scores. The following paragraphs show how guidance should be limited for assessment purposes.

Planning

In order to assess this criterion, students should be given an open-ended problem to investigate; for example, variations in water quality (pollution), along a named, small stretch of stream.

Although teachers may provide a general aim or context, students must individually identify a problem or research question. For example, students may decide to investigate variations or changes in species distribution, water temperature, oxygen content, light levels etc. and identify the factors that may be responsible for the pattern, and design a method for collecting data.

Aspect 1: Defining the problem and selecting variables
The problem or research question should be clearly stated, possibly in the form of a hypothesis (e.g. there is a difference between the number and type of species located upstream and downstream of a sewage outlet). Students must clearly state the relevant variables in the investigation (e.g. light, temperature, dissolved oxygen, water chemistry) including those to be measured and the control – in this example, the upstream readings unaffected by the sewage outlet.

Aspect 2: Controlling variables
It is not always possible to control all variables, but students should still identify such variables and, where possible, attempt to minimize their influence.

Aspect 3: Developing a method for collection of data
The method should enable students to collect enough relevant data. However, what is considered to be enough depends on the nature of the investigation and the time available to students. Some variables may vary seasonally (e.g. water temperature and stream discharge).

Data collection and processing

The collection, recording and processing of data is a key part of developing students' understanding of the interaction between environment and society. Investigations can be based on either primary and/or secondary data.

Aspect 1: Recording data
When data collection is carried out in group work, the actual recording and processing of data should be carried out independently.

Data may be quantitative and/or qualitative and may consist of numerical measurements, observations, photographs, results of questionnaires or interviews, drawings and/or maps. Primary data may be collected through fieldwork, surveys or laboratory investigations. Use of secondary data may be the only way to investigate some topics (e.g. time-based surveys of vegetation succession) but in this situation students must select the relevant data for themselves. If the data is selected for students by others (e.g. teachers or field centre staff), no credit can be awarded.

Students who systematically collect relevant data and record it clearly will obtain full marks in this section. Students who collect relevant data, but use incorrect units, only partially fulfill this aspect. Students who collect little or no data, and whose results are difficult or impossible to understand, do not fulfill this aspect at all, and would score 0 marks.

Aspect 2: Processing data

Processing data refers to the manipulation of raw data before it is finally presented. It is important to use an investigation that requires data processing. This might include grouping elements from raw data, calculation of mean values, percentages, indices or statistical tests. For example, a correlation may be used to show the relationship between two sets of data, or a t-test to show the mean and standard deviation of two data sets.

Aspect 3: presenting processed data

It is important to select a method of presentation that displays the data to best effect and aids interpretation. Presentation of data may take many forms, including graphical models such as dispersion diagrams, sketch maps, charts, flow diagrams or annotated drawings.

A high level of neatness and precision, use of scientific conventions and clear headings and labels aid effective presentation. Repetitive presentation of the same data set in a variety of formats is inappropriate and will not receive extra marks.

Discussion, evaluation and conclusion

Once the data has been processed and presented in a suitable form, the results should be discussed and analysed, and conclusions are made. In analysing, evaluating and concluding, students should discuss the broader significance of their results.

Although teachers may lead class discussions on group projects, students must be able to produce independent discussions, evaluation and conclusions for assessment purposes.

Aspect 1: Discussing and reviewing

In the discussion, students should review and analyse their results and consider them in relation to relevant literature and accepted scientific understanding/models. Analysis should include identification of trends, patterns and/or anomalies that may or may not agree with established theory.

Aspect 2: Evaluating procedure(s) and suggesting improvements

Students should evaluate their investigation in a constructive and reflective way, recognizing strengths, weaknesses and limitations. This should enable them to suggest realistic improvements to the study. Students may consider sampling design, limitations and use of equipment, time constraints, data quality (accuracy and precision) and relevance.

Aspect 3: Concluding

Students should provide a clear and concise conclusion that is supported by evidence from their data.

Personal skills

This criterion is assessed summatively once only at the end of the course.

Aspect 1: Carrying out techniques

Effective students should be able to carry out a range of techniques competently, follow instructions, and assemble and use equipment with precision and accuracy.

Aspect 2: Working in a team

Effective teamwork includes recognizing the contribution of others. This will allow the exchange and discussion of ideas.

Aspect 3: Working safely and ethically

Students should adhere to safe and ethical working practices, citing secondary sources, and avoiding plagiarism. Due attention to environmental impact should be shown, such as avoidance of waste, safe waste disposal, and minimizing damage to local environments.

ADVICE ON THE EXTENDED ESSAY

The Extended Essay is an in-depth study of a focussed topic that promotes intellectual discovery, creativity and writing skills. It provides you with an opportunity to explore and engage with an academic idea or problem in your favourite International Baccalaureate diploma subject. It will develop your research skills (something needed at universities and tertiary education in general), and provide you the opportunity to produce an individualized and personal piece of work. The essay is a major piece of structured writing that is formally presented. Many students find the Extended Essay a valuable stimulus for discussion in interviews for university or employment. You are expected to spend approximately 40 hours on the project, and the finished piece of work should be no more than 4000 words.

You will have a supervisor for your essay, who will help you to decide on a suitable topic, and check that you are keeping to the timing and regulations. You can meet with your supervisor for 3 to 5 hours over the course of your essay: several short meetings are recommended (e.g. once a fortnight for 30 minutes) rather than a few long ones, as this will help you and your supervisor to exchange ideas and feedback on a regular basis. Your supervisor will:

- give you a copy of the assessment criteria and subject specific details (available from the IBO)
- give you advice on the skills of undertaking research
- help you with shaping your research question and the subsequent structure and content of your essay
- give you examples of excellent Extended Essays from the IBO
- read and comment on your work (but cannot edit it)
- give you advice on the format of the bibliography, the abstract and referencing
- conduct a short concluding interview (viva voce) with you once you have finished the essay.

To make the most of your Extended Essay, you need to make sure you:

- undertake the work agreed by you and your supervisor
- keep appointments and deadlines
- are honest about your progress and any problems you may be facing
- pace yourself so you do not have a lot of work at the last minute.

The Extended Essay is marked according to certain assessment criteria which you will receive from your supervisor. The maximum total number of marks you can receive is 36, and you can see from the criteria how many marks are allotted to each aspect of your Essay (there are 11 different marking criteria).

Details specific to ESS are outlined below. These give examples of specific topics and research questions.

Bibliography (references)

A bibliography should be in alphabetical order according to author's surname. It should be on a separate sheet of paper with a title at the top. You must make sure you consider

To learn more about how to cite different sources in the *Chicago Manual of Style* format, go to www.pearsonhotlinks. com, insert the express code 2630P and click on activity EE.1.

whether any source you use is likely to be reliable; this is especially true for internet resources, where there are relatively few quality controls. If at all possible, you should therefore include the author of any article from the web. You should also include the date a web page was accessed. The references in your Extended Essay should follow the *Chicago Manual of Style* (Footnotes).

Detail specific to Environmental systems and societies

An Extended Essay in this course will provide you with the opportunity to explore an environmental topic or issue of particular interest to you and your locality. As this is an interdisciplinary subject, you will need to integrate theory from the course with practical methodologies which are relevant to your topic. A systems approach is particularly effective and, as this is something emphasized throughout the course, this should be familiar to you. You will be expected to show appreciation and use of this approach in the analysis and interpretation of the data gathered.

The course focuses on the interaction and integration of natural environmental systems and human societies, and your essay needs to achieve this as well. It should not deal exclusively with ecological processes or with societal activities, but instead should give significant (though not necessarily equal) weight to both these dimensions. For example, while the environmental systems and societies syllabus includes a study of pure ecological principles, in an Extended Essay it would have to be explored within the context of some human interaction with the environmental system. A specific natural system needs to be studied, rather than general systems that have been covered in the course.

If your aims are to obtain largely descriptive or narrative data, of the type produced in the human sciences, a group 3 essay may be more appropriate. If you are only going to collect quantitative data typical of the experimental sciences, then a group 4 essay may be more appropriate. An ESS essay must cover both group 3 and group 4 criteria and be fully transdisciplinary in nature.

A crucial feature of any suitable topic is that it must be open to analytical argument. For example, rather than simply describing a given nature reserve, you would also need to evaluate its relationship with a local community, or compare its achievement with original objectives, or with a similar initiative elsewhere. The topic must leave room for you to be able to form argument that you both construct and support, using analysis of your own data, rather than simply reporting analysed data obtained from other sources. Certain topics should be avoided for ethical or safety reasons (e.g. experiments likely to inflict pain on living organisms, cause unwarranted environmental damage, or put pressure on others to behave unethically). Experiments that pose a threat to health (e.g. using toxic or dangerous chemicals, or putting oneself at physical risk during fieldwork) should also be avoided unless adequate safety apparatus and qualified supervision are available.

Focus

Essential to a successful Extended Essay is the focus of the topic chosen. If a topic is too broad, it can lead you into superficial treatment and it is unlikely you will be able to produce any fresh analysis, or novel and interesting conclusions of your own. So, for example, topics on the left of Table 1 are better than topics on the right.

TABLE 1 FOCUSING THE TOPIC OF YOUR ESSAY	
Focussed	Unfocussed
The ecological recovery of worked-out bauxite quarries in Jarrahdale, Western Australia	Environmental effects of mining
A comparison of the energy efficiency of grain production in The Netherlands and Swaziland	Efficiency of world food production
The comparative significance of different sources of carbon dioxide pollution in New York and Sacramento	Impacts of global warming
Managing the environmental impact of paper use at a Welsh college	Paper recycling

Topics with a sharper focus enable you to channel your research to produce interesting and original conclusions and discussions. A short and precise statement outlining the overall approach of your investigation is also helpful in determining the focus of your essay, and making sure you stick to it. For example, if your topic is an examination of the ecological footprint of your school canteen, the research question could be: From the major inputs and outputs of the school canteen, what overall estimate of its environmental impact can be made in terms of an ecological footprint? The approach would include an analysis of the records and practical measurements that assess the inputs and outputs of the canteen, and an analysis of data into a holistic environmental footprint model that indicates environmental impact. For some investigations, particularly those that are experimental, a clearly stated hypothesis may be just as acceptable as, and possibly better than, a research question.

An Extended Essay in Environmental Systems and Societies may be investigated either through primary data collection (i.e. from fieldwork, laboratory experimentation, surveys or interviews) or through secondary data collection (i.e. from literature or other media). It may even involve a combination of the two. However, given the limited time available and the word limit for the essay, the emphasis should be clearly with one or the other to avoid the danger of both becoming superficial. Experience shows that data based on questionnaires and interviews are to be avoided, as such data are difficult to analyse and conclusions difficult to arrive at. Fieldwork and lab experiments are a more reliable way to gather data for your essay.

If the essay is focussed largely on the collection of primary data, you must check carefully with the literature to make sure you select the most appropriate method for obtaining valid quantitative data. You must ensure you reference these secondary sources of information in your bibliography. If the essay is focussed on secondary data, you need to take great care in selecting sources, ensuring that there is a sufficient quantity and range, and that they are all reliable. The internet and other media contain a great many unfounded and unsupported claims that you need to be wary of – checking information from several different sources will help you evaluate its value and accuracy. You must sort through your sources and use only those that have some academic credibility. For an essay of this type, you are expected to produce a substantial bibliography and not be limited to just a few sources.

Once you have assembled your data, you must produce your own analysis and argue your own conclusions. This will happen more naturally if the essay is based on primary data since such data has not been previously analysed. A source of secondary data, may come with its own analysis and conclusions. If you use secondary data, it is essential that you further manipulate it, or possibly combine it with other sources, so that there is clear evidence in the essay of your personal involvement in analysis and drawing of conclusions. You are expected to be academically honest in your essay – plagiarism (direct copying) is a very serious matter which the IBO deals with severely.

A central theme in the syllabus for Environmental Systems and Societies is the systems approach. This should be reflected to some degree in your essay which should include an attempt to model, at least partially, the system or systems in question. The term 'model' can be applied in its broadest sense to include, for example, mathematical formulae, maps, graphs and flow diagrams. Systems terminology (e.g. input, output, processes) should be used where appropriate.

Assessment criteria

Details of the assessment criteria will be provided by your supervisor. Specific points relating to Environmental Systems and Societies are summarized below.

Criterion A: research question

A sharply focussed research question defining the purpose of the essay must be stated clearly. It is acceptable to formulate the research question as a clearly stated hypothesis. This may be particularly appropriate, for example, in experimental investigations. A hypothesis will always lead to clear critical arguments concerning the extent to which the results support or refute it.

Criterion B: introduction

The introduction should set the research question or hypothesis in context. Theoretical principles can be outlined, and the history or geography of the location central to the issue under discussion given.

Criterion C: investigation

If the essay involves experimentation or practical fieldwork, a detailed description of your methods is needed (ideally with diagrams and photos). Careful attention should be given to the design of experiments to include use of, for example, quantification, controls, replication and random sampling, where appropriate. The selection of techniques should be explained and justified, and any assumptions on which they depend should be clearly stated. If secondary data are used, you need to make sure the sources are reliable. Sources must be referenced. You should indicate how the secondary data were generated.

Criterion D: knowledge and understanding of the topic studied

You must demonstrate sound understanding of the Environmental Systems and Societies course, and that you have read beyond the syllabus and carried out your own independent study. You need to have sufficient knowledge of the topic to handle the issues and arguments effectively. You need to show links between your study and previous work from references you have found. You also need to use theoretical knowledge to underpin your essay.

Criterion E: reasoned argument

There should be a clear step-by-step logical argument linking the raw data to the final conclusions. Each step should be defended and supported with evidence.

Criterion F: application of analytical and evaluative skills appropriate to the subject

You need to use your analytical skills to manipulate and present your data. You must evaluate you data and comment on its reliability and validity. You should include a model of the system studied and use the correct terminology when discussing it.

Criterion G: use of language appropriate to the subject

You must use terminology appropriate to the subject throughout your essay. Both scientific and systems terminology should be used.

Criterion H: conclusion

This section should be separated with its own heading within the essay. It should contain a brief summary of the direct conclusions of your research question or hypothesis, supported by evidence and arguments already presented. It should not contain new evidence or discussion. You should also identify any outstanding gaps in your research or new questions that have arisen which you think would deserve further attention.

Criterion I: formal presentation

You must check with the assessment criteria to make sure that you have met all the formal requirements for the Extended Essay. Particular attention should be paid to the use of graphs, diagrams, illustrations and tables of data. These should all be appropriately labelled with a figure or table number, a title, a citation where appropriate, and be located in the body of the essay, as close as possible to their first reference.

Criterion J: abstract

This is a brief summary of the essay. It is judged on the clarity of the overview it presents, and not on the quality of the research, arguments, or conclusions.

Criterion K: holistic judgment

You should demonstrate personal engagement, initiative and insight in your topic. This will be easier if you have direct experience of the environmental issue under discussion. A major theme of this subject is the interrelatedness of systems and components within them. An essay that recognizes these underlying principles and the interrelatedness of components will most clearly demonstrate an element of the 'insight and depth of understanding' referred to in this criterion.

ADVICE ON EXAMINATION STRATEGIES

Command terms and definitions

You need to become familiar with the command words listed and defined below. They are all found in International Baccalaureate Environmental Systems and Societies examination questions – and misinterpretation of these terms is one of the main ways in which marks are lost in exams.

The command terms indicate the level of detail needed for a given question and relate to course assessment objectives 1–5 (page 318). Objectives 1 and 2 are about lower order skills, whereas objectives 3, 4 and 5 relate to higher order skills.

Objective 1

- *Demonstrate* an understanding of information, terminology, concepts, methodologies and skills with regard to environmental issues.

  Define – Give the precise meaning of, for example, a word, phrase, concept or physical quantity.

  Draw – Represent by means of a labelled, accurate diagram or graph, using a pencil. A ruler (straight edge) should be used for straight lines. Diagrams should be drawn to scale. Graphs should have points correctly plotted (if appropriate) and joined in a straight line or smooth curve.

  Label – Add labels to a diagram.

  List – Give a sequence of brief answers with no explanation.

  Measure – Obtain a value for a quantity.

  State – Give a specific name, value or other brief answer without explanation or calculation.

Objective 2

- *Apply and use* information, terminology, concepts, methodologies and skills with regard to environmental issues.

  Annotate – Add brief notes to a diagram or graph.

  Apply – Use an idea, equation, principle, theory or law in relation to a given problem or issue.

  Calculate – Obtain a numerical answer showing the relevant stages of working.

  Describe – Give a detailed account.

  Distinguish – Make clear the differences between two or more concepts or items.

  Estimate – Obtain an approximate value.

  Identify – Find an answer from a number of possibilities.

  Outline – Give a brief account or summary.

Objectives 3, 4 and 5

- *Synthesize, analyse and evaluate* research questions, hypotheses, methods and scientific explanations with regard to environmental issues.
- Using a holistic approach, *make reasoned and balanced judgments* using appropriate economic, historical, cultural, socio-political and scientific sources.
- *Articulate and justify* a personal viewpoint on environmental issues with reasoned argument while appreciating alternative viewpoints, including the perceptions of different cultures.

Analyse – Break down in order to bring out the essential elements or structures.

Comment – Give a judgment based on a given statement or result of a calculation.

Compare and contrast – Give an account of similarities and differences between two (or more) items or situations, referring to both (or all) of them throughout.

Construct – Display information in a diagrammatic or logical form.

Deduce – Reach a conclusion from the information given.

Derive – Manipulate a mathematical relationship to give a new equation or relationship.

Design – Produce a plan, simulation or model.

Determine – Obtain the only possible answer.

Discuss – Offer a considered and balanced review that includes a range of arguments, factors or hypotheses. Opinions or conclusions should be presented clearly and supported by appropriate evidence.

Evaluate – Make an appraisal by weighing up the strengths and limitations.

Examine – Consider an argument or concept in a way that uncovers the assumptions and interrelationships of the issue.

Explain – Give a detailed account, including reasons or causes.

Justify – Give valid reasons or evidence for an answer or conclusion.

Predict – Give an expected result.

Solve – Obtain the answer(s) using algebraic and/or numerical methods and/or graphical methods.

Suggest – Propose a solution, hypothesis or other possible answer.

To what extent – Consider the merits or otherwise of an argument or concept. Opinions and conclusions should be presented clearly and supported with empirical evidence and sound argument.

Strategies

International Baccalaureate examinations for Environmental Systems and Societies are dominated by data-based questions and open-ended or free-response questions.

Strategy for success when answering data-based questions

Data-based questions present you with data in some form and ask you questions about it. Some questions will ask you to read the data displayed and some will ask you to draw conclusions from it.

Pay close attention to the number of marks for each question. The examiner is comparing your answer to acceptable answers on a mark-scheme. You can write as much as you like but be guided by the number of marks available and do not contradict yourself. Marking is positive, so you will not be penalized if you say something wrong.

You are expected to use the data provided in the question. Try to get into the habit of using the data when you practise data-based questions. This will make it natural to do the same when sitting the exam. Become familiar with unit expressions such as $kJ\,m^{-2}\,yr^{-1}$ (read as kilojoules per metre squared per year). If you are not comfortable with the unit expressions you see in data-based questions, see your teacher for help.

Questions which use the command term 'compare' require you to relate the *similarities* as well as *differences* between two sets of data. In most cases, where the answer involves numeric data, you will not achieve a mark unless you provide a unit.

Use a ruler when answering data-based questions since the graphs are often small and the degree of precision required in your answers is often quite demanding. Practise the questions given at the end of each chapter in this book. A mark-scheme is provided towards the end of the book. Compare your answer with the suggested answer, and look at the mark-bands.

Strategy for success when answering open-ended questions

You must be familiar with all the command terms. It is extremely important that you know these terms and what is expected in response to each of them. Make sure you devote more time to questions that receive more marks.

If you are asked to 'Discuss' you should identify and present at least two alternative views. If you are asked to 'List three factors' you will not gain any extra credit for listing more than three factors.

Remember these tips.
- The examiner does not know you. You must communicate fully what you know and not expect the examiner to do your thinking for you.
- State the obvious in your answers. Many of the items in a mark-scheme will be information that is very basic in relation to the question.
- Do not use abbreviations that may be unfamiliar to someone else. Always use the full words first and put the abbreviations in brackets. Be clear and concise with your choice of words.
- If your handwriting is very small or unclear, print your response. If the examiner cannot read your writing, you will not get any marks.
- Make sure to use extra paper if you need it.

Remember that the written papers form only part of the overall assessment. The internal assessment is graded by your teacher and moderated by an examiner.

During the exam use your time appropriately.
- Read each question twice before beginning to write.
- Plan your time – allocate time according to the number of marks per question.
- If you have time at the end, re-read your answers and make sure you have said exactly what you want to say.

APPENDIX: BASIC STATISTICS AND DATA ANALYSIS

Sampling

A sample is a representative body of data. A large number of items (the total population) can be represented by a small sub-section (the sample) when it is impractical or impossible to measure the total population. Sampling is therefore an efficient use of time and resources which makes it possible to make statements about the total population while using a representative section. Sampling makes fieldwork investigations manageable.

There are different types of sampling which have their own strengths and weaknesses. In general, there are two main types of sampling – spatial sampling and temporal sampling. Spatial sampling refers to samples that vary in where they are taken from. Temporal sampling refers to samples that are taken over different time periods. Both can be used – for example monitoring water quality changes above and below a sewage outlet between summer and winter.

Both temporal and spatial sampling can be sub-divided into three main sub-types: random, systematic and stratified (Figure 13.1).

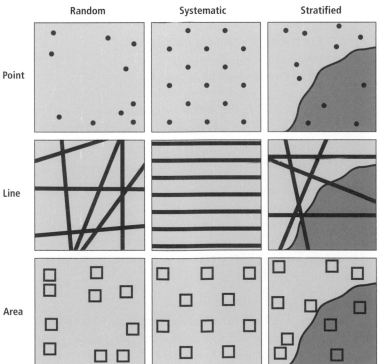

Figure 13.1
Random, systematic and stratified sampling.

Before selecting one or more types of sampling, a number of questions should be considered.
- What is the population being studied and in what area/time?
- What is the minimum size of sampling needed to produce reliable information and results?
- What is the most appropriate form of sampling for the enquiry?

Random sampling

In a random sample, each item has an equal chance of being picked. Samples are often picked by using a random number table (Table 13.1). This is a table with no bias in the sequence of numbers. Once a number is chosen, it can be related to a map, a grid reference, an angular direction and distance. Although fair, the random sample may miss important parts of the survey area. It is also very time-consuming to do properly (page 31).

TABLE 13.1 RANDOM NUMBER TABLE											
17	42	28	23	17	59	66	38	61	02	10	78
33	53	70	11	54	48	63	50	90	37	21	46
77	84	87	67	39	95	85	54	97	37	33	41
61	05	92	08	29	94	19	96	50	01	33	85
50	14	30	85	38	97	56	37	08	12	23	07
27	26	08	79	61	03	62	93	23	29	26	04
03	64	59	07	42	95	81	39	06	41	29	81
17	08	72	87	46	75	73	00	26	04	66	91
40	49	27	56	48	79	34	32	81	22	60	53

Systematic sampling

Systematic sampling is much quicker and easier than random sampling. Items are chosen at regular intervals (e.g. every five metres, every tenth person, and so on). However, it is possible that a systematic sample will miss out important features. For example, in a survey of soil moisture and temperature in a ploughed field, if samples are taken on every ridge (or every furrow) and disregard other important microclimates, the results will be biased. The major problem with this type of sampling is that it can easily give a biased result because the sample is too small and, as a result, large areas are not included in the sample.

Stratified sampling

If it is known that there are important sub-groups in an area, for example different rock types which could influence soil types or farming types, it is possible to make a representative sample that takes into account all the sub-groups in the study area. It is also possible to weight the sample so that there is a proportionate number of samples related to the relative size of each sub-group.

Sample size

Determining the appropriate size of a sample is a critical matter. It depends on the nature and aims of the investigation but also on the time available (and other practical considerations such as access, land ownership, safety and so on). There are statistical formulae that can be used to determine sample size for a survey. Such statistical tests often depend on confidence limits (i.e. the statistical limits of probability that tell you how significant your results are likely to be). These are shown opposite in Table 13.2. For example, suppose in a survey of vegetation in an area with a sample of 100 points, 90% of the points were seen to be occupied by deciduous woodland, the true figure (at the 95% confidence level) is 90% ± 6% (i.e. between 84% and 96%). The larger the sample size, the narrower the limits of the true population.

Percentage calculated	Sample size 25	Sample size 50	Sample size 100
98% or 2%	5.6	4.0	2.8
97% or 3%	6.8	4.9	3.4
96% or 4%	7.8	5.6	3.9
95% or 5%	8.7	6.2	4.4
94% or 6%	9.5	6.8	4.8
92% or 8%	10.8	7.7	5.4
90% or 10%	12.0	8.5	6.0
85% or 15%	14.3	10.1	7.1
80% or 20%	16.0	11.4	8.0
75% or 25%	17.3	12.3	8.7
70% or 30%	18.3	13.0	9.2
65% or 35%	19.1	13.5	9.5
60% or 40%	19.6	13.9	9.8
55% or 45%	19.8	14.1	9.9
50%		20.0	14.2

TABLE 13.2 RANGE OF ERROR OF ESTIMATES OF POPULATION WITH ONE CHARACTERISTIC* AT 95% CONFIDENCE LIMIT

* For example, the proportion of deciduous woodland in a survey of vegetation types in an area.

Confidence limits are based on normal probability (page 339). This assumes that 50% of the values are above the average (mean) and 50% are below. It also assumes that most of the values are within one standard deviation (page 336–37) of the mean. Probability states that in a normal distribution:

- 68% of samples lie within ± 1 standard deviation of the mean
- 95% of samples lie within ± 2 standard deviations of the mean
- 99.9% of samples lie within ± 3 standard deviations of the mean.

In other words, there is less than a 1 in 100 chance that the mean lies outside the sample mean ± 3 standard deviations, and less than a 1 in 20 chance that the true population mean lies outside the sample mean ± 2 standard deviations.

 95% confidence limits are used in ecological investigations.

Descriptive statistics

There are many types of statistics, some of them extremely easy and some very complex. At the most basic, there are simple descriptive statistics. These include the mean or average, the maximum, minimum, range (maximum–minimum), the mode (most frequently occurring number, group or class) and the median (middle value when all the numbers are placed in ascending or descending rank order).

There are also three different types of data.
- Nominal data refer to objects which have names, such as rock types, land-uses, dates of floods, famines, and so on.
- Ordinal or ranked data are placed in ascending or descending order, for example settlement hierarchies are often expressed in terms of ranks. Spearman's rank correlation coefficient (pages 340–42) is used to compare two sets of ranked data such as infant mortality rate and purchasing power parity (page 340).
- Interval or ratio data refer to real numbers – interval data has no true zero (as in the case of temperature which can be in °C or °F) whereas ratio data possess a true zero (as in the case of rainfall).

Summarizing data

The mean or average is found by totalling (Σ) the values (x) for all observations and then dividing by the total number of observations (n), thus Σx is divided by n. In Table 13.3, the average carbon dioxide emission per country is $\frac{21\,804.8}{20} = 1090.24$

TABLE 13.3 CARBON DIOXIDE EMISSIONS FOR SELECTED COUNTRIES

Country	Million tonnes of carbon dioxide
USA	6044.0
China	5005.7
Russia	1523.6
India	1341.8
Japan	1256.8
Germany	808.0
Canada	638.8
UK	586.7
South Korea	465.2
Italy	449.5
Mexico	437.6
South Africa	436.6
Iran	433.2
Indonesia	377.9
France	373.4
Brazil	331.5
Spain	330.2
Ukraine	329.7
Australia	326.5
Saudi Arabia	308.1
Total (Σ)	21 804.8

Source: Economist Pocket World In Figures, 2009

The mode refers to the group or class which occurs most often. In Table 13.3, every value occurs once, so there is no mode. If, however, there were two values of 436 (for instance), the mode would be 436.

The median is the middle value when all the data are placed in ascending or descending order. In Table 13.3, there are two middle values (the 10th and 11th values), so we take the average of these two. In this case, the values are 449.5 and 437.6, so the median value is 443.55, which is not actually a value in the data set.

Summarizing groups of data

In some cases, the data we collect are in the form of groups (e.g. daily rainfall, slope angles or ages). Such data may be recorded as 0–4, 5–9, 10–14, 15–19, etc.

Table 13.4 shows daily rainfall in an area of rainforest. To make recording simpler, groups of 5 mm rainfall have been used. Finding an average or mean is slightly more difficult. We use the mid-point of the group, multiply it by the frequency and then proceed as before. So, from Table 13.4, $n = 100$ and $\Sigma x = 870$. The mean is $\frac{870}{100} = 8.7$.

TABLE 13.4 DAILY RAINFALL FOR AN AREA OF TROPICAL RAINFOREST			
Daily rainfall / mm	Mid-point	Frequency	Mid point × frequency
0–4	2	20	40
5–9	7	42	294
10–14	12	24	288
15–19	17	12	204
20–24	22	2	44
Total		100	870

The modal group is the one which occurs with the most frequency (i.e. 5–9 mm). The median or middle value is the average of the 50th and 51st values when ranked: these are both in the 5–9 mm group.

Measures of dispersion

The range is the difference between the maximum (largest) and the minimum (smallest) value. Going back to Table 13.3, the maximum is 6044.0 and the minimum is 308.1, hence the range is 6044.0 – 308.1 = 5735.9. An alternative measure is the inter-quartile range (IQR). This is similar to the range but gives only the range of the middle half of the results – by this the extremes are omitted. The IQR is found by removing the top and bottom quartiles (quarters) and stating the range that remains. The top quartile is found by taking the 25% highest values and then finding the mid-point between the last of the top 25% and the next point. The lower quartile is found by taking the 25% lowest values and finding the mid-point between the first of these and the next highest value. The first quartile is termed Q1, and the third quartile Q3.

Hence the IQR in the case of carbon dioxide emissions (Table 13.3) is from mid-way between the 5th and 6th values (i.e. half way between 1256.8 and 808 = 1032.4) to mid-way between the 15th and 16th values (i.e. half-way between 373.4 and 331.5 = 352.45). The result is 1032.4 – 352.45 = 679.95 – a much smaller variation than when all values (including extremes) are included.

Not every case is as easy! For example, there may be a number of observations not divisible by 4. In those situations, we have to make an informed guess at where the quartile would be.

If we add the figure for Poland (307.0 million tonnes) to Table 13.3, we get 21 observations. The quartiles are then at $5\frac{1}{4}$ and $15\frac{3}{4}$ (as each quarter is $5\frac{1}{4}$ in size).

The principle is the same as before. Find the values which represent 25% and 75% of the values. Then, find half the difference between the bottom of the top 25% and the next value below. Then find half the difference between the top of the lowest 25% and the next value above.

The 25% value is now found a quarter of the way between 1256.8 and 808.0, while the 75% value lies three-quarters of the way between 331.5 and 330.2. Thus, the first quartile is found by subtracting one-quarter of the difference of 1256.8 and 808.0 from 1256.8.

$$1256.8 - \frac{(1256.8 - 808.0)}{4} = 1144.6$$

Q1 is mid-way between 1144.6 and 808.0: 976.3.

The 75% value is found by taking three-quarters of the difference of 331.5 and 330.2 from 331.5.

$$331.5 - 3 \frac{(331.5-330.2)}{4} = 330.525$$

Q3 is located midway between 330.52 and 331.5: 331.0125

Thus, the IQR is 976.3 − 331.0125 = 645.2875.

Suppose we now add the figure for 22nd largest producer of carbon dioxide, Thailand (267.8 million tonnes) to the table. There are now 22 observations.

The 25% and 75% values now are found at $5\frac{1}{2}$ and $16\frac{1}{2}$ (as each quarter is $5\frac{1}{2}$ in size, i.e. $\frac{22}{4}$). Thus the 25% value is found half-way between the 5th and 6th figures, 1256.8 and 808.0: 1032.4. The 75% value is found half-way between the 17th and 18th values, 330.2 and 329.7: 329.95). Hence Q1 is found half-way between the 25% value and the next value below, midway between 1032.4 and 808.0, namely 920.2. Q3 is found half-way between the 75% value and the next value above, the midpoint between 329.95 and 330.2 namely 330.075.

Thus the IQR in this case is 920.2 − 330.075 = 590.125.

Standard deviation

Another way of showing grouping around a central value is by using the standard deviation. This is one of the most important descriptive statistics because:

- it takes into account all the values in a distribution
- it is necessary for probability and for more complex statistics.

Standard deviation measures the dispersal of figures around the mean, and is calculated by first measuring the mean and then comparing the difference of each value from the mean.

Standard deviation is based on the ideas of probability. If a number of observations are made, then we would expect most to be quite close to the average, a few to be very much larger or smaller, and equal proportions above and below the mean.

The formula for the standard deviation (s) is:

$$s = \sqrt{\frac{\Sigma(x - \bar{x})^2}{n}}$$

where x refers to each observation, $\bar{x}$ to the mean, n is the number of points, and $(x - \bar{x})^2$ tells us to subtract the mean from each observation, and then to square the result.

Table 13.5 (opposite) shows the values worked out for $\bar{x}$, $(x - \bar{x})$ and $(x - \bar{x})^2$.

Standard deviation is found by putting the figures into the formula.

$$s = \sqrt{\frac{46\,724\,131.81}{20}} = \sqrt{2\,336\,206} = 1528 \text{ approx.}$$

Thus the average deviation of all values around the mean (1090.24) is 1528. This gives a much more accurate figure than the range or IQR, as it takes into account all values and is not as affected by extreme values. Given normal probability, we would expect that about 68% of the observations fall within 1 standard deviation of the mean, about 95% within 2 standard deviations of the mean, and about 99% within 3 standard deviations (Figure 13.2). Here we can see quite clearly that the rich countries are well above average (and some are over the mean plus two standard deviations, whereas the poorer countries are much more similar in income – they are all within one standard deviation of the mean).

TABLE 13.5 WORKING OUT THE VALUES TO CALCULATE STANDARD DEVIATION				
Country	Millions of tonnes of carbon dioxide, x	$\bar{x}$	$(x - \bar{x})$	$(x - \bar{x})^2$
USA	6044.0	1090.24	4953.76	24 539 738.14
China	5005.7	1090.24	3915.46	15 330 827.01
Russia	1523.6	1090.24	432.76	1 87 281.2176
India	1341.8	1090.24	251.56	63 282.4336
Japan	1256.8	1090.24	166.56	27 742.2336
Germany	808.0	1090.24	−282.24	79 659.4176
Canada	638.8	1090.24	−451.44	203 798.0736
UK	586.7	1090.24	−507.54	257 596.8516
South Korea	465.2	1090.24	−625.04	390 675.0016
Italy	449.5	1090.24	−640.74	410 547.7476
Mexico	437.6	1090.24	−652.64	425 938.9696
South Africa	436.6	1090.24	−653.64	427 245.2496
Iran	433.2	1090.24	−657.04	431 701.5616
Indonesia	377.9	1090.24	−712.34	507 428.2756
France	373.4	1090.24	−716.84	513 859.5856
Brazil	331.5	1090.24	−758.74	575 686.3876
Spain	330.2	1090.24	−760.04	577 660.8016
Ukraine	329.7	1090.24	−760.54	578 421.0916
Australia	326.5	1090.24	−763.74	583 298.7876
Saudi Arabia	308.1	1090.24	−782.14	611 742.9790
Σ				46 724 131.81

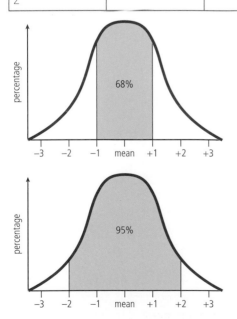

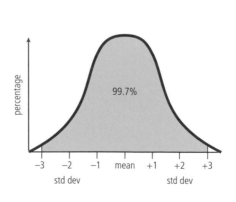

◀ **Figure 13.2**
Standard deviations from the mean.

Inferential statistics

Inferential statistics use results from surveys to make estimates or predictions (i.e. they make an inference about the total population or about some future situation). To understand inferential statistics, it is important to grasp three related concepts: probability, sampling and significance.

Probability

One of the main tasks of inferential statistics is to establish the likelihood of particular event or value occurring – this is known as probability. Probability is measured on a scale from 0 to 1. The value 1 represents absolute certainty (e.g. everyone will eventually die), whereas the value 0 represents absolute impossibility (a non-American citizen will become President of the USA). In statistics, probability (p) is often expressed as a percentage:

- $p = 0.05$ (a 1-in-20 chance) is a 95% level of probability;
- $p = 0.01$ (a 1-in-100 chance) is a 99% level of probability;
- $p = 0.001$ (a 1-in-1000 chance) is a 99.9% level of probability.

Sampling

See pages 331–32 for a discussion of sampling methods. The key aspect here is to decide how reliable our sample size is and how accurately it allows us to predict (i.e. what is the probability that our sample is truly representative?).

Significance

Significance relates to the probability that a hypothesis is true. In statistics, it is the convention to use a null hypothesis (a negative statement that we aim to disprove). A null hypothesis might state, for example, that there is no difference in the water quality above and below a sewage outlet. The alternative hypothesis (aka the research hypothesis) would state that there is a difference between the water quality above and below a sewage outlet. The probability at which at which it is decided to reject the null hypothesis is known as the significance level. The significance level indicates the number of times that the observed differences could be caused by chance. The practice is to refer to results as 'significant', 'highly significant' and 'very highly significant' respectively at the 95%, 99% and 99.9% levels of significance (Figure 13.3). This means there is a 1 in 20, 1 in 100 and 1 in 1000 chance (probability) of the result occurring by chance.

Ecology uses the 95% significance level (a 1 in 20 chance of a result occuring by chance) this correlates with the 95% (p = 0.05) probability level occurring by chance.

Figure 13.3
Probability and significance scales.

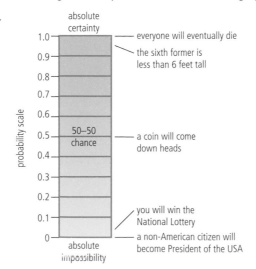
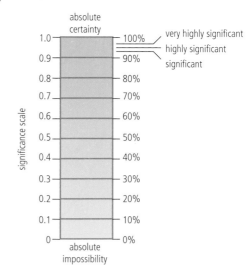

Sampling error or standard error

This statistic provides an estimate of the true population mean (i.e. the likely value we would get if we were able to measure all individuals in a population). It is based on two concepts – probability and normal distribution. In general, we would expect in a large population very few very large values and very few very small values. Most values would tend to group around the mean (Figure 13.4). So, any estimate that we make is likely to be somewhere near the true population mean. Our estimates are less likely to be very much smaller or larger than the population mean. Thus, it is possible, within certain limits to estimate where the true population mean lies.

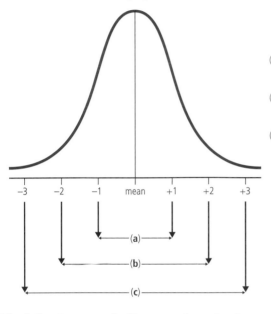

(**a**) 68% of values are within ± 1 standard deviation of the mean

(**b**) 95% of values are within ± 2 standard deviation of the mean

(**c**) 99% of values are within ± 3 standard deviation of the mean

The following example illustrates the point. In a survey of vegetation characteristics on the Isle of Purbeck (UK), a sample of 100 observations found that 50% of the area was farmland, 14% heathland, 12% woodland and 24% other. From these figures, it is possible to state that the true population mean for woodland is somewhere around 12%. The formula for sampling error or standard error is:

$$\sqrt{\frac{P(100-p)}{n}}$$

Where P refers to the proportion of (in this case) woodland

$(100 - p)$ refers to the proportion that is not (in this case) woodland

n refers to the sample size.

Thus, our estimate of the proportion of woodland that exists on the Isle of Purbeck is:

$$12\% \pm \sqrt{\frac{12 \times 88}{100}} = 12\% \pm 3.2\% = \text{from } 8.8\% \text{ to } 15.2\%$$

We are stating that we know that our own survey may not be totally accurate and that the true population mean is likely to lie somewhere between these limits.

The larger the sample, the more accurate the estimate. In the above example, if the proportion of woodland were still 12% but the sample size was 1000, the standard error or sampling error would be:

$$12\% \pm \sqrt{\frac{12 \times 88}{1000}} = 12\% \pm 1.0\%$$

Equally, given our results from our sample of 100 we can say that:
- one standard error = 12% ± 3.2% = a range from 8.8% to 15.2%
- two standard errors = 12% ± 6.4% = a range from 5.6% to 18.4%
- three standard errors = 12% ± 9.6% = a range from 2.4% to 21.6%

Confidence limits

Confidence limits are based on the ideas of probability and assume the data being sampled have a normal distribution. They are usually established at the 95% and 99% levels . These levels are found by multiplying the standard error by 1.96 and 2.58 (i.e. 2 and 3 standard deviations above and below the mean – see Figure 13.4).

Going back to the survey on the Isle of Purbeck, the sample mean was 12% and the standard error was 3.2%. So, at the 95% confidence level, the actual confidence level for the woodland would be:

$$12\% \pm (3.2 \times 1.96) = 12\% \pm 6.27 = 5.63\text{–}18.27\%$$

At the 99% confidence level, the limits would be:

$$12\% \pm (3.2 \times 2.56) = 12\% \pm 8.19 = 3.81\text{–}20.19\%.$$

We could express this in a slightly different way and say that if the actual woodland mean were 12% , we would expect that:
- 95% of the surveys would record the mean as lying between 5.63% and 18.27%
- 99% of surveys would record the mean as lying between 3.81% and 20.19%.

Spearman's rank correlation coefficient (Rs)

Spearman's rank correlation coefficient (Rs) is one of the most widely used statistics in social and environmental sciences. It is relatively quick and easy to do and only requires that data are available on the ordinal (ranked) scale. More complex data can be transformed into ranks very simply. It is called a rank correlation because only the ranks are correlated not the actual values. The use of Rs allows us to decide whether or not there is a significant statistical correlation (relationship) between two sets of data. In some cases, it is clear whether a correlation exists or not. However, in most cases it is not so clear cut and to avoid subjective comments, we use Rs to bring in a certain amount of objectivity.

Purchasing power parity (PPP) and infant mortality rates (IMR)

Procedure

1. State null hypothesis (H_0) – there is no relationship between IMR and PPP. The alternative hypothesis (H_1) is that there is a relationship between IMR and PPP. (Note that this example uses secondary data.)
2. Rank both sets of data from high to low (highest value is rank 1, second highest 2, and so on) as in Table 13.6. In the case of joint or tied ranks, find the average rank (if two values occupy positions 2 and 3 they both take on rank 2.5. If three values occupy positions 4, 5 and 6, they all take rank 5).
3. Work out the correlation using the formula:

$$Rs = 1 - \frac{6\Sigma d^2}{n^3 - n}$$

where d refers to the difference between ranks and n the number of observations.

Country	PPP / $	IMR / ‰	Rank / PPP	Rank / IMR	Difference	Difference²
Afghanistan	800	151.9	10	1	9	81
Bangladesh	1 500	59.2	9	2	7	49
Brazil	10 100	22.5	4	6	−2	4
China	6 000	20.2	6	7	−1	1
India	2 800	30.1	7	5	2	4
Kenya	1 600	54.7	8	3	5	25
Mexico	14 200	18.4	3	8	−5	25
South Africa	10 000	44.4	5	4	1	1
UK	36 600	4.6	2	9	−7	49
USA	47 000	6.3	1	10	−9	81
						320

TABLE 13.6 RANKED DATA FOR PPP AND IMR

$$Rs = 1 - \frac{6\Sigma d^2}{n^3 - n} = 1 - \frac{6 \times 320}{10^3 - 10} = 1 - \frac{1920}{990} = 1 - 1.94 = -0.94$$

4   Compare the computed Rs with the critical values for a given level of significance (normally 95% in ecological studies) in the statistical tables (Table 13.7). If the computed value exceeds the critical values in the table, we can say that we are 95% or 99% sure that there is a relationship between the sets of data. In other words, there is only a 5% or 1% chance that there is no relationship between the data.

n	Significance level	
	95%	99%
4	1.00	–
5	0.90	1.00
6	0.83	0.94
7	0.71	0.89
8	0.64	0.83
9	0.60	0.78
10	0.56	0.75
12	0.51	0.71
14	0.46	0.65
16	0.43	0.60
18	0.40	0.56
20	0.38	0.53
22	0.36	0.51
24	0.34	0.49
26	0.33	0.47
28	0.32	0.45
30	0.31	0.42

TABLE 13.7 LEVELS OF SIGNIFICANCE FOR SPEARMAN'S RANK CORRELATION

It is convention to accept 95% and 99% levels of significance. From the table, for a sample of 10 (as in our example), these values are 0.56 for 95% significance and 0.75 for 99% significance. In this example, our computed value is −0.94 (the minus sign can be ignored), so there is more than 99% chance that there is a relationship between the data.

The fact that the correlation is negative shows that it is an inverse relationship (as one variable increases the other decreases). Thus as PPP increases goes up, infant mortality rate decreases (Figure 13.5). The next stage would be to offer explanations for the relationship.

Figure 13.5
Scatter graph to show the relationship between PPP and IMR.

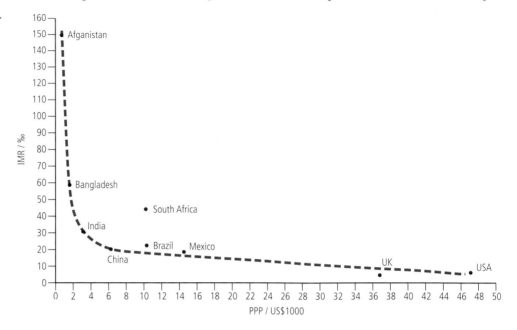

It is important to realize that Spearman's rank has its weaknesses. It has a number of limitations which must be considered.
- It requires a sample size of at least seven.
- It tests for linear relationships (Figure 13.6a and b) and would give an answer of zero for data such as river discharge and frequency, which follows a curvilinear pattern, with few very low or very high flows and a large number of medium flows (Figure 13.6c).
- It is easy to make false correlations, as between summer temperatures in the UK and infant mortality rates in India. A significant relation is not necessarily a causal one.
- The question of scale is always important. As shown in Figure 13.6d, a survey of distance downstream and tubifex worms for the whole of a drainage system may give a strong correlation whereas analysis of just a small section gives a much lower result.

Figure 13.6
Spearman's rank graphs.
(a) Linear relationship, Rs = +1.0.
(b) Linear relationship, Rs = −1.0.
(c) Curvilinear relationship, Rs = 0.0.
(d) Mixed relationship, Rs = +1.0 for complete data set; Rs = 0.0 for subset.

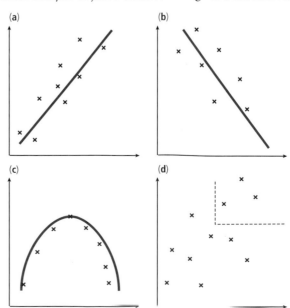

As always, statistics are tools to be used. They are only part of the analysis, and we must be aware of their limits.

There are other correlation coefficients – the Pearson product moment correlation coefficient is a more powerful correlation but it requires more sophisticated data. However, it is available on many computer packages. The principles are the same as for Spearman's rank, but the data need to be interval or ratio (real numbers) rather than just ranked data. Again, the correlation tests for a linear relationship.

The nearest neighbour index (NNI)

Part of the study of ecosystems (and vegetation) is concerned with distributions in space and over time. The spatial distribution of vegetation in an area can be described by looking at a map. This may lead us to conclude that the some types of vegetation (or ecosystems) are scattered, dispersed or concentrated. However, the main weakness with the visual method is that it is subjective and individuals differ in their interpretation of the pattern. Some objective measure is required and this is provided by the NNI.

There are three main types of pattern which can be distinguished: uniform or regular, clustered or aggregated, and random. These are shown in Figure 13.7. The points may represent individual trees, etc. If the pattern is regular, the distance between any one point and its nearest neighbour should be approximately the same as from any other point. If the pattern is clustered, then many points will be found a short distance from each other and there will be large areas of the map without any points. A random distribution normally has a mixture of some clustering and some regularity.

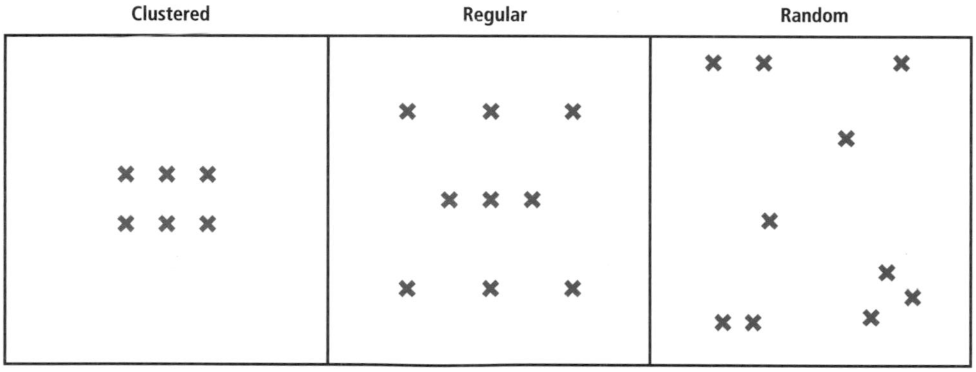

Figure 13.7
Nearest neighbour patterns.

NNI is the technique most commonly used to analyse these patterns. It is a measure of the spatial distribution of points, and is derived from the average distance between each point and its nearest neighbour. This figure is then compared to computed values which state whether the pattern is regular (NNI = 2.15), clustered (NNI = 0) or random (NNI = 1.0). Thus, a value below 1.0 shows a tendency towards clustering, whereas a value of above 1.0 shows a tendency towards uniformity.

The formula for the NNI looks somewhat daunting at first, but, like most statistics, is extremely straightforward providing care is taken.

$$\text{NNI or Rn} = 2\overline{D}\sqrt{\frac{N}{A}}$$

where $\overline{D}$ is the average distance between each point and its nearest neighbour and is calculated by finding $\sum\frac{d}{N}$ (d refers to each individual distance), N the number of points under study and A the size of the area under study. It is important that you use the same units for distance and area (e.g. metres or km but not a mixture).

For example, a survey of the distribution of vegetation types in the Camley Street Natural Park in London was undertaken to plot the distribution of deciduous trees and marsh species. The results are shown in Figure 13.8 and Tables 13.8 and 13.9. The area of the nature reserve is approximately 13 200m².

Figure 13.8
Distribution of vegetation in Camley Street Natural Park.

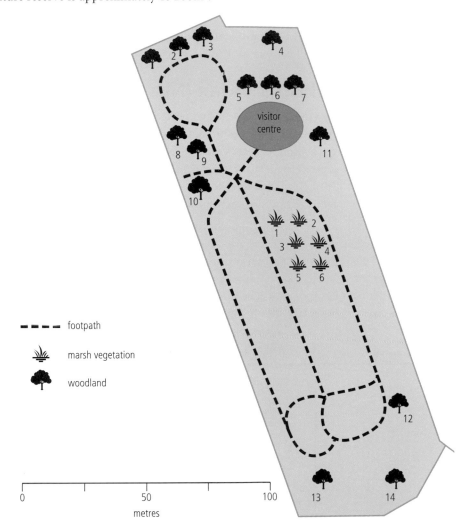

TABLE 13.8 NEAREST NEIGHBOUR DISTANCES FOR MARSHLAND VEGETATION

Vegetation	Nearest neighbour	Distance / m
1	2	10
2	1, 3	10
3	2, 4, 5	10
4	3, 6	10
5	3, 6	10
6	4, 5	10
Σd		60

$$\text{NNI or Rn} = 2\bar{D}\sqrt{\frac{N}{A}}$$

$$\bar{D} = \sum\frac{d}{N} = \frac{60}{6} = 10$$

$$Rn = 2 \times 10 \times \sqrt{\left(\frac{6}{13\,200}\right)} = 0.43$$

This answer suggests a significant degree of clustering (Figure 13.9).

TABLE 13.9 NEAREST NEIGHBOUR DISTANCES FOR WOODLAND VEGETATION		
Vegetation type	Nearest neighbour	Distance / m
1	2	14
2	3	10
3	2	10
4	6	20
5	6	10
6	5, 7	10
7	6	10
8	9	10
9	8	10
10	9	20
11	7	22
12	14	30
13	14	30
14	13	30
Σd		236

$$\text{NNI or } Rn = 2\overline{D}\sqrt{\frac{N}{A}}$$

$$\overline{D} = \sum \frac{d}{N} = \frac{236}{14} = 16.86$$

$$Rn = 2 \times 16.86 \times \sqrt{\left(\frac{14}{13\,200}\right)} = 1.10$$

This answer suggests regular spacing (Figure 13.9).

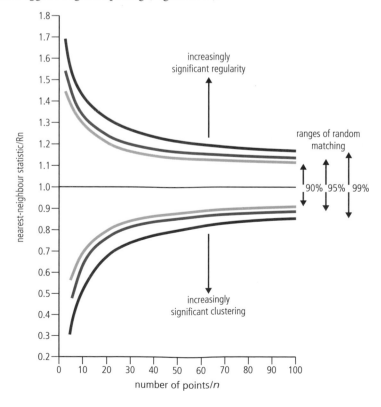

Figure 13.9
NNI significance ranges.

There are important points to bear in mind when using NNI.
- Two or more sub-patterns (one clustered, one regular) may suggest a random result.
- What is the definition of, for example, a tree? Do you include all individuals – or just those above a certain size?
- Why do we take the nearest neighbour? Why not the third or fourth nearest?
- The choice of the area, and the size of the area studied, can completely alter the result. and make a clustered pattern appear regular and vice-versa.
- Although the NNI may suggest a random pattern, if a controlling factor (e.g. soil type or altitude) is randomly distributed, the vegetation is in fact anything but randomly distributed.

Graphical techniques: charts

Bar charts

Bar charts are one of the simplest ways of representing data (Figure 13.10). Each bar in a bar chart is of a standard width, but the length or height is proportional to the value being represented. There is a range of bar chart types. A simple bar chart shows a single factor. A multiple bar chart can be used to show changing frequency over time (e.g. monthly rainfall figures). A compound bar chart involves the sub-division of simple bars. For example, a bar might be proportional to sources of pollution and be sub-divided on the basis of its composition. A combination of compound and multiple bar graphs may show how sources of pollution change over time.

Figure 13.10
Bar charts showing percentage cover of vegetation in 3 years.

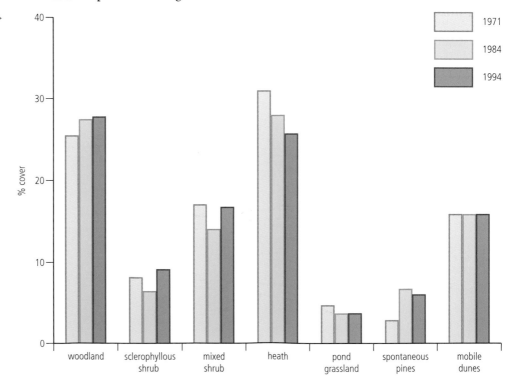

Pie charts

Pie charts are sub-divided circles (Figure 13.11). They are used to show proportional variations in the composition of a feature (e.g. the proportion of sand, silt and clay in a soil).

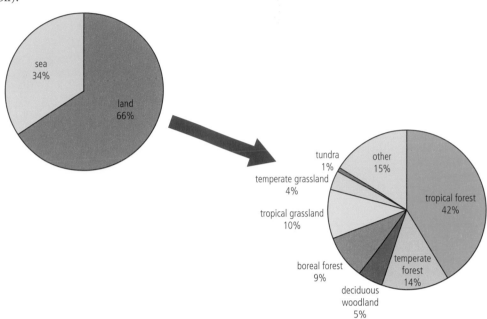

Figure 13.11
Pie charts showing global carbon fixing.

The following steps should be taken when making a pie chart:

1 Convert the data into percentages.
2 Convert the percentages into degrees by multiplying by 3.6 and rounding up or down to the nearest whole number.
3 Draw the appropriately located circles on a map or diagram.
4 Subdivide the circle into sectors using the figures obtained in step 2.
5 Differentiate the sectors by means of different shading.
6 Draw a key explaining the scheme of shading and/or colours.
7 Give the diagram a title.

Dispersion diagrams

A dispersion diagram is a very useful diagram for showing the range of a data set, the tendency to group or disperse, and for comparing two sets of data (Figure 13.12). It involves the plotting the values of a single variable on a vertical axis. The horizontal axis shows the frequency. The resulting diagram shows the frequency distribution of a data set. They can also be used to determine the median value, modal value and the inter-quartile range.

Kite diagram

A kite diagram is a form of chart which allows you to view the relative distribution of different species along a transect (Figure 13.13). It is commonly used to show variations in sand dune succession, for example. Distribution is shown on the *y*-axis, species on the *x*-axis, and the abundance of each species by the width of the columns. First, plot a series of bars representing the relative abundance of each species at each location. Then join the ends of the bars to form the kite shape.

Figure 13.13
Kite diagram showing vegetation succession on Studland Beach, UK.

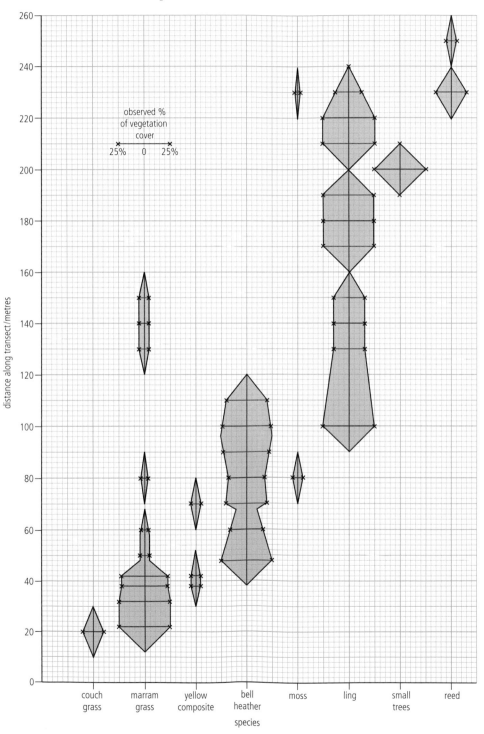

Graphical techniques: graphs

Line graphs

Line graphs can be quite simple graphs which are used to show changes over time (e.g. temperature change elated to the enhanced greenhouse effect) or over distance (e.g. variations in the populations of planktonic krill (Euphausiids), shrimps and crabs (decapods), ostracods and fish in the North Atlantic, Figure 13.14)

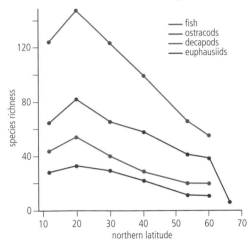

Figure 13.14
Line graphs showing species richness and latitude.

In all line graphs, there is an independent variable and a dependent variable. In this example, the line of latitude is the independent variable and each species is a dependent variable. The independent variable is plotted on the horizontal or x-axis while the dependant variable is plotted on the vertical or y-axis. Nearer the equator there is more energy, more plankton and hence more developed food chains.

Multiple or compound line graphs can show changes in more than one variable, for example changes in energy use over time. Such diagrams can reveal interesting relationships between the variables. On such graphs, data can be plotted in a number of different forms – in absolute terms, relative terms, percentage terms or cumulative terms.

Flow-lines

Flow lines show the volume of transfer between different groups or places. A good example is energy flow in an ecosystem (Figure 13.15). Alternatively, migration rates and direction could be shown using flow lines. In many cases, absolute data are used (Figure 13.15) but it is possible to use relative data.

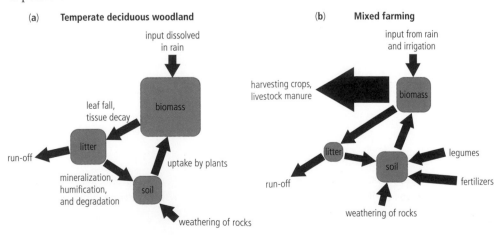

Figure 13.15
Flow chart showing nutrient cycles for (**a**) a temperate deciduous woodland and (**b**) an area nearby where the woodland has been cleared for mixed farming.

349

As with all graphical techniques, it is important to:
- keep the background as simple as possible so as to avoid clutter
- choose an appropriate scale, so that extreme values can be shown without any loss of clarity
- provide a key, and give a title to the diagram.

Triangular graphs

Triangular graphs are used to represent data that can be divided into three parts (e.g. soil consists of sand, silt and clay; population consists of the young, adult and elderly). These graphs require that the data have been converted into percentages, and that the percentages add up to 100%. On Figure 13.16, point A has 70% silt, 10% sand and 20% clay. The main advantage of a triangular graph is that it allows a large amount of data to be shown on one diagram. In many cases, once the data have been plotted onto a triangular graph, groupings become evident. In the case of soil texture, there are established soil textural groups. Triangular graphs can be tricky to construct. However, with care they can provide a reliable way of classifying large amounts of data which have three components.

Figure 13.16
Triangular graphs showing soil structure.

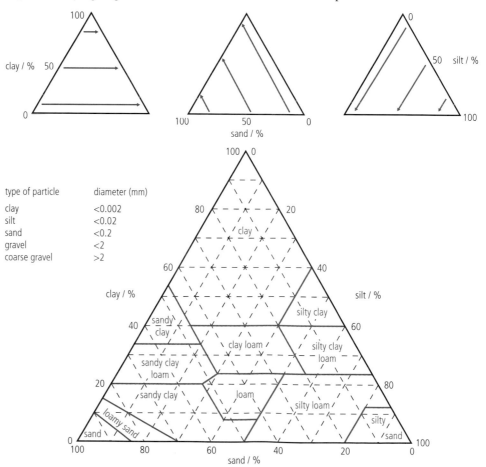

Semi-log and double log graphs

Semi-log and double log graphs can be daunting at first. They allow scientists to compare small-scale features with large-scale ones, and be relative growth over time. This would not be as easy on an ordinary line graph.

The logarithmic scale compresses the range of values. It gives more space to smaller values but compresses the space available for the larger values – look at the space available for large and small values on the line graph and semi-log graph in Figure 13.17.

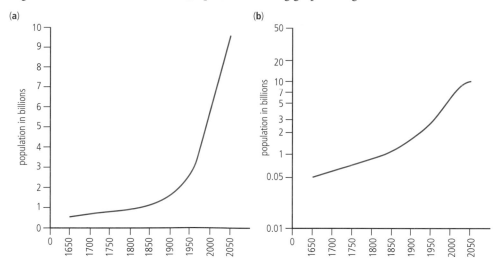

Figure 13.17
(a) Line graph and (b) semi-log graph showing numbers of survivors and lifespan.

Source: Huggett, R. *Fundamentals of biogeography*, Routledge, 1998, Fig. 4.6, p. 93

In a semi-log graph (aka as log-normal), one scale is logarithmic – usually the vertical one – while the other is a normal linear scale – usually the horizontal one. In the logarithmic parts of the scale, each of the cycles is logarithmic. This means that each cycle on the scale increases by the power of 10. For example, in the first cycle, values may be 1, 2, 3, 4, etc., whereas in the second cycle they would be 10, 20, 30, 40, etc., and in the third cycle 100, 200, 300, 400, etc. and so on.

It is important to realize that the logarithmic axis does not begin at 0 but some factor of 1 (e.g. 0.1, 100, 100 etc.); the horizontal axis can begin at any number and could even be nominal data such as the names of the months of the year.

ADDITIONAL QUESTIONS FOR CHAPTERS 2 AND 3

Chapter 2

PRACTICE QUESTIONS

1 The figure below shows the numbers of known species in a range of animal and plant groups. Also included on the same figure is the estimated total number of species for each group, this includes the species that have yet to be discovered.

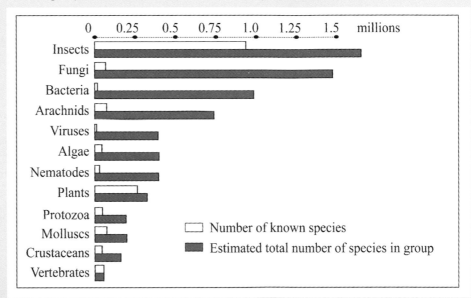

Source: UNEP printed in the *Economist*, 21 March 1998, page 12

(a) (i) State which group contains the most known species.   [1]

    (ii) State which group has the greatest difference between known number and estimated total number of species.   [1]

(b) (i) Suggest **one** reason why it is so difficult for scientists to state exactly how many species exist in a group.   [1]

    (ii) Suggest why the number of known vertebrate species may so closely match the estimated total number.   [1]

(c) Outline a field technique you might use for collecting species diversity data for one of the groups listed in the figure above.   [3]

© International Baccalaureate Organization [2006]

2 The figure below shows the numbers of wood mice and bank voles collected from traps. The number **above** the trapping point (●) represents wood mice and the number **below** the trapping point (●) represents bank voles.

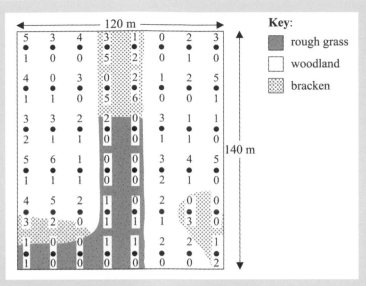

Key:
- ▨ rough grass
- □ woodland
- ▒ bracken

Source: A Cadogen and G Best, *Environment and Ecology*, page 51, Blackie and Sons Ltd, 1992

(a) Complete the table by calculating the numbers of wood mice and bank voles found in bracken. *[1]*

	Rough grass	Woodland	Bracken
wood mice	6	50	
bank voles	3	15	

(b) Suggest **two** reasons for the relationship between rodent numbers and habitat shown in the figure and table above. *[2]*

(c) Explain why the rodents were marked and released after capture. *[1]*

© International Baccalaureate Organization [2007]

3 The data table below shows the nitrogen content of a temperate forest and a tropical forest.

Component	Nitrogen / $g\,m^{-2}$	
	Temperate forest	Tropical forest
leaves	12.4	52.6
wood*	18.5	41.2
roots	18.4	28.2
surface litter	40.9	3.9
soil**	730.9	85.3
total	821.1	211.2

* living wood only   ** does not include roots

Source: Adapted from Odum E P. *Fundamentals of Ecology*. Saunders College Publishing, 1971, page 375

(a) (i) Calculate the total nitrogen content in biomass (excluding surface litter) for temperate and tropical forests. *[1]*

  (ii) Calculate the percentage of total nitrogen present in biomass (excluding surface litter) for temperate and tropical forests. Give your answer to the nearest 0.1%. *[1]*

(b) Determine which of the two biomes contains a proportionally larger amount of nitrogen in its soil. Support your answer with appropriate calculations. *[2]*

(c) Suggest a possible explanation for the difference in nitrogen content in surface litter between the two biomes. [1]

(d) Using the table above, list for both temperate forest and tropical forest, the following ecosystem components, in terms of their importance as nitrogen storages, in ascending order: biomass, surface litter, soil. [1]

(e) In terms of the impact on nitrogen storage, deduce which ecosystem would suffer more from clear cut forestry practices (complete removal of all tree cover). Explain your answer. [2]

(f) Using the data in the table above, and your knowledge of biotic and abiotic conditions in tropical and temperate forests, explain which of the two biomes would be a better choice for growing crops. [2]

© International Baccalaureate Organization [2004]

4 Explain the relationship between climate and net primary productivity in two contrasting biomes you have studied. [7]

© International Baccalaureate Organization [2005]

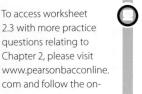

To access worksheet 2.3 with more practice questions relating to Chapter 2, please visit www.pearsonbacconline.com and follow the on-screen instructions.

5 Explain the present distribution of desert and tundra and discuss the factors controlling their relative productivity. [6]

© International Baccalaureate Organization [2008]

6 (a) How does ploughing affect soil nitrogen and carbon levels? [6]

(b) How does deforestation affect soil carbon levels? [4]

Chapter 3

PRACTICE QUESTIONS

1 (a) Define the term *sustainability* [2]

(b) Identify the equation that is used to calculate sustainable yield (SY): [1]

$$SY = \left(\frac{\text{total biomass}}{\text{energy}} \text{ at time } t+1 \right) - \left(\frac{\text{total biomass}}{\text{energy}} \text{ at time } t \right)$$

$$SY = \left(\frac{\text{total biomass}}{\text{energy}} \text{ at time } t \right) - \left(\frac{\text{total biomass}}{\text{energy}} \text{ at time } t \right)$$

$$SY = \left(\frac{\text{total biomass}}{\text{energy}} \text{ at time } t \right) + \left(\frac{\text{total biomass}}{\text{energy}} \text{ at time } t \right)$$

(c) Outline **two** factors that may undermine the ability of a country to maintain or develop a policy of sustainable development. [3]

© International Baccalaureate Organization [2003]

2 The table below gives data for recruitment and growth, and harvesting of salmon (*Salmo salar*) over a 10-year period.

Year	Recruitment and growth / tonnes	Harvesting / tonnes	Yield / tonnes
1	23 400	23 250	150
2	23 425	23 300	?
3	24 450	23 400	1 050
4	24 560	23 500	1 060
5	22 345	23 400	−1 055
6	24 356	?	−144
7	23 450	25 000	−1 500
8	22 900	25 125	−2 225
9	21 000	24 600	−3 600
10	21 210	24 300	3 090

(a) Calculate the missing values for year 2 and year 6. [1]

The yield data from the table above is shown in the following graph.

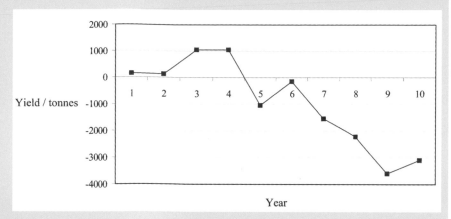

(b) Identify the year in which harvesting first becomes unsustainable. [1]

(c) Predict what will happen if the apparent trend shown in the graph continues. [1]

(d) Outline **two** factors that cause humans to use resources unsustainably. [2]

3 The table below shows renewable energy alternatives, how the energy is produced and their limitations.

Alternative renewable energy source	How the energy is produced	Major limitation
tidal power	Energy is produced by using the ebbing and/or flooding tide to turn turbines and produce electricity.	
wind power	Wind turbines are driven by available wind energy. The wind energy is turned into electrical energy via a generator. The electrical energy is supplied to an electrical grid to do work.	Dependent on the wind: no wind equals no energy.
biofuel		Produces emissions and requires large areas to grow biofuel crop.

(a) State **one** other form of alternative renewable energy source not listed above. [1]

(b) Complete the table above for tidal power and biofuel. [2]

(c) Most MEDCs are still dependent on non-renewable forms of energy. Suggest reasons why MEDCs have not adopted renewable energy sources. [3]

4 The figures below show a farming system and the activities for the farm in areas A, B and C over a year.

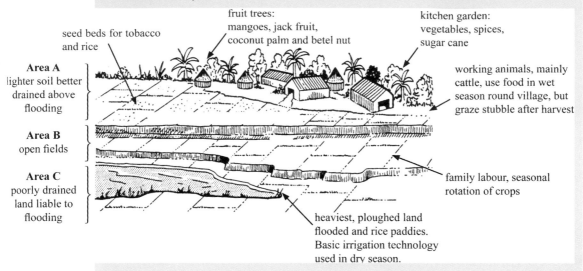

Month	March	April	May	September		March
Season	Pre–monsoon		Wet season	Dry season		
Area A	cattle in yard, mangoes, vegetables			repairing and thatching, green coconuts, betel nuts		
Area B	jute			wheat, tobacco, mustard		
Area C	grazing, rice (flooding)			grazing		

Source: Adapted from M Carr, Patterns, *Process and Change in Human Geography*, Macmillan, (1987), page 142

(a) State, giving **two** reasons whether this system is more typical of farming in a more economically developed country (MEDC) or a less economically developed country (LEDC). *[2]*

(b) Complete the systems diagram below to show **three** inputs, processes and outputs for the farming system shown in the figures. *[3]*

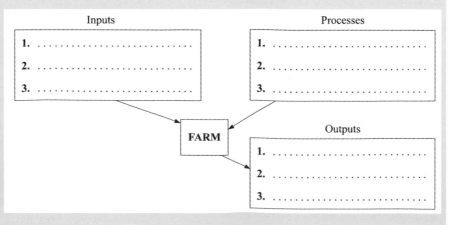

(c) With reference to the figures, describe **two** ways in which the farming system has been developed in response to variations in the local environment. [2]

© International Baccalaureate Organization [2006]

5 The data in Table 1 show the ecological footprints for people in various countries of the world. A five-hectare footprint would mean that five hectares of biologically productive space (including land and sea) are in constant production to support the average individual of that country.

Available capacity is the total amount of biologically productive space for each country. If the footprint exceeds the biologically productive area of the country, the country has an ecological deficit.

TABLE 1				
Country	Population in 1997	Ecological footprint / headperson^{-1}	Available capacity / headperson^{-1}	Ecological difference (deficit if negative) / headperson^{-1}
Australia	18 550 000	9.0	14.0	5.0
Ethiopia	58 414 000	0.7	0.5	−0.3
Germany	81 845 000	5.3	1.9	−3.4
India	790 230 000	0.8	0.5	−0.3
Indonesia	203 631 000	1.4	2.6	1.2
Japan	125 672 000	4.3	0.9	
Norway	4 375 000	6.2	6.3	0.1
Russian Federation	146 381 000	6.0	3.7	−2.3
Singapore	2 899 000	7.2	0.1	−7.1
USA	268 189 000		6.7	−3.6
UK	58 587 000	5.2	1.7	−3.5
Venezuela	22 777 000	3.8	2.7	−1.1
World	5 892 480 000	2.8	2.1	−0.7

Source: The Earth Council. *Ranking the Ecological Impact of Nations.* www.ecouncil.ac.cr

(a) (i) Calculate the ecological deficit for Japan [1]

(ii) Calculate the ecological footprint for a person in the USA [1]

(iii) If the Earth's resources were equally shared, there would be a total of 2.1 hectares of space available for each person. State how many countries in Table 1 have an available capacity greater than 2.1 hectares. [1]

(iv) Suggest why Indonesia is not in ecological deficit despite the fact that its population is so large. [2]

(**b**) Gross Domestic Product (GDP) is a measure of the economic wealth of a country divided by the number of people in that country. Table 2 shows the GDP for various countries.

TABLE 2	
Country	GDP per person in 1999 / US$
Australia	21 300
Ethiopia	560
Germany	22 100
India	1 720
Indonesia	2 830
Japan	23 100
Norway	24 700
Russian Federation	4 000
Singapore	23 300
USA	31 500
UK	21 200
Venezuela	8 500

Source: based on data from the 1999 *CIA World Factbook*. www.photius.com

(**i**) Complete Table 3, using the data from Tables 1 and 2 to rank the countries according to the size of their ecological footprints and GDP. [2]

TABLE 3		
Rank	Size of ecological footprint (country with largest footprint first)	GDP (country with highest GDP first)
1		USA
2	Australia	Norway
3		Singapore
4		
5	Russian Federation	
6	Germany	
7	UK	
8		
9		
10		Indonesia
11	India	
12		Ethiopia

(**ii**) State what relationship (if any) your ranking in Table 3 shows between ecological footprint and GDP. [1]

(**iii**) Explain how it is possible for some countries, such as Singapore, to have such a high GDP despite the fact that they have so little biologically productive space. [2]

(**c**) (**i**) Using data from Table 1 only, state whether or not the current global use of resources is sustainable. Justify your answer [2]

(**ii**) Describe **two** ways in which a country might be able to decrease its ecological footprint through technological development. [4]

© International Baccalaureate Organization [2005]

6 The graph below shows the estimated world water withdrawals from 1960 to 2000.

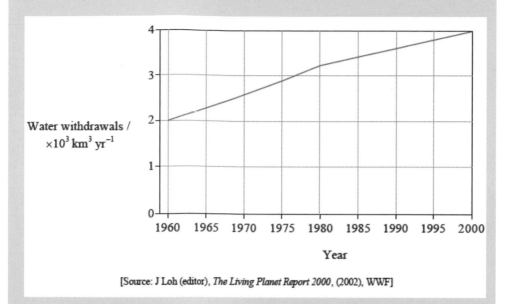

[Source: J Loh (editor), *The Living Planet Report 2000*, (2002), WWF]

(a) Calculate the percentage increase in world water withdrawals from 1960 to 2000.

[2]

(b) Suggest **three** reasons for the increase in water withdrawals during the period 1960 to 2000.

[3]

© International Baccalaureate Organization [2004]

7 (a) Define the term *carrying capacity*. [1]

(b) Define the terms *over-population*, *under-population* and *optimum population*. [3]

(c) Using a diagram, show how under-population, optimum population and over-population can be defined. [3]

(d) Outline the characteristics of regions that are considered to be:

(i) over-populated [2]

(ii) under-populated. [2]

To access worksheet 3.5 with more practice questions relating to Chapter 3, please visit www.pearsonbacconline.com and follow the on-screen instructions.

ANSWERS

In the following mark-schemes:

- a semi colon (;) between answers suggests *different* marking points
- a solidus (/) between answers suggests *alternative* marking points
- marks are shown by the number in square brackets, there are no half marks
- information in brackets (...) is not needed to score the mark
- notes in italics are a guide on what to accept / reject in marking
- *OWTTE* is the abbreviation for 'Or words to that effect'
- marks for expression of ideas are awarded thus:
  - *[0]* no expression of relevant ideas
  - *[1]* expression and development of relevant ideas is limited
  - *[2]* ideas are relevant, satisfactorily expressed and reasonably well developed
  - *[3]* ideas are relevant, very well expressed and well developed.

Chapter 1

1 (a) interval between 1st and 2nd peak is about 90 days and interval between 2nd and 3rd peak is approximately 75 days;

$$\frac{90 + 75}{2} = 82.5/80 \ (\pm 4 \text{ days}) / 15 \text{ January} + 80 \text{ days}$$

$\approx$ 20 April ($\pm$5 days) *[2]*

(b) *T. occidentalis*: 7; ($\pm$1)
E. sexmaculatus: 1550; ($\pm$50) *[1]*
Both needed for [1].

(c) (i) 25 to 30 September; ($\pm$3 days) *[1]*
(ii) 10 December; ($\pm$2 days) *[1]*

(d) (i) 15 days; ($\pm$5 days) *[1]*
(ii) the predator population takes some days to take advantage of the increase in prey; availability of food facilitates reproduction of prey; predator cannot increase in number without access to food and so must wait for increase in prey; *[1 max]*

(e) (i) the increase in prey leads to a corresponding increase in predator which corrects the trend towards increase in prey; the decrease in prey leads to a corresponding decrease in predator which corrects the trend towards decrease in prey; the periodic nature of the population curves indicates a feedback controlled interaction; *[2 max]*

(ii) elimination of predators / competitors; modern medicine decreasing effect of disease; elimination of density-dependent limiting factors; importation of food or resources from other areas to overcome shortages; increased efficiency in utilization of resources; our ability to colonize almost any habitat; tools and technology; *[3 max]*

(f) melting of polar ice caps causes lowering of planetary albedo thus increasing amount of solar energy at Earth's surface, leading to increase in temperature; melting of tundra through warming causes release of methane causing more warming; increased evaporation leading to increased precipitation at poles triggering net cooling; *[2 max]*

2 (a) energy is neither created nor destroyed / energy is conserved / *OWTTE*; *[1]*

(b) 1000 kJ − 100 kJ (10%) = 900 kJ;
output = 900 kJ − 135 kJ (15%) = 765 kJ; *[2]*

3 (a) a simplified description; designed to show the structure or workings of an object, system or concept; require approximations to be made; *[2 max]*

(b) (i) growth of human population depends (at a simple level) on birth rates and death rates; from this rates of natural increase can be calculated and population total predicted; population pyramids enable policy makers to chart what proportion of the population are in the fertile age bracket helping to predict likely birth rates; demographic transition model shows how population growth is linked to economic development; enables the reasons for population growth to be understood; but not all countries conform to the stages identified; models are hugely simplified, and may not reflect the complex

(ii) ecological footprints can be effective for comparing environmental impacts of different societies; able to provide a quantitative estimate of human carrying capacity; a quantification of what can be a very complex set of factors; can be useful tools for getting people to think about their impact; stresses the systems approach and interconnectedness of eco and social systems; very difficult to calculate figures e.g. per capita CO_2 emissions; *[3 max]*

To receive full marks answers must have a balance of strengths and weaknesses. Award credit if other relevant models are evaluated.

4 (a) 1 = evaporation;
2 = transpiration / evapotranspiration;
3 = precipitation;
4 = run-off / infiltration; *[2]*

Four correct [2], three or two correct [1].

(b) too simplistic / no values / no indication of time / two dimensional; *[1]*

5 (a) (i) feedback that tends to damp down / neutralize / counteract any deviation from an equilibrium, and promotes stability; *[1]*
(ii) feedback that amplifies / increases change (it leads to exponential deviation away from equilibrium); *[1]*

(b) most ecosystems contain inbuilt checks and balances;without internal balance an ecosystem would spiral out of control; without negative feedback no ecosystem could be self-sustaining *[1 max]*

Chapter 2

1 (a) trophic level 3 / tertiary trophic level / secondary consumer / carnivore; *[1]*

(b) amount of leaves / algae in the stream could increase as no longer consumed; with knock-on effect on abiotic conditions / impact on species in the food web as visibility is reduced; less food for fish so they may eat other things, knock-on effect on other prey species; decline in numbers of bats / spiders / birds / frogs that depend on invertebrates (emergent phase) as food source; *[2 max]*

2 (a) producers convert solar energy into chemical energy through photosynthesis; one of the main contributors to organic matter in soil; through symbiotic bacteria, producers are significant in fixing nitrogen; provide habitat for other organisms; *[2 max]*

Accept other reasonable statements that show ecological knowledge.

(b) e.g. Chilean matorral

producer	primary consumer	secondary consumer
Chilean thorn tree $\rightarrow$	rodent $\rightarrow$	Chilean wild cat
Acacia caven	*Octodon degus*	*Felis guigna*

[3]

Award [1] for appropriately labelled trophic levels, [2] for three appropriate species or [1] for two appropriate species. Do not accept rabbit, fox etc., unless there is some identifying feature e.g. snowshoe hare and arctic fox.

(c) pyramid of biomass represents biomass at a given time; whereas pyramid of productivity represents rate at which stocks are being generated; pyramid of biomass is measured in units of mass / energy / $J\,m^{-2}$ / $g\,m^{-2}$; pyramid of productivity is measured in units of flow / $J\,m^{-2}\,yr^{-1}$ / $g\,m^{-2}\,yr^{-1}$; *[2]*

3 $N(N-1) = 5235 \times 5234 = 27\,399\,990$;
$\Sigma n(n-1) = 552 + 20 + 30 + 2\,248\,500 + 1\,438\,800 + 6\,247\,500 = 9\,935\,402$;
$D = \dfrac{27\,399\,990}{9\,935\,402} = 2.8 / 2.76$; *[3]*

4 (a) (i) population numbers decrease from October until June; mean mass increases (exponentially) from September until March and then slows down / *OWTTE*; *[2]*

Answer should make reference to the data in the table and graphs.

(ii) stream A demonstrates a slow decline in population size whereas stream B shows a dramatic exponential decline / *OWTTE*; the maxima for population size and mean mass are higher for stream A; *[2]*

Accept other valid answers.

Answer should make reference to the data in the table and graphs.

(iii) $\dfrac{6350 - 44}{6350} \times 100 = 99.3\%$; *[1]*

(b) the mass of organic material in organisms or ecosystems (usually per unit area); *[1]*

(c) (i) e.g. using electro-fishing techniques / netting a significant number of trout could be caught, tagged and released; important to ensure that the capture and tagging does not stress / harm the fish; later (next day) the capture exercise would be repeated using the same effort and time as before; the fish caught would be noted as tagged or untagged and the Lincoln index applied; *[3]*

Award [1] for concept of capture–mark–release–recapture without giving an outline of the method.

(ii) *Award [1] for each factor with an explanation,* e.g. oxygen content – the amount of oxygen in the water will influence the ability of organisms to respire / high levels of oxygen – high respiration potential; pH – the pH of the water will affect the stream chemistry which in turn will affect the plants and animals / extremes of acid and alkaline conditions will stress both plants and animals / pH will influence the species types present; temperature – water temperature affects both plant and animal biochemistry / warmer water suits some species and not others / extreme temperatures may alter water chemistry and oxygen content; *[3 max]*

Accept other reasonable answers.

5 (a) (i) the orderly process of change over time in a community; changes in the community of organisms cause changes in the physical environment; this allows another community to become established and replace the former through competition; leading often to greater complexity; *[2 max]*

(ii) time; distance (from sea); *[1 max]*

(iii) soils will become more mature; soils will be deeper; contain more organic material; become more complex; develop distinct horizons; *[2 max]*

(b) positive feedback; *[1]*

(c) as succession occurs soils become better structured and more fertile; this will support greater diversity of producers and larger producers; therefore gross productivity / primary productivity will increase; numbers of niches will increase and food webs will become more complex; diversity will increase; as food webs become more complex net productivity will increase; gross primary productivity, net

primary productivity and diversity will stabilize as ecosystem reaches climatic climax; *[5 max]*

Award [3 max] if no case study is used.

Chapter 3

1 (a)

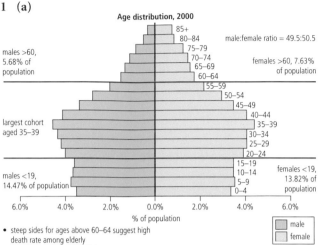

* steep sides for ages above 60–64 suggest high death rate among elderly
* wide base suggests high birth rate

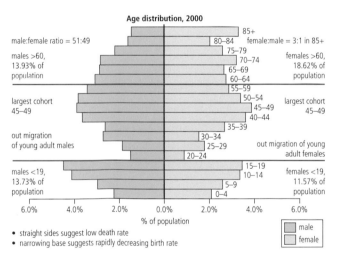

* straight sides suggest low death rate
* narrowing base suggests rapidly decreasing birth rate

[6]

(b) Area A – urban; Area B – rural; *[2]*

(c) large loss of males and females aged 20–39 suggests out-migration of young adults from Area B – probably due to a lack of jobs in a rural environment; increasing size of cohorts in the 20–39 year groups in Area A suggests in-migration of workers to an urban area where there are more jobs; *[4]*

(d) out-migration leads to: loss of young people; decline in number of educated / innovative people; ageing population with increased death rates and reduced birth rates; size of the local market (population) also declines; increased need for specialized health services for the elderly; [4]

in-migration may lead to: over-crowding; youthful population; high birth rate; low death rate; need for education services; crèches; child-care etc.; [4]

2 (a) (i) cheapest = gas;
most expensive = wind offshore; [1]

Both needed for [1].

(ii) gas is cheap because it is relatively plentiful; it can be burned directly without the need for refining; technology is already in place to access the gas and burn it in existing gas fired power stations; [1 max]

wind offshore technology is still at the experimental stage; easily disrupted by rough seas; can interrupt shipping lanes; [1 max]

(b) organic waste decomposes and gives off methane gas which can be burned; waste can be burned directly to generate energy e.g. burning straw; [2]

(c) (i) likely to be much higher; [1]

Accept lower if justification given in (ii) is appropriate e.g. better technology; new reserves discovered; price subsidized by governments to enable fossil fuels to compete with renewables.

(ii) as stocks become depleted, easiest / most accessible resources will already have been mined; leaving resources most difficult to access which are more costly to reach; scarcity of resources will push costs up; environmental taxes to compensate for global warming will make fossil fuels more expensive; [2 max]

(d) *advantages:* HEP does not involve release of pollutants; turbines can be switched on whenever energy is needed; dams may be multipurpose *e.g.* for leisure, irrigation or fishing; renewable source (*i.e.* will not run out); relatively cheap to run (once initial construction completed);

disadvantages: vast areas may be flooded involving loss of habitats, farmland and / or displacement of people; cost of building dams may be high leading to huge debts; dams may restrict flows of sediment affecting ecosystems or farming downstream; may disrupt fish migratory paths; may lead to increased erosion rates downstream; dams silt up; [4 max]

[2 max] for advantages and [2 max] for disadvantages.

(e) the more renewable energy resources that are used, the smaller the ecological footprint of a population; because in calculating ecological footprint amount of land required for absorbing waste carbon dioxide from fossil fuels is included; [2]

3 (a) natural soils have a variable organic content – high (7%) in the A horizon but absent in the B horizon; agricultural soils have a uniform organic content (3–5%) mixed in the plough horizon; [2]

(b) nitrate levels are higher in agricultural soils than in natural soils due to the addition of nitrate fertilizers; [1]

(c) carbonates are low in the upper horizons of natural soils but rich in the lower horizons because they are carried down by percolating water; in agricultural soils, there are carbonates throughout the soil due to the addition of fertilizers and the action of ploughing; [2]

(d) levels of calcium and hydrogen are higher in natural soils; phosphorus and potassium are higher in farmed soils; this is largely due to use of NPK fertilizers which add (nitrates and) phosphorus and potassium to the soil; consequently, the percentage of other minerals in the soil decreases; [4]

4 (a) water consumption has increased at a faster rate than population growth; [1]
Figures are not needed.

(b) increased demand for domestic goods / luxury items e.g. washing machines and swimming pools; increased economic development so more water used in industry; agricultural development so greater use of water in irrigation (for intensive) farming; cultural change towards greater personal hygiene; [2 max]

Chapter 4

1 (a) *Award [1] for each factor identified. Specific ecosystem examples must be included e.g. Australian coral reef, Brazilian tropical rainforest, for full marks. If no examples given [3 max] can be awarded.*

natural hazard events e.g. in montane forest loss of species due to eruption of Mount St Helens; global catastrophic events e.g. meteor impact and extinction of dinosaurs; habitat degradation, fragmentation and loss e.g. pandas and bamboo forest in China; introduction and / or escape of non-native and genetically modified species; monoculture e.g. loss of wild grass species and insects in North American grain belt; pollution e.g. DDT and loss of bird species in North America in 1970s; hunting or collecting e.g. shooting of large predators in tropical savannah; harvesting e.g. cod population in North Atlantic Ocean; *[6 max]*

(b) more diverse ecosystems are generally more stable and therefore are less fragile; due to their variety of nutrient and energy pathways; species have a greater choice of food sources if one species becomes extinct; biodiversity includes diversity of habitat as well as diversity of species; more diverse ecosystems are better able to cope with natural threats to their survival and therefore less fragile;

[5]

Credit given for different interpretations of 'fragility' though concept of fragility must still be valid within an understanding of ecosystem functioning.

(c) many groups are involved in loss of biodiversity and therefore education to a wide audience is important; people who are often the direct cause of biodiversity loss (e.g. through hunting) need to be educated as to the longer-term value of preserving ecosystems; as they will play a central role in their conservation (producer); other communities may indirectly play a role (e.g. as a market for tropical hardwoods) and so should be educated to help reverse destructive practices (consumer); education can have a huge, immediate impact when damage is inadvertent; e.g. coral reef education programmes for divers; education is the first step in increasing lobbying of governments to ensure environmentally sustainable practice (policy makers); education is not the only factor – legislation plays a vital part in establishing e.g. conservation areas; and international treaties to control trade in endangered species and agreements over pollution; proper finance is vital to run conservation areas and ensure enforcement of international agreements; *[7 max]*

Give credit to candidates who link their response to the statement in the question e.g. by use of terms such as producer, consumer etc. Answers which fail to recognize that education alone is not enough to reverse loss of biodiversity should be awarded

[5 max].

2 (a) *species diversity:* the variety of species per unit area (this includes both the number of species present and their relative abundance); *(Glossary definition)*

The response must have concept of unit area and / or relative abundance for the mark. 'Number of species' is insufficient.

habitat diversity: the range of different habitats in an ecosystem; often associated with the variety of ecological niches / OWTTE; *[2 max]*

(b) *description [1 max]:* city has by far the highest biomass per square km; city has highest density of population; city has lowest biodiversity as absolute number of species and expressed as index; i.e. a small number of common species are very abundant; forest has lowest biomass; and population; forest biodiversity is high, but not as high as farmland; i.e. a wide variety of species, none of which is very abundant; farmland has much lower biomass than city, higher than forest; farmland has lower population than city, higher than forest;

explanation: city is a specialized environment that a few species can exploit very well; food from gardens. rubbish (garbage), etc. may be available to support some species; city has low habitat diversity / low number of ecological niches; forest is a multi-layered habitat, with a variety of plant species, so habitat diversity is high; farmland may have highest habitat diversity of all, having both natural and artificial habitats; some food from human sources may be available in farmland (crops); the diversity index of the three environments takes account of the species diversity and the relative abundance of the species hence farmland highest; *[4 max]*

(c) (i) the process through which new species form / OWTTE (*Glossary*) / the process by which change in the frequency of genetic trait occurs (in response to environmental pressures); *[1]*

(ii) individual organisms in a population vary; natural selection = the tendency of those organisms most adapted to / fittest for environment to survive; and therefore to pass their characteristics to their progeny; thus organisms become increasingly adapted to their environment; a changing environment may affect speciation / evolution; mutations may affect rate of speciation; appropriate example; *[2 max]*

Reward any two of the above points or any other reasonable points.

(iii) isolation of a small sub-group of the original population may encourage / accelerate speciation; through impossibility of interbreeding / exchange of genetic material with original population; and adaptations to new environment; entirely new endemic species / unique species not found elsewhere may appear; e.g. unique finches / tortoises / iguanas on Galapagos Islands; *[2 max]*

Any other reasonable point.

3 (a) past extinctions occurred suddenly over relatively short time periods; caused by definitive environmental catastrophies e.g. meteorite strike, volcanic eruption, earthquakes, etc.; animals / plants died from both initial event and the short term environmental turmoil that followed (or given example e.g. climate change and cooling of planet that occurred following meteor strike / volcanic eruption); or due to more gradual environmental change leading to more gradual species extinction; climate induced change is the most likely cause; the most notable example being the extinctions caused by glaciations *[4 max]*

(b) previous mass extinctions caused by physical (abiotic) factors whereas current one due to humans (biotic factors); current extinctions happening over human lifespan to hundreds of years whereas past extinctions happened over long time-spans, often millions of years; *[2]*

(c) *e.g. tiger (in danger of extinction):* endangered because of habitat (forest) loss due to agriculture; loss of food source as traditional food source is being used by humans; hunting for hides, trophies, medicine; destroyed because regarded as a nuisance / pest; ecological role is as top carnivore; loss would lead to increase in herbivorous mammals; ethical issues surrounding loss (rights of future generations, rights of the species);

e.g. crocodile (brought back from extinction): was endangered due to excessive hunting for skins, meat, trophies; and due to threat to humans and livestock; and due to habitat degradation (loss of water quality); ecological role as top carnivore; loss would lead to imbalance in food pyramid; no longer under threat of extinction because of education (no longer seen as 'evil'); ban on hunting; legal protection; *[7 max]*

4 (a) *Answer should be balanced to include both examples of animals that are prone to extinction and those that are not.*

Factors which may leave an animal prone to extinction include: small population size e.g. blue whale – influences reproductive success / prone to disease / inbreeding / susceptible to environmental change; reduced genetic pool – prone to mutations due to inbreeding / genetic weakness leading to physical weakness; over-hunting e.g. rhino; loss of habitat e.g. panda / fragmented habitat – lack of food resources / lack of space;

Factors that may lead to an animal being less prone to extinction include: large population e.g. cockroach – less affected by predation / large genetic pool; extensive geographical range – less susceptible to individual habitat loss; non-specialist existence e.g. the rat – survives in many environments; *[5 max]*

(b) global volcanic eruption leading to rapid climate change / hostile environment; catastrophic events such as meteorite impact leading to rapid climate change / hostile environment; over-hunting of large mammals by man (in the Holocene) to the extent that populations became reproductively unviable / wiped out; *[2 max]*

Do not accept Ice Age.

(c) population size; reduction in population size; numbers of mature individuals; geographic range and degree of fragmentation; quality of habitat; area of occupancy; probability of extinction; *[6 max]*

Award [1] for the name of each factor and [1] for the explanation plus a named example, e.g. Tasmanian wolf is now extinct as a result of over-hunting / habitat loss; giant panda is presently endangered due to habitat loss / disturbance.

(d) *collecting:* using legislation to prevent moving / import of endangered species; education about impact of collecting to change behaviour; encouraging non-destructive collection by photography rather than digging up; *[2 max]*

overgrazing: fencing / cordoning off sensitive habitats / biological hotspots; reducing herd sizes; providing alternative grazing; supplementing income through nature tourism; *[2 max]*

Accept other choices of threat and reasonable strategies.

Expression of ideas: [3]

Total = [20]

5 **(a)** the Albufera has such high diversity due to a wide range of habitat types; therefore, many niches for many species; the area is physically large; there is a mix of aquatic and terrestrial environments; the area is preserved and the biodiversity is proactively protected and encouraged; *[3 max]*
Award credit if data is cited.

(b) *Answers need four of the following threats to receive [2 max]. If only two of the following threats are addressed, award [1 max].*
power station producing terrestrial and atmospheric pollution; agriculture / run-off pollution and drainage; tourist pressure causing disturbance and pollution; road / road kill / disturbance; further development; dune erosion / habitat loss; *[2 max]*

(c) (i) site 1 will have a greater range of species; species community more complex at site 1; will include trees, shrubs and ground cover; *[2 max]*

(ii) site 1 more mature; site 1 older; site 5 newer, not gone through full succession; site 1 more stable, greater range of niches; *[2 max]*

(d) site 2 would demonstrate a much higher diversity index than site 4; site 2 is much more mature and has a range of habitats with a large range of niches for insects; site 4 may be a monoculture favouring few species; chemical pesticides may limit species in site 4; *[2 max]*

(e) reserves are often controlled by the principle of island geography; good reserves need to be large (as the Albufera marsh is); small reserves have problems supporting biodiversity; larger animals need large areas; biodiversity is high due to multiple habitat types; background environmental conditions are good e.g. water quality; organisms safely move in and out of the marsh; multiple habitats have many edges, edges provide new niches thus higher diversity; *[4 max]*

(f) high profile / charismatic species catch public attention both nationally and internationally (e.g. tiger – India); however, species-based conservation favours charismatic organisms and is less successful in saving 'non-cuddly' species; saving a named species requires preserving the animals' habitat, this benefits all other organisms in that habitat; however, a species can be artificially preserved (e.g. in a zoo) whilst its natural habitat is destroyed (e.g. giant panda); *[3 max]*
Award any three of the above points [1] each or any other suitable suggestions.

Chapter 5

1 **(a)** *water quality:* the physical and chemical characteristics of a river;
pollution: the contamination of the Earth–atmosphere system to such an extent that normal environmental processes are adversely affected;
discharge: the volume of water passing a set point in a given time e.g. $m^3 s^{-1}$; *[3]*

(b) likely to be a line graph;
oxygen content increases rapidly between sites 4 and 5; this is due to the presence of a weir, which causes turbulent flow in the river and helps oxygenate the water; *[6]*

(c) temperatures are lower upstream of the sewage outlet but increase significantly (4–5 °C) downstream; *[3]*

(d) (i) pH measures the proportion of exchangeable hydrogen;

(ii) logarithmic scale;

(iii) pH of stream affected by a number of factors other than the sewage outlet: the underlying geology, pH of rainwater, local industries and their emissions, run-off from fields, fertilizers or detergents that are used locally; hence, there may be little variation noticeable on account of the sewage works; *[3]*

(e) personal fieldwork: students will probably conclude (*i*) that it is difficult to monitor water quality along the length of a stream and (*ii*) that it is difficult to trace the source of the pollution; *[3]*

2 **(a)** a day when the air pollution index is 100 or lower; *[1]*

(b) an irregular pattern – the API is largely between 80 and 120 during 2003 but gradually it becomes more variable; for example, in 2006 it varied between 70 and 178; it varies less after 2006, and also begins to fall; it reaches its lowest in 2008 when it briefly fell below 60; *[4]*

(c) evidence is contradictory; e.g. January 2004 and Jan 2006 have low APIs, whereas Jan 2005, 2007 and 2008 have quite high APIs; January 2009 is relatively high; summer months are generally low (e.g. 2004–06) although the summers of 2007–08 are relatively high; *[3]*

(d) it would be expected that the API is higher in winter due to the more widespread burning of coal, and high pressure conditions; however, if industry is becoming cleaner, air quality should be improving; moreover, energy for heating is just one source of pollutants; vehicle emissions, industrial and municipal emissions are present throughout the year; but these are more likely to increase in winter when it is colder; this coincides with calm, high pressure conditions; [4]

3 the benefits of using DDT were in health and farming; in health, DDT was used to control lice that spread typhus, and mosquitoes that spread malaria; in farming, it was used to control pests; however DDT can build up in the food chain (bioaccumulation and biomagnification); consequently, top predators may accumulate very high concentrations of DDT – enough to have an impact on their survival chances; similarly, among humans there is evidence that DDT can have a negative impact on health; [5]

4 (a) nutrient enrichment (eutrophication) caused by human activities (cultural); [1]

(b) discharge of untreated sewage; discharge of treated sewage; dissolving of nitrogen oxides from internal combustion engines and furnaces; discharge of detergents; [2]

(c) natural runoff of nitrates and phosphates; [1]

(d) eutrophication occurs when increased amounts of nitrogen and / or phosphorus are carried in streams, lakes and groundwater causing nutrient enrichment; this leads to an increase in algal blooms as plants respond to the increased nutrient levels; however, the increase in algae and plankton shade the water below, cutting off the light supply for submerged plants; the prolific growth of algae, especially in autumn results in anoxia (oxygen starvation in the water); the increased plant biomass and decomposition – which leads to a build-up of dead organic matter – also leads to a change in species composition; [5]

5 (a) likely to be a bar chart; [5]

(b) there are great variations in the amount of landfill in Europe; on average, 58% of waste is taken to landfill; this varies from 99% in Ireland and 94% in Greece; to 18% in Denmark and 24% in Luxembourg; [4]

(c) in the European Union, recycling accounts for 10% of materials, on average; this ranges from 28% in Luxembourg and 22% in Denmark and Germany to 1% in Ireland, Portugal and Spain; reasons for variable rates of recycling may include: government policy and incentives to recycle, such as weekly and fortnightly collections from households; level of education – people with higher educational achievements may be more inclined to recycle; cost / level of well-being – those who are better off recycle more than those who are poor; level of urbanization – it is easier to collect from urban areas than arrange collections when people are dispersed in the countryside; [4]

(d) 5% of waste in the EU is composted, this varies from 15% in the Netherlands to 1% in Denmark and Luxembourg and minimal amounts in Ireland, Greece, Italy and the UK; it might be expected that agricultural countries might compost more, although the figures for Ireland and Greece do not support this; urban industrialized countries might not use as much composting, apart from domestic sources; nevertheless, up to 10% of waste in Germany is composted; government policy is likely to be a very important factor; e.g. the Netherlands composts 15% of its waste and recycles a further 17%; [5]

6 (a) it shields the earth from ultraviolet radiation; [1]

(b) refrigerants; propellants; [2]

(c) CFCs are stable compounds that persist in the atmosphere for decades; under the influence of ultraviolet radiation they break down and release halogen atoms such as chlorine; these begin to break down the ozone; [3]

7 (a) the ozone hole is an area of reduced ozone concentration in the atmosphere; it varies from place to place and over the course of a year, and from year to year; [1]

(b) in 1980, the ozone hole was largely confined to Antarctica and the thickness of the stratospheric ozone was about 240–280 Du (Dobson units); by 1991, the ozone hole was wider and deeper; it had reached as far as South America and had got as low as 160–180 Du over Antarctica; [3]

(c) cataracts and blindness; skin cancer; reduced plant productivity; damage to phytoplankton, fish eggs and shallow water species; [4]

Chapter 6

1 (a) a simplified description of reality; designed to show the structure or workings of an object, system or concept; [2]

(b) oceanic circulation / ice / human activity / land and terrestrial features; *[1]*

[1] for any two correct.

(c) nitrogen / oxygen / carbon dioxide / water vapour / methane / ozone / other named trace gases; *[2]*

Four correct [2], three or two correct [1].

(d) solar inputs will be short wavelength, and radiation outputs will be long wavelength; *[1]*

(e) pollutant emissions leading to photochemical smogs; increased global temperatures through burning fossil fuels; altering chemistry of precipitation through sulfur dioxide / SO_2 and nitrogen oxide / NO_x emissions; depletion of stratospheric ozone increasing input of UV light; reducing rainfall through deforestation; *[3 max]*

(f) *strengths*: it stresses the interactions (feedback) within the system; represents the complex atmosphere as a system with inputs, outputs and transfers;

Accept other reasonable strengths.

limitations: nature of the interactions is not really shown; some categories are too broad to be helpful *e.g.* atmospheric circulation; some interactions are not shown; relative importance of different parts of the system not shown; *[4 max]*

Answer must refer to both strengths and limitations for full marks.

2 **(a)** *Answer should demonstrate an understanding of atmospheric insulation and how this is achieved within the atmosphere. Particular reference should be made to the role of carbon dioxide, which is transparent to incoming radiation and absorbs outgoing radiation.*

greenhouse gases transparent to incoming short-wave solar radiation; out-going long-wave radiation trapped / reflected by greenhouse gases; gases include: CO_2, CH_4, N_2O, O_3, H_2O and CFCs;

Two correct gases needed for [1].

creates a 'thermal blanket'; maintains an average Earth temperature of about 15 °C; *[4 max]*

(b) *Answer should address biomes, global agriculture and human society.*

biomes: north / south shift in biomes relative to the equator (latitude shift); movement of biomes up slope (altitude shift);

agriculture: crop zones move north / south from equator; e.g. wheat belt in North America may move north; cultivation patterns will change; crop types may change; water resources will change and limit / expand crop production; changing global weather patterns will influence rain patterns and alter crop production dynamics;

society: national resources base will change; water resources will change; which will drive economic, social and cultural change; sea level rise may cause economic and social stress due to loss of land and resources (including migration); *[7 max]*

Accept any other reasonable answers.

All of the above should be supported by case study evidence or examples.

(c) *Award [3 max] for any three of the following.*

systems models are not always accurate; model is less complex than reality; data series too short for confident predictions; not all elements are known or understood; *[3 max]*

Award [1] for each of the following.

present trend based on data collected since industrial revolution; long-term data (10 000 years) show climate fluctuation cycles not overall rise; some models predict future rise others argue for future cooling; *[3 max]*

Accept any other reasonable answers.

Expression of ideas max [3 marks].

Total [20 max]

3 **(a)** *description*: steady increase / exponential growth in carbon dioxide concentration until 1990; carbon dioxide concentration increased from about 315 ppm in 1960 to about 370 ppm in 2000 / increased by about 50 ppm over 40 years / increased by about 1 ppm per year; slight acceleration of rate of increase between 1985 and 1990; *[2 max]*

Accept any other reasonable points.

explanation: carbon dioxide increased mainly by human activity (e.g. mostly burning of fossil fuels); human population has increased significantly since 1960 which has increased human activity; electricity demand has increased steadily since 1960, increasing fossil fuel use in power stations; car ownership / road traffic increased dramatically since 1960, increasing fossil fuel use; forests cleared for agriculture / timber / development; standard of living increased markedly, since 1960, increasing fossil fuel use in industry / homes; [4 max]

Accept any other reasonable explanations.

(b) increased global warming / greenhouse effect; sea level rise / flooding of low lying lands; melting of icecaps / retreat of glaciers; which reduces planetary albedo; and further increases warming, which is a positive feedback effect; increased frequency of hurricanes; some areas become cooler and some hotter than before; some areas becoming drier and some wetter; effects of climate change on biomes and ecosystems; possible famine as food production is affected; examples of changes in distribution of named species; greater rate of photosynthesis; therefore accelerated plant growth; which may act as negative feedback effect to reduce carbon dioxide levels; [6 max]

Accept any other reasonable point.

(c) international agreements; more efficient appliances e.g. low energy light bulbs; insulation of buildings to reduce heating / cooling needed; replanting of trees / reforestation; use of more nuclear power; use of more renewable energy sources; carbon emission trading; more use of public transport; [5 max]

Accept any other reasonable points.

Expression of ideas [3 max].

Total [20 max]

4 (a) *Award [1] for any three of the following.*

CO_2, CO, CH_4, CFCs, water (vapour), N_2O, NO_2, NO_X, SO_2, ozone; [1 max]

Accept either names or formulas.

(b) *Answers must state more than 'fossil fuels' to achieve the mark.*

e.g. increased CO_2, through increased combustion of fossil fuels (oil, coal, natural gas); e.g. increased CO_2, through increased use of private cars; e.g. increased CH_4, through incomplete decomposition of organic materials from some agricultural activities / farm stock / padi fields; [1 max]

NB There is some evidence that efforts to bring about the reduction in the use of CFCs are now being successful, so allow: 'restrictions on the use of CFCs as propellants and in refrigerators / air conditioners, leading to reductions in the amounts entering the atmosphere'.

(c) increase in global temperatures / global warning; trapping of heat in the lower atmosphere, by preventing long-wave radiation escaping; thermal expansion of the oceans; melting of ice-caps (e.g. Greenland / Antarctica); retreat of valley glaciers (Alps, New Zealand); long-term rise in sea-level / flooding of lowland areas / low islands; change in the distribution of world biomes; change in the pattern of agricultural production; [2 max]

Any other reasonable point.

Award [0] for 'greenhouse effect' alone. Reject 'Health effects on humans'.

5 *Responses to this question will depend on the candidate's own personal viewpoint but examples could be:*

example 1:
stating viewpoint: global warming is the biggest threat to life on Earth ever and we are heading for catastrophe; [1 max]

evidence: evidence for heating of the Earth is overwhelming; evidence from increasing greenhouse gases caused by human activities; ice caps retreating; glaciers retreating; sea levels rising; more floods; hurricanes increase in severity; [3 max]

example 2:
stating viewpoint: global warming may be occurring but has throughout the life of the Earth and will bring benefits to many people; [1 max]

evidence: shift of biomass towards the poles will mean crops can grow where they could not before; more rainfall in some areas is a good thing; if the Arctic ice melts, we can mine for minerals and oil under the Arctic sea; large areas of Siberia and Canada will be warmer and easier to live in; [3 max]

Award up to [3 max] for any three pieces of evidence. Accept any other reasonable suggestions.

6 (a) feedback refers to knock-on effects; positive feedback refers to an accelerating increase whereas negative feedback is a self-regulating change; [1]

(b) positive feedback could occur as rising temperatures cause ice to melt, thereby reducing the albedo (reflectivity) of the Earth's surface, which increases absorption of solar radiation; this increases warming which could release methane from permafrost; methane is a greenhouse gas which can increase warming; [3]

(c) global dimming refers to a decreasing amount of sunlight reaching the Earth's surface; could be caused by increased cloud and dust in the atmosphere; source of the dust could be natural (e.g. volcanic) or anthropogenic – made by humans – (e.g. emissions of soot); consequences include reduced plant growth, lower temperatures, and reduced effectiveness of solar power; [6]

(d) some causes of climate change are natural e.g. volcanic eruptions and variations in the earth's orbit; solar output varies (sunspot activity); the atmosphere is very complex and interacts with the oceans, land and human processes; not all feedback mechanisms are understood; many processes are long term and the impacts of climate change have not yet occurred; [3]

7 (a) (i) Kyoto Protocol, 1997; [1]
   (ii) it gave legally binding cuts in emissions based on 1990 levels (e.g. the EU agreed to cut emissions by 8%, the USA by 7% and Japan by 6%); [3]

(b) not all countries sign up; those that do may feel disadvantaged if they reduce emissions but other countries do not; [3]

(c) *carbon trading:* an attempt to create a market where permits to emit carbon dioxide can be traded; in Europe the market is called the Emissions Trading System (ETS); permits are issued by governments; governments set targets for the amount of carbon dioxide that can be emitted nationally; the amount is divided between the various industries and permits issued; industries likely to exceed their limits must buy permits from others; targets are set to reduce pollution; it is working but not very well; [3]

carbon taxes: carbon taxes are used to encourage producers to reduce emissions of carbon dioxide; they can be implemented by taxing companies that burn fossil fuels, in relation to the carbon content of the fuel(s) burnt; such a measure would work best if implemented internationally, but can operate at a national level; [3]

(d) grow your own food; eat locally produced products; use energy efficient products; reduce your heating / weatherproof your home; unplug appliances not in use; turn off lights; reduce use of air conditioning and refrigerants; use a manual lawnmower not an electric or diesel one; turn off taps; take showers not baths; walk more; ride a bike; use public transport; use biofuels; eat lower down the food chain (vegetables rather than meat);

buy organic food; get involved in local political action; [6]

8 (a) greenhouse gases help to insulate the earth by retaining long-wave radiation and maintaining temperatures; increases in the concentration of greenhouse gases in the atmosphere are correlated with / cause / believed to cause increasing global temperatures; [2]

(b) some societies more affected than others due to their geographical location; e.g. increased sea levels will not be an issue for landlocked countries / some countries will be flooded or disappear; e.g. heavily glaciated areas may suffer more from melting / flooding with increase in global temperatures; e.g. the ozone layer is thinner in higher latitudes; e.g. for some areas, impacts may be positive, such as increased temperature / rainfall may improve farming / tourism in dry cold areas; the same impacts may affect societies differently because of socio-economic factors; e.g. LEDCs that depend heavily on farming may be harder hit than countries that can afford to import their food if climate is affected; e.g. MEDCs with better health and education may be able to protect population better against skin cancers from increased UV; e.g. MEDCs with greater wealth and technological development can mitigate against climate change more readily (through constructing sea defences / hurricane warning systems); [6 max]

Award credit for any other answers of equivalent validity, relevance and substance.

(c) *preventive stategies:* reducing emissions of carbon dioxide, methane, HCFCs / HFCs, nitrogen oxides through changes to current practice; reducing fossil fuel use e.g. through developing alternative energy sources e.g. renewables / nuclear; technology to improve energy efficiency e.g. in buildings / transport; changing farming practice e.g. reducing cattle farming (methane) / artificial fertilizer use (nitrogen oxides); incentives provided through e.g. international targets / carbon taxes; increasing natural recycling of carbon, by reducing deforestation / increasing afforestation; high technology solutions e.g. climate engineering / phytoplankton farms / carbon sequestration; plans to suspend small mirrors in space between the sun and the Earth to deflect solar radiation; plans to add sulfur to jet fuel to increase sulfur dioxide in atmosphere (adding particulates) so reducing solar radiation reaching Earth; [3 max]

reactive strategies: engineering works to protect coastal areas from flooding; improving prediction and warning systems to reduce impact of increased natural hazards e.g. hurricanes; migration of people to cooler / wetter areas; land use planning, reducing the densities of people living in most vulnerable areas; contingency planning, investing in emergency services / stockpiling food stores to offset disaster in emergency situations; *[3 max]*

evaluation of strategies: preventive might be more important because they are trying to stop the problem happening in the first place; however, reactive might be more important, because even if we stop releasing greenhouse gases today, the argument is that the effects will still be felt from gases emitted in the past; reactive might be more cost effective, because we are not sure exactly what effects will be felt where, and so money can be targeted when real problems emerge; preventive may be more important because if we reduce greenhouse gas emission now we can offset the worst effects of climate change; preventive might be more important because they depend on international cooperation, and countries working together are more likely to bring about effective change; *[4 max]*

Award [4 max] if no distinction is made between preventative and reactive.

Expression of ideas [2 max].

Total: [20]

9 **(a)** the addition of various atmospheric pollutants from industry may have changed our atmosphere (and as a consequence climate); heat produced by human activity (industry, urban living) may have changed atmospheric systems (leading to global climate change); change in our natural environment / albedo by humans including deforestation / agricultural activity / urbanization may have changed climate indirectly; CO_2 from burning fossil fuels is a greenhouse gas; methane from rice growing / cattle farming is a greenhouse gas; *[1 max]*

Answers must specifically identify the link between humans and climate for mark to be awarded. 'Atmospheric pollution' would not be acceptable; however, 'atmospheric pollution caused by industry' would gain a mark.

(b) sketch graph of temperature against time / years showing temperature fluctuations over the past 2000 years, both high and low points (*accuracy in*

the position of points is not essential); a steady rise over the last 100 years; annotation e.g. industrial revolution / little ice age; *[3]*

(c) changes in the Earth's orbit around the Sun changing the amount of available incoming radiation thus influencing global climate; changes in the Sun's radiation output, e.g. sunspot activity; plate tectonics shift position of land masses; plate tectonics causing mountain building and affecting air flows; volcanic activity leading to changes in atmospheric composition; natural dynamic variation in the atmospheric system leading to climate change; ocean current changes leading to global energy change; *[2 max]*

(d) (i) e.g. UK climate becoming warmer and wetter / Ethiopia becoming hotter and drier; *[1]*

(ii) e.g. UK: climate change will cause policy change which will change behaviour and influence footprint size; due to increased temperature more energy used for air conditioning thus larger footprint; warmer temperatures may require less heating thus smaller footprint; dealing with changing climate conditions, e.g. more flooding, may require more flood defences and thus more resources, thus larger footprint; new climate may require new building styles, which require resources which may increase footprint size; warmer temperatures may increase productivity of local natural vegetation and therefore reduce footprint size; warmer temperatures may increase productivity of local agriculture and therefore reduce footprint size; *[2 max]*

Chapter 7

1 **(a)** technocentrist because they tend to argue that economic development should precede environmental protection; and argue that society can find solutions for environmental problems through technology which comes when the economy is strong; would point to 'success' stories like Canada and Scandinavia who have good environmental records and are economically developed; *[2 max]*

(b) *arguments in favour of the statement*: costly to change technology to more environmentally sustainable forms e.g. new power stations or investment in renewable technologies such as solar; often LEDCs rely on weak pollution laws to attract multinationals to locate there; so if they set environmental controls they will lose jobs and income vital for development; rights to emit CO_2 for example can be bought and sold (richer countries can afford to buy the right to emit more CO_2) which has implications for industrial development; often countries with best record of environmental protection are the most developed economically e.g. Scandinavia; people in poverty will often be forced to act with short term perspective e.g. unsustainable use of forests in order to survive; it is not fair to expect LEDCs to protect the environment, as richer countries didn't when they were going through their industrial revolutions;

arguments against: some of the most economically developed countries have huge ecological footprints and are very wasteful e.g. US, UK, Japan; unsustainable use of the environment will only bring short-term economic growth not long-term economic growth; often the most sensible users of the environment are people who are considered 'undeveloped economically'; e.g. indigenous tribes in Amazonia / street kids recycling waste; people in poverty are often more intimately dependent on their environment – vital to protect it to help them; surely we can and should learn from the mistakes made by richer countries?; (very anthropocentric view) what about the rights of other living species to be unmolested?; environmental damage will have a knock-on effect on human societies that cannot wait until everyone has developed before we address it e.g. loss of species diversity, once gone its gone; environment is the source of our resources for development so it is vital that the two go hand in hand – sustainable development;

[10 max]

(c) (i) technology and scientific techniques used to overcome soil degradation problems thus conserving soil; modern ploughing technology and practice, e.g. contour ploughing; the use of new crop strains, e.g. genetically modified grain; the development of new devices, e.g. windbreaks and strategic shelter belts; *[3 max]*

Accept other reasonable answers.

(ii) ecocentric approach conservative; reluctant to adopt new technology; adopt solutions that are holistic and environmentally friendly;

e.g. application of organic fertilizers / crop rotations / shelter belts / farming on a smaller scale / non-industrial farming; reluctance to use heavy machinery due to soil compaction and energy issues; *[3 max]*

Accept other reasonable answers.

No credit should be given for naming the farming system. However, if farming system is not named award [5 max].

2 (a) *This can be argued either way, although it is more probable that Kuan Tzu was an ecocentrist. Give credit for strong justification.*

ecocentrist because: the proverb seems to be advising taking a long-term view; clearly advocates education and ecocentrism stresses importance of self-reliant communities; through education people will arguably learn to value the environment and use resources sustainably; refers to 'the people' and this perhaps suggests a lack of faith in elites / authorities; *[4]*

or

technocentrist because: education will help lead to technological development; through technology we will find longer-term solutions to environmental problems; we need to understand natural processes in order to control them; faith in the ability of people to overcome obstacles; *[4]*

(b) education – level and type will affect environmental awareness; economic conditions – will shape views towards environment e.g. short-term or long-term view; political context – will affect e.g. how groups in society are organized / treated; cultural views – will affect predominant attitudes to the environment; religious view – holy texts / doctrine may dictate relationship between people and creation / nature; *[2 max]*

(c) Perhaps cartoonist is suggesting that politicians / society refuse to act because they claim that more research needs to be done first; despite the fact that evidence (falling birds) is in front of their eyes; *[2]*

3 (a) the technocentric manager approach to water resource management would suggest that future needs can be met by technology, innovation and the ability to use 'untapped' reserves; technocentric managers would support desalination, iceberg capture and transport, wastewater purification, synthetic water production, rain seeding, deep aquifer extraction; would also look at innovative

ways to reduce water use per se, both in industry and at a domestic level;

the ecocentric manager approach would highlight the overuse and misuse of water; encourage the conservation of water; encourage greater recycling; encourage water use within sustainable level; encourage water use that had few detrimental impacts on habitat, wildlife and the environment; monitoring use to remain within sustainable limits; encouraging industry and society to use less water;

[8 max]

(b) ecocentrism involves an holistic world view; this implies individuals / local groups making changes which affect the whole; it also means working with natural processes; ecocentric involves self-imposed restraint e.g. reuse of bath water; ecocentric involves emphasis on small-scale e.g. local tube well; ecocentric involves emphasis on community involvement e.g. locally built micro-dams; ecocentric involves education e.g. local awareness campaigns; ecocentric focuses on basic needs of those below subsistence e.g. low technology irrigation; *[5 max]*

Award [2 max] if ecocentrism is discussed without reference to local application.

Features of ecocentrism do not need to be stated explicitly as the choice of strategy may imply these.

(c) *description:* irrigation using pumped ground water reserves; genetically modified plant species, disease resistant cereals; rice with genes to produce more proteins and vitamins; hydroponics is a good example of a technological solution; mechanization; agribusiness / industrial agriculture; fertilizers / pesticides; *[3 max]*

Award [1 max] for any statement which explains what a technocentric strategy might be.

evaluation: techno solutions may represent the only way to increase yield to meet demand; may have environmental costs / not be environmentally sustainable; high economic outlay, and therefore not an option for LEDC; may include both engineering solutions and biotechnology solutions;

[3 max]

[6 max], award [4 max] if there is no evaluation.

4 *Answers must be balanced and two appropriate societies contrasted. An answer which merely summarizes the differences between ecocentric and technocentric paradigms should not be awarded more than [6 max].*

e.g. indigenous shifting cultivator farmers in the Amazonian rainforest in Brazil and urban elites in Brasilia.

shifting cultivators: lifestyle and practices are much more closely bound up with their natural environment; i.e. live 'in tune' with the forest, utilizing forest materials for construction of their homes, canoes and for medicines; understanding of how the forest works so adapt farming practices e.g. use agroforestry to mimic layering of the forest and protect ground crops from harsh sunlight and heavy downpours; recognition that soil is often infertile so farmers shift and allow small pockets of forest to regenerate before returning to the plot some 50 years later; spiritual role of forest is also a feature of their cultural lives leading to respect for trees and other species; in conclusion a less destructive and closer connection between social systems and ecological systems; can crudely and broadly be generalized as 'ecocentric'; *[5 max]*

urban (capitalist) elites: rainforest seen as a resource for development, a source of cash; lack of understanding for how the natural systems works mean political decisions can lead to wasteful / damaging actions e.g. construction of dams, which then become silted up; establish policies, which encourage urban shanty dwellers to migrate and use the deforested land, but farming is unsuccessful because of lack of fertility of the soil; political prestige projects and ideology (e.g. the frontier mentality about the interior of Brazil) can lead to 'standing' value of rainforest being underestimated by urban elites; can crudely and broadly be generalized as 'technocentric'; *[5 max]*

Obviously within these groups there will be subsets and individuals with different environmental paradigms.

5 (a) it has no economic value / not easy to quantify; value of resource usually measured in economic terms; need to consider aesthetic or intrinsic value which is subjective; views can be diverse and hard to assess; *[2 max]*

(b) *Award [1] for stating two societies which demonstrate significant differences.*

Award [5 max] for each society.

e.g. the Dogon people in West Africa and industrial capitalism of Western Europe: the Dogon operate a mixed farming system with cultivation of millet and tobacco, livestock herding and hunter gathering; the ecosystem (bushland) surrounding their settlement is seen as the source of all the resources (food, building materials, fuel and medicine) that they need; subsistence depends on harnessing the power of the bush through work; but the bush is also the home of potentially vindictive spirits; respect is an essential part of the relationship between the Dogon and their environment; trees are particularly respected, wood is not wasted and wooden objects are left to deteriorate once no longer useful;

in industrial capitalism economic growth (and the consumption patterns that sustain growth) can be idealized / worshipped in place of the spiritual dimension of an ecosystem; just as in the Dogon system, ecosystems are seen as economic resources which can be exploited through work in order to develop economies / meet needs; but the scale and technological power of these systems means that in the past this has led to exploitation of resources at unsustainable rates e.g. the massive deforestation of ancient forests in Europe for fuel and building materials; but increasingly it is being argued that ecosystems should be seen as natural capital which can yield an income if exploited sustainably; and so quotas are set, for example for fishing catches, to preserve the natural capital;   *[10 max]*

Award [5 max] if no attempt is made to relate the value system to how the resources are used.

Award [5 max] if no attempt is made to compare the societies.

Chapter 2 – additional answers

1 (a) (i)   insects;   *[1]*

      (ii)   fungi;   *[1]*

  (b) (i)   many species simply have not been discovered yet (large areas of tropical forest / deep ocean unexplored for example); rate of extinction is so rapid that some species become extinct before we have discovered them; small organisms hard to find / capture / identify;   *[1 max]*

      (ii)   vertebrates are larger, so are easier to find / catch and classify; there are fewer species of vertebrate, so the chance of finding all of them is higher;   *[1 max]*

  (c) e.g. for insects, use a large sweep net to capture; and then identify using keys the number of species;

count number of individuals in each species; use Simpson's diversity index (involves total number of insect species and number of individuals); number of species must be recorded within a given area (e.g. number of species in a quadrat / hectare);   *[3 max]*

2 (a) wood mice in bracken 7, bank voles in bracken 23;   *[1]*

    Both figures needed to receive [1].

  (b) species' preference for nesting / shelter sites; preferred food sources located in particular habitats; rough grassland marginal for both species because it offers little shelter from predators; mice and voles occupy different niches;   *[2 max]*

  (c) so that when the animals are recaptured population size / Lincoln index can be calculated;   *[1 max]*

3 (a) (i)   *temperate forest*: 12.4 + 18.5 + 18.4 = 49.3 g m^{-2};

        tropical forest: 52.6 + 41.2 + 28.2 = 122.0/122 g m^{-2} *[1]*

        Both needed for [1].

    (ii)   *temperate forest*: $\frac{49.3}{821.1} \times 100 = 6.0\%$

        tropical forest: $\frac{112}{211.2} \times 100 = 57.8\%$ *[1]*

  (b) *temperate forest*: $\frac{730.9}{821.1} \times 100 = 89.0\%$

    tropical forest: $\frac{85.3}{211.2} \times 100 = 40.4\%$

    temperate forests have a larger proportion of nitrogen stored in the soil;   *[2]*

    Award [0] if temperate forest is stated without supporting calculations.

  (c) high temperatures and year round availability of water in tropical forests allow for continuous breakdown of nitrogen containing compounds; resulting in very rapid turn around and reabsorption; presence of mycorrhizae in tropical rain forest tree roots increases rate of organic matter breakdown; leading to rapid reabsorption of nitrogen, so very little found in soil; in temperate forests breakdown slows down significantly during winter months, causing nitrogen build up in soil;   *[1 max]*

  (d) *temperate forest*: 1 surface litter; 2 biomass; 3 soil;

    tropical forest: 1 surface litter; 2 soil; 3 biomass   *[1]*

    Both lists needed for [1].

(e) tropical rainforest would suffer more from clear cutting; a larger proportion of nitrogen is stored in living tissue which would be lost through clear cutting; climatic conditions in tropical rainforests would wash away soil quicker / leach the soil of nutrients; *[2 max]*

(f) (temperate forests) because: tropical forests have some of the highest rates of primary productivity but have relatively poor soils; temperate forests have lower primary productivity rates but far more fertile soils; climatic factors are not limiting in TRF but nutrients (nitrogen) may be; cleared land in tropics is exposed to washing away of thin soil and leaching of nutrients; temperate forests have higher nitrogen content in the soil; temperate forests store nitrogen as a result of incomplete breakdown of organic matter resulting in availability of nitrogen for crops; *[2 max]*

Do not credit final point if already given in (c). For 'temperate forest' on its own award [0].

4 *Candidates may choose any contrasting biomes. Award [3 max] if specific biomes are not mentioned.*

climate determines the global distribution the productivity of biomes; climate is a limiting factor as it controls the amount of photosynthesis which can occur in plants; water availability, light and temperature are the key climate controls; photosynthesis is a chemical reaction, therefore temperature will also affect rates of photosynthesis; this is why e.g. tropical rainforests, which have high constant temperatures (typically 26 °C) and rainfall (over 2500 mm p.a.) throughout the year; have high rates of NPP; e.g. hot deserts have high temperatures, but low precipitation (typically under 250 mm p.a.); therefore rates of NPP are very low; *[7 max]*

Give credit if appropriate diagrams are included.

5 *explanation for distribution*: deserts are found in a band approximately 30 degrees latitude; tundra is found at high latitudes/adjacent to ice margins; climate is the controlling factor; and is determined largely by Hadley cells/tricellular model; deserts found where rainfall is less than 250 mm a year; tundra also has little rainfall but low productivity is due to low insolation/sunlight; and low temperatures; soil may be permanently frozen (permafrost) in tundra; vegetation is low scrubs/grasses so productivity is low; in deserts productivity is low due to low/unevenly distributed rainfall; *[6 max]*

6 (a) *carbon*: increased ploughing leads to increased air/oxygen in soil; which leads to increased activity of aerobic microbes/decomposers/bacteria/fungi; which

leads to increased oxidation of carbon compounds/organic compounds/humus; *[3]*

nitrogen: increased ploughing leads to decreased waterlogging; which leads to leads to increased air/oxygen in soil; which leads to increased nitrification and decreased denitrification; which lead to increased nitrate ions in soil; *[3]*

(b) removal of trees leads to increased soil temperature (because decreased shade); which leads to increased rate of respiration of aerobic microbes; which leads to increased rate of decomposition/breakdown of organic matter; which leads to decreased carbon in soil (because output to atmosphere as carbon dioxide); *[4]*

Chapter 3 – additional answers

1 (a) use of a resource at a rate which allows for natural regeneration; while minimizing damage to the environment; *[2]*

(b) $SY = \left(\dfrac{\text{total biomass}}{\text{energy}} \text{ at time } t+1 \right) - \left(\dfrac{\text{total biomass}}{\text{energy}} \text{ at time } t \right)$ *[1]*

(c) *A range of answers may be acceptable e.g.* war; countries resources are diverted to armies rather than invested in education / agriculture / development projects; population expansion; more resources must be put into sustaining the population rather than development; national debt; paying off heavy foreign debts leans less money left over for inward investment; cultural inertia; culture may not have a philosophy of sustainability (consumerist culture of west or nomadic culture of Africa); political unrest; short-term thinking predominates but sustainable development is a long-term goal; *[3 max]*

[1] for both factors and [1] each for brief description of each factor.

2 (a) *year 2*: 125;
year 6: 24 500; *[1]*
Both needed for [1].

(b) year 5; *[1]*

(c) the population will ultimately crash; *[1]*

(d) over population leading to unrealistic demands for limited resources; financial motives (greed) – exploitation of resources beyond sustainable limits for short-term financial gain (cod fishing); use of resource beyond sustainable limits due to lack of knowledge of resource's sustainable level; *[2 max]*

3 (a) wave power / solar radiation / heat pumps / water wheels; *[1]*

Accept other suitable answers if appropriate.

(b) *tidal power, limitation*: good tidal range required / right shape of coastline / interferes with navigation / impact on wildlife / expensive; *[1]*

Only 1 limitation required.

biofuel, energy production: plant material burnt directly to produce heat / transformed into ethanol (used as a fuel) / converted to methane (methane digestion); *[1]*

Only 1 limitation required.

Award [2] if both answers are correct and [1 max] if one or two partial answers are correct.

(c) MEDCs traditionally / culturally dependent on fossil fuels; fossil fuels are energy efficient / easy to transport / relatively cheap; changing to renewable energy on a large scale requires massive capital investment / cultural inertia against change to renewables / many renewables depend on environmental conditions that are not constant (e.g. wind, sunshine, waves); *[3]*

4 (a) LEDC (*no mark*)

basic/lack of technology generally; rice farming is typical of LEDCs / where rice is often the staple crop; cash crops for export such as sugar cane, tobacco; houses look fairly simple and made from local / cheap materials / thatched roofs; dependence on working animals; labour intensive (family labour); mixed cropping on small scale; *[2 max]*

(b) *inputs*: water / technology / cattle (livestock) / sunlight / rain / manure / seed / labour / soil; *[1 max]*

processes: planting / ploughing / harvesting / irrigating / repair / respiration / run-off / labour; *[1 max]*

outputs: jute / vegetables / mangoes / Jack fruit / palm / coconut / sugar cane / spices / crops/ waste / income / energy / rice / food / betel nuts / tobacco / cattle (livestock) / heat / oxygen / carbon dioxide / wheat / mustard; *[1 max]*

(c) different crops planted at different levels; rotation of crops to match seasonal rainfall patterns; monsoonal climate so main crop is rice; irrigation technology used in dry season; livestock fed

differently at different times of year; different jobs done at different times of year; *[2 max]*

5 (a) (i) Japan = −3.4 hectares person^{-1} (units not required); *[1]*

Answer may appear in table.

(ii) United States = 10.3 hectares person^{-1} (units not required); *[1]*

Answer may appear in table.

(iii) 6; *[1]*

(iv) a high proportion of people exist below the poverty line (i.e. they do not have all the resources they need); soil is particularly fertile (volcanoes) and so they are able to support a lot of people by using the land very intensively; very low rates of pollution per person perhaps because of high proportion of people in agriculture; relatively low dependence on fossil fuels especially in terms of transport; *[2 max]*

Do not accept 'because they have a lot of available capacity', as other countries have similar amounts of land, smaller populations, but are in deficit.

(b) (i) *rank for footprints*: US, Australia, Singapore, Norway, Russian Federation, Germany, UK, Japan, Venezuela, Indonesia, India, Ethiopia; *[1]*

rank for GDP: USA, Norway, Singapore, Japan, Germany, Australia, UK, Venezuela, Russian Federation, Indonesia, India, Ethiopia; *[1]*

(ii) countries with highest GDPs generally have the largest footprints; *[1]*

(iii) they depend on imports for resources; they are sufficiently wealthy that they can afford to buy these resources in from abroad; they have a developed economy that is not based on primary industries; *[2 max]*

(c) (i) no, it is not sustainable; *[1]*

world footprint is 2.8 hectares person^{-1} and there is only 2.1 hectares person^{-1} available; Earth currently in ecological deficit −0.7 hectares person^{-1}; we are looking at *global* footprint so cannot offset larger footprints against smaller ones as you can when looking at whether individual nations are sustainable; *[2 max]*

If no justification is attempted award [0].

Figures not necessary if candidate has demonstrated conceptual understanding.

(ii) using technology to remanufacture or recycle can reduce the overall amount of resources consumed and so ecological footprint is reduced; e.g. through bottle banks; absolute reductions in energy and material use can reduce ecological footprint; e.g. energy efficiency initiatives; reduction in pollution by technological advances; e.g. through renewable / alternative energy technologies instead of fossil fuels; use of technology to intensify and therefore maximize production from available land; e.g. through GM crops;
[4 max]

Each way of decreasing footprint must be adequately described for [2].

6 (a) $1960 = 2 \times 10^3 \text{ km}^3 \text{ yr}^{-1}$
$2000 = 4 \times 10^3 \text{ km}^3 \text{ yr}^{-1}$;
$\frac{4 - 2}{2} \times 100 = 100\%$;   [2]

Correct answer on its own, award [2]

(b) increasing global population requiring more water; industry expanding and requiring more clean water (cooling processes, etc.); globally, greater use of water for irrigation; increase in water use by developing countries;   [3]

Accept other reasonable answers.

7 (a) *carrying capacity*: the maximum number of species (or load) that can be sustainably supported by a given environment;   [1]

(b) *over-population*: there are too many people relative to the resources and technology locally available to maintain an adequate standard of living; *under-population*: there are far more resources (e.g. food production, energy and minerals) in an area than can be used by the people living there; *optimum population*: the number of people which, when working with all available resources, will produce the highest per capita economic return, the highest standard of living and quality of life;   [3]

(c) see Figure 3.54 on page 154;   [3]

(d) *characteristics of over-populated areas (e.g. Bangladesh, Somalia and parts of Brazil and India)*: insufficient food and materials; low incomes leading to poverty, poor living conditions and a high level of emigration;   [2]

characteristics of under-populated areas (e.g. Canada and Australia): can export their surplus food, energy and mineral resources; have high levels of immigration; possible that standard of living would increase through increased production if population increased;   [2]

GLOSSARY

The IBO ESS syllabus contains a glossary with key words you need to know. Additional words that will increase your understanding and appreciation of the subject are highlighted throughout the book and defined here.

Acid rain Any precipitation which is distinctly more acid than normal rainfall (pH 5.5–6.0). It is caused by emissions of sulfur dioxides and/or oxides of nitrogen.

Agenda 21 Outcome of the 1992 Rio Earth Summit. A blueprint for action to achieve sustainable development worldwide (the number 21 refers to an agenda for the 21st century).

Agribusiness Farming based on the desire to maximize productivity and profit in order to compete in a global market. Involves large-scale monocultures, intensive use of fertilizers and pesticides, mechanized ploughing and harvesting, and food production geared to mass markets, including export.

Albedo The amount of incoming solar energy reflected back into the atmosphere by the Earth's surface.

Altruism Unselfish concern for the welfare of others.

Anoxia A total decrease in levels of oxygen – very low levels of oxygen.

Anthropocentric Human-centred worldview where nature exists and is used for human benefit.

Bioaccumulation Pesticides build up in the body tissue (mainly fats) of primary consumers.

Biomagnification Pesticides become concentrated in animal tissues at each successive trophic level of a food chain.

Birth rate, age-specific (ASBR) The number of births per 1000 women of any specified year groups.

Buffer zone Areas of habitat, which may be either disturbed or managed, that surround conservation areas.

Carnivore An organism that feeds on animals.

Carnivory The process of an organism feeding on an animal.

CITES An international agreement between governments that aims to ensure international trade in specimens of wild animals and plants does not threaten their survival.

Competition, interspecific Competition between different species.

Competition, intraspecific Competition within a species.

Conservation, ex situ Helping to protect a species in zoos.

Conservation, in situ Helping to protect a species within its habitat.

Consumers Organisms that eat other organisms to obtain their food.

DDT Dichloro-diphenyl-trichloroethane. A synthetic pesticide that is strongly absorbed by soils. It is not very soluble in water but is very soluble in lipids (fats), and so builds up in the fatty tissue of organisms.

Decomposers Bacteria and fungi that feed on dead and decaying organisms.

Density-dependent factors Factors that lower the birth rate or raise the death rate as a population grows in size.

Density-independent factors Factors that affect a population irrespective of population density (e.g. environmental change).

Deposition, dry A form of acid rain – dry deposition is the deposition on surfaces of dry gases/ particles in the atmosphere.

Deposition, wet A form of acid rain – wet deposition is the deposition on surfaces of dissolved substances and particles formed by any form of precipitation.

Diffusion Describes the spread of species at the edge of their ranges into new areas. Diffusion often follows jump dispersal events.

Diversity The number of species and their relative abundance in a given area or sample.

Ecocentric A worldview that sees nature as having an inherent value.

Ecological deficit Relates to the available capacity of a country. If the ecological footprint of the country exceeds the biologically productive area then the country has an ecological deficit.

Ecological footprint Represents the hypothetical area of land required by a society, group or individual to fulfil all their resource needs and assimilation of wastes.

Edge effects Changed environmental conditions at the edge of reserves.

Equilibrium, stable Where a system returns to the original equilibrium following disturbance.

Equilibrium, static Systems where there is no input or output of energy or matter, and there is no change in the system over time.

Equilibrium, steady-state Despite constant inputs and outputs of energy and matter, the overall stability of the system remains.

Equilibrium, unstable Where a system does not return to the same equilibrium following disturbance but forms a new equilibrium.

Export subsidies Government policy to encourage export of goods and discourage sale of goods on the domestic market through low-cost loans or tax relief for exporters.

Extinctions, mass Periods when a large proportion of the total number of species on the Earth at the time have been wiped out.

Farming, commercial Production of crops or animals for profit. Often involves the production of one crop.

Farming, extensive Farms that are large in comparison to the money and labour put into them (e.g. the cattle ranches of central Australia, where only a few workers are responsible for thousands of acres of land).

Farming, intensive Farms that take up a small area of land but aim to have very high output (through large inputs of capital and labour).

Farming, shifting cultivation Rotational system where a small area of land is cleared for crops. Also known as 'slash-and-burn' reflecting the way land is cleared. Once land has been exhausted a new area is used. Old land can be returned to once the fertility has recovered.

Farming, subsistence Produces only enough food to feed the family or small community working it, and not for profit. Typically uses no machines and follows the polyculture approach.

Fertility rate, general The number of births per thousand women aged 15–49 years.

Fertility rate, total The average number of births per women of child-bearing age.

Field capacity The maximum amount of water that a soil can hold.

Flows Movement through a system in the form of inputs and outputs. Can be either transfers or transformations.

Global dimming The effect of small droplets (aerosols) that reflect solar energy, blocking light from entering the lower atmosphere, thereby having a cooling effect on the Earth.

Goods Marketable commodities derived from natural capital such as timber and grain.

Grain equivalent Allows comparison between different food types, where food can be converted into grain equivalents – the mass of grain needed to produce the equivalent amount of a given food type.

Herbivore An organism that feeds on plants.

Herbivory The process of an organism feeding on a plant.

Holism The view that a system has properties that can only be perceived by looking at the inter-relationships of its components, and the functioning of the whole system.

Import tariffs Taxes imposed on imports to a country that make them more expensive.

Inertia Resistance of an ecosystem to being altered.

J-curve Population growth curve which shows exponential growth. Growth is initially slow then increasingly rapid, and does not slow down.

Jump dispersal Long-distance dispersal of species to remote areas by one or a few individuals.

Life expectancy (E_0) The average number of years that a person can be expected to live, given that demographic factors remain unchanged.

Limit, liquid Occurs when there is sufficient water to reduce cohesion between the soil particles.

Limit, plastic Occurs where each soil particle (ped) is surrounded by a film of water sufficient to act as a lubricant.

Limit, shrinking The state at which the soil passes from having a moist to a dry appearance.

Macrophyte A plant that grows in or near water.

Mortality rate, age-specific (ASMR) The number of deaths per 1000 population of a specific age group (e.g. under 1 year old, under 5 years old etc.).

Mortality rate, infant (IMR) The total number of deaths of children aged <1 year per 1000 live births.

Mortality rate, standardized (SMR) Death rate per thousand people of a particular age group (e.g. under 1 year, over 60 years, etc.). Infant mortality rate is an example of SMR.

Mutualism An interaction in which two organisms live together and both species benefit from the relationship.

Neonatal deaths Deaths that occur between birth and 7 days.

Optimum population The number of people which, when working with all the available resources, will produce the highest per capita economic return.

Organizations, governmental (GOs) Bodies established through international agreements to bring together governments to work on an international scale (e.g. the United Nations Environment Program, UNEP).

Organizations, non-governmental (NGOs) Bodies not run by, funded by, or influenced by governments of any country (e.g. Greenpeace; the World Wide Fund for Nature, WWF).

Over-population Occurs when there are too many people relative to the resources and technology locally available to maintain an adequate standard of living.

Paradigm A model or template based on evidence or experience.

Parasitism Interaction where one organism (the parasite) benefits at the expense of another.

Percentage cover The proportion of a quadrat covered by a species, measured as a percentage.

Percentage frequency The percentage of the total number of quadrats that a species was present in.

Perinatal deaths Deaths that occur after the first week of life but before the end of the first four weeks of life (i.e. 8–28 days).

Phase out Cessation of production – which may occur in a series of stages.

Photochemical smog A pollution cloud at ground level caused by a mixture of nitrogen oxides and volatile organic compounds (VOCs).

Photosynthesis The process by which green plants convert light energy from the Sun into useable chemical energy stored in organic matter. It requires carbon dioxide, water, chlorophyll and light.

Plagioclimax Interrupted succession where interference halts the process of succession so that the climax community is not reached; often a result of human activities.

Polyculture Farming system that uses many crop species.

Post-neonatal period Deaths that occur after the first week of life and before the end of the first year (i.e. 8–365 days).

Population density The number of individuals of each species per unit area.

Predation Process of an animal eating another animal.

Producers Organisms that can produce their own food (i.e. glucose).

Pyramid of biomass The amount of biomass present at each trophic level at a certain point in time, and represents the standing stock of each trophic level measured in units such as grams of biomass per square metre ($g\,m^{-2}$). Biomass may also be measured in units of energy, such as $J\,m^{-2}$.

Pyramid of numbers The number of organisms (producers and consumers) coexisting in an ecosystem. Quantitative data for each trophic level are drawn to scale as horizontal bars arranged symmetrically around a central axis.

Pyramid of productivity Show the rate of production over a period of time. Each level represents energy per unit area per unit time. Productivity is measured in units of flow ($g\,m^{-2}\,yr^{-1}$ or $J\,m^{-2}\,yr^{-1}$). These pyramids show the flow of energy through a food chain.

Resilience The ability of an ecosystem to recover after a disturbance.

Respiration The process that releases energy from glucose and other organic molecules inside all living cells.

S-curve Population growth curve which shows an initial rapid growth (exponential growth) and then slows down as the carrying capacity is reached.

Sampling, continuous Every organism along a transect is recorded.

Sampling, random Used when habitat is homogeneous (the same) throughout an area. A random-number generator can be used to produce coordinates.

Sampling, stratified random Used when two very different habitats are sampled, with samples taken at random from both areas.

Sampling, systematic Samples are taken at fixed distances along a transect.

Secular migration Dispersal of species over geological timescales (e.g. thousands to millions of years).

Services Ecological services derived from natural capital (e.g. flood and erosion protection; climate stabilization; maintenance of soil fertility).

Species richness The number of species in a given area or sample.

Storages The stock or reservoir of energy and matter in a system.

Strategists, *K*- Individuals with lower reproductive rates but better competitive ability.

Strategists, *r*- Individuals with a high reproductive rate and rapid development.

Sustainable yield, maximum (MSY) The largest yield (or catch) that can be taken from a species' stock over an indefinite period. MSY aims to maintain the population size at the point of maximum growth rate by harvesting the individuals that would normally be added to the population, allowing the population to continue to be productive indefinitely. It is the point where the highest rate of recruitment can occur.

Succession The orderly process of change over time in a community.

Succession, primary Succession occurring on a previously uncolonized substrate.

Succession, secondary Occurs in places where a previous community has been destroyed (e.g. after forest fires).

Technocentric A worldview that sees technology as providing solutions to environmental problems even when human effects push natural systems beyond their normal boundaries.

Transect, belt A band of chosen width (usually 0.5–1 m) along an environmental gradient.

Transect, continuous Sample where the whole transect is sampled (in either a belt or line through the habitat). *See also* **continuous sampling**.

Transect, interrupted Samples taken at points of equal distance along the gradient. *See also* **systematic sampling**.

Transfer Movement that does not involve a change of form or state.

Transformation Movement that involves a change in form or state.

Transpiration The evaporation and diffusion of water from leaves.

Trent biotic index A measurement of levels of pollution in aquatic ecosystems, based on indicator species which tend to disappear from a river as the level of organic pollution increases.

Turnover time Time for a water molecule to enter and leave a part of the system (i.e. the time taken for water to completely replace itself in part of the system).

Under-population Occurs when there are far more resources (e.g. food production, energy and minerals) in an area than can be used by the people living there.

Use, consumptive The harvesting of resources (e.g. food products, timber for fuel or housing, medicinal products and the hunting of animals) for consumption.

Use, direct Ecosystem goods and service that are directly used by human populations.

Use, indirect Values derived from ecosystem services that provide benefits outside the ecosystem itself (e.g. natural water filtration which may benefit people far downstream).

Use, non-consumptive Uses that include the enjoyment of recreational and cultural activities that do not require the harvesting of resources.

Values, optional Values derived from to potential future use of ecosystem goods and services which are not currently used.

Values, existence (also known as **non-use values**) Aesthetic and intrinsic values.

Values, recreational Natural resources that have a value in terms of holiday destinations and as places for people to relax and take time away from their daily lives.

Value system, environmental Set of criteria through which personal environmental issues are judged.

Xerophytes Plants adapted to dry conditions (e.g. desert plants).

Index

and eutrophication 231
tropical rainforest 37, 38
New York World summit 206–7
NGOs (non-governmental organizations)
204, 209
strengths and weaknesses 205
niches 20
and competition 21
and habitat diversity 176
nitrates in tap water 234
nitrogen cycle 44, 49–50, 51
nitrogen and eutrophication 232
nitrogen oxides 249, 250–1, 252, 253, 257
nomadic herding 140
non-renewable resources 97, 98–9
energy 108, 120, 121
North America
cereal farming 139
ecological footprint 162–3
fossil fuel use 162
human-induced land degradation 130
population predictions 84
see also Canada; United States
Norway: fish farming 140–1
nuclear accidents 74–6, 217, 291
nuclear fission 100, 113
nuclear fusion 100
nuclear power 108, 109, 119–20, 273
advantages and disadvantages 113–14
risks 114
nutrient cycles 50–1

O

Odum, Howard 47
oil 97, 108, 109, 119, 120
pollution 61, 112
oil palm plantations 118–19, 203
omnivore 15
open systems 3–4, 5
open-cast mining 112
orang-utans 209
organic farming 146
organisms; estimating abundance 30–2
Our Common Future 104, 105, 207, 292
over-fishing 195
overgrazing 129
oxygen meter 28
ozone 242, 243
effect on forests and crops 249–50
effect on human health 250
and halogenated organic gases 244–5
hole 98, 244–5, 248, 260
tropospheric 249–50, 251, 252–3
and ultraviolet radiation 243
ozone-depleting substances 98, 244, 246, 247–8

P

padi fields 144, 264
Palestinian territories 150–1
palm oil *see* oil palm
parasitism 22, 23
particulates
and Beijing Olympics 226, 227
sizes 226
peat 123, 124

Penan forest people 204
percentage cover in quadrat 31–2
permafrost 40, 41
personal value systems 295–7
questionnaire 295
shades of green 297
social influences 296
Peru: ecological footprint 163, 165
pesticides 136
and agribusiness 145
DDT 18, 198–9, 228–9, 230
and food chains 18
loss of diversity 188
pollution by 149
pH measures 26
philosophies, environmental 74
creationism 179
eutrophication 236
and EVSs 284–6
of industrial nations 218
protected areas 210
range of 284–5, 286–7
and resources 102
value of environment 100
waste management 241
zoos 213
see also ecocentric; technocentric
phosphorus and eutrophication 232
photoautotrophs 43
photochemical smog 250–1, 252
photosynthesis 44–5
and biomes 35–6
energy transformation 9, 45
and food chain 15
as process 2
photosynthetic bacteria 16
phytoplankton 15, 16, 245
pioneer communities 185, 187
pitcher plant 22
plagioclimax 70–2
plankton and UV-B light 98
plants
abundance 31–2
photosynthesis 2, 9, 15, 44, 45
temperature adaptations 56
plastic limit of soil 126
plate tectonics 181–4
polar cell 36–7, 43
pollution 223, 313
air 220, 226–8, 241, 249–52, 276–7
computer equipment 225, 238
costs 218
defined 217
detection and monitoring 219–23
and extinctions 191
and fish farming 141
and low diversity 33
major sources 218
natural 313
non-point source 217–18, 313
oil from Hurricane Katrina 61
point source 217–18
polluter pays 313
soil 129, 219
water 149, 150, 219, 220–21
pollution management 223–8

cleaning up 225–6
human activities 224–5
social factors 226–8
polyculture 134, 139, 141–2
Popolucas' farming, Mexico 134
population 31
carrying capacity 55, 57, 58–9
defined 19–20
density-dependent/independent factors 58, 60–2
explosion-crash cycle 58
growth as positive feedback 7
interactions 21–3
J- and S-curves 57–9, 154
limiting factors 55–7, 58, 60–2
human 153, 155, 156–7
internal and external factors 61–2
tolerance 55–6
population, human
ageing of 95
death rates 87–8
demographic transition models 90–1
doubling times 87
exponential growth 83, 84, 152–3
fertility 84–7
and improving technology 156, 157
limiting factors 153, 155, 156–7
limits-to-growth model 152–3
natural increase 88
optimum 154, 156
over- and under-population 154–5, 156
policies 165–6
population pyramids 88–90
population-resource ratios 171–2
predictions 84, 93–4
pyramids 89, 90, 92, 173
and resources 306–7
and technology 171–2
world 83
positive feedback 7–9
poverty 167–8
prairie, tall grass 186
precipitation 36–7, 242
acid rain 253–7, 288, 313
and soil degradation 129, 131
see also rainfall; water
predator-prey interaction 8, 22
as density-dependent control 60
negative feedback 22
and survivorship rates 63
pressure groups 290–1
primary consumers 15, 16
primary productivity 52–4
pronatalist policies 170–1
processes 1–2
producers 14, 15, 16
estimating biomass 33
pyramid models 16–17
role of 43–4
production:respiration ratio 68
productivity
diagrams 47
gross 53–4
net (NP) 53–4
primary and secondary 52–4
pyramids of 16, 17, 19